Pocatello Trail Guide

HIKING, BIKING, and CROSS-COUNTRY SKIING
over 300 miles of trails around The Gate City

Pocatello Trail Guide

HIKING, BIKING, and CROSS-COUNTRY SKIING
over 300 miles of trails around The Gate City

Ryan Byers

Lost River Publishing LLC

WARNING! Spending time outdoors carries inherent risks. Each route described in this book presents its own challenges and dangers. Users of this guidebook must accept full responsibility for their safety and well-being. While every effort has been made to ensure the accuracy of the trail descriptions, conditions can change rapidly due to weather, erosion, or other factors. Trails may differ from what is described here. This guidebook is not a substitute for experience, sound judgment, or prudent decision-making. It is essential to prepare adequately for your adventure and to remain vigilant to unexpected circumstances. Remember, safety is paramount—be cautious, stay informed, and always be prepared for the unexpected.

Pocatello Trail Guide: HIKING, BIKING, and CROSS-COUNTRY SKIING over 300 miles of trails around The Gate City
© 2024 Ryan Byers

Cover and interior design: Ryan Byers
Photos, maps, and elevation profiles: Ryan Byers
Editor: Mary Byers
Cover image: Mary Byers ascending one of BLM T351's rocky hills

International Standard Book Number: 979-8-9876471-2-7
Library of Congress Control Number: 2024912838

First Edition. Updated February 2025.
Published by Lost River Publishing LLC
lostriverpublishing.com

Lost River Publishing LLC

This book is dedicated to all the pets of the world, and in particular, to my faithful writing companion, Mister Kitty. Life has been less vibrant without you.

Regions & Trail Locations

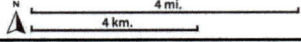

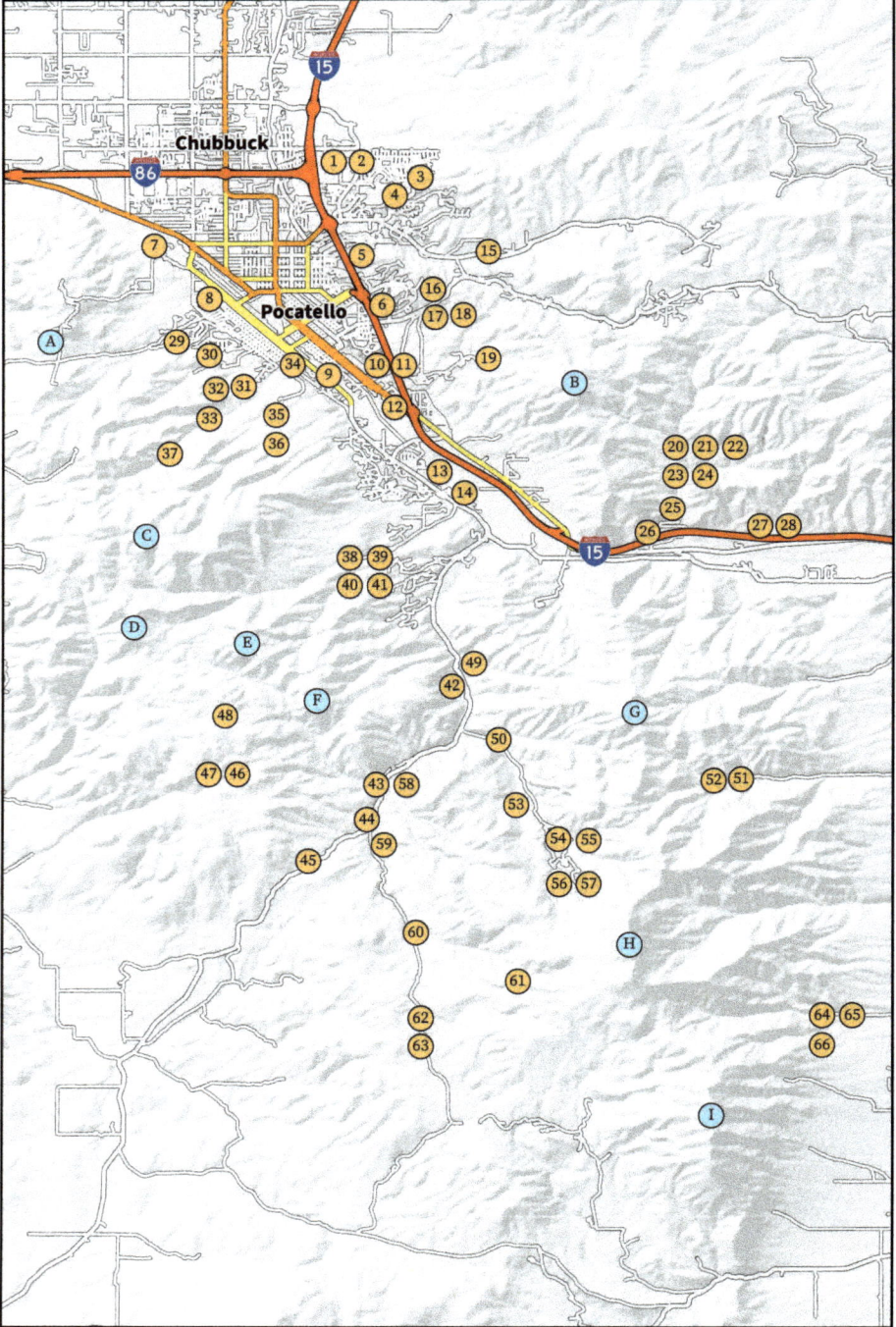

N
4 mi.
4 km.

Chubbuck

15

86

Pocatello

A

B

C

D

E

F

G

H

I

15

15

Regions & Trail Locations

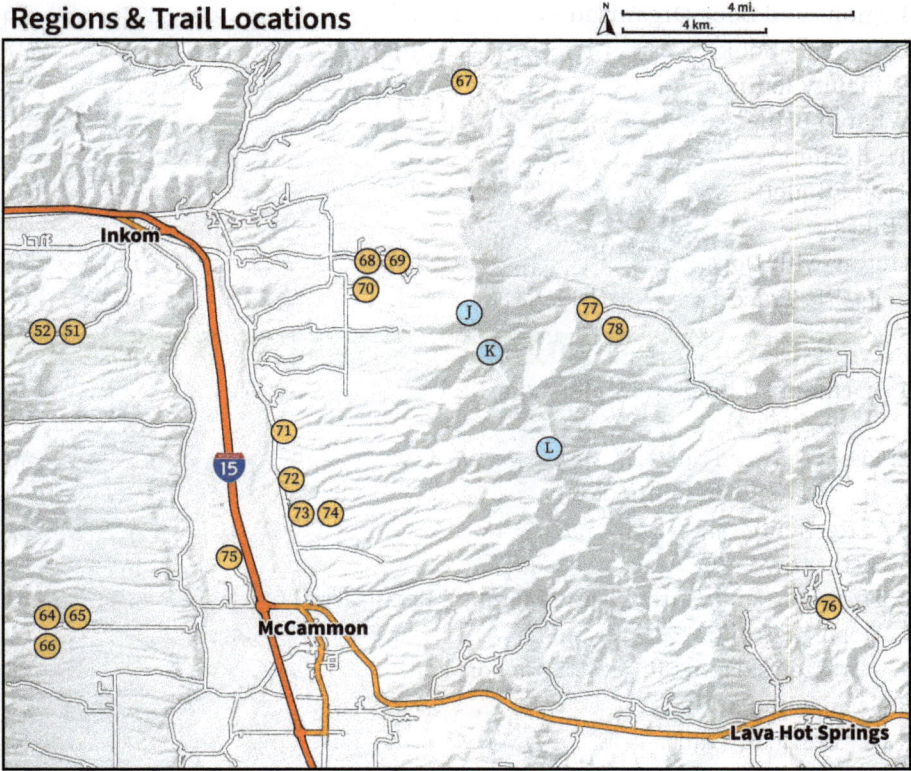

Contents

Mountains

Map Legend

P	Free parking	⊶ Gate or cattle guard		BLM land
P	Paid or restricted parking	⇌ Bridge		
🏠	Trailhead	① Numbered bridge		State land
🚻	Restroom	① or junction		
⛵	Portneuf River access point	City Creek Management Area or relevant City property		Forest Service land
🏕	Campground			
🏚	Shelter			Park
🎿	Ski lift	Portneuf Wildlife Management Area		
🛝	Playground			Golf course

Wildflowers along Sullivan's (City Creek Management Area).

Acknowledgements

When I began working on this project, I thought it would be a much easier undertaking compared to my previous guidebook, "Idaho Twelvers." After all, hiking City Creek Trail is far easier than climbing to the top of Borah Peak's 12,662-foot summit, so naturally, the project would be a breeze. Boy, was I wrong! I was unprepared for and am continually impressed by the breadth of Pocatello's trail systems. From those of you who joined me out on the trails, all the way to the proofreaders, I am forever thankful. I want to give a shout out to Mary Byers, John Byers, Steve Byers, David Sprawls, Bruce Olenick, Cary Rhodes, Tony Razo, Greg Roberts, Adrianna Mason, Rob Kleffner, Samantha Solomon, Kim Obele, Robert Harris, Nels Rasmussen, Manuel Camacho, Sage Rice, Hannah Sanger, Andrea Faust, Allison Radmall, Dana Kmetz, Blaine Newman, Ian Wilson, Tyler Peterson, Jason Beck, Chris Wagner, Brian Sagendorf, Daniel Wells, Adria Mead, Jessica Quinn, Tedi Razo, Mark Norrell, and Crystal Anderson. I want to give my mom, Mary Byers, an extra shoutout. In addition to editing the book, she joined me on many of these trails. It was fun seeing her progress to become a strong hiker.

pocatellotrailguide.com

Have you discovered something new on the trails not covered in this guidebook? Let me know! Visit pocatellotrailguide.com to submit feedback and help me improve future editions with the most up-to-date trail information.

On the website, you'll find GPX files for each trail, providing extra assistance during your outdoor adventures. You can also find Pocatello outdoor gear for sale, including stickers and hats, to show your love for exploring the area's beautiful trails.

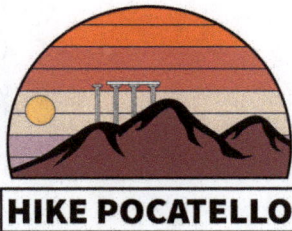

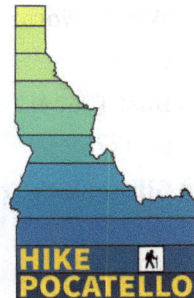

HIKE POCATELLO   **HIKE POCATELLO**   **HIKE POCATELLO**

Best Hikes

Best Hikes with Kids

Best Forest Hikes

Best Wildflower Hikes

Best Hikes for Fall Colors

Best Hikes with Views

Best Hikes Under 1.5 Hours

11 **Red Hill Ridge Trail**
(p. 77)

34 **City Creek Trail**
until bridge 10 (p. 162)

39 **Gibson Jack Trail**
until the bridge (p. 182)

43 **West Fork Mink Creek Trail**
(until the second bridge)
(p. 198)

73 **North Quinn Creek Road**
(p. 313)

Best Hikes Under 3 Hours

17 **Wiggle Worm Trail**
(p. 104)

49 **Kinney Creek Trail**
(p. 222)

57 **East Fork Mink Creek Trail**
turn around at the pond
(p. 252)

60 **Wendigo Trail**
(p. 263)

72 **Robbers Roost Canyon Loop**
(p. 309)

Best Challenging Hikes

38 **Sterling Justice Trail**
(p. 178)

52 **South Walker Creek Trail**
(p. 234)

55 **Crestline Trail**
(p. 245)

68 **Pebble Creek Ski Area**
(p. 293)

78 **Robbers Roost Trail**
(p. 328)

Community Favorites

19 **BLM 301 (Barton Road)**
(p. 111)

34 **City Creek Trail**
(p. 162)

39 **Gibson Jack Trail**
(p. 182)

43 **West Fork Mink Creek Trail**
(p. 198)

57 **East Fork Mink Creek Trail**
(p. 252)

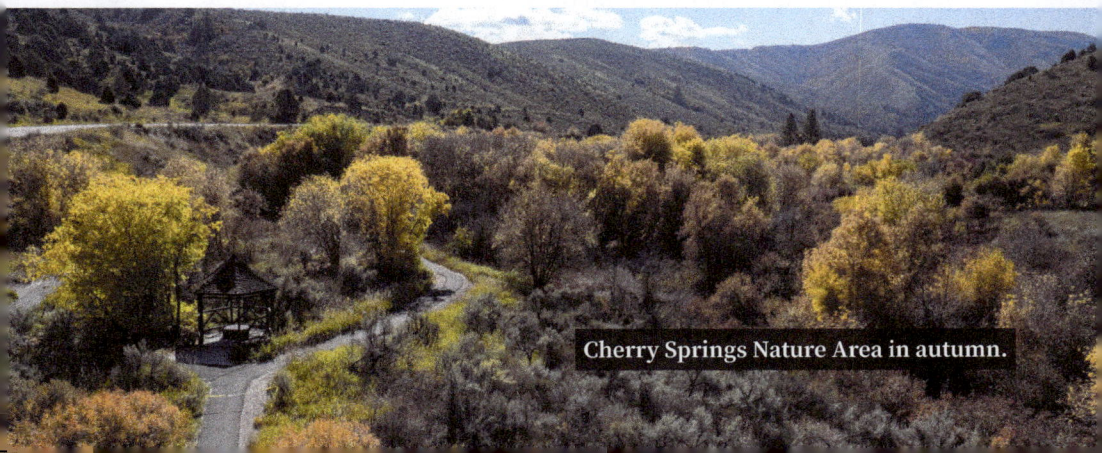
Cherry Springs Nature Area in autumn.

Best Rides

Easy Routes

Bench Loop (pp. 410, 421, 419)
(Bench Trail > Rim Trail > Lifeflight)
A short singletrack loop above the City Creek Trail. Perfect for beginners.
▽ 2.3-mile loop   ▽ 340 feet of elevation gain

Elk Meadows Loop (p. 214)
A rocky but generally easy-to-ride 4x4 road with great scenery.
▽ 5.6-mile loop   ▽ 550 feet of elevation gain

City Creek Road (p. 156)
A wide dirt road with plenty of access points for various mountain bike trails.
▽ 4.6 miles out-and-back   ▽ 600 feet of elevation gain

Intermediate Routes

Gibson Jack to West Fork Mink Creek (pp. 182, 214, and 198)
(Gibson Jack Trail > Elk Meadows > West Fork Mink Creek)
Two popular singletrack trails that are bridged together with the north-east section of the Elk Meadows Loop. A shuttle car is recommended.
▽ 9 miles one-way   ▽ 1,100 feet of elevation gain

Pioneer Ridge Loop (p. 96)
Designed with mountain bikers in mind, this singletrack loop offers easy-to-climb trails in northern Pocatello.
▽ 8.2-mile loop   ▽ 1,250 feet of elevation gain

Valve House Loop (pp. 256, 263, and 260)
(Valve House Trail > Wendigo Trail > South Fork Mink Creek Road > South Fork Mink Creek Trail)
A mix of singletrack and doubletrack trails on the largely forested slopes of Scout Mountain. South Fork Mink Creek Trail has a couple very steep hills, so newer riders may prefer to take South Fork Mink Creek Road back to the Valve House Trailhead instead.
▽ 10.2-mile loop   ▽ 1,900 feet of elevation gain

Hard Routes

Over the Top Loop (p. 166)
(Cusick Creek Road > Serengeti > Over the Top > Sullivan's > Serengeti > Cusick Creek Road)

A tough climb that has some of the best views in the City Creek area. The trail can be narrow and rocky in places, especially near the top of the route. It is usually ridden clockwise.

▽ 7.2-mile loop ▽ 1,140 feet of elevation gain

Corral Creek Loop (pp. 205 and 202)
(Crystal Summit Road > Corral Creek > Mink Creek Road)

A fast and forested singletrack with a great view of Scout Mountain. Bikers often ride up and down Corral Creek as an out-and-back ride, though I recommend parking at the Corral Creek Trailhead, riding up Mink Creek Road, and then using Crystal Summit Road to access the top of Corral Creek for a more enjoyable climb.

▽ 6.6-mile loop ▽ 1,090 feet of elevation gain

Slate Mountain Loop (pp. 190, 198, 214, and 182)
(West Fork Gibson Jack > Slate Mountain Trail > Slate Mountain - West Fork Connector > West Fork Mink Creek > Elk Meadows > Gibson Jack Trail)

A lengthy loop that travels through a variety of classic Pocatello trails. The views from high on the Slate Mountain Trail make the incline worth it. I recommend using the Slate Mountain - West Fork Connector to dodge the steep southeastern stretch of Slate Mountain Trail and loop back toward the trailhead.

▽ 13.9-mile loop ▽ 2,550 feet of elevation gain

Cave Trail (p. 101)
An interweaving mix of technical community made trails not far from the city center. This short and dusty set of trails is best for experienced riders who like a bit of a thrill.

▽ 1 mile out-and-back ▽ 190 feet of elevation gain

Hikers on Bell Marsh - Walker - Goodenough Trail.

Introduction

Located between two mountain ranges and bordered by thousands of acres of national forest, Pocatello provides easy access to hundreds of miles of varied trails perfect for any outdoor enthusiast. From evergreen covered peaks high above grassy meadows, to crumbling basalt cliffs amidst a sea of sagebrush, the area's environment is wonderfully dynamic and provides enjoyable trails for all types of hikers. As I grew up enjoying the many outdoor opportunities Pocatello provides, the city and the surrounding wilderness hold a special place in my heart. The goal of this book is to highlight these trail systems so that anyone can enjoy and connect with the natural beauty that Pocatello and Southeast Idaho have to offer.

To ensure the data in this book was accurate, I spent many hours exploring the trails to gather GPS coordinates, simplify directions, and capture photos. As the book is designed for a variety of trail users, I made sure to travel the trails using various methods such as hiking, biking, trail running, and cross-country skiing. Some of the trails were familiar to me, while others were new discoveries. It was an exhausting but rewarding experience to navigate the network of trails in the area. Much of my difficulty in navigating these trails was due to the disjointed nature of the available information. Some websites, apps, and maps are excellent for one trail system, but lacking for another. I hope that the content of this book will simplify the process and assist you in your own adventures in and around Pocatello.

Choosing which trails to feature in the book was challenging due to the large number of trails in the area. In the end, I selected trails based on specific criteria. The trailheads had to be accessible by standard passenger vehicles, with only a few exceptions. Moreover, the trails had to be officially recognized. This unfortunately eliminates several popular community-made trails, particularly in the City Creek and Elk Meadows areas. Trails that traverse private property were evaluated on a case-by-case basis. Lastly, the trails had to be navigable. Several trails can be found on official maps; however, they have disappeared through lack of use. In general, I selected trails that are easy to access, official, and enjoyable.

Brief Human History of the Area

Hundreds of years before Manifest Destiny changed the landscape of the American West, the Shoshone and Bannock Native American Tribes called the Pocatello region home. These tribes shared a similar language and traveled stretches of Idaho, Utah, Montana, Wyoming, and into Canada, hunting wild game, fishing the many rivers and streams, and gathering native plants and roots. Petroglyphs created by the Shoshone-Bannock Tribes can still be found etched into the basalt cliffs and boulders around Pocatello. For those interested in the history of the tribes, the Shoshone-Bannock Tribal Museum in Fort Hall, Idaho, is well worth the visit.

Fur trappers and explorers began venturing into the region in the 1800s, signifying the start of the United States' western expansion. Fort Hall, an important trading post about 30 miles north of Pocatello near the Snake River, was built in 1834. In the 1840s, the fort became an essential stop for immigrants resupplying on the Oregon and California Trails. Although the original fort no longer exists, the Fort Hall Replica, located in Pocatello's Upper Ross Park near the Bannock County Historical Museum, offers history buffs a glimpse into Pocatello's pioneer past.

Thousands of pioneers walked along these two trails as they passed through the area. Most had no intention of settling in Idaho and continued on their way farther west. It was not until the 1860s gold rush that pioneers began settling in what was then known as the "Idaho Territory." The arrival of the settlers also brought about the necessity for a railway in the region. Pocatello's unique position on the Snake River Plain's eastern edge and at the Portneuf Canyon's opening proved to be a prime route for a railway. The location was optimal for maneuvering a railway from Wyoming through the Rocky Mountains into the Northwest, hence earning the city nicknames, "The Gate City" or "The Gateway to the Northwest."

During the expansion in 1868, the Fort Hall Indian Reservation was established, which at the time included the current-day location of Pocatello. The inception of the Reservation goes back to the 1850s when disputes between Native Americans and settlers were escalating in this region. Shoshone Chief Pocatello (also known in Shoshoni as Tonaioza or "Buffalo Robe"), to protect historically Native lands, came into conflict with settlers and eventually the U.S. Army. The fighting ended with the Fort Bridger Treaty of 1868, which saw Chief Pocatello lead his people to the newly established Fort Hall Indian Reservation.

In 1878, the Utah & Northern Railway was granted permission to build a railroad across the Reservation, cementing the area as a transportation hub. Initially known as "Pocatello Junction," this early settlement of tents and boxcars was confined to a narrow 40-acre area along the railroad. As the railway brought more people into the area, conflict over land borders began between the workers and the Reservation, with workers frequently trespassing on Reservation lands. In 1887, the Reservation agreed to sell a townsite to the United States government. This resulted in 1,840 acres becoming available for settlement. Finally, in 1889, with a population of about 3,000 people, the city of Pocatello was founded. A year later, in 1890, Idaho became the 43rd state.

Pocatello has progressed well beyond being a simple rail camp. Today, Pocatello has grown to a population of almost 60,000 people, and is home to Idaho State University. The railroad is still a prominent landmark that runs through the heart of the city, though it is no longer the sole driver of the local economy. With beautiful hiking trails, biking paths, rock climbing, and river access available within 10 minutes of the city center, it is no wonder why people choose to call Pocatello home.

The Portneuf Gap from BLM T352.

Bonneville Flood

As you explore Pocatello's trails, you will come across the dark brown cliffs that run alongside the Portneuf River in the southern part of the city. A hot spot for local rock climbers, these smooth basalt flows in the Portneuf Valley originate from an eruption that occurred in the Gem Valley about 600,000 years ago. Alongside these rock walls, you will often find boulders up to 12 feet across, such as those in Ross Park. Both the smoothness of the basalt cliffs and the placement of these large "Bonneville Boulders" can be traced back to the Bonneville Flood.

Lake Bonneville was a massive pluvial lake that covered much of Utah and parts of Nevada and Idaho during the Pleistocene period (otherwise known as the Ice Age). About 17,400 years ago, the lake broke through a natural dam at Red Rock Pass near Downey, Idaho. This resulted in a catastrophic flood that lasted for over a year. The outflow of water poured north following the current-day path of the Portneuf River, eventually slamming into a narrow canyon between Inkom and Pocatello at over 300 feet in height and traveling at 60 miles per hour. This canyon, now known as the Portneuf Gap, was stripped of basalt and other material as the floodwaters continued into Pocatello. The churning and fast-moving water acted as a rock tumbler, smoothing over any exposed basalt and depositing boulders in the Portneuf Valley as the flood traveled into the Snake River Plain.

To learn more about Pocatello's geologic past, I recommend visiting the Idaho State University Museum of Natural History.

Mountain Ranges

Pocatello is nestled in the Portneuf Valley between two mountain ranges, the Bannock Range on the west, and the Portneuf Range on the east. The Portneuf Range has a sub-range that runs alongside Pocatello on the east which is called the Pocatello Range. For most of the trails in this book, an easy way to determine which range you are in is by checking which side of the railroad tracks you are on. If you are west of the railroad, you will be in the Bannock Range. If you are on the east side, you will be in the Portneuf Range. If you are on the east side and alongside Pocatello, you are in the Pocatello Range.

Bannock Range

Located on the west side of Pocatello, the Bannock Range runs north to south, spanning 65 miles and starting just below American Falls and ending in northeast Utah near the Bear River. These forested peaks contain many of Pocatello's most popular trail systems, including City Creek, Gibson Jack, and West Fork Mink Creek. The range is home to the scenic Scout Mountain, one of the area's most popular climbs and recreation areas. The range is named after the indigenous Bannock Native American tribe.

Summits in the Bannock Range featured in this book are listed below.

Mountain Name	Elevation	Page
Old Tom Mountain	8,733 feet	382
Scout Mountain	8,710 feet	374
Indian Mountain	7,298 feet	367
Rock Knoll	7,268 feet	353
Kinport Peak	7,222 feet	347
Slate Mountain	6,980 feet	361
Gibson Mountain	6,775 feet	357
Howard Mountain	5,841 feet	336

Portneuf Range

Named after the Portneuf River that flows below the range's rounded summits, the Portneuf Range runs about 60 miles north to south, from Blackfoot to Preston. The stretch of peaks in this range near Inkom are the highest in the book, providing beautiful views of Southeast Idaho. Bonneville Peak, the highest summit in this range, is home to the Pebble Creek Ski Area. The word "Portneuf" is derived from "Port Neuf," which is French for "New Port."

Summits in the Portneuf Range featured in this book are listed below.

Mountain Name	Elevation	Page
Bonneville Peak	9,271 feet	388
Snow Peak	9,132 feet	392
Haystack Mountain	9,033 feet	399

Pocatello Range

A small offshoot of the Portneuf Range, the Pocatello Range runs from north to south directly east of Pocatello, covering about 22 miles. This subrange starts just north of Chubbuck and ends south of Pocatello at the Inkom Gap. This range's close proximity to the city provides easy access to many well-marked trailheads, such as those in the Chinese Peak-Blackrock Canyon Trail System. Chinese Peak, the range's highpoint, dominates the skyline of Pocatello, and is easily accessible from the city center. Those looking to climb the peaks north of Chinese Peak will be disappointed to learn private property restricts access to these Bureau of Land Management summits. The range is named for the city it runs alongside, which itself is named after Chief Pocatello, a 19th-century Shoshone leader.

Summits in the Pocatello Range featured in this book are listed below.

Mountain Name	Elevation	Page
Chinese Peak	6,791 feet	340

The Bannock Range from BLM 319.

Caribou-Targhee National Forest

Many of the trails featured in this book are located in the Caribou-Targhee National Forest, which surrounds much of Pocatello. The Caribou-Targhee National Forest contains over three million acres of protected forest land in Idaho, Wyoming, and Utah, including areas adjacent to Yellowstone National Park and Grand Teton National Park. Although originally established as separate forests in 1891, the Caribou and Targhee National Forests now operate as one. The forest is administered by the U.S. Forest Service.

In the Bannock Range southwest of Pocatello, the Caribou-Targhee National Forest protects over 60,000 acres of land, while in the Portneuf Range east of Inkom, over 70,000 acres are protected. The trails found in these forests are some of the most scenic in the area, and make one appreciate that they were set aside for conservation and recreation.

City Creek Management Area (CCMA)

The City Creek Management Area is a tract of land owned by the City of Pocatello to the west of historic downtown Pocatello, serving as a ground and surface water protection area. The initial 1,915 acres were purchased from the Federal Government by the City of Pocatello in 1920. However, subsequent purchases, trades, and donations from the Federal Government, U.S. Forest Service, and private landowners have increased that number to the 3,000 acres managed today.

As the name suggests, the CCMA is home to the City Creek Trail System. It is also the location of both the perennial City Creek and the seasonal Cusick Creek. Both streams enter the Portneuf River shortly after passing under South Grant Avenue. The CCMA exists to protect this valuable watershed and the collection of trails contained within it.

As you access the many trails in this area, be sure to respect the environment and other trail users. In particular, be aware that preventing trail erosion and maintaining water quality are essential to the city. Avoid going off-trail on unofficial trails when traveling in the City Creek Trail System. Also, remember to pick up any human or pet waste to help keep this ecosystem healthy.

Portneuf Wildlife Management Area

Located between Inkom and McCammon, the Portneuf Wildlife Management Area (WMA) provides a critical winter range for mule deer and a habitat for sharp-tailed grouse. The WMA was established in 1970 by the Idaho Department of Fish and Game and encompasses 3,950 acres of sagebrush steppe and aspen forests between the Portneuf River and Haystack Mountain. When hiking in the WMA, it is important to keep in mind how vital these protected spaces are for the ecosystem. The area is utilized by hunters during hunting season, so be alert when accessing the trails contained within it. Also, be aware that gathering antler sheds in the WMA is not allowed year round, so make sure to obey any posted signage.

Cattle on the Trails

In 1964, the 88th Congress passed and President Lyndon B. Johnson signed the Wilderness Act into law. The purpose of the act was to "To establish a National Wilderness Preservation System for the permanent good of the whole people, and for other purposes." This monumental act of conservation resulted in over 111 million acres of pristine wilderness becoming governmentally protected land and has been a benefit for both the United States and all who visit these natural areas.

As you explore these scenic and protected natural areas, you may wonder why cattle are allowed in them. The answer lies within the Wilderness Act. The act stipulates "the grazing of livestock, where established prior to the effective date of this Act, shall be permitted to continue subject to such reasonable regulations as are deemed necessary by the Secretary of Agriculture." In short, cattle are allowed on the trails in these areas.

The presence of cattle on the trails may not be ideal for those looking to experience untrampled nature, but it is the reality of the situation when hiking in national forests. When entering areas with cattle, be respectful of the animals. Make sure to always leave gates as you find them unless posted signage says otherwise.

Regions and Book Organization

This book is a comprehensive guide to the trails in the Pocatello area, classified according to their proximity to the city center. For easy reference, the trails are grouped into five distinct regions, starting with the urban hikes located in the heart of Pocatello and progressively expanding outwards. Within each region, the trails are arranged by their proximity to one another, generally in a north-to-south fashion. The five regions are as follows:

1. **Portneuf Greenway and Urban Trails**: Trails 1 - 14

2. **Pocatello Range**: Trails 15 - 28

3. **Bannock Range (North)**: Trails 29 - 48

4. **Bannock Range (South)**: Trails 49 - 66

5. **Portneuf Range**: Trails 67 - 78

Organizing the book was challenging, given the many outdoor recreation options available in the area. Most of this book focuses on individual trails designed primarily for hiking and mountain biking. However, additional sections were necessary to ensure the content was clear and organized. Thus, I included three additional sections to provide a comprehensive guide to the outdoor recreation options available in the Pocatello area. These sections are:

6. **Mountains**: This section is designed for those looking to summit the many peaks in the Pocatello area. It provides detailed information and guidance for those seeking to climb to the tops of the area's peaks.

7. **City Creek and Pioneer Ridge Trail Overviews**: The City Creek Trail System and the Pioneer Ridge Trail System are featured in the book's main section. However, both trail systems offer many mountain biking trails that deserve a stand-alone section to showcase all of the different trails within them. This section of the book is primarily intended for mountain bikers, but hikers and trail runners may also find the information useful.

8. **Cross-Country Skiing**: This section highlights the excellent cross-country skiing and snowshoeing options available in the Caribou-Targhee National Forest, such as the East Mink Creek Nordic Center and the Idaho Park N' Ski program.

Using This Book

Hiking a new trail can feel daunting. To make the experience less intimidating, the hikes in this book include the following details:

Overview: A brief description of the route along with any interesting information that might be relevant to trail users.

Quick Facts: Useful attributes to help prepare for your outing (listed below).

Getting There: The driving directions for reaching the trailhead. The majority of trailheads can be accessed by passenger vehicles, though there are a few trails, particularly in the Elk Meadows and Caddy Canyon areas, where high clearance may be required.

The Hike: The detailed route description to help navigate the trail. Typically includes a mix of trail conditions, directions, and scenery.

Keep Going: Several trails start from within existing trails. In such cases, the Keep Going category comes in handy. This section helps to identify additional trails that are not commonly used, but are accessible from the described route. It also suggests fun loop variants that can be added to the featured trail.

Notes: Information about the area's history and useful tips for the trails will appear in colored boxes throughout the book.

Map and Elevation Profile: Visual aids to help showcase the route.

Quick Facts include:

▶ **Distance:** The length of the trail in miles, dependent on whether the route is a loop, one-way, out-and-back, or lollipop loop (out-and-back with a loop on one end). The mileage estimates were gathered using a handheld Global Positioning System (GPS) unit in tandem with a wrist-based GPS unit. You will likely see variations when using your own device, though the distances should be close.

▶ **Elevation Gain:** The total elevation gained on the route.

▶ **Difficulty:** The overall difficulty of the route, depending on activity type. For more information on the calculation of the difficulty rating, refer to the Difficulty Ratings section on page 29.

- ▶ **Hiking Time:** The estimated time to fully complete the trail on foot for a moderately fit hiker.
- ▶ **Nearest Town:** The location of the nearest town.
- ▶ **Trail Surface:** The type of material that makes up the trail, such as pavement or dirt.
- ▶ **Wheelchair Access:** Indicates whether the trail and trailhead are accessible for wheelchairs.
- ▶ **Dog-Friendly:** Applicable leash laws for the trail.
- ▶ **Amenities:** The availability of restrooms, water, etc.
- ▶ **Contact:** Phone number or website of the appropriate landowners.
- ▶ **Trailhead GPS Coordinates:** The GPS coordinates for locating the trailhead.
- ▶ **Trail User Icons:** Icons that depict the types of users allowed on the trail.

🚶	**Foot Traffic**	🚲 ALL	**All eBikes**
🐎	**Horses**	🏍 <24"	**Vehicles 24" or Less in Width**
🚲	**Mountain Bikes**	🏍 <50"	**Vehicles 50" or Less in Width**
🚲 Class 1	**Class 1 eBikes**	🏍 ALL	**All Vehicles**

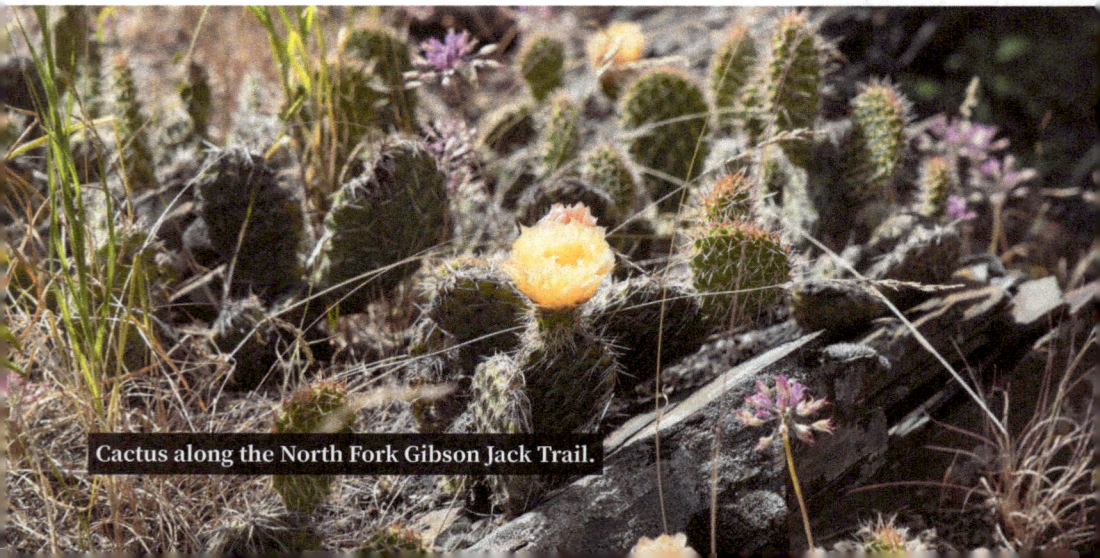

Cactus along the North Fork Gibson Jack Trail.

Difficulty Ratings

As the book has different sections dedicated to hiking, mountain biking, cross-country skiing, and mountain climbing, I chose to include several systems for rating the difficulty of the various trails.

Hiking

The Shenandoah's Hiking Difficulty scale is the equation that the National Park Service often uses to determine trail difficulty. I used this scale to rate the routes in this book. The equation uses a numeric rating to assign the difficulty of a hike. The numerical rating is derived from the following equation:

The Square Root of (Elevation Gain x 2 x distance (in miles))

The Shenandoah Hiking Difficulty ratings are classified by the National Park Service as follows:

► **< 50 (Easiest):** A hike that is generally suitable for anyone who enjoys walking. Mostly level or with a slight incline. Generally less than three miles.

► **50 - 100 (Moderate):** A moderate hike is generally suitable for novice hikers who want a bit of a challenge. The terrain will involve a moderate incline and may have some steeper sections. Generally three to five miles.

► **100 - 150 (Moderately strenuous):** Moderately strenuous hikes will generally be challenging for an unconditioned person. The terrain will involve a steady and often steep incline. Generally five to eight miles.

► **150 - 200 (Strenuous):** Strenuous hikes will challenge most hikers. The hike will generally be longer and steeper, but may be deemed "Strenuous" because of the elevation gain. Generally seven to ten miles.

► **> 200 (Very strenuous):** Only well-conditioned and well-prepared hikers should attempt very strenuous hikes. The hike will generally be long and steep, and may include rock scrambling, stream crossings, and other challenging terrain. Generally eight or more miles.

Mountain Biking

For the City Creek and Pioneer Ridge Trail Overviews, I used the International Mountain Bicycling Association (IMBA) Trail Difficulty Rating System. Before getting too hung up on the ratings, it is important to remember that the ratings are relative to the overall difficulty of the trail system they are contained in. A black diamond in one trail system is not the same as a black diamond in another. With that in mind, the rating system is as follows:

▶ **Green Circle (Easy):** Trails suitable for beginners, featuring wide paths, gentle slopes, minimal obstacles, and few technical challenges.

▶ **Blue Square (Intermediate):** Trails appropriate for riders with some experience, offering moderate challenges such as steeper climbs and descents, narrow sections, and occasional obstacles like roots and rocks.

▶ **Black Diamond (Advanced):** Trails designed for experienced riders, featuring steep gradients, technical sections, significant obstacles like large rocks, roots, drops, and narrow passages. These trails may also include optional advanced features or jumps.

Cross-Country Skiing

Cross-country ski trails are rated similarly to the mountain bike trails, using a three-tier color-based system relative to the trail system they are a part of. Given that a groomed ski trail has fewer obstacles than a rocky bike trail, the ratings are slightly less scientific. The steepest part of a route and average grade generally determines the difficulty. The ratings are as follows:

▶ **Green (Easy):** These are runs with minimal elevation changes, making them suitable for beginners or those who prefer a relaxed skiing experience.

▶ **Blue (Intermediate):** These runs may have moderate hills and are usually manageable for skiers who are comfortable on their skis.

▶ **Black (Advanced):** These runs have extended moderate to steep hills and are best suited for experienced skiers.

Mountain Climbing

The hikes featured in the Mountains section of the book include two ratings. The first is Shenandoah's Hiking Difficulty rating, which shows the relative effort for the route. The second is the Yosemite Decimal System (YDS) rating. The YDS is used to rate the difficulty of hikes, climbs, and scrambles in mountainous terrain on a 5-class rating system. While the routes to the summits in this book do not exceed the Class 2 rating, all five classes are listed below:

▶ **Class 1:** A maintained hiking trail. Little to no exposure.

▶ **Class 2:** A rough hiking trail with some exposure that may require use of hands for balancing, such as crossing a large field of boulders. Route finding may be required.

▶ **Class 3:** Steep scrambling with moderate exposure that requires the use of handholds to progress. Falls could lead to serious injury or death.

▶ **Class 4:** Steep scrambling and minor rock climbing with severe exposure. Falls may be fatal. Ropes are often used during the hike.

▶ **Class 5:** Technical rock climbing. Ropes and anchors are needed to ascend safely. Only experienced rock climbers should attempt these routes.

What To Bring

Rather than listing specific items to bring, the current mindset in the outdoor community is to instead suggest a list of ten item categories that are recommended for everyone planning on spending time in the wilderness.

1. **Hydration** - Water and/or water filtration. When in doubt, bring more water than you plan on needing.

2. **Nutrition** - Granola bars, fruit snacks, anything to keep energy levels high. This is especially important when hiking with kids.

3. **Insulation** - Be prepared for a variety of weather conditions. Getting caught in a sudden downpour without a rain jacket is a quick way to learn the importance of this category.

4. **Illumination** - A headlamp or flashlight. Racing the setting sun to the bottom of a trailhead without a flashlight is stressful. Simply having a charged cell phone with a flashlight app can make a world of difference.

5. **First Aid** - A general-purpose first aid kit to help you or others in emergencies.

6. **Sun Protection** - Due to its high desert location, many of the trails in Pocatello offer very little natural sun protection along the route. This is especially true for trails in the Blackrock Canyon area, as well as for summit hikes. At a minimum, bring and apply SPF-30 or higher sunscreen. I would also recommend sunproof layers, sunglasses, hats, and lip balm.

7. **Fire Starters** - Waterproof matches or weatherproof fire starters.

8. **Emergency Shelter** - Something to protect you from the elements in an emergency. Emergency blankets are great, but even a large rain poncho can help.

9. **Repair Kit** - Duct tape, multitool, knife, extra pack buckles, etc. For mountain bikers, extra tubes, patch kits, and cycling multitools are recommended.

10. **Navigation** - A map, compass, or GPS. If you can justify the extra weight, this book is a perfect resource to bring with you on the trails.

> One item that always joins me on the trails is a canister of bear spray (or if in-town, a small runner's pepper spray). The peace of mind it offers knowing I can defend myself against any mammal is worth the extra weight.

Trail Safety

Although hiking is generally safe, going into the wilderness carries some degree of risk. To stay safe, it is essential to be prepared for a variety of situations that could arise. While the categories covered below are important, a non-negotiable is to always tell someone where you are going and when you are expected to return.

Sun Exposure

Going out for a hike on a sunny day is a wonderful way to spend your leisure time. However, it is necessary to protect yourself from the harmful effects of prolonged exposure to the sun. Even on a cloudy day, the sun's ultraviolet (UV) rays can penetrate clouds and harm your skin. The trails in this book that lead to mountain summits in particular put you at a greater risk for sun damage. Here are some useful items that can help prevent sun damage:

▶ Sunscreen rated SPF-30 or higher

▶ Lightweight, long-sleeved clothes made of UV-blocking materials

▶ SPF lip balm

▶ A hat or headscarf

▶ Sunglasses with UV-blocking lenses

Hydration

Keeping hydrated is essential to staying active while outdoors. A good rule of thumb is to drink at least one quart (one liter) of water an hour while hiking. In addition to water, electrolyte beverages or electrolyte packets are a great way to prevent dehydration. If you fail to replace the water lost through sweat, it can lead to heat exhaustion.

▶ Heat Exhaustion: When the body overheats and cannot cool down, typically through excessive sweating. Symptoms include:

▽ Heavy sweating   ▽ Clammy skin

▽ Dizziness   ▽ Nausea and vomiting

▽ Fatigue   ▽ Weak pulse

Temperature and Weather

This book features trails that pass through various landscapes, including open mountain ridges, forested creek ravines, dry sage fields, and paved river walks. Knowing the terrain on which you will be traveling allows you to bring the right gear and clothing. The season and time of day also have a significant impact on the trail conditions. Spring and fall hikes can have harsher temperature swings than summer hikes. When hiking with dogs, it is important to be aware of surface types as they have different thermal storage. For example, unshaded blacktops during the heat of a summer day may be too hot for dogs' paws.

Checking the weather forecast before heading out is another necessary step when preparing for a hike. Is a significant wind chill expected? Will a rain or snowstorm sneak up on you? If it rained earlier, will the trail be too muddy? Mountain tops, in particular, are more exposed to changing weather patterns and temperatures. You must bring the correct clothing to avoid dangerous situations.

▶ Hypothermia: When your body loses heat faster than it can produce it, you are at risk for hypothermia. Symptoms include:

▽ Shivering   ▽ Memory loss

▽ Exhaustion   ▽ Slurred speech

▽ Confusion   ▽ Drowsiness

▽ Fumbling hands

▶ Frostbite: Damage to the skin and underlying tissue due to exposure to cold and freezing. Symptoms include:

▽ Numbness

▽ A white or grayish-yellow skin area

▽ Skin that feels unusually firm or waxy

Lightning

When overcast skies transform into lightning storms, it is best to stay inside and avoid being outdoors. If a storm develops while you are out on the trails, quickly get below the tree line. If you have a choice between a tall stand of trees or a low stand, head for the low stand. Avoid open meadows or isolated trees. If caught in a storm, get low and squat on the balls of your feet. If you are hiking with others, spread out by at least 15 feet from one another to prevent a group strike. Hikers looking to summit mountains need to be extra vigilant about the possibility of developing thunderstorms.

Wildlife

Southeast Idaho's diverse high desert landscape provides a natural habitat for a wide variety of wildlife. The trails in this book pass through land home to many animals, such as mule deer, bobcats, coyotes, yellow-bellied marmots, red-tailed hawks, great horned owls, and many more. Spotting a wild animal during a hike can be a thrilling experience, but it is important to remember that these creatures are wild and must be treated with respect. In rare cases, you might encounter a species that can be dangerous to humans. Knowing how to handle such situations is crucial for your safety, particularly when you're miles away from civilization.

▶ **Black Bears:** Black bears are uncommon on Pocatello's trails, though they are known to visit the area occasionally. One of my favorite Pocatello anecdotes is that in 2018, a black bear broke into the city's zoo! Rare as these animals might be in this area, it is possible to see them. In most cases, black bears will flee from any meetings with a human. If you encounter one who does not flee, remain calm and slowly back away while making lots of noise. If attacked, fight back. The advice for playing dead does not apply to black bear encounters.

▶ **Mountain Lions:** The elusive mountain lion, commonly called a cougar, is no stranger to the forested hills and rocky cliffs found in Southeast Idaho. These solitary hunters avoid humans when possible and usually run off when encounters occur. While the odds of being attacked by one are low, it never hurts to take precautions when in mountain lion country. Avoid using the trails after dusk and before dawn when cougars are most active. Keep pets and small children under control and close by at all times. If you come across a cougar, don't run, as it can trigger its instinct to chase. This instinct is why mountain bikers are more likely to be targeted and why they should take extra precaution. Maintain eye contact and make yourself look as large and threatening as possible. Never turn your back on a mountain lion. If the cat does decide to attack, fight back with everything you have.

▶ **Moose:** Around Pocatello, the animal I am most nervous about encountering is a moose, particularly in the Gibson Jack, West Fork Mink Creek, and Scout Mountain areas. These giant herbivores may seem docile, but they can be aggressive if they feel threatened. If you encounter one, give it plenty of space. Keep dogs on leashes when hiking in moose territory. Moose perceive dogs as a threat and they can respond aggressively. If a moose charges, quickly get behind cover, such as a tree or large rock.

Be aware that moose are not found exclusively in low wetlands. I was recently surprised to see a moose on the dry, grassy summit of Chinese Peak!

▶ **Rattlesnakes:** Two types of rattlesnakes live in Idaho: the prairie rattlesnake and the western rattlesnake. Of the two, the western rattlesnake is more common. You are most likely to encounter them on the trails between April and October. If you encounter a rattlesnake, move away and give it plenty of space. They avoid humans and only bite when threatened.

While the adrenaline-inducing sound of the rattle is appreciated by all who almost step on these serpents, be aware that not every rattlesnake will rattle when threatened. I have had several close calls with rattlesnakes where they never made a sound. If you have a dog, it's especially important to be careful when letting them run off-leash.

▶ **Ticks:** These pesky parasites can spread diseases and are found in the grassy and wooded areas that the trails in this book pass through. When you are on wide trails that are well maintained, such as any of the Greenway trails, you are unlikely to encounter these arachnids. Be cautious on more rugged and narrow paths, particularly those that take you through sagebrush. Be sure to check for ticks after finishing a hike.

Trail Etiquette

Sharing the trails is a key component of enjoying time outdoors. Regardless whether one is hiking, biking, or riding a motorized vehicle, treating others with respect should be a core tenet of anyone heading out into nature. Adhering to the following set of rules ensures a positive experience for all who utilize these trail systems:

▶ Know when to yield the trail. Motorized vehicles yield to foot traffic, bikers, and equestrians. Bikers yield to foot traffic and equestrians. Foot traffic yields to equestrians. When encountering downhill traffic of the same user type, the user moving uphill has the right of way. While hikers generally have the right of way when encountering mountain bikers, it often makes sense for hikers to yield to allow bikers to maintain momentum. Hikers, use your best judgment and step aside if it's easy to do so.

▶ Avoid blocking the trail. Check behind you periodically to allow faster trail users to pass you.

▶ Leave gates as you find them unless signage says otherwise.

▶ Stay on the trail when possible, and do not create new trails. When hikers or dogs go off-trail or cut between switchbacks, it can damage the environment and cause erosion. Similarly, do not use the trails when they are muddy.

▶ Do not disturb wildlife. These natural spaces are their home; we are just visitors.

▶ Maintain control of your dog and clean up after it.

▶ Do not throw rocks, especially when on hillsides or mountains.

eBikes

Electric bikes, also known as eBikes, are becoming increasingly popular among biking enthusiasts as they offer a convenient way to stay active and explore the outdoors. However, it is worth noting that landowners have their own set of rules regarding the use of eBikes on their trails. I have included the relevant eBike status for each trail in this book. It is essential to note that some of the trails in this book only allow specific classes of eBikes. The eBike class ratings are as follows:

▶ Class 1: eBikes that are pedal-assist only and do not use throttle. The maximum assisted speed is 20 mph.

▶ Class 2: eBikes that are throttle-assisted. Maximum assisted speed is 20 mph.

▶ Class 3: eBikes that are pedal-assist only that do not use throttle. The maximum assisted speed is 28 mph.

Hiking with Dogs

Dogs can be an excellent companion when exploring the outdoors. Man's best friend can turn an isolated trail into an enjoyable opportunity to connect with nature, providing physical and mental benefits to both the dog and the owner. When out on the trails with your furry best friend, it is essential to follow basic trail etiquette. Not every person or dog on the trail wants to interact with your canine. Do not let your dog chase wildlife. Make sure to have control of your dog at all times, including when off-leash. If an off-leash dog does not return to its owner when verbally called, it would not be considered to be under control. Dogs hiking off-trail cause erosion. Make sure to bring waste bags to collect your dog's waste, and equally important, be sure to dispose of the bags properly.

Keeping the dog safe is another essential factor to consider. In addition to the unknown temperament of other dogs on the trail, Pocatello's wildlife can be hazardous. Ticks are often found in the grasses and shrubs along these trails and can spread Lyme Disease. Coyotes and mountain lions are always a threat to dogs that stray too far from their owner. Rattlesnakes, too, can be a danger to unobservant dog owners. Be extra cautious when traveling on trails known for harboring moose, as the presence of dogs can aggravate them, causing the moose to attack both the dog and the owner.

Leash Laws

Trails have differing rules regarding dogs, depending on the landowner and applicable surface management agency. For instance, the City of Pocatello requires dogs to be leashed at all times, while the U. S. Forest Service and Bureau of Land Management are more lenient. The applicable leash laws for each trail are included in the Quicks Facts sections.

Environmental Impact of Dog Waste

A common claim is that it is acceptable to leave dog waste in the remote wilderness. People argue that other animals do it, and it is away from other humans and popular trails. The reality is that unlike wild animal feces, dog waste is harmful to the environment. Wild animals consume food from their home environment. Nutrients within the ecosystem are ingested by native animals, such as birds, squirrels, and deer, and are later returned to the ecosystem as waste. The ecosystem operates as a closed loop, with no gain or loss of nutrients.

On the other hand, dog food is rich in nutrients that are not part of the ecosystem being visited. This nutrient-rich food is excellent for the dog's health but bad for the environment. When pet waste is not picked up, it leads to excess nitrogen and phosphorus buildup, which can lead to unstable conditions in many ecosystems. This can damage the health of forests, soils, and waterways by causing toxic algae blooms in waterways or by creating conditions ideal for invasive plants to thrive.

Dog feces also contain harmful bacteria, such as E. coli, and parasites that are harmful to wildlife and humans. According to the Environmental Protection Agency, a single gram of pet waste contains an average of over 23 million fecal coliform bacteria. When left on the trail, these bacteria and parasites make their way into the creeks and streams, polluting the area.

For all these reasons, please always pick up after your dog, regardless of what trail you are on. All of this applies to humans as well, so make sure to properly dispose of or pack out your waste too.

Leave No Trace

With the ever-increasing amount of people heading out into the Idaho wilderness, we must strive to help preserve and maintain these environments for everyone to enjoy. Leave No Trace, a nonprofit organization whose core principles were built in collaboration with the U.S. Forest Service, National Park Service, and Bureau of Land Management, has developed seven principles to help minimize our outdoor impact. These principles are:

1. **Plan Ahead and Prepare**
   - ▶ Know the regulations and special concerns for the area you'll visit.
   - ▶ Prepare for extreme weather, hazards, and emergencies.
   - ▶ Schedule your trip to avoid times of high use.
   - ▶ Visit in small groups when possible. Consider splitting larger groups into smaller groups.
   - ▶ Repackage food to minimize waste.
   - ▶ Use a map and compass or GPS to eliminate the use of marking paint, rock cairns or flagging.

2. **Travel and Camp on Durable Surfaces**
   - ▶ Durable surfaces include maintained trails and designated campsites, rock, gravel, sand, dry grasses or snow.
   - ▶ Protect riparian areas by camping at least 200 feet from lakes and streams.
   - ▶ Good campsites are found, not made. Altering a site is not necessary.

▽ In popular areas:

- ◉ Concentrate use on existing trails and campsites.
- ◉ Walk single file in the middle of the trail, even when wet or muddy.
- ◉ Keep campsites small. Focus activity in areas where vegetation is absent.

▽ In pristine areas:

- ◉ Disperse use to prevent the creation of campsites and trails.
- ◉ Avoid places where impacts are just beginning.

3. Dispose of Waste Properly

▶ Pack it in, pack it out. Inspect your campsite, food preparation areas, and rest areas for trash or spilled foods. Pack out all trash, leftover food and litter.

▶ Utilize toilet facilities whenever possible. Otherwise, deposit solid human waste in catholes dug six to eight inches deep, at least 200 feet from water, camp and trails. Cover and disguise the cathole when finished.

▶ Pack out toilet paper and hygiene products.

▶ To wash yourself or your dishes, carry water 200 feet away from streams or lakes and use small amounts of biodegradable soap. Scatter strained dishwater.

4. Leave What You Find

▶ Preserve the past: examine, photograph, but do not touch cultural or historic structures and artifacts.

▶ Leave rocks, plants and other natural objects as you find them.

▶ Avoid introducing or transporting non-native species.

▶ Do not build structures, furniture, or dig trenches.

5. Minimize Campfire Impacts

▶ Campfires can cause lasting impacts to the environment. Use a lightweight stove for cooking and enjoy a candle lantern for light.

▶ Where fires are permitted, use established fire rings, fire pans, or mound fires.

- ▶ Keep fires small. Only use down and dead wood from the ground that can be broken by hand.
- ▶ Burn all wood and coals to ash, put out campfires completely, then scatter cool ashes.

6. **Respect Wildlife**

- ▶ Observe wildlife from a distance. Do not follow or approach them.
- ▶ Never feed animals. Feeding wildlife damages their health, alters natural behaviors (habituates them to humans), and exposes them to predators and other dangers.
- ▶ Protect wildlife and your food by storing rations and trash securely.
- ▶ Control pets at all times, or leave them at home.
- ▶ Avoid wildlife during sensitive times: mating, nesting, raising young, or winter.

7. **Be Considerate of Other Visitors**

- ▶ Respect other visitors and protect the quality of their experience.
- ▶ Be courteous. Yield to other users on the trail.
- ▶ Step to the downhill side of the trail when encountering pack stock.
- ▶ Take breaks and camp away from trails and other visitors.
- ▶ Let nature's sounds prevail. Avoid loud voices and noises.

©Leave No Trace: www.LNT.org

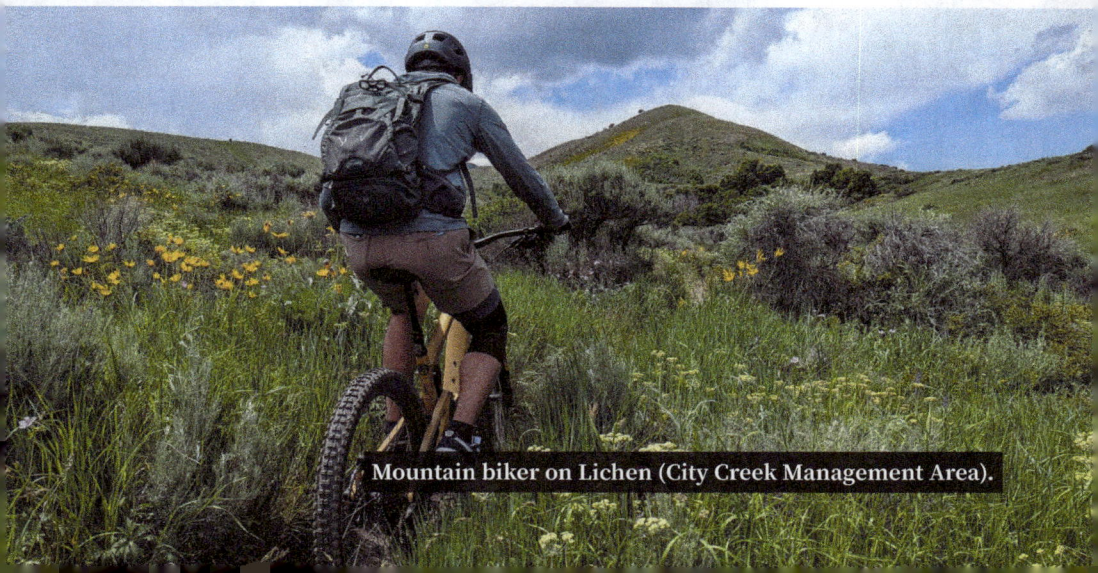

Mountain biker on Lichen (City Creek Management Area).

Portneuf Greenway and Urban Trails

Located in the heart of Pocatello, the Portneuf Greenway is a network of over 27 miles of scenic paved paths for walking, trail running, and biking throughout the city, providing easy access to the outdoors. These paths take you through a variety of environments, from Ross Park's basalt cliffs to the Portneuf River, and offer stunning views of the city and surrounding mountains. Alongside the river, the trails provide Portneuf River Access Points, giving kayakers and rafters areas to drop off and pick up their gear. These non-motorized trails are an excellent option for families looking for a fun activity, as some are located close to the city parks.

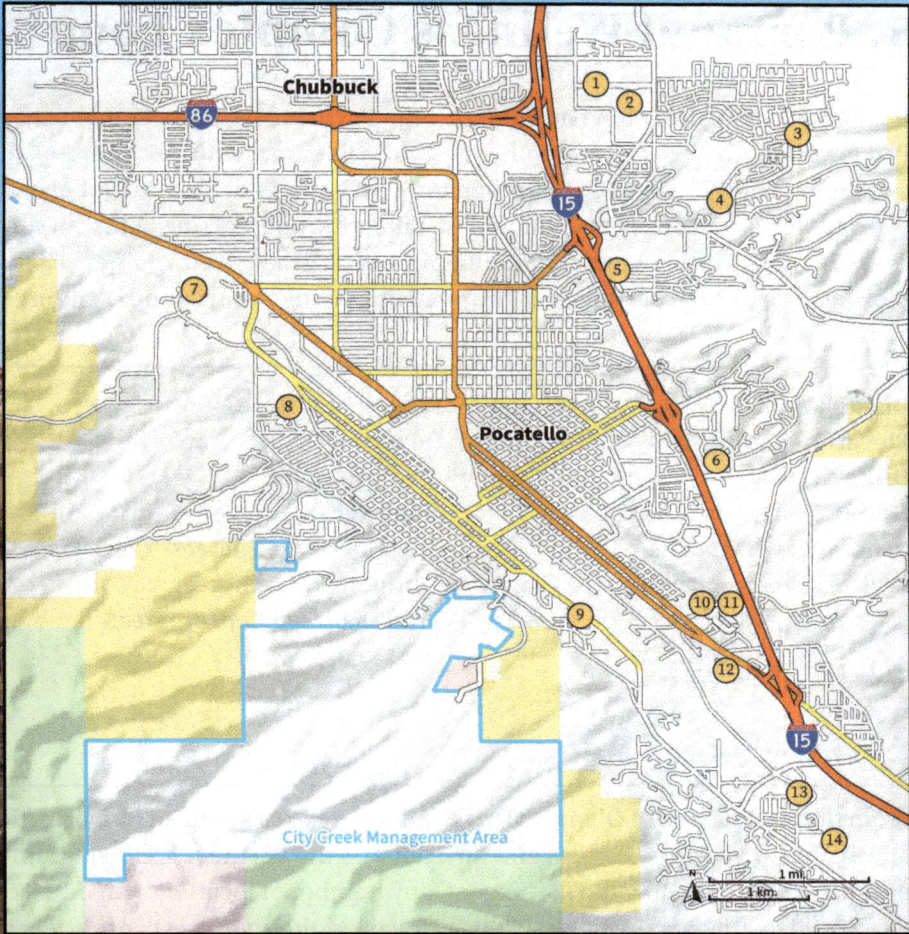

Map Legend

The pillars atop the Red Hill Ridge Trail.

1. Portneuf Wellness Complex Loop

If you are looking for a fun day outdoors, the Portneuf Wellness Complex has you covered. There's something for everyone to enjoy, with a 6.5-acre lake, swimming beach, fishing docks, seven multi-use sports fields, four volleyball courts, two basketball courts, a mountain bike park, and walking paths, all surrounding an 11,000-person outdoor amphitheater. The paved Wellness Complex Loop circles the perimeter of the complex, giving a preview of all the area has to offer.

Distance: 1.3-mile loop
Elevation Gain: 70 feet
Difficulty: Easy
Hiking Time: About 30 minutes
Nearest Town: Pocatello
Trail Surface: Pavement

Wheelchair Access: Yes
Dog-Friendly: Yes; must be on a leash at all times
Amenities: Restrooms and water are available at the Wellness Complex.
Contact: portneufgreenway.org
Trailhead GPS Coordinates: N42° 55.029' W112° 26.181'

Getting There

From the intersection of Olympus Drive and Pocatello Creek Road, drive north on Olympus Drive for 1.3 miles and turn left into the Portneuf Wellness Complex parking lot. Once in the parking lot, any number of locations can be used to start this path. For the book, I chose to start in the southwest corner near Fairground Drive.

The Hike

From the southwest corner of the loop, head north on the paved trail, which crosses by the rocky western edge of the pond shortly into the hike. Once the trail moves beyond the pond and the surrounding rocks, it crosses a small road and merges with the sidewalk. Continue on the sidewalk as it passes to the left of the pavilion. At about 0.2 miles, the sidewalk makes a right (east) turn and transitions back into the blacktop path.

This northern stretch of the trail passes the amphitheater and the mountain bike course. A large berm blocks the amphitheater from view. At about 0.7

A summer day at the Portneuf Wellness Complex.

miles, the path reaches the complex's northeast corner, where it turns to the right (south) and travels between the sports fields and Olympus Drive. (Just a few yards into this turn, there is an opening in the fence for the mountain bike path. If you want to connect to the Parrish Trail, which is just across Olympus Drive to the north, there is a crosswalk nearby.)

At 0.9 miles, the trail reaches the southeast corner of the loop, where it makes a right (west) turn toward the parking lot. The southern stretch of the path travels below the sports fields and volleyball courts until it reaches the pond at 1.2 miles. There are many side paths around the pond that are fun to explore. The route hugs the parking lot's sidewalk until it ends back in the southwest corner.

Keep Going

Located on the eastern side of Olympus Drive across from the northeast corner of the Wellness Complex, the **Parrish Trail** travels between typical Southeast Idaho desert landscapes on the north and residential backyards on the south. This eastbound paved path climbs uphill alongside power lines, gaining 170 feet over 0.8 miles. The trail ends when it reaches Hiskey Street.

It may come as a surprise to know that the pond within the Wellness Complex is named the Bannock Reservoir. In addition to swimming and paddleboarding, fishermen use the pond to catch rainbow trout.

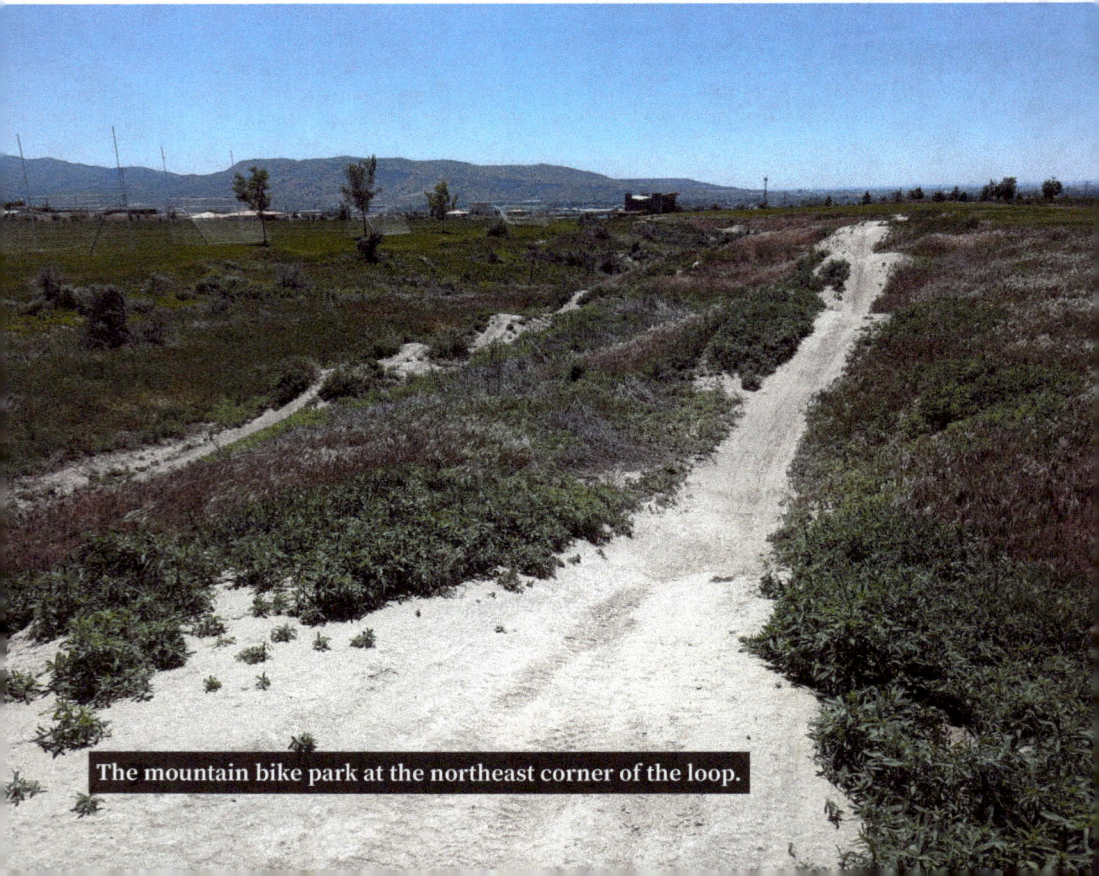

The mountain bike park at the northeast corner of the loop.

Portneuf Wellness Complex Loop

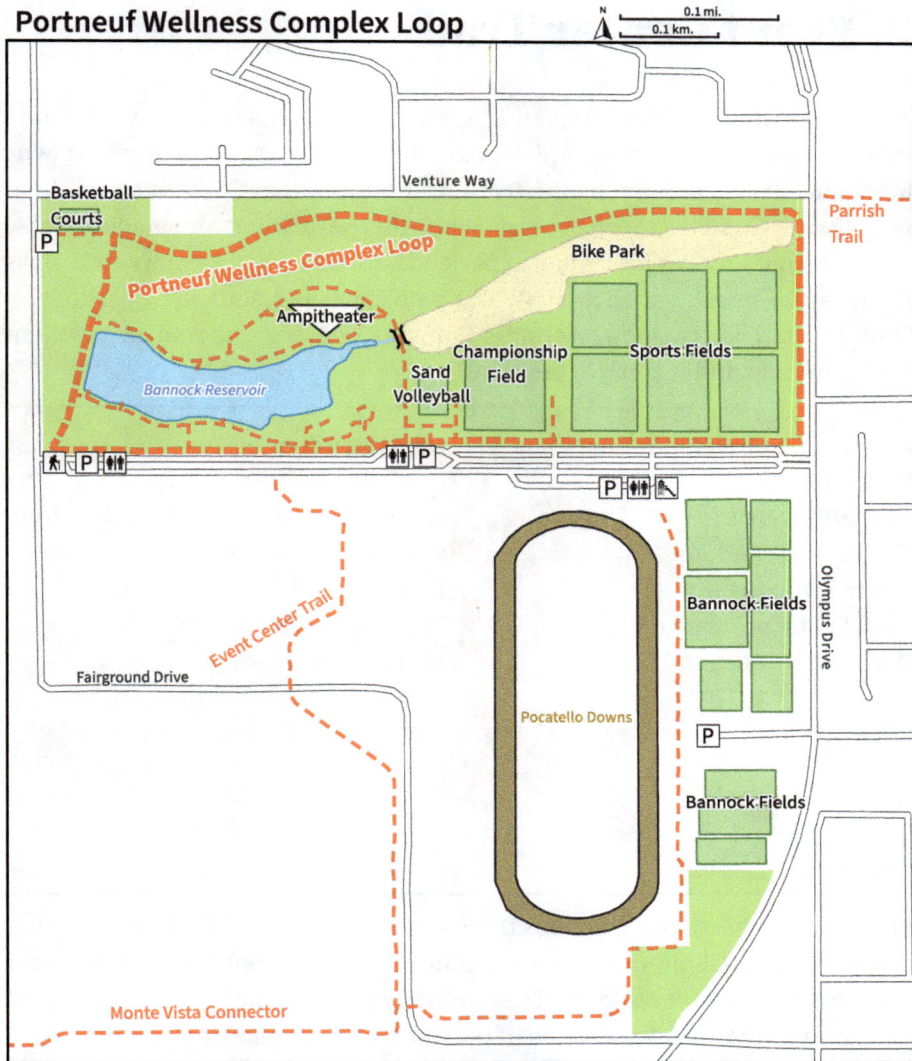

N
0.1 mi.
0.1 km.

Venture Way

Basketball
Courts
P

Parrish
Trail

Portneuf Wellness Complex Loop

Bike Park

Ampitheater

Championship
Field

Sports Fields

Bannock Reservoir

Sand
Volleyball

Event Center Trail

Fairground Drive

Bannock Fields

Olympus Drive

Pocatello Downs

P

Bannock Fields

Monte Vista Connector

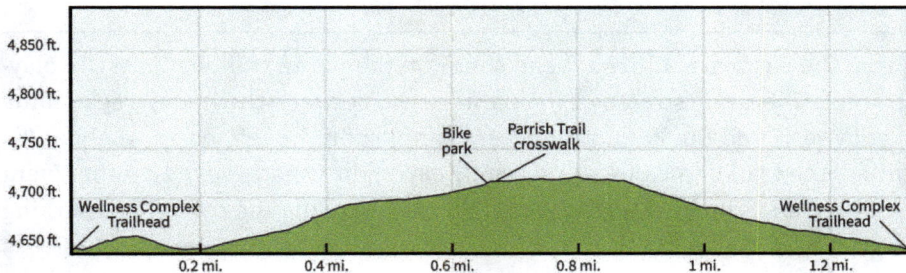

Bike
park

Parrish Trail
crosswalk

Wellness Complex
Trailhead

Wellness Complex
Trailhead

4,850 ft.
4,800 ft.
4,750 ft.
4,700 ft.
4,650 ft.

0.2 mi.   0.4 mi.   0.6 mi.   0.8 mi.   1 mi.   1.2 mi.

2. Event Center Trail

The Event Center Trail provides an alternate stretch of the Greenway to explore in the Portneuf Wellness Complex area. This path tours the Pocatello Downs horse race track, passing by the Bannock County Event Center and the Bannock Soccer Complex in the process. When there are no soccer games or horse races, the path makes for a quiet experience, though when event season picks up, it can be buzzing with activity. The path starts just across the parking lot from the popular Portneuf Wellness Complex, making this trail an excellent option to keep things fresh in the area.

Distance: 1.2 miles one-way
Elevation Gain: 50 feet
Difficulty: Easy
Hiking Time: About 30 minutes
Nearest Town: Pocatello
Trail Surface: Pavement
Wheelchair Access: Yes

Dog-Friendly: Yes; must be on a leash at all times
Amenities: Restrooms and water are available at the Wellness Complex.
Contact: portneufgreenway.org
Trailhead GPS Coordinates:
Eastern Trailhead
N42° 54.978' W112° 25.725'
Western Trailhead
N42° 55.008' W112° 26.015'

Getting There

From the intersection of Olympus Drive and Pocatello Creek Road in Pocatello, drive north on Olympus Drive for 1.3 miles and turn left into the Portneuf Wellness Complex parking lot. The eastern trailhead is behind a pavilion and playground to your left at the end of the last Bannock soccer field.

The Hike

From the eastern trailhead, head south on the paved trail just past the playground. This early stretch of the path travels between the horse track on the right (west) and the Bannock Soccer Complex on the left (east). At about 0.4 miles, the trail comes to a junction. Keep right (west) to stay on the Event Center Trail. From that turn, the trail skirts around the edge of a gravel parking lot.

At 0.6 miles, the path crosses to the west side of Fairground Drive. Once on the other side, turn right (north) and continue alongside the road. This stretch of trail travels near the large tent-like Bannock County Event Center Indoor Arena and the Center's RV park. At about 0.9 miles, the path once again crosses Fairground Drive, this time to the north side of the street.

The final stretch of the trail runs along the outside of another large gravel parking lot. The path ends at the western trailhead back in the Portneuf Wellness Complex parking area across from the pond, about 0.2 miles from the starting point.

Keep Going

The **Monte Vista Connector**, located at the southwest corner of the Event Center Trail, is a new path designed to link the Wellness Complex area with the Farm Bureau and Hospital Trails. This paved trail extends for about 0.3 miles before it dead ends near the interstate, but there are plans to expand it in the future.

Idaho's state horse, the Appaloosa, can reach a top speed of 41 mph.

The Event Center Trail alongside the Bannock Soccer Complex.

Event Center Trail

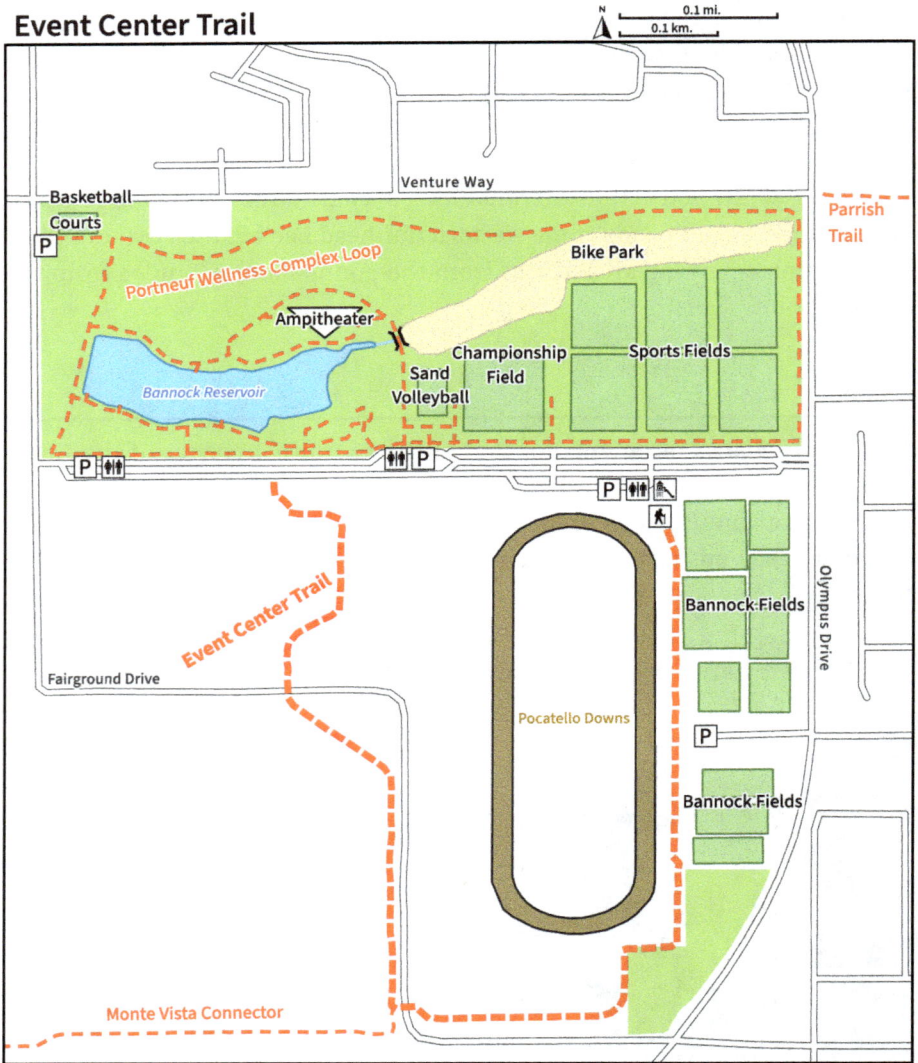

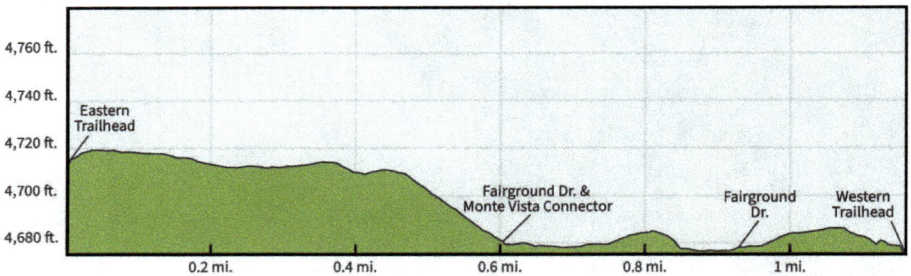

N
0.1 mi.
0.1 km.

Venture Way

Basketball
Courts

P

Parrish
Trail

Portneuf Wellness Complex Loop

Bike Park

Ampitheater

Championship
Field

Sand
Volleyball

Bannock Reservoir

Sports Fields

P

P

P

Event Center Trail

Fairground Drive

Pocatello Downs

Bannock Fields

Olympus Drive

P

Bannock Fields

Monte Vista Connector

4,760 ft.

4,740 ft.

4,720 ft.   Eastern
              Trailhead

4,700 ft.

4,680 ft.

                                    Fairground Dr. &   Fairground   Western
                                    Monte Vista Connector Dr.   Trailhead

        0.2 mi.   0.4 mi.   0.6 mi.   0.8 mi.   1 mi.

3. Satterfield Trail

The Satterfield Trail is a short hiking and biking path with a well-marked trailhead that leads from the residential Satterfield neighborhood into a juniper-sided gully. Only a quarter mile of what people typically travel on is on public land. Many paths (such as Rollercoaster and Bluebird Ravine) continue onto private property from this trail, though I am not including them. If you choose to hike in this area, obey any posted signage whenever traversing private property.

Distance: 0.5 miles out-and-back
Elevation Gain: 80 feet
Difficulty: Easy
Hiking Time: About 20 minutes
Nearest Town: Pocatello
Trail Surface: Dirt, rock

Wheelchair Access: None
Dog-Friendly: Yes; must be on a leash at all times
Amenities: None
Contact: City of Pocatello Parks & Recreation 208-234-6232
Trailhead GPS Coordinates: N42° 54.643' W112° 24.572'

Getting There

From the junction of Pocatello Creek Road and Satterfield Drive, head east on Satterfield Drive for 1.2 miles. The trailhead is south of Lois Lane on the east side of Satterfield Drive. No parking area exists. Park along the street.

The Hike

From the trailhead, head to the east on the singletrack trail. The first part of the hike crosses an open field before reaching a juniper forest. Although some side trails intersect with the main path, keep heading east to stay on route. The section of the trail covered here ends at about a quarter of a mile, where it meets the border of private property. The trail unofficially continues to the east from there, but the increasing construction in the area and unclear trail designation prevented me from covering it.

In 1889, Pocatello was established. The next year, Idaho officially became the 43rd state.

Satterfield Trail shortly past the trailhead.

Satterfield Trail

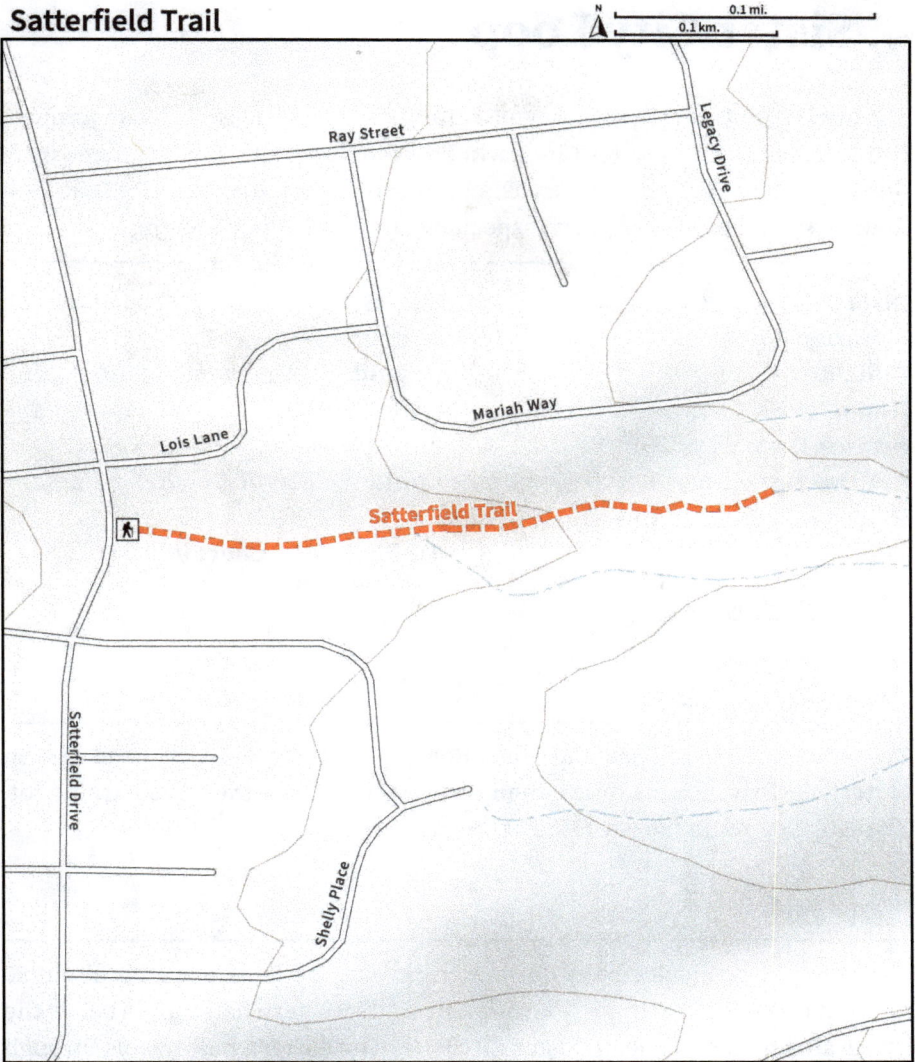

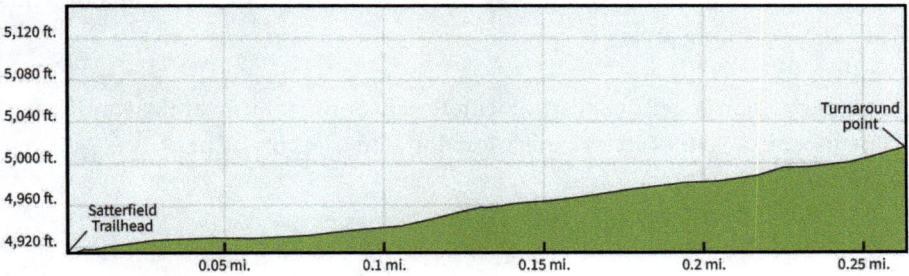

N

0.1 mi.

0.1 km.

Ray Street

Legacy Drive

Lois Lane

Mariah Way

Satterfield Trail

Satterfield Drive

Shelly Place

5,120 ft.

5,080 ft.

5,040 ft.

5,000 ft.

4,960 ft.

4,920 ft.

Satterfield
Trailhead

Turnaround
point

0.05 mi.   0.1 mi.   0.15 mi.   0.2 mi.   0.25 mi.

4. Sister City Loop

The Sister City Loop is a pleasant 0.5-mile walk among sagebrush and junipers just below the grassy Sister City Park. This loop provides a brief escape from the residential neighborhoods. The path traverses the Sister City Disc Golf Course, so hikers must be alert, especially during summer evenings.

Distance: 0.5-mile loop
Elevation Gain: 50 feet
Difficulty: Easy
Hiking Time: About 20 minutes
Nearest Town: Pocatello
Trail Surface: Gravel
Wheelchair Access: None

Dog-Friendly: Yes; must be on a leash at all times
Amenities: A portable restroom and water hookups are available at the Sister City Park.
Contact: City of Pocatello Parks & Recreation 208-234-6232
Trailhead GPS Coordinates: N42° 54.129' W112° 25.076'

Getting There

From the junction of Pocatello Creek Road and Satterfield Drive, head east on Satterfield Drive for 0.4 miles, then turn left down into the large parking lot. The loop begins on the west side of the parking area.

The Hike

Whether you go clockwise or counterclockwise, the loop descends about 50 feet as it makes its southward journey. The trail's western half travels below the dry, grassy hillside beneath Sister City Park. The eastern half travels through sage and scattered juniper trees. The southernmost point of the loop makes a U-turn near Satterfield Drive. Stay on the wide dirt trail until the loop ends back at the parking area.

The park's name derives from Pocatello's Sister City in Iwamizawa, Japan. The Japanese Sister City organization donated trees in the park.

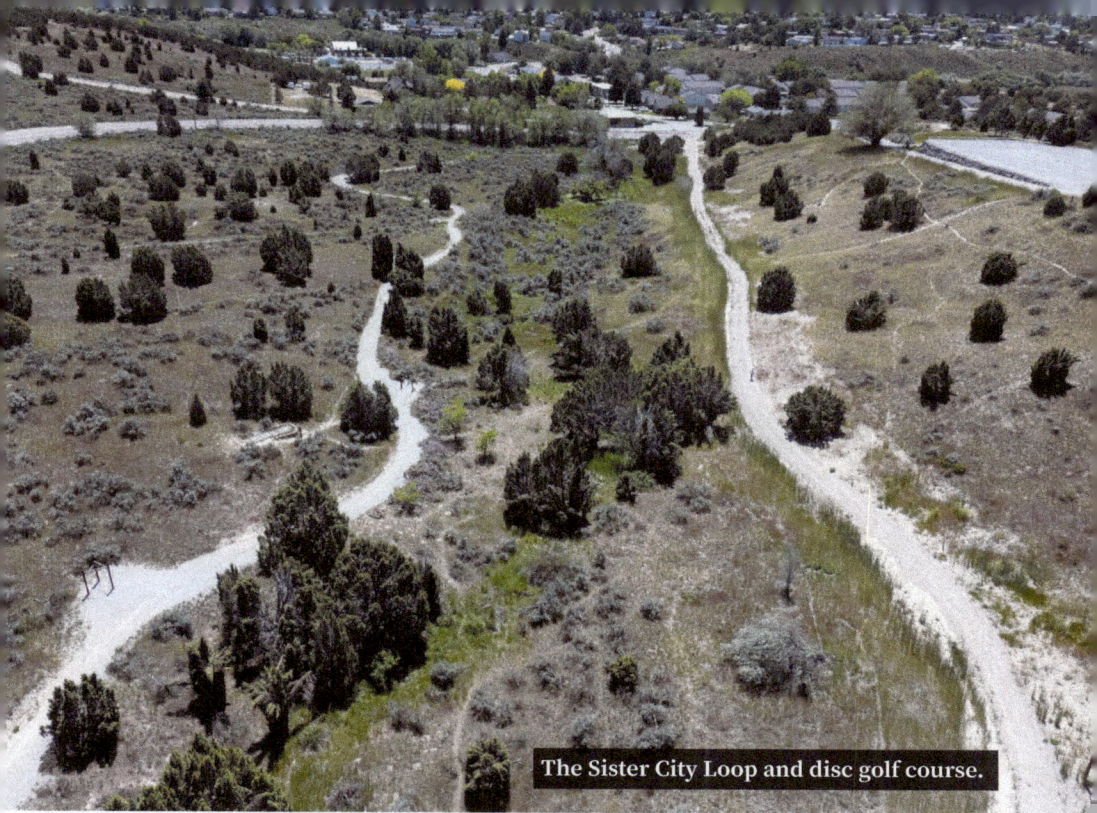
The Sister City Loop and disc golf course.

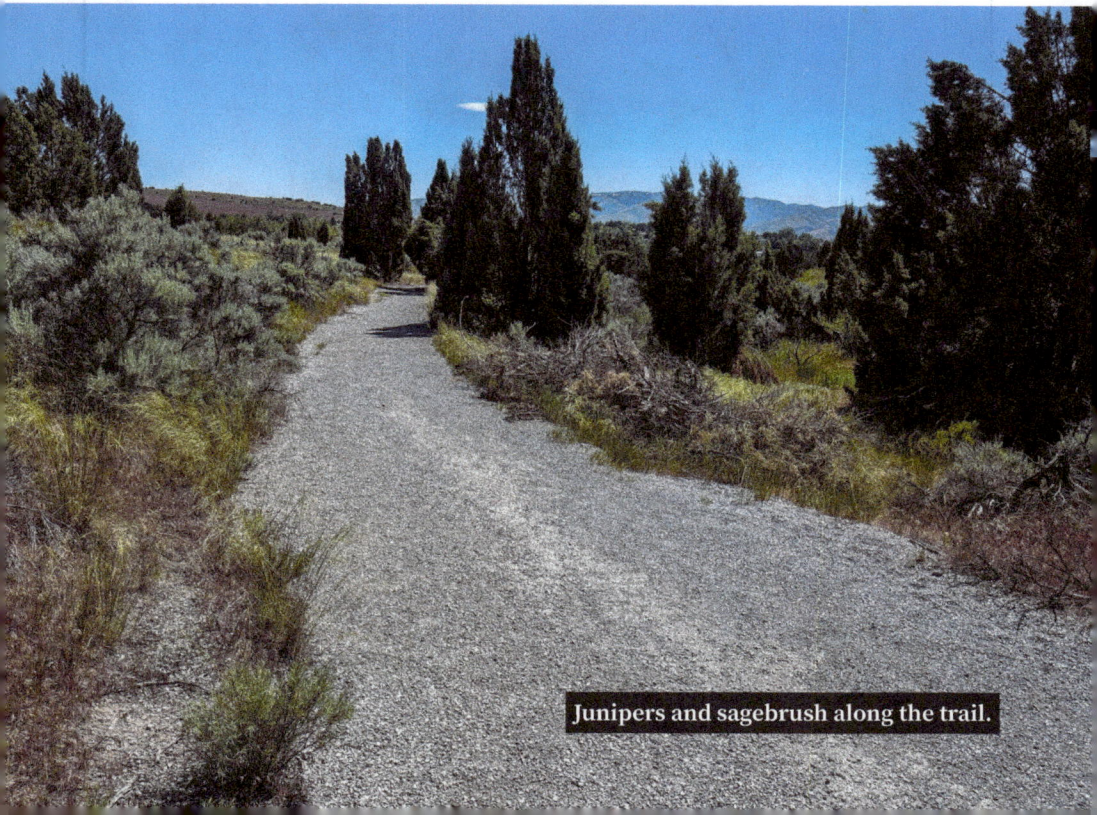
Junipers and sagebrush along the trail.

Sister City Loop

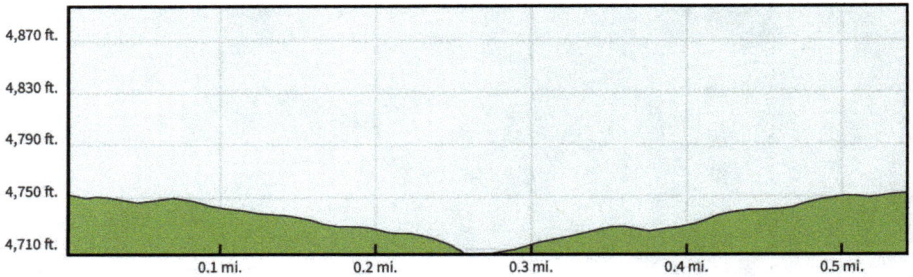

N

0.05 mi.
0.05 km.

P

Michelle Street

Marilyn Street

Satterfield Drive

Sister City Park

P

Sister City Loop

Pocatello Creek Road

4,870 ft.

4,830 ft.

4,790 ft.

4,750 ft.

4,710 ft.

0.1 mi.   0.2 mi.   0.3 mi.   0.4 mi.   0.5 mi.

5. Farm Bureau Insurance and Marshall Racine Trail

The northern stretch of the trail travels a bit too close to the noisy I-15. However, the middle and southern portions of the trail offer a pleasant hillside walk toward the Farm Bureau Insurance building. Overall, this is an enjoyable urban trail that offers elevated views of the interstate.

Distance: 2 miles out-and-back
Elevation Gain: 190 feet
Difficulty: Easy
Hiking Time: About 45 minutes
Nearest Town: Pocatello
Trail Surface: Pavement
Wheelchair Access: Yes

Dog-Friendly: Yes; must be on a leash at all times
Amenities: None
Contact: portneufgreenway.org
Trailhead GPS Coordinates:
Cedar Street Trailhead
N42° 53.543' W112° 25.947'
Farm Bureau Trailhead
N42° 52.827' W112° 25.590'

Getting There

From the intersection of Jefferson Avenue and East Alameda Road, drive east on East Alameda Road for 0.3 miles. Turn left onto Monte Vista Drive. In 0.3 miles, after crossing over the interstate, turn right onto Renee Avenue, and then make another right turn onto Cedar Street. There is no parking lot, though there is plenty of street parking. The trail is on the west side of Cedar Street.

If you choose to start the hike from the south end of the trail, parking is available in the Farm Bureau Parking lot, though it is restricted to employee-only parking Monday through Friday from 7 a.m. to 5 p.m.

The Hike

The first one-third of this paved path travels south between the quiet Cedar Street and the busy interstate, making for an uneventful urban walk. However, at 0.3 miles, the trail leaves the highway noise behind and begins climbing up a small hill, providing a pleasant experience on a grassy, dry hillside. The last half of the path has a bit of elevation change, gaining and losing about 100 feet, though it is not steep. The path ends along a new stand of trees below the Farm Bureau Insurance building.

> How hot is too hot for a dog's feet on pavement? According to the American Kennel Club, if the temperature is 85 degrees or more and the pavement hasn't had an opportunity to cool, it may be too hot to walk a dog safely.

The trail winding toward the Farm Bureau Insurance building.

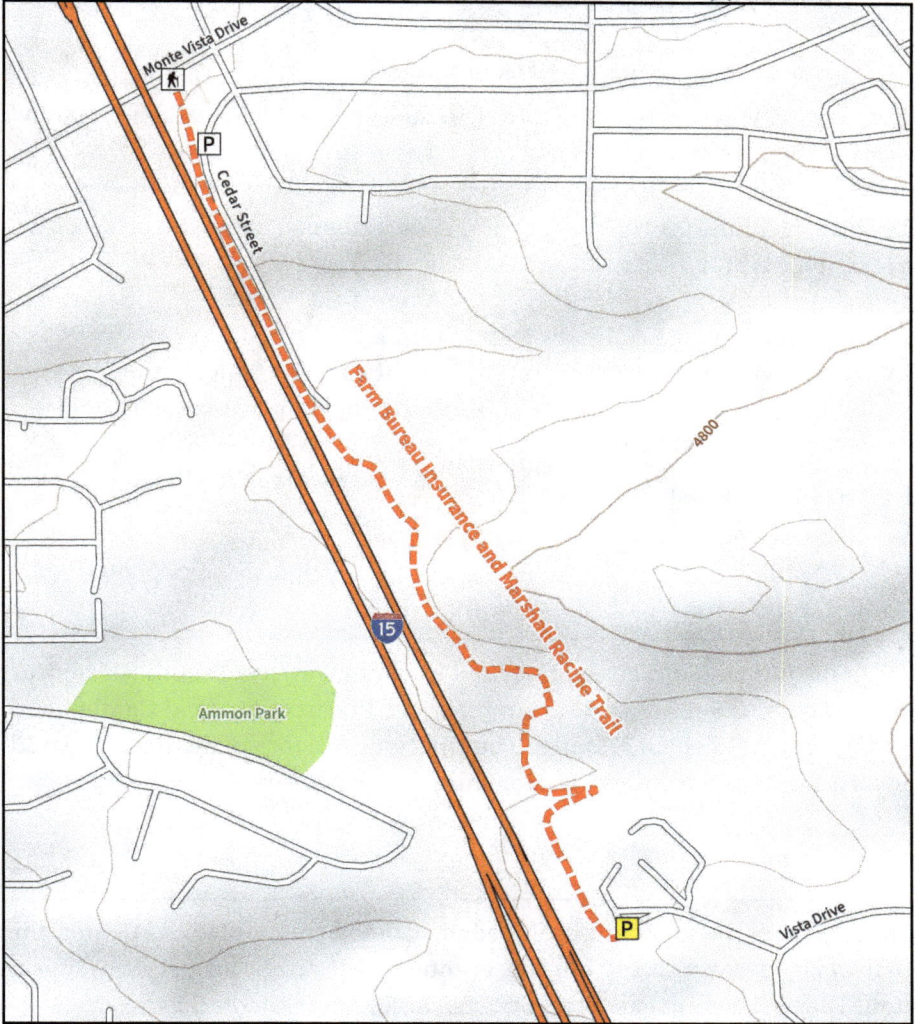

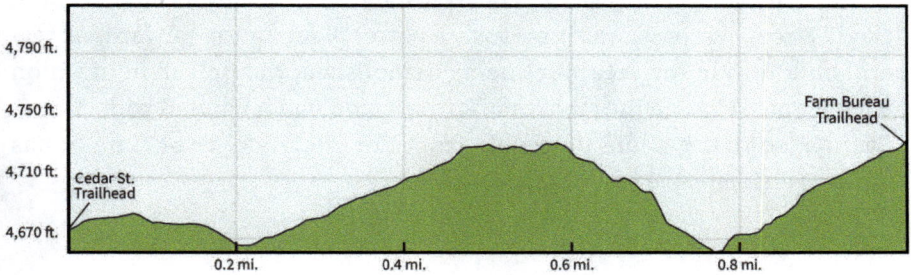

Farm Bureau Insurance and Marshall Racine Trail

N   0.1 mi.
0.1 km.

Monte Vista Drive

Cedar Street

Farm Bureau Insurance and Marshall Racine Trail

4800

I5

Ammon Park

Vista Drive

P

P

4,790 ft.

4,750 ft.   Farm Bureau
Trailhead

4,710 ft.   Cedar St.
Trailhead

4,670 ft.

0.2 mi.   0.4 mi.   0.6 mi.   0.8 mi.

6. Hospital Trail

This short, no-frills path offers a nice view of the area's mountains. The trail's proximity to Franklin Middle School and the Portneuf Medical Complex allows users a much-needed reprieve in an otherwise busy area.

Distance: 1.1 miles out-and-back
Elevation Gain: 100 feet
Difficulty: Easy
Hiking Time: About 30 minutes
Nearest Town: Pocatello
Trail Surface: Pavement
Wheelchair Access: Yes

Dog-Friendly: Yes; must be on a leash at all times
Amenities: None
Contact: portneufgreenway.org
Trailhead GPS Coordinates:
Portneuf Medical Center Trailhead
N42° 52.301' W112° 25.245'
East Terry Street Trailhead
N42° 52.040' W112° 25.175'

Getting There

From the junction of Center Street and Hospital Way, head southeast on Hospital Way for 0.5 miles and turn right at the Portneuf Medical Center south entrance sign. In about 0.1 miles, you will come to a fork in the road. The trailhead is located directly across from this fork. Street parking is available.

The Hike

Starting from the northern trailhead near the Portneuf Medical Center, this path gently descends a dry hillside, eventually passing by an electrical substation. The trail ends at East Terry Street near Franklin Middle School.

The Union Pacific smokestack, a tall freestanding chimney located near the Gould Street overpass, was previously a power plant for the railyard. As several buildings in the area were being demolished, the president of Union Pacific opted to keep the smokestack intact, and had it painted with "Union Pacific," so that it could be visible from the interstate. Over time, it has become an iconic part of the city's skyline.

The trail below the Portneuf Medical Center.

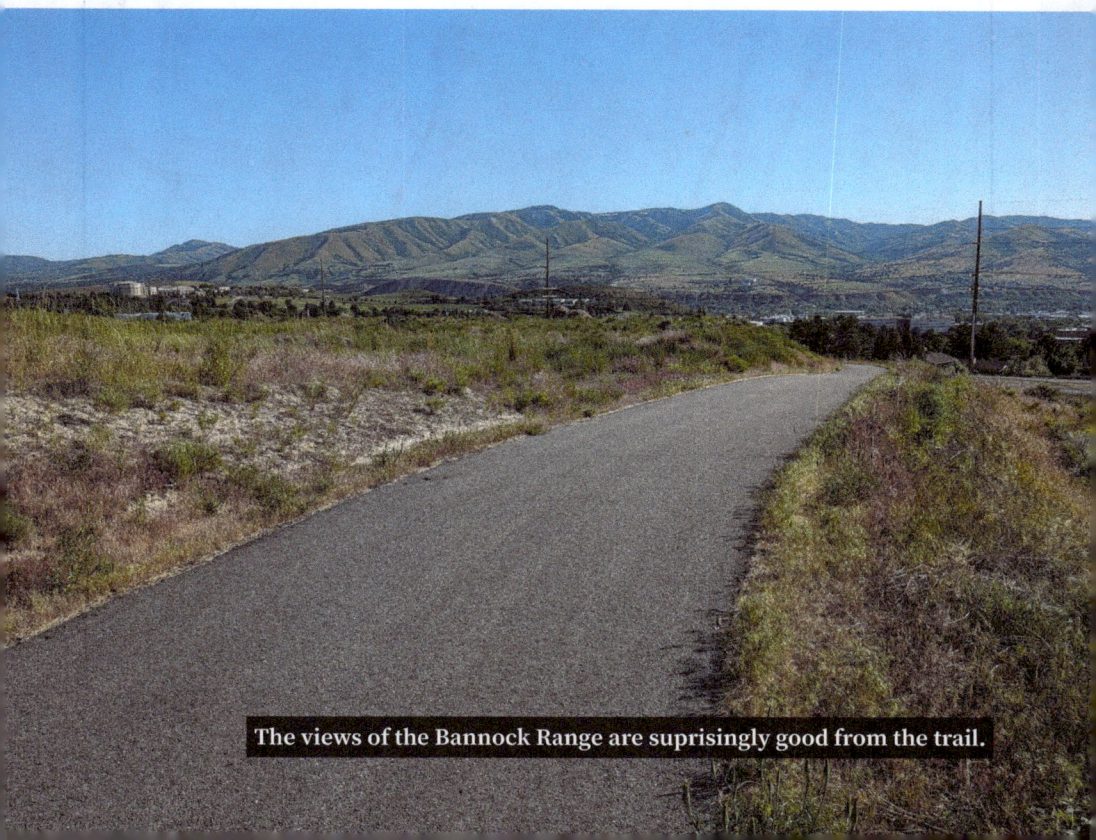

The views of the Bannock Range are suprisingly good from the trail.

Hospital Trail

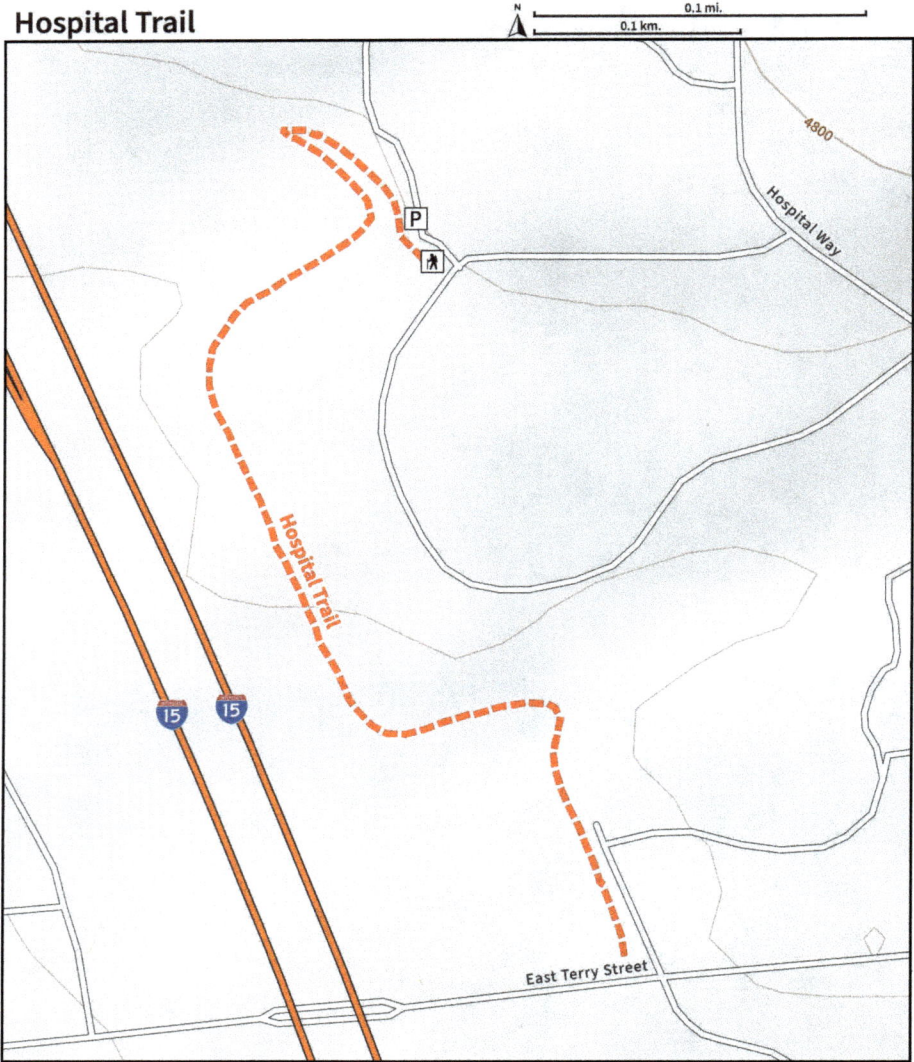

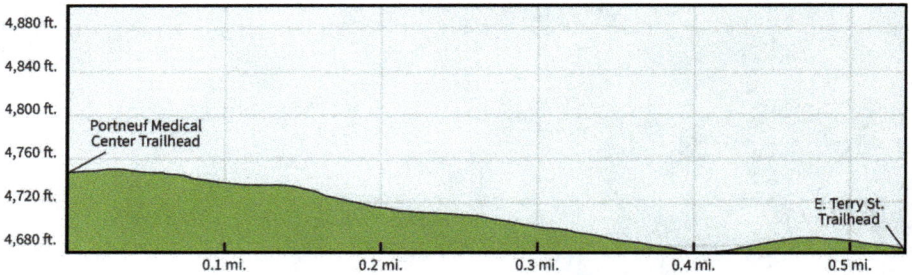

N

0.1 mi.

0.1 km.

4800

Hospital Way

P

Hospital Trail

15   15

East Terry Street

4,880 ft.

4,840 ft.

4,800 ft.

4,760 ft. — Portneuf Medical
Center Trailhead

4,720 ft.

E. Terry St.
Trailhead

4,680 ft.

0.1 mi.   0.2 mi.   0.3 mi.   0.4 mi.   0.5 mi.

7. Abraszewski and Simplot / Swanson Trail

Located between the scenic Portneuf River on one side and the industrial Great Western Malting Plant on the other, the Abraszewski and Simplot/Swanson Trail places you in the center of contrasting environments. Don't let that dissuade you, though; the trail is surprisingly tranquil and offers a quiet hiking experience in northwest Pocatello.

Distance: 2.5 miles out-and-back
Elevation Gain: 20 feet
Difficulty: Easy
Hiking Time: About 1 hour
Nearest Town: Pocatello
Trail Surface: Pavement

Wheelchair Access: Yes
Dog-Friendly: Yes; must be on a leash at all times
Amenities: None
Contact: portneufgreenway.org
Trailhead GPS Coordinates: N42° 53.449' W112° 29.134'

Getting There

From the intersection of North Main Street and North Kraft Road in Pocatello, head west on North Kraft Road for 0.8 miles. Once you cross a bridge over the Portneuf River the signed trailhead and plentiful parking are to your left (west). The trail begins at the southern end of the parking area.

The Hike

For the first 0.4 miles, this shaded and generally flat path travels northwest alongside the Portneuf River. About 0.3 miles in, the Abraszewski Trail transitions into the Simplot/Swanson Trail, where it soon departs the shady river for a more traditional Pocatello desert experience. The remainder of the path is generally in the sagebrush away from the river, though this riparian scenery has its own charm. The path ends at a dead end next to the river.

The early stretch of the Abraszewski Trail provides plenty of cooling shade.

As you start down the Abraszewski Trail, you will come across an inscribed rock dedicated to the memory of Dr. Paul Abraszewski, a local cardiologist for whom the trail is named.

Abraszewski and Simplot / Swanson Trail

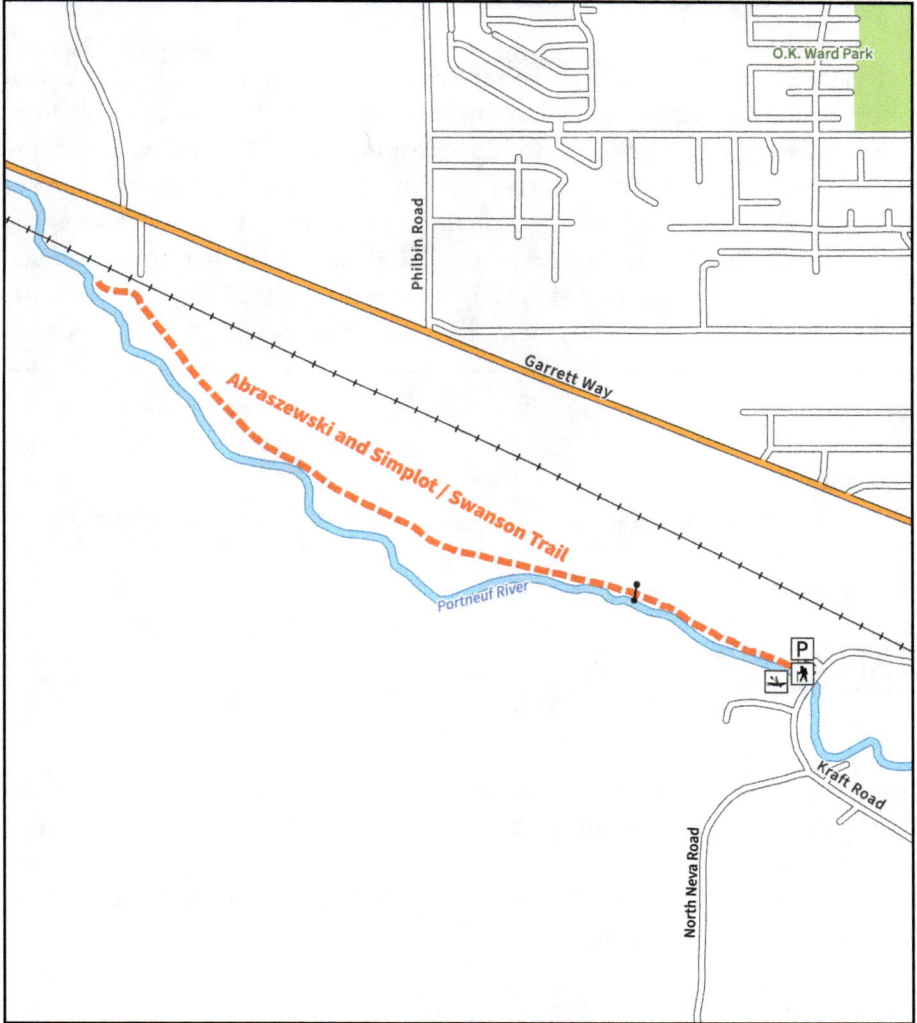

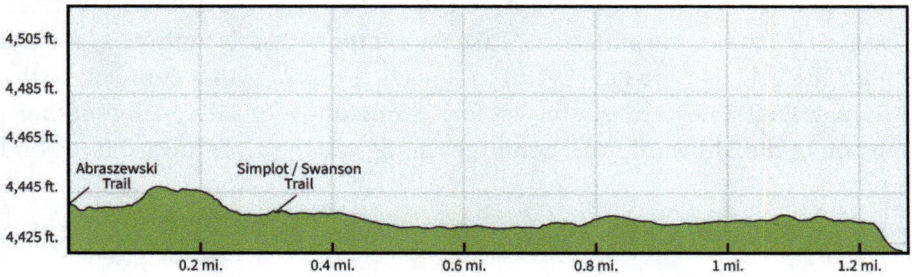

N
0.25 mi.
0.25 km.

O.K. Ward Park

Philbin Road

Garrett Way

Abraszewski and Simplot / Swanson Trail

Portneuf River

P

Kraft Road

North Neva Road

Abraszewski
Trail

Simplot / Swanson
Trail

4,505 ft.

4,485 ft.

4,465 ft.

4,445 ft.

4,425 ft.

0.2 mi.   0.4 mi.   0.6 mi.   0.8 mi.   1 mi.   1.2 mi.

8. Sacajawea Park

Sacajawea Park is a beautiful riverside recreation area in west Pocatello that offers a variety of paved trails to explore. The area has a disc golf course, educational signage, and river access for floating and fishing. For bird watchers, the park is an excellent location to view waterfowl. For photographers, the trees alongside the river glow with colors in the autumn. The easiest way to view the park is by walking along the Sacajawea Trail, a short loop that explores much of the area. The western half of the loop travels through tall grass, whereas the eastern stretch travels directly alongside the river under deciduous trees.

Distance: 0.9-mile loop
Elevation Gain: 20 feet
Difficulty: Easy
Hiking Time: About 20 minutes
Nearest Town: Pocatello
Trail Surface: Pavement

Wheelchair Access: Yes
Dog-Friendly: Yes; must be on a leash at all times
Amenities: A portable restroom is available at the trailhead.
Contact: portneufgreenway.org
Trailhead GPS Coordinates: N42° 52.563' W112° 28.319'

Getting There

From the junction of South Garfield Avenue and West Carson Street, head southwest on West Carson Street for 0.2 miles. Once you cross the bridge, turn right onto Riverside Drive, and in 0.4 miles, turn right onto Aspen Lane. The trailhead will be on your right in 0.2 miles.

The Hike

From the parking lot, head south on the paved trail. At 0.1 miles, keep left (east). At 0.2 miles, the path forks. Take the center path as it continues east and under the bridge. (The left (north) fork leads to a bridge that connects to the Brennan Trail. The right (southeast) fork, sometimes considered the southern portion of the Millward Mile, continues alongside the river toward Raymond Park.)

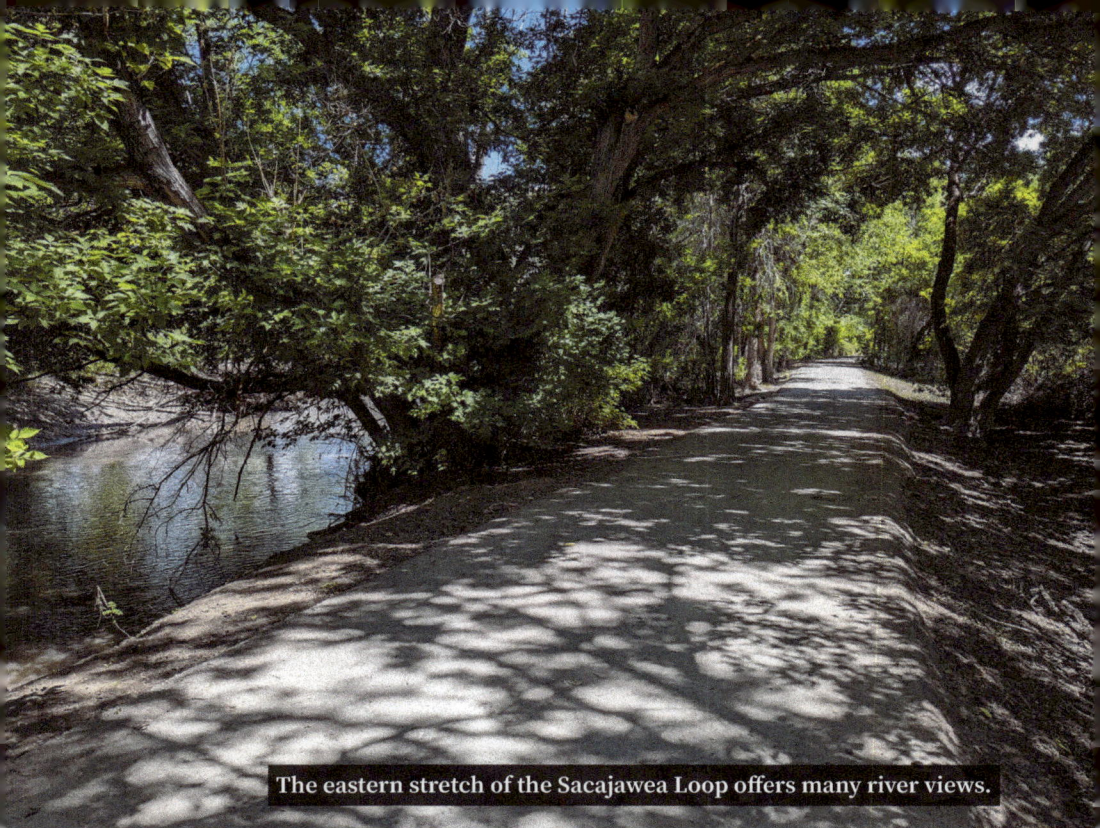

The eastern stretch of the Sacajawea Loop offers many river views.

After emerging from the bridge, the path travels along the Portneuf River as it heads north. At about 0.4 miles, continue straight (north), avoiding the path to the left (west) that cuts through the center of the loop from the parking lot. At about 0.6 miles, the path departs the river and makes a left (southwest) turn. Shortly beyond this turn, the trail passes by the Millward Mile Trail to the right (north). Continue left (south) to finish the loop and return to the parking area.

Sacagawea was a Shoshone Native American who played an instrumental role as a translator on the Lewis and Clark Expedition. There are various English spellings of her name that you may encounter including Sacajawea, Sacagawea, and Sakakawea.

Keep Going

Two additional Greenway Trails begin from Sacajawea Park. The first, the **Brennan Trail**, is located on the east side of the Portneuf River and provides an alternative riverwalk for those looking for a quieter experience. A straightforward hike, this northbound trail parallels the river, with the path staying a short distance away from the tree-lined river in the first half before entering the shaded foliage in the second. The 0.6-mile one-way trail ends just short of the North Arthur Avenue Bridge. A pedestrian bridge to connect Brennan Trail with Millward Mile is scheduled for construction, but for now, if you wish to continue, walk the 60 or so yards across the vehicle bridge.

The second Greenway Path that connects with Sacajawea Park is the **Millward Mile**. The trail begins north of the park at a small signed parking area off North Main Street and connects with Sacajawea Park after 0.6 miles. There isn't an official endpoint for this path, though arguably, the Millward Mile continues through Sacajawea Park, following alongside the river until the path ends at Riverside Drive. This extended version of the trail is about 1.3 miles one-way. The stretch of the Millward Mile north of Sacajawea Park is a pleasant trail that has a nice bridge over the river, though the Kraft Road crossing near the trailhead can be dangerous, as vehicles often turn off of North Main Street onto Kraft Road going 50 mph.

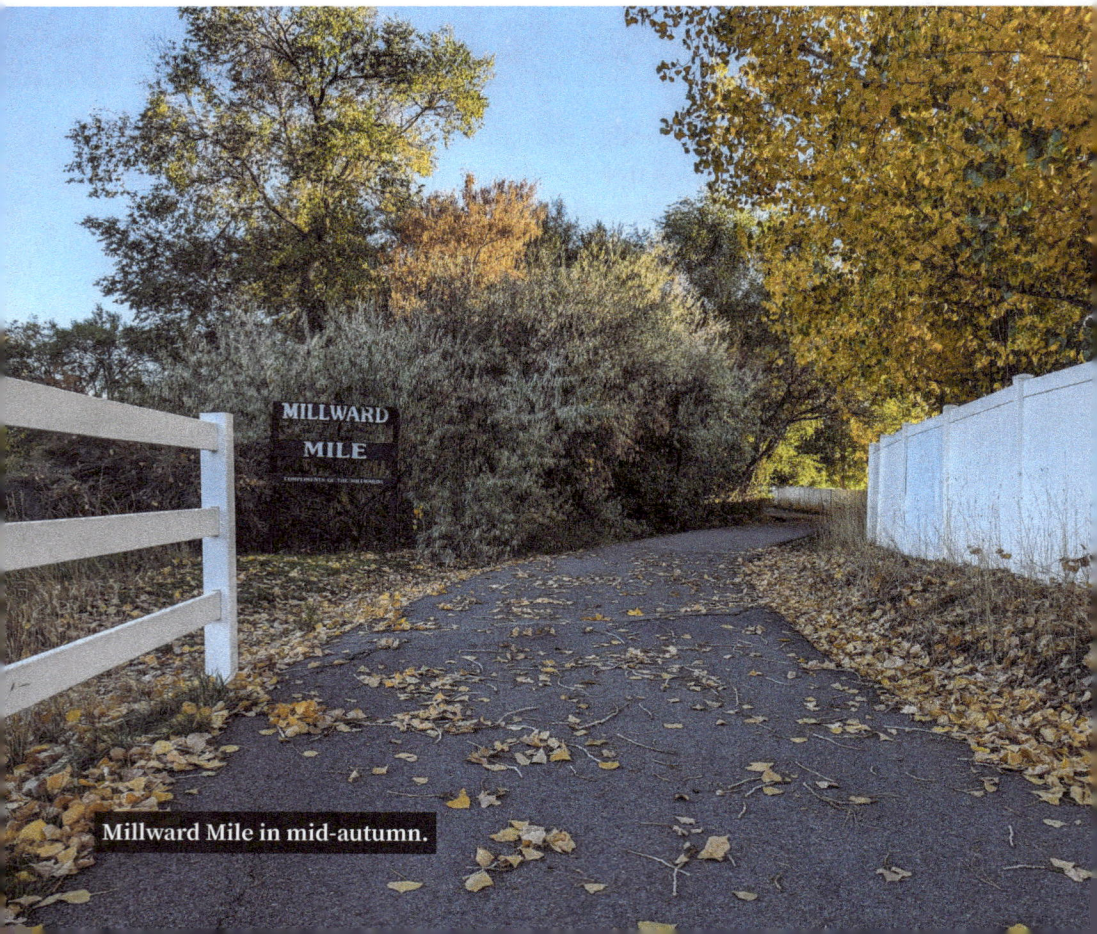

Millward Mile in mid-autumn.

Sacajawea Park

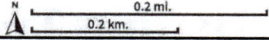

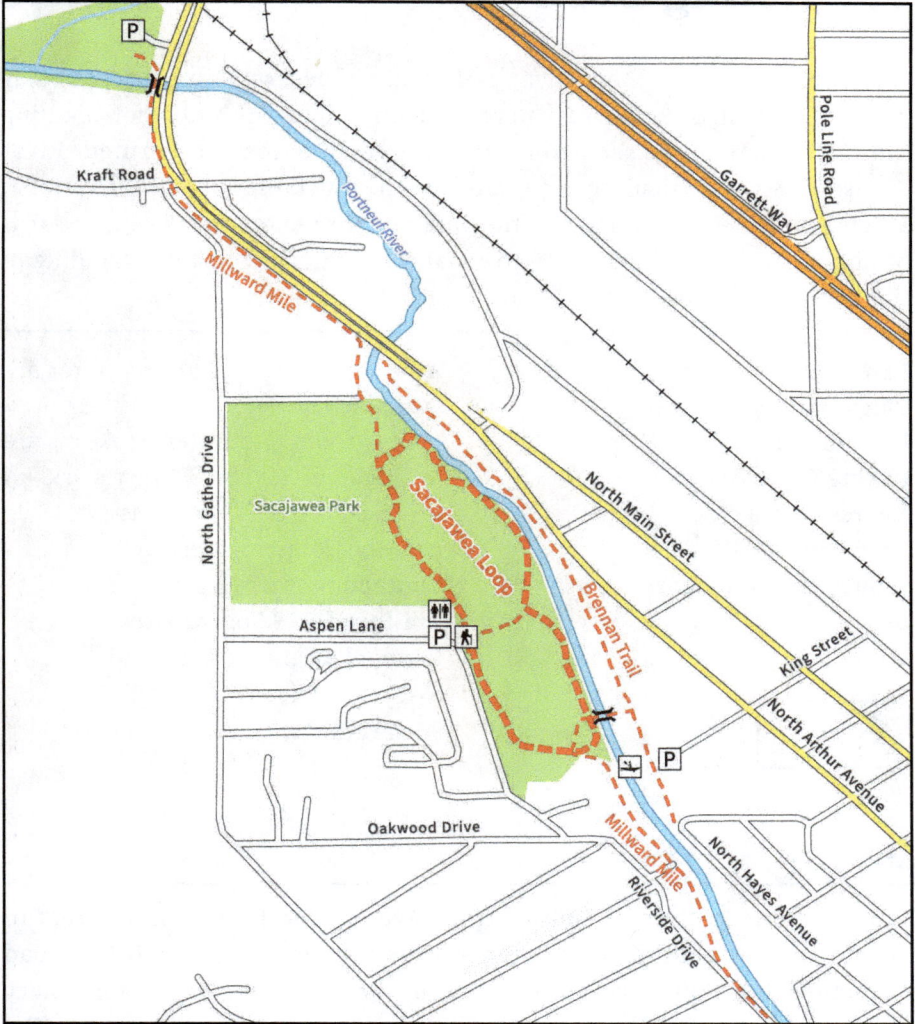

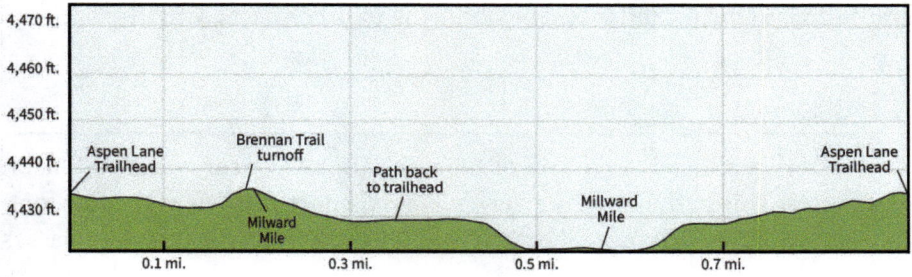

Map labels:

P (parking, top left)

Kraft Road

Portneuf River

Millward Mile

North Gathe Drive

Sacajawea Park

Sacajawea Loop

Aspen Lane

P

Garrett Way

Pole Line Road

North Main Street

Brennan Trail

King Street

North Arthur Avenue

Oakwood Drive

Milward Mile

North Hayes Avenue

Riverside Drive

P

0.2 mi.

0.2 km.

Elevation profile labels:

4,470 ft.
4,460 ft.
4,450 ft.
4,440 ft.
4,430 ft.

Aspen Lane Trailhead

Brennan Trail turnoff

Milward Mile

Path back to trailhead

Milward Mile

Aspen Lane Trailhead

0.1 mi.   0.3 mi.   0.5 mi.   0.7 mi.

9. Hirning Trail

With views of the Portneuf River and plenty of access points near popular parks, the Hirning Trail is easy to recommend. Kayakers and others floating the river can often be seen from the path utilizing the two Portneuf River Access Points. A particularly nice feature of the trail is the Spaulding Overlook, a viewpoint where you can watch the untamed river enter into the Army Corps of Engineers-constructed concrete canal of downtown Pocatello. Floating in this concrete channel is prohibited.

Distance: 2 miles out-and-back
Elevation Gain: 40 feet
Difficulty: Easy
Hiking Time: About 45 minutes
Nearest Town: Pocatello
Trail Surface: Pavement
Wheelchair Access: Yes
Dog-Friendly: Yes; must be on a leash at all times

Amenities: Restrooms and water are available at Centennial Park. A portable restroom and water hook-ups are available at Taysom Rotary Park. A life jacket loaner station is available near the Centennial Bridge.
Contact: portneufgreenway.org
Trailhead GPS Coordinates:
Bannock Highway Trailhead
N42° 50.943' W112° 26.117'
West Halliday Street Trailhead
N42° 51.433' W112° 26.869'

Getting There

From the intersection of South Arthur Avenue and East Benton Street in Pocatello, head southeast on South Arthur Avenue for 0.8 miles (the road becomes South Main Street at 0.4 miles) and turn right into the Taysom Rotary Park parking lot. There are plenty of parking spots in the parking area. The Hirning Trail is just through the park on the south side, though the eastern trailhead is about 0.1 miles east of where the park connects with the trail.

The Hike

The eastern trailhead begins off of Bannock Highway near two metal bison sculptures. This path hugs the river as it travels northwest near the low foothills of the Bannock Range. Shortly into the path, at 0.1 miles, the trail passes

A walker enjoying the views along the Hirning Trail.

the Taysom Rotary Park on its right (north) and a Portneuf River Access Point on its left (south). Around 0.6 miles, the path passes by a bridge to Centennial Park on its left (south) and a parking area near the Pocatello Community Charter School to its right (north). This is also the location of the last Portneuf River Access Point before the river enters the concrete channel.

At 0.9 miles, the paved trail passes by the Spaulding Overlook and a bridge across the river on its left (south). The path ends shortly past that overlook at West Halliday Street.

The Portneuf River is 124 miles long, starting in Caribou County and ending at the Snake River near American Falls. In recent years, floating the river has become a popular activity in Pocatello.

Keep Going

Two pleasant parks are located off the Hirning Trail that are worth exploring. The **Taysom Rotary Park**, located near the southeast trailhead, has plenty of open grass and a shaded pavilion and makes for a relaxed place to take a break. **Centennial Park**, located across the large bridge in the northwest stretch of the path, has a large shaded pavilion, a playground, and a restroom. This park sits just below the Lower City Creek Trailhead and is a popular area for mountain bikers to park.

The Centennial Bridge connecting the Hirning Trail to Centennial Park.

Hirning Trail

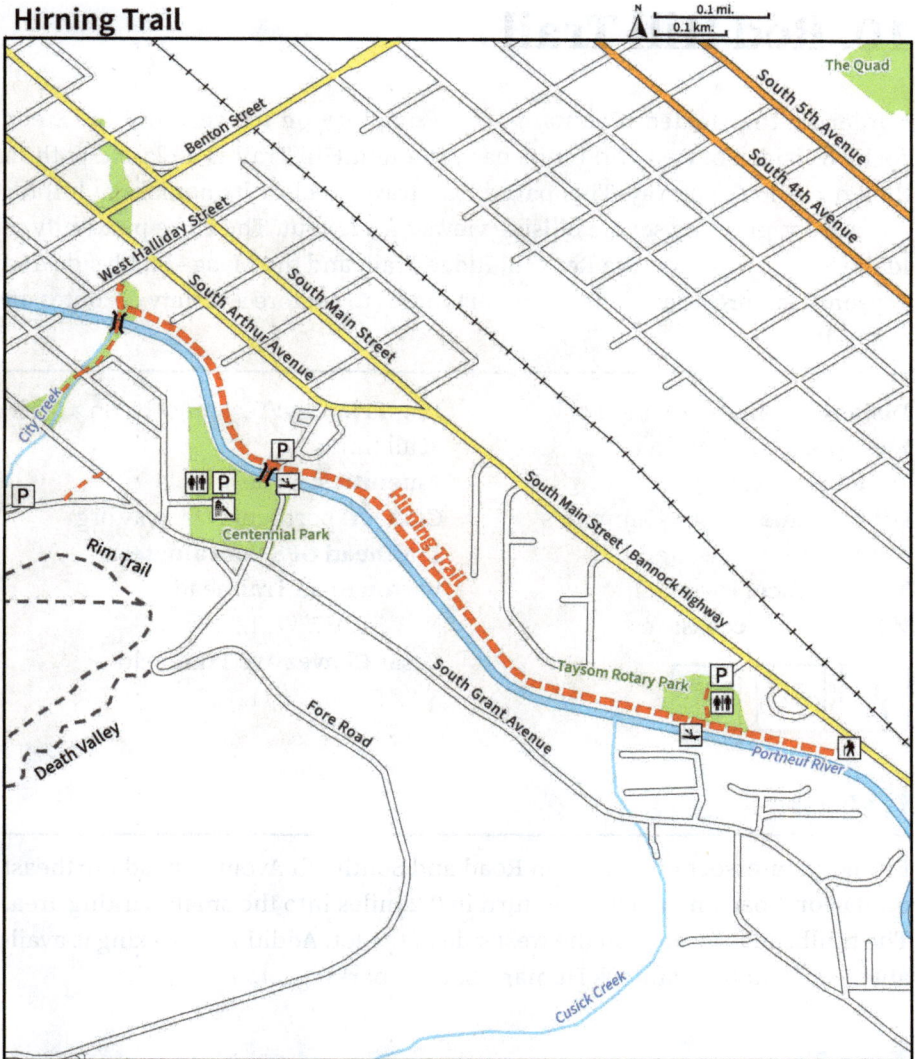

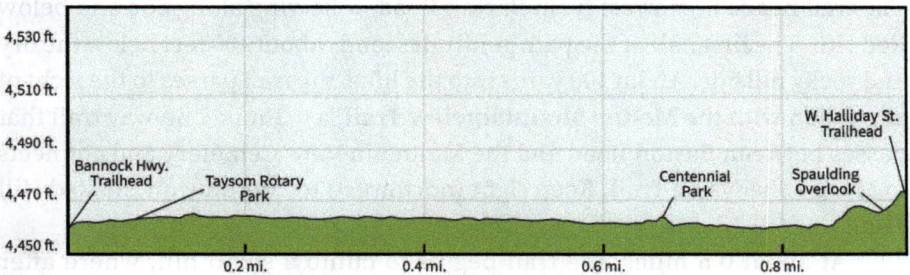

N
0.1 mi.
0.1 km.

The Quad

South 5th Avenue

South 4th Avenue

Benton Street

West Halliday Street

South Arthur Avenue

South Main Street

City Creek

Centennial Park

Rim Trail

P

P

Hirning Trail

South Main Street / Bannock Highway

Fore Road

South Grant Avenue

Taysom Rotary Park

P

Death Valley

Portneuf River

Cusick Creek

4,530 ft.

4,510 ft.

4,490 ft.

4,470 ft.

4,450 ft.

Bannock Hwy.
Trailhead

Taysom Rotary
Park

Centennial
Park

Spaulding
Overlook

W. Halliday St.
Trailhead

0.2 mi.   0.4 mi.   0.6 mi.   0.8 mi.

10. Red Hill Trail

Bordering the shaded Mountain View Cemetery on its west and the steep rocky hillsides of Red Hill on its east, the Red Hill Trail is a classic path in the Pocatello Greenway. This paved trail travels below its namesake hill for its entirety, granting scenic hillside views throughout. The close proximity to Idaho State University, the Red Hill Ridge Trail, and the Maag - Shadyside and Taysom Trail provides plenty of opportunities to explore a variety of routes off this path.

Distance: 2 miles out-and-back
Elevation Gain: 160 feet
Difficulty: Easy
Hiking Time: About 45 minutes
Nearest Town: Pocatello
Trail Surface: Pavement
Wheelchair Access: Yes

Dog-Friendly: Yes; must be on a leash at all times
Amenities: None
Contact: portneufgreenway.org
Trailhead GPS Coordinates:
Barton Road Trailhead
N42° 51.057' W112° 25.182'
Cesar Chavez Ave Trailhead
N42° 51.669' W112° 25.921'

Getting There

From the intersection of Barton Road and South 5th Avenue, head northeast on Barton Road and make a left turn in 0.2 miles into the small parking area. The trailhead is located on the west side of the lot. Additional parking is available nearby at the Bannock Humane Society parking lot.

The Hike

The trail heads northwest from Barton Road, following alongside and below Red Hill. The first half of the path gently descends about 100 feet below the dry and rocky hillside. About 100 yards into the hike, the trail passes to the right of a junction with the **Melton Mountainview Trail**, a 0.3-mile one-way trail that passes between Barton Road and the Mountain View Cemetery and connects to Maag - Shadyside Trail. Keep right (northwest) to continue on the Red Hill Trail.

At about 0.5 miles, the trail begins to climb a small hill, where after

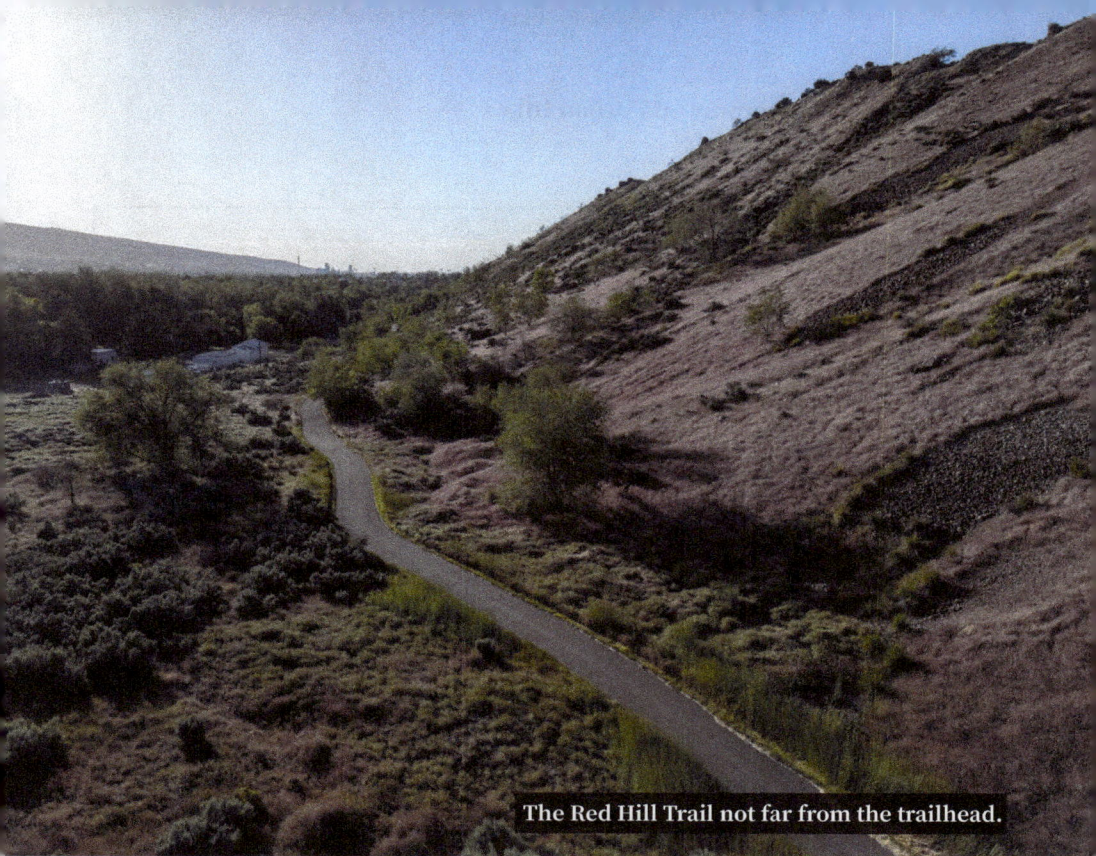

The Red Hill Trail not far from the trailhead.

climbing 80 feet you will reach the top at 0.8 miles, with Davis Field off to the trail's left (west). At 0.9 miles, the trail passes by a connecting path to the Red Hill Ridge Trail on the right (southeast) side of the path. The trail ends at Cesar Chavez Avenue on the ISU campus across from the Bengal Theater.

Idaho State University has gone through several name changes in its history. It was founded in 1901 as the Academy of Idaho, but was renamed the Idaho Technical Institute in 1915. In 1927, it became the University of Idaho - Southern Branch, and in 1947 it was known as Idaho State College. Finally, in 1963, it was given its current name, Idaho State University.

Keep Going

Given that both trails share the same parking lot, pairing the paved Red Hill Trail with the rugged Red Hill Ridge Trail makes for a varied loop. There is a turnoff at the end of the Red Hill Trail at 0.9 miles which connects to the Red Hill Ridge Trail. Traveling one way atop the rocky ridge and the other way on the blacktop trail below it can make for a fun workout.

Red Hill Trail

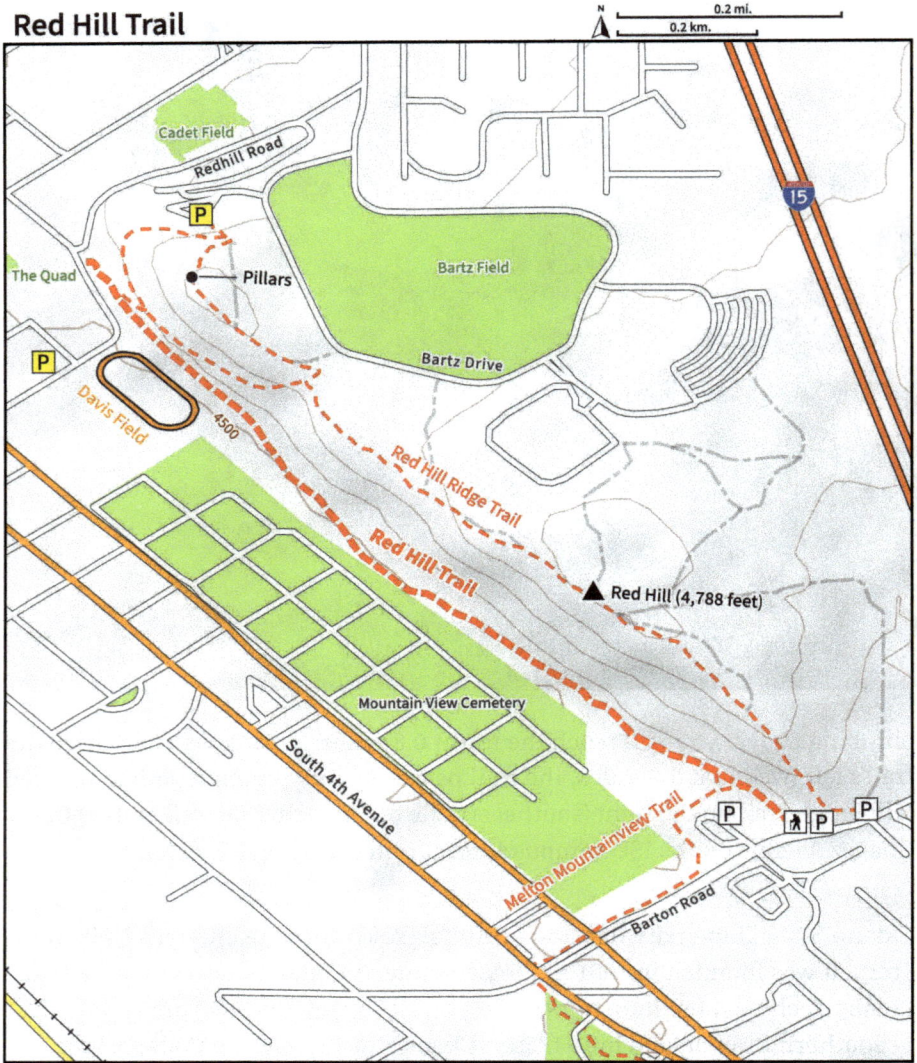

N

0.2 mi.
0.2 km.

Cadet Field

Redhill Road

P

The Quad

Pillars

Bartz Field

Bartz Drive

P

Davis Field

4500

Red Hill Ridge Trail

Red Hill Trail

▲ Red Hill (4,788 feet)

Mountain View Cemetery

South 4th Avenue

Melton Mountainview Trail

P

P P

I-15

Barton Road

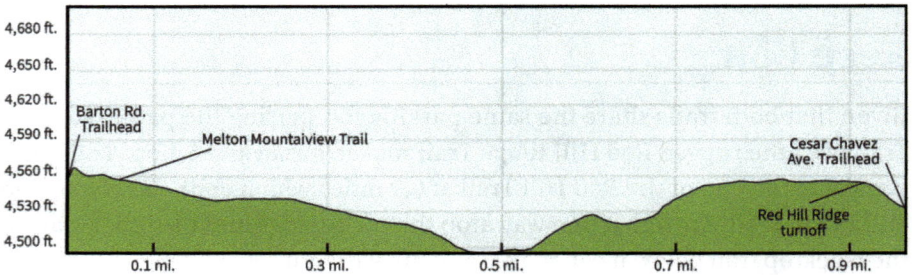

4,680 ft.
4,650 ft.
4,620 ft.
4,590 ft.
4,560 ft.
4,530 ft.
4,500 ft.

Barton Rd.
Trailhead

Melton Mountainview Trail

Cesar Chavez
Ave. Trailhead

Red Hill Ridge
turnoff

0.1 mi.   0.3 mi.   0.5 mi.   0.7 mi.   0.9 mi.

11. Red Hill Ridge Trail

A beautiful ridge walk easily accessible from Idaho State University, the Red Hill Ridge Trail has several moderate hill climbs before ending at the iconic pillars that overlook campus. The trail runs above Mountain View Cemetery's forest treetops for most of the hike, making it an excellent choice for an autumn outing. This rocky path is exposed to the sun, so be sure to bring sun protection.

Distance: 2.2-mile lollipop loop
Elevation Gain: 600 feet
Difficulty: Moderate
Hiking Time: About 1 hour
Nearest Town: Pocatello
Trail Surface: Dirt, rock
Wheelchair Access: None

Dog-Friendly: Yes; must be on a leash at all times
Amenities: None
Contact: Idaho State University, 208-282-4636
Trailhead GPS Coordinates:
Barton Road Trailhead
N42° 51.071' W112° 25.109'
Red Hill Drive Trailhead
N42° 51.711' W112° 25.798'

Getting There

From the intersection of Barton Road and South 5th Avenue, head northeast on Barton Road and turn left in 0.3 miles onto the dirt road and small parking area. The trailhead is located on the west side of the parking area. Additional parking is available nearby at the Red Hill Trailhead, as well as at the Bannock Humane Society parking lot.

If you are looking to climb directly to the pillars, there is a parking area on the west side of the route near Bartz Field off Red Hill Drive. This large parking lot has a staircase that leads to the route, though it requires an Idaho State University parking pass unless you are accessing it on the weekend or in the evenings.

The Hike

The trail climbs a steep and rocky hill from the parking area, following the ridgeline northwest. This first hill is the largest on the hike, gaining 240 feet in

The Red Hill Ridge Trail with the Mountain View Cemetery in the background.

0.4 miles. At 0.2 miles, the trail forks. Keep left (northwest) to stay on the main route, which soon climbs up a short but steep incline. (If you were to go right instead, you would bypass this incline on a more gradual trail).

Once atop the hill at 0.4 miles, which is the high point of Red Hill (4,788 feet), you will have a good view of the pillars at the far end of Red Hill in the distance. Continue northwest on the spine of the ridge, staying left near the steep hillside whenever confronted with a side trail. This ridge walk has a few small hills to climb, though it is never enough to dampen the experience. After a small but steep decline, you will reach a junction at 0.8 miles.

At the junction between the north and south ridges of Red Hill, make a right (northeast) turn and then make the first left (northwest) turn to begin the final climb toward the pillars. The pillars are 100 vertical feet from the junction and 0.2 miles away. At about 0.9 miles, keep left (northwest) at the fork. Once at the pillars, you will have views of ISU's campus, Davis Field, Bartz Field, and the Stephens Performing Arts Center. Many people turn around here, though the full loop actually continues down the north side.

Pass under the pillars and continue on the trail northeast as it descends down the north side of Red Hill. At about 1.0 mile, the trail makes a left (west) turn, passing by a set of stairs leading to a parking lot. This lower stretch of Red Hill hugs the hillside as it eventually travels across the west side of the hill below the large ISU "I." Make sure to continue straight (southeast) at 1.2 miles to pass by a connecting trail to the paved Red Hill Trail. At about 1.4 miles, the trail connects back to the original route at the junction between the hilltops. Turn right (southeast) to retrace your steps back to the southern trailhead.

The four pillars on top of Red Hill were originally part of the McHan Funeral Home, established in 1916 and located in Historic Downtown Pocatello. The funeral home eventually became the McHan-Henderson Funeral Home. After relocating to a new location, the original building was demolished in 1966, though the pillars were preserved. The McHan-Henderson Funeral Home donated them to ISU, and in 1970, they were placed atop Red Hill.

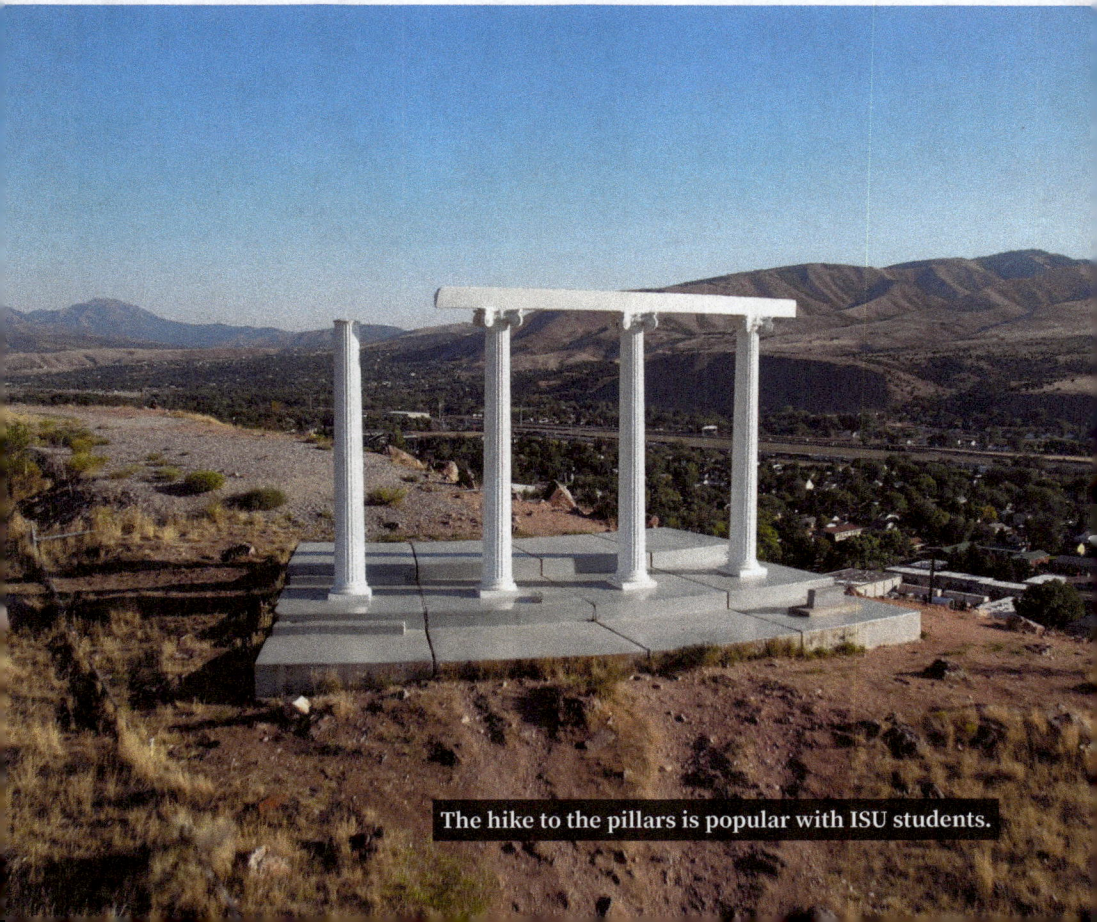

The hike to the pillars is popular with ISU students.

The Red Hill Ridge Trail with the pillars in the distance.

Red Hill Ridge Trail

N

0.2 mi.
0.2 km.

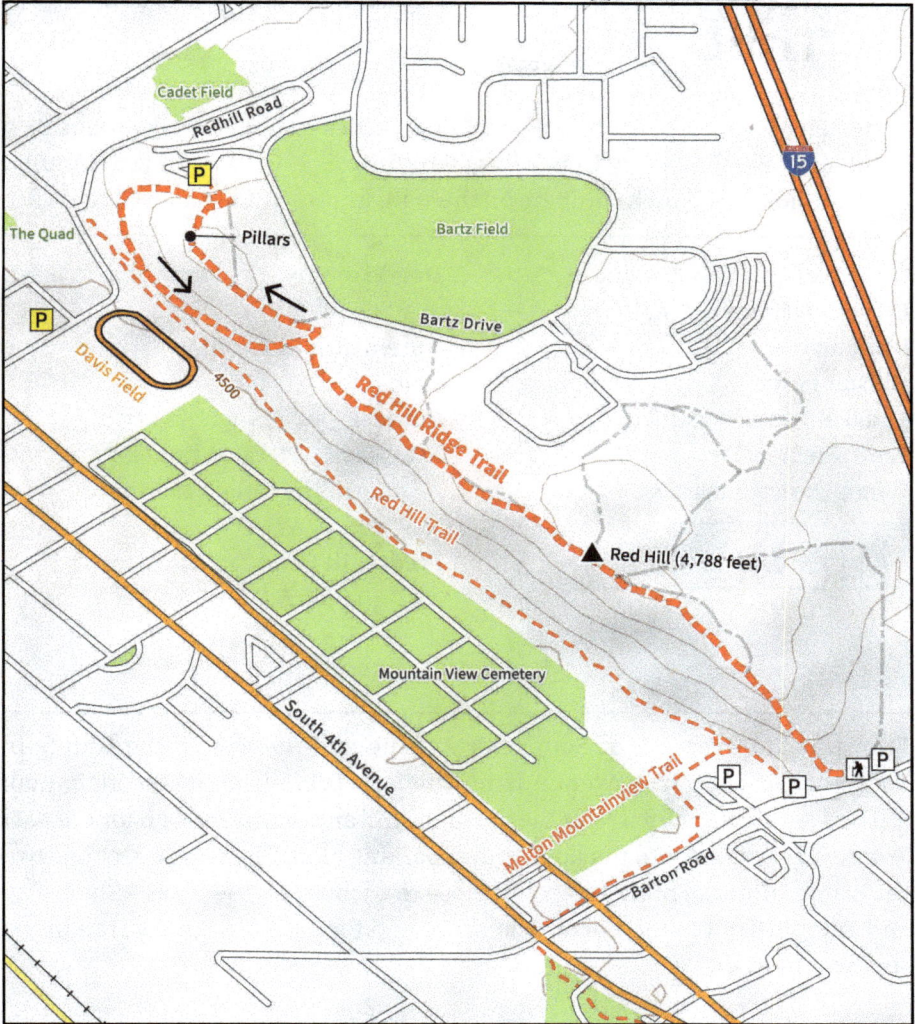

Cadet Field
Redhill Road
Bartz Field
The Quad
P
Pillars
Bartz Drive
P
Davis Field
4500
Red Hill Ridge Trail
Red Hill Trail
Red Hill (4,788 feet)
Mountain View Cemetery
South 4th Avenue
Melton Mountainview Trail
P
P
P
Barton Road
I-15

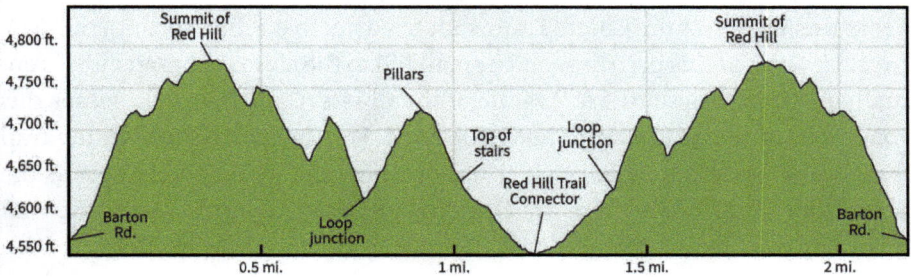

4,800 ft.
4,750 ft.
4,700 ft.
4,650 ft.
4,600 ft.
4,550 ft.

Summit of Red Hill
Pillars
Top of stairs
Loop junction
Summit of Red Hill
Barton Rd.
Loop junction
Red Hill Trail Connector
Barton Rd.

0.5 mi.   1 mi.   1.5 mi.   2 mi.

12. Maag - Shadyside and Taysom Trail

The Maag - Shadyside and Taysom Trail provides a shaded walk alongside a basalt cliff and the grassy Upper Ross Park Disc Golf Course. In the summer, it is common to see rock climbers on the wall, known as the Shady Side Wall.

Distance: 1.1 miles out-and-back
Elevation Gain: 40 feet
Difficulty: Easy
Hiking Time: About 30 minutes
Nearest Town: Pocatello
Trail Surface: Pavement
Wheelchair Access: Yes

Dog-Friendly: Yes; must be on a leash at all times
Amenities: Restrooms and water are available at Upper Ross Park.
Contact: portneufgreenway.org
Trailhead GPS Coordinates:
Avenue of the Chiefs Trailhead
N42° 50.571' W112° 25.021'
Fredregill Road Trailhead
N42° 50.883' W112° 25.445'

Getting There

From the intersection of South 5th Avenue and Avenue of the Chiefs in Pocatello, head south on Avenue of the Chiefs for 0.1 miles as it ascends a small hill between basalt cliffs. Near the top of the hill and just past a sign for the AMI Trailhead, turn left into the large gravel parking area. The parking lot has two separate trailheads branching off it close to each other, the Maag - Shadyside and Taysom Trail in the northeast corner and the AMI / Kirkham Trail in the southeast corner.

The Hike

From the Avenue of the Chiefs Trailhead, head north on the Taysom Trail. The first 200 yards of this path descend a small hill to the side of a basalt cliff, eventually reaching the southern Avenue of the Chiefs. Once the trail crosses this road, it becomes the Maag - Shadyside Trail. For the next 0.2 miles, the trail travels alongside the dark basalt cliffs, which rock climbers will know as the Shady Side Wall. While there are climbing routes all along this wall, the trail passes by two climber-specific areas at 0.2 and 0.3 miles, respectively.

The Shady Side Wall is popular with climbers during the heat of the summer.

Just past the second rock climbing wall, the trail leaves the cliffs and runs across the Upper Ross Park Disc Golf Course. This grassy area is nice to walk through, but you should be alert for disc golfers. Toward the end of the disc golf course, the path crosses the northern Avenue of the Chiefs. Not far beyond that crossing, the trail ends at a sidewalk by Fredregill Road.

Keep Going

There are plenty of fun sites just off the Shadyside Trail. In addition to the rock climbing walls and disc golf course, Upper Ross Park is home to the Fort Hall Replica, Bannock County Historical Complex, the Southeast Idaho Veterans Memorial, a roofed pavilion, and a playground. Just a stone's throw from the disc golf course, across South 4th Avenue, you will find the Rotary Rose Garden, the Pocatello Visitor Center, and a statue of Chief Pocatello.

The Pocatello Pump, the longest-running rock climbing competition in the United States, takes place in Ross Park along the Shady Side Wall and at the Sunny Side Wall, which is located off of South 2nd Avenue.

Maag - Shadyside and Taysom Trail

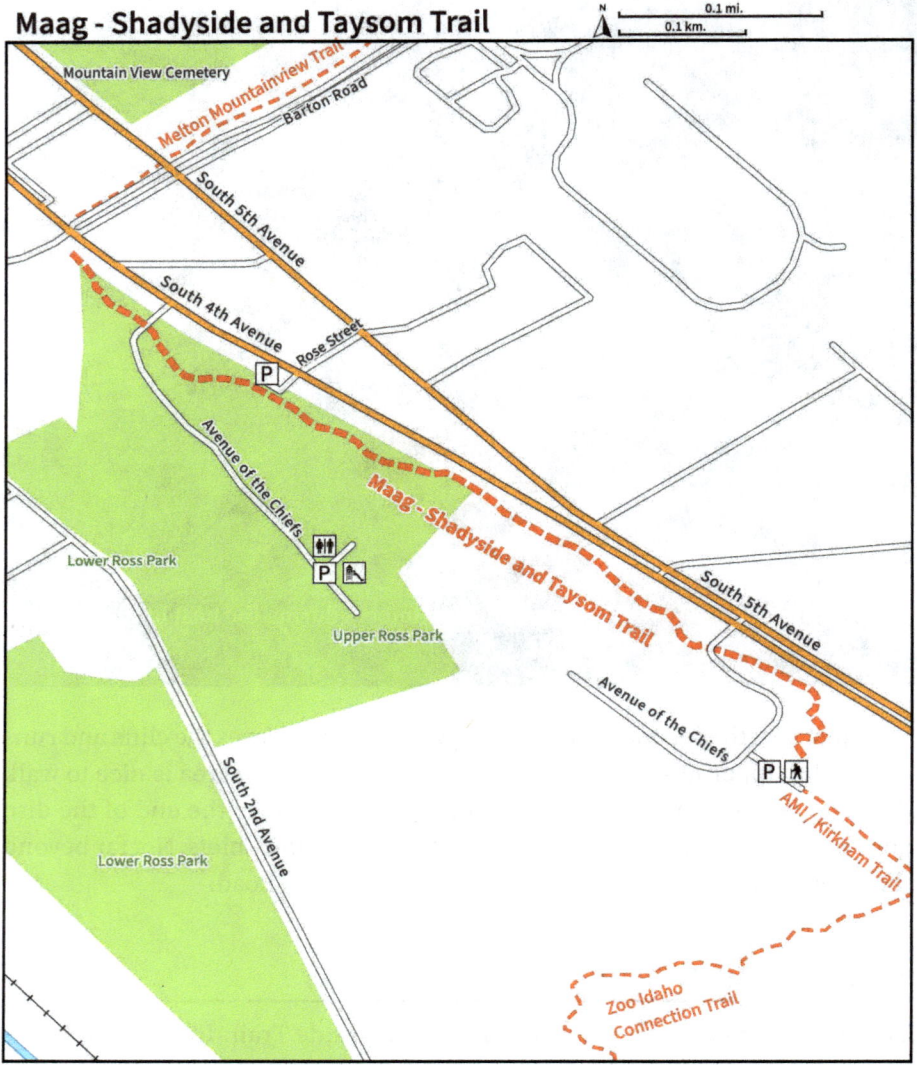

Mountain View Cemetery
Melton Mountainview Trail
Barton Road
South 5th Avenue
South 4th Avenue
Rose Street
P
Avenue of the Chiefs
Lower Ross Park
P
Maag - Shadyside and Taysom Trail
Upper Ross Park
South 5th Avenue
Avenue of the Chiefs
South 2nd Avenue
P
Lower Ross Park
AMI / Kirkham Trail
Zoo Idaho
Connection Trail

0.1 mi.
0.1 km.

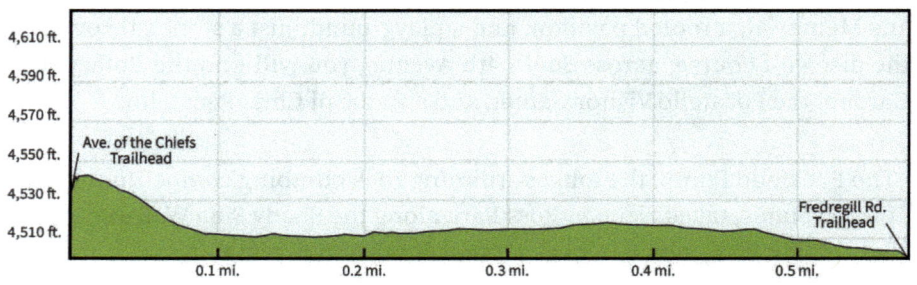

4,610 ft.
4,590 ft.
4,570 ft.
4,550 ft.
4,530 ft.
4,510 ft.

Ave. of the Chiefs
Trailhead

Fredregill Rd.
Trailhead

0.1 mi.   0.2 mi.   0.3 mi.   0.4 mi.   0.5 mi.

13. AMI / Kirkham Trail

Sitting atop basalt flows covered in sagebrush and dry grass, the AMI / Kirkham Trail offers a glimpse into the area's largely unaltered native landscape while providing excellent views of the surrounding mountains. This section of the Greenway is a popular gateway to connect the southern part of town to the ISU area. It is well-used by everyone from rollerbladers to dog walkers, many of whom come from Pocatello Animal Services, located near the trail's northern trailhead. This is a largely shadeless trail, so early morning or early evening start times are recommended in the heat of the summer.

Distance: 2.4 miles out-and-back
Elevation Gain: 60 feet
Difficulty: Easy
Hiking Time: About 45 minutes
Nearest Town: Pocatello
Trail Surface: Pavement
Wheelchair Access: Yes

Dog-Friendly: Yes; must be on a leash at all times
Amenities: None
Contact: portneufgreenway.org
Trailhead GPS Coordinates:
North 2nd Avenue Trailhead
N42° 49.688' W112° 24.511'
Avenue of the Chiefs Trailhead
N42° 50.559' W112° 25.016'

Getting There

North 2nd Avenue Trailhead: From the junction of Bannock Highway and South Valley Road, head northeast on South Valley Road for 0.5 miles. Turn right (southeast) onto Kirkham Road. In 0.2 miles, make a left (east) at the stop sign onto North 2nd Avenue and then take the first left (north) into the AMI/Kirkham Trail parking lot. The trail begins at the northwest corner of the parking lot.

Avenue of the Chiefs Trailhead: From the intersection of South 5th Avenue and Avenue of the Chiefs in Pocatello, head south on Avenue of the Chiefs for 0.1 miles as it ascends a small hill between basalt cliffs. Near the top of the hill and just past a sign for the AMI Trailhead, turn left (south) into the large gravel parking area. The AMI / Kirkham Trail begins in the southeast corner.

AMI / Kirkham Trail surrounded by sagebrush.

The Hike

From the North 2nd Avenue Trailhead, take the trail north as it heads up a small hill, keeping right (north) at the fork about 0.1 miles in. (If you were to take the left (northwest) path, you would end up atop the South Valley Connector.)

This early section of the path moves through basalt cliffs, eventually passing through an underpass that places you on the north side of the South Valley Connector. Once you emerge from the underpass, you will find the crumbling Atlas Powder Company Dynamite Cache and a sheltered picnic bench on the trail's right (north) side. Beyond this point, the basalt cliffs open up to sagebrush fields.

For the next 0.9 miles, the trail travels northwest in the sage, ending in a couple of long straightaways. The trail ends in a gravel parking lot, which it shares with the Maag - Shadyside Trail.

The southern stretch of the trail among the basalt cliffs.

Keep Going

Two optional side paths split off the AMI / Kirkham Trail, as well as a full Greenway trail. The first side path, an unnamed alternate path off of the main trail, occurs just over 0.3 miles into the hike. This right (east) turn places you on a secluded unpaved trail among the sage and cactus that eventually wraps its way back onto the main AMI / Kirkham Trail further north. This side trail is 0.5 miles long.

The second optional path is the **Zoo Idaho Connection Trail**. This 0.5-mile one-way trail ends at a pleasant sitting area overlooking the railyard and Riverside Golf Course. For rock climbers, this path provides easy access to the top of the Sunny Side Walls, specifically the Main Wall. The trail begins just 0.1 mile south of the northern AMI / Kirkham Trailhead and is a southwest turn onto a rough dirt trail. About a quarter mile in, this dirt trail connects with the narrow paved Zoo Idaho Connection Trail. No dogs are allowed on this trail.

The **South Valley Connector Trail** is a unique part of the Greenway in southern Pocatello that is easily accessible from AMI / Kirkham Trail's southern parking lot. The 1.0-mile one-way trail travels atop the South Valley Connector, gaining 90 feet and hugging the road for the entirety of its journey as it climbs from Bannock Highway over the Portneuf River and railroad onto the basalt lava flows and eventually ends at South 5th Avenue. The southwest portion of the path has pretty views of the river, railroad, and hills of southwest Pocatello. In contrast, the northeast section that traverses under the interstate, sided by sagebrush and rock, is more desolate, but does provide a view of Chinese Peak. The trail is often used as a connecting path between AMI / Kirkham Trail and the Edson Fichter Nature Area.

Those curious about Pocatello's railroad history will be interested in the Atlas Powder Company Dynamite Cache found in the trail's southern section. The Atlas Powder Company was an explosives and chemical company that was a major supplier of explosives to the Union Pacific Railroad. Explosives such as TNT, black powder, and dynamite were stored in the cache, whose location was chosen due to its position away from downtown Pocatello.

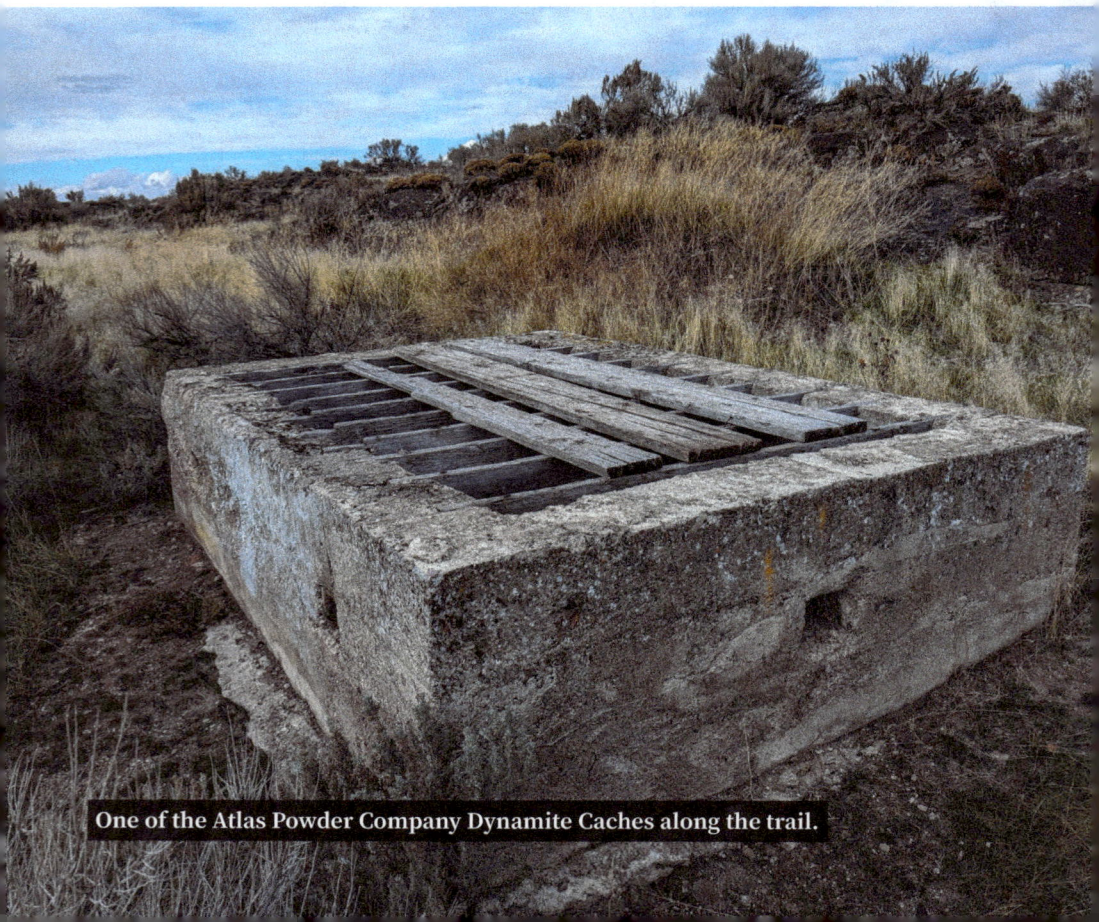

One of the Atlas Powder Company Dynamite Caches along the trail.

AMI / Kirkham Trail

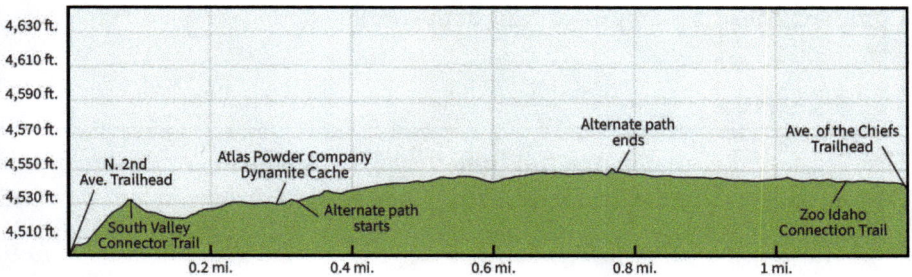

0.25 mi.
0.25 km.

N

Maag - Shadyside and Taysom Trail

South 5th Avenue

Avenue of the Chiefs Trailhead

Lower Ross Park

Zoo Idaho Connection Trail

15

South 5th Avenue

Alternate Path

AMI / Kirkham Trail

South 2nd Avenue

Riverside Golf Course

Portneuf River

South Valley Road

Bannock Highway

South Valley Connector Trail

Indian Hills Trail

North 2nd Avenue Trailhead

4,630 ft.					
4,610 ft.					
4,590 ft.					
4,570 ft.			Alternate path ends		Ave. of the Chiefs Trailhead
4,550 ft.	Atlas Powder Company Dynamite Cache				
4,530 ft.	N. 2nd Ave. Trailhead	Alternate path starts			Zoo Idaho Connection Trail
4,510 ft.	South Valley Connector Trail				

0.2 mi.   0.4 mi.   0.6 mi.   0.8 mi.   1 mi.

14. Edson Fichter Nature Area

With a family-friendly fishing pond and beautiful river access, the Edson Fichter Nature Area offers a bounty of outdoor opportunities. The main Edson Fichter Loop is the best way to navigate this riparian zone. Educational displays highlighting the area's ecosystem are located along this paved path, making the walk fun for all age groups. A particularly cool feature of the area is the Monarch Waystation, which provides energy and shelter to monarch butterflies as they migrate through North America. Dog owners will be happy to learn that the southeast portion of the path (which has a standalone dog pond) allows off-leash dogs.

Distance: 1-mile loop
Elevation Gain: 20 feet
Difficulty: Easy
Hiking Time: About 30 minutes
Nearest Town: Pocatello
Trail Surface: Pavement
Wheelchair Access: Yes

Dog-Friendly: Yes; on-leash at the trailhead and while on the main trail. Off-leash if under control is allowed east of the dog pond.

Amenities: Restrooms and water available nearby at the Indian Hills Soccer Complex. A life jacket loaner station is available at the trailhead.

Contact: portneufgreenway.org

Trailhead GPS Coordinates: N42° 49.324' W112° 24.370'

Getting There

From the intersection of Bannock Highway and Cheyenne Avenue in Pocatello, head north on Cheyenne Avenue for about 0.2 miles. Turn right shortly past Cherokee Street, following the signs for Edson Fichter Nature Area. The well-marked trailhead is at the east end of this road past the Indian Hills Soccer Complex. There is plenty of parking at the trailhead.

The Hike

Head east up the small paved hill from the signed trailhead. At the top of this hill, you will pass by the Edson Fichter / Indian Hills Trail on your left. Descend the other side of the hill and continue straight, where you will pass an outdoor

The Edson Fichter Pond sits in the heart of this paved trail system.

amphitheater on your left and the Beverly Trail on your right. At about the 0.1-mile mark, make a right (southeast) turn and cross a bridge over the Portneuf River. Take a right turn once across the bridge to start the loop, which is about 0.8 miles in total. Stay right at every paved junction to complete the loop back to this bridge.

The first half of the loop travels southeast, spending most of its time alongside the river. At 0.3 miles, you will come to a pleasant river viewing area where two small forks of the Portneuf rejoin. This is an excellent spot to take a break and cool off in the water on a hot summer day.

You will pass by the dog pond's southern end shortly after this river view-point, where the off-leash zone begins. About half a mile into the main hike, the path makes a northwestern U-turn, trading the river for the railway. Once the trail reaches the dog pond's northern end, the off-leash stretch of the hike is over.

The last section of the hike runs alongside the fishing pond. After reaching the northern tip of the pond, the trail turns south. Make the next right turn at the paved junction to return to the starting bridge.

Keep Going

The area is filled with small trails that can be a fun way to change up the main loop. If you are looking for something more substantial that stays close to the main Edson Fichter Loop, I recommend the **Beverly Trail**. Starting near the trailhead on the main loop's right (south) side, this 0.9-mile out-and-back trail hugs the southern side of the Portneuf River, providing an excellent alternate river walk from the main loop.

The **Edson Fichter and Indian Hills Trail** is a 0.9-mile one-way trail that travels northwest above the Portneuf River. The trail begins on the left (north) side of the Edson Fichter Main Loop near the parking lot, at the top of the small hill. In addition to great views of the river, this path serves as a connector for those looking to access the AMI / Kirkham Trail from the Edson Fichter Area.

Anglers will be excited to know that Edson Fichter's fishing pond is stocked with rainbow trout. Three docks extend into the pond, making this a great spot for fishermen to cast their rods.

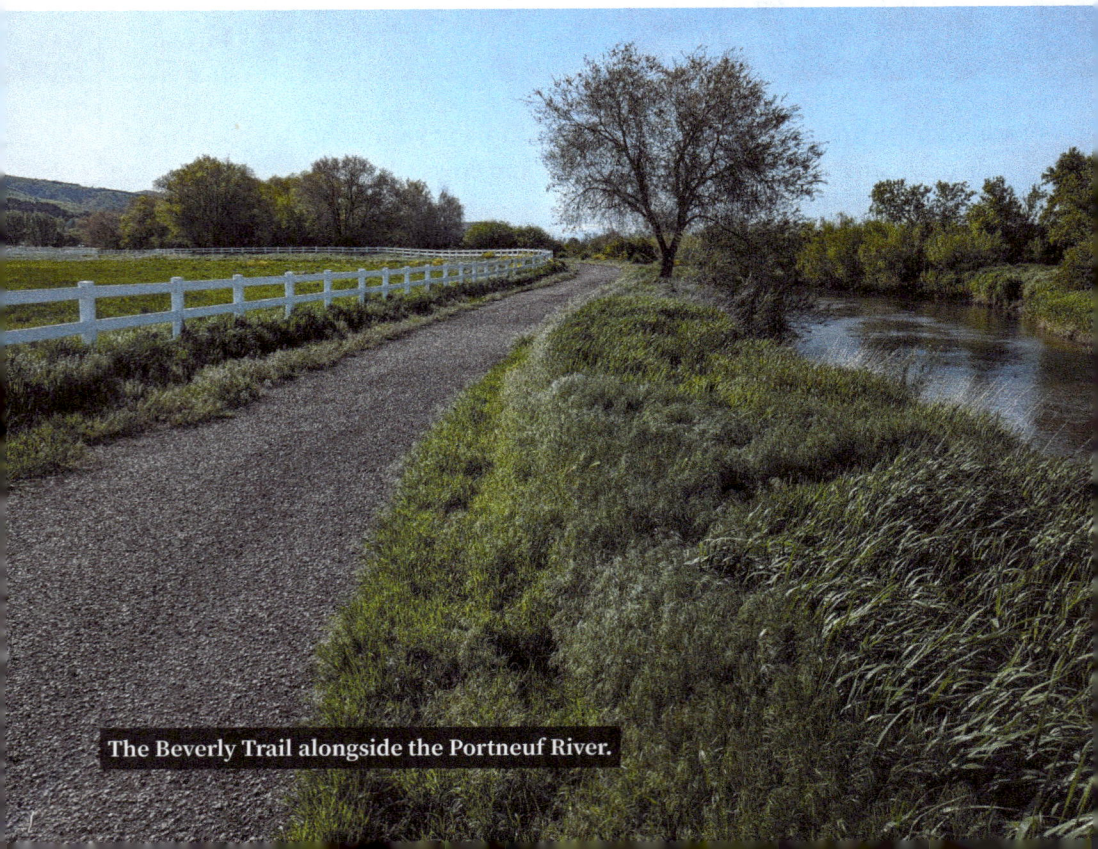

The Beverly Trail alongside the Portneuf River.

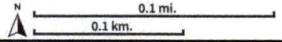

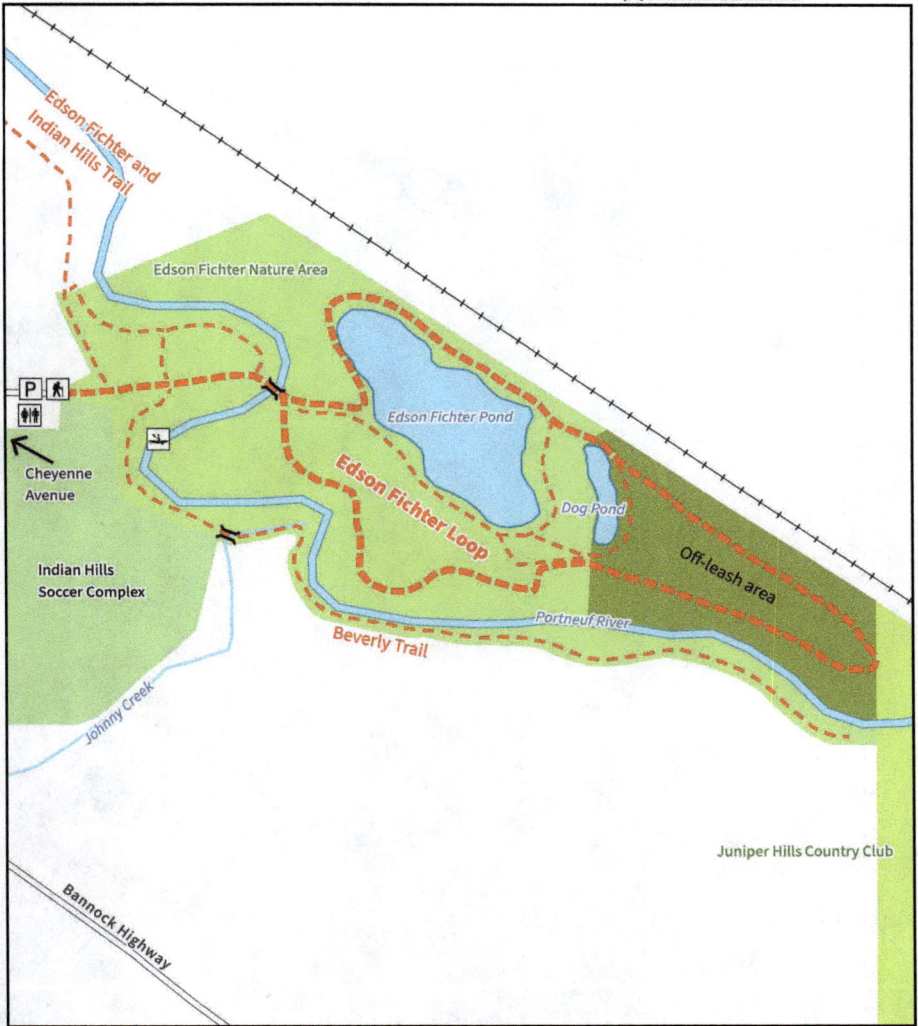

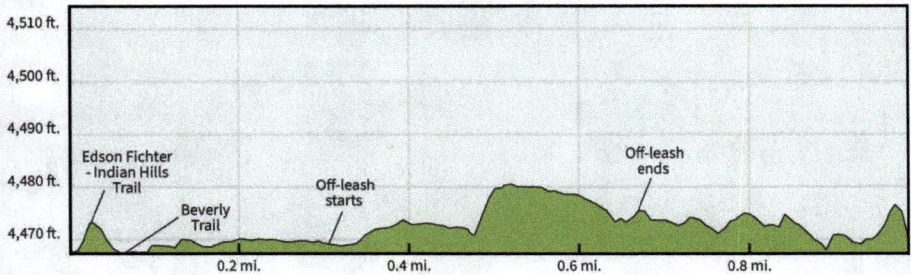

Edson Fichter Nature Area

N
0.1 mi.
0.1 km.

Edson Fichter and
Indian Hills Trail

Edson Fichter Nature Area

Edson Fichter Pond

Edson Fichter Loop

Dog Pond

Off-leash area

P

Cheyenne
Avenue

Indian Hills
Soccer Complex

Beverly Trail

Portneuf River

Johnny Creek

Bannock Highway

Juniper Hills Country Club

4,510 ft.
4,500 ft.
4,490 ft.
4,480 ft.
4,470 ft.

Edson Fichter
- Indian Hills
Trail

Beverly
Trail

Off-leash
starts

Off-leash
ends

0.2 mi.   0.4 mi.   0.6 mi.   0.8 mi.

Pocatello Range

Located to the east of the city, the Pocatello Range boasts a robust trail system that is easily accessible from town. One of the highlights of this region is the Chinese Peak - Blackrock Trail System, which offers a variety of interconnected trails for hikers, bikers, and motorized users on Bureau of Land Management land. The newly developed Pioneer Ridge Trail System is another highlight, providing a well-designed hiking and mountain biking system in the northeast part of the city with open vistas of the town and the Snake River Plain.

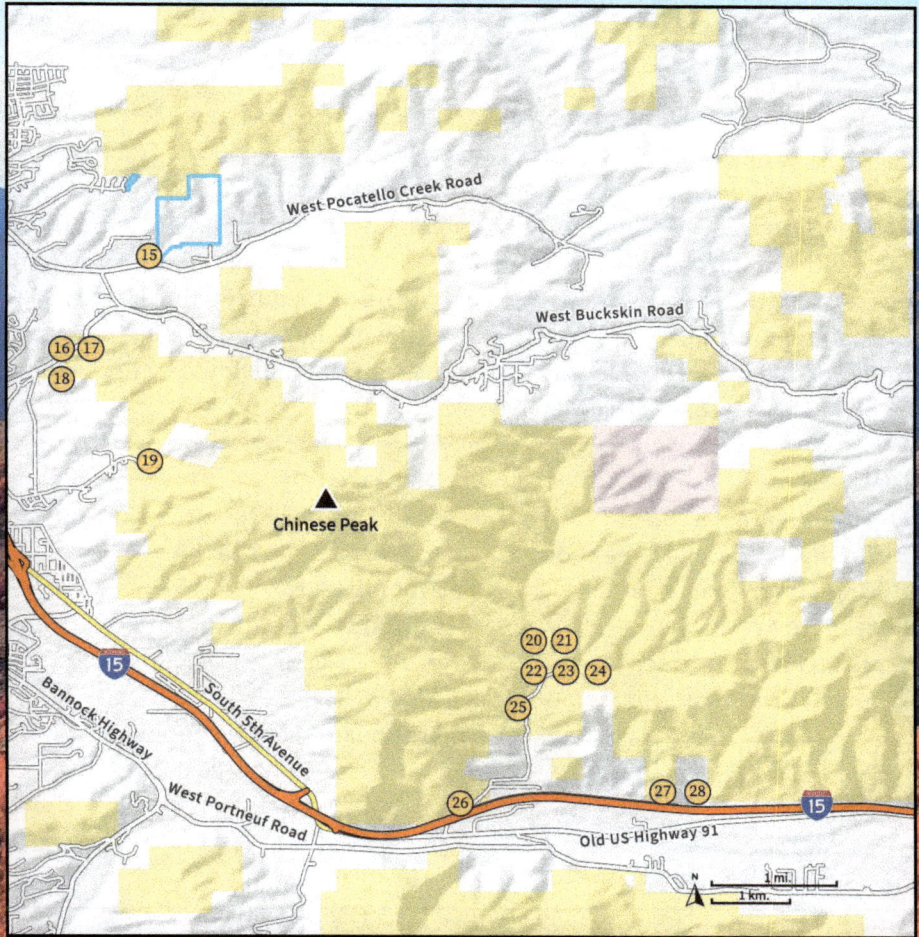

West Pocatello Creek Road

West Buckskin Road

⑮

⑯ ⑰
⑱

⑲

▲
Chinese Peak

⑳ ㉑
㉒ ㉓ ㉔
㉕

Bannock Highway
South 5th Avenue
15

West Portneuf Road

㉖

㉗ ㉘
15

Old US Highway 91

N
1 mi.
1 km.

The eastern slopes of Chinese Peak in autumn.

15. Pioneer Ridge Loop

The Pioneer Ridge Loop gives hikers a chance to explore the wilderness in the northeastern part of the city. This sage and juniper-sided loop climbs high on the hills overlooking the city, granting excellent views of the Snake River Plain and the Satterfield residential area. The first mile of the trail (also called Top of the First) runs through a rehabilitated section of the old landfill, so it is important to stay on the path for environmental concerns during this stretch. The system is close to many residential areas, though the only official access point is off Pocatello Creek Road. For an overview of the individual trails, visit the Pioneer Ridge Trail Overview on page 427.

Distance: 8.2-mile lollipop loop
Elevation Gain: 1,250 feet
Difficulty: Moderately strenuous
Hiking Time: About 4 hours
Nearest Town: Pocatello
Trail Surface: Dirt, rock
Wheelchair Access: None

Dog-Friendly: Yes; on-leash at the trailhead. May be off-leash if under control once on the trail
Amenities: None
Contact: Bureau of Land Management, Pocatello Field Office 208-478-6340
Trailhead GPS Coordinates: N42° 53.304' W112° 23.335'

Getting There

From the intersection of Olympus Drive and Pocatello Creek Road, head east on Pocatello Creek Road for 2.5 miles. Turn left onto Archery Club Lane (also called Little Pocatello Creek), where you will immediately find a small parking turnoff near a gate. The trail begins just past the gate to the north.

The Hike

From the small parking area, head north, passing by the gate on a trail to its right. Once on the other side, you will continue north on the wide Little Pocatello Creek Road. At 0.2 miles, next to the Junction 1 sign, the trail leaves the wide dirt road for a singletrack path on the left (north). This singletrack path, also known as Top of the First, winds up through a juniper forest, reaching a gate at 0.3 miles. Continue northeast through the gate on the trail as it

travels alongside the junipers.

For the next three-quarters of a mile, the trail climbs 250 feet as it makes its way north through sage and juniper forests toward the central Pioneer Ridge Trail System. At mile 1.0, the trail comes to a gate, where the trail transitions from the City of Pocatello property to BLM land. Once on BLM land, there are many intersecting trails, so keep an eye out for trail signage.

Continue north through the gate until you reach Junction 2 at 1.1 miles, signifying the end of the Top of the First. Turn right (northeast) onto Wacko's Way, which wraps around a hillside through the junipers. At about 1.2 miles, the trail comes to a series of intersecting paths. Continue north on the center path for about 70 yards, where you will then make a right (northeast) turn. At 1.4 miles, continue straight (east) across the intersecting trail.

At about 1.5 miles, cross over an intersecting path and continue north on the singletrack trail. From here, the trail switchbacks a few times across a grassy hillside intermixed with junipers. At 1.7 miles, at Junction 3, the trail ends its initial large stretch of incline at a junction with the main Pioneer Ridge Loop. Follow the loop clockwise by taking the left (southwest) path onto South Paw. (If you wish to walk the loop counterclockwise, turn right (north) onto the Line Drive Trail.)

The area offers plenty of fun trails for both hikers and mountain bikers.

About 30 yards on South Paw, continue west across an intersecting trail. The trail continues on the hillside above a dry drainage, providing excellent views of Chinese Peak to the southeast. A little over 1.9 miles in, continue south across an intersecting trail. At 2.0 miles, again, continue through an intersecting trail, this time to the west. At 2.1 miles, make a slight right to stay on the main loop.

At 2.2 miles, the trail crosses over to the northwest side of a 4x4 trail. The trail travels high on a dry hillside for the next half mile as it makes its way north. At 2.7 miles, at Junction 11, the trail turns right (north), beginning Around the Horn. Shortly onto Around the Horn, the trail crosses two wide 4x4 paths, both variations of the Lower Missing Springs Trail. Continue northeast through both of these paths.

Around the Horn is a rather scenic stretch of the loop, providing excellent views of the hillsides and the residential area to the west. At about 3 miles, you will pass the Otta Here (Junction 10) on the trail's right (east) side. (Otta Here connects with Line Drive, allowing for a shorter loop option.) About a quarter of a mile past Otta Here, the trail enters a juniper forest and passes through a couple of drainages. After crossing the second drainage, the trail makes a left (southwest) turn out of the forest and continues along the hillside.

At about 3.4 miles, the trail turns north, crossing over a hillside toward the water tank. As the path nears the water tank, several other 4x4 trails cross over the path, which can be confusing. The first of these rogue paths begins at 3.5 miles. Whenever confronted with one of these 4x4 trails, continue on the singletrack to the north. At 3.6 miles, the path continues to the northeast as it crosses Upper Missing Springs Road. Shortly beyond that dirt road crossing, continue northeast, crossing two singletrack paths until the trail enters the forest. You will pass by Junction 9 in this forest.

At 3.7 miles, the trail comes to a fork at Junction 8. The right path is the beginning of Four Bagger, which shortens the loop and ends at the top of Line Drive. To continue the main loop, take the left path, which begins Frozen Rope. About a quarter of a mile into Frozen Rope, you will pass through Junction 7. At about 4.0 miles, the trail crosses to the northeast side of a 4x4 trail. About 120 yards from there, the trail crosses another 4x4 trail, this time to the east side. The remainder of Frozen Rope travels across the northern tip of the loop. The trail here is sided by sagebrush and has excellent views of the landscape to the north.

At 4.7 miles, Frozen Rope ends at Junction 6. To the left (north) is the Pickle, which connects to a private trail on which the Pocatello Pioneers race team practices. To the right (south) is the Hit for the Cycle, which you continue on to stay in the loop. Shortly onto Hit for the Cycle, the path crosses to the south side of the doubletrack Lower Pocatello Road. The trail winds across sagebrush hillsides and occasional juniper forests for the next mile as it makes its way southwest.

At 5.7 miles, the path crosses a cattle guard and comes to Junction 5. On the path's right (west) side, you will find Four Bagger Trail, which heads west across the 4x4 trail. To the south (roughly straight ahead across a rough 4x4 trail), you will find the beginning of Line Drive Trail. Continue on Line Drive as it heads south. Line Drive descends about 150 feet for the next half-mile until it connects with Wacko's Way. At about 6.1 miles, you will pass through Junction 4, avoiding Otta Here on the trail's right (west) side.

At 6.3 miles, you will reach Junction 3, completing the main loop. Make the left (northeast) turn onto Wacko's Way and retrace your path back to the trailhead.

Pioneer Ridge was conceived and designed by Bruce Olenick. The trail system is named after the local middle school and high school mountain bike team, the "Pocatello Pioneers," who practice in the area.

Pioneer Ridge Loop

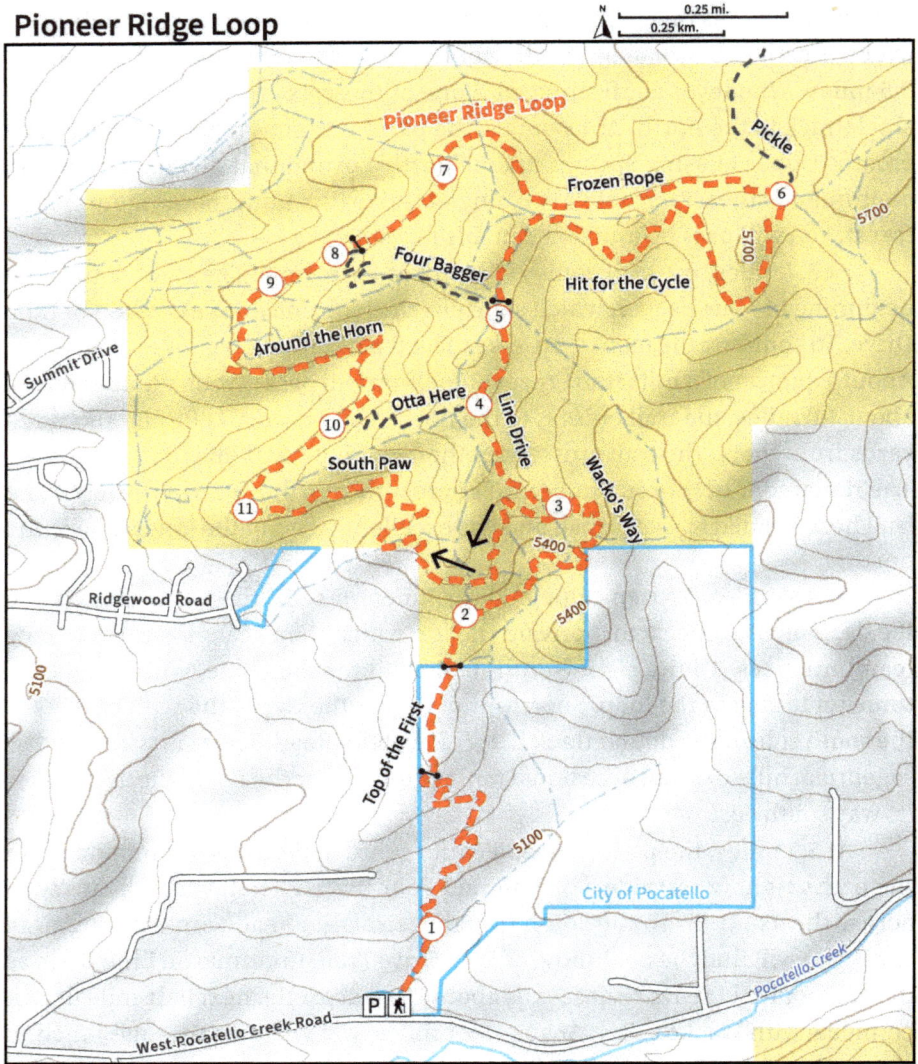

N

0.25 mi.
0.25 km.

Pioneer Ridge Loop

Pickle

7

Frozen Rope

6

5700

5700

8

Four Bagger

Hit for the Cycle

9

5

Around the Horn

Otta Here

4

Line Drive

Summit Drive

10

Wacko's Way

South Paw

3

11

5400

Ridgewood Road

2

5400

5100

Top of the First

5100

City of Pocatello

1

Pocatello Creek

P

West Pocatello Creek Road

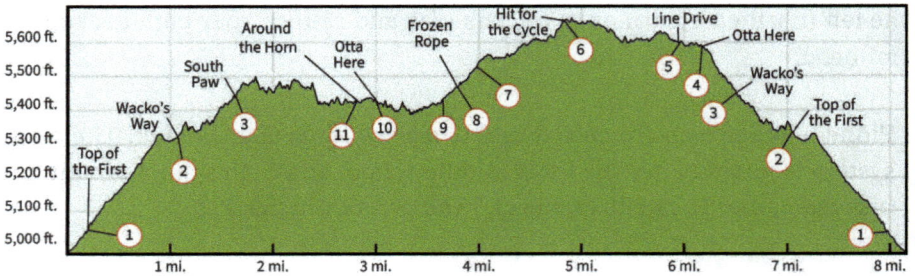

Elevation profile:

Elevation	Labels
5,600 ft.	
5,500 ft.	Around the Horn, Otta Here, Frozen Rope, Hit for the Cycle, Line Drive, Otta Here
5,400 ft.	South Paw, Wacko's Way
5,300 ft.	Wacko's Way
5,200 ft.	Top of the First, Top of the First
5,100 ft.	
5,000 ft.	

1 mi.   2 mi.   3 mi.   4 mi.   5 mi.   6 mi.   7 mi.   8 mi.

16. Cave Trail

The Cave Trail mini-trail system is a challenging set of interconnected technical mountain bike trails that feature many jumps, gaps, ramps, and other obstacles built by the community. These trails are located below Buckskin Road and run through rocky sage and juniper hills in a dry drainage. Hikers should be careful, as the trails are mainly used by mountain bikers. The main path passes through the heart of the Cave Trail system, and while it is not technical, veering off it may lead to challenging terrain. Cave Trail is situated on Idaho State University land, and even though the University does not maintain these trails, they have generously permitted their inclusion in this book.

Distance: 1 mile out-and-back
Elevation Gain: 190 feet
Difficulty: Easy; Black diamond for mountain bikers
Hiking Time: About 30 minutes
Nearest Town: Pocatello
Trail Surface: Dirt, rock

Wheelchair Access: None
Dog-Friendly: Yes; Must be on a leash at all times
Amenities: None
Contact: Idaho State University, 208-282-4636
Trailhead GPS Coordinates: N42° 52.271' W112° 24.421'

Getting There

From the junction of S. 5th Avenue and E. Carter Street, head northeast on E. Carter Street for 0.2 miles. Turn right onto S. 8th Avenue, then turn left at the light onto Martin Luther King Jr Way. Continue on Martin Luther King Jr Way for 0.3 miles until it transitions into E. Terry Street at the light. Continue on E. Terry Street for 1.3 miles. Once past American Road, turn left into a small unnamed parking area, where you can find the trail on the north side.

The Hike

Starting from the trailhead, head northeast on the singletrack trail, which leads down into the drainage. For the initial 0.4 miles, the trail travels northeast through a series of intersecting trails that zigzag. I recommend staying on the well-defined path and avoid taking any trails toward the left (west) onto the hillside or the right (east) into the juniper forest to avoid technical terrain.

At around 0.4 miles, the path turns toward the left (northwest). The remaining 0.1 or so mile of the trail is rockier as it ascends toward a juniper forest. Although there is no visual indicator, the official trail ends at the half-mile mark before continuing onto private property.

Cave Trail is unofficially named after a small cave located about 0.2 miles from the trailhead toward the left (north) of the main path. Spelunkers should not get their hopes up as the cave is very small.

Some of the area's many interweaving trails.

Cave Trail

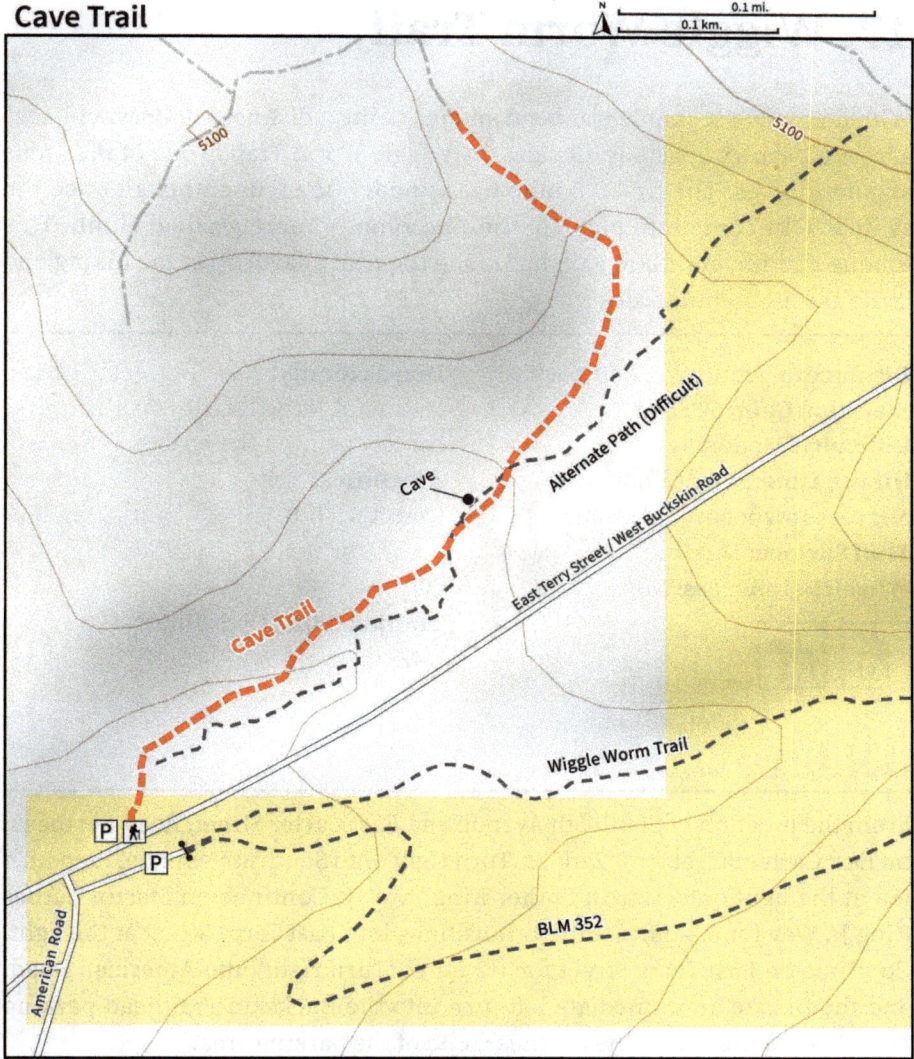

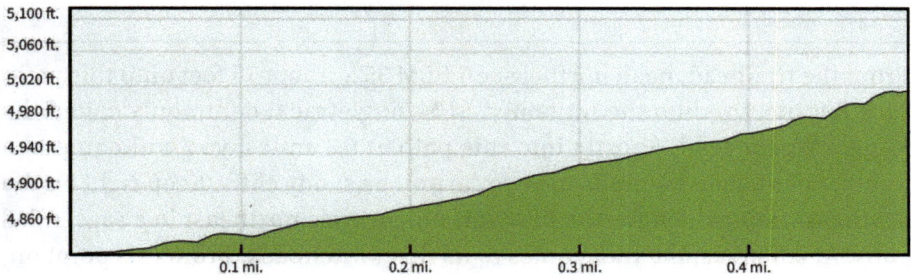

17. Wiggle Worm Trail

With an easily accessible trailhead and featuring a distinct set of switchbacks across a beautiful juniper hillside, the Wiggle Worm Trail is one of the area's standout hikes. The first 0.8 mile has a moderate incline, though once the switchbacks come into play, the trail becomes a more gradual climb. This unique and fun elevation gain has made the trail a favorite in the hiking and trail running communities.

Distance: 5.9 miles out-and-back
Elevation Gain: 600 feet
Difficulty: Moderate
Hiking Time: About 3 hours
Nearest Town: Pocatello
Trail Surface: Dirt, rock
Wheelchair Access: None

Dog-Friendly: Yes; on-leash at the trailhead. May be off-leash if under control once on the trail
Amenities: None
Contact: Bureau of Land Management, Pocatello Field Office 208-478-6340
Trailhead GPS Coordinates: N42° 52.259' W112° 24.391'

Getting There

From the junction of South 5th Avenue and East Carter Street, head northeast on East Carter Street for 0.2 miles. Turn right onto South 8th Avenue, then turn left at the light onto Martin Luther King Jr. Way. Continue on Martin Luther King Jr. Way for 0.3 miles until it transitions into East Terry Street at the light. Continue on East Terry Street for 1.2 miles. Turn right onto American Road, and then make an immediate left turn into the Buckskin Trailhead parking area. The trailhead is at the northeast end of the parking area.

The Hike

From the trailhead, head northeast on BLM 352. About 70 feet onto this path, turn left (north) onto the unnamed BLM singletrack, commonly called the Wiggle Worm Trail. Shortly into this path at 0.1 miles, you will come to a jumble of intersecting trails near some unique sandy cliffs. Keep right on the southeast trail, which for the first half mile travels northeast in a sage-sided gully. At 0.6 miles, the trail comes to its first switchback. From this point on, the trail earns its Wiggle Worm name, beginning a seemingly endless stretch of switchbacks.

For the next 2.3 miles, the trail gradually climbs 400 feet through open hillsides in the south and juniper forests in the north. When in the forests, be careful not to take any unofficial small paths that cut between switchbacks. Similarly, don't get confused by a compelling-looking fork when on the southern end of the trail, keep left to stay on the well-traveled Wiggle Worm Trail.

As you climb higher on this route, the switchbacks become more prolonged, and the views of the hillsides and ravine more striking. The trail ends at about 2.9 miles, when it joins with the doubletrack BLM 352 Trail. You can either retrace your footsteps back to the trailhead, or turn right (west) onto BLM 352, which ends back at the parking lot in 1.1 miles.

> Contrary to what you may see online, Wiggle Worm Trail does not allow mountain bikers.

Wiggle Worm Trail's unique switchbacks.

Wiggle Worm Trail

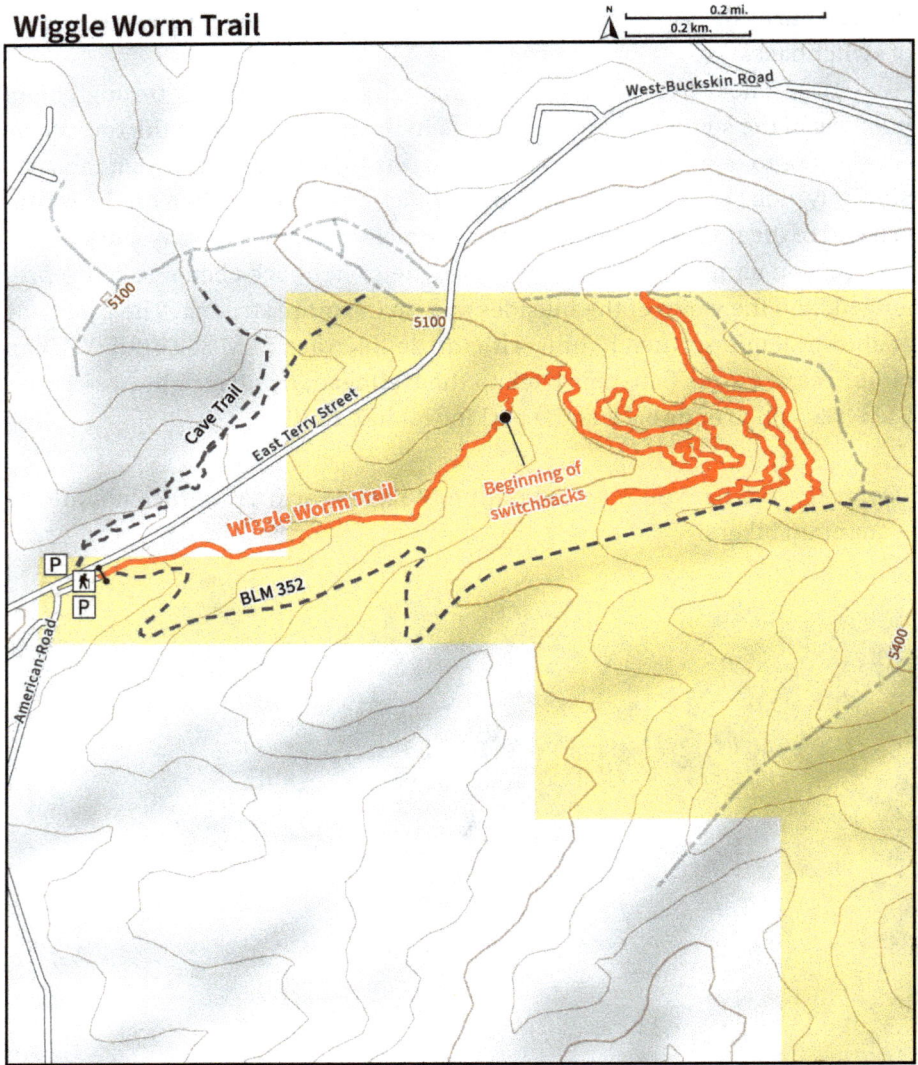

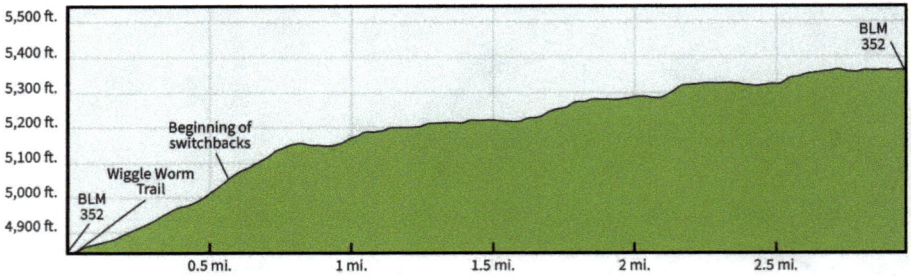

N

| 0.2 mi. |
| 0.2 km. |

West-Buckskin Road

5100

5100

Cave Trail

East Terry Street

Wiggle Worm Trail

Beginning of switchbacks

BLM 352

P

P

American Road

5400

5,500 ft.								BLM 352
5,400 ft.								
5,300 ft.								
5,200 ft.								
5,100 ft.	Beginning of switchbacks							
5,000 ft.	Wiggle Worm Trail							
4,900 ft.	BLM 352							

0.5 mi.   1 mi.   1.5 mi.   2 mi.   2.5 mi.

18. BLM 352

A notoriously steep hill in the middle of this route may turn away casual hikers, but those who push through are rewarded with an excellent ridge walk and scenic views of Chinese Peak. The early stretch of the path before the incline is also a nice hike, with views of the Buckskin area for those not looking for a strenuous climb. As both this trail and the popular Wiggle Worm Trail share the same parking lot, they are frequently used in tandem.

Distance: 6.8 miles out-and-back
Elevation Gain: 1,980 feet
Difficulty: Strenuous
Hiking Time: About 4 hours
Nearest Town: Pocatello
Trail Surface: Dirt, rock
Wheelchair Access: None

Dog-Friendly: Yes; on-leash at the trailhead. May be off-leash if under control once on the trail
Amenities: None
Contact: Bureau of Land Management, Pocatello Field Office 208-478-6340
Trailhead GPS Coordinates: N42° 52.259' W112° 24.391'

Getting There

From the junction of South 5th Avenue and East Carter Street, head northeast on East Carter Street for 0.2 miles. Turn right onto South 8th Avenue, then turn left at the light onto Martin Luther King Jr. Way. Continue on Martin Luther King Jr. Way for 0.3 miles until it transitions into East Terry Street at the light. Continue on East Terry Street for 1.2 miles. Turn right onto American Road, and then make an immediate left turn into the Buckskin Trailhead parking area. The trailhead is at the northeast end of the parking area.

The Hike

From the trailhead, head northeast on the 4x4 path. For the next 1.2 miles, the trail climbs about 550 feet up a gradual incline through a dry hillside. This section occasionally has large ruts, though they are usually easy to navigate. At 1.1 miles, the trail passes by the endpoint of Wiggle Worm Trail, which is located on the left (north) side of the path. At 1.2 miles, the trail comes to the top of a small hill. At this point, a few unofficial trails emerge from the trail's left

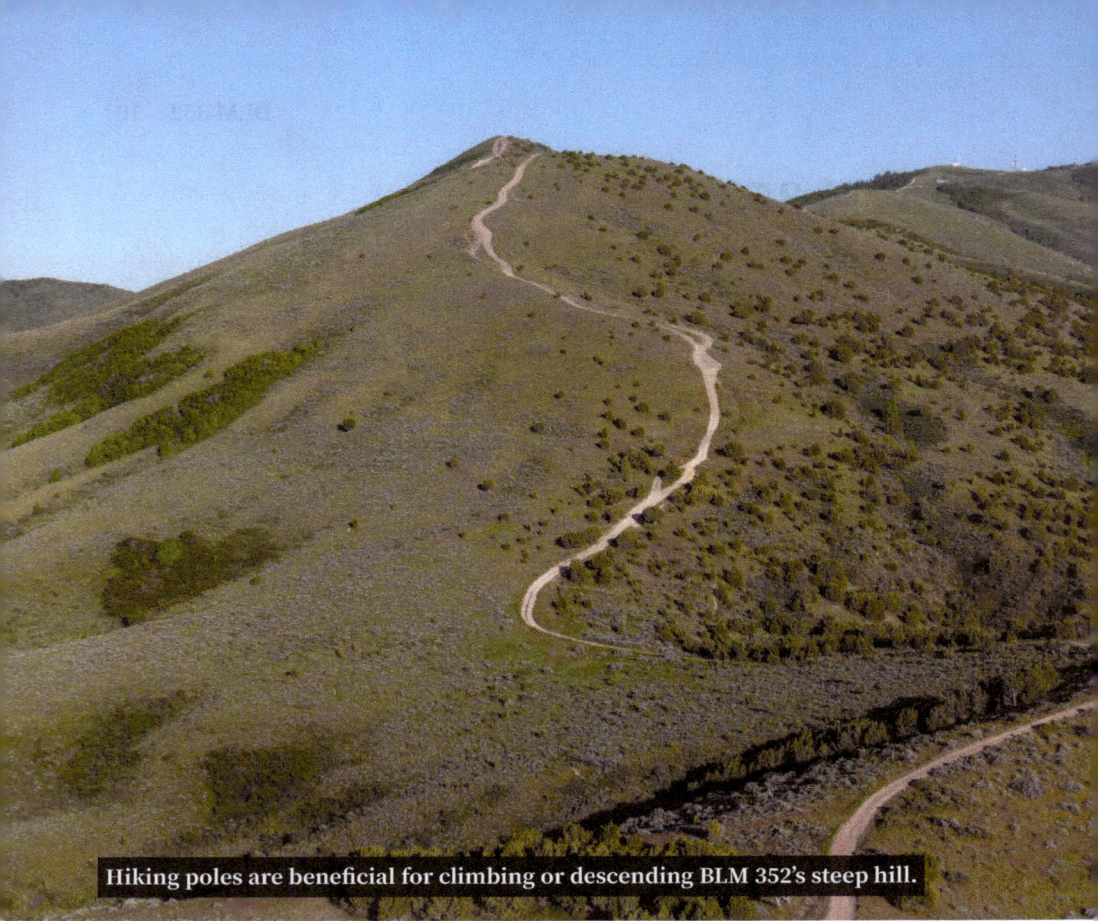

Hiking poles are beneficial for climbing or descending BLM 352's steep hill.

(north) side. Continue past them on the well-used path to the east/southeast down through the junipers.

At 1.4 miles, the trail reaches the top of another small hill, where you will have an excellent view of the upcoming steep hillside to the southeast. For those looking for a casual hike, this is a fine spot to turn around; otherwise, continue toward the steep climb, which gains over 550 feet in about 0.4 miles. After this grueling climb, you will reach the top of the incline at 2.0 miles. Be sure to check out the excellent vista behind you!

While the most strenuous climb of the hike is done, there is one last hill to ascend before reaching the ridge walk. This next hill climbs about 200 feet in 0.2 miles on a rocky path, so be prepared for another tough climb. At 2.3 miles, you will come to the top of the incline, where you will have many views of Chinese Peak's northwest ridge and the upcoming ridge walk. At 2.5 miles, keep right (south) to avoid an unofficial trail. At 2.8 miles, you will come to a fork. Either option works, though I recommend the left (southeast) path.

At 3.0 miles, the trail increases in steepness, gaining about 250 feet in a quarter of a mile. At 3.1 miles, continue straight (south), avoiding an unofficial trail on the path's right (west) side. At 3.4 miles, keep right (southwest) at the fork. (If you go left, you eventually reach the mountain's summit on a steep, rocky trail. You would also pass by BLM T355, which heads east and connects to Blackrock Canyon.)

The trail ends when it connects to BLM 301. If you would like to summit the mountain, turn left (northeast) onto BLM 301, which, after a quarter mile, reaches the top of Chinese Peak.

Just north of Pocatello, the Snake River Plain stretches across southern Idaho like a smile. The eastern half of the plain was primarily formed by the movement of tectonic plates over the Yellowstone Hotspot, resulting in the flat landscape we see today.

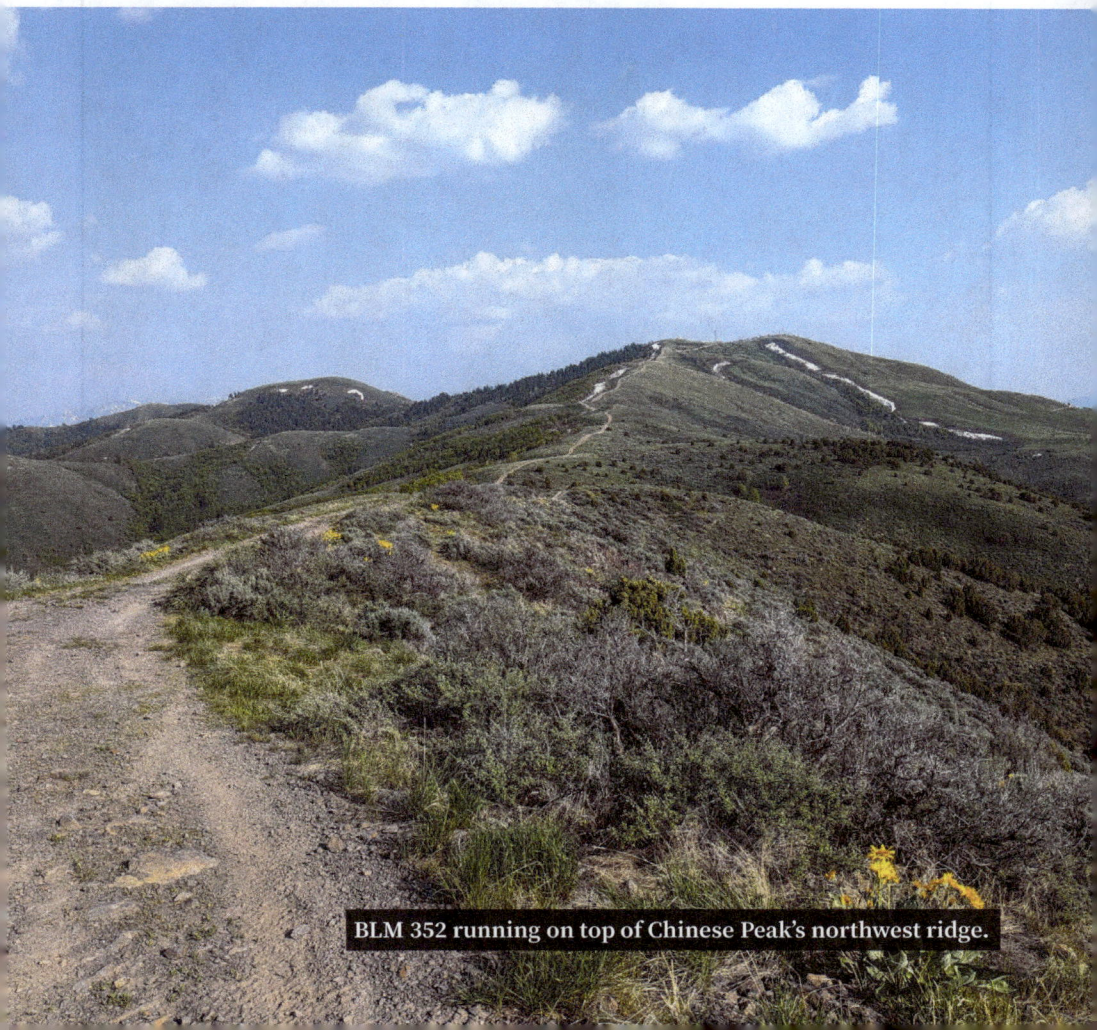

BLM 352 running on top of Chinese Peak's northwest ridge.

BLM 352

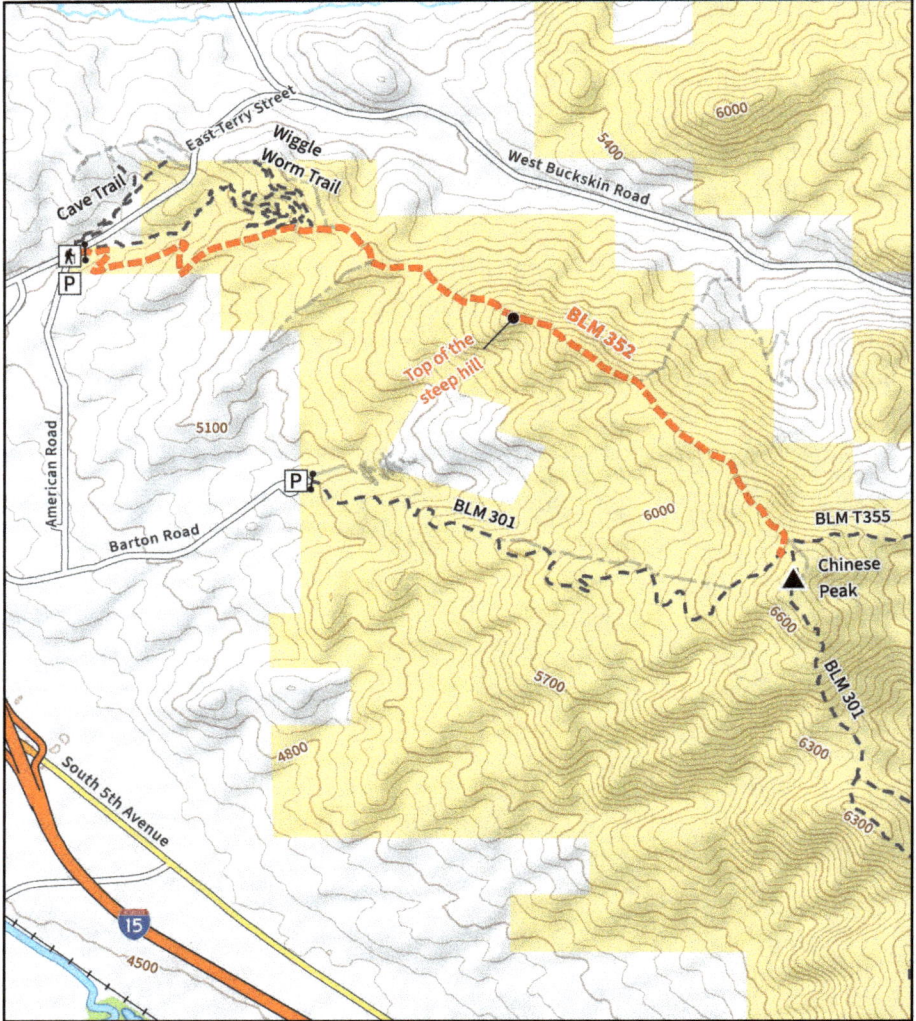

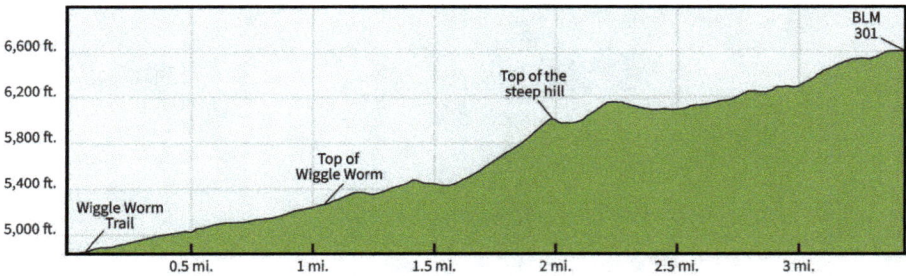

19. Chinese Peak via Barton Road (BLM 301)

This uncomplicated path to the top of Chinese Peak is one of Pocatello's classic trails, providing hikers with an excellent workout, passing through sun-exposed sage hillsides and scattered juniper forests before rewarding them with unmatched views of the area. With easy access from the city, this well-maintained path is one of the area's most popular routes. While this is a recommended hike, it should be noted that vehicles are allowed on this dirt road, so stay alert for approaching cars.

Distance: 5.5 miles out-and-back
Elevation Gain: 1,680 feet
Difficulty: Moderately strenuous
Hiking Time: About 3 hours
Nearest Town: Pocatello
Trail Surface: Dirt, rock
Wheelchair Access: None

Dog-Friendly: Yes; on-leash at the trailhead. May be off-leash if under control once on the trail
Amenities: None
Contact: Bureau of Land Management, Pocatello Field Office 208-478-6340
Trailhead GPS Coordinates: N42° 51.383' W112° 23.541'

Getting There

From the junction of South 5th Avenue and Barton Road, head northeast on Barton Road for 1.8 miles, until you reach a large gravel parking lot. The trailhead is located at the east end of the parking area.

The Hike

The route to the summit is straightforward. From the trailhead, head east past the gate on the signed BLM 301 Road. Stay on the wide dirt path as it snakes its way uphill until it reaches the summit at 2.8 miles. To make it more interesting, the hike can be divided into two halves, "the lower mountain" and "the upper mountain."

The first half, or "the lower mountain," travels at a consistently moderate incline through scattered juniper forests and climbs almost 900 feet in about 1.5 miles. While the trail does pass through low juniper trees, there is

Chinese Peak's towered summit.

no shade. At 1.5 miles, the trail climbs to a vantage point, giving superb views of Pocatello and the Snake River Plain. This viewpoint marks the end of "the lower mountain."

The second half of the climb, or "the upper mountain," is defined by barren hillsides with excellent city views. It begins with a gentler incline before becoming steep at 2.1 miles. At 2.4 miles, this sun-beaten trail enters a high deciduous forest, giving a nice, albeit brief, change of scenery. Shortly past this forest at 2.5 miles, keep right (northeast) to pass by BLM 352, located on the trail's left (northwest) side.

At about 2.7 miles, you will reach several junctions. Make a slight right (southwest) at this first junction, then keep left (south) up the steep forest-lined hill at the second junction. Chinese Peak's summit is at the top of that hill.

If you look toward the northwest from the trail, you will see three isolated mountains rising out of the Snake River Plain. These three buttes, Big Southern Butte, Middle Butte, and East Butte, were formed by volcanic eruptions long ago. The youngest and largest of the three, Big Southern Butte, was formed 300,000 years ago and is one of the largest rhyolite domes in the world.

Chinese Peak via Barton Road (BLM 301)

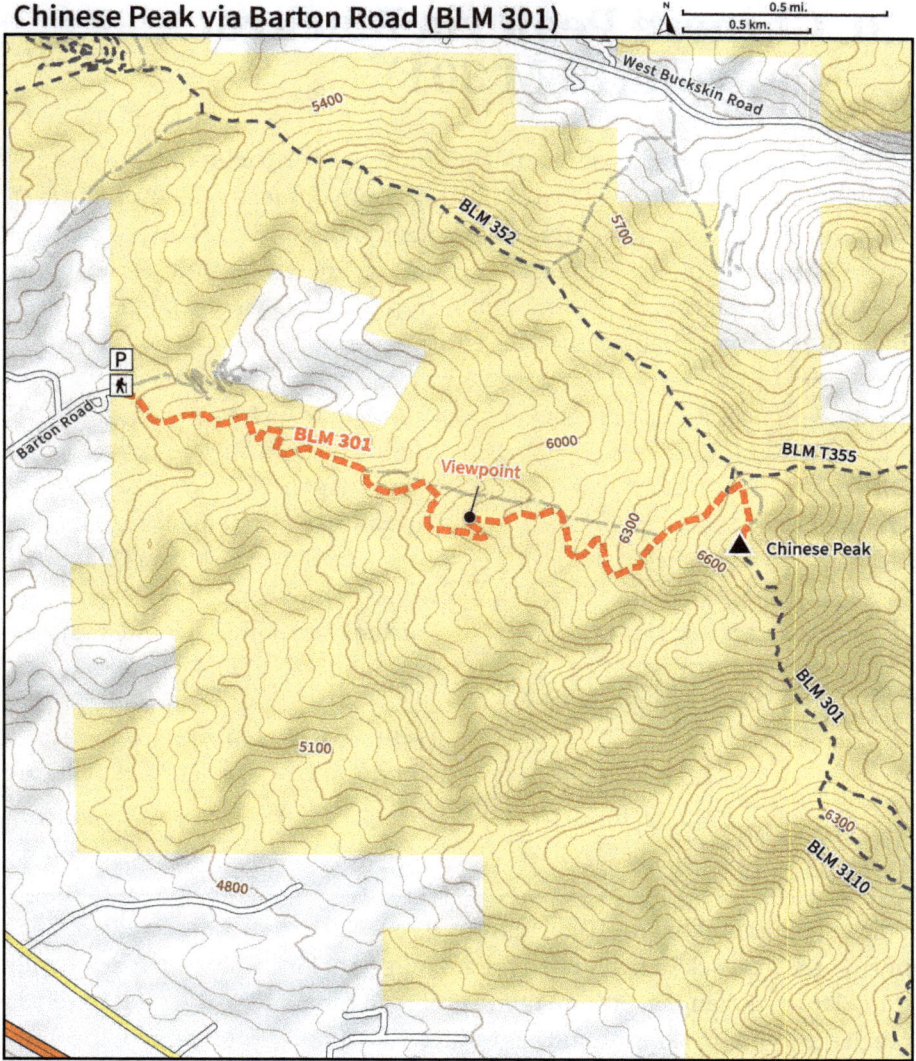

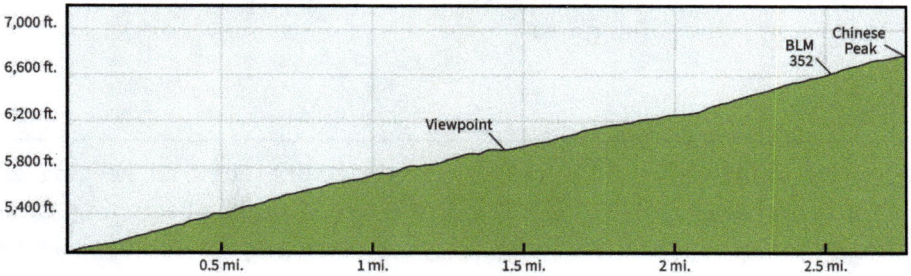

N

0.5 mi.

0.5 km.

West Buckskin Road

5400

BLM 352

5700

P

Barton Road

BLM 301

Viewpoint

6000

BLM T355

6300

6600

Chinese Peak

BLM 301

5100

6300

BLM 3110

4800

7,000 ft.

6,600 ft.

6,200 ft.

5,800 ft.

5,400 ft.

Viewpoint

BLM 352

Chinese Peak

0.5 mi.   1 mi.   1.5 mi.   2 mi.   2.5 mi.

20. Chinese Peak via Blackrock Canyon (BLM 301)

One of the more popular trails in the Chinese Peak - Blackrock Trail System, BLM 301 gives hikers a chance to climb high onto Chinese Peak from the east, rewarding those who make this strenuous uphill climb with expansive city vistas from the mountain's summit. Even if you are not summiting the mountain, climbing to Chinese Peak's southern ridge takes you through beautiful high forest scenery and is worth the effort.

Distance: 6.4 miles out-and-back
Elevation Gain: 1,920 feet
Difficulty: Strenuous
Hiking Time: About 4 hours
Nearest Town: Pocatello
Trail Surface: Dirt, rock
Wheelchair Access: None

Dog-Friendly: Yes; on-leash at the trailhead. May be off-leash if under control once on the trail
Amenities: Vault toilets are available at the Upper and Lower Blackrock Canyon Trailheads.
Contact: Bureau of Land Management, Pocatello Field Office
208-478-6340
Trailhead GPS Coordinates:
N42° 49.248' W112° 19.672'

Getting There

From the junction of West Old Highway 91 and Blackrock Canyon Road, head north on Blackrock Canyon Road for 2.3 miles, making a slight left at 1.0 mile into Blackrock Canyon. Stay on this gravel road for another 1.3 miles until you reach the upper parking area. The trailhead is 0.1 miles southwest of the parking lot. There are two trails that begin off this section of the road about 50 yards from each other. Directions here are for the southernmost trail - the second right turn from the parking area.

The Hike

From the trailhead, head northwest on the signed BLM 301 Trail, keeping left at the fork shortly into the hike. The trail is steep from the beginning, gaining over 1,200 feet in 1.9 miles atop a dry hill, so be prepared for a strenuous

BLM 301's steep climb from above the saddle.

few miles. At 0.8 miles, continue straight, passing by BLM 3112 on the trail's left (south) side. At 1.4 miles, keep left (west) to avoid a steep shortcut. Not far beyond that, at 1.7 miles, stay right (north) to continue past BLM 3111.

At 1.9 miles, the trail levels out in a deciduous forest, which turns a fiery shade of red in the autumn. This relatively flat and shady stretch of trail is a refreshing change of pace and makes for a worthwhile destination. At 2.4 miles, the forested trail emerges onto Chinese Peak's southern ridge (6,120 feet) at a junction with BLM 3110 on the left (south) side of the trail. This location is an excellent spot to take in the views. For those not looking to summit the mountain, it is a good location to turn around.

From this junction, over 650 feet of climbing remains before reaching the top of the mountain. Head north on the trail, which, after a brief descent, begins the steep and rocky climb toward the summit. Mountain bikers should be warned that this section will almost certainly require walking your bike. For hikers, hiking poles are beneficial during this stretch.

At about 3.0 miles, you will arrive at the southernmost tower on Chinese Peak. From here, the summit is about 0.2 miles away. At 3.2 miles, make a right (north) turn, which will take you to the mountain's true summit (6,791 feet).

Chinese Peak via Blackrock Canyon (BLM 301)

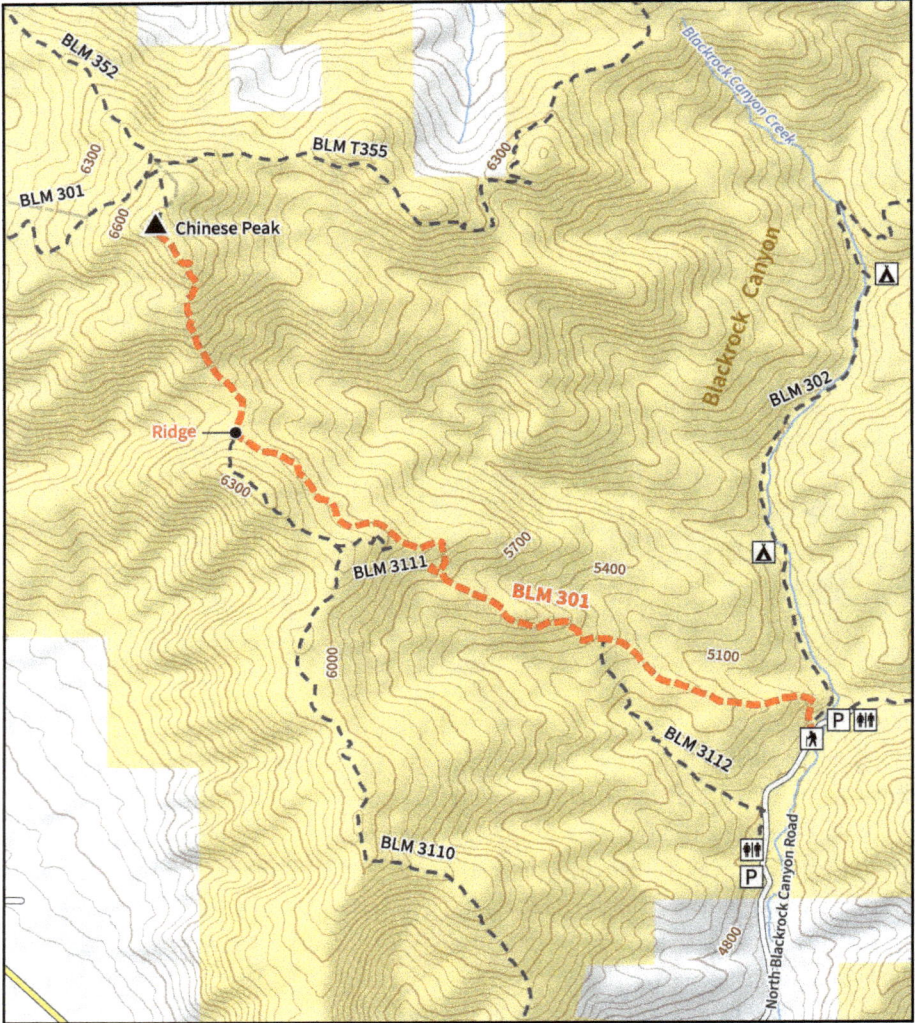

N
0.5 mi.
0.5 km.

BLM 352
BLM T355
BLM 301
6300
6600
Chinese Peak
6300
Ridge
BLM 3111
BLM 3110
6000
5700
5400
BLM 301
5100
BLM 3112
Blackrock Canyon Creek
Blackrock Canyon
BLM 302
4800
North Blackrock Canyon Road

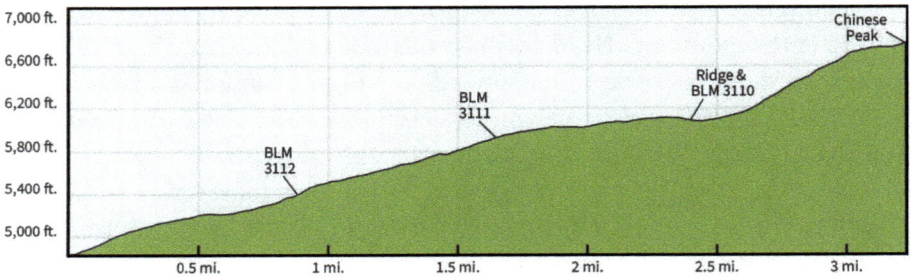

7,000 ft.
6,600 ft.
6,200 ft.
5,800 ft.
5,400 ft.
5,000 ft.

Chinese Peak
Ridge & BLM 3110
BLM 3111
BLM 3112

0.5 mi.   1 mi.   1.5 mi.   2 mi.   2.5 mi.   3 mi.

21. BLM 302

BLM 302 is a well-maintained 4x4 trail that runs alongside a shady creek before climbing high onto Blackrock Canyon's northern hills. With only a moderate incline and excellent area views, I recommend this trail for both hikers and mountain bikers.

Distance: 7.7 miles out-and-back
Elevation Gain: 1,340 feet
Difficulty: Moderately strenuous
Hiking Time: About 4 hours
Nearest Town: Pocatello
Trail Surface: Dirt, rock
Wheelchair Access: None

Dog-Friendly: Yes; on-leash at the trailhead. May be off-leash if under control once on the trail
Amenities: Vault toilets are available at the Upper and Lower Blackrock Canyon Trailheads.
Contact: Bureau of Land Management, Pocatello Field Office 208-478-6340
Trailhead GPS Coordinates: N42° 49.248' W112° 19.672'

Getting There

From the junction of West Old Highway 91 and Blackrock Canyon Road, head north on Blackrock Canyon Road for 2.3 miles, making a slight left at 1.0 mile into Blackrock Canyon. Stay on this gravel road for another 1.3 miles until you reach the upper parking area. The trailhead is 0.1 miles southwest of the parking lot. Directions here are for the southernmost starting point (the second right turn from the parking area).

The Hike

From the trailhead, head northeast on the 4x4 trail, continuing down the middle path when arriving at a fork immediately into the hike, following signs for BLM 302. The beginning stretch of the hike gradually climbs northward in a drainage beneath sage-covered hillsides. At 0.7 miles, you will pass the Lower Blackrock Campsite on the trail's left (west) side. Shortly past that turnoff, the trail enters the forest along a pleasant creek. At 1.9 miles, the trail passes the Upper Blackrock Campsite on the path's right (east) side.

BLM 302 and Blackrock Canyon in the early summer.

At about 2.2 miles, the trail makes a sharp right (southeast) turn as it begins to climb out of the creek, gaining 550 feet in 1.2 miles. This upper section of the hike can be a bit of a workout, though the great views of Chinese Peak's forested eastern foothills are worth it. At about 3.3 miles, the trail reaches its highest point (5,930 feet) at a junction with BLM T355, located on the trail's left (north) side. Continue right (east) to stay on BLM 302.

At 3.4 miles, about 100 yards past the previous junction, you will come to an intersection with BLM 319 on the trail's right (east) side. I actually recommend turning around at this junction, as the final 0.4 miles of BLM 302 descends 250 feet on a poorly maintained trail in a forest until it ends at a gate.

Two campsites are located alongside the trail near the creek for those looking for an extended stay in Blackrock Canyon.

Keep Going

Two outstanding trails, BLM 319 and BLM T355, originate from the top of BLM 302 in Blackrock Canyon.

BLM 319

Located 3.4 miles into BLM 302 on the right (east) side of the trail, BLM 319 is a 2.7-mile one-way trail that stays high atop the northeast hills and ridgetops of Blackrock Canyon. This 4x4 trail has a moderate elevation change throughout, gaining 600 feet and losing 350 feet as it moves southeast atop the ridgeline. In the early season, wildflowers line large stretches of the path, making the views of the Portneuf Range and Blackrock Canyon even more rewarding.

BLM T355

Located 3.3 miles into BLM 302 on the left (north) side of the trail, BLM T355 is a 3.9-mile one-way trail that climbs to the top of Chinese Peak. This non-motorized and rocky 4x4 trail has excellent views of Chinese Peak's eastern forests, though it only moves through tree cover occasionally. This hike has a significant elevation change; it gains over 1,250 feet and loses about 600 feet. The trail is straightforward, though be sure to continue straight (south) at 1.5 miles to avoid an unofficial side trail. BLM T355 ends near the top of Chinese Peak on a path between BLM 352 and BLM 301.

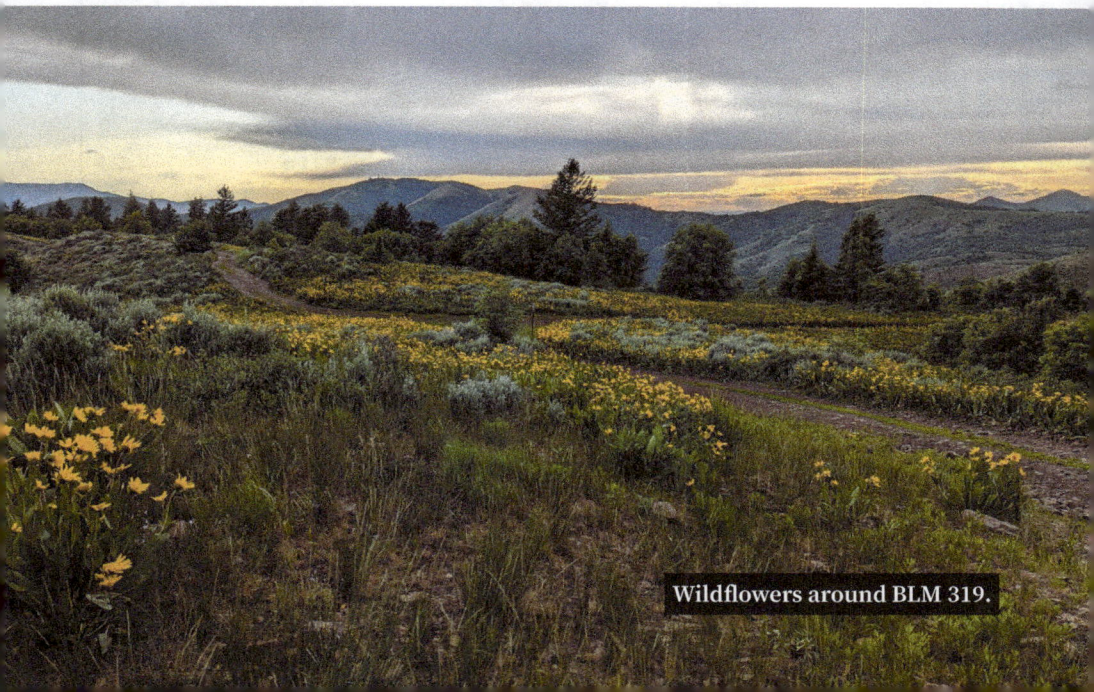

Wildflowers around BLM 319.

BLM 302

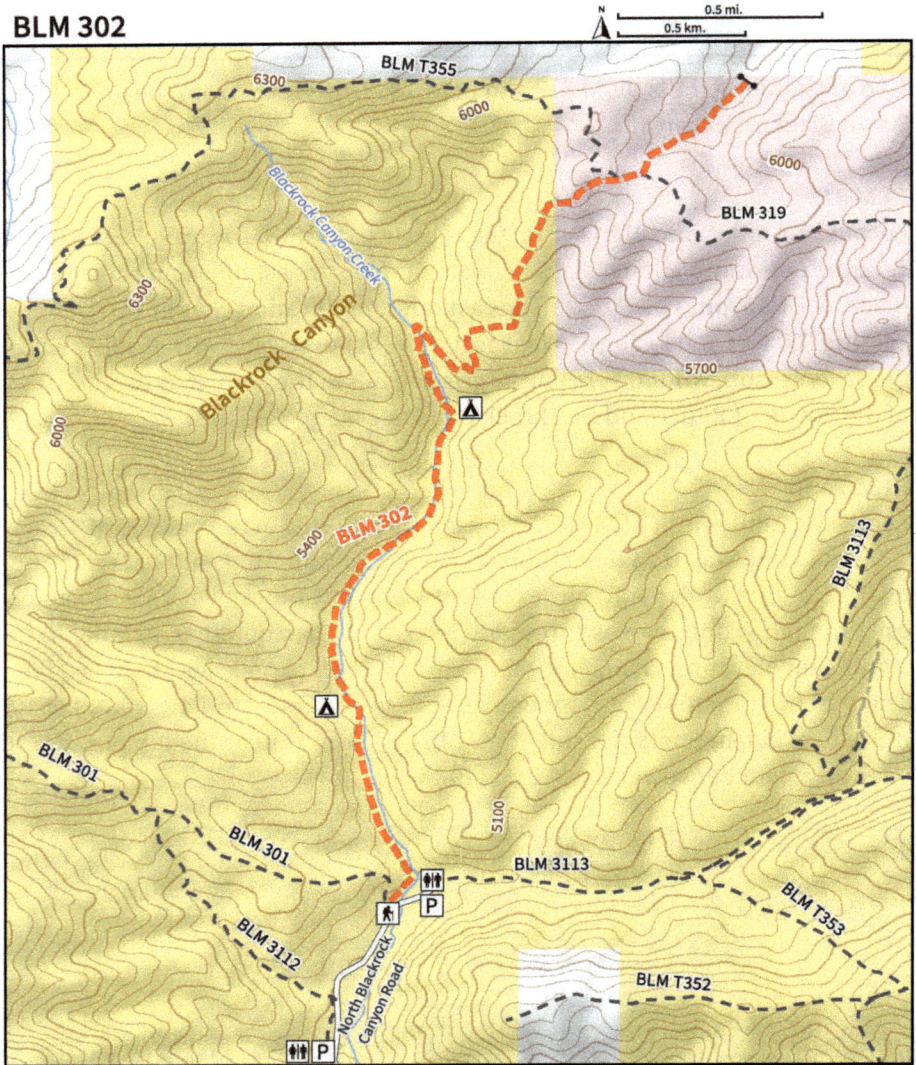

Map of BLM 302 route through Blackrock Canyon, with scale 0.5 mi. / 0.5 km., showing contour lines at 6300, 6000, 5700, 5400, 5100, and trails BLM T355, BLM 319, BLM 301, BLM 3112, BLM 3113, BLM T353, BLM T352, North Blackrock Canyon Road, and Blackrock Canyon Creek.

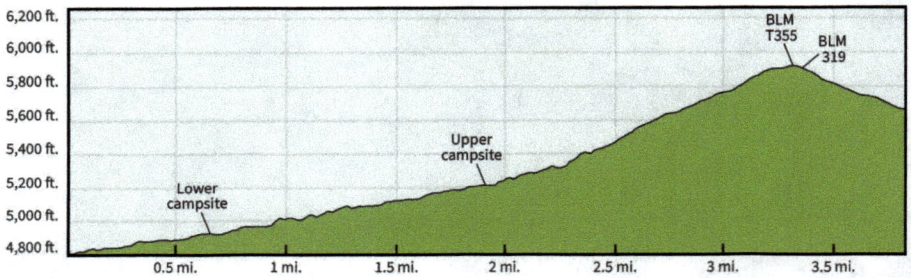

Elevation profile from 4,800 ft. to 6,200 ft. over 3.5 mi., marking Lower campsite, Upper campsite, BLM T355, and BLM 319.

22. BLM 3113

This well-used 4x4 road runs atop a prominent ridge in the heart of the Blackrock Canyon Trail System, providing excellent views for much of the hike. Advanced mountain bikers that are comfortable with rocks may enjoy descending this trail, though the rocky uphill will be challenging.

Distance: 5.8 miles out-and-back
Elevation Gain: 1,420 feet
Difficulty: Moderately strenuous
Hiking Time: About 3.5 hours
Nearest Town: Pocatello
Trail Surface: Dirt, rock
Wheelchair Access: None

Dog-Friendly: Yes; on-leash at the trailhead. May be off-leash if under control once on the trail
Amenities: Vault toilets are available at the Upper and Lower Blackrock Canyon Trailheads.
Contact: Bureau of Land Management, Pocatello Field Office 208-478-6340
Trailhead GPS Coordinates: N42° 49.335' W112° 19.543'

Getting There

From the junction of West Old Highway 91 and Blackrock Canyon Road, head north on Blackrock Canyon Road for 2.3 miles, making a slight left at 1.0 mile into Blackrock Canyon. Stay on this gravel road for another 1.3 miles until you reach the upper parking area. The trailhead is located at the north end of the parking area.

The Hike

From the trailhead, head northeast on the sage-sided BLM 3113. At about 0.6 miles, keep left (northeast) at the fork, avoiding BLM T353 on the right (east). At 0.8 miles, continue straight, passing the turnoff for BLM T354 on the trail's right (east) side. For the next 0.5 miles, the trail continues northeast, paralleling BLM T354 on the west side of a forested creek.

At about 1.4 miles, the trail makes a sharp U-turn at a junction. The trail to the right (north) is an unofficial trail. Keep left (southwest) to continue on BLM 3113. At about 1.7 miles, the path begins a steep northeast climb atop a ridge, gaining 800 feet in 1.1 miles. This shadeless wide path can be strenuous,

BLM 3113 near the junction with BLM 319.

though the views of the ravines on either side are well worth it.

The trail tops out at about 2.8 miles, merging with another ridge south of a forest. After a brief but pleasant walk, the trail ends when it connects with BLM 319.

The Chinese Peak - Blackrock Trail System offers over 40 miles of trails only 15 minutes south of Pocatello.

BLM 3113

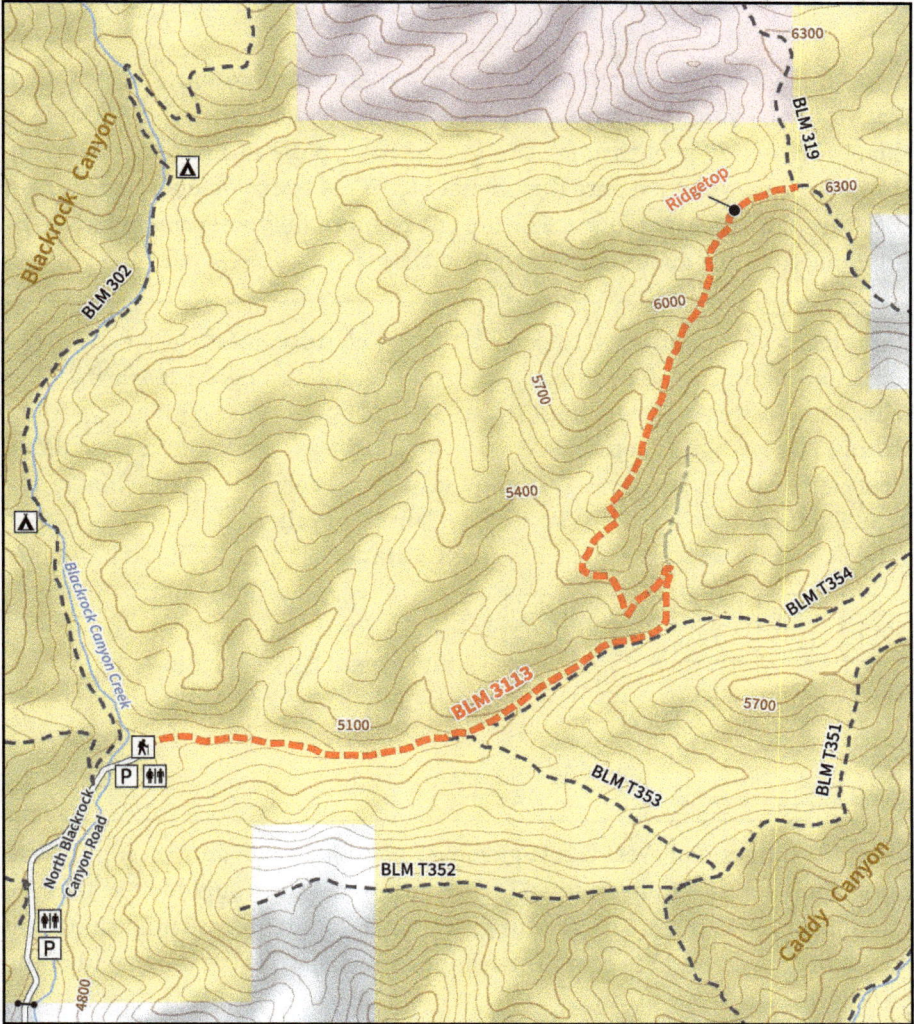

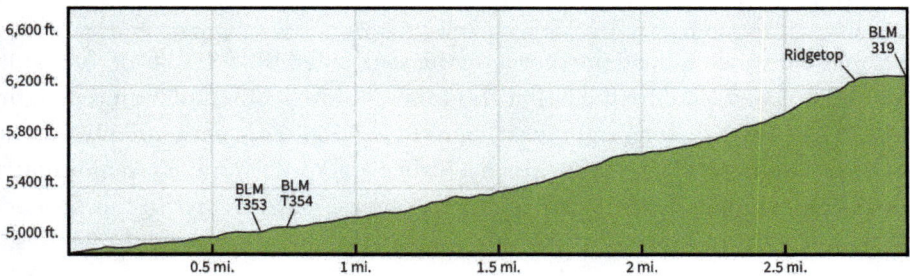

23. BLM T354

If you are looking for a bit of solitude while still remaining centrally located in Blackrock Canyon, this may be the path for you. The first quarter of the hike travels on a wide trail through the sagebrush typical of Blackrock Canyon. However, once you turn onto the official BLM T354 trail, you enter a narrower path through a pleasant forest. The top can be incredibly steep and rocky, so be prepared for a strenuous climb.

Distance: 5.1 miles out-and-back
Elevation Gain: 1,220 feet
Difficulty: Moderately strenuous
Hiking Time: About 3 hours
Nearest Town: Pocatello
Trail Surface: Dirt, rock
Wheelchair Access: None

Dog-Friendly: Yes; on-leash at the trailhead. May be off-leash if under control once on the trail
Amenities: Vault toilets are available at the Upper and Lower Blackrock Canyon Trailheads.
Contact: Bureau of Land Management, Pocatello Field Office 208-478-6340
Trailhead GPS Coordinates: N42° 49.335' W112° 19.543'

Getting There

From the junction of West Old Highway 91 and Blackrock Canyon Road, head north on Blackrock Canyon Road for 2.3 miles, making a slight left at 1.0 mile into Blackrock Canyon. Stay on this gravel road for another 1.3 miles until you end at the upper parking area. The trailhead is located at the north end of the parking area.

The Hike

From the trailhead, head northeast on the sage-sided BLM 3113 trail. At about 0.6 miles, keep left (northeast) at the fork, avoiding BLM T353 on the right (east). At 0.8 miles, turn right (east) onto BLM T354. This path quickly enters a creekside forest. The forest can be a little overgrown at times, so mountain bikers should make sure to have eye protection. The trail stays in this shaded drainage, intermittently opening into sagebrush slopes for the next 1.2 miles.

At 1.9 miles, the trail makes a right (south) turn and climbs to a ridge. Once on the ridge, the path resumes its northeastern journey, becoming steeper in the process. The remainder of the hike ascends 550 feet in about 0.7 miles on a rocky ridge. As you climb higher on this trail, the rockier and steeper it becomes, with the top being especially difficult for bikers. The trail ends once it connects with BLM 319.

> The city of Chubbuck is named after Walter Elmer Chubbuck, a railroad conductor who spent 50 years with Union Pacific Railroad.

Early summer wildflowers along BLM T354.

BLM T354

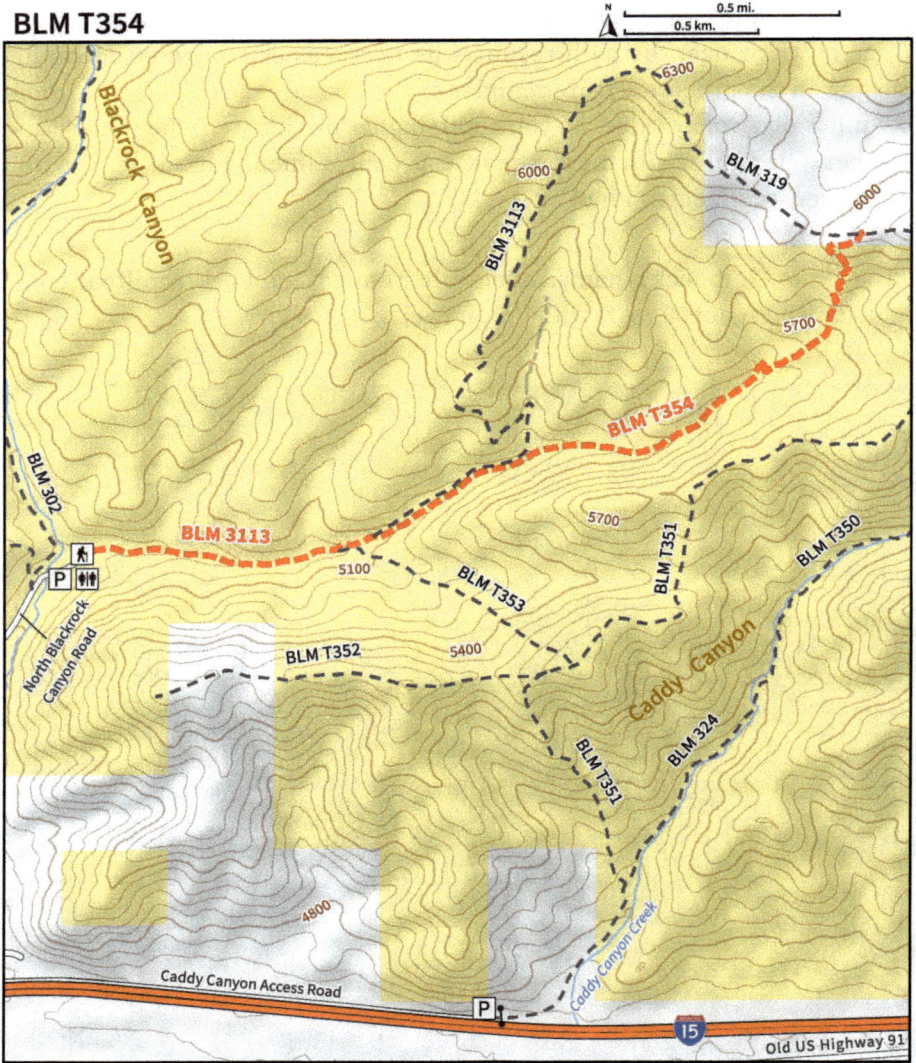

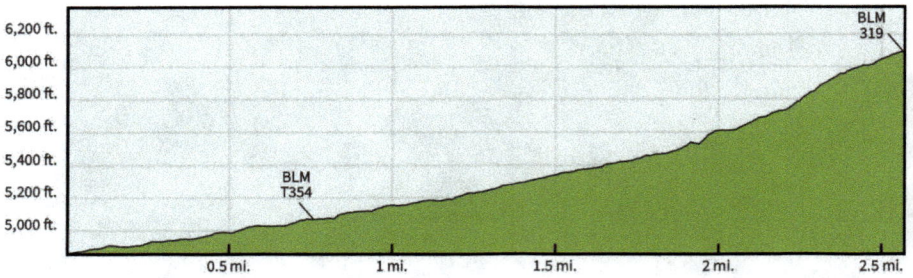

24. BLM T352 & T353

BLM T352 and T353 are two individually short trails that, when combined, form a route to a hilltop overlook of Blackrock Canyon. The steep BLM T353 climbs through a scenic sage hillside, joining T352 once at the top. The latter half of the climb is a series of small rocky hills, eventually rewarding you with great views of the area.

Distance: 4.8 miles out-and-back
Elevation Gain: 1,430 feet
Difficulty: Moderately strenuous
Hiking Time: About 3 hours
Nearest Town: Pocatello
Trail Surface: Dirt, rock
Wheelchair Access: None

Dog-Friendly: Yes; on-leash at the trailhead. May be off-leash if under control once on the trail
Amenities: Vault toilets are available at the Upper and Lower Blackrock Canyon Trailheads.
Contact: Bureau of Land Management, Pocatello Field Office 208-478-6340
Trailhead GPS Coordinates: N42° 49.335' W112° 19.543'

Getting There

From the junction of West Old Highway 91 and Blackrock Canyon Road, head north on Blackrock Canyon Road for 2.3 miles, making a slight left at 1.0 mile into Blackrock Canyon. Stay on this gravel road for another 1.3 miles until you end at the upper parking area. The trailhead is located at the north end of the parking area.

The Hike

From the trailhead, head northeast on the sage-sided BLM 3113 trail. At about 0.6 miles, keep right (east) at the fork, continuing past the fence to begin the signed BLM T353. Once on BLM T353, the trail's incline increases, gaining over 650 feet in 0.7 miles. While the trail will give you a challenging workout, the views are excellent, especially of the wooded hill on the right (south) side of the trail. If you are hiking BLM T352 later in the route, you will soon find yourself atop that hill.

The trail peaks at 1.4 miles (5,700 feet), where you will come to a junction with BLM T351. At the intersection, veer right (southwest) onto BLM T351, which you will stay on for about 400 feet until you come to a junction with BLM T352. Continue right (west) to begin BLM T352. This rocky path, which is 1.0 mile one-way, heads west, moving up and down several small hills. This dry path can be repetitive due to the false hope each subsequent hill gives of being the endpoint, though the views are enjoyable throughout.

The trail ends at 2.4 miles at the edge of a rounded hill, where you will have an excellent view of the Portneuf Gap.

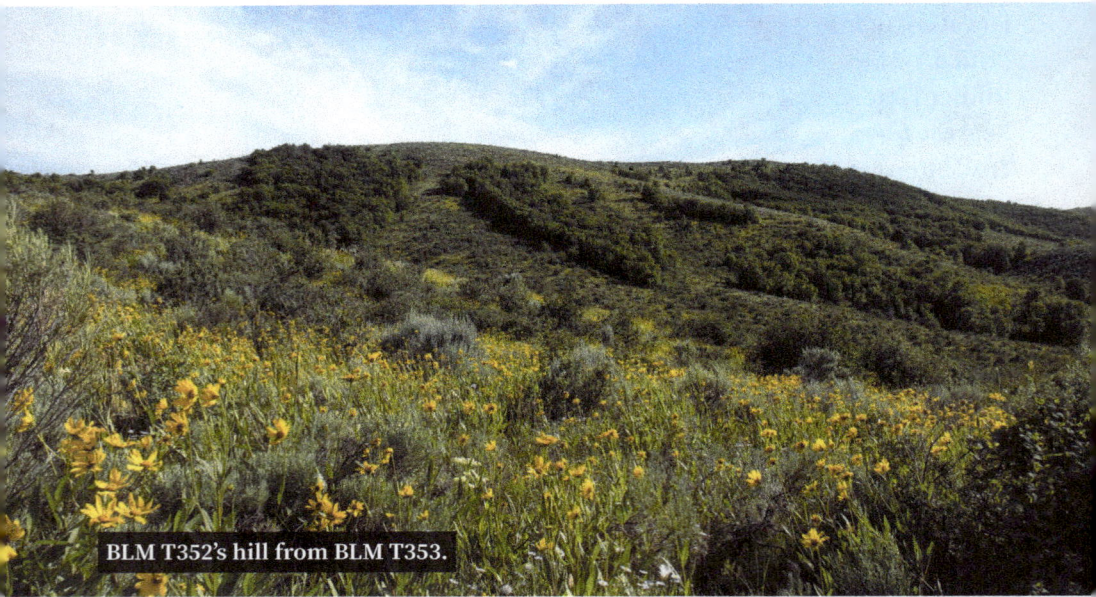

BLM T352's hill from BLM T353.

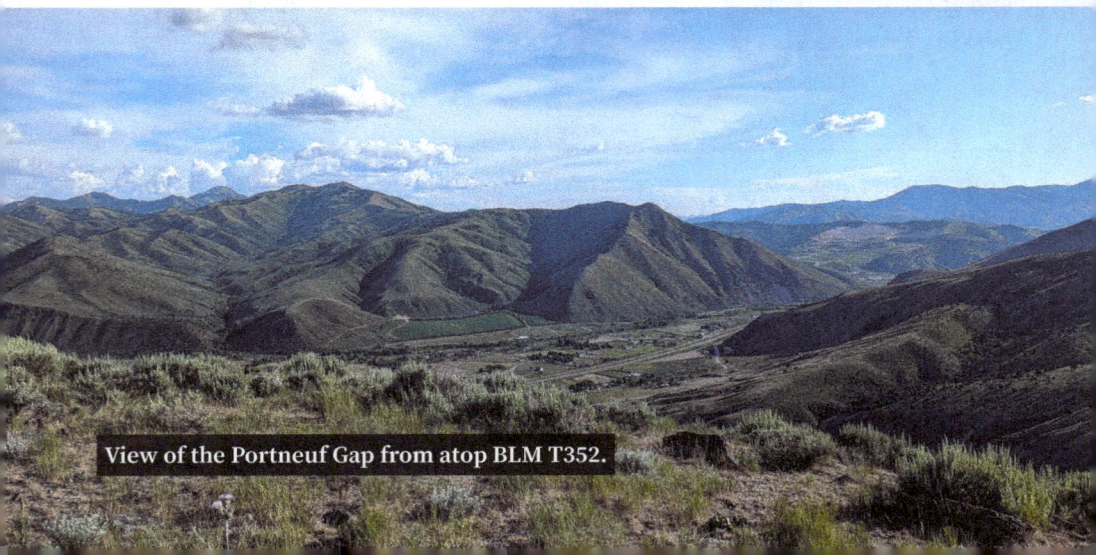

View of the Portneuf Gap from atop BLM T352.

BLM T352 & T353

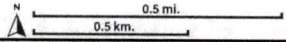

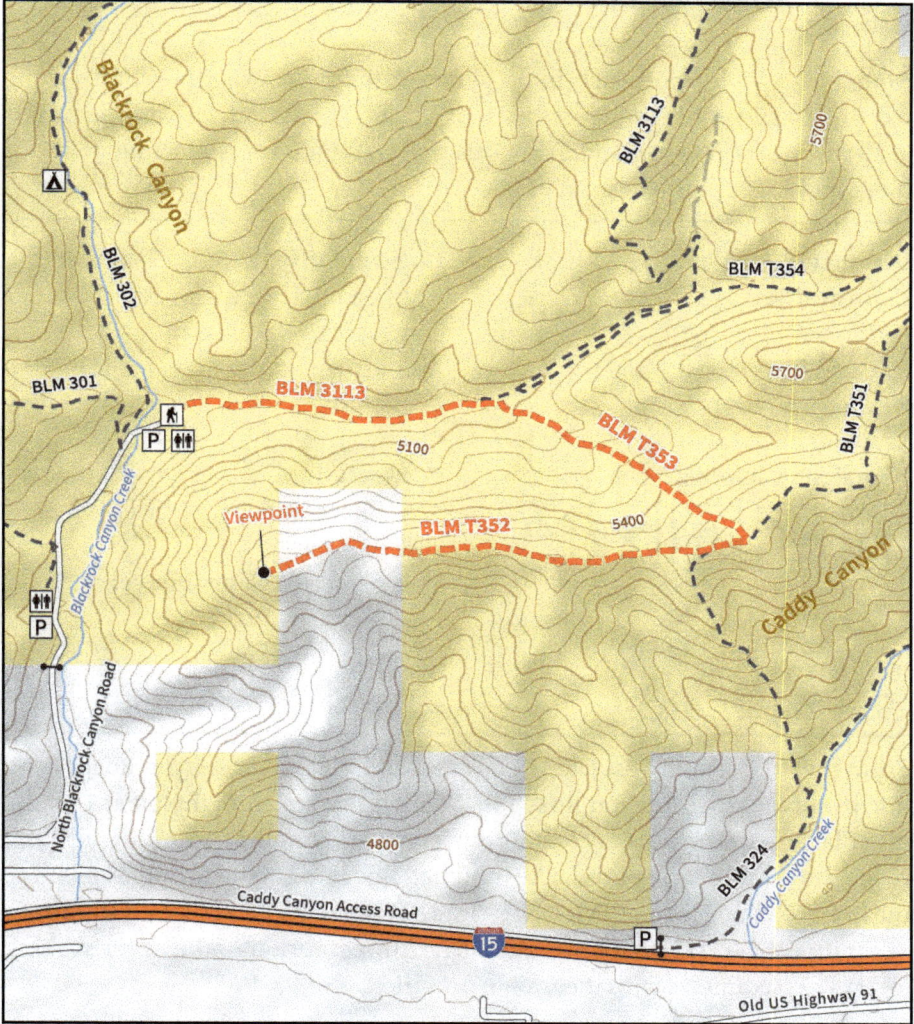

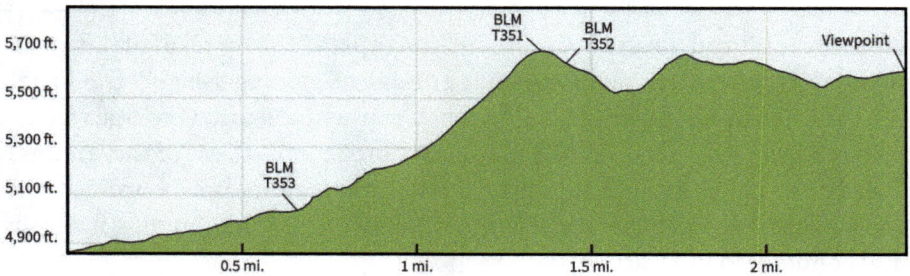

25. BLM 3112

Dotted with wildflowers early in the summer, the short BLM 3112 climbs along a dry drainage until it connects with BLM 301. The last quarter of the trail is very steep, so I recommend using this trail as an alternate starting point for those looking to climb high on BLM 301.

Distance: 1.7 miles out-and-back
Elevation Gain: 500 feet
Difficulty: Moderate
Hiking Time: About 1 hour
Nearest Town: Pocatello
Trail Surface: Dirt, rock
Wheelchair Access: None

Dog-Friendly: Yes; on-leash at the trailhead. May be off-leash if under control once on the trail
Amenities: Vault toilets are available at the Upper and Lower Blackrock Canyon Trailheads.
Contact: Bureau of Land Management, Pocatello Field Office 208-478-6340
Trailhead GPS Coordinates: N42° 49.000' W112° 19.826'

Getting There

From the junction of West Old Highway 91 and Blackrock Canyon Road, head north on Blackrock Canyon Road for 1.7 miles, making a slight left at 1.0 mile into Blackrock Canyon. Stay on this gravel road for another 0.7 miles until you reach the lower parking area. The trailhead is located about 0.2 miles north of the lower parking lot on the left (west) side of the road. Alternatively, there is a 4x4 trail, BLM A3112, that begins at the northwest corner of the lower parking lot and also connects with the trail in 0.2 miles.

The Hike

From the trailhead, head northwest on the 4x4 path. The first half of this steep-sided trail travels alongside a sage-filled drainage, gaining over 200 feet in half a mile. At 0.5 miles, the trail enters a small copse of trees that emerges from a forested drainage, making for a nice shade break in the heat of the summer. Shortly beyond that small copse at 0.6 miles, the trail makes a northern turn and becomes steeper. The final 0.3 miles climbs over 250 feet, ending when the trail connects to BLM 301.

Consider using BLM 3112 as an alternate starting point for climbing Chinese Peak.

Many birds were in consideration to be Idaho's state bird, including the bald eagle, western tanager, and sage hen. Ultimately, the mountain bluebird won the critical schoolchildren's vote and was designated the state bird in 1931.

BLM 3112

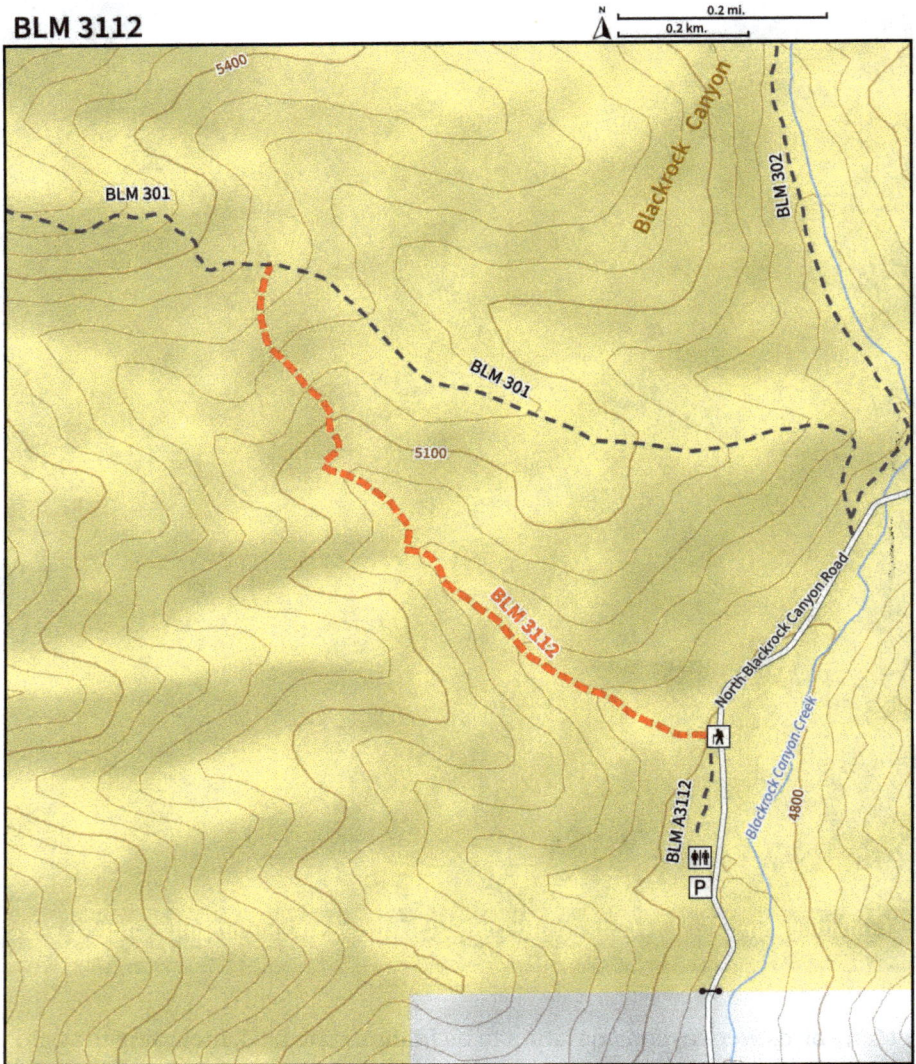

N

0.2 mi.

0.2 km.

BLM 301

Blackrock Canyon

5400

BLM 302

BLM 301

5100

BLM 3112

North Blackrock Canyon Road

Blackrock Canyon Creek

4800

BLM A3112

P

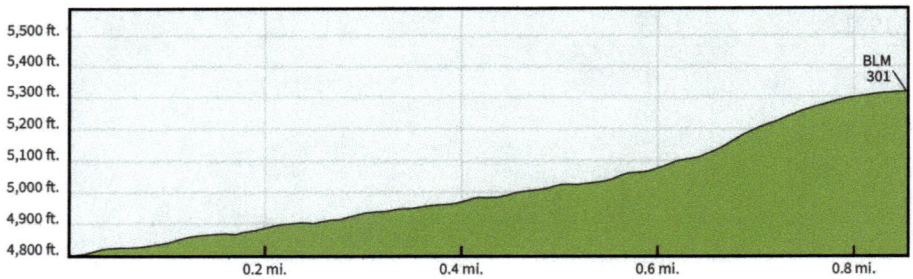

5,500 ft.						
5,400 ft.						BLM 301
5,300 ft.						
5,200 ft.						
5,100 ft.						
5,000 ft.						
4,900 ft.						
4,800 ft.						

0.2 mi.   0.4 mi.   0.6 mi.   0.8 mi.

26. BLM 3110

A steep and rocky climb high onto a ridge on Chinese Peak, BLM 3110 is a strenuous trail that rewards hikers with stunning views of the area and a beautiful ridge walk. There are several intersecting BLM trails once atop the ridge, making this an excellent start for a loop hike.

Distance: 7.7 miles out-and-back
Elevation Gain: 2,260 feet
Difficulty: Strenuous
Hiking Time: About 5 hours
Nearest Town: Pocatello
Trail Surface: Dirt, rock
Wheelchair Access: None

Dog-Friendly: Yes; on-leash at the trailhead. May be off-leash if under control once on the trail
Amenities: None at the trailhead. Vault toilets are available nearby at the Upper and Lower Blackrock Canyon Trailheads.
Contact: Bureau of Land Management, Pocatello Field Office 208-478-6340
Trailhead GPS Coordinates: N42° 47.962' W112° 20.465'

Getting There

From the junction of West Old Highway 91 and Blackrock Canyon Road, head north on Blackrock Canyon Road for 0.3 miles. Once under the interstate, the parking area and trailhead will be to your right at a gate.

The Hike

From the signed trailhead, head west through the gate on the 4x4 trail, which parallels the interstate for the first 0.2 miles before making a right (north) turn into a dry drainage. At about 0.6 miles, the trail turns to the right (southeast), where you begin switchbacks as the trail approaches a ridge. Once atop the ridge at 0.9 miles, the trail turns to the north and becomes steeper, climbing over 800 feet in three-quarters of a mile. This rocky path can be strenuous, but you will be treated to excellent views of Indian Mountain's foothills across the interstate.

At 1.6 miles, the trail briefly levels out in a sage hillside, providing a moment to rest before climbing the remaining 240 feet to the top of the ridge.

At 2.0 miles, the trail crests the ridge, providing views of southern Pocatello, Blackrock Canyon, and the Bannock Range. With most of the trail's incline out of the way, you are rewarded with a beautiful northbound ridge walk as you head toward Chinese Peak. There are occasional ups and downs, but this is a pleasant experience overall.

At about 2.9 miles, you will come to a fork in the road. You can take either trail, as they rejoin in about 0.2 miles. For this route's mileage, I took the left path. At 3.1 miles, you will come to the base of a small hill, requiring about 130 feet of climbing. Once on the other side of the hill at 3.3 miles, you will come to an intersection with BLM 3111 on the right (east) side of the path. Continue northwest to stay on BLM 3110, which shortly climbs a 200-foot hill.

At 3.8 miles, you will reach the route's high point (6,350 feet) at the top of the hill, with a view of Chinese Peak. If you are not planning on summiting Chinese Peak, I recommend turning around at this point to avoid a steep descent. If you choose to continue forward, hiking poles are encouraged. The route ends at the bottom of the hill at a junction with BLM 301.

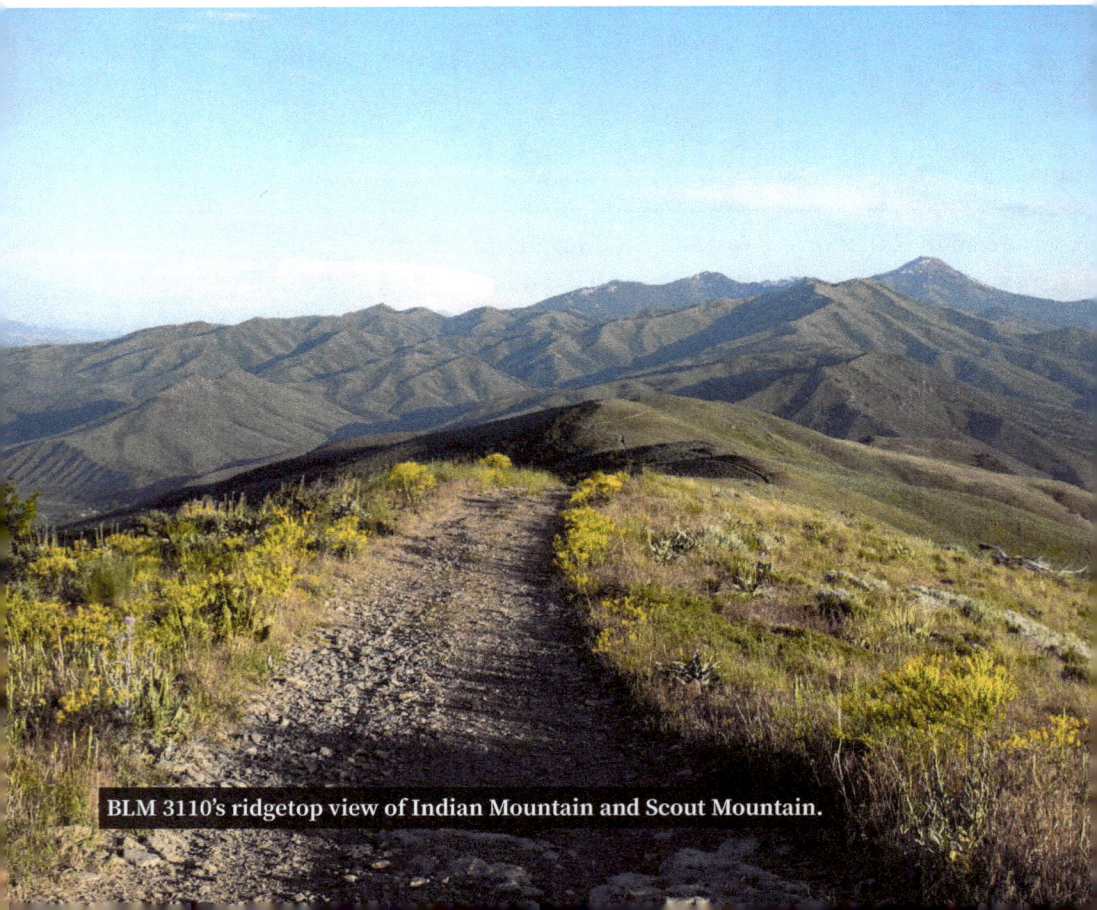

BLM 3110's ridgetop view of Indian Mountain and Scout Mountain.

Wildflowers along BLM 3110's ridgewalk.

Keep Going

There are a couple of fun loop options on this trail. At 3.3 miles, turning right (east) will begin the **BLM 3111 Trail**. This short 0.3-mile one-way 4x4 trail descends 200 feet, connecting BLM 3110 with BLM 301. Once on BLM 301, descend it back to the Blackrock Canyon parking area, and then hike south on the main road back to the trailhead.

You can also hike to the endpoint of BLM 3110 and turn right (southeast) directly onto BLM 301. While you have to descend a steep hill to get to that junction, you then walk through a nicely forested section of BLM 301.

For trail runners or anyone looking for an adventurous hike, one of my favorite custom routes in town starts at BLM 3110. Take BLM 3110 to its endpoint, merging onto BLM 301. Continue north on BLM 301, summiting Chinese Peak and then staying on the route as it descends the mountain's western side. At the junction with BLM 352, head north onto BLM 352, which eventually ends at the Buckskin Trailhead. This route, which I have dubbed the "Portneuf Ridge," is about 8.5 miles one way and ascends 3,000 feet.

BLM 3110

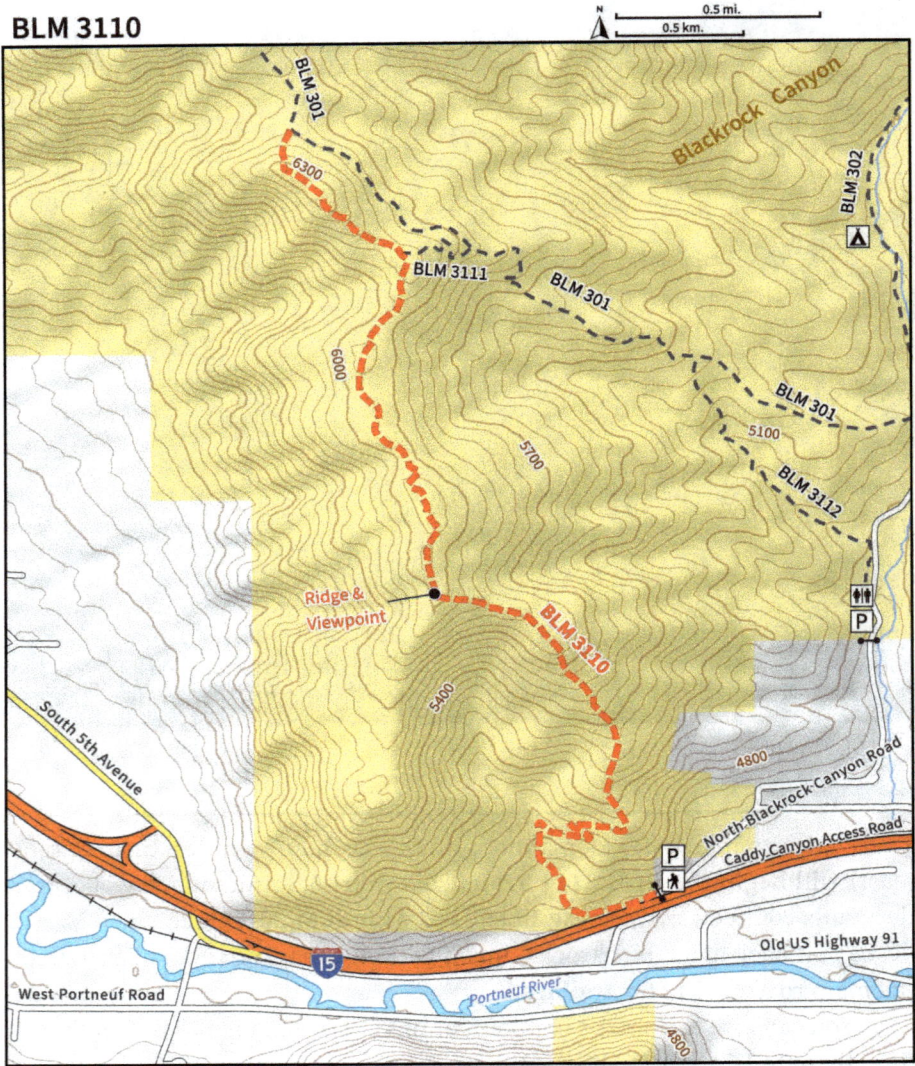

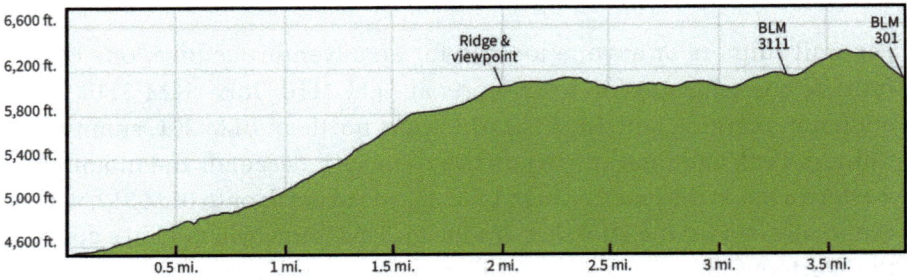

27. BLM T351

A ridgetop companion to the nearby BLM 324 and BLM T350 trails, BLM T351 has views of both Caddy Canyon and the Blackrock Canyon areas. This tough hike climbs a series of four hills atop a ridge and can be steep and rocky in parts, so hiking poles are recommended. The trail spends most of its time high on a grassy and sagebrush-sided ridge, so sun protection is recommended.

Distance: 7.1 miles out-and-back
Elevation Gain: 2,180 feet
Difficulty: Strenuous
Hiking Time: About 4.5 hours
Nearest Town: Pocatello
Trail Surface: Dirt, rock
Wheelchair Access: None

Dog-Friendly: Yes; on-leash at the trailhead. May be off-leash if under control once on the trail
Amenities: None at the trailhead. Vault toilets are available nearby at the Upper and Lower Blackrock Canyon Trailheads.
Contact: Bureau of Land Management, Pocatello Field Office 208-478-6340
Trailhead GPS Coordinates: N42° 48.036' W112° 18.399'

Getting There

From the junction of West Old Highway 91 and Blackrock Canyon Road, head north on Blackrock Canyon Road for 0.3 miles. Once you pass under the interstate, turn right (east) onto Caddy Canyon Access Road, a dirt 4x4 road. Continue on this dirt road for 1.8 miles until you get to the parking area just past a gate. This dirt road is full of large ruts, so a vehicle with good ground clearance is recommended. Caddy Canyon Access Road is a nightmare when muddy, so plan your hike accordingly. The trail begins at the east end of the parking area.

The Hike

From the trailhead, head east through the gate on BLM 324. At 0.6 miles, you will come to a clearing, where on the left (northwest) side, past a few cattle water troughs, you will find BLM T351. Once on the trail, it immediately begins a steep climb, gaining over 840 feet over about 0.8 miles. The trail starts out

A hiker ascending one of BLM T351's rocky hill climbs.

easy enough but becomes filled with rocks the higher you climb, which may be difficult for mountain bikers.

At about 1.4 miles, you will pass by BLM T352 on the trail's left (west) side. Shortly beyond that, at 1.5 miles, you will pass by T353 on the left (northwest) side of the trail, which also happens to be the top of the first large hill (5,700 feet). From there, the trail plateaus before descending a steep decline.

At 1.9 miles, the trail bottoms out before beginning the second of the route's steep hill climbs, with this one climbing about 240 feet in 0.3 miles. At 2.3 miles, you will reach the top of the hill (5,730 feet), where you again are given a chance to rest your legs as the trail levels out. The trail gradually climbs atop a ridge with excellent views for the next quarter mile.

At 2.6 miles, you will come to the base of the third hill climb. This hill is the shortest of the climbs, gaining 200 feet in under 0.2 miles. At 2.7 miles, you will reach the top (5,950 feet) and find an excellent view of Caddy Canyon's forests to the east. Continue northeast on the trail, where you will descend 150 feet before beginning the last of the hills.

This final incline begins at 3.0 miles and climbs over 350 feet in 0.4 miles. Once the hill tops out at 3.4 miles (6,160 feet), the end of the route is visible. The trail ends at a junction with BLM T350 and BLM 319.

BLM T351

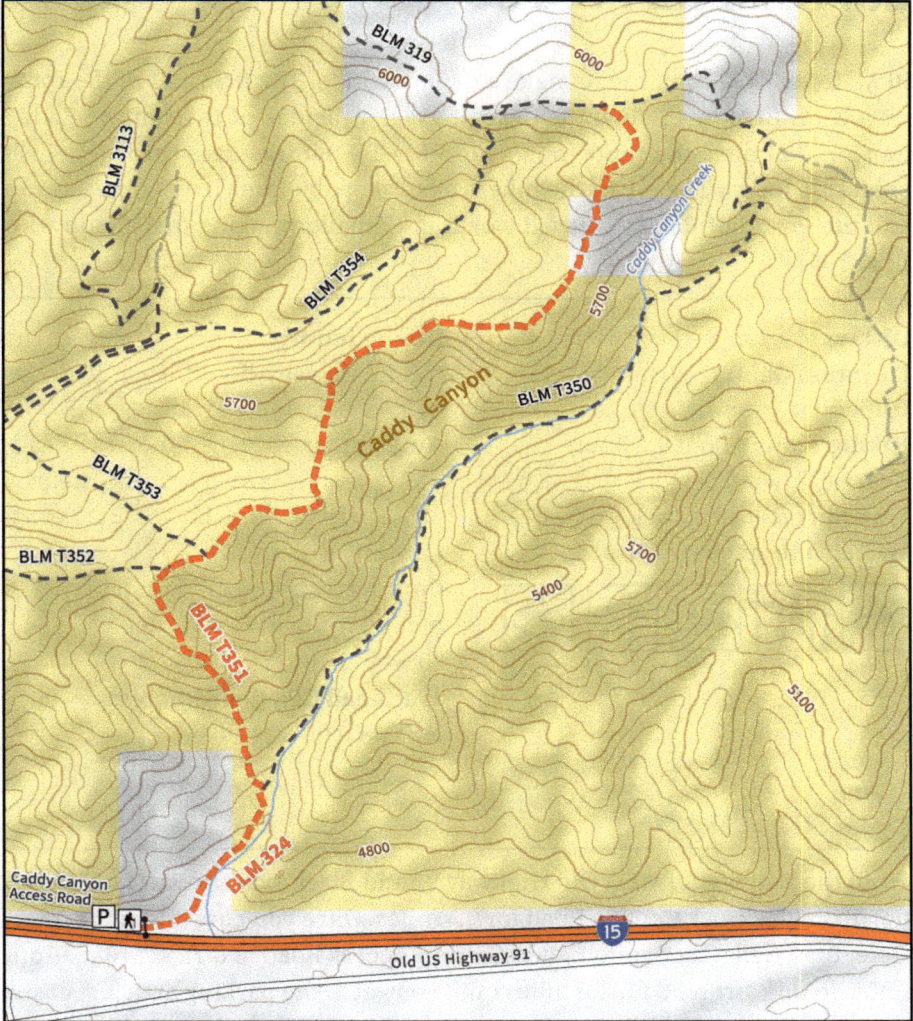

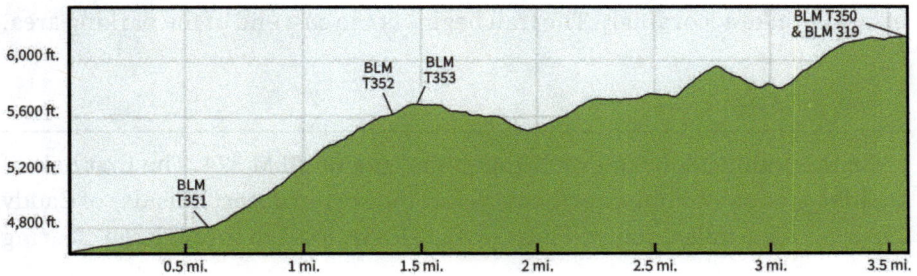

28. BLM 324 & T350

BLM 324 & T350 combine to make a dynamic hike. The first half of the route travels on BLM 324 below the desolate sage hillsides of the remote Caddy Canyon, but once the route joins onto BLM T350 it traverses through a lush creekside forest. The top of the hike is a bit steep, but the views of the canyon and the Portneuf Range are well worth it. Consider making this a loop with BLM T351.

Distance: 7.7 miles out-and-back
Elevation Gain: 1,950 feet
Difficulty: Strenuous
Hiking Time: About 4.5 hours
Nearest Town: Pocatello
Trail Surface: Dirt, rock
Wheelchair Access: None

Dog-Friendly: Yes; on-leash at the trailhead. May be off-leash if under control once on the trail
Amenities: None at the trailhead. Vault toilets are available nearby at the Upper and Lower Blackrock Canyon Trailheads.
Contact: Bureau of Land Management, Pocatello Field Office 208-478-6340
Trailhead GPS Coordinates: N42° 48.036' W112° 18.399'

Getting There

From the junction of West Old Highway 91 and Blackrock Canyon Road, head north on Blackrock Canyon Road for 0.3 miles. Once you pass under the interstate, turn right (east) onto Caddy Canyon Access Road, a dirt 4x4 road. Continue on this dirt road for 1.8 miles until you get to the parking area just past a gate. This dirt road is full of large ruts, so a vehicle with good ground clearance is recommended. Caddy Canyon Access Road is a nightmare when muddy, so plan your hike accordingly. The trail begins at the east end of the parking area.

The Hike

From the trailhead, head east through the gate on BLM 324. The first half of the hike gradually climbs northeast below the barren desert hillsides of Caddy Canyon. At 0.6 miles, you will pass by BLM T351, located through the clearing

A particularly rocky stretch of BLM T350 in the evening.

on the trail's left (northwest) side. At 1.7 miles, the trail transitions from BLM 324 to BLM T350, which also sees the scenery transition from dry sagebrush to a lush creekside forest.

At about 2.8 miles, the trail begins to climb out of the creek onto the dry hillside. After a couple of switchbacks at 3.3 miles, you will come to a junction between two hilltops. Take the left (northwest) path to stay on route. The right (southeast) path is an unnamed trail not part of the Chinese Peak - Blackrock Trail System.

Once in the forest past the junction, the trail begins a steep, rocky hill climb, gaining 250 feet in about 0.3 miles. At the top of the hill (6,290 feet), the trail makes a left (southwest) turn, beginning the final stretch of the hike. Before starting the final stretch, be sure to take a minute and enjoy the views of the area, particularly those of the Putnam Mountains to the northeast. The trail ends at a junction with BLM T351 and BLM 319.

A view of the Bannock Range from high on BLM T350.

Zoo Idaho is located in Pocatello's Ross Park. It serves as a sanctuary for various native species of the Intermountain West region that are either injured or orphaned and would not have survived in the wild. The zoo offers a convenient opportunity to observe animals commonly found in Yellowstone National Park, including bears, cougars, eagles, elk, and many more.

BLM 324 & T350

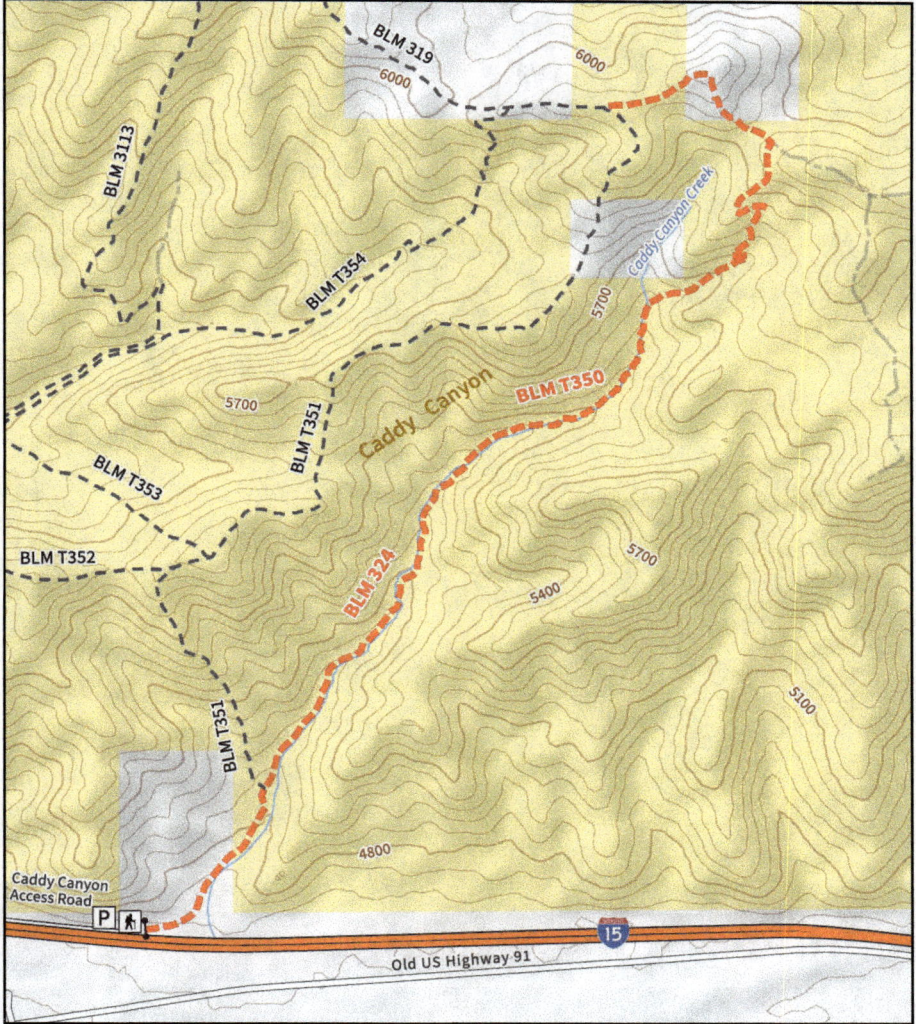

0.5 mi.
0.5 km.

BLM 319
6000
6000
BLM 3113
BLM 354
Caddy Canyon Creek
5700
BLM T351
Caddy Canyon
BLM T350
5700
BLM T353
5400
BLM T352
5700
BLM 324
5100
BLM T351
4800
Caddy Canyon
Access Road
P
Old US Highway 91
I 15

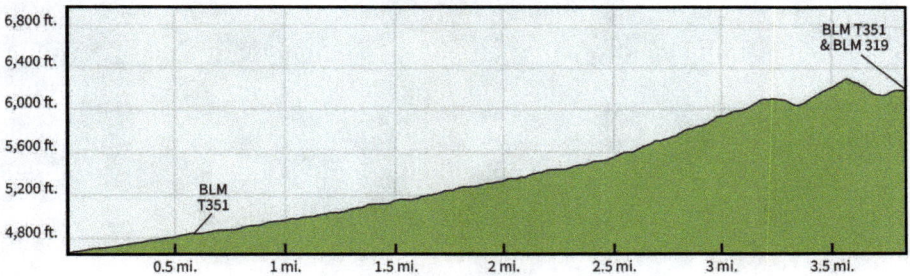

6,800 ft.
6,400 ft.
6,000 ft.
5,600 ft.
5,200 ft.
4,800 ft.

BLM T351 & BLM 319

BLM T351

0.5 mi. 1 mi. 1.5 mi. 2 mi. 2.5 mi. 3 mi. 3.5 mi.

Bannock Range (North)

The northern part of the Bannock Range is home to several of the most popular trailheads in the region. These include City Creek, Gibson Jack, and West Fork Mink Creek. With a little bit of planning beforehand, hikers and mountain bikers can link all these trail systems together, creating endless routes for their excursions. From picturesque creekside walks to breathtaking mountaintop paths, it's no wonder why the northern stretch of the Bannock Range has become a favorite destination for outdoor enthusiasts in the area.

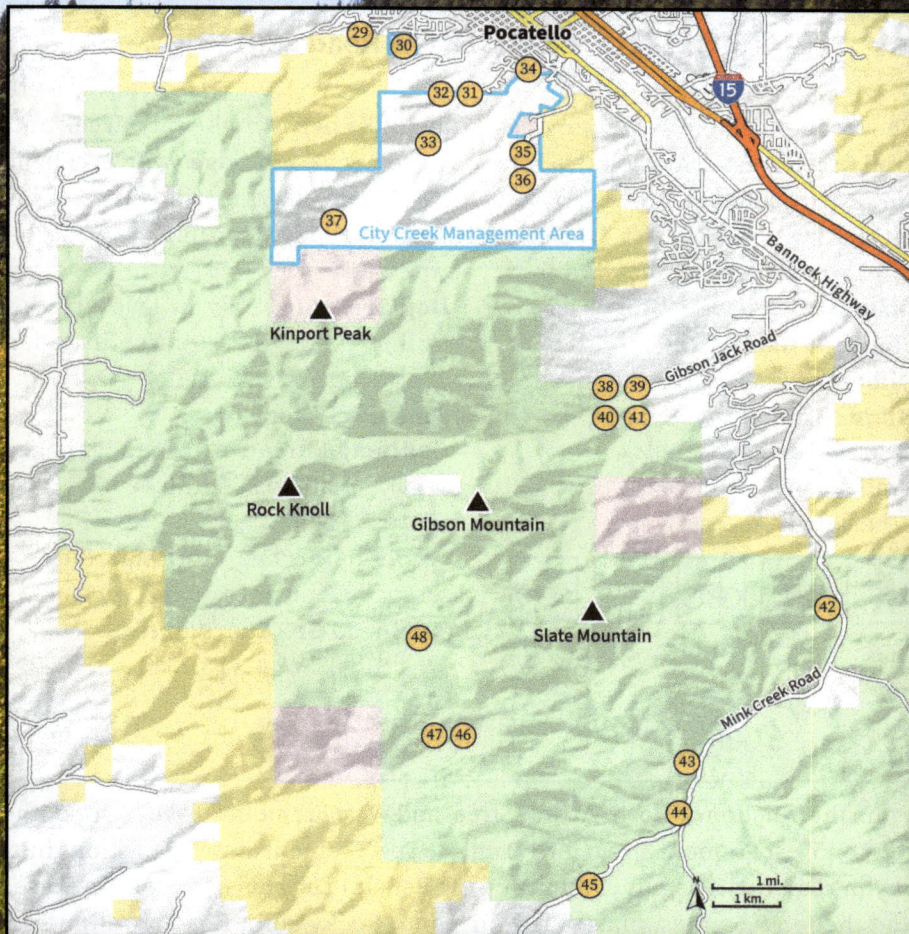

Pocatello

City Creek Management Area

Kinport Peak

Gibson Jack Road

Rock Knoll

Gibson Mountain

Slate Mountain

Mink Creek Road

Bannock Highway

1 mi.
1 km.

A field of wildflowers along the Elk Meadows Loop.

29. Ridgeline Track (FS Road 280)

The steep Ridgeline Track provides a quiet hike between the City Creek and Trail Creek areas. The rocky trail travels on top of barren ridges with excellent views, particularly of Howard Mountain. Mountain bikers may prefer combining this trail with Old Two Track to dodge an incredibly steep hill.

Distance: 6 miles out-and-back
Elevation Gain: 1,800 feet
Difficulty: Moderately strenuous
Hiking Time: About 4 hours
Nearest Town: Pocatello
Trail Surface: Dirt, rock
Wheelchair Access: None

Dog-Friendly: Yes; on-leash at the trailhead. May be off-leash if under control once on the trail
Amenities: None
Contact: Bureau of Land Management, Pocatello Field Office 208-478-6340; Caribou-Targhee National Forest, Westside Ranger District 208-236-7500
Trailhead GPS Coordinates: N42° 51.533' W112° 28.756'

Getting There

From the junction of North Arthur Street and West Fremont Street, head southwest on West Fremont Street for 1.0 mile. (West Fremont Street transitions into Skyline Drive as it begins climbing up the Bench.) Turn left onto Canyon Drive, and then in 0.5 miles, make a left turn onto Rocky Point Road. Continue on Rocky Point Road for 0.2 miles, and then make a right onto Lupine Drive. The trail begins at the west end of Lupine Drive. There is limited street parking.

The Hike

The path zigzags up a steep hillside from the trailhead until it reaches a junction at 0.4 miles. Keep right (west) at the intersection, and then make a short left (southwest) turn about 200 feet beyond that. The trail enters a juniper forest as it makes its way to the top of a small ridge, reaching it at 1.0 mile, almost 700 feet above the parking area. This is a great spot to take a water break and prepare for the incredibly steep hill you see before you.

Continue south, following the steep trail as it heads straight up the hill, gaining 360 feet in 0.4 miles. At 1.1 miles, keep left to avoid Old Two Track.

View of Pocatello from high on the Ridgeline Track.

Once at the top of the hill (1.4 miles), you will have excellent views of Howard Mountain to the northwest. Descend and keep left at 1.8 miles to avoid the end-point of Old Two Track. The trail begins another significant incline shortly past the junction, gaining 450 feet in half a mile.

At 2.1 miles, you will pass by the endpoint of Water Tank Ridge on the left (east) side of the path. The trail reaches the top of the ridge at 2.3 miles (6,160 feet), ending in a pleasant ridge walk with scenic views. At 2.9 miles, keep right (west). The trail ends connecting with East Wild Horse Mountain Trail near an unnamed road.

The city of American Falls, which is situated west of Pocatello along I-86, was relocated to its current location in 1925 prior to the construction of the first American Falls Dam. The original location of the city now rests below the reservoir. When the water level is low, some of the old town's buildings and foundations become visible.

Keep Going

The end of Ridgeline Track places you onto the **East Wild Horse Mountain Trail** (Forest Service Trail 004) near its starting point. The East Wild Horse Mountain Trail is a 2.0-mile one-way doubletrack that travels south atop a ridgeline, eventually ending high on a ridge (7,070 feet) not far from Kinport Peak's summit. This path is an excellent way to connect from the Ridgeline Track to Midnight Ridge Road, making for scenic loop options. The trail climbs over 1,200 feet on a rocky trail, with the last half mile being particularly steep, though the views of Kinport Peak and the surrounding hills are well worth the climb. At about 0.6 miles, the trail passes through a barbed wire gate. The trail ends at Midnight Ridge Road.

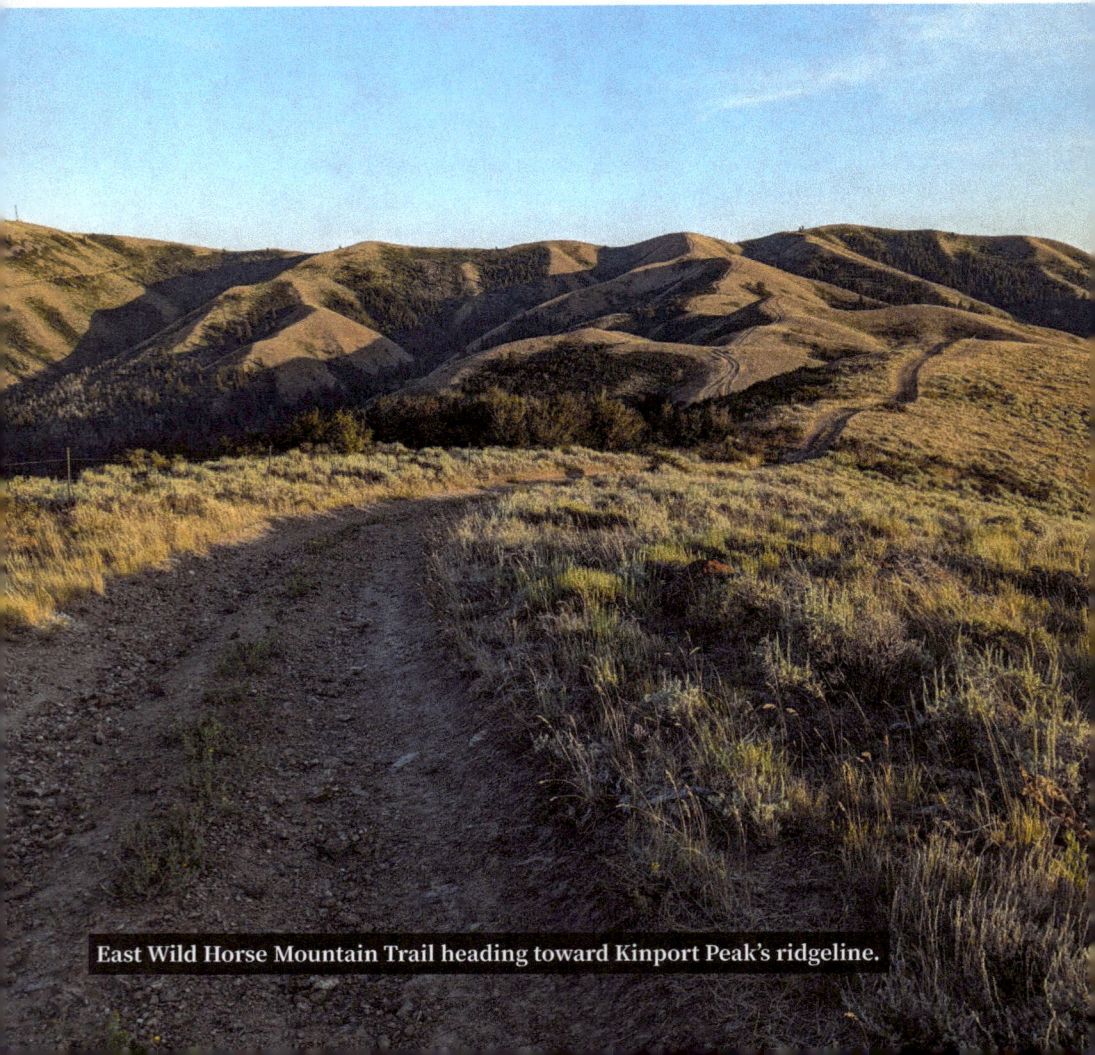

East Wild Horse Mountain Trail heading toward Kinport Peak's ridgeline.

Ridgeline Track

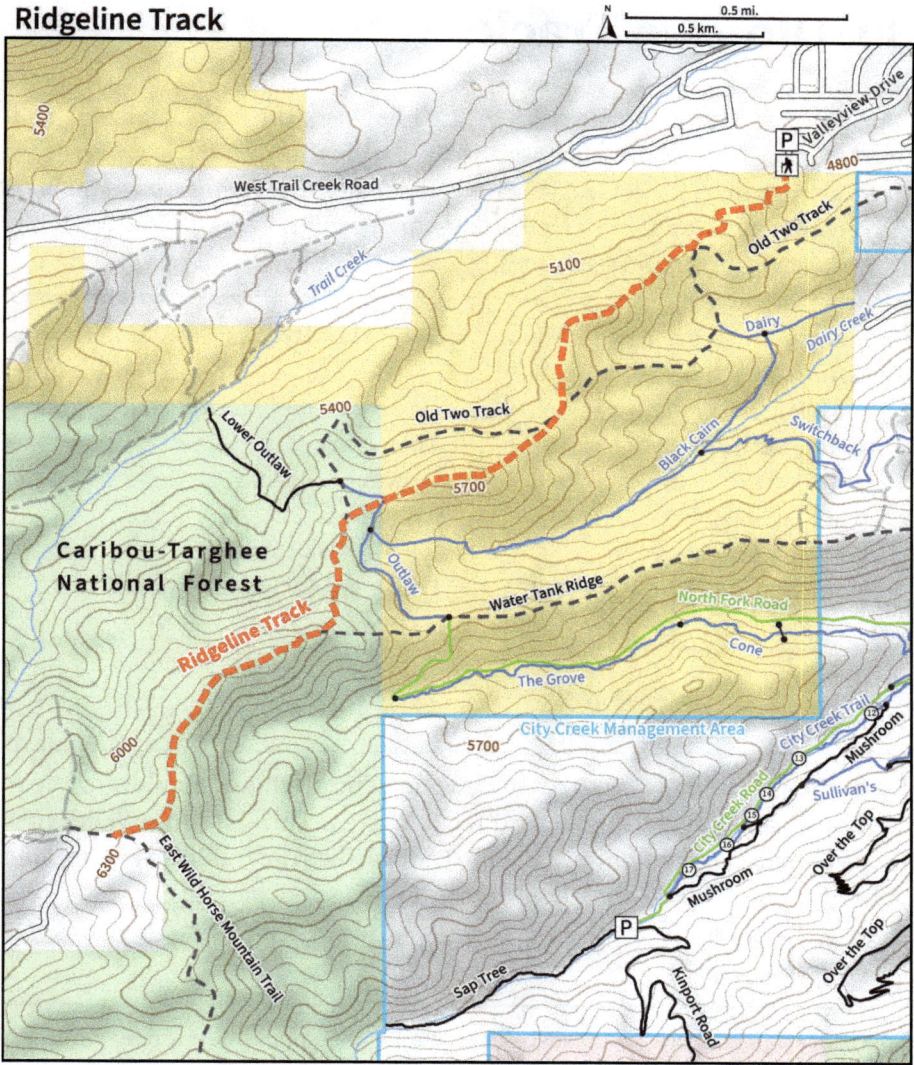

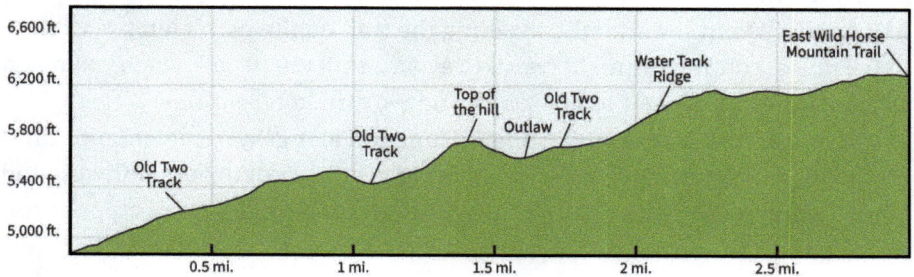

0.5 mi.

0.5 km.

5400

West Trail Creek Road

4800

Valleyview Drive

Trail Creek

5100

Old Two Track

Dairy

Dairy Creek

Old Two Track

Switchback

Lower Outlaw

5400

Black Cairn

5700

Outlaw

Caribou-Targhee
National Forest

Water Tank Ridge

North Fork Road

Ridgeline Track

Cone

The Grove

6000

City Creek Management Area

City Creek Trail

Mushroom

5700

Sullivan's

6300

City Creek Road

Mushroom

East Wild Horse Mountain Trail

Over the Top

Sap Tree

Kinport Road

Over the Top

Elevation profile:

6,600 ft.

East Wild Horse
Mountain Trail

6,200 ft.

Water Tank
Ridge

5,800 ft.

Top of
the hill

Old Two
Track

Old Two
Track

Outlaw

5,400 ft.

Old Two
Track

5,000 ft.

0.5 mi.   1 mi.   1.5 mi.   2 mi.   2.5 mi.

30. Old Two Track

Old Two Track is an unusual trail located between the City Creek and Trail Creek areas. The beginning 1.5 miles are confusing and occasionally very steep, though once it intersects the Ridgeline Track it becomes a pleasant hike. My recommendation for this trail is to use it in conjunction with the Ridgeline Track to navigate around a steep hill.

Distance: 5.1 miles out-and-back
Elevation Gain: 1,480 feet
Difficulty: Moderately strenuous
Hiking Time: About 3 hours
Nearest Town: Pocatello
Trail Surface: Dirt, rock
Wheelchair Access: None

Dog-Friendly: Yes; leash is required for the first 0.3 mile. After 0.3 mile, may be off-leash if under control.
Amenities: None
Contact: Bureau of Land Management, Pocatello Field Office 208-478-6340
Trailhead GPS Coordinates: N42° 51.396' W112° 28.330'

Getting There

From the junction of North Arthur Avenue and Highland Boulevard, head southwest on Highland Boulevard for 0.9 miles. Turn left onto Valleyview Drive, then in 0.7 miles, turn right onto Sandy Lane. The trailhead is at the end of Sandy Lane on the south side. There is limited street parking.

The Hike

The trail begins by heading west through an unusual wooden fence, where in about 230 feet, it turns to the right (north). The early stretch of this trail travels briefly through a juniper forest before entering onto a sage-covered hillside. At 0.1 miles, continue straight, avoiding the trail on the path's left (west) side. At 0.2 miles, continue straight (west) to avoid a trail on the left. Once you reach the junction with Ridgeline Track at 0.8 miles, turn left (south).

The trail descends south from the junction alongside a metal fence until it reaches a dry drainage. Once in the drainage, the trail turns southwest and climbs an incredibly steep hill, gaining 280 feet in 0.2 miles. Once atop the hill

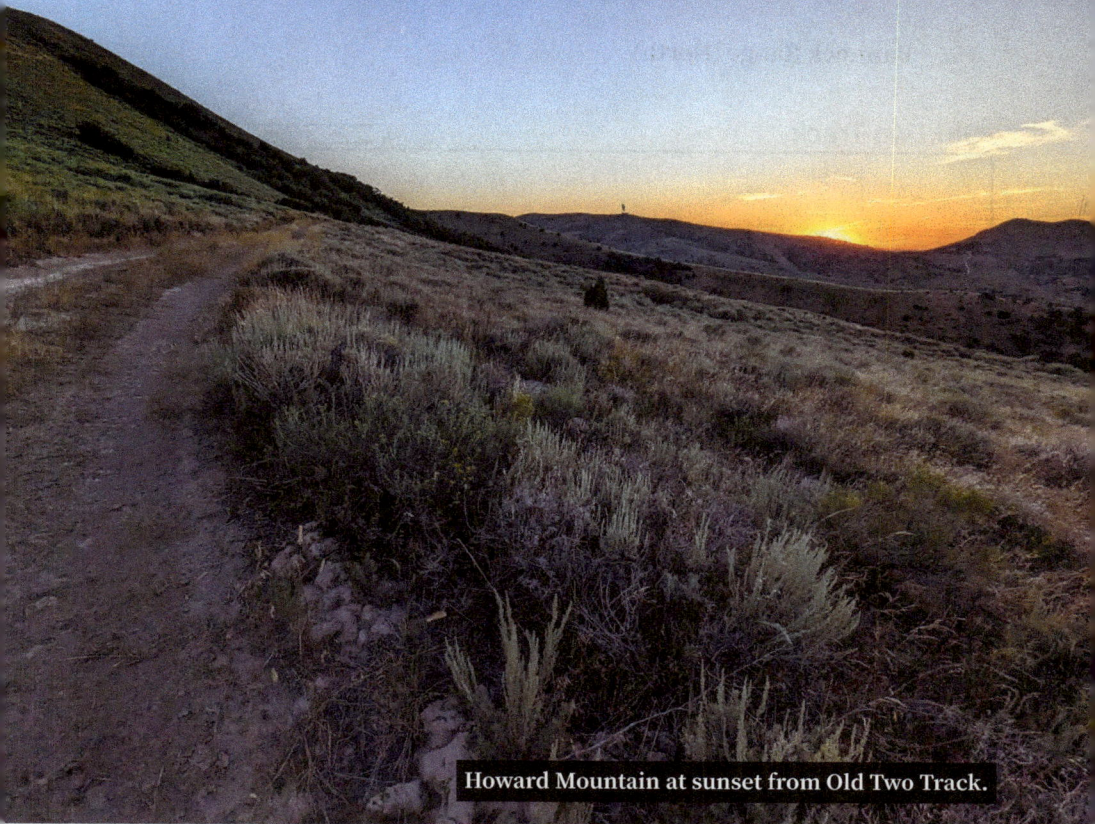

Howard Mountain at sunset from Old Two Track.

at 1.3 miles, the incline becomes much more gradual, and the trail turns to the west.

At 1.6 miles, the trail intersects with Ridgeline Track. Join it briefly as it heads southwest before making a right (west) turn at a fork. The goal from here is to circumnavigate the steep hill to your left (southwest) and connect with Ridgeline Track on the other side. Old Two Track travels to the west on the slopes of that hill, crossing a few forests before making a sharp left (southwest) turn at about 2.2 miles at a junction.

The trail climbs about 130 feet from that junction to the top of a hill, where you will keep left (south) at a small junction. After another hill climb, the trail ends when it connects with Ridgeline Track (5,700 feet).

Originally constructed in 1892, Pocatello High School was destroyed by a fire in 1914. The school has a rich historical background, having been visited by notable figures such as Theodore Roosevelt in 1903, William Howard Taft in 1911, and John F. Kennedy in 1960. The school is sometimes cited as one of the most haunted locations in America.

Old Two Track

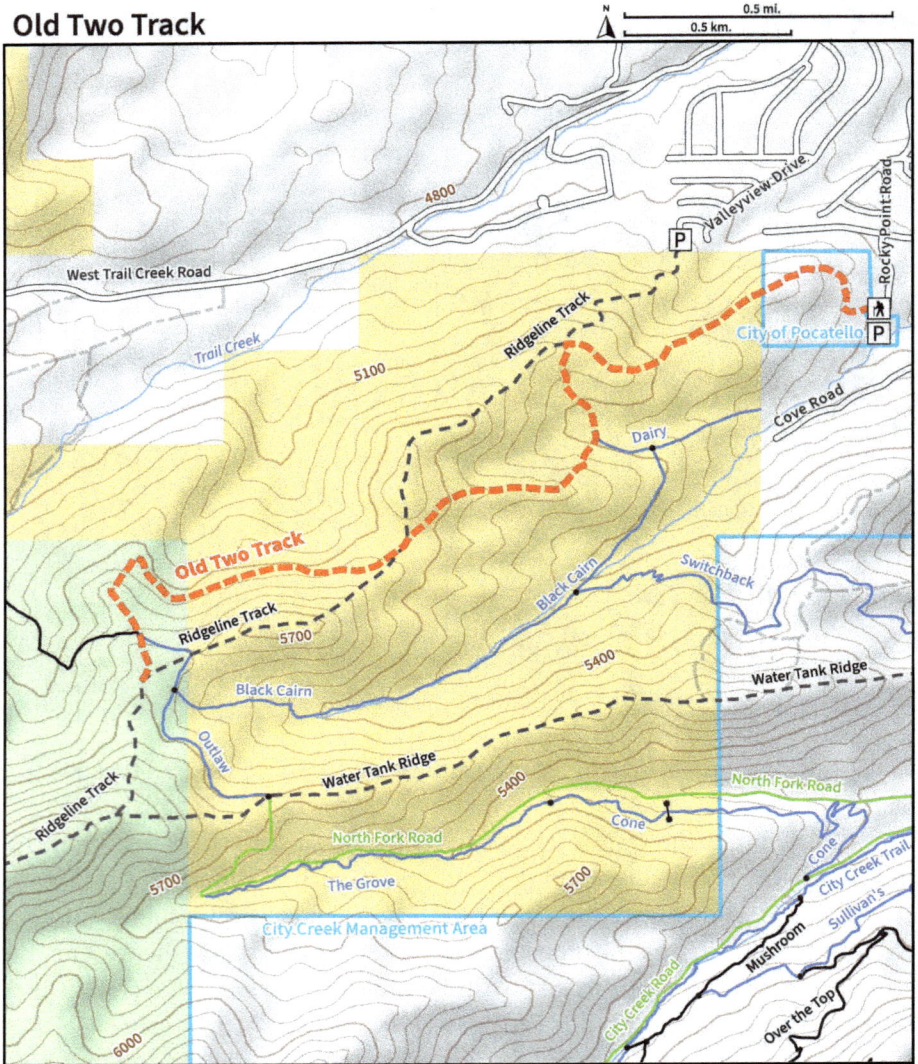

0.5 mi.
0.5 km.

N

4800

Valleyview Drive

Rocky Point Road

West Trail Creek Road

P

Trail Creek

City of Pocatello

P

5100

Ridgeline Track

Dairy

Cove Road

Old Two Track

Ridgeline Track

5700

Black Cairn

Switchback

Black Cairn

5400

Water Tank Ridge

Outlaw

Water Tank Ridge

5400

North Fork Road

Ridgeline Track

North Fork Road

Cone

Cone

City Creek Trail

The Grove

5700

Sullivan's

5700

City Creek Management Area

Mushroom

City Creek Road

Over the Top

6000

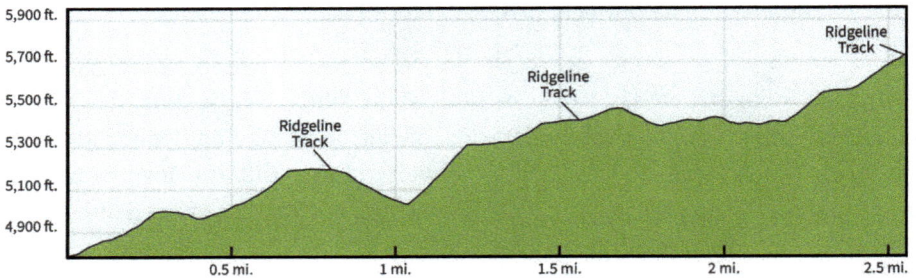

5,900 ft.

5,700 ft.

5,500 ft.

5,300 ft.

5,100 ft.

4,900 ft.

Ridgeline Track

Ridgeline Track

Ridgeline Track

0.5 mi.   1 mi.   1.5 mi.   2 mi.   2.5 mi.

31. Water Tank Ridge

Easily accessible from the Upper City Creek Trailhead, Water Tank Ridge is a moderately strenuous and sun-exposed hike that rewards those who climb the steep hill with a fun rollercoaster of a ridge walk and unsurpassed views of the area. The trail can be incredibly rocky, especially during the initial significant incline, so mountain bikers are in for a challenging ride. Hikers are encouraged to bring poles.

Distance: 5 miles out-and-back
Elevation Gain: 1,700 feet
Difficulty: Moderately strenuous
Hiking Time: About 3 hours
Nearest Town: Pocatello
Trail Surface: Dirt, rock
Wheelchair Access: None

Dog-Friendly: Yes; leash is required for the first 1.3 miles. After 1.3 miles, may be off-leash if under control.
Amenities: None
Contact: Bureau of Land Management, Pocatello Field Office 208-478-6340;
City of Pocatello Parks & Recreation 208-234-6232
Trailhead GPS Coordinates: N42° 50.861' W112° 27.635'

Getting There

From the junction of South 4th Avenue and Benton Street, head southwest on Benton Street for 0.7 miles. Turn right onto South Grant Avenue, and then make a left on West Whitman Street. After a couple of blocks, turn left onto South Lincoln Avenue, and then in 0.5 miles, turn left onto City Creek Road, following a sign for the City Creek Trails. You will reach the Upper City Creek Trailhead at the end of this road in 0.5 miles, where you will find plenty of parking. The route begins on the south side of the parking area.

The Hike

From the trailhead, head south through the gate on City Creek Road, where in about 200 feet, you will turn right onto the path for Water Tank Ridge. At about 0.4 miles, you will come to a large water tank that overlooks City Creek. Keep left, following the tank clockwise, avoiding the first left turn, and then taking

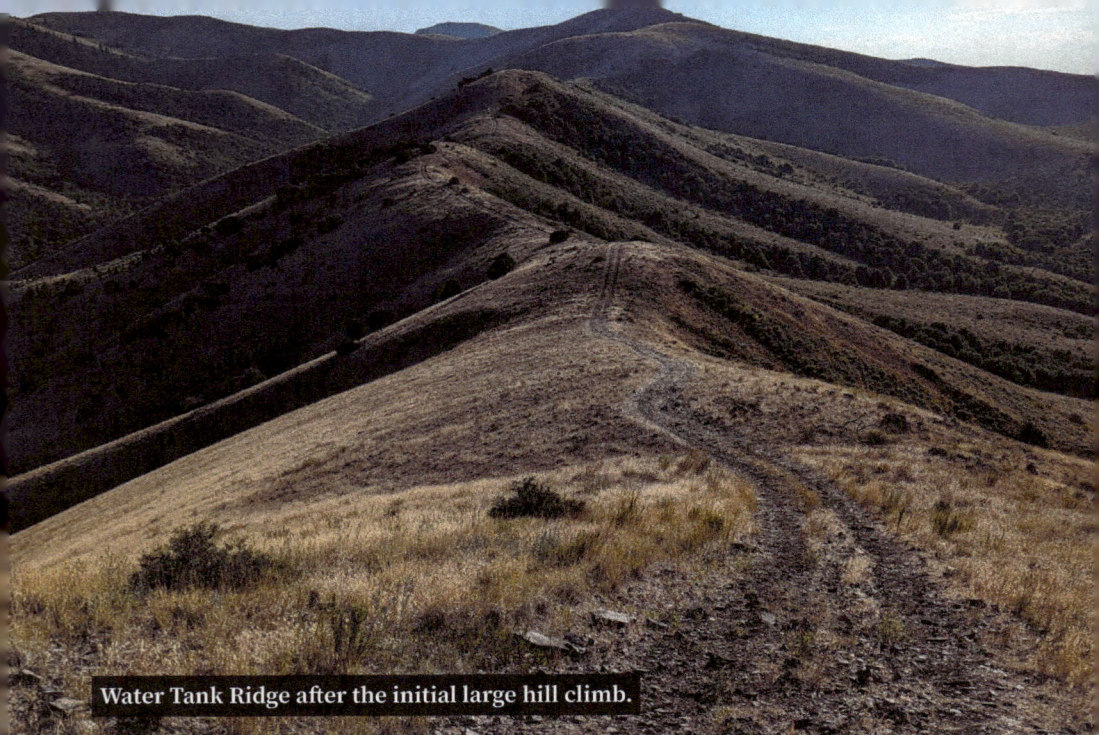
Water Tank Ridge after the initial large hill climb.

the second one that heads west. From here, the rocky trail climbs 700 feet in 0.8 miles to the top of a ridge, making for a moderately challenging climb.

Once atop the ridge, at about 1.3 miles, you will have excellent views of the City Creek Management Area as you catch your breath. With the significant incline out of the way, the trail continues west on top of the ridge, following it as it climbs and descends several small but steep hills. Keep straight (west) to avoid an unofficial 4x4 trail to the right (north) at 1.3 miles. After descending a small hill, the trail intersects with the North Fork Road at 2.2 miles. Keep straight (west) through the intersection to continue on Water Tank Ridge. If you are not looking to connect to the Ridgeline Track, this junction is a fine place to either turn around or join another trail.

Once past the intersection, the trail begins a steep climb, gaining 300 feet in 0.3 miles. Avoid the rough side path that emerges on the left side of this climb. The trail ends once it comes to an intersection with the Ridgeline Track (6,000 feet).

Keep Going

Once at the endpoint, you have several options to make this path into a loop. I recommend making a left (south) turn at 2.2 miles onto North Fork Road. From there, you can take The Grove and descend to City Creek Road, and eventually, the Upper City Creek parking lot.

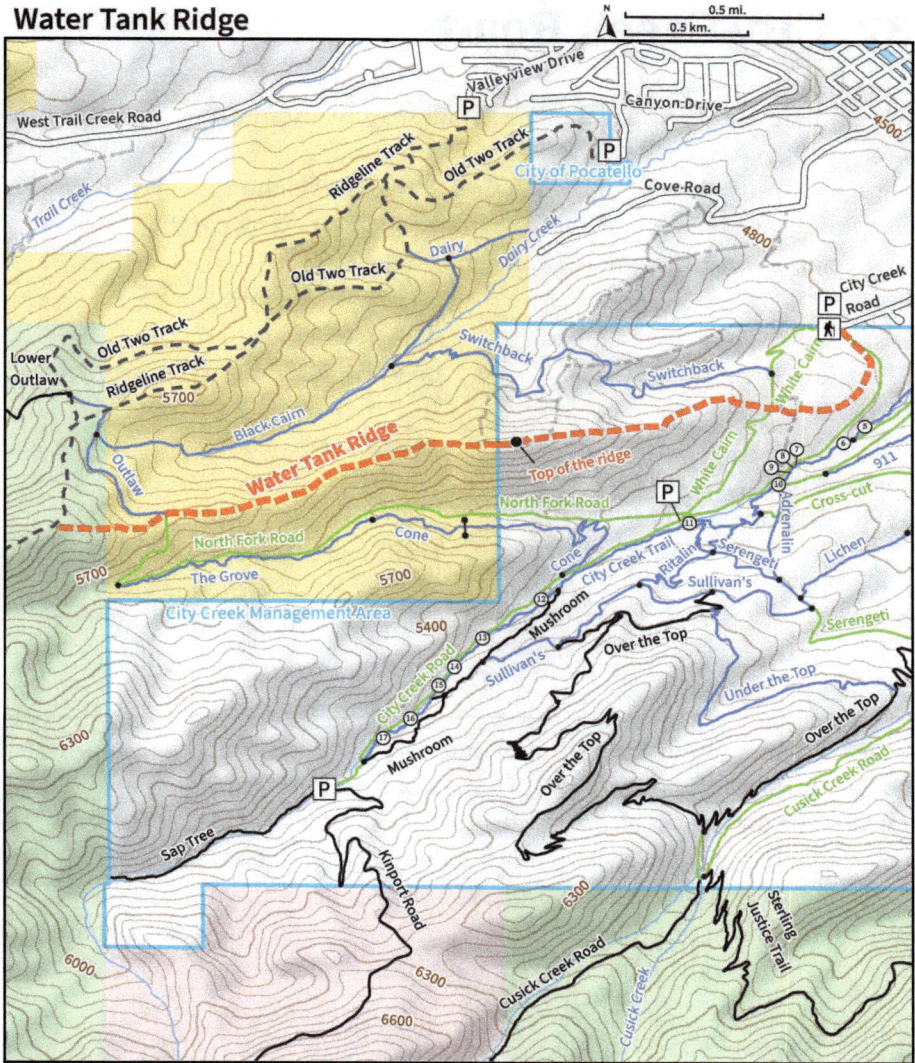

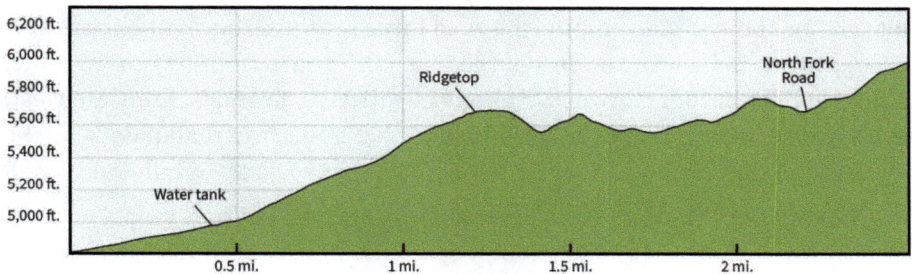

Water Tank Ridge

N

0.5 mi.

0.5 km.

West Trail Creek Road

Valleyview Drive

Canyon Drive

4500

Ridgeline Track

Old Two Track

City of Pocatello

Cove Road

Trail Creek

Old Two Track

Dairy

Dairy Creek

4800

City Creek Road

Old Two Track

Switchback

Switchback

White Cairn

Lower Outlaw

Ridgeline Track

5700

Black Cairn

Water Tank Ridge

Top of the ridge

White Cairn

911

Outlaw

North Fork Road

Cross-cut

Adrenalin

Lichen

North Fork Road

Cone

City Creek Trail

Ritalin

Serengeti

5700

The Grove

5700

Cone

Mushroom

Sullivan's

Serengeti

City Creek Management Area

5400

City Creek Road

Sullivan's

Over the Top

Under the Top

6300

Mushroom

Over the Top

Over the Top

Sap Tree

Kinport Road

Cusick Creek Road

6300

Sterling Justice Trail

6000

Cusick Creek Road

Cusick Creek

6300

6600

6,200 ft.
6,000 ft.
5,800 ft.   Ridgetop
5,600 ft.
5,400 ft.
5,200 ft.
5,000 ft.
        Water tank

North Fork Road

0.5 mi.   1 mi.   1.5 mi.   2 mi.

32. City Creek Road

A well-maintained dirt road that runs above and parallel to City Creek, City Creek Road is easy to follow and dotted with parking areas that provide access to several trails. While the shaded City Creek Trail is the more popular hike, this sunny road is a fun trail with pleasant scenery in its own right. Just be sure to keep an eye out for vehicles while enjoying it.

Distance: 4.6 miles out-and-back
Elevation Gain: 600 feet
Difficulty: Moderate
Hiking Time: About 2.5 hours
Nearest Town: Pocatello
Trail Surface: Dirt, rock

Wheelchair Access: None
Dog-Friendly: Yes; must be on a leash at all times
Amenities: None
Contact: City of Pocatello Parks & Recreation 208-234-6232
Trailhead GPS Coordinates: N42° 50.861' W112° 27.635'

Getting There

From the junction of South 4th Avenue and Benton Street, head southwest on Benton Street for 0.7 miles. Turn right onto South Grant Avenue, and then make a left on West Whitman Street. After a couple of blocks, turn left onto South Lincoln Avenue, and then in 0.5 miles, turn left onto City Creek Road, following a sign for City Creek Trails. You will reach the Upper City Creek Trailhead at the end of this road in 0.5 miles, where you will find plenty of parking. The hike begins on the south side of the parking area.

The Hike

The road begins by moving southeast through the Upper City Creek parking lot gate. In about a quarter mile, the road turns southwest and runs above City Creek, which it does for the rest of the hike. This is a very sun-exposed route, though it does become forested at about 1.7 miles. At 0.9 miles, keep left (west) at the fork, passing by North Fork Road. At 2.2 miles, the road passes by the endpoint of the City Creek Trail to the left. The road ends at 2.3 miles in a small parking area before the Kinport Road gate.

As you travel southwest on City Creek Road, you will pass by four small parking areas that provide direct access to the City Creek Trail.

▶ Parking Area 1: Located at 0.6 miles. Provides access to Bridge 7.

▶ Parking Area 2: Located at 0.7 miles. Provides access to Bridges 9 and 10.

▶ Parking Area 3: Located at 1 mile, just past the North Fork Road turnoff. Provides access to Bridge 11. This is the largest of the parking areas and is a common starting point for many trails.

▶ Parking Area 4: Located just before the Kinport Road gate at 2.3 miles. Provides access to Kinport Road and is a popular dropoff location for downhill mountain bikers.

City Creek Road in autumn.

City Creek Road

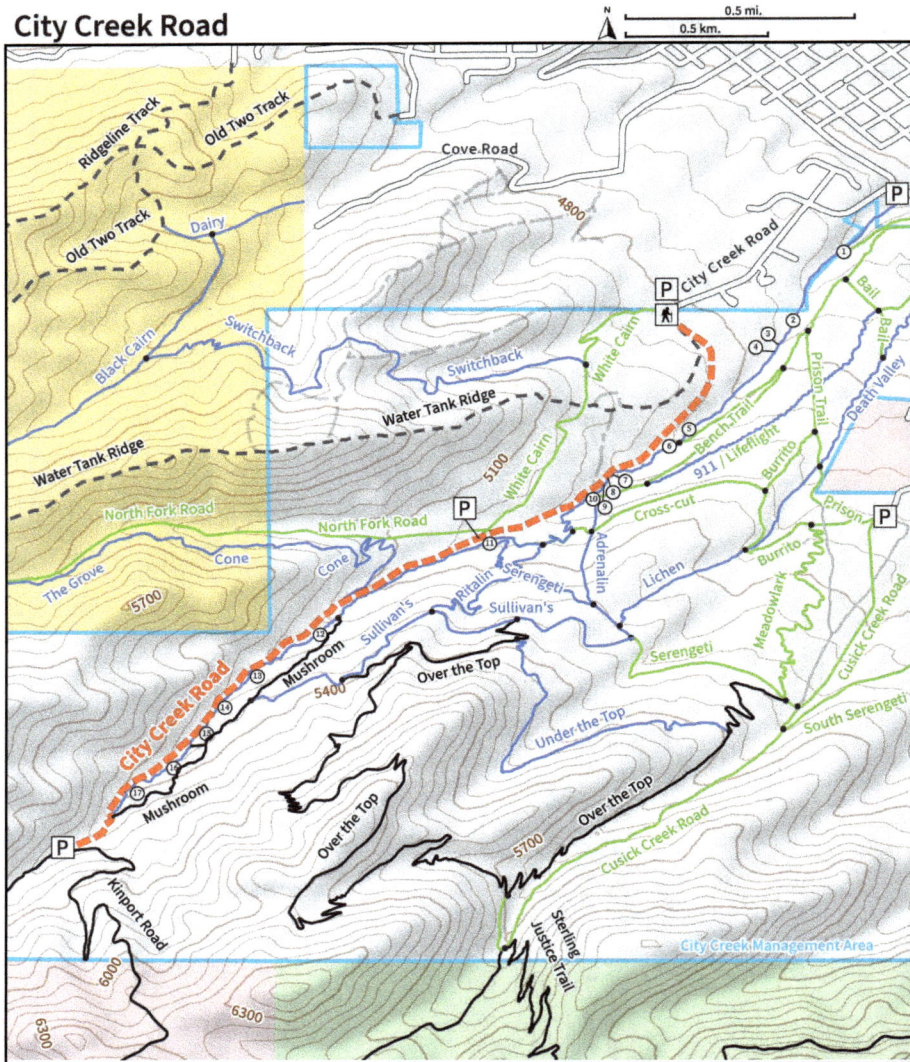

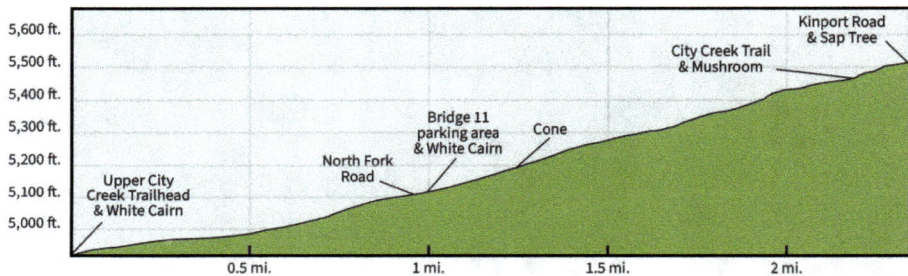

N

0.5 mi.

0.5 km.

Cove Road

4800

City Creek Road

Ridgeline Track

Old Two Track

Old Two Track

Dairy

Black Cairn

Switchback

Switchback

Water Tank Ridge

White Cairn

White Cairn

Prison Trail

Bail

Bail

Death Valley

Water Tank Ridge

North Fork Road

North Fork Road

5100

Bench Trail

911 / Lifeflight

Burrito

Prison

The Grove

Cone

Cone

Cone

Cross-cut

Adrenalin

Lichen

Burrito

Meadowlark

Cusick Creek Road

5700

Ritalin

Serengeti

Sullivan's

Sullivan's

Serengeti

South Serengeti

City Creek Road

Mushroom

Mushroom

5400

Over the Top

Under the Top

Over the Top

Over the Top

Kinport Road

Over the Top

5700

Cusick Creek Road

Sterling Justice Trail

City Creek Management Area

6000

6300

6300

Elevation profile

5,600 ft.				Kinport Road & Sap Tree
5,500 ft.				City Creek Trail & Mushroom
5,400 ft.				
5,300 ft.		Bridge 11 parking area & White Cairn	Cone	
5,200 ft.		North Fork Road		
5,100 ft.				
5,000 ft.	Upper City Creek Trailhead & White Cairn			

0.5 mi.   1 mi.   1.5 mi.   2 mi.

33. North Fork Road

The motorized North Fork Road makes for a straightforward hike through a steep-sided drainage. The dirt road is usually in good condition, though occasional ruts and seasonal ponds can make driving on it difficult. This isn't the most sought-after path for hikers due to the nearby shaded Grove Trail, though this does have its merits as a wide 4x4 road that connects to a useful junction.

Distance: 3.8 miles out-and-back
Elevation Gain: 650 feet
Difficulty: Moderate
Hiking Time: About 2 hours
Nearest Town: Pocatello
Trail Surface: Dirt, rock
Wheelchair Access: None

Dog-Friendly: Yes; leash is required for the first 0.5 mile. After 0.5 mile, may be off-leash if under control.
Amenities: None
Contact: City of Pocatello Parks & Recreation 208-234-6232; Bureau of Land Management, Pocatello Field Office 208-478-6340
Trailhead GPS Coordinates: N42° 50.288' W112° 28.084'

Getting There

From the junction of South 4th Avenue and Benton Street, head southwest on Benton Street for 0.7 miles. Turn right onto South Grant Avenue, and then make a left on West Whitman Street. After a couple of blocks, turn left onto South Lincoln Avenue, and then in 0.5 miles, turn left onto City Creek Road, following a sign for City Creek Trails. You will reach the Upper City Creek Trailhead at the end of this paved road in 0.5 miles. From the Upper City Creek Trailhead, continue south on the dirt City Creek Road for 1.0 mile, until you reach a parking area along City Creek Trail. North Fork Road is just 200 feet to the northeast of this parking area.

The Hike

The path heads west from where the road splits off City Creek Road, paralleling The Grove and an intermittent stream. At 1.6 miles, the road makes a sharp northeast turn, departing the stream and heading up a rocky ridge. The trail ends at a junction (5,700 feet) with Water Tank Ridge and Outlaw.

City Creek originates from the northwest side of Kinport Peak and flows for 4.7 miles before joining the Portneuf River.

North Fork Road in the early summer.

North Fork Road

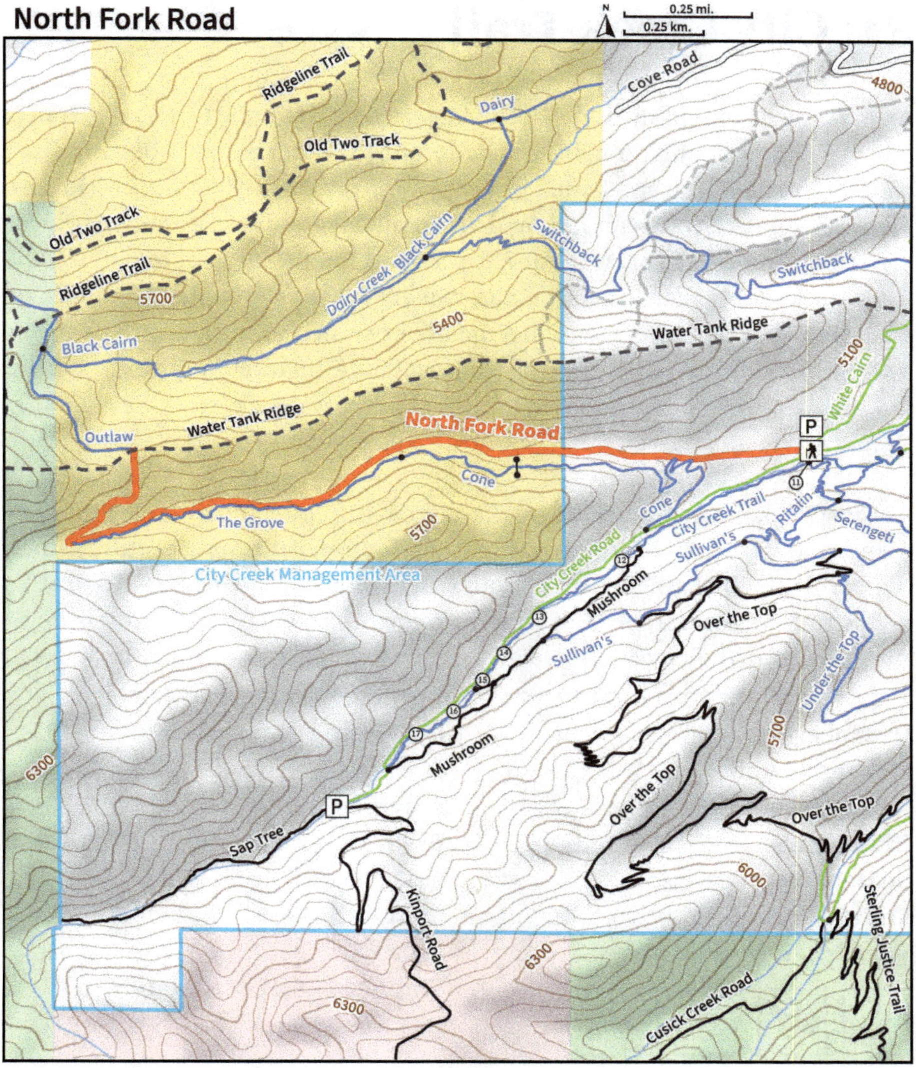
N
0.25 mi.
0.25 km.
Cove Road
4800
Ridgeline Trail
Dairy
Old Two Track
Old Two Track
Ridgeline Trail
5700
Dairy Creek
Black Cairn
Switchback
Switchback
5400
Black Cairn
Water Tank Ridge
5100
White Cairn
Water Tank Ridge
Outlaw
North Fork Road
P
Cone
The Grove
5700
Cone
City Creek Trail
Ritalin
Serengeti
City Creek Road
Sullivan's
City Creek Management Area
Mushroom
Over the Top
Sullivan's
Under the Top
5700
Mushroom
6300
Over the Top
P
Sap Tree
Over the Top
Kinport Road
6000
Sterling Justice Trail
6300
Cusick Creek Road
6300

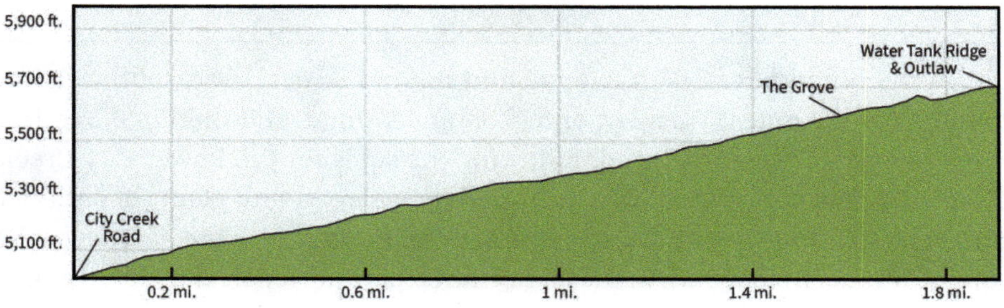
5,900 ft.
5,700 ft.
5,500 ft.
5,300 ft.
5,100 ft.
City Creek Road
The Grove
Water Tank Ridge & Outlaw
0.2 mi.
0.6 mi.
1 mi.
1.4 mi.
1.8 mi.

34. City Creek Trail

As the crown jewel of the City Creek Management Area, the City Creek Trail is one of the most popular trails in Pocatello, and for good reason. A beautiful and well-maintained lush creek walk just minutes from the city center, the trail is a favorite for hikers, trail runners, and mountain bikers alike. Seventeen bridges cross over the creek, making for a fun way to track your progress along the route. Mountain bikers, in particular, will enjoy the seemingly countless side trails that allow for fresh loops on almost every visit. In the autumn, the area is awash with vibrant colors, making it a popular destination for photographers. For an overview of the individual trails in the City Creek Area, visit the City Creek Management Area Trail Overview on page 405.

As City Creek is a narrow singletrack trail that is frequented by large groups of hikers and mountain bikers, it is important for everyone to respectfully share the trail. Avoid blocking the trail. Mountain bikers, be careful going fast on this pedestrian-heavy trail. And of course, if you are traveling with your dog, be sure to pick up their waste as you go.

Distance: 6 miles out-and-back
Elevation Gain: 950 feet
Difficulty: Moderately strenuous
Hiking Time: About 3 hours
Nearest Town: Pocatello
Trail Surface: Dirt, rock, gravel
Wheelchair Access: None

Dog-Friendly: Yes; must be on a leash at all times
Amenities: None at the trailhead. Restrooms and water are available nearby at Centennial Park.
Contact: City of Pocatello Parks & Recreation 208-234-6232
Trailhead GPS Coordinates: N42° 51.173' W112° 27.019'

Getting There

From the junction of S. 4th Avenue and Benton Street, head southwest on Benton for 0.7 miles. Turn left onto S. Grant Avenue, and then in 0.3 miles, turn right onto the gravel road, following the signs for the Lower City Creek Trailhead. The trailhead is at the end of this gravel road with plenty of parking. Alternate parking can be found at Centennial Park, just to the east across S. Grant Avenue. Do not park in the large church parking lot off S. Grant Avenue.

City Creek Trail's Bridge 11.

The Hike

From the signed trailhead, head southwest on the singletrack path. The initial stretch of the trail is on gravel, though in general the path is on dirt intermixed with rocks and occasionally roots. About 0.2 miles into the hike, you will come to a fork in the road, where you will keep right and cross over Bridge 1. At about 0.7 miles, you will come to a fork, where you can take either path. At 0.9 miles, the trail crosses Bridge 5, entering into a lovely stretch of the hike with tall deciduous trees and horsetail along the creek.

At 1.1 miles, keep left at the fork. At 1.2 miles, you will come to a junction, with Bridge 10 on your right. Continue straight (southwest) to begin the Upper City Creek Trail. At about 1.3 miles, the trail turns left at a fence. Behind the fence is the old City Creek Trail path that is being restored. Due to this trail restoration, the next stretch can be confusing as you are rerouted from the creek onto Cross-cut, a trail frequently used by mountain bikers, until you reconnect with the Upper City Creek Trail at 1.7 miles. To keep things simple, make every right turn until you are back on the main trail.

Once back on the main path, the route hugs the shaded creek for the remainder of the hike. Just past 1.7 miles, you will come to a junction. Continue straight (southwest), passing by Bridge 11 on the right side of the trail. At about 2.3 miles, you will come to a fork where you can take either path. Around 2.7 miles, you will pass through a junction near a bench, where you will continue to the right (southwest). The trail ends once it connects with City Creek Road.

The City Creek Trail is technically divided into two sections, Upper and Lower City Creek Trails. The Lower City Creek Trail, the most highly trafficked portion of the trail, begins at the Grant Street Parking Lot and ends at Bridge 10. Mountain bikers must remember that the area between Bridges 1 - 5 is designated as One-Way Uphill Only. Upper City Creek Trail consists of the stretch of trail between Bridge 10 and the endpoint at City Creek Road.

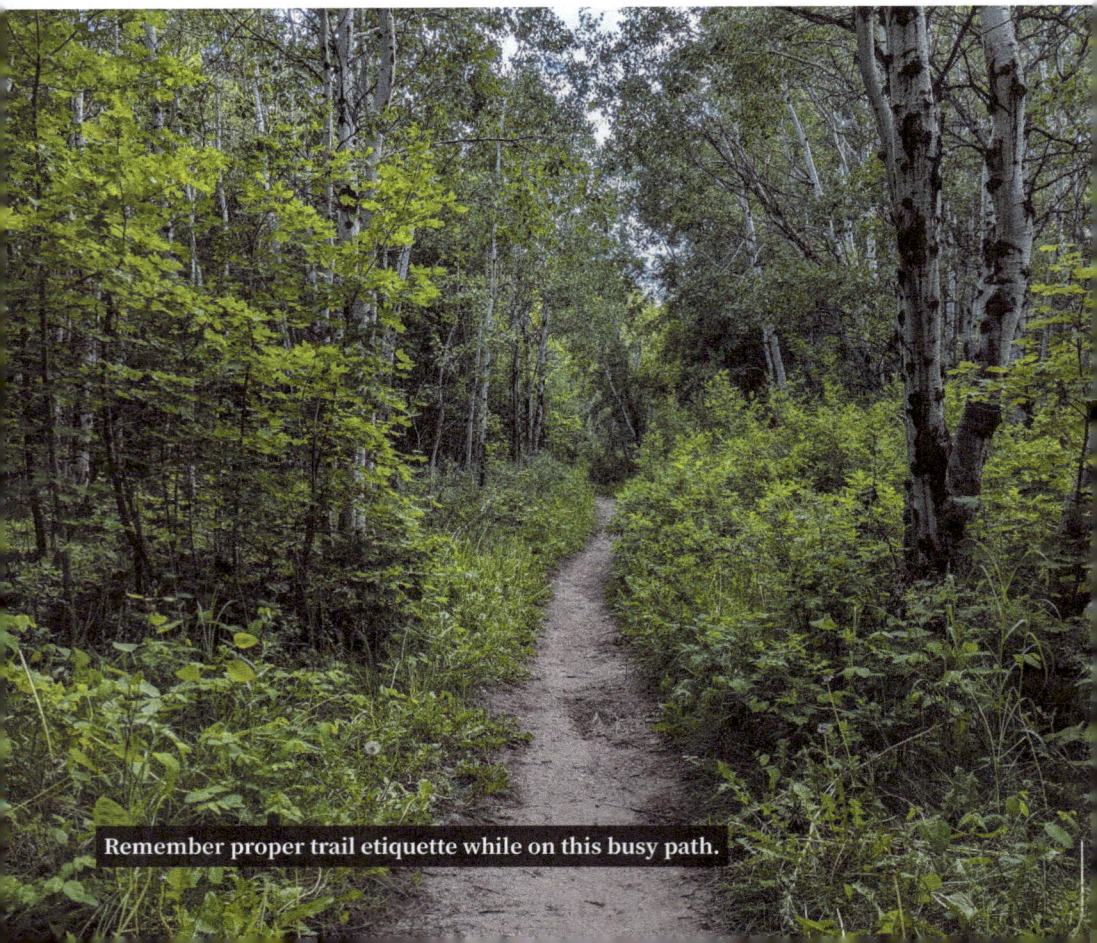

Remember proper trail etiquette while on this busy path.

City Creek Trail

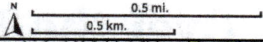

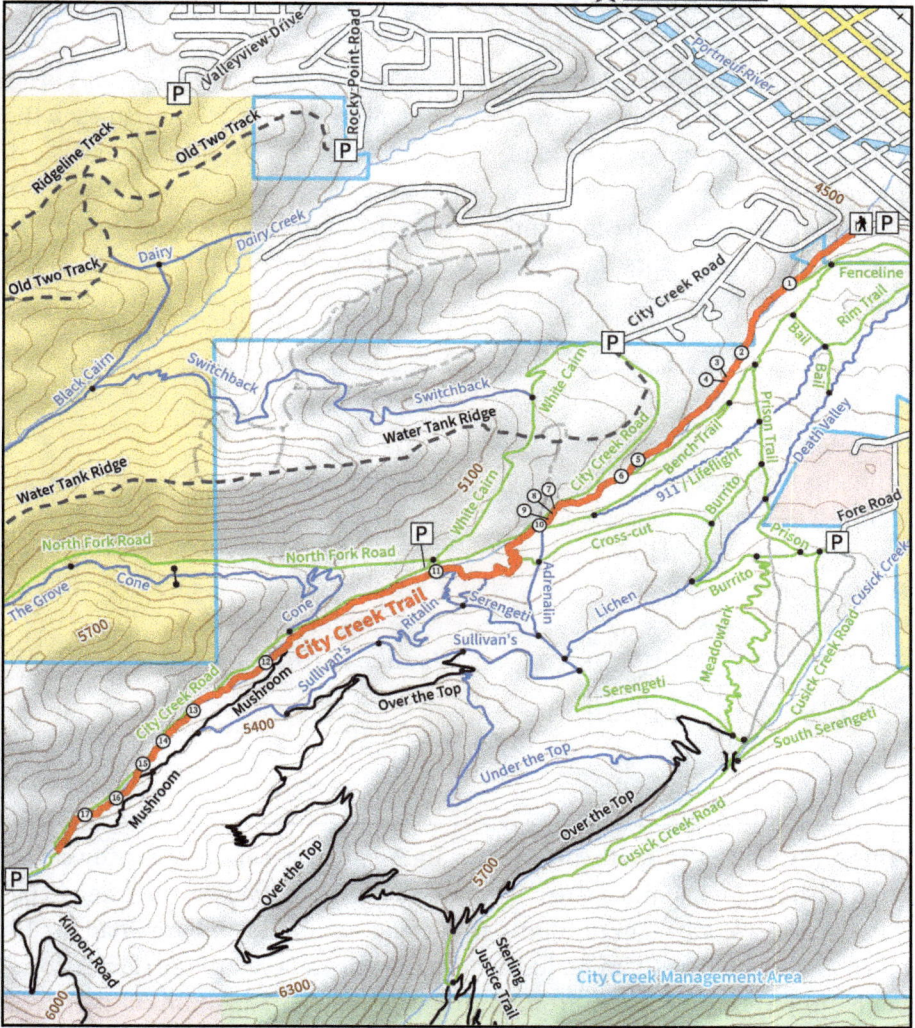

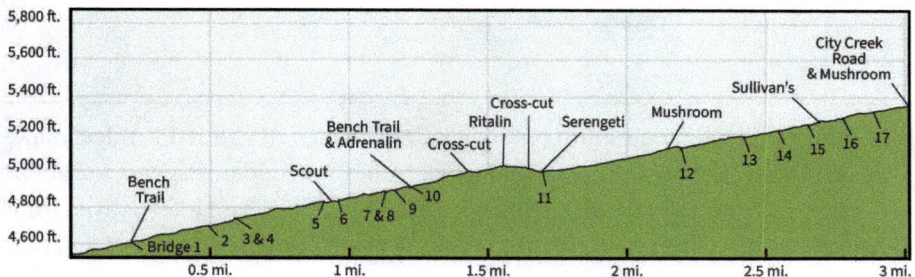

N

0.5 mi.
0.5 km.

Valleyview Drive

Rocky Point Road

Ridgeline Track

Old Two Track

Old Two Track

Portneuf River

4500

Dairy

Dairy Creek

City Creek Road

Fenceline

Black Cairn

Switchback

Rim Trail

Ball

Ball

Switchback

Water Tank Ridge

White Cairn

Bench Trail

Prison Trail

Death Valley

Water Tank Ridge

5100

White Cairn

City Creek Road

911 / Lifeflight

Burrito

Prison

Fore Road

North Fork Road

North Fork Road

Cross-cut

Lichen

Burrito

Cusick Creek

The Grove

Cone

5700

Cone

City Creek Trail

Mushroom

Sullivan's

Ritalin

Serengeti

Adrenalin

Sullivan's

Meadowlark

Cusick Creek Road

City Creek Road

5400

Mushroom

Over the Top

Serengeti

South Serengeti

Under the Top

Over the Top

Over the Top

Cusick Creek Road

Kinport Road

Over the Top

5700

Sterling Justice Trail

City Creek Management Area

6000

6300

Elevation profile:

5,800 ft.
5,600 ft.
5,400 ft.
5,200 ft.
5,000 ft.
4,800 ft.
4,600 ft.

Bench Trail

Scout

Bench Trail & Adrenalin

Cross-cut

Ritalin

Cross-cut

Serengeti

Mushroom

Sullivan's

City Creek Road & Mushroom

Bridge 1   2   3 & 4   5   6   7 & 8   9   10   11   12   13   14   15   16   17

0.5 mi.   1 mi.   1.5 mi.   2 mi.   2.5 mi.   3 mi.

35. Over the Top Loop

Traveling through forested ravines, grassy hillsides, and rocky ridges, the Over the Top Loop gives hikers a chance to experience a variety of landscapes in the City Creek Management Area. The midpoint of this moderate climb takes you high onto a ridge below Kinport Peak, giving spectacular views of both Cusick Creek and City Creek. In the autumn, this trail is a must for anyone looking to see incredible fall colors. This loop travels through several popular mountain bike paths, so be sure to stay alert to avoid getting hit and allow uphill bikers to pass you.

Distance: 7.2-mile lollipop loop
Elevation Gain: 1,140 feet
Difficulty: Moderately strenuous
Hiking Time: About 4 hours
Nearest Town: Pocatello
Trail Surface: Dirt, rock
Wheelchair Access: None

Dog-Friendly: Yes; must be on a leash at all times
Amenities: None at the trailhead. Restrooms and water are available nearby at Centennial Park.
Contact: City of Pocatello Parks & Recreation 208-234-6232
Trailhead GPS Coordinates: N42° 50.325' W112° 27.084'

Getting There

From the junction of South 4th Avenue and Benton Street, head southwest on Benton Street for 0.7 miles. Turn left onto South Grant Avenue, and then in 0.4 miles, make a slight right turn onto Fore Road. Continue on Fore Road for 1.4 miles, turning left at 1.0 mile, just before the Pocatello Women's Correctional Center to stay on Fore Road. From that turn, Fore Road transitions into a gravel road, where in 0.4 miles, you will find the Cusick Creek Trailhead and plenty of parking.

The Hike

From the trailhead, head south on Cusick Creek Road. At about 0.7 miles, make a right (northwest) turn onto a singletrack trail. Continue northwest for about 150 feet until you join the doubletrack Serengeti Trail. Just a few yards onto Serengeti, turn left (northwest) off the doubletrack onto the Over the Top Trail.

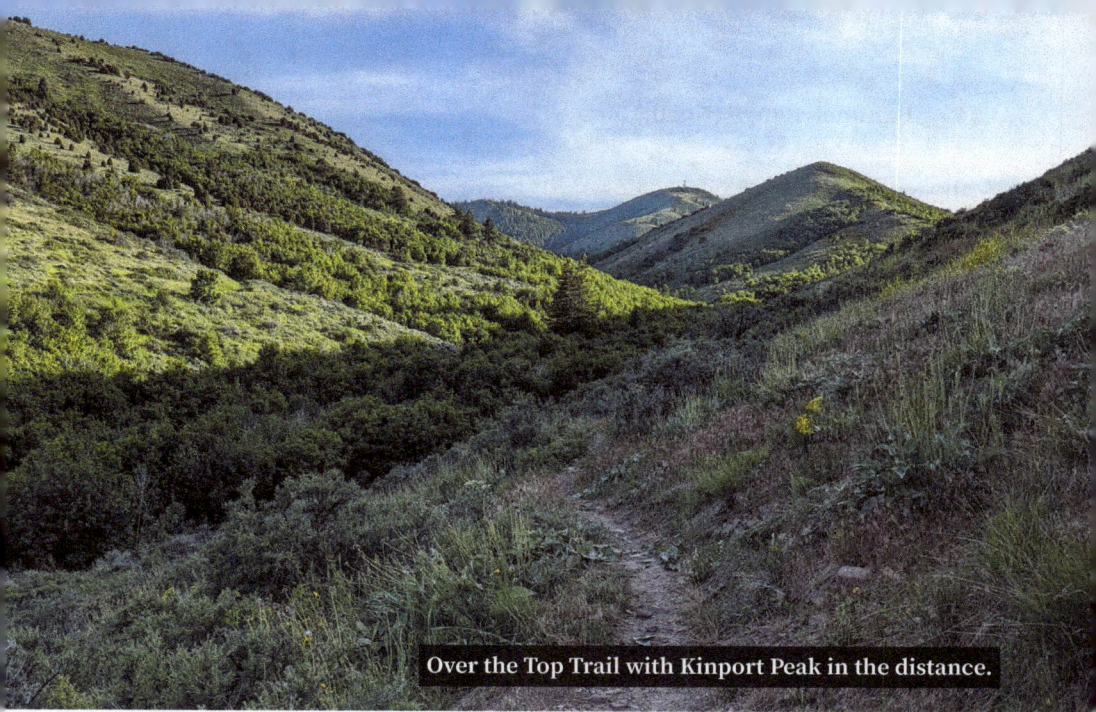

Over the Top Trail with Kinport Peak in the distance.

The early stretch of the Over the Top Trail winds its way up a grassy hillside on a series of switchbacks. At 1.1 miles, keep left (southwest) at the junction to avoid Under the Top Trail. From this junction, the trail heads across an open hillside with beautiful views of Cusick Creek to the left. At 1.7 miles, the trail begins another set of switchbacks, where you will keep right at every junction to stay on the route. At about 2.0 miles, keep right (north) to stay on the trail, avoiding a connecting trail to the south that leads to Sterling Justice Trail.

The path soon leaves the switchbacks behind and, at 2.2 miles, enters a deciduous forest above the creek. At about 2.5 miles, shortly after leaving the forest, the trail reaches the top of a small ridge with excellent views of the area. There are a couple of wild, unofficial side trails at this point, so be sure to stay on the well-used Over the Top Trail as it continues to the west.

From the small ridge, the trail makes its final push for the high ridgeline, gaining over 250 feet in 0.7 miles. Continue on the trail as it crosses a dry hillside and a low forest. If you are hiking this trail early in the season, there is often a snow bank over the trail just below the ridgetop, so hiking poles are recommended. At about 3.2 miles, you will come to the top of a ridge, which is the high point of the route (6,090 feet). This is an excellent place to take a well-earned break and grab a few pictures. You will find two unofficial side trails at this point, so to continue the route, head northeast on the well-used trail toward the city.

The trail travels northeast on the dry ridge for about the next half mile, occasionally crossing a few rocky stretches. Be sure to look behind you periodically to take in the excellent view of Kinport Peak. At about 3.8 miles, the trail crosses over to the north side of the ridge and heads southwest, beginning the rocky descent toward City Creek. At 4.2 miles, you will reach the top of several short switchbacks. This can be challenging to mountain bikers, though hikers won't have much of an issue.

Once the switchbacks end, at about 4.4 miles, the trail heads northeast across the dry hillside and occasionally passes through scattered forests. At about 4.6 miles, the trail comes to a fork. Either option works, though the left option is easier on the legs. At about 5.0 miles, the trail comes to another fork. Keep right (northeast) to stay on the route. (The left (southwest) path continues to the upper portion of Sullivan's.)

Once past that fork, the trail's incline levels out, making for a more leisurely hike. At about 5.4 miles, keep left at two back-to-back junctions with Under the Top Trail, and then at 5.5 miles, keep right at two more junctions to merge onto Sullivan's. Stay on Sullivan's as it continues east. At about 5.9 miles, keep right (south) to merge onto Serengeti. Continue southeast for about 0.6 miles, passing by Over the Top and reconnecting with the Cusick Creek Road, which you will follow back down to the trailhead.

> The Over the Top Trail Race is an annual trail run organized by the Pocatello Running Club in the spring. The race, which began in 2017, offers participants multiple distances to choose from, all of which travel within the City Creek Trail System. The 10-mile and 25-kilometer courses include a climb on the Over the Top Trail, making it a challenging experience for the racers.

Trail runners on Over the Top's late spring snow bank.

Over the Top Loop

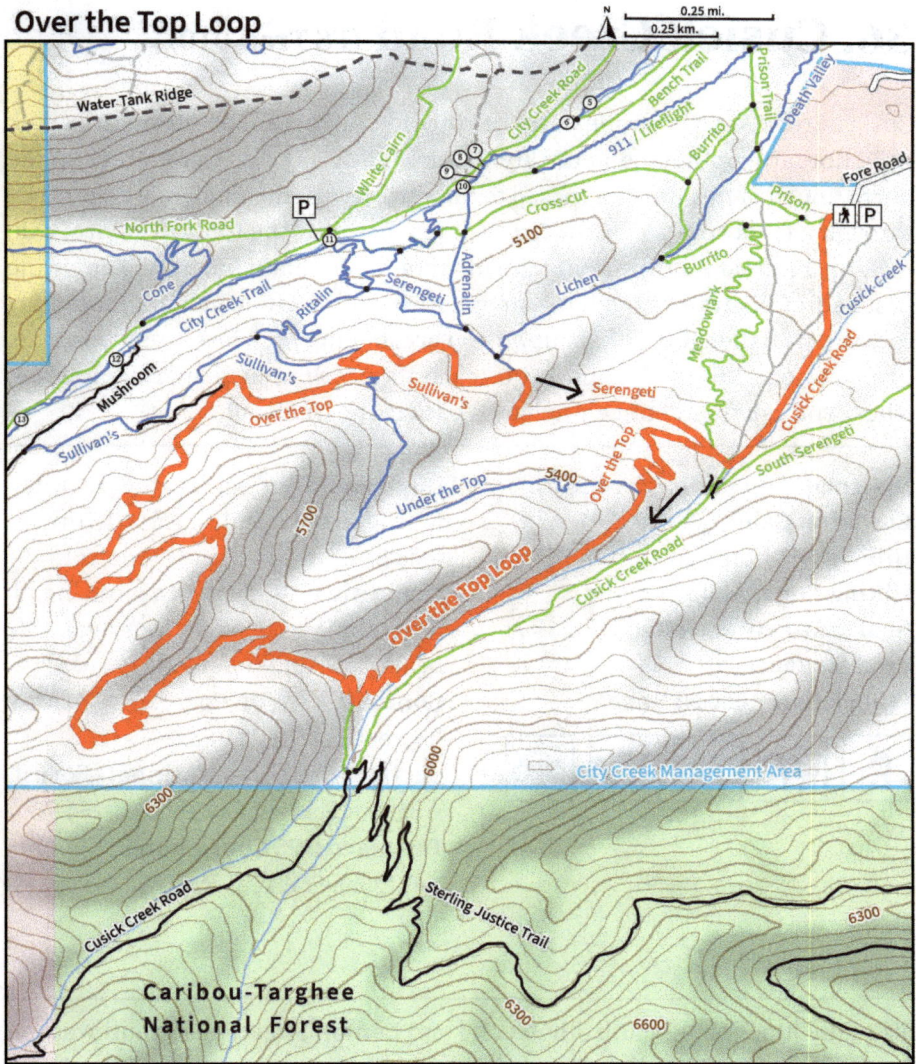

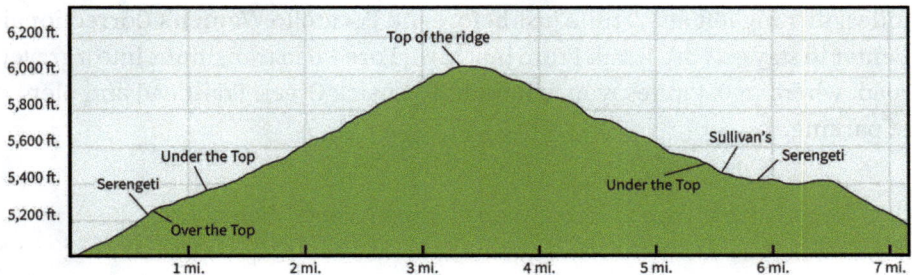

0.25 mi.
0.25 km.

Water Tank Ridge

City Creek Road

Bench Trail

Prison Trail

Death Valley

White Cairn

911 / Lifeflight

Burrito

Fore Road

Cross-cut

North Fork Road

Prison

5100

P

Burrito

Cone

City Creek Trail

Ritalin

Serengeti

Adrenalin

Lichen

Meadowlark

Cusick Creek Road

Cusick Creek

Mushroom

Sullivan's

Over the Top

Sullivan's

Serengeti

Over the Top

South Serengeti

Sullivan's

Under the Top

5400

5700

Over the Top Loop

Cusick Creek Road

6000

City Creek Management Area

6300

Cusick Creek Road

Sterling Justice Trail

6300

6300

6600

Caribou-Targhee
National Forest

6,200 ft.			Top of the ridge					
6,000 ft.								
5,800 ft.								
5,600 ft.						Sullivan's		
5,400 ft.	Under the Top					Serengeti		
5,200 ft.	Serengeti					Under the Top		
	Over the Top							

1 mi.   2 mi.   3 mi.   4 mi.   5 mi.   6 mi.   7 mi.

36. Cusick Creek Road (FS Trail 010)

Cusick Creek Road is a wide path that provides an excellent alternative creek walk not far from the popular City Creek Trail. Unlike its sister creek to the north, much of this trail is exposed to the sun, though the final mile does travel through a thick conifer forest. The trail finishes near the top of Kinport Peak, making it a great way to summit the mountain. Mountain bikers will enjoy the first half of the trail, though the steep forests of the latter half are incredibly rocky and challenging to bike up. If you are looking for a less strenuous hike, I recommend hiking this until you reach the Sterling Justice Trail junction, where you can then retrace your steps back to the trailhead.

Distance: 7 miles out-and-back
Elevation Gain: 2,090 feet
Difficulty: Strenuous
Hiking Time: About 4 hours
Nearest Town: Pocatello
Trail Surface: Dirt, rock
Wheelchair Access: None

Dog-Friendly: Yes; leash is required for the first 1.7 miles. After 1.7 miles, may be off-leash if under control.
Amenities: None at the trailhead. Restrooms and water are available nearby at Centennial Park.
Contact: City of Pocatello Parks & Recreation 208-234-6232; Caribou-Targhee National Forest, Westside Ranger District 208-236-7500
Trailhead GPS Coordinates: N42° 50.325' W112° 27.084'

Getting There

From the junction of South 4th Avenue and Benton Street, head southwest on Benton Street for 0.7 miles. Turn left onto South Grant Avenue, and then in 0.4 miles, make a slight right turn onto Fore Road. Continue on Fore Road for 1.4 miles, turning left at 1.0 mile just before the Pocatello Women's Correctional Center to stay on Fore Road. From that turn, Fore Road transitions into a gravel road, where in 0.4 miles, you will find the Cusick Creek Trailhead and plenty of parking.

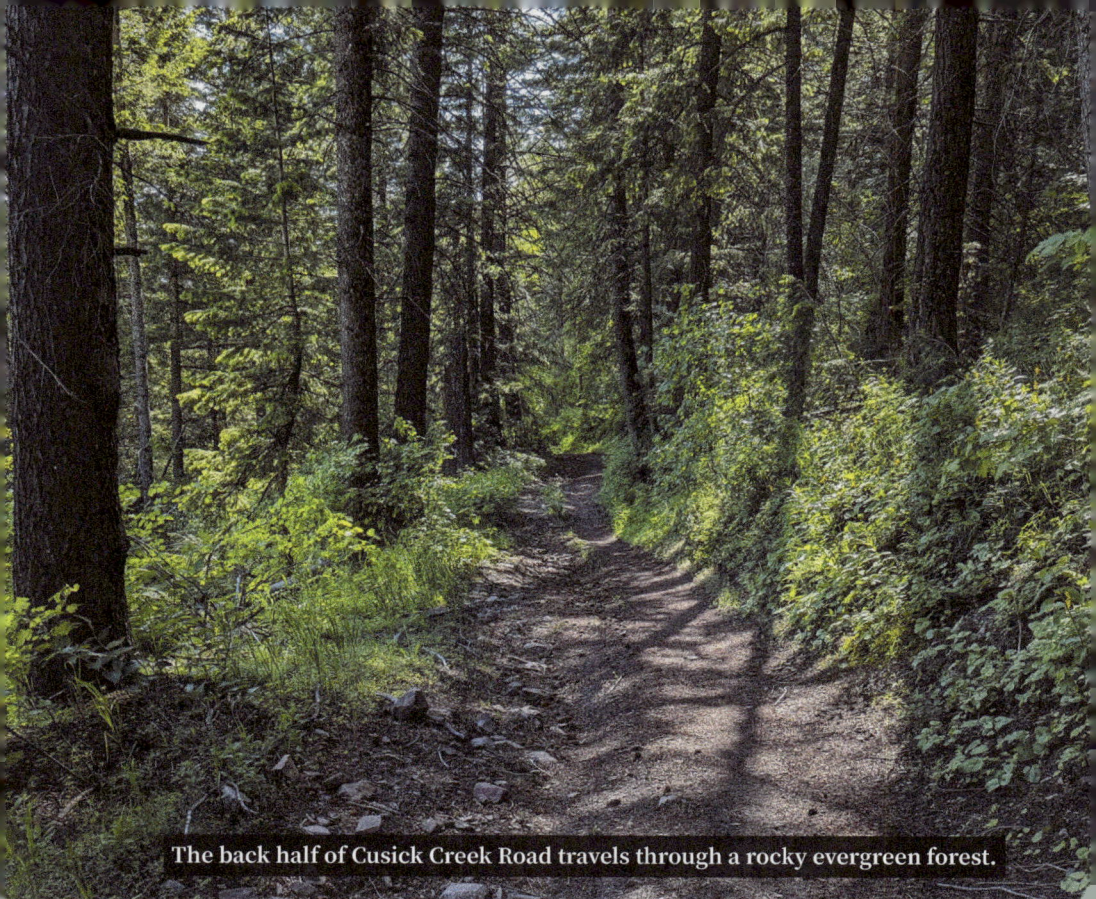
The back half of Cusick Creek Road travels through a rocky evergreen forest.

The Hike

The first stretch of the hike from the trailhead travels south through tall grass until it reaches the west side of Cusick Creek, where it then follows the creek upstream. At about 0.7 miles, the trail passes by Serengeti on its right (north) side and then crosses over a small bridge to the east side of the creek. Once across the creek, turn right (southwest) to continue following the creek upstream. (Turning left across the bridge would take you on South Serengeti.) The trail becomes a bit rockier once past the bridge, though the shade from the low trees makes it enjoyable.

At about 1.7 miles, the trail comes to a junction with the Sterling Justice Trail on the left (east) and the Sterling Justice to Over the Top Connector to the right (west). Continue on the 4x4 trail south as it crosses Cusick Creek. Past the creek, the trail becomes steeper and is often covered in large rocks, making for a challenging mountain bike ride.

As you climb higher on the trail, the surrounding vegetation becomes thicker, with the final stretch of the trail traveling through a rocky evergreen forest. Starting at 2.6 miles, the final stretch of the trail climbs 700 feet in 0.9 miles on a series of switchbacks. At 3.3 miles, you pass through a gate shortly before the trail exits the forest. The trail ends at a junction with Johnny Creek Road (7,080 feet).

Keep Going

Found at the end of Cusick Creek Road, **Johnny Creek Road** (Forest Service Road 294) is a 1.8-mile one-way 4x4 trail that travels atop Kinport Peak's high ridges, ending at Wild Horse Mountain (7,200 feet). The trail gains 190 feet and loses 260 feet on an often rocky road that heads east. Cusick Creek Road joins Johnny Creek Road 0.2 miles from its actual start off of Kinport Road. At 1.1 miles, there is a shortcut road on the left (north), though if you choose to continue on the main route, you will find great views of the Portneuf Gap. The trail ends on a rocky ridge with excellent views of Kinport Peak to the west.

Cusick Creek originates from the east side of Kinport Peak and flows for 3.8 miles before joining the Portneuf River.

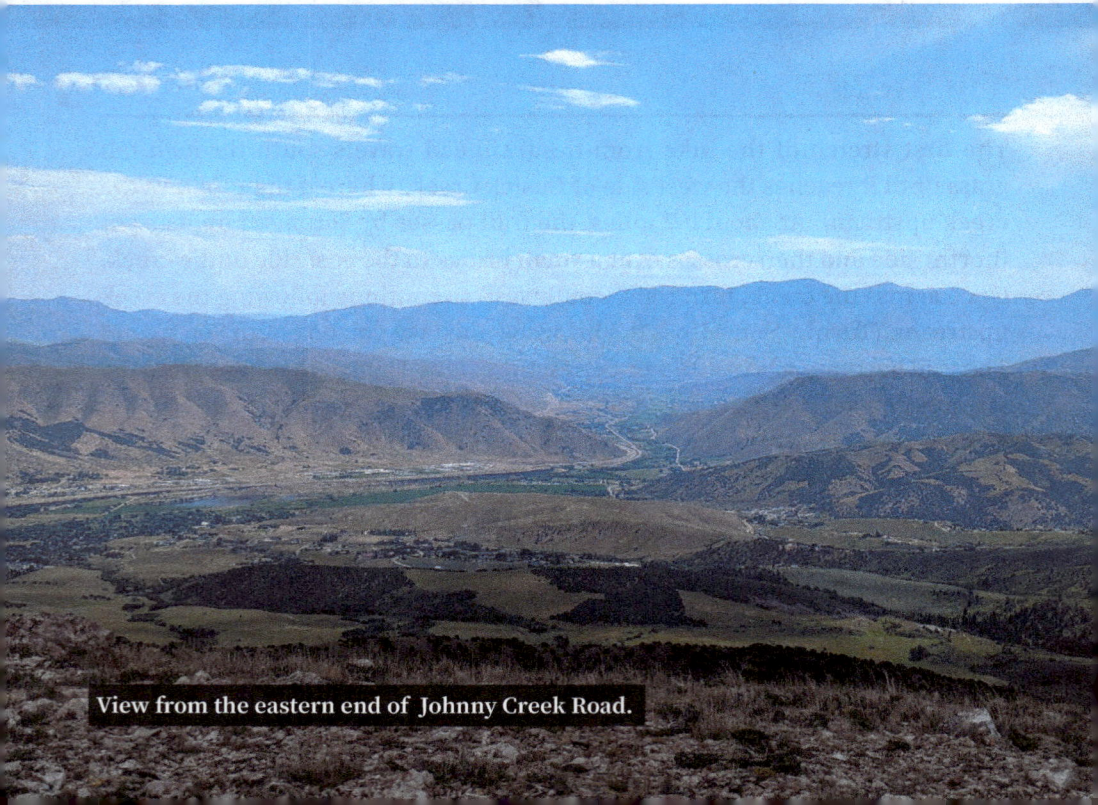

View from the eastern end of Johnny Creek Road.

Cusick Creek Road

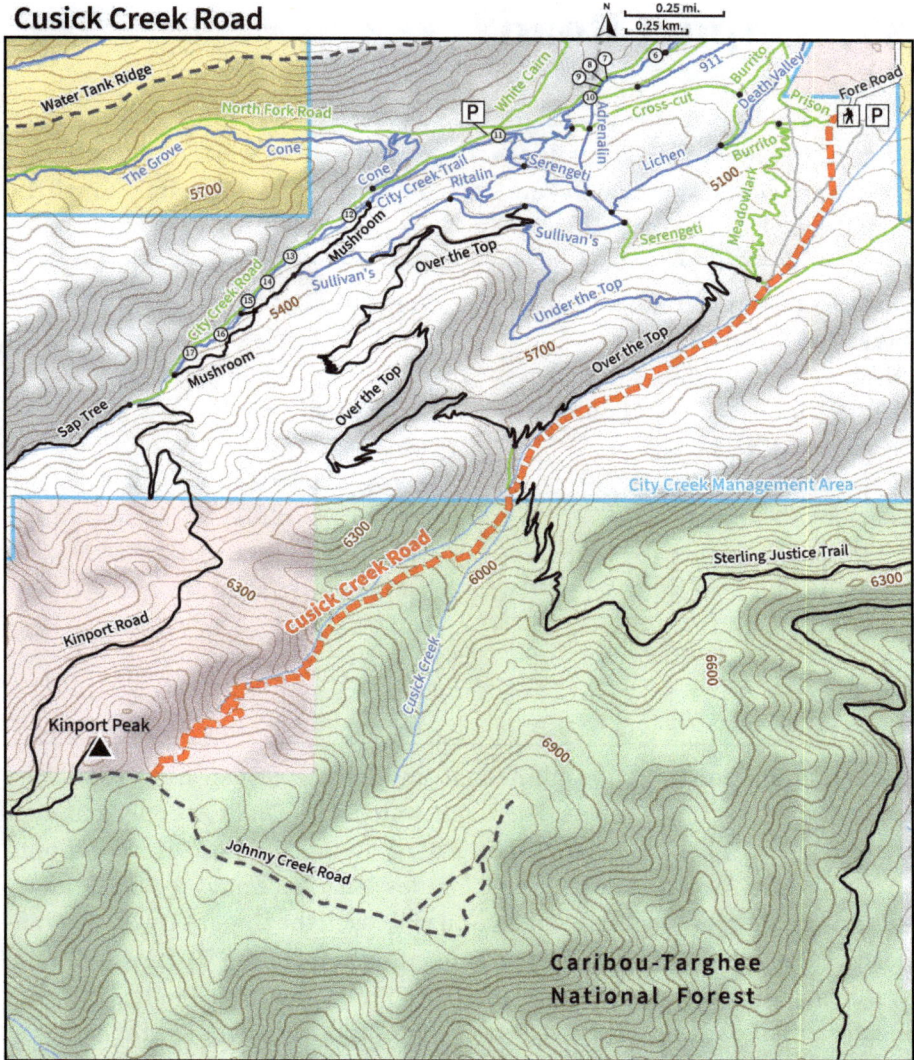

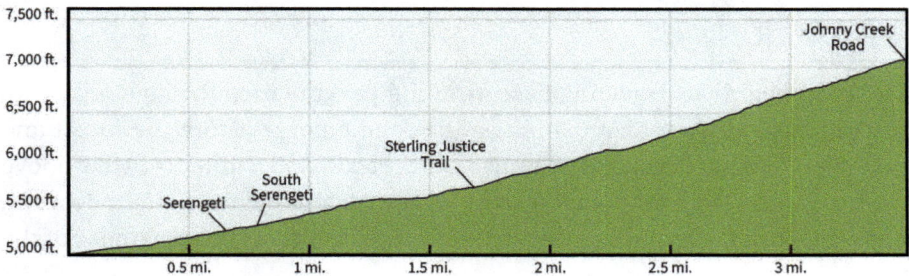

N

0.25 mi.
0.25 km.

Water Tank Ridge

North Fork Road

The Grove

Cone

5700

Cone

Cone

White Cairn

Adrenalin

Cross-cut

911

Burrito

Death Valley

Prison

Fore Road

P

P

City Creek Trail

Mushroom

Ritalin

Serengeti

Lichen

5100

Burrito

Meadowlark

Sullivan's

Serengeti

Mushroom

Sullivan's

Over the Top

Under the Top

5400

City Creek Road

Over the Top

Over the Top

5700

Over the Top

Sap Tree

Mushroom

City Creek Management Area

6300

Cusick Creek Road

Sterling Justice Trail

6300

Kinport Road

6300

6000

Cusick Creek

6900

Kinport Peak

6900

Johnny Creek Road

Caribou-Targhee
National Forest

7,500 ft.

7,000 ft.

Johnny Creek
Road

6,500 ft.

6,000 ft.

Sterling Justice
Trail

5,500 ft.

South
Serengeti

Serengeti

5,000 ft.

0.5 mi.　1 mi.　1.5 mi.　2 mi.　2.5 mi.　3 mi.

37. Kinport Road

A rocky dirt road that winds its way to the summit of Kinport Peak, Kinport Road gives hikers a steep challenge that rewards those who complete it with panoramic views. Mountain bikers will enjoy descending this path, though the upper stretch can be incredibly rocky.

Distance: 5.6 miles out-and-back
Elevation Gain: 1,800 feet
Difficulty: Moderately strenuous
Hiking Time: About 3.5 hours
Nearest Town: Pocatello
Trail Surface: Dirt, rock
Wheelchair Access: None

Dog-Friendly: Yes; leash is required for the first mile. After one mile, may be off-leash if under control.
Amenities: None
Contact: City of Pocatello Parks & Recreation 208-234-6232; Caribou-Targhee National Forest, Westside Ranger District 208-236-7500
Trailhead GPS Coordinates: N42° 49.440' W112° 29.175'

Getting There

From the junction of South 4th Avenue and Benton Street, head southwest on Benton Street for 0.7 miles. Turn right onto South Grant Avenue, and then make a left on West Whitman Street. After a couple of blocks, turn left onto South Lincoln Avenue, and then in 0.5 miles, turn left onto City Creek Road, following a sign for City Creek Trails. You will reach the Upper City Creek Trailhead at the end of this paved road in 0.5 miles. From the Upper City Creek Trailhead, continue south on the dirt City Creek Road for 2.3 miles until you reach a small parking area just before the Kinport Road gate. Kinport Road begins at that gate.

The Hike

The road begins by traveling east from the parking area through a gate up through a steep forest. At 0.3 miles, the road emerges from the forest and passes to the right (south) of an unnamed 4x4 trail. At 0.6 miles (420 feet above the trailhead), the trail makes a sharp east turn and begins a slight descent. Enjoy this brief downhill, as the incline is consistent for the remainder of the hike.

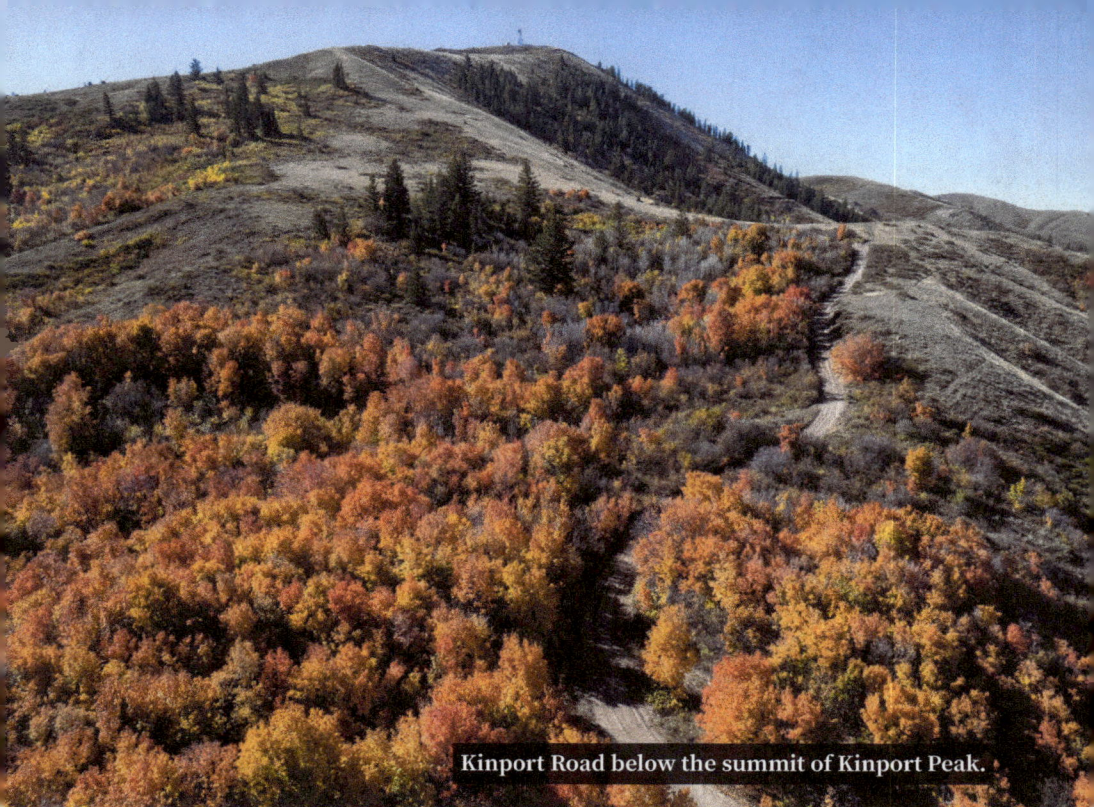
Kinport Road below the summit of Kinport Peak.

After several turns atop a small ridge, the trail reaches a fork at about 1.2 miles. Keep right (southeast) at this fork to avoid an unofficial trail. Not far beyond that at 1.4 miles, keep left (south). At 1.4 miles, you will pass by an unofficial path on the road's left (east) side that steeply climbs to the summit. This is an excellent place to take a break before beginning the very rocky upper stretch of the mountain.

The next mile of the hike climbs 650 feet as the road traverses across the northern face of Kinport Peak, with the eventual goal of circling to the south side of the summit. The initial stretch of the path past 1.4 miles is a more gradual incline that passes through a small forest, though it becomes steeper and rockier once out of the trees. At 2.4 miles, the trail reaches a junction (7,050 feet) with the Midnight Ridge Road on a ridge southwest of the summit. Keep left (east) to stay on Kinport Road.

The summit is about 160 vertical feet from the junction and 0.4 mile away. Continue east on the road, keeping left (north) at the back-to-back forks starting at 2.6 miles. (The first of these junctions is the beginning of Johnny Creek Road, which can be found on p. 172.) Kinport Road ends shortly after these junctions at a radio tower. The actual summit of the mountain (7,216 feet) is about 50 yards to the southeast, though the northernmost set of radio towers provides the best views of the area and is typically where people end the hike.

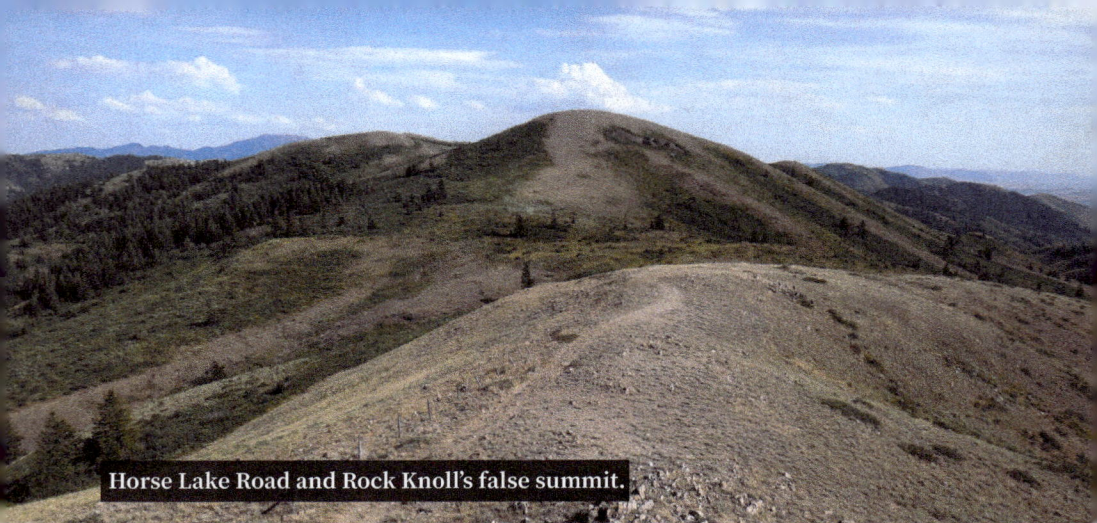
Horse Lake Road and Rock Knoll's false summit.

Keep Going

At the junction 2.4 miles into Kinport Road, you will find the start of the **Midnight Ridge Road** (Forest Service Road 290) to the right (west). This 4.2-mile one-way road travels atop Kinport Peak's high ridges and hills, gaining and losing about 650 feet as it travels south, though half of that elevation gain is found on one 300-foot steep hill climb at the very end of the route. The trail, which travels between thick brush and open hillsides, has excellent views of the area and is a great way to access a few remote trails, which are listed below.

At 0.7 miles, the Midnight Ridge Road passes by East Wild Horse Mountain Trail (p. 148) on the trail's right (north) side.

At a pond 1.3 miles into Midnight Ridge Road, the path passes by **Horse Lake Road** (Forest Service Road 287) on the left (east) side of the trail. Horse Lake Road is a wild 1.3-mile one-way 4x4 trail that heads toward Rock Knoll on a dry hillside. On U.S. Forest Service maps, Horse Lake Road connects to a singletrack trail that traverses just below Rock Knoll's summit, though this path may not exist due to lack of use. While it may not be ideal for a through hike, there are some interesting views on this trail, especially of Rock Knoll, so if you are in the area it can be a worthwhile excursion.

At about 1.9 miles, Midnight Ridge Road comes to a fork. Keep right (south) to stay on Midnight Ridge Road. Going left (southeast) begins the **Midnight Creek Trail** (Forest Service Trail 058), which is a 2.5-mile one-way doubletrack that descends 790 feet alongside a creek. The route has plenty of shade and is rarely aggressively steep, making for a fun mountain bike ride, especially when combined with Pole Canyon (Monument Gulch) (p. 217), found at the end of this trail. Technically, Midnight Creek Trail continues for another 0.9 miles past the Pole Canyon (Monument Gulch) junction on a singletrack, though it is so wild I can't recommend it.

Kinport Road

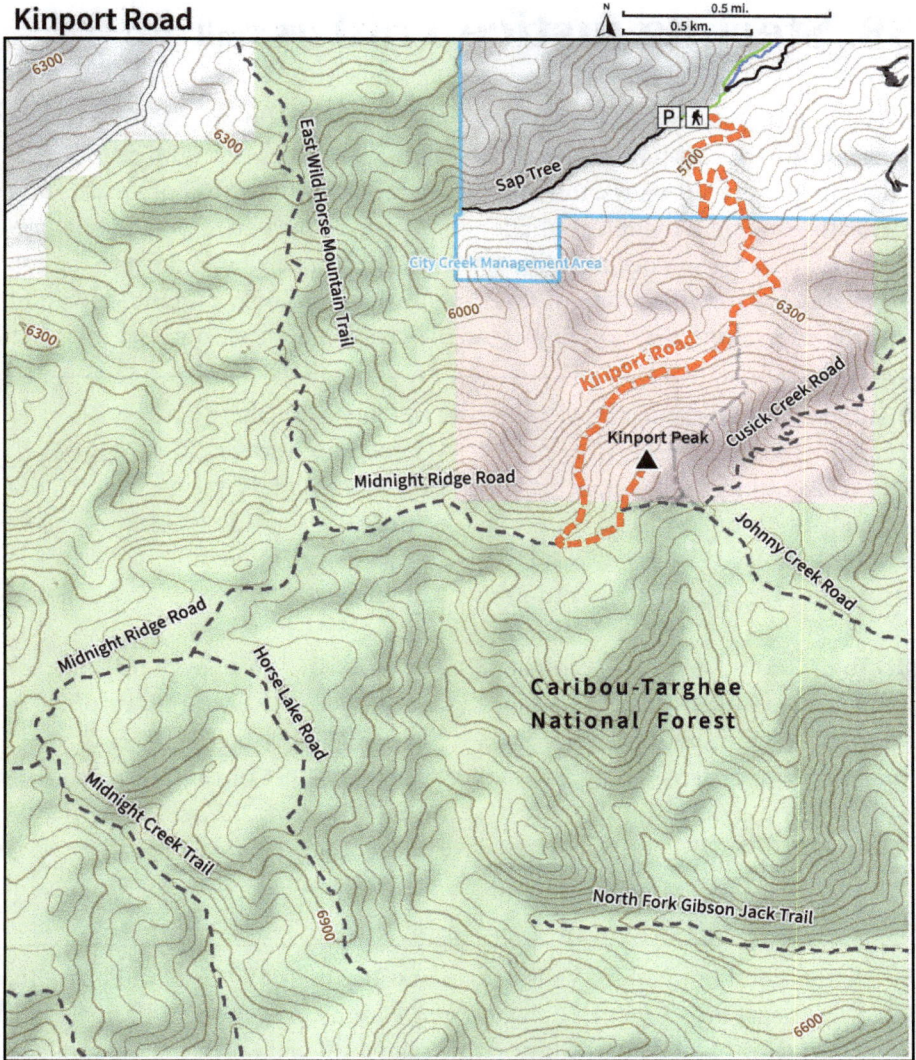

N

0.5 mi.

0.5 km.

6300

6300

East Wild Horse Mountain Trail

Sap Tree

5700

P

City Creek Management Area

6000

6300

Kinport Road

Cusick Creek Road

Kinport Peak

Midnight Ridge Road

Johnny Creek Road

Midnight Ridge Road

Horse Lake Road

Caribou-Targhee National Forest

Midnight Creek Trail

6900

North Fork Gibson Jack Trail

6600

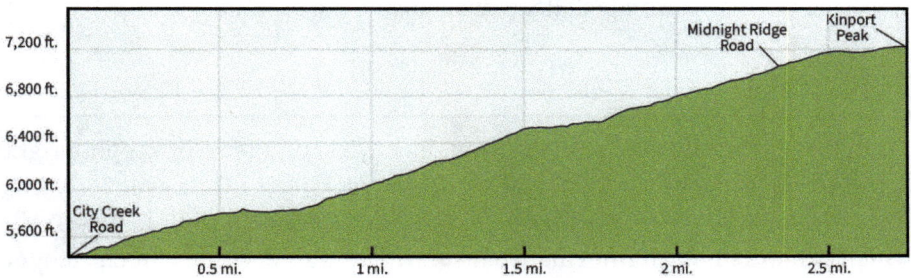

7,200 ft.

6,800 ft.

6,400 ft.

6,000 ft.

5,600 ft.

City Creek Road

Midnight Ridge Road

Kinport Peak

0.5 mi.   1 mi.   1.5 mi.   2 mi.   2.5 mi.

38. Sterling Justice Trail (FS Trail 505)

Located in the mountains high above southern Pocatello, the Sterling Justice Trail is one of the city's most rewarding outdoor experiences. With rugged hillsides and panoramic views, the trail is easy to recommend for both hikers and bikers looking for a moderate challenge. Bikers, in particular, need to be prepared for a rocky and occasionally narrow ride. Those who make it to the top of the trail are rewarded with the Sterling Justice Overlook, a scenic viewpoint with an informative display labeling all the visible points of interest.

Distance: 7.7 miles one-way; 9.3 miles round trip for the overlook

Elevation Gain: 1,330 feet; 1,310 feet round trip for the overlook

Difficulty: Moderately strenuous; Strenuous for the overlook out-and-back

Hiking Time: About 4.5 hours; 5 hours for the overlook out-and-back

Nearest Town: Pocatello

Trail Surface: Dirt, rock

Wheelchair Access: None

Dog-Friendly: Yes; on-leash at the trailhead. May be off-leash if under control once on the trail

Amenities: A vault toilet is available at the trailhead.

Contact: Caribou-Targhee National Forest, Westside Ranger District 208-236-7500

Trailhead GPS Coordinates: N42° 47.575' W112° 25.887'

Getting There

From the junction of South Valley Road and Bannock Highway in Pocatello, head southeast on Bannock Highway for 1.4 miles, where you will turn right onto West Gibson Jack Road. Stay on this road until you reach the Gibson Jack Trailhead in 2.3 miles, which has plenty of parking. The trail begins on the west side of West Gibson Jack Road, just outside the parking lot.

The Hike

From the signed Gibson Jack Trailhead, head west on the trail, keeping right at the fork to avoid the wide West Fork Gibson Jack Trail a little over 100 yards from the start. At 0.7 miles, turn right (north) onto the Sterling Justice Trail, which is marked by an informative display. The trail becomes much steeper

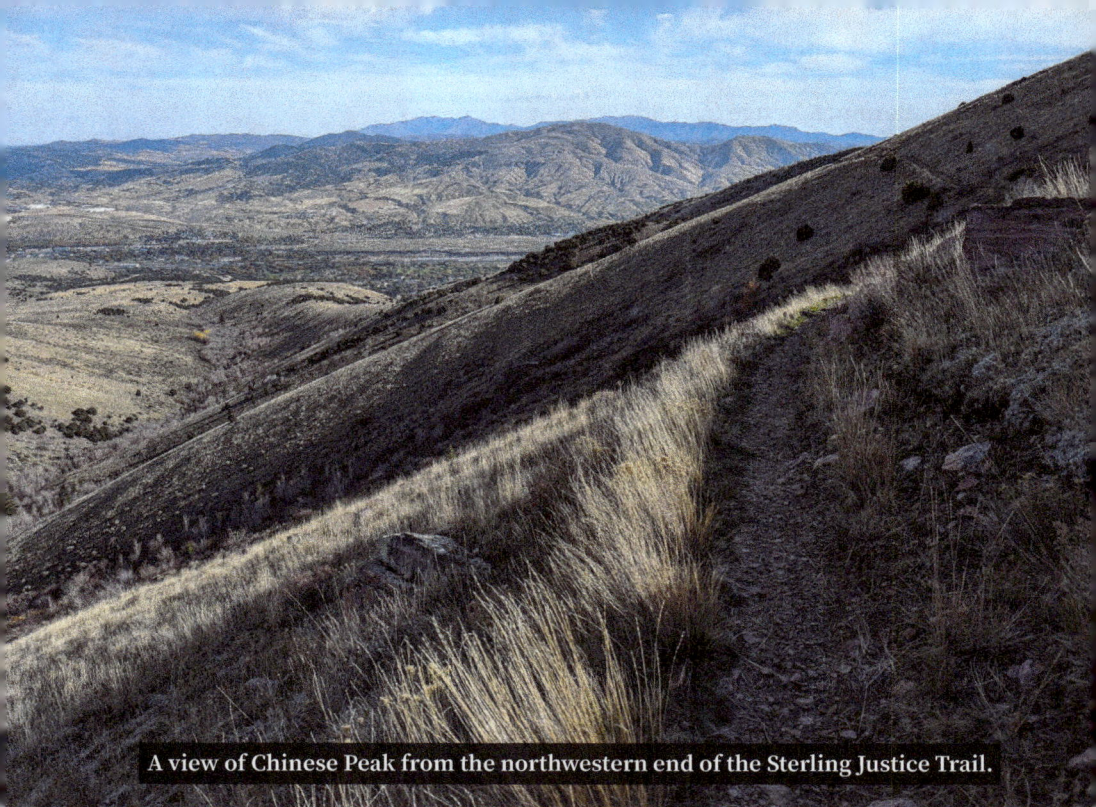

A view of Chinese Peak from the northwestern end of the Sterling Justice Trail.

once you make this turn, gaining about 500 feet in just over a mile on a few switchbacks.

The trail winds uphill from this turnoff through sagebrush and mountain shrubs, eventually reaching a northern turn at 1.7 miles, where the trail levels out. With a large portion of the route's incline behind you, this upper section of the path provides a pleasant up-and-down northbound walk through exposed hillsides and intermittent forests. At 2.2 miles, you will pass through a small forest with a rope swing with skis used as a seat. This is an excellent place for a water break, and an incredible location to photograph Gibson Mountain in the autumn.

At 3.0 miles, the trail shifts to the northwest, contouring around two forested ravines. The trail turns east once you emerge from the second forested ravine at about 3.8 miles. This stretch of trail can be difficult for mountain bikers as it cuts through rocky terrain filled with large boulders. At about 4.4 miles, the trail turns left (north), leaving the steep hillside for a more gradual hilltop climb.

At about 4.6 miles, you will come to the turnoff for the Sterling Justice Overlook, located on the trail's right (north) side. The overlook is about 0.1 miles away from the turnoff and offers stunning views of the city and surrounding mountains. A sizable panoramic display at the overlook labels the points of interest visible from this viewpoint. For those not looking to connect with Cusick Creek Road, I recommend turning around at this point.

Back at the Sterling Justice Overlook junction, continue on the main trail heading west. For the next 1.5 miles, the trail cuts through the steep hillside high above a remote drainage. This level stretch of the trail can be slightly overgrown and rocky, so bikers may have to mind their speed.

At about 6.0 miles, the trail turns north and begins its 500-foot descent into Cusick Creek. A series of switchbacks that cut into the steep hillside can be fun to bike down; just remember to make noise at any blind turn to alert other uphill hikers or bikers. The trail ends at Cusick Creek Road.

The trail is named after Sterling Justice (1884-1980), a renowned U.S. Forest Service Ranger of the Pocatello District. The trail's development took over five years and was completed in 2013 by members of the local "PedalFest" organization. The organization is an association of mountain bikers from the Portneuf Valley whose sole purpose is to promote the sport of mountain biking through racing, education, trail building/maintenance, and resource protection.

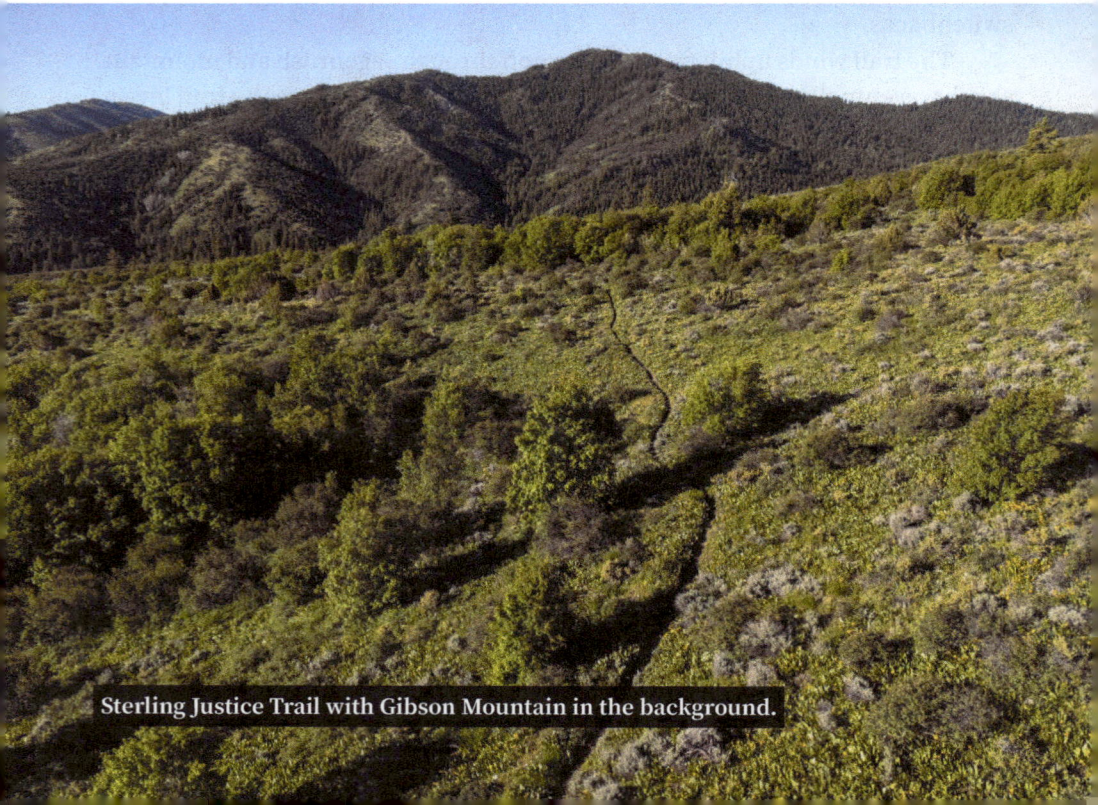

Sterling Justice Trail with Gibson Mountain in the background.

Sterling Justice Trail

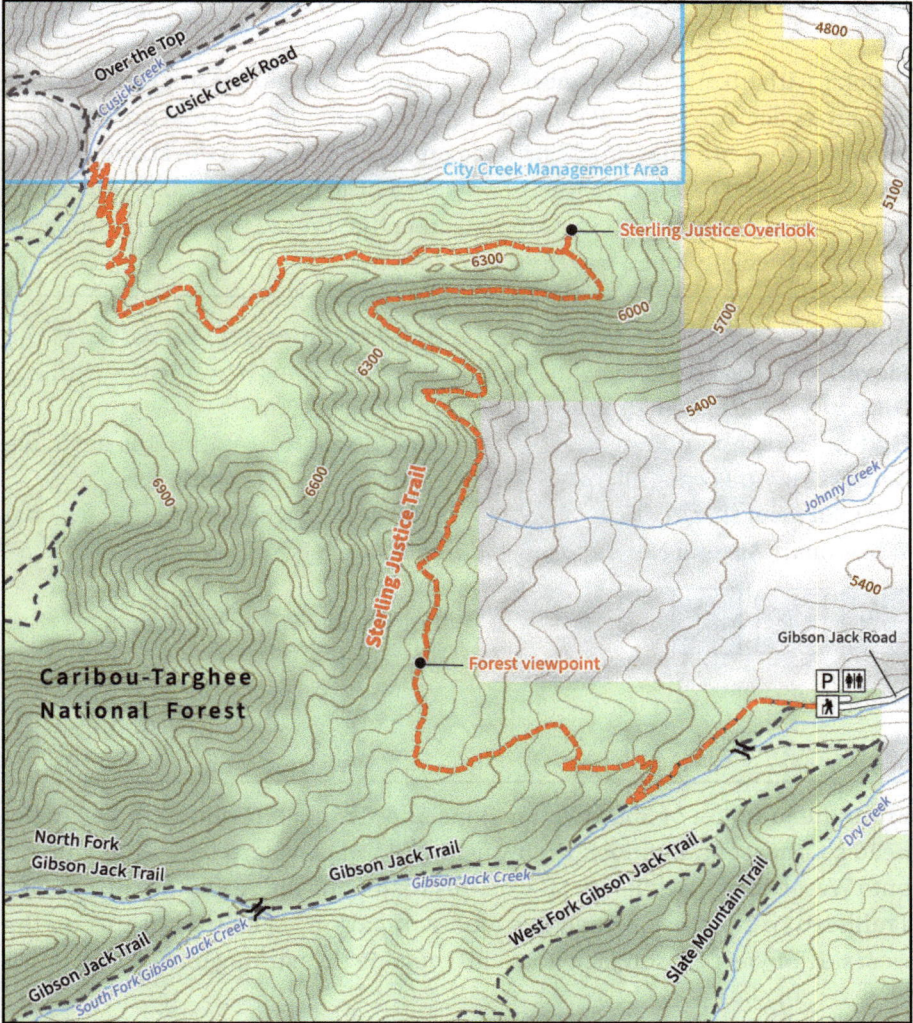

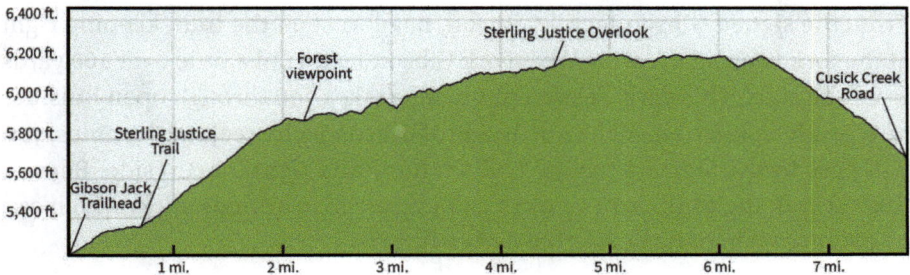

N

0.5 mi.

0.5 km.

Over the Top

Cusick Creek

Cusick Creek Road

4800

5100

City Creek Management Area

5700

Sterling Justice Overlook

6300

6000

5400

6300

Johnny Creek

Sterling Justice Trail

6600

6900

5400

Gibson Jack Road

P

Forest viewpoint

Caribou-Targhee
National Forest

North Fork
Gibson Jack Trail

Gibson Jack Trail

Gibson Jack Creek

West Fork Gibson Jack Trail

Dry Creek

Slate Mountain Trail

Gibson Jack Trail

South Fork Gibson Jack Creek

6,400 ft.

6,200 ft.

6,000 ft.

5,800 ft.

5,600 ft.

5,400 ft.

Forest
viewpoint

Sterling Justice Overlook

Cusick Creek
Road

Sterling Justice
Trail

Gibson Jack
Trailhead

1 mi.   2 mi.   3 mi.   4 mi.   5 mi.   6 mi.   7 mi.

39. Gibson Jack Trail (FS Trail 014)

Popular with hikers, trail runners, and mountain bikers, Gibson Jack Trail has earned its acclaim in the Pocatello outdoor community. Aspen groves, evergreens, grassy hillsides, and a pristine creek, all resting in the shadow of the heavily forested Gibson Mountain, provide a little bit of everything one could hope for in a day hike. It is important to note that moose frequent this area, so be alert, especially when traveling with dogs.

Distance: 7.2 miles out-and-back
Elevation Gain: 1,240 feet
Difficulty: Moderately strenuous
Hiking Time: About 3.5 hours
Nearest Town: Pocatello
Trail Surface: Dirt, rock
Wheelchair Access: None

Dog-Friendly: Yes; on-leash at the trailhead. May be off-leash if under control once on the trail
Amenities: A vault toilet is available at the trailhead.
Contact: Caribou-Targhee National Forest, Westside Ranger District 208-236-7500
Trailhead GPS Coordinates: N42° 47.575' W112° 25.887'

Getting There

From the junction of South Valley Road and Bannock Highway in Pocatello, head southeast on Bannock Highway for 1.4 miles, where you will turn right onto West Gibson Jack Road. Stay on this road until you reach the Gibson Jack Trailhead in 2.3 miles, which has plenty of parking. The trail begins on the west side of West Gibson Jack Road, just outside the parking lot.

The Hike

From the signed Gibson Jack Trailhead, head west on the trail, keeping right at the fork to avoid the wide West Fork Gibson Jack Trail a little over 100 yards from the start. This early section of the hike takes you through open hillsides on a gently uphill trail on the north side of Gibson Jack Creek. At 0.7 miles, you will pass by the Sterling Justice Trail on the trail's right (north) side. Beyond this turnoff, the trail narrows from a doubletrack to a singletrack, which can be overgrown in parts during the early summer.

Wildflowers along Gibson Jack Trail.

Stay on the trail, lined with shrubs, wildflowers, and small trees, until you reach a bridge at about 1.7 miles. You will notice a small trail to the right (north) just before this bridge. This trail is the **North Fork Gibson Jack Trail** (Forest Service Trail 017). It is an incredibly wild and marshy trail directly alongside (and often on) the North Fork Gibson Jack Creek. Adventurous hikers may enjoy the many plank walks in the first stretch of the trail, though others may be uncomfortable navigating the vegetation. I recommend hiking this trail only as long as you enjoy its wild nature.

At the bridge located at 1.7 miles, cross over the creek (which becomes the South Fork Gibson Creek past the bridge) and continue on the Gibson Jack Trail. The incline increases once beyond the bridge, but only a little. For the remainder of this southwestern moving trail, thick evergreens overflow on the slopes of Gibson Mountain to your left (south), while the open hillsides remain on your right side. As you progress on the trail, you will enter mixed pine and aspen forests, providing pleasant shade on a hot day.

At about 3.4 miles, in an aspen grove, the trail turns south. A short, steep hill at that grove's end signifies the trail's final push. At the top of the hill, you will find a pink gate. Go through the gate and descend the short hill, where the trail ends, connecting to Elk Meadows.

Keep Going

If you are looking to switch up the route back to the trailhead, I recommend turning left (east) once at Elk Meadows and hiking over to the West Fork Gibson Jack Trail. This rocky hike, which is featured on page 186, provides excellent views of the area, including views of the Gibson Jack Trail you just hiked.

Moose are the largest type of deer in the world and the tallest mammal in North America. They can grow to be quite massive, weighing up to 1,600 pounds and standing at a height of six feet at their shoulders. Interestingly, the word "moose" comes from the Algonquian words "moosu" and "moz," meaning "twig eater" or "bark stripper."

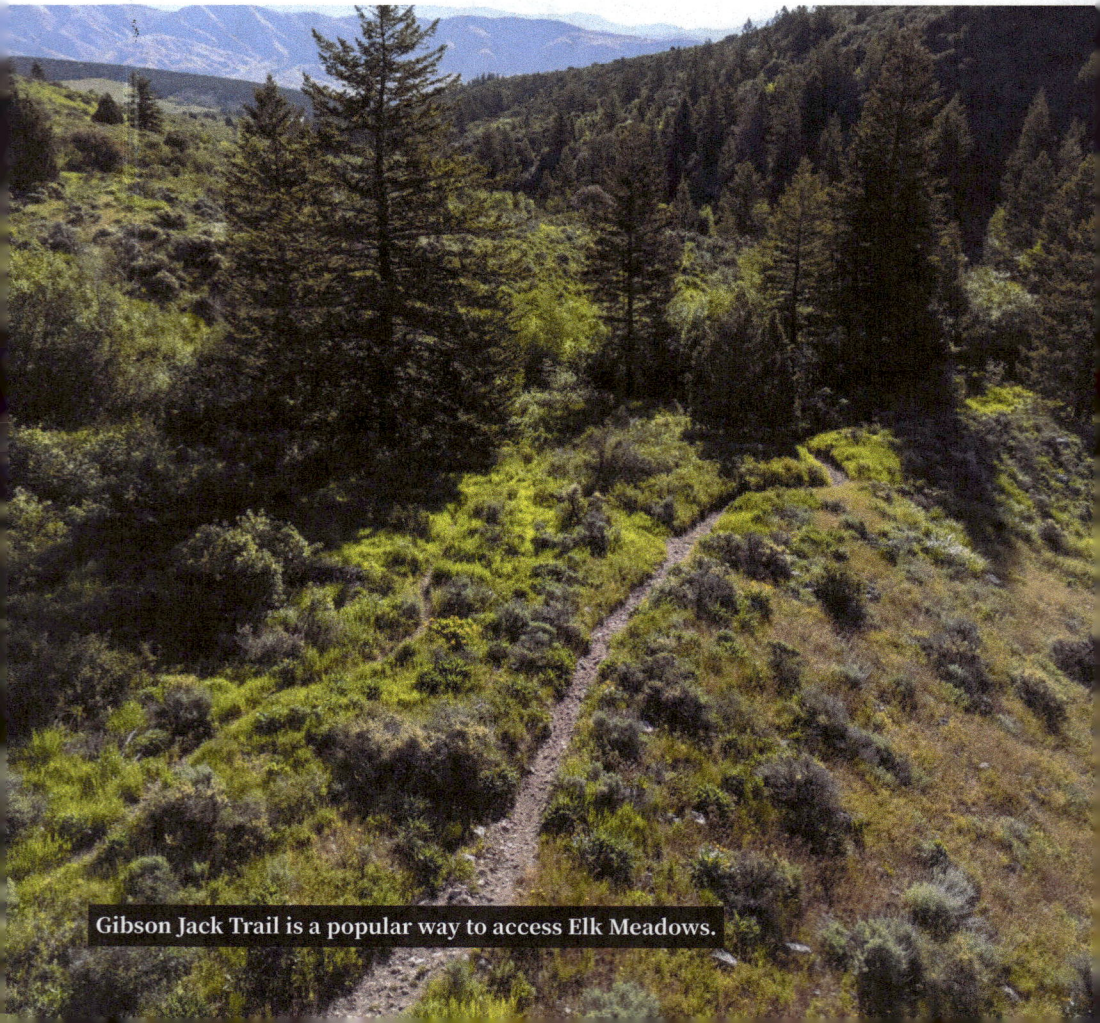

Gibson Jack Trail is a popular way to access Elk Meadows.

Gibson Jack Trail

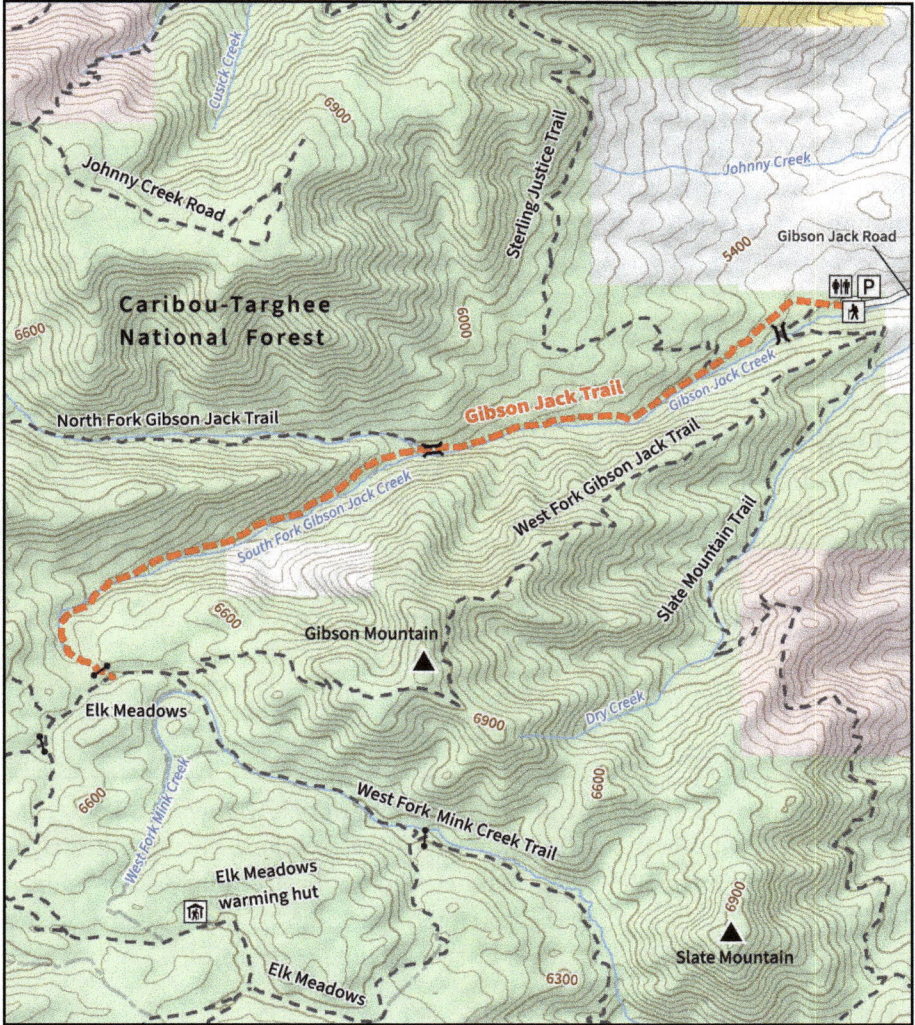

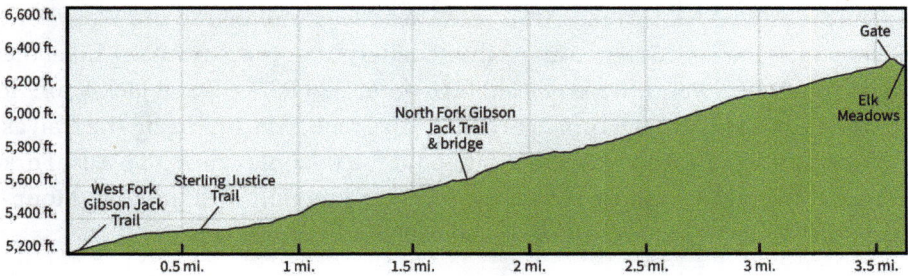

N

0.5 mi.

0.5 km.

Cusick Creek

6900

Johnny Creek Road

Sterling Justice Trail

Johnny Creek

5400

Gibson Jack Road

Caribou-Targhee National Forest

6600

6000

Gibson Jack Trail

North Fork Gibson Jack Trail

Gibson Jack Creek

West Fork Gibson Jack Trail

South Fork Gibson Jack Creek

Slate Mountain Trail

6600

Gibson Mountain

6900

Dry Creek

West Fork Mink Creek Trail

6600

West Fork Mink Creek

6600

Elk Meadows

6900

Elk Meadows warming hut

Elk Meadows

6300

Slate Mountain

6,600 ft.

6,400 ft.

6,200 ft.

6,000 ft.

5,800 ft.

5,600 ft.

5,400 ft.

5,200 ft.

Gate

Elk Meadows

North Fork Gibson Jack Trail & bridge

West Fork Gibson Jack Trail

Sterling Justice Trail

0.5 mi. 1 mi. 1.5 mi. 2 mi. 2.5 mi. 3 mi. 3.5 mi.

40. West Fork Gibson Jack Trail
(FS Trail 015)

The West Fork Gibson Jack Trail is a formidable companion to the nearby Gibson Jack Trail. It offers hikers great views as a reward for completing this steep dry ridge walk. Mountain bikers are in for a challenging ride due to steep inclines and a consistently rocky trail. I recommend combining this route with the Gibson Jack Trail, which starts at the same trailhead.

Distance: 4.7 miles one-way
Elevation Gain: 1,840 feet
Difficulty: Moderately strenuous
Hiking Time: About 3.5 hours
Nearest Town: Pocatello
Trail Surface: Dirt, rock
Wheelchair Access: None

Dog-Friendly: Yes; on-leash at the trailhead. May be off-leash if under control once on the trail
Amenities: A vault toilet is available at the trailhead.
Contact: Caribou-Targhee National Forest, Westside Ranger District 208-236-7500
Trailhead GPS Coordinates: N42° 47.575' W112° 25.887'

Getting There

From the junction of South Valley Road and Bannock Highway in Pocatello, head southeast on Bannock Highway for 1.4 miles, where you will turn right onto West Gibson Jack Road. Stay on this road until you reach the Gibson Jack Trailhead in 2.3 miles, which has plenty of parking. The trail begins on the west side of West Gibson Jack Road just outside the parking lot.

The Hike

From the signed Gibson Jack trailhead, head west, following the West Fork Gibson Jack Trail #015 sign. Almost immediately after the start of the hike, the trail forks, where you will make a left turn onto West Fork Gibson Jack Trail. At 0.3 miles, you will cross a bridge over Gibson Creek, continuing on the trail as it ascends a small forested hillside. At about the 0.6 mile mark, the West Fork Gibson Trail makes a sharp southwest turn at a junction with the Slate Mountain Trail. Keep right to continue on the West Fork Gibson Jack Trail.

West Fork Gibson Jack Trail is sometimes referred to as "Upper Gibson."

From that u-turn, the trail begins the climb atop a dry, broad ridge toward Gibson Mountain, which is 1,500 vertical feet away from this point. The first half mile on this ridge is a moderate incline but becomes steep just past the 1-mile mark. This extremely rocky trail can be challenging to bike up, so be prepared to walk much of this path. About 1.5 miles in, the trail enters an open juniper forest. At 1.7 miles (6,030 feet), the trail flattens out briefly, making for an excellent resting spot before climbing the next 1,000 feet to the top.

Continue on this steep and rocky trail, which becomes lined with ever-greens the higher you climb. Make sure to pause periodically to catch your breath and enjoy the views of Dry Creek to the left (east) and Gibson Creek to the right (west). At about 2.9 miles (6,750 feet), an unofficial narrow path forks off to the right (west). Keep left to stay on the West Fork Gibson Jack Trail, which leaves the ridge to cut across the eastern face of Gibson Mountain.

At 3.4 miles, the trail sharply turns to the right (west) at a wooden fence. Shortly past this point, at 3.5 miles, the trail reaches its highest elevation (7,010 feet), with incredible vistas of West Fork Mink Creek and Elk Meadows. At 3.7 miles, the trail enters the last of the high conifer forests on the route. Once you emerge from the forest at about 3.9 miles, the trail begins its western descent to the northern tip of Elk Meadows. After descending a dry ridge, the trail passes through a small forest, where it ends once it connects with the Elk Meadows Loop.

Dark cliffs on the valley floor are common along the Portneuf River, especially in Inkom and southern Pocatello. These cliffs are composed of basalt, a volcanic rock formed when basaltic lava cools rapidly.

The early stretch of the hike until the bridge is popular with local photographers.

West Fork Gibson Jack Trail

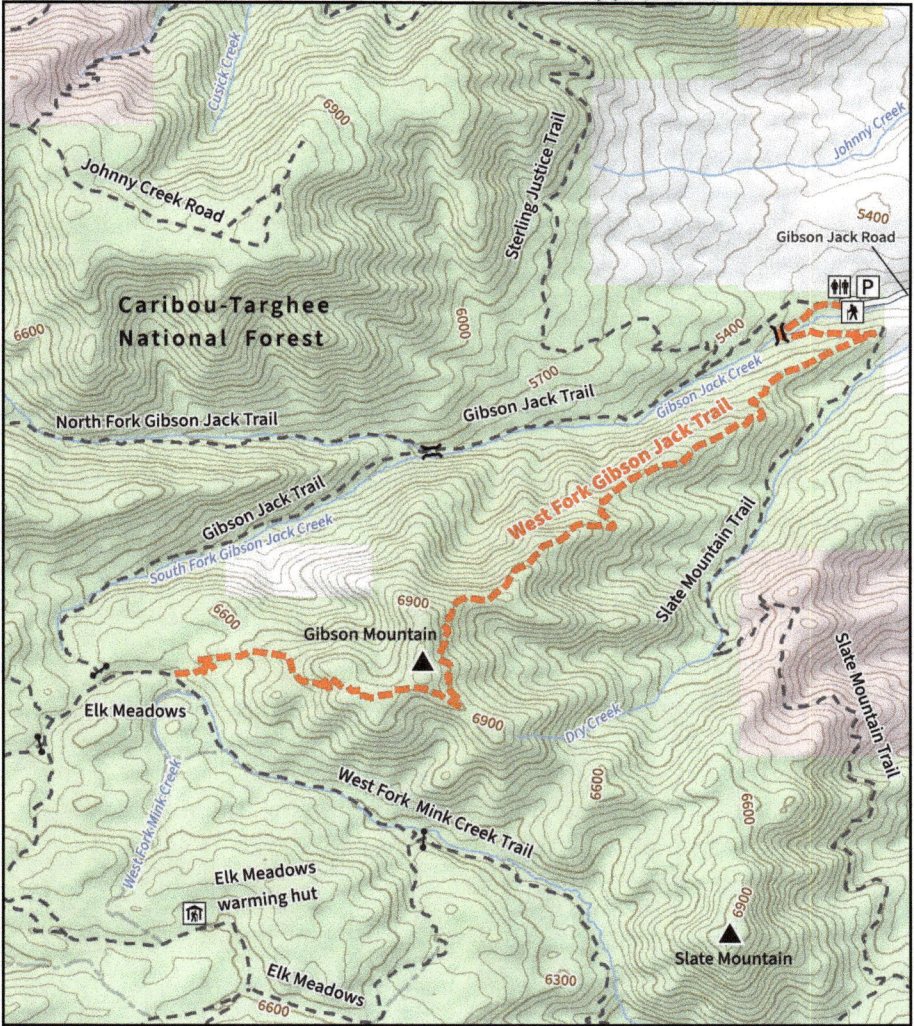

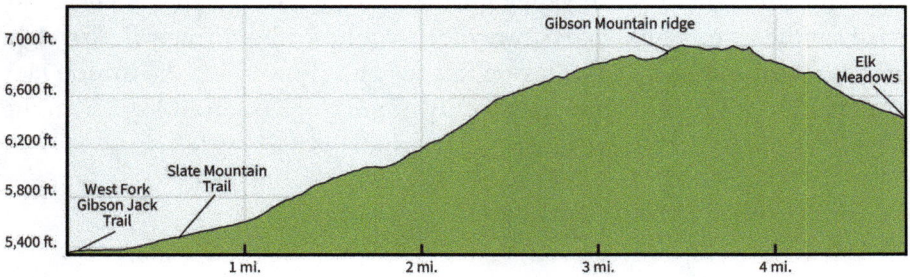

N

0.5 mi.

0.5 km.

Cusick Creek

6900

Johnny Creek Road

Sterling Justice Trail

Johnny Creek

Gibson Jack Road

5400

Caribou-Targhee
National Forest

6600

6000

5400

5700

Gibson-Jack Creek

North Fork Gibson Jack Trail

Gibson Jack Trail

West Fork Gibson Jack Trail

Gibson Jack Trail

South Fork Gibson-Jack Creek

6600

6900

Gibson Mountain

▲

Slate Mountain Trail

Slate Mountain Trail

Elk Meadows

West Fork Mink Creek

6900

Dry Creek

6600

6600

6900

West Fork Mink Creek Trail

Elk Meadows
warming hut

🏠

Elk Meadows

6300

Slate Mountain

▲

6600

Elevation profile:

7,000 ft.

6,600 ft.

6,200 ft.

5,800 ft.

5,400 ft.

Gibson Mountain ridge

Elk
Meadows

Slate Mountain
Trail

West Fork
Gibson Jack
Trail

1 mi.   2 mi.   3 mi.   4 mi.

41. Slate Mountain Trail (FS Trail 018)

Offering panoramic views in the Bannock Range, the Slate Mountain Trail is a classic trail for both hikers and bikers. The trail travels through the forested Dry Creek before climbing up a rocky hillside. Once high above the creek, the trail maintains its altitude, cutting into the side of the scenic Slate Mountain for a series of ups and downs alongside rock outcroppings. The final stretch of the hike is a steep descent on loose rock, which can be fun for downhill bikers but becomes a slog for uphill riders. The official trail does not summit Slate Mountain, though a turnoff onto a smaller trail about 2.6 miles into the hike does provide summit access (p. 362). If possible, I recommend parking a shuttle car at the end of the trail at the Slate Mountain Parking Lot and making this a one-way hike.

Distance: 8.2 miles one-way
Elevation Gain: 1,800 feet
Difficulty: Moderately strenuous
Hiking Time: About 5 hours
Nearest Town: Pocatello
Trail Surface: Dirt, rock
Wheelchair Access: None
Dog-Friendly: Yes; on-leash at the trailhead. May be off-leash if under control once on the trail

Amenities: A vault toilet is available at the Gibson Jack trailhead.
Contact: Caribou-Targhee National Forest, Westside Ranger District 208-236-7500
Trailhead GPS Coordinates:
Gibson Jack Trailhead
N42° 47.575' W112° 25.887'
Slate Mountain Trailhead
N42° 44.025' W112° 24.448'

Getting There

From the junction of South Valley Road and Bannock Highway in Pocatello, head southeast on Bannock Highway for 1.4 miles, where you will turn right onto West Gibson Jack Road. Stay on this road until you reach the Gibson Jack Trailhead in 2.3 miles, which has plenty of parking. The trail begins on the west side of West Gibson Jack Road, just outside the parking lot.

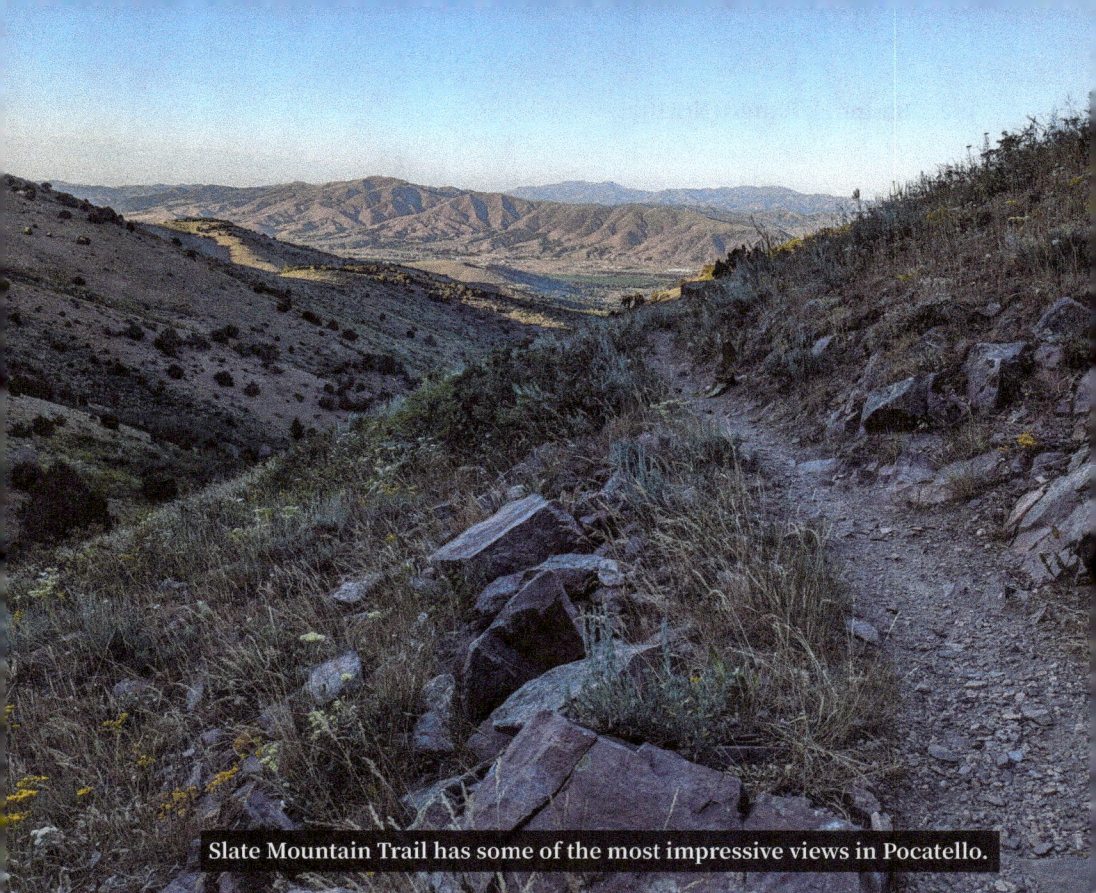
Slate Mountain Trail has some of the most impressive views in Pocatello.

The Hike

While the actual Slate Mountain Trailhead is located off of Mink Creek Road, I recommend approaching this trail from the north at the Gibson Jack Trailhead. This northern half of the hike offers a more gradual climb along a scenic creek and allows for various route options utilizing the West Fork Mink Creek and Gibson Jack trails.

From the Gibson Jack trailhead, head west, following the Slate Mountain Trail sign. Almost immediately after the start of the hike, the trail forks, where you will make a left turn onto the wide West Fork Gibson Jack Trail. At 0.3 miles, you will cross a bridge over Gibson Creek, continuing on the trail as it ascends a small forested hillside. At around the 0.6 mile mark, the West Fork Gibson Trail makes a sharp southwest turn at a junction with the official Slate Mountain Trail.

Turn left (northeast) onto the singletrack Slate Mountain Trail, which makes a sharp turn to the south after a couple hundred feet. For the next 1.9 miles, this southbound trail ascends alongside the forested Dry Creek, which is especially colorful in the autumn. For those mountain biking, tall grass and brush can overtake the trail in parts, and there are occasional roots in the path, but this is a fun stretch to ride. Depending on the season, several small creek crossings may usually be stepped over without getting your boots wet.

At about 2.5 miles, the trail turns to the left (east) and begins climbing out of the creekbed. Not far from that turn, at about 2.9 miles, a rocky alternate path appears on the trail's right (east) side. This trail cuts off about 0.2 miles from the route, though I recommend staying on the main path unless you are in a rush. Once you reach the 3.3-mile mark, you will have an excellent view of Indian Mountain. This point also marks the end of the constant incline. Just past this viewpoint, a small singletrack path splits off to the right (southwest) of the main path. This small path is where you would begin the 1.5-mile climb to Slate Mountain's summit (p. 362). The official Slate Mountain Trail does not summit Slate Mountain, so keep left at this fork.

With the constant incline out of the way, the trail shifts into a refreshing mix of uphills and downhills, contouring below Slate Mountain between cliffed hillsides and thick forests, all with beautiful views of the area. Mountain bikers, in particular, will enjoy this portion of the path, though be warned

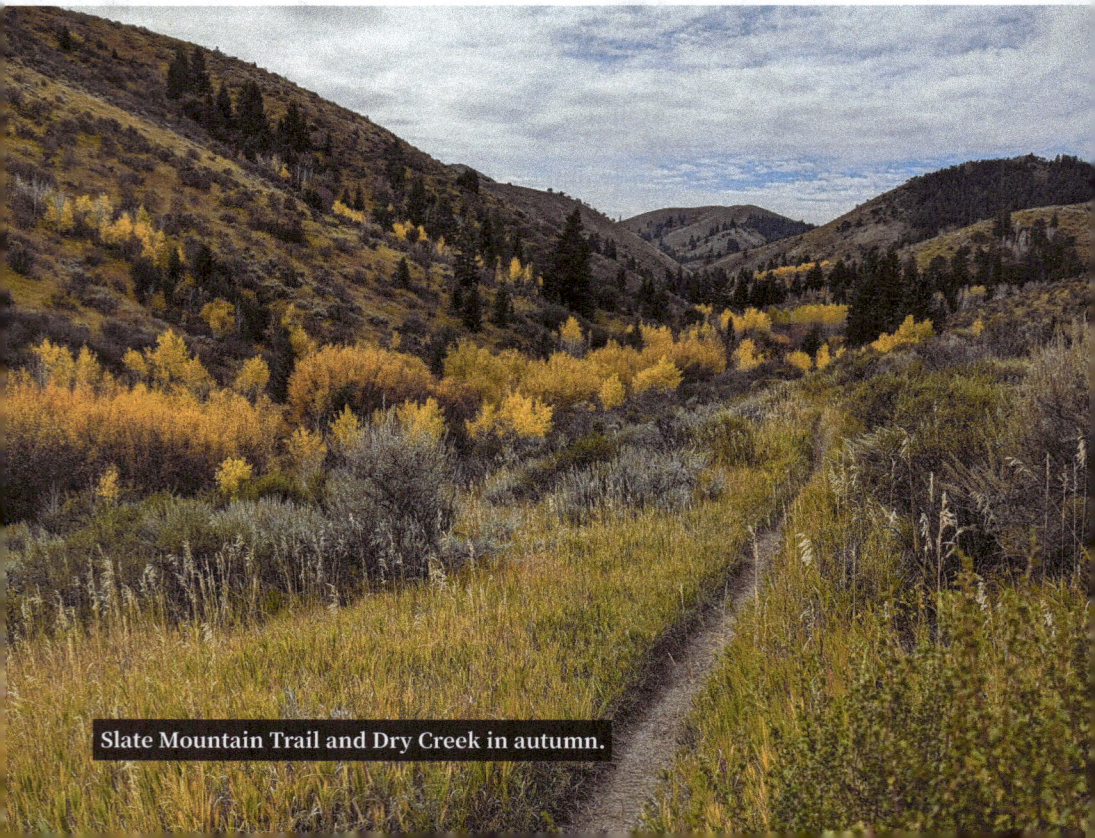

Slate Mountain Trail and Dry Creek in autumn.

Slate Mountain Trail with Scout Mountain in the background.

that the trail can be rocky. At about 5.7 miles, the trail turns east, and a trail appears on the right (south) side of the path. Keep left at this junction to stay on the Slate Mountain Trail. (The trail to the right, the West Fork to Slate Mountain Connector, is about 0.9 miles long and connects to the West Fork Mink Creek Trail.)

At about 6.0 miles, you will reach the top of the southern section of the trail. This stretch of the path is primarily a steep descent on loose rock among juniper trees. At about 7.1 miles, the trail turns left (northeast), followed by a right (south) turn at 7.3 miles. The remainder of the path descends a dry drainage on a rutted trail, which can be difficult to bike. The trail ends just past a bridge crossing at the Slate Mountain parking lot.

Keep Going

Located just before the bridge 30 yards west of the Slate Mountain Trailhead, the **Slate Mountain - Valve House Connector** (Forest Service Trail 048) is a one-mile one-way trail that climbs about 200 feet, connecting the Slate Mountain Trail to the Valve House Trail. The path starts as an overgrown singletrack, but once it crosses over to the south side of Mink Creek Road, it becomes a well-maintained 4x4 trail. While not the most exciting trail, this path does provide an off-road route to connect Slate Mountain with the trails on Scout Mountain.

Slate Mountain Trail

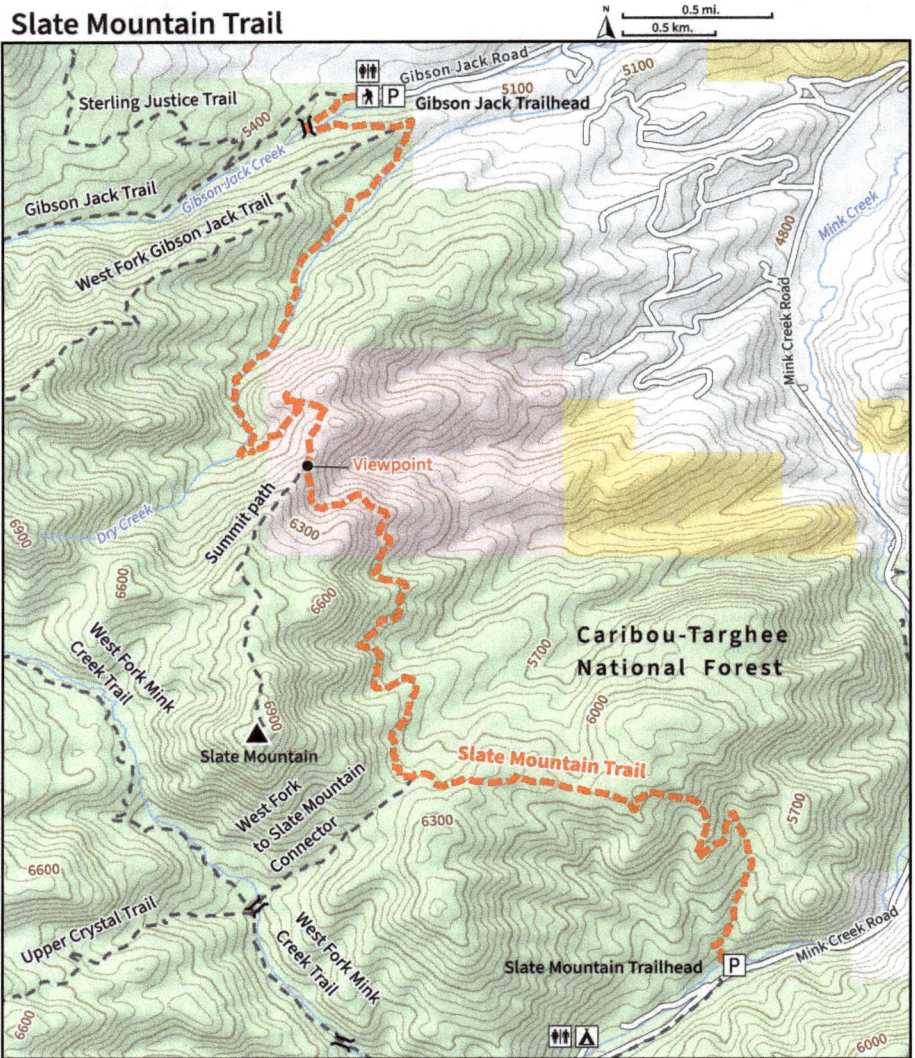

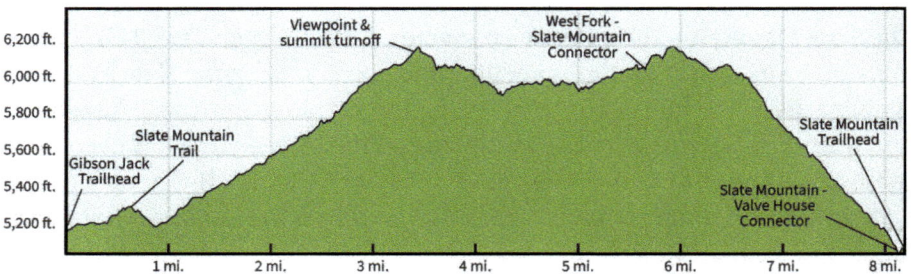

Sterling Justice Trail

Gibson Jack Road
5100
5100
Gibson Jack Trailhead

5400
Gibson Jack Trail
Gibson Jack Creek
West Fork Gibson Jack Trail

Mink Creek
4800

Mink Creek Road

Dry Creek
6900

Viewpoint

Summit path
6300

6600

West Fork Mink Creek Trail
6600

Slate Mountain

West Fork to Slate Mountain Connector

5700

6000

Caribou-Targhee National Forest

Slate Mountain Trail

6300

5700

Upper Crystal Trail
6600

West Fork Mink Creek Trail

Slate Mountain Trailhead
Mink Creek Road

6600

6000

Elevation profile:

- 6,200 ft.
- 6,000 ft.
- 5,800 ft.
- 5,600 ft.
- 5,400 ft.
- 5,200 ft.

Gibson Jack Trailhead

Slate Mountain Trail

Viewpoint & summit turnoff

West Fork - Slate Mountain Connector

Slate Mountain Trailhead

Slate Mountain - Valve House Connector

1 mi. 2 mi. 3 mi. 4 mi. 5 mi. 6 mi. 7 mi. 8 mi.

42. Cherry Springs Nature Area
(FS Trails 035 & 036)

The paved Cherry Springs Nature Area is a family-friendly path that explores the riparian habitat of Mink Creek. With plenty of educational signage about wildlife, vegetation, and the area's history, this shady hike is easy to recommend to anyone looking for a short trip into Pocatello's wilderness. The area is especially pleasant in the autumn when the many deciduous trees make the area a favorite for photographers.

Distance: 2 miles out-and-back. (Both the north and south trails are 0.5 miles one way.)
Elevation Gain: 150 feet
Difficulty: Easy
Hiking Time: About 1 hour
Nearest Town: Pocatello
Trail Surface: Pavement

Wheelchair Access: Yes
Dog-Friendly: Yes; must be on-leash at all times
Amenities: A vault toilet is available at the trailhead.
Contact: Caribou-Targhee National Forest, Westside Ranger District 208-236-7500
Trailhead GPS Coordinates: N42° 45.060' W112° 23.643'

Getting There

From the junction of South Valley Road and Bannock Highway in Pocatello, head southeast on Bannock Highway for 6.0 miles (the road becomes Mink Creek Road after 2.3 miles). Turn right when you get to the large Cherry Springs Nature Area sign, where you will find the large parking area. To begin the southern trail from the parking lot, head south on the paved trail to the left of the three-panel wooden display. The northern trail begins to the right of that same wooden display.

The Hike

There are two Cherry Springs trails, Cherry Springs North and Cherry Springs South, though they are seamlessly connected. Both trails are about 1-mile round trip and end in small loops, with the Cherry Springs South forested loop being a particularly scenic highlight. The northern trail passes by the newly

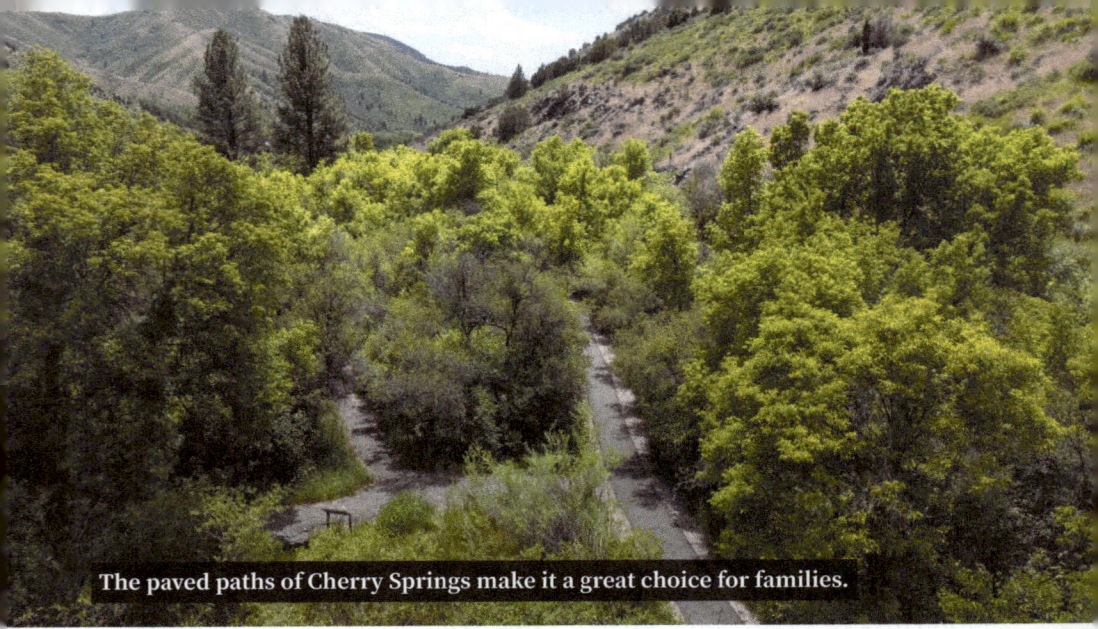
The paved paths of Cherry Springs make it a great choice for families.

renovated Cherry Springs Amphitheater, about 0.1 miles from the parking lot. Various small sub-trails emerge from both trails, making the area fun to explore.

The Cherry Springs Nature Area was created by the Civilian Conservation Corps (CCC) in the 1930s and was originally used as a tent campground. The CCC was a work relief program established in the United States during the Great Depression. This program was part of President Franklin D. Roosevelt's New Deal initiatives and aimed to provide employment opportunities for young men while also addressing conservation and natural resource management needs.

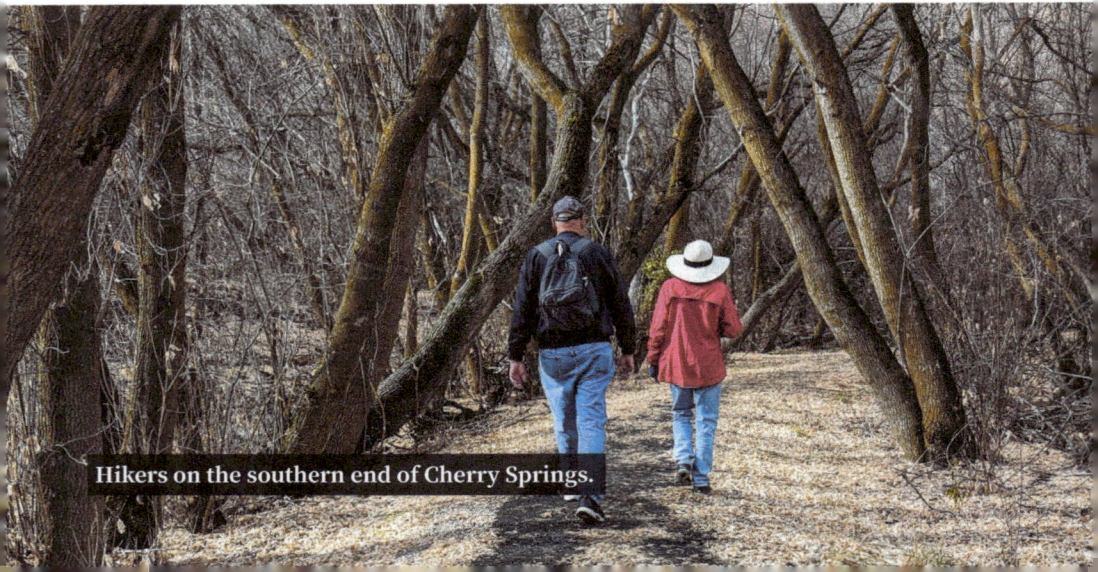
Hikers on the southern end of Cherry Springs.

Cherry Springs Nature Area

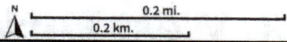

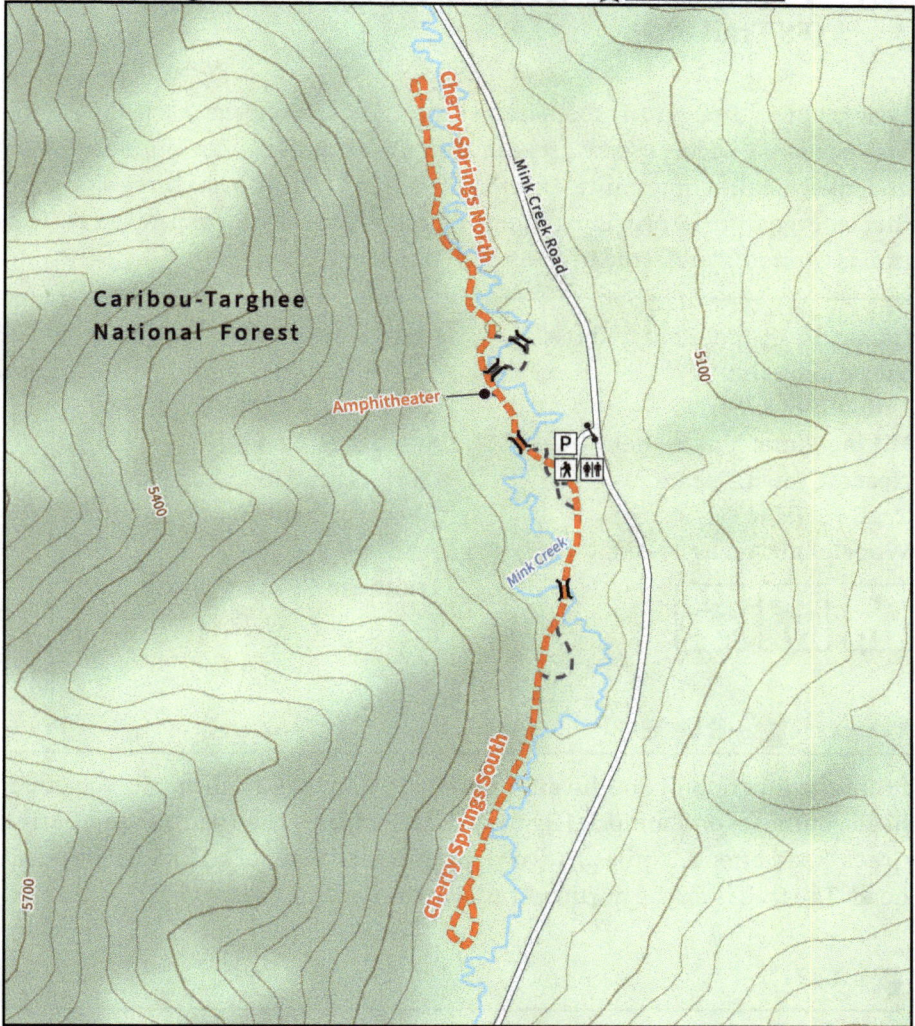

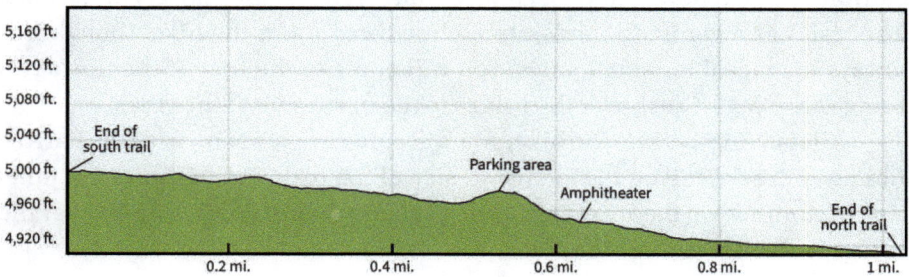

N

0.2 mi.

0.2 km.

Cherry Springs North

Mink Creek Road

5100

Caribou-Targhee
National Forest

Amphitheater

P

Mink Creek

5400

Cherry Springs South

5700

5,160 ft.

5,120 ft.

5,080 ft.

5,040 ft.

End of
south trail

5,000 ft.

Parking area

4,960 ft.

Amphitheater

End of
north trail

4,920 ft.

0.2 mi.   0.4 mi.   0.6 mi.   0.8 mi.   1 mi.

43. West Fork Mink Creek Trail
(FS Trail 059)

Beaver ponds, Douglas-fir stands, and aspen groves alongside a trickling creek have made the widely used West Fork Mink Creek Trail a go-to option for bikers and hikers in the community. This forested uphill trail also has three side trails that emerge from it, providing a good amount of variety for repeat users. This trail is commonly referred to as simply "West Fork."

Distance: 7.5 miles out-and-back
Elevation Gain: 1,070 feet
Difficulty: Moderate
Hiking Time: About 4 hours
Nearest Town: Pocatello
Trail Surface: Dirt, rock
Wheelchair Access: None

Dog-Friendly: Yes; on-leash at the trailhead. May be off-leash if under control once on the trail
Amenities: None
Contact: Caribou-Targhee National Forest, Westside Ranger District 208-236-7500
Trailhead GPS Coordinates: N42° 43.355' W112° 25.163'

Getting There

From the junction of South Valley Road and Bannock Highway in Pocatello, head southeast on Bannock Highway for 8.7 miles. (The road becomes Mink Creek Road after 2.3 miles.) Turn right into the West Fork Mink Creek Trailhead. The trail is on the northwest side of the parking area.

The Hike

From the signed trailhead, head west on the wide trail as it enters the forested canyon, which follows the West Fork of Mink Creek for the entirety of the hike. The trail has a gentle to moderate incline throughout the hike, though it is always manageable. At 0.4 miles, you will come to the first of the trail's two bridge crossings. Cross over the bridge to the north side of the creek.

About 0.6 miles into the hike, you will come to a junction with the narrow Chimney Creek Trail on the left (west) side of the path. Stay right on this junction to continue on the West Fork Mink Creek Trail. At 0.9 miles, cross over the bridge to the west side of the creek.

West Fork Mink Creek Trail in the summer.

At about 1.6 miles, you will pass between a junction with two other trails: Upper Crystal Trail on the left (west) and the West Fork to Slate Mountain Connector to the right (east). Stay on the middle path (north). For the next mile or so, the trail becomes rockier, steeper, and narrower, making for a challenging climb on a bike. At about 2.7 miles, the incline decreases, and the creek opens up into a series of meadows and beaver ponds.

For the remainder of the hike, the trail travels between thick forests on the left (west) and the creek on the right (east). At 3.7 miles, the trail leaves the creek and enters the forest, ending just past a gate at the Elk Meadows Loop.

Keep Going

In addition to the Elk Meadows Loop (p. 214), which is located at the end of the trail, three side trails branch off the West Fork Mink Creek Trail.

The first side trail you will come across is the **Chimney Creek Trail** (Forest Service Trail 052), which appears 0.6 miles into the hike as an unmarked singletrack path on the left side of the trail. This 0.5-mile one-way trail gains 300 feet and follows Chimney Creek through a shaded side drainage in the West Fork area. Two small bridges are on this path, one almost immediately into the hike and another at 0.2 miles. The official trail ends near an old wellhouse over the creek, though an unofficial trail continues for another 1.2 miles, climbing 700 feet until it reaches the top of Corral Creek Trail.

The second trail that emerges off West Fork is Upper Crystal Trail (p. 208). This 1.7 mile one-way trail provides a nice forested climb to Crystal Summit Road and is a popular ride for mountain bikers. It begins 1.6 miles into the West Fork Mink Creek Trail on the left side of the path.

The **West Fork to Slate Mountain Trail Connector** (Forest Service Trail 045) is the last path that emerges from the West Fork Trail. This trail begins after about 1.6 miles on the right (east) side of West Fork. It is 0.9 miles one-way and climbs 500 feet through a largely shadeless gully. As the name suggests, the trail ends connecting to the Slate Mountain Trail. The path begins nice and wide, but after a bridge crossing shortly into the hike, it becomes a narrow singletrack.

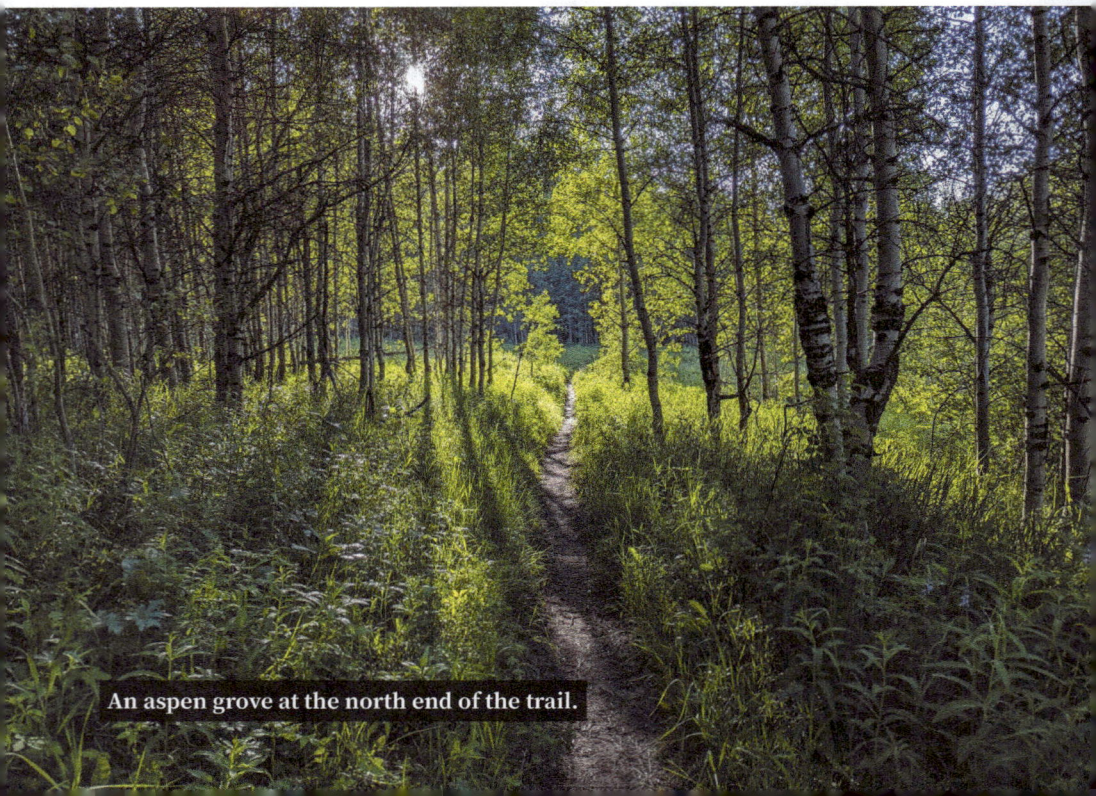

An aspen grove at the north end of the trail.

West Fork Mink Creek Trail

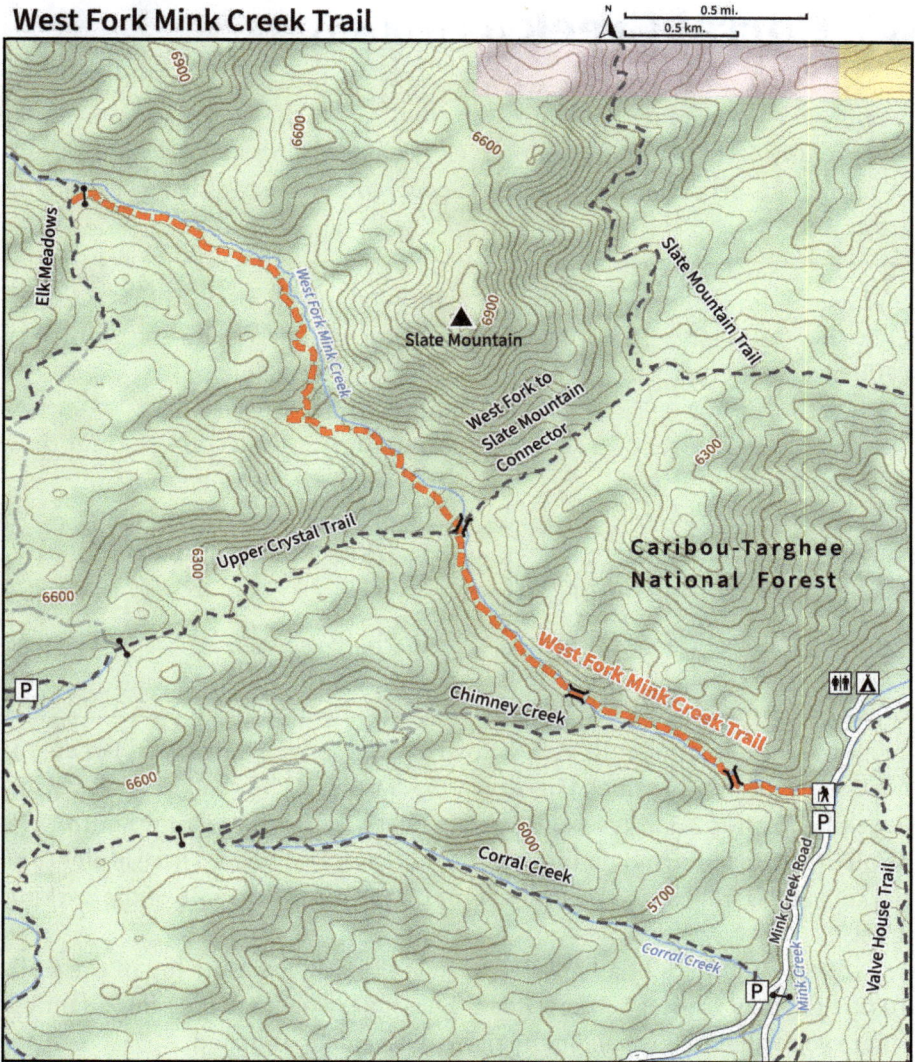

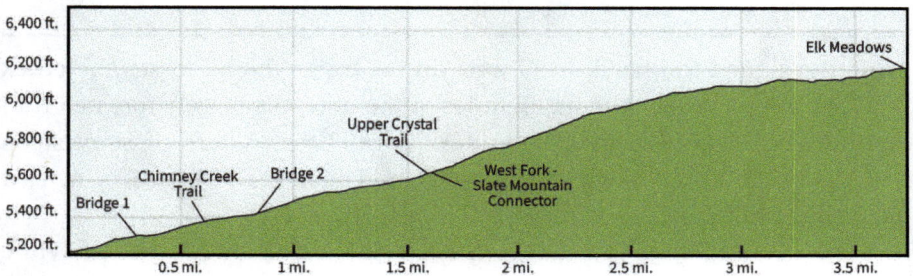

N

0.5 mi.

0.5 km.

Elk Meadows

6900

6600

6600

West Fork Mink Creek

Slate Mountain Trail

Slate Mountain

6900

West Fork to Slate Mountain Connector

6300

Caribou-Targhee National Forest

Upper Crystal Trail

6300

6600

West Fork Mink Creek Trail

Chimney Creek

6600

P

6600

6000

Corral Creek

5700

Mink Creek Road

P

P

Corral Creek

Mink Creek

Valve House Trail

6,400 ft.							Elk Meadows
6,200 ft.							
6,000 ft.							
5,800 ft.		Upper Crystal Trail					
5,600 ft.	Chimney Creek Trail	Bridge 2	West Fork - Slate Mountain Connector				
5,400 ft.							
5,200 ft.	Bridge 1						

0.5 mi.   1 mi.   1.5 mi.   2 mi.   2.5 mi.   3 mi.   3.5 mi.

44. Corral Creek (FS Trail 061)

A favorite in the mountain bike community, Corral Creek is a moderately used forest path, descending in a wild creek drainage. This speedy ride is also a pleasant hike, providing a nice view of Scout Mountain near the top, especially at sunset.

Distance: 5.1 miles out-and-back
Elevation Gain: 1,190 feet
Difficulty: Moderately strenuous
Hiking Time: About 2.5 hours
Nearest Town: Pocatello
Trail Surface: Dirt, rock
Wheelchair Access: None

Dog-Friendly: Yes; on-leash at the trailhead. May be off-leash if under control once on the trail
Amenities: None
Contact: Caribou-Targhee National Forest, Westside Ranger District 208-236-7500
Trailhead GPS Coordinates: N42° 42.712' W112° 25.376'

Getting There

From the junction of South Valley Road and Bannock Highway in Pocatello, head southeast on Bannock Highway for 9.5 miles. (The road becomes Mink Creek Road after 2.3 miles.) At 9.5 miles, just past the turnoff for South Fork Mink Creek Road, turn right into the Corral Creek Trailhead. There is plenty of parking at the trailhead. The trail begins on the northwest side of the parking area.

Many mountain bikers prefer to start the ride from the top of the trail. To do this, take Crystal Summit Road (Forest Service Road 006) for 3.3 miles, where you will find the trail on the right (east) side of the road.

The Hike

From the signed trailhead, head west on the trail, which crosses the creek in about 140 yards. For the first 2 miles of the hike, the largely forested trail steadily climbs uphill on the north side of Corral Creek. There are some steep and rocky segments, though they are small and manageable on a bike, at least on the downhill.

About 2.0 miles in, you will reach a bend in the trail at a rocky shelf. While

Corral Creek can be rocky in places, especially near the top.

not quite the end of the incline, this challenging-to-ride rock pile makes for a great place to pause and catch your breath.

At 2.2 miles, the trail crosses over a cattle guard in a field. The remainder of the hike descends alongside sage and deciduous trees until it connects with Crystal Summit Road.

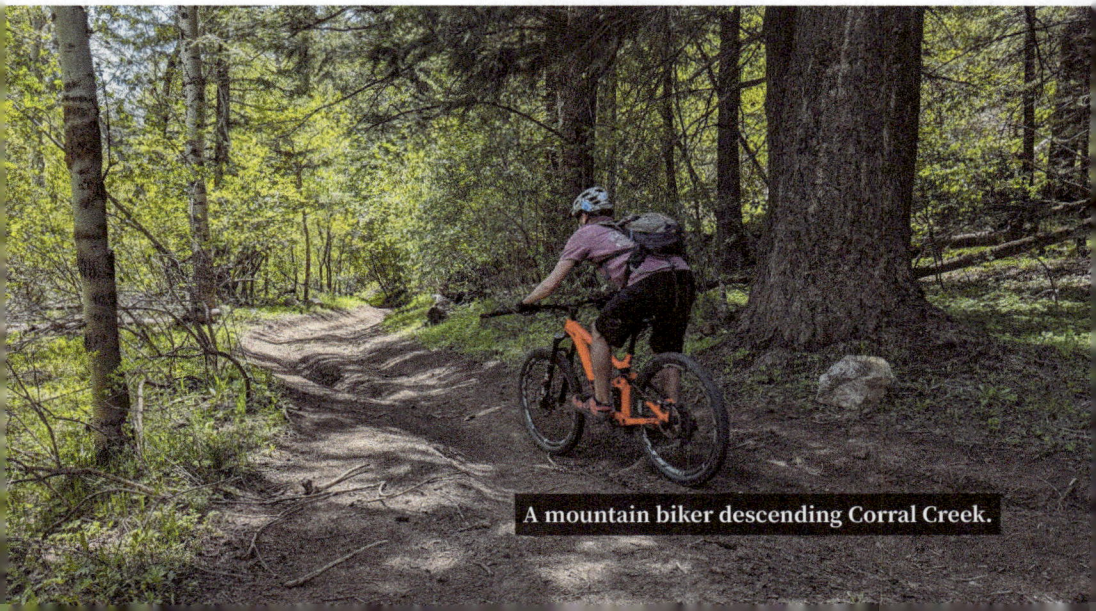

A mountain biker descending Corral Creek.

Corral Creek

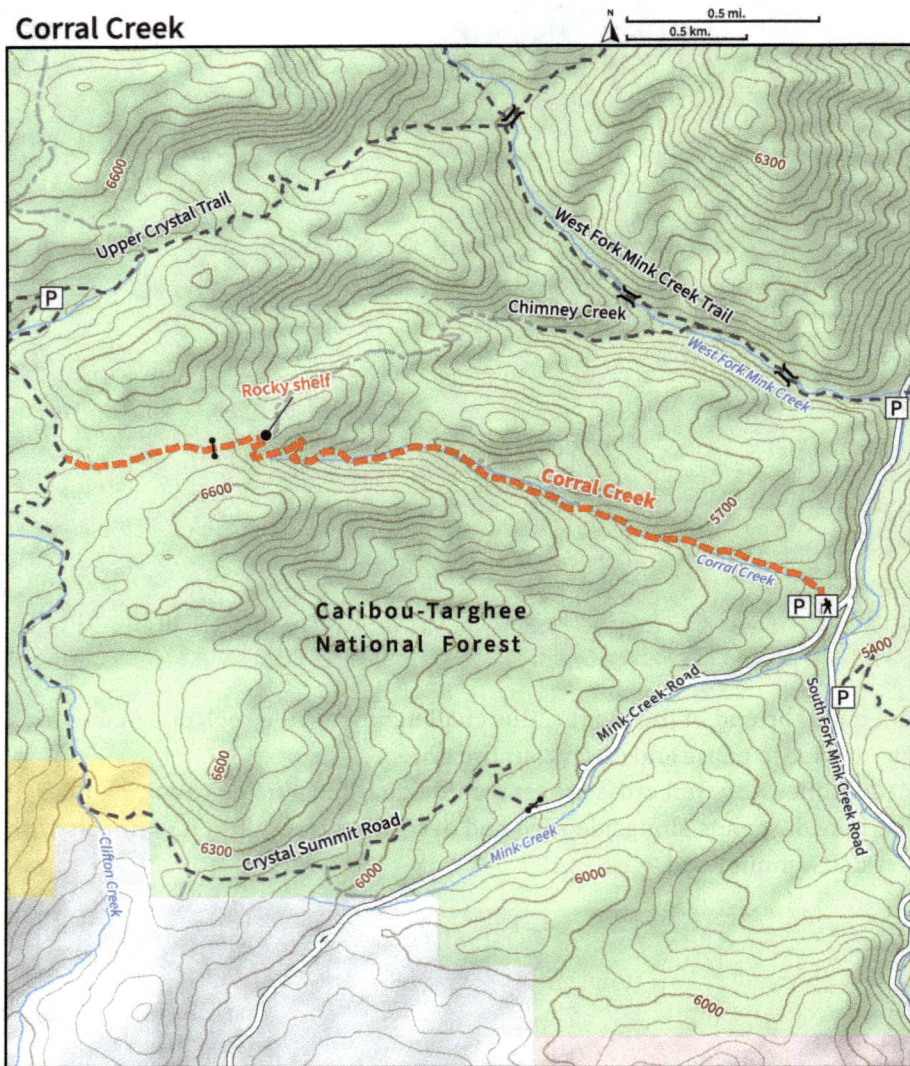

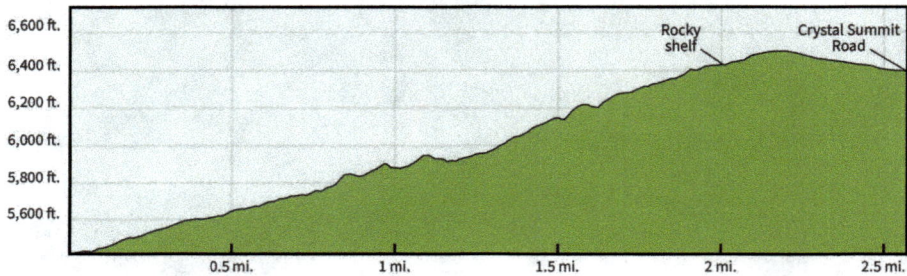

45. Crystal Summit Road (FS Road 006)

Crystal Summit Road is frequently used by motorized vehicles to access trails, including Elk Meadows and Corral Creek. However, this shouldn't deter you from enjoying what can be a beautiful hike in its own right. The first 4 miles are a pleasant mix of open meadows and evergreen forests, but the final 1.7 miles can be challenging for vehicles due to the rugged terrain.

Distance: 11.4 miles out-and-back
Elevation Gain: 1,560 feet
Difficulty: Strenuous
Hiking Time: About 6.5 hours
Nearest Town: Pocatello
Trail Surface: Dirt, rock
Wheelchair Access: None

Dog-Friendly: Yes; on-leash at the trailhead. May be off-leash if under control once on the trail
Amenities: None
Contact: Caribou-Targhee National Forest, Westside Ranger District 208-236-7500
Trailhead GPS Coordinates: N42° 42.088' W112° 26.259'

Getting There

From the junction of South Valley Road and Bannock Highway in Pocatello, head southeast on Bannock Highway for 10.6 miles. (The road becomes Mink Creek Road after 2.3 miles.) Turn right just before the turnoff to park alongside the road.

The Hike

From the parking area, head northwest, following the signs for Forest Service Road 006. For the first 1.2 miles, the trail steadily gains 500 feet as it makes its way west. At 1.2 miles, the trail shifts to the north and becomes more level. At 2.9 miles, keep right (north) to stay on route. After crossing a small meadow surrounded by forests, keep left (northwest) at 3.3 miles to avoid merging onto Corral Creek Trail.

At 4.0 miles, keep left (west), passing Upper Crystal Trail on the right (east) and Crystal Creek Trail on the left (southwest). Past that junction, the path becomes a little more rugged, entering thicker forests and becoming rockier. At 5.7 miles, the road ends at a small parking area and cattle guard.

Keep Going

Crystal Summit Road is the closest you can get to Elk Meadows in a passenger vehicle. At the road's endpoint, you can continue north on **Forest Service Trail 44,** a rugged and rocky trail about half a mile long. Forest Service Trail 44 ends when it connects with Elk Meadows.

Crystal Summit Road passing through an evergreen forest.

Crystal Summit Road

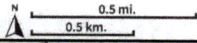

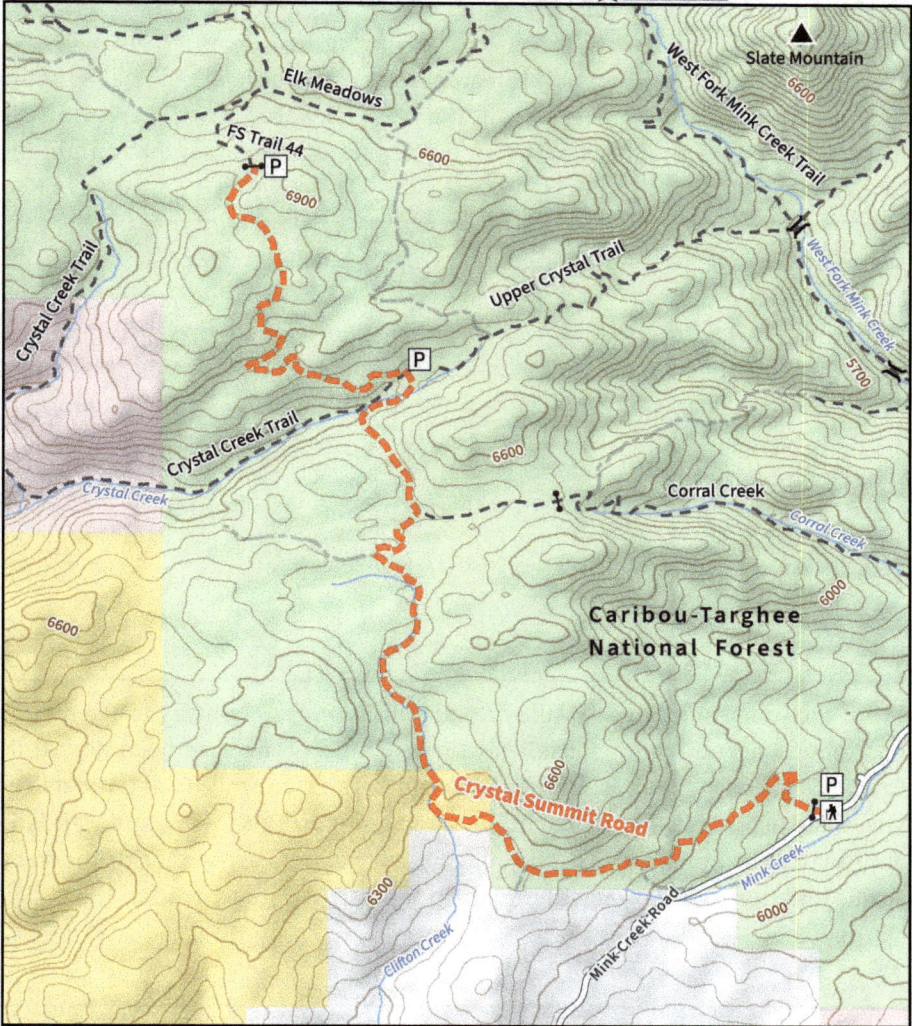

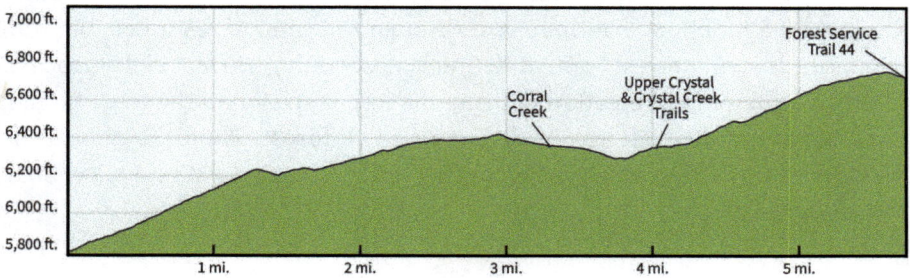

N

0.5 mi.
0.5 km.

Elk Meadows

FS Trail 44

P

6900

6600

Slate Mountain

6600

West Fork Mink Creek Trail

West Fork Mink Creek

5700

Upper Crystal Trail

P

Crystal Creek Trail

6600

Crystal Creek Trail

Crystal Creek

Corral Creek

Corral Creek

6600

Caribou-Targhee
National Forest

6000

6600

6600

Crystal Summit Road

P

Mink Creek

6300

Mink Creek Road

6000

Clifton Creek

Elevation profile:

7,000 ft.
6,800 ft.
6,600 ft.
6,400 ft.
6,200 ft.
6,000 ft.
5,800 ft.

Corral
Creek

Upper Crystal
& Crystal Creek
Trails

Forest Service
Trail 44

1 mi.   2 mi.   3 mi.   4 mi.   5 mi.

46. Upper Crystal Trail (FS Trail 060)

The Upper Crystal Trail is not only a great route that connects Crystal Summit Road to West Fork Mink Creek Trail, but it is also a trail worth exploring on its own. It offers a fun descent through a dense conifer forest that mountain bikers in particular will enjoy.

Distance: 3.4 miles out-and-back
Elevation Gain: 850 feet
Difficulty: Moderate
Hiking Time: About 2 hours
Nearest Town: Pocatello
Trail Surface: Dirt, rock
Wheelchair Access: None

Dog-Friendly: Yes; on-leash at the trailhead. May be off-leash if under control once on the trail
Amenities: None
Contact: Caribou-Targhee National Forest, Westside Ranger District 208-236-7500
Trailhead GPS Coordinates: N42° 43.708' W112° 27.756'

Getting There

From the junction of South Valley Road and Bannock Highway in Pocatello, head southeast on Bannock Highway for 10.6 miles. (The road becomes Mink Creek Road after 2.3 miles.) Turn right onto Crystal Summit Road (Forest Service Road 006). This dirt road can be rough going, so AWD is recommended. Stay on this road for 4 miles until you reach a junction. Park alongside the road at this junction, where you will find the trail on the southwest side.

The Hike

From the trailhead junction, head northeast on the 4x4 road, which transitions into a singletrack trail shortly into the hike. At 0.4 miles, the trail comes to a gate at a junction. Continue east through the gate. At 0.5 miles, the trail begins its descent to West Fork Mink Creek, descending 840 feet in the process. There are a few small meadows during the upper stretch of the trail, though the majority of the trail travels through a thick forest. The trail ends at the West Fork Mink Creek Trail, just below the junction with the West Fork to Slate Mountain Connector.

Wildflowers along Upper Crystal Trail.

The Caribou-Targhee National Forest occupies over 3 million acres of protected forest land in Idaho, Wyoming, and Utah, including areas next to Yellowstone National Park and Grand Teton National Park.

Upper Crystal Trail

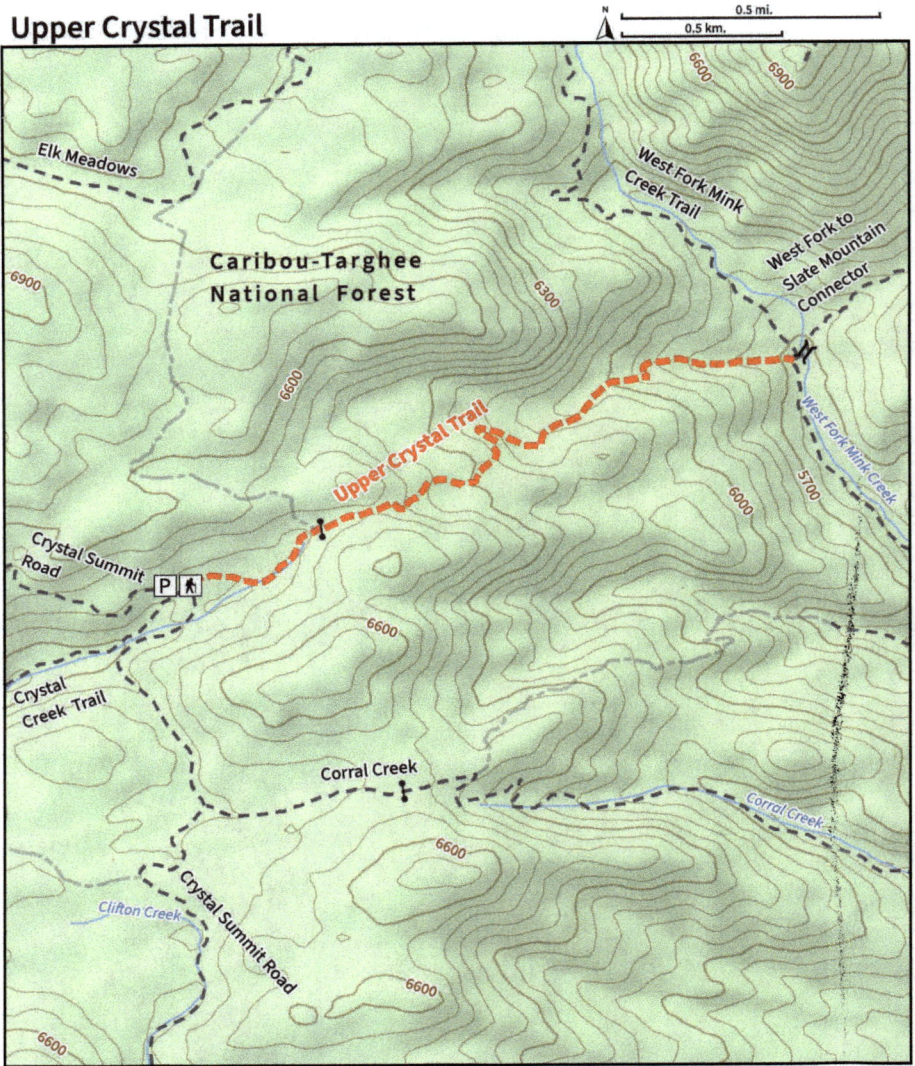

Elk Meadows

Caribou-Targhee
National Forest

6900

6600

6300

West Fork Mink
Creek Trail

West Fork to
Slate Mountain
Connector

6600

6900

West Fork Mink Creek

5700

Upper Crystal Trail

6000

Crystal Summit
Road

P

6600

Crystal
Creek Trail

Corral Creek

Corral Creek

Crystal Summit Road

Clifton Creek

6600

6600

6600

N

0.5 mi.

0.5 km.

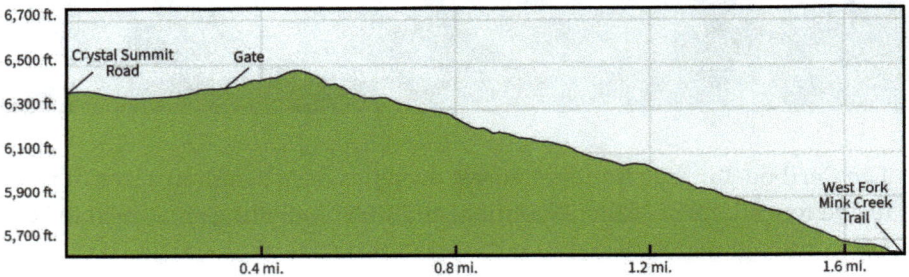

6,700 ft.			
6,500 ft.	Crystal Summit Road	Gate	
6,300 ft.			
6,100 ft.			
5,900 ft.			West Fork Mink Creek Trail
5,700 ft.			

0.4 mi.   0.8 mi.   1.2 mi.   1.6 mi.

47. Crystal Creek Trail (FS Trails 024 & 064)

Crystal Creek Trail gives hikers the opportunity to travel alongside a forested creek, marshy meadows, and scenic ponds on a beautiful and lesser-used trail in the Bannock Range. The path can be overgrown at places, so be prepared for a bit of route finding at times. The trail makes for a great loop hike with Crystal Summit Road.

Distance: 3.6 miles one-way
Elevation Gain: 650 feet
Difficulty: Moderate
Hiking Time: About 2 hours
Nearest Town: Pocatello
Trail Surface: Dirt, rock
Wheelchair Access: None

Dog-Friendly: Yes; on-leash at the trailhead. May be off-leash if under control once on the trail
Amenities: None
Contact: Caribou-Targhee National Forest, Westside Ranger District 208-236-7500
Trailhead GPS Coordinates: N42° 43.708' W112° 27.756'

Getting There

From the junction of South Valley Road and Bannock Highway in Pocatello, head southeast on Bannock Highway for 10.6 miles. (The road becomes Mink Creek Road after 2.3 miles.) Turn right onto Crystal Summit Road (Forest Service Road 006). Stay on this road for 4 miles until you reach a junction. Park alongside the road at this junction, where you will find the trail on the southwest side.

The Hike

From the trailhead, head southwest on the singletrack trail, which, for the first 1.4 miles, gradually descends alongside the scenic Crystal Creek between evergreen forests. At 0.4 miles, keep left (west) at the fork. At 1.4 miles, keep right (northwest) at the fork. This fork marks the beginning of the trail's incline.

For the next 1.9 miles, the trail winds its way northeast, gaining 800 feet in the process. This stretch of the hike travels through a pristine drainage that often has seasonal ponds. During this stretch, keep an eye out for moose. The trail is often rocky, so mountain bikers may be in for a rough climb.

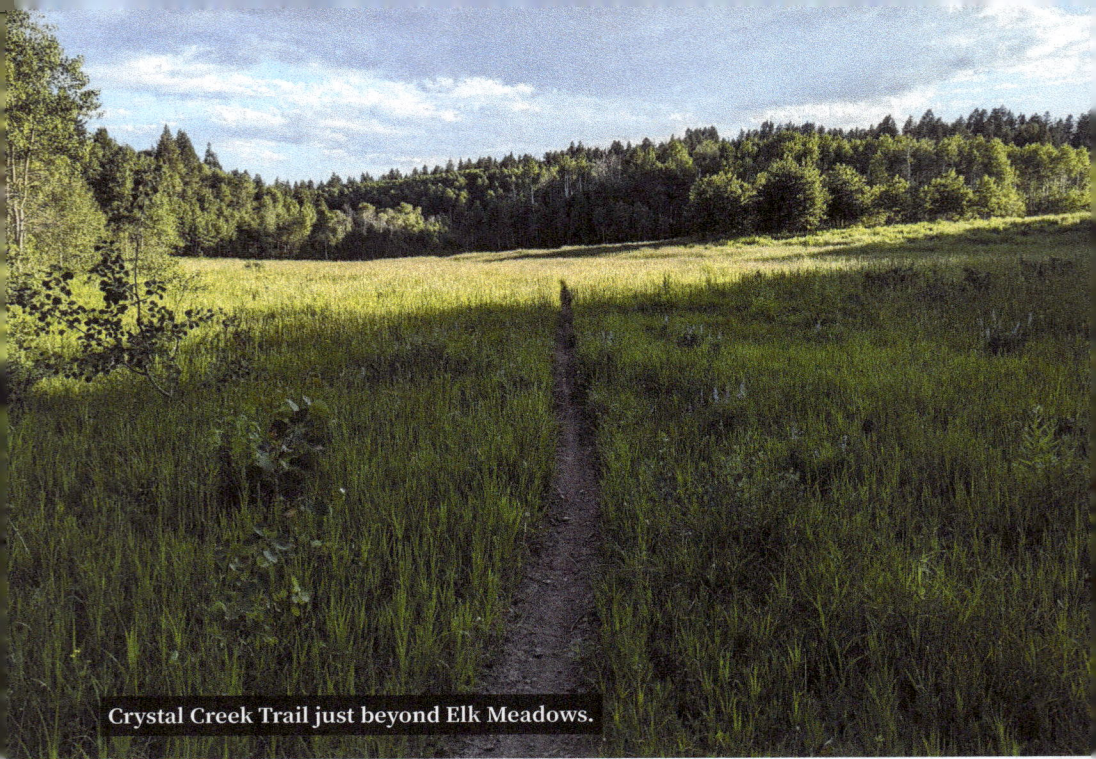
Crystal Creek Trail just beyond Elk Meadows.

At 3.2 miles, in the middle of a meadow, make a slight right (northeast) at the fork. Not far past the fork, the path tops out in the woods at 3.3 miles and begins its descent toward Elk Meadows to the east. At 3.5 miles, the trail can be challenging to follow as it disappears into a grassy meadow. Just keep moving northeast, and you will eventually reach Forest Service Trail 44. The trail ends when it connects with Forest Service Trail 44, shortly before the beginning of the Elk Meadows Loop.

Keep Going

I recommend making this route into a loop by utilizing Crystal Summit Road and Forest Service Trail 44. This loop option is about 5.7 miles round trip.

Did you know that it is illegal not to smile in Pocatello? In 1948, the Mayor of Pocatello passed an ordinance making it illegal not to smile. As a result, the City has earned the nickname "U.S. Smile Capital."

Crystal Creek Trail

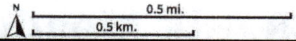

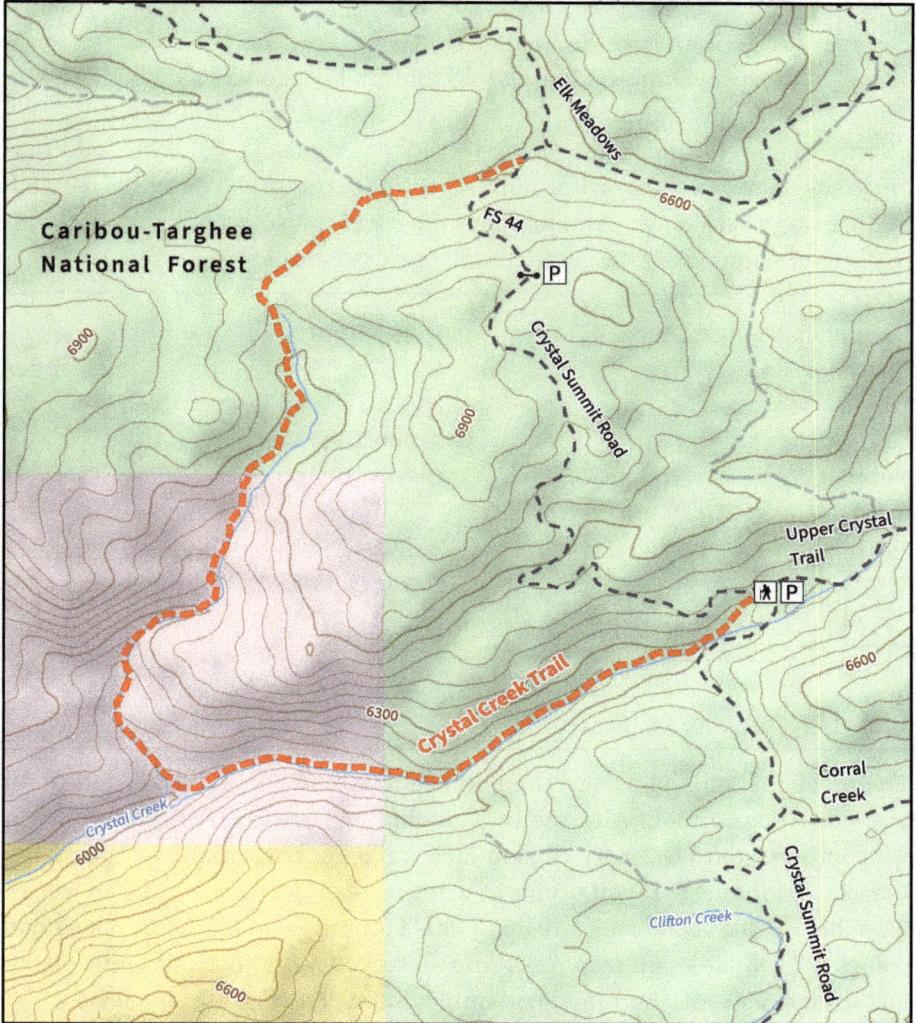

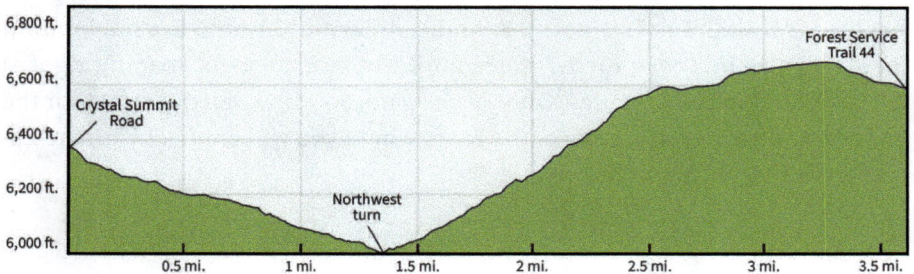

N

0.5 mi.

0.5 km.

Elk Meadows

6600

FS 44

P

Caribou-Targhee
National Forest

6900

Crystal Summit Road

6900

Upper Crystal
Trail

P

6600

Crystal Creek Trail

6300

Corral
Creek

Crystal Creek

6000

Clifton Creek

Crystal Summit Road

6600

Elevation profile:

6,800 ft.

6,600 ft.

Forest Service
Trail 44

6,400 ft.

Crystal Summit
Road

6,200 ft.

Northwest
turn

6,000 ft.

0.5 mi.   1 mi.   1.5 mi.   2 mi.   2.5 mi.   3 mi.   3.5 mi.

48. Elk Meadows Loop (FS Trail 022)

The Elk Meadows Loop is a highly versatile trail in the Bannock Range. As a standalone trail, Elk Meadows is a well-traveled pathway through conifer forests, aspen groves, and beautiful sage meadows, blanketed gold with wildflowers in the summer. Those who complete the entire loop will experience much of the beauty Southeast Idaho provides. The trail is also good for those choosing to hike segments of it to connect with separate trails.

Distance: 5.6-mile loop
Elevation Gain: 550 feet
Difficulty: Moderate
Hiking Time: About 3 hours
Nearest Town: Pocatello
Trail Surface: Dirt, rock
Wheelchair Access: None

Dog-Friendly: Yes; on-leash at the trailhead. May be off-leash if under control once on the trail
Amenities: None
Contact: Caribou-Targhee National Forest, Westside Ranger District 208-236-7500
Trailhead GPS Coordinates: N42° 44.752' W112° 28.259'

Getting There

The most challenging part of the Elk Meadows Loop is getting to it. Several popular trails connect with the loop, including the West Fork Mink Creek, Gibson Jack, and West Fork Gibson Jack trails, making hiking or biking the best access method. If you prefer to drive instead, your best bet is to use an All-Wheel-Drive vehicle to drive up Crystal Summit Road (Forest Service Road 006) to the vehicle stopping point. From there, you must hike half a mile on the last stretch of Crystal Summit Road until it intersects with Elk Meadows.

From the junction of South Valley Road and Bannock Highway in Pocatello, head southeast on Bannock Highway for 10.6 miles. (The road becomes Mink Creek Road after 2.3 miles.) Turn right onto Crystal Summit Road. Stay on this road for 5.7 miles until you reach a gate, keeping right at 2.9 miles and left at 4.0 miles. Once at the gate, continue north on foot for the last remaining rugged stretch of the road, where you will connect with the Elk Meadows Loop in about half a mile.

The Elk Meadows Loop is the end destination for many popular trails.

The Hike

The hike begins at the southern end of the loop, where it connects with Forest Service Trail 44. Moving around the loop counter-clockwise, head east on the 4x4 trail as it gradually moves downhill below a sagebrush hillside. At 0.5 miles, you will come across a small pond, where the trail turns left (north) beginning the eastern stretch of Elk Meadows.

After turning past the pond, you will cross through a field, which, depending on the season, may be glowing with wildflowers. Continue on this mostly downhill and forested trail for the next mile. At about 1.6 miles, you will pass by the gated and well-signed end point of the West Fork Mink Creek Trail. Shortly beyond the West Fork Mink Creek turnoff, the trail makes a northwestern turn, signifying the end of the downhill and the beginning of almost three miles of gradual incline.

This northwestern trail moves within and alongside aspens and conifer trees before emerging into a meadow at about 2.5 miles. You will come to the signed West Fork Gibson Jack Trail at about 2.9 miles at the northeast tip of the loop.

The rocky southwest portion of the Elk Meadows Loop.

The trail turns west from here as it crosses over the northern tip of the loop, passing by the signed Gibson Jack Trail at 3.1 miles. Past this trailhead, the path turns southwest, moving between conifers and aspens. At about 3.4 miles, you will pass by a lightly used turnoff to your right (northwest) that leads to Rock Knoll. Beyond that, at 3.5 miles, you will come to the signed Pole Canyon (Monument Gulch) Trail.

Thick forests line the trail on this western and slightly steeper side of the loop. At about 4.4 miles, the trail leaves the forest and turns southeast onto a rocky hill. Shortly past this southeast turn, you will come across an unnamed 4-wheeler trail to the left (north) of the main trail. This alternate trail is far smoother and stays in the shade of the forest, though you miss scenic views by skipping the main loop.

Stay right to avoid the alternate path and climb the rocky hill. This rugged section is brief and the last of the trail's incline. At 5.3 miles, you will pass by a trail to the Elk Meadows warming hut. At 5.4 miles, the trail turns south onto the final stretch through a large meadow, which, depending on the season, can be quite marshy.

Keep Going

While Gibson Jack, West Fork Gibson Jack, and West Fork Mink Creek are popular trails that branch off of Elk Meadows, there is one other prominent trail worth mentioning: **Pole Canyon (Monument Gulch)** (Forest Service Trail 029). This is a 1.0 mile one-way doubletrack trail located on the northwest side of Elk Meadows (3.6 miles counterclockwise or 2.2 miles clockwise). Pole Canyon (Monument Gulch) travels west, descending 530 feet in a heavily forested canyon. The first 0.6 miles gently climbs uphill before beginning a steep descent, which makes for a fun mountain bike ride. The trail ends at a junction with Midnight Creek Trail.

A forest descent on the Pole Canyon (Monument Gulch) Trail.

The Elk Meadows area in autumn.

Elk Meadows Loop

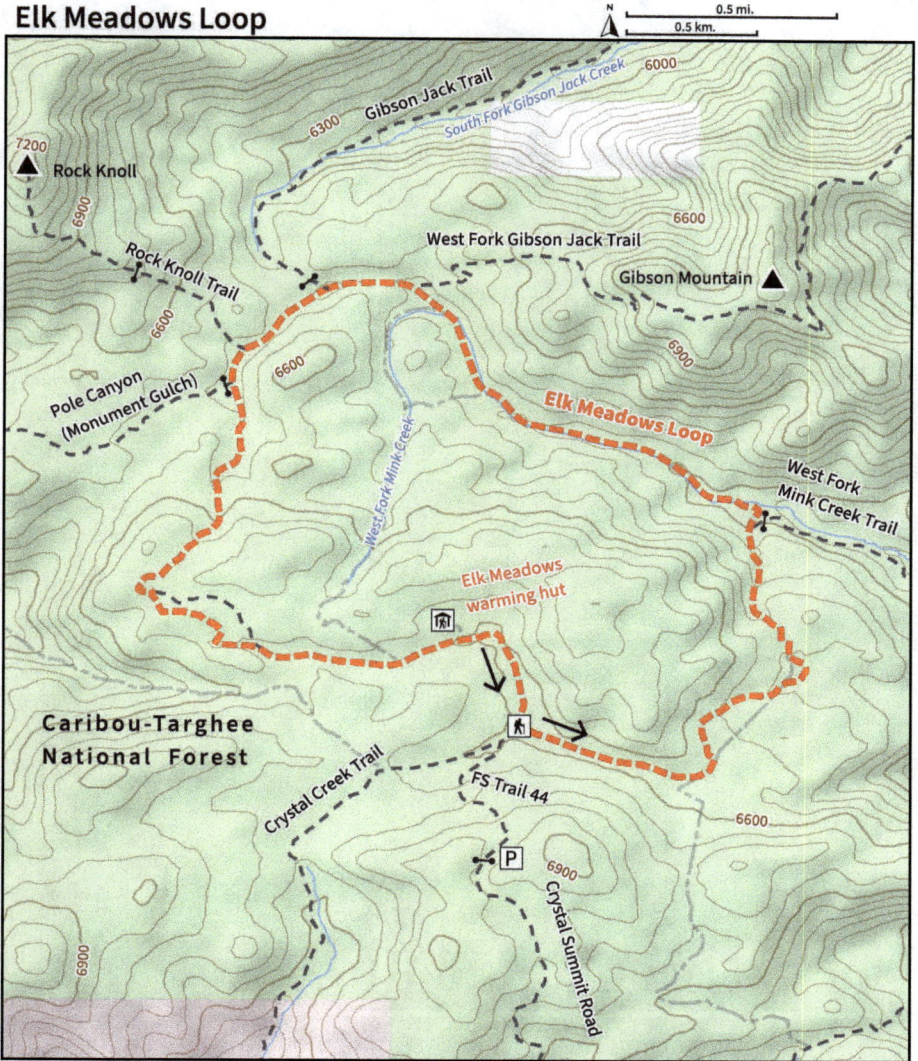

0.5 mi.
0.5 km.

Rock Knoll
7200

6300
Gibson Jack Trail
South Fork Gibson Jack Creek
6000

6900

West Fork Gibson Jack Trail
6600
Gibson Mountain

Rock Knoll Trail

6600

Pole Canyon
(Monument Gulch)

6600

6900

Elk Meadows Loop

West Fork
Mink Creek Trail

West Fork Mink Creek

Elk Meadows
warming hut

Caribou-Targhee
National Forest

Crystal Creek Trail

FS Trail 44

6600

P

6900

6900

Crystal Summit Road

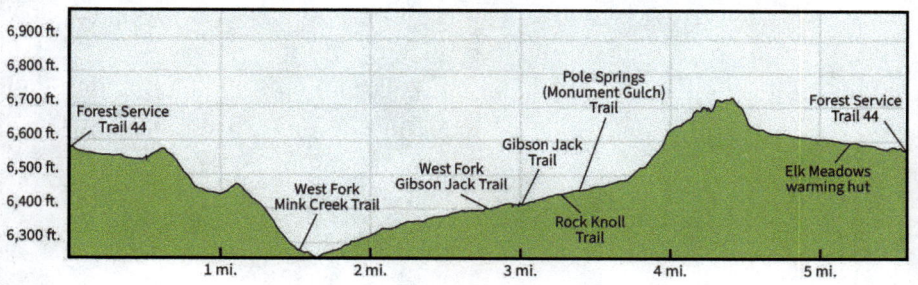

6,900 ft.
6,800 ft.
6,700 ft.
6,600 ft.
6,500 ft.
6,400 ft.
6,300 ft.

Forest Service
Trail 44

West Fork
Mink Creek Trail

West Fork
Gibson Jack Trail

Gibson Jack
Trail

Pole Springs
(Monument Gulch)
Trail

Rock Knoll
Trail

Elk Meadows
warming hut

Forest Service
Trail 44

1 mi.   2 mi.   3 mi.   4 mi.   5 mi.

Bannock Range (South)

The heavily forested and rugged Scout Mountain looms over the network of trails in the southern half of the Bannock Range. These trails offer breathtaking views and are generally more secluded, taking hikers through dense evergreen forests, high wildflower meadows, and rocky ridges. The two campgrounds in this range, Scout Mountain Campground and Goodenough Creek Campground, serve as great starting points for those who wish to spend more time outdoors. Many of the routes in this area allow for motorized travel, making them a popular choice for ATVs and dirt bikers.

An evergreen forest along Indian Creek Trail.

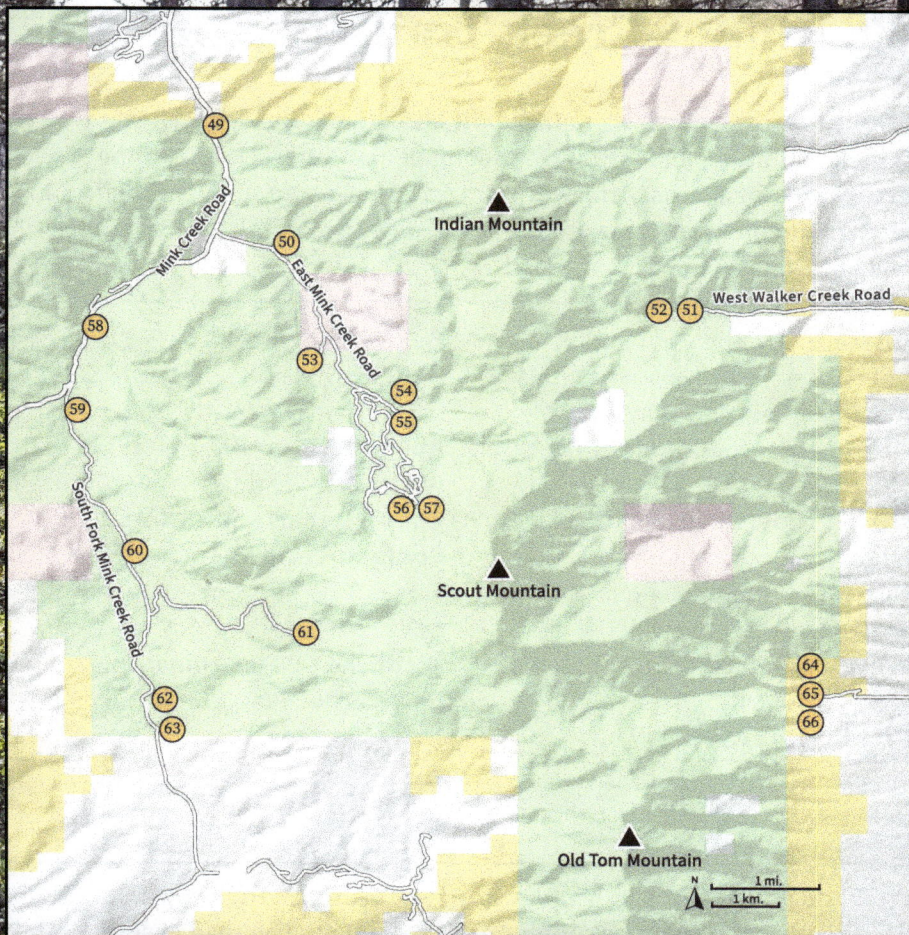

Map labels:
- 49 Mink Creek Road
- 50 East Mink Creek Road
- Indian Mountain
- 58
- 53
- 59
- 54
- 55
- 52 51 West Walker Creek Road
- South Fork Mink Creek Road
- 60
- 56 57
- Scout Mountain
- 61
- 64
- 65
- 66
- 62
- 63
- Old Tom Mountain

N
1 mi.
1 km.

49. Kinney Creek Trail (FS Trail 292)

With an easily accessible trailhead off Mink Creek Road, excellent views of Indian Mountain, and a well-traveled path along a creek, the Kinney Creek Trail makes for a pleasant hike. If you are not looking to summit Indian Mountain, I recommend turning around at 1.8 miles, which will take off almost 700 feet of elevation gain from the total.

Distance: 4.9 miles out-and-back; 3.6 miles round trip to creek crossing
Elevation Gain: 1,390 feet; 730 feet
Difficulty: Moderately strenuous; Moderate
Hiking Time: About 3 hours; about 2 hours
Nearest Town: Pocatello
Trail Surface: Dirt, rock
Wheelchair Access: None

Dog-Friendly: Yes; on-leash at the trailhead. May be off-leash if under control once on the trail
Amenities: None at the trailhead. A vault toilet is available nearby at the Cherry Springs Nature Area.
Contact: Caribou-Targhee National Forest, Westside Ranger District 208-236-7500
Trailhead GPS Coordinates: N42° 45.636′ W112° 23.808′

Getting There

From the junction of South Valley Road and Bannock Highway in Pocatello, head southeast on Bannock Highway for 5.4 miles. (The road becomes Mink Creek Road at 2.3 miles.) Once you see the large Caribou National Forest sign, turn left into the small Kinney Creek Trailhead. The trail is located on the east side of the trailhead.

The Hike

From the Kinney Creek Trailhead, head east past the gate on the singletrack path. This easy-to-follow trail gradually climbs uphill on the north side of the creek, often with views of Indian Mountain in the distance. The early stretch has a bit of shade, but most of the hike is exposed to the sun. At 0.4 miles, you will cross over a cattle guard. At 1.8 miles, the trail comes to a junction at a creek crossing that can be hard to see. Both trail options increase substantially

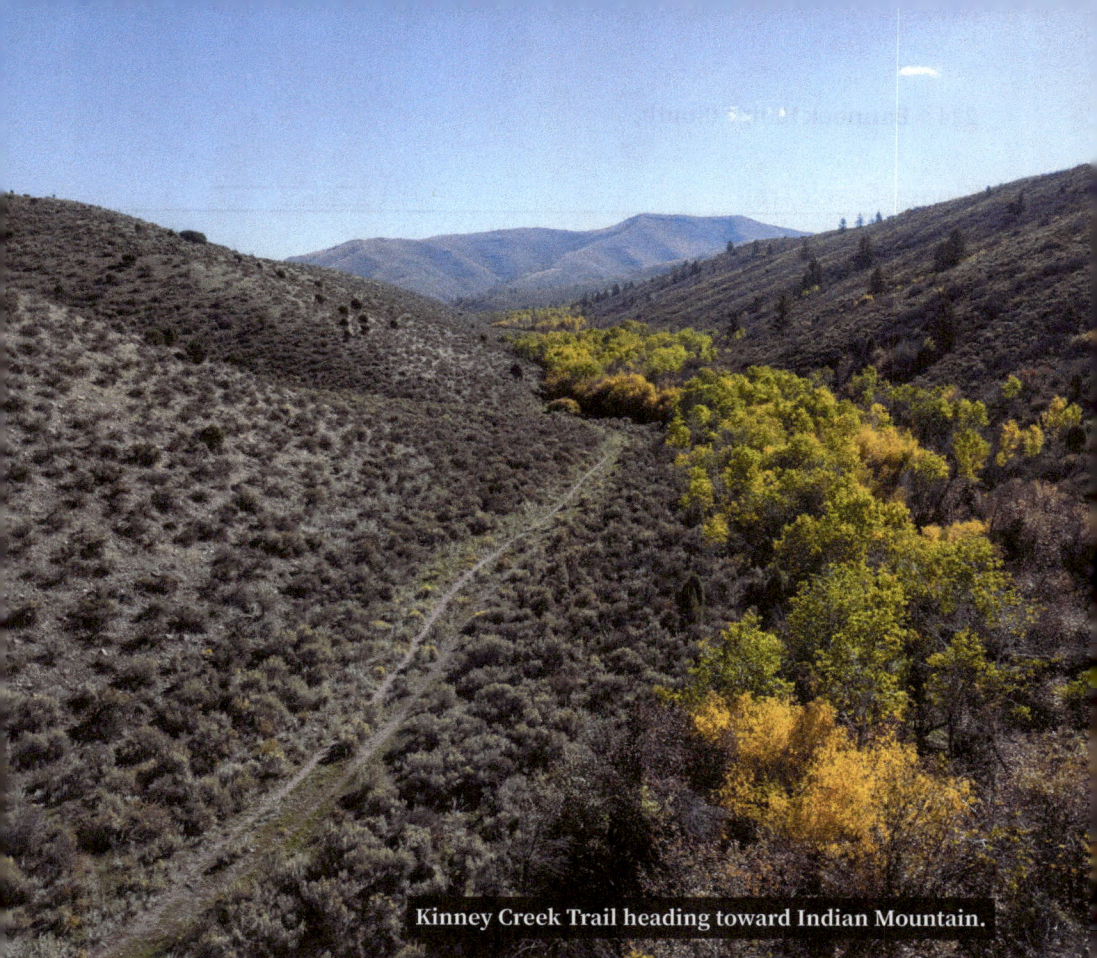

Kinney Creek Trail heading toward Indian Mountain.

in steepness, so unless you intend to summit Indian Mountain, I recommend turning around at this point.

Make a southeast turn across the creek at the junction to stay on the Kinney Creek Trail. (The path that continues on the north side of the creek is an unnamed trail that eventually leads to the summit of Indian Mountain. For more information on this unnamed trail, go to page 368.)

Past the creek, the trail climbs through dense sagebrush onto a ridge. The views of Kinney Creek are quite pretty, so even if you do not summit, the hike is a worthwhile experience. At 2.2 miles, the trail becomes even steeper, climbing over 450 feet until it ends in 0.3 miles. Technically, the trail ends at 2.5 miles, though an unofficial trail continues up the ridge and eventually onto the summit.

Kinney Creek, originating from the west side of Indian Mountain, is a 2.6-mile tributary of Mink Creek.

Kinney Creek Trail

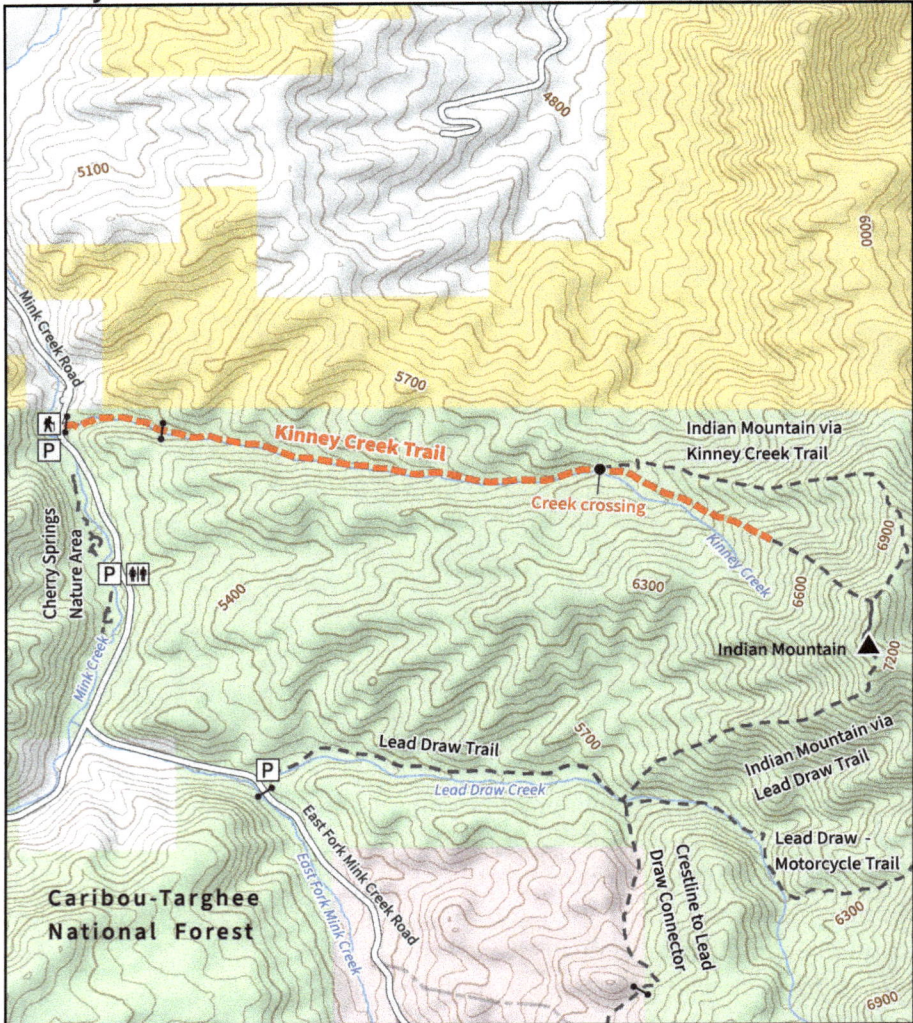

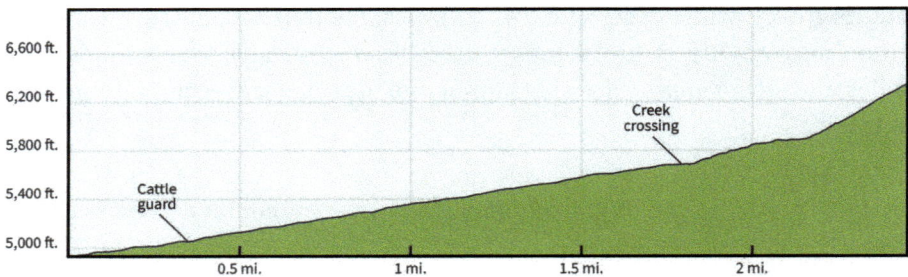

N
0.5 mi.
0.5 km.

Mink Creek Road

4800

5100

6000

5700

Kinney Creek Trail

Indian Mountain via
Kinney Creek Trail

Creek crossing

Kinney Creek

6900

Cherry Springs
Nature Area

P

P

5400

6300

6600

Mink Creek

Indian Mountain

7200

Lead Draw Trail

5700

Indian Mountain via
Lead Draw Trail

P

Lead Draw Creek

Lead Draw -
Motorcycle Trail

East Fork Mink Creek Road

East Fork Mink Creek

Crestline to Lead
Draw Connector

6300

**Caribou-Targhee
National Forest**

6900

6,600 ft.

6,200 ft.

Creek
crossing

5,800 ft.

5,400 ft.

Cattle
guard

5,000 ft.

0.5 mi.   1 mi.   1.5 mi.   2 mi.

50. Lead Draw Trail (FS Trail 109)

A short and sun-exposed path through sagebrush and cattle country, the Lead Draw Trail may interest hikers looking for a simple offering in the Scout Mountain area. A junction with three unique paths at the end of this trail does make things more interesting, especially for trail runners and mountain bikers looking to get some serious miles in. It is important to note that there is a shooting range shortly into this hike. Please be careful when crossing this range, especially when hiking with children and dogs.

Distance: 2.6 miles out-and-back
Elevation Gain: 450 feet
Difficulty: Easy
Hiking Time: About 1.5 hours
Nearest Town: Pocatello
Trail Surface: Dirt, rock
Wheelchair Access: None

Dog-Friendly: Yes; on-leash at the trailhead. May be off-leash if under control once on the trail
Amenities: None
Contact: Caribou-Targhee National Forest, Westside Ranger District 208-236-7500
Trailhead GPS Coordinates: N42° 44.278' W112° 23.036'

Getting There

From the junction of South Valley Road and Bannock Highway in Pocatello, head southeast on Bannock Highway for 6.8 miles. (The road becomes Mink Creek Road after 2.3 miles.) Turn left onto East Fork Mink Creek Road. In 0.6 miles, turn left into the signed Lead Draw Trailhead, which has plenty of parking. The trail is located on the east side of the trailhead.

The Hike

From the Lead Draw parking lot, cross over the cattle guard on the east end of the lot onto the 4x4 trail. At around the 0.2 mile mark, the trail leaves the sagebrush and enters the shooting range clearing. While shooters are not supposed to shoot across the trail, I recommend everyone use extreme caution when entering this clearing. There are a few lightly used 4x4 trails in this area, but the one you want to stay on is northeast across the clearing and hugs the hills.

The trail enters the sagebrush past the clearing, traveling below Indian

Sagebrush are a common sight along the Lead Draw Trail.

Mountain's barren foothills and dry drainages. Continue on this gradual uphill path as it travels east. This area is often filled with cattle, so keep an eye out for them relaxing in the shade near the creek on hot summer days. At around 1.3 miles, a rough singletrack path begins on the left (north) side of the trail. This path ascends to the top of Indian Mountain (that route is featured on page 371). The old ski lodge also sits shortly up this path on the right (east) side.

Keep right (southeast) to stay on the Lead Draw Trail, which, after a brief creek crossing, ends in a large field that is a junction with the Lead Draw Motorcycle Trail and the Crestline to Lead Draw Connector.

Keep Going

If you are looking for a longer hike, I recommend continuing onto the Lead Draw - Motorcycle Trail (p. 229) at the end of the Lead Draw Trail. At 1.7 miles on that trail (or 3 miles from the Lead Draw Trailhead), you will come to a beautiful viewpoint that overlooks the area. It can be quite a steep climb, so be prepared for some incline.

Lead Draw was once a downhill skiing destination in Southeast Idaho. In the 1930s, the Civilian Conservation Corps (CCC) built the Lead Draw Recreation Area as part of Franklin Roosevelt's New Deal. The area had a small ski lodge, a rope tow, and probably the only ski jump in Southeastern Idaho at that time. However, the ski hill closed after World War II due to a lack of snow for several years. Its closure helped lead to the creation of the Pebble Creek Ski Area on the nearby Bonneville Peak. The remains of the ski lodge are still visible today. They are located at the end of the route, just before the creek crossing, shortly up a steep trail to the north.

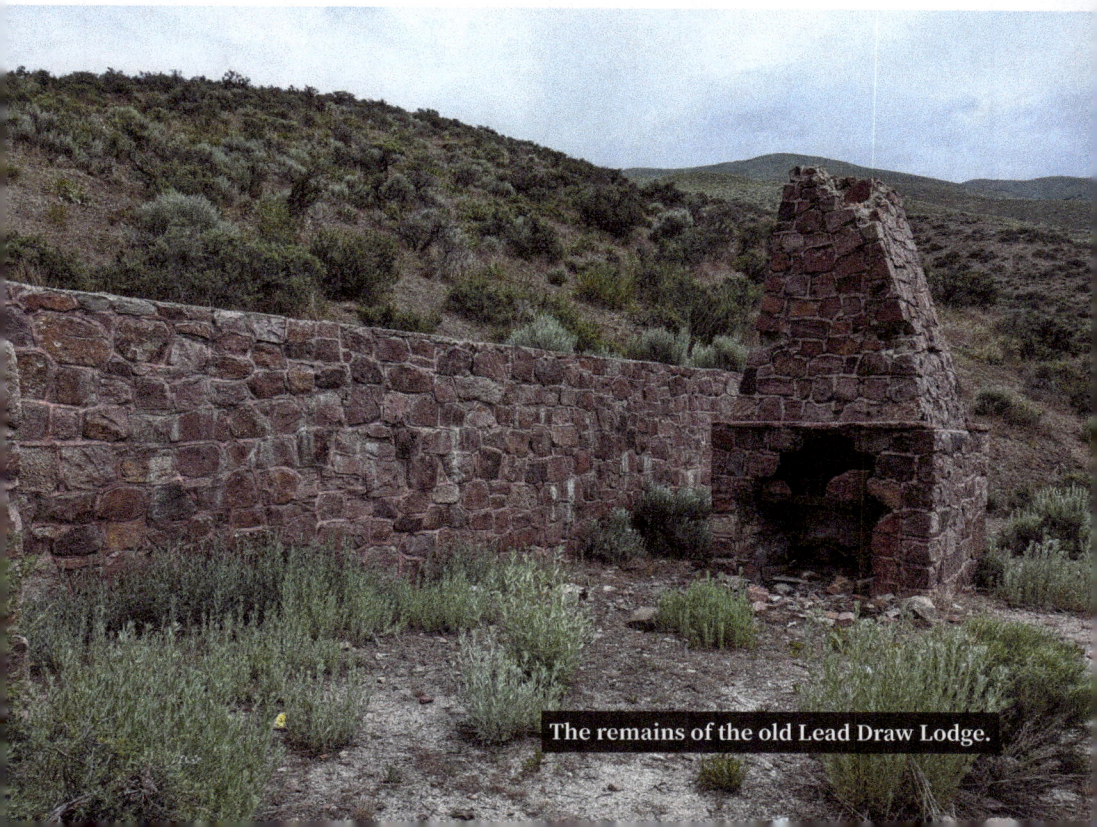

The remains of the old Lead Draw Lodge.

Lead Draw Trail

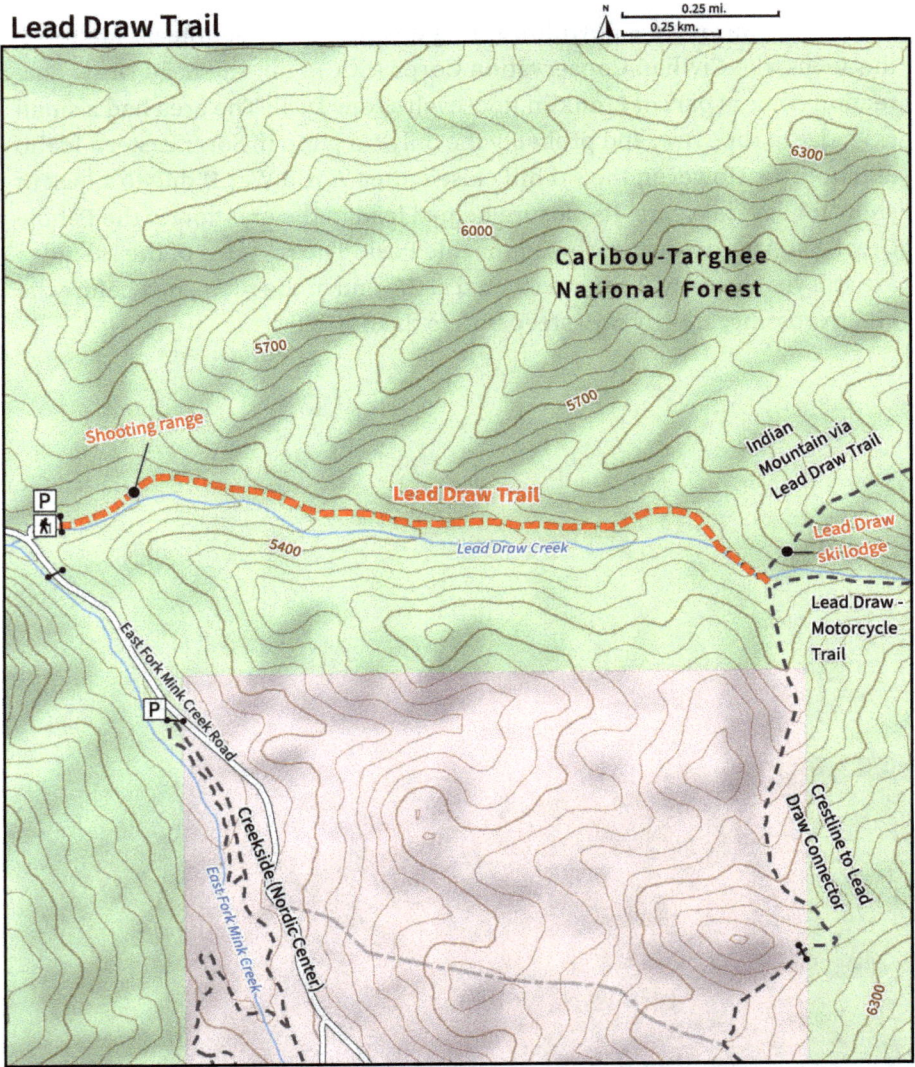

N

0.25 mi.
0.25 km.

Caribou-Targhee
National Forest

6300

6000

5700

5700

Shooting range

P

Lead Draw Trail

5400

Lead Draw Creek

Indian
Mountain via
Lead Draw Trail

Lead Draw
ski lodge

Lead Draw -
Motorcycle
Trail

East Fork Mink Creek Road

P

Creekside (Nordic Center)

East Fork Mink Creek

Crestline to Lead
Draw Connector

6300

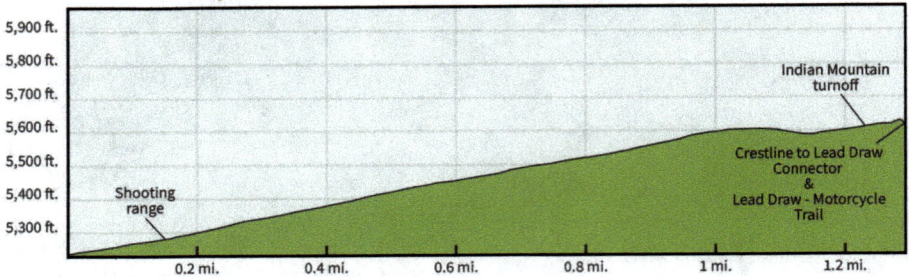

5,900 ft.
5,800 ft.
5,700 ft.
5,600 ft.
5,500 ft.
5,400 ft.
5,300 ft.

Shooting
range

Indian Mountain
turnoff

Crestline to Lead Draw
Connector
&
Lead Draw - Motorcycle
Trail

0.2 mi.   0.4 mi.   0.6 mi.   0.8 mi.   1 mi.   1.2 mi.

51. Lead Draw - Motorcycle Trail
(FS Trail 110)

An underappreciated trail in the Pocatello trail system, the Lead Draw - Motorcycle Trail offers two unique experiences, depending on which side you start from. The western approach, easily accessible from the Lead Draw Trailhead, follows a steep, dusty trail alongside sagebrush and low forests to the top of a high ridge on Indian Mountain. The eastern approach, which is more difficult to access due to its location on the east side of the Bannock Range, follows a lush creek through evergreen and aspen forests on its way to the ridge. The usual advice is to start from the Lead Draw Trailhead, but I suggest driving to the eastern trailhead off West Walker Creek Road, due to its more enjoyable and shaded path.

Distance: 7.6 miles one-way; 4.1 miles round trip to ridge

Elevation Gain: 1,140 feet; 1,100 feet

Difficulty: Moderately strenuous; Moderate

Hiking Time: About 4.5 hours; about 2.5 hours

Nearest Town: Inkom

Trail Surface: Dirt, rock

Wheelchair Access: None

Dog-Friendly: Yes; on-leash at the trailhead. May be off-leash if under control once on the trail

Amenities: None

Contact: Caribou-Targhee National Forest, Westside Ranger District 208-236-7500

Trailhead GPS Coordinates: N42° 43.572' W112° 18.572'

Getting There

From I-15 south of Pocatello, take Exit 58 for Inkom. Turn right on I-15BL/Old Highway 30 West. In 0.7 miles, turn right onto Park Street, and then in 0.2 miles, make a left onto West Portneuf Road. Continue on West Portneuf Road for 5.2 miles. Turn right onto West Walker Creek Road. Stay on West Walker Creek Road for 3.9 miles until you reach the trailhead at an open parking area. While the first half-mile of West Walker Creek Road is paved, the remaining 3.4 miles are on a dirt road. All-Wheel-Drive is not required, but it does make the drive quite a bit easier. The trailhead is past a gate on the southwest side of the parking area.

The Lead Draw - Motorcycle Trail passing through a forest.

The Hike

From the trailhead, head west on the 4x4 trail past the gate. At about 0.2 miles, you will come to a junction with the South Walker Creek Trail on your left (south). Keep right at this junction and cross the creek to the singletrack trail.

For the next mile, the trail continues alongside the creek. There are five creek crossings on this eastern stretch of the route, season-dependent. There are no bridges, but the crossings are usually easy to navigate without getting wet. Continue on the path as it moves between tall conifers mixed in with abundant aspens, creating a beautiful setting.

At about 1.3 miles, keep left to pass by the Indian Creek Trail, which is located on the right (north) side of the path. From there, the narrow trail becomes steeper, leaving the evergreens behind as it climbs toward the ridge. The higher you go on this trail, the rockier it becomes. At 1.7 miles, the trail begins to climb out of the forested creek onto a bushy hillside as it makes its final push for the ridge, which is about 350 vertical feet away.

About 2.1 miles into the hike, you will reach the top of the ridge (6,640 feet) at a barbed wire fence. Continue on the trail west past the fence, ignoring any trails to your left or right. Shortly past the fence, the trail shifts to the southwest as it gradually contours downhill across the open hillside, with remarkable vistas of the area.

At about 2.5 miles, just past a short forest, the trail begins its steep almost 900-foot descent to the Lead Draw area. (This spot is an excellent turnaround point for those not looking to connect with the Lead Draw Trail or the Crestline to Lead Draw Trail.) Continue down the trail as it descends below a ridge into a drainage, with the hillside on its right and the forest on its left. Bring eye protection if you are mountain biking, as low branches often encroach on the path.

At 3.0 miles, the decline lessens as the trail turns to the northwest. The next 0.8 miles continue along the creek, crossing it a few times beginning around 3.4 miles. The trail ends in a large opening at a junction with the Lead Draw Trail on the right (northwest) and the Crestline - Lead Draw Connector on the left (south).

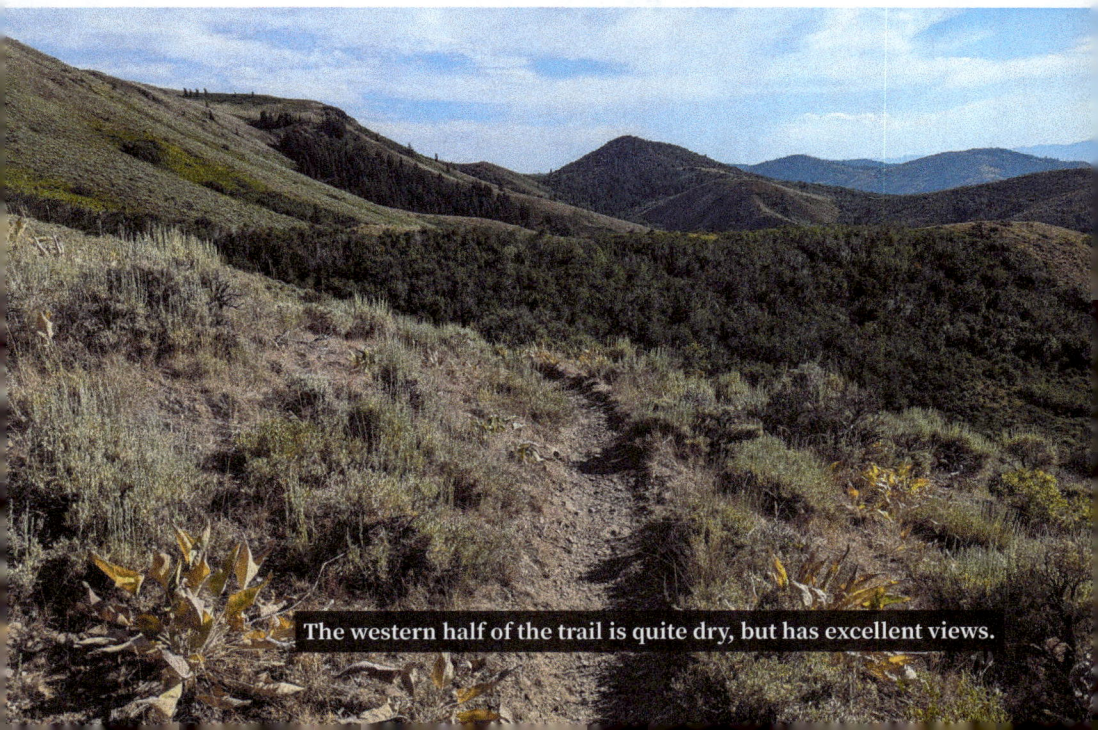

The western half of the trail is quite dry, but has excellent views.

Keep Going

At 1.3 miles into the hike, you will come to the **Indian Creek Trail** (Forest Service Trail 106) on the right (north) side of the path. This 3.3-mile one-way singletrack climbs 450 feet on a barren trail over a ridge and then descends 1,100 feet in an evergreen forest, ending at a fence separating U.S. Forest Service land and private property. The trail can be overgrown with foliage and often has deadfall to navigate, but it provides a calmer experience for those looking for a bit of isolation.

About 2.0 miles into the Indian Creek Trail, you will come across the **North Fork Indian Creek Trail** (Forest Service Trail 103) to the left (west) of the path. This 1.6-mile one-way singletrack climbs 1,050 feet to a ridge high on Indian Mountain. This lightly used trail can be hard to follow, but it offers excellent views of Blackrock Canyon and the Indian Creek areas. The beginning 0.3 miles travel alongside the creek on a visible trail before departing northwest up the sage-covered hill just past a distinct rock formation. At about 0.5 miles, the trail becomes visible again as you travel alongside a fence to the west atop a ridge. As you climb higher on this route, the trail will disappear for long stretches. Just stay on top of the ridge and you will be going in the right direction. The trail ends on a random sub-ridge 300 feet below the main Indian Mountain ridge, though there is a lightly used unofficial trail that climbs another 300 feet over the top to the mountain's west side.

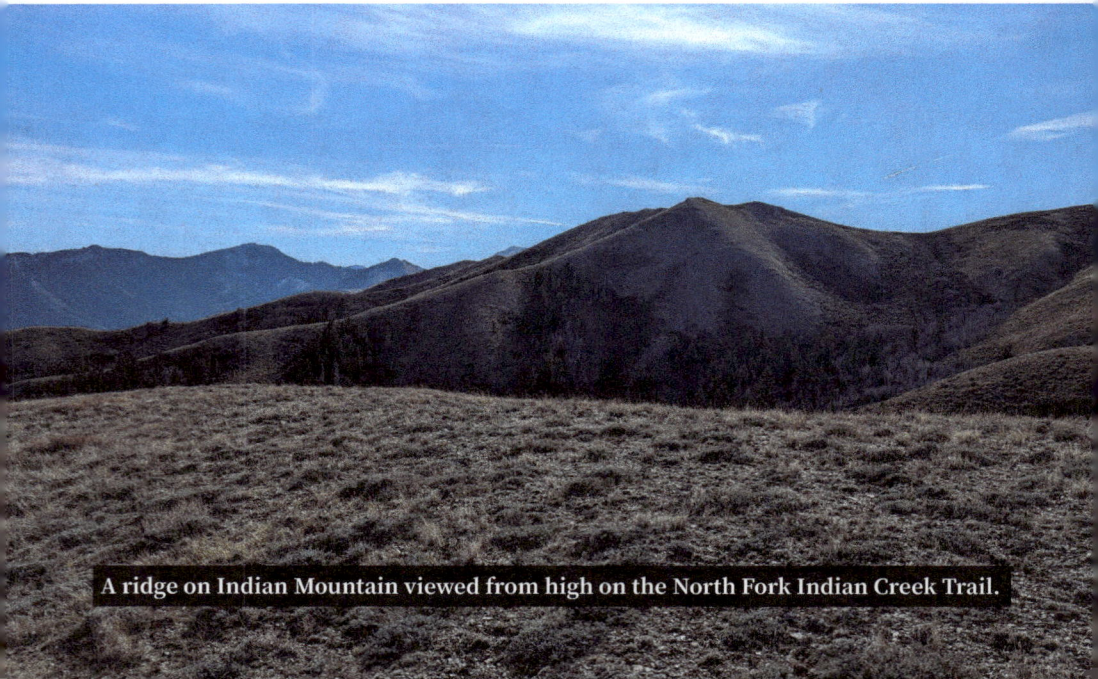

A ridge on Indian Mountain viewed from high on the North Fork Indian Creek Trail.

Lead Draw - Motorcycle Trail

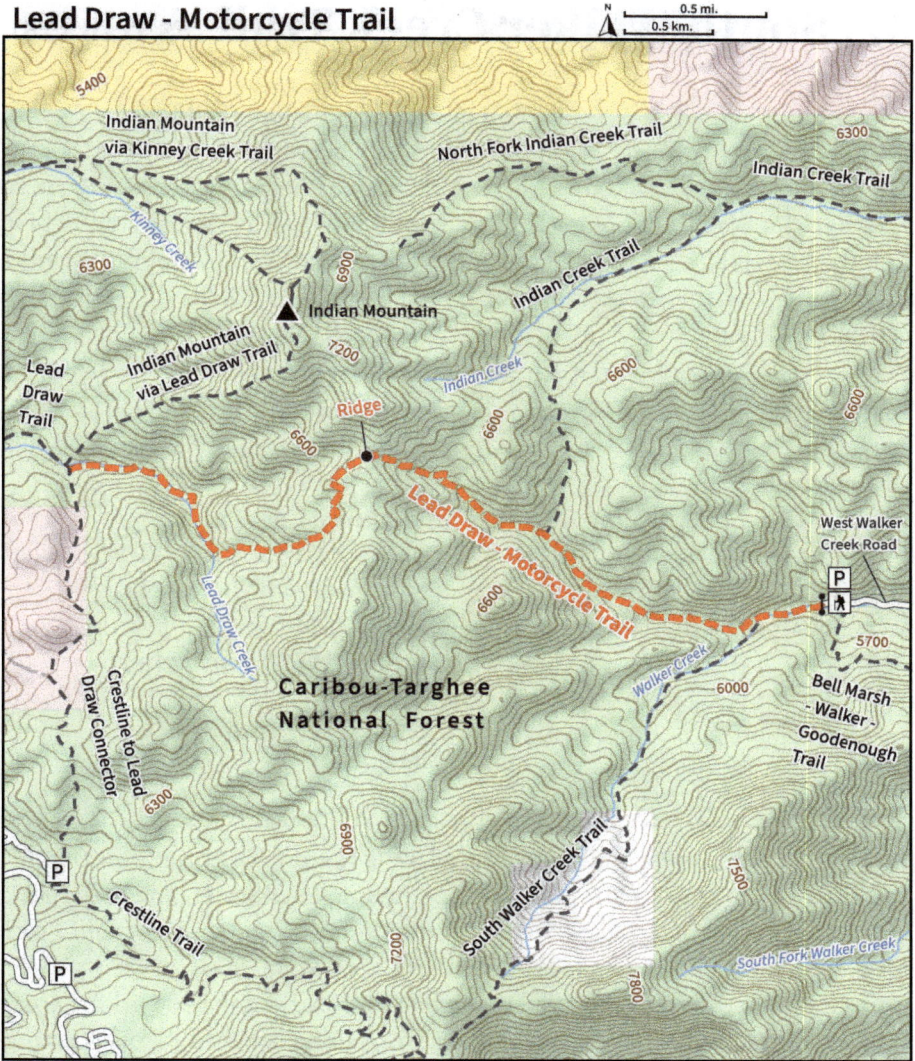

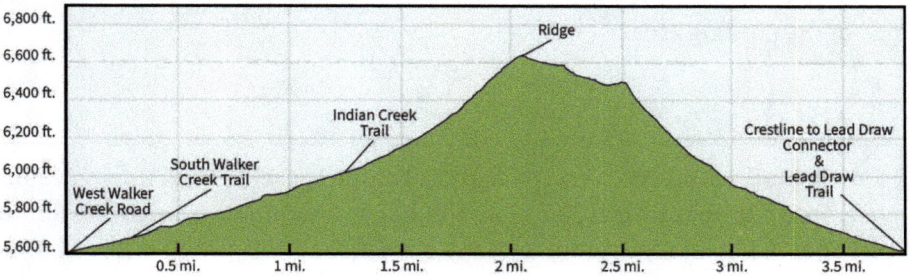

N
0.5 mi.
0.5 km.

Indian Mountain
via Kinney Creek Trail

North Fork Indian Creek Trail

Indian Creek Trail

6300

5400

Kinney Creek

6300

6900

▲ Indian Mountain

Indian Creek Trail

Indian Mountain
via Lead Draw Trail

7200

Indian Creek

Lead
Draw
Trail

6600

6600

Ridge

6600

6600

6600

Lead Draw - Motorcycle Trail

West Walker
Creek Road

P

Lead Draw Creek

6600

5700

Crestline to Lead Draw Connector

Caribou-Targhee
National Forest

Walker Creek

6000

Bell Marsh
- Walker -
Goodenough
Trail

6300

6900

South Walker Creek Trail

7500

P

Crestline Trail

7200

7800

South Fork Walker Creek

P

6,800 ft.

Ridge

6,600 ft.

6,400 ft.

Indian Creek
Trail

6,200 ft.

Crestline to Lead Draw
Connector
&
Lead Draw
Trail

6,000 ft.

South Walker
Creek Trail

5,800 ft.

West Walker
Creek Road

5,600 ft.

0.5 mi.   1 mi.   1.5 mi.   2 mi.   2.5 mi.   3 mi.   3.5 mi.

52. South Walker Creek Trail (FS Trail 115)

The South Walker Creek Trail is a challenging hike alongside the forested Walker Creek that eventually rewards you with a beautiful view of Scout Mountain. While there is an almost constant incline, the beginning half of the hike is rather pleasant as the route follows a wide 4x4 trail. The last half of the hike follows a steep and wild singletrack, which can be difficult to follow. About 1 mile of the trail crosses private property. During that stretch of the hike, it is crucial to stay on the trail and practice proper trail etiquette.

Distance: 6.2 miles out-and-back
Elevation Gain: 2,240 feet
Difficulty: Strenuous
Hiking Time: About 4.5 hours
Nearest Town: Inkom
Trail Surface: Dirt, rock
Wheelchair Access: None

Dog-Friendly: Yes; on-leash at the trailhead. May be off-leash if under control once on the trail
Amenities: None
Contact: Caribou-Targhee National Forest, Westside Ranger District 208-236-7500
Trailhead GPS Coordinates: N42° 43.572' W112° 18.572'

Getting There

From I-15 south of Pocatello, take Exit 58 for Inkom. Turn right on I-15BL/ Old Highway 30 West. In 0.7 miles, turn right onto Park Street, and then in 0.2 miles, make a left onto West Portneuf Road. Continue on West Portneuf Road for 5.2 miles. Turn right onto West Walker Creek Road. Stay on West Walker Creek Road for 3.9 miles until you reach the trailhead at an open parking area. While the first half-mile of West Walker Creek Road is paved, the remaining 3.4 miles are on a dirt road. All-Wheel-Drive is not required, but it does make the drive quite a bit easier. The trailhead begins past a gate on the southwest side of the parking area.

The Hike

From the trailhead, head west through the gate on the wide Lead Draw - Motorcycle Trail. At about 0.2 miles, you will come to a junction with the South Walker Creek Trail on your left (south). Keep left at this junction to join onto

A hiker on the high ridge of South Walker Creek Trail.

the South Walker Creek Trail. The trail travels southwest for the next 1.2 miles alongside the heavily forested Walker Creek. While there is consistent elevation gain, this is an enjoyable, occasionally rocky, stretch of the hike.

At 1.4 miles, the trail passes to the left of a green gate, signifying the transition from U.S. Forest Service land to private property. The trail makes a right (west) turn at 1.7 miles as it leaves the creek to cross over a ridge, where once on the other side of the ridge, the trail levels out. At about 2.1 miles, the 4x4 path turns to the left (southeast) and stops at a dead end. As you continue toward the dead end, look for a wild singletrack trail on the southeast (right) side of the 4x4 trail that leads into the forest. This is the path you will merge onto to continue on the South Walker Creek Trail.

Once on the singletrack trail, the path begins to climb, gaining 500 feet in 0.4 mile as it climbs through a steep and rocky forest. The trail levels out at about 2.4 miles, just before crossing over to the west side of Walker Creek.

Once across the creek at about 2.5 miles, the trail transitions back to U.S. Forest Service land, ending the private property stretch of the hike. Just past the creek, turn left (southwest) to stay on route as the trail enters a steep forest.

The trail gains 400 feet from the creek in 0.3 miles, until it crests atop a high ridge. Before you reach the ridge, the path can be hard to follow, so be sure to go slowly to stay on route. The trail reaches the top of the ridge at about 2.8 miles, where you will find your first view of Scout Mountain. This makes for a great spot to take a break and enjoy the excellent views. To continue on the South Walker Creek Trail, ignore the unofficial trail that crosses to the east and west atop the ridge between two hills. Instead, look for a singletrack trail that heads southwest across the hillside toward Scout Mountain.

With most of the route's incline out of the way, the remainder is a pleasant walk with great views of the area. At 3.2 miles, the trail reaches another ridge before descending west. The trail ends when it connects with the Crestline Trail.

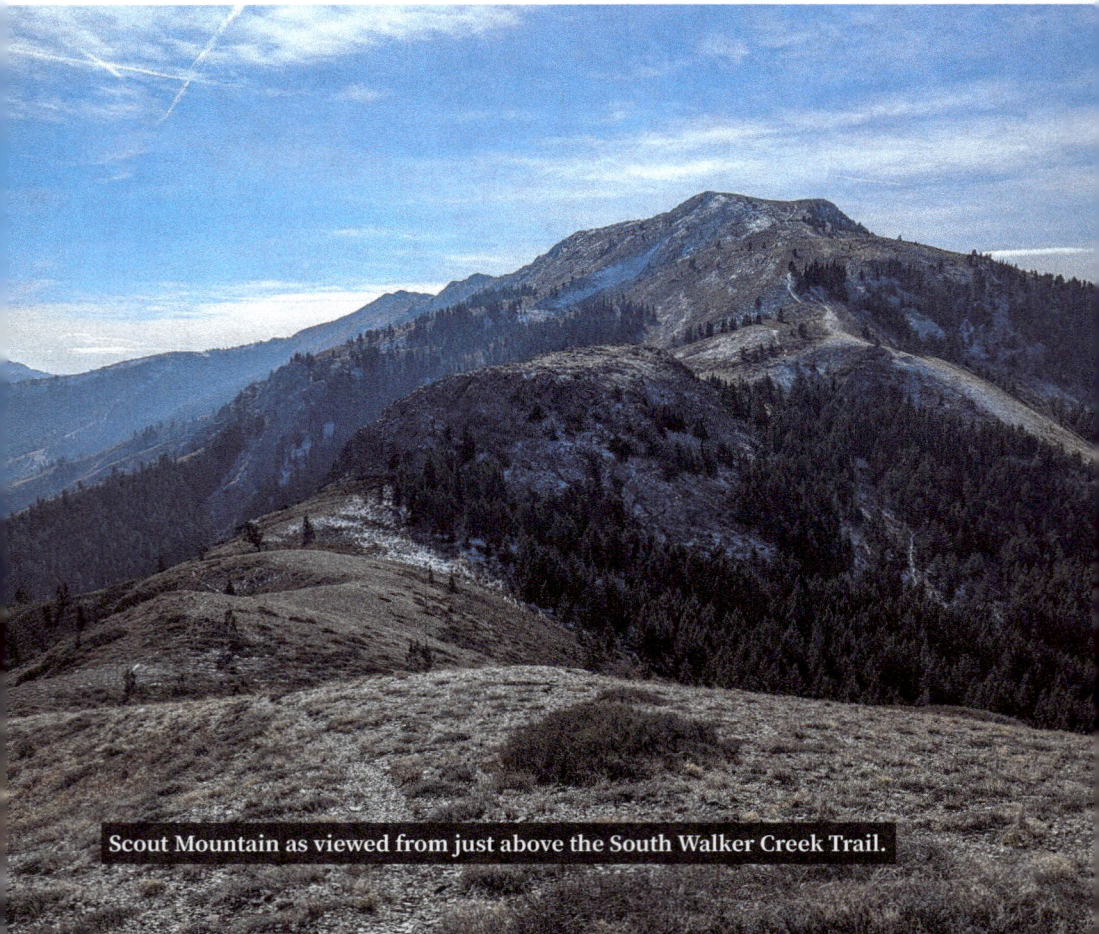

Scout Mountain as viewed from just above the South Walker Creek Trail.

South Walker Creek Trail

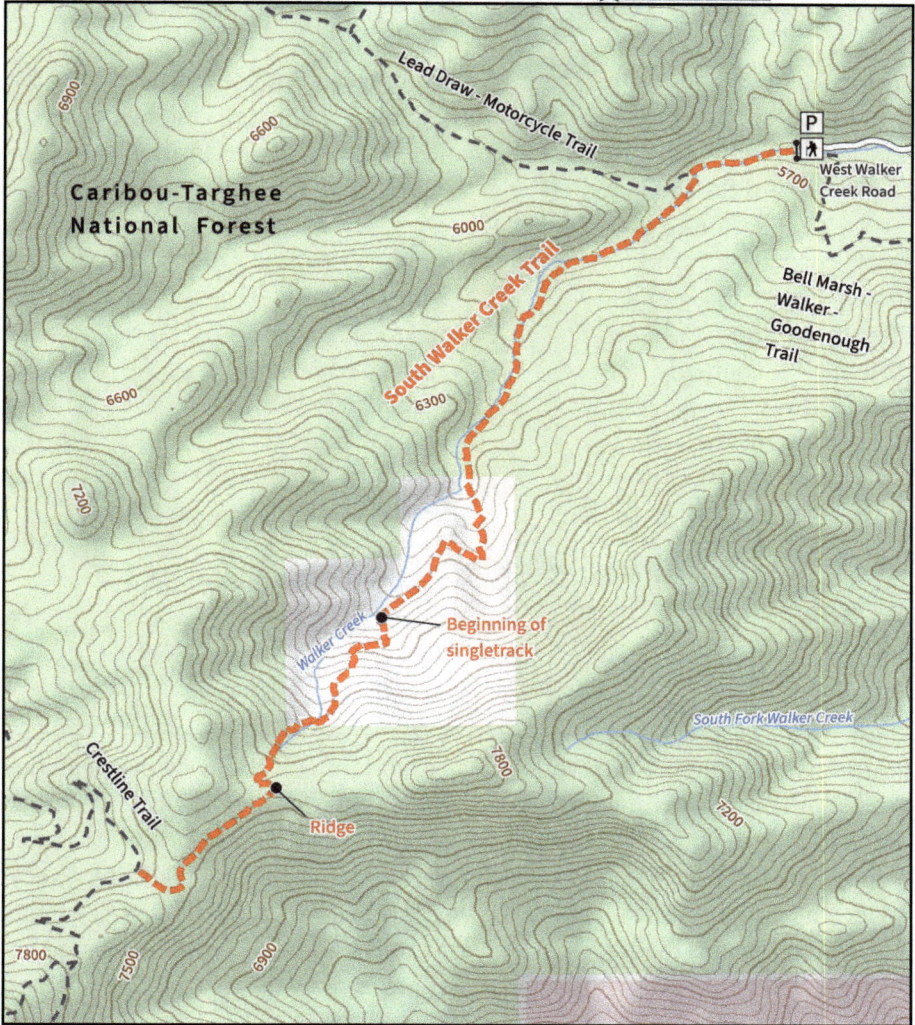

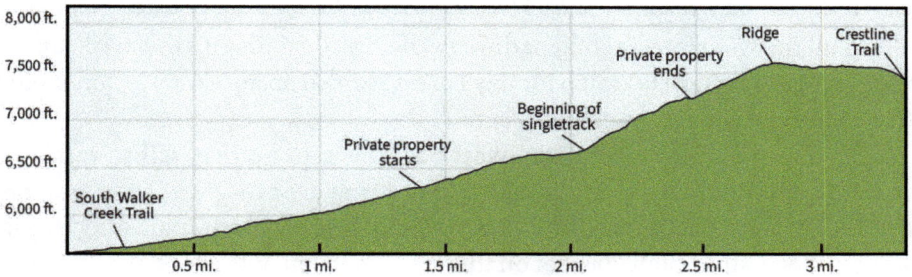

N

0.5 mi.

0.5 km.

Lead Draw - Motorcycle Trail

6900

6600

Caribou-Targhee
National Forest

6000

P

West Walker
Creek Road

5700

Bell Marsh -
Walker -
Goodenough
Trail

South Walker Creek Trail

6300

6600

7200

Walker Creek

Beginning of
singletrack

South Fork Walker Creek

7800

7200

Crestline Trail

Ridge

7800

7500

6900

Elevation profile

8,000 ft.

7,500 ft.

7,000 ft.

6,500 ft.

6,000 ft.

South Walker
Creek Trail

Private property
starts

Beginning of
singletrack

Private property
ends

Ridge

Crestline
Trail

0.5 mi.   1 mi.   1.5 mi.   2 mi.   2.5 mi.   3 mi.

53. Blind Springs Trail (FS Trail 127)

Featuring unique views of Scout Mountain and an opportunity to traverse cross-country ski slopes in the summer, the Blind Springs Trail is a pleasant hike that links the Valve House Trail to the East Mink Creek Nordic Center. For an overview of the individual trails at the East Mink Creek Nordic Center, visit the East Mink Creek Nordic Center Trail Overview on page 434.

Distance: 4.9 miles out-and-back
Elevation Gain: 1,130 feet
Difficulty: Moderately strenuous
Hiking Time: About 3 hours
Nearest Town: Pocatello
Trail Surface: Dirt, rock
Wheelchair Access: None

Dog-Friendly: Yes; on-leash at the trailhead. May be off-leash if under control once on the trail
Amenities: Vault toilets are available at the trailhead.
Contact: Caribou-Targhee National Forest, Westside Ranger District 208-236-7500
Trailhead GPS Coordinates: N42° 43.010' W112° 22.708'

Getting There

From the junction of South Valley Road and Bannock Highway in Pocatello, head southeast on Bannock Highway for 6.8 miles. (The road becomes Mink Creek Road at 2.3 miles.) Following the sign for the Mink Creek Nordic Center, turn left past the prominent corner mailboxes onto East Fork Mink Creek Road, which you will stay on for 1.8 miles. Turn right onto Forest Service Road 524, which reaches the large parking area in 0.4 miles. The trail is located on the west side of the parking area past the gate.

The Hike

Given all the wide intersecting pathways, the first 0.8 miles on this trail can be confusing, so be sure to watch for any Forest Service posts with "127" on them. This will keep you on the correct route.

From the parking lot, head west past the gate on the trail toward the Nordic Center. When you enter the large clearing near the yurt, head west on the trail to the right of the white garage. There will be a sign indicating this is a snowshoe path. About 300 feet on this trail, keep left at the fork, where at 0.2

Hikers on Blind Springs Trail.

miles, you will emerge at a junction. Join the trail on your left, which skiers will recognize as the Red Fox ski trail, and continue heading uphill to the west.

At 0.5 miles, keep right (northwest) at the fork, onto a path that skiers will recognize as Deer Trail. At 0.6 miles, you will come to a junction. Continue straight (northwest) on the trail, which skiers will recognize as Lagomorph. At 0.8 miles, turn left (southwest) at the "127" sign.

With the maze of forested trails behind you, continue on this rocky and shadeless stretch of trail, enjoying the views of the Nordic area and Scout Mountain to the southeast. At about 1.2 miles, you will reach the high point near a gate between two hills. Continue on the trail past the gate as it descends a sage and grass ravine toward Blind Spring.

Once the trail enters the forest, watch for a right (northwest) turn at around 1.7 miles. Make the right turn, avoiding the Upper Blind Springs Trail that continues south. The remainder of the hike descends alongside the trickling Blind Spring. At 1.9 miles, pass through a cattle gate. Beyond that gate, the trail passes below a large rock outcropping on the path's right (north) side. The trail ends when it connects with the Valve House Trail.

Keep Going

At the 1.7-mile mark, continuing straight (south) instead of turning right (west) would begin the **Upper Blind Springs Trail** (Forest Service Trail 140). This lesser-used 4x4 road is 0.9-miles long and connects to the Overlook Trail near a junction with Valve House Trail. The first half of this path can be steep as it climbs 250 feet out of the creek, but once atop the sage hillside, you have lovely views of the evergreen forest surrounding Valve House Trail.

The Pocatello Sunrise Lions Club Disc Golf Complex, situated at the East Mink Creek Nordic Center, features two 18-hole disc golf courses. With Scout Mountain as the backdrop, the course makes for a scenic summer escape from the city.

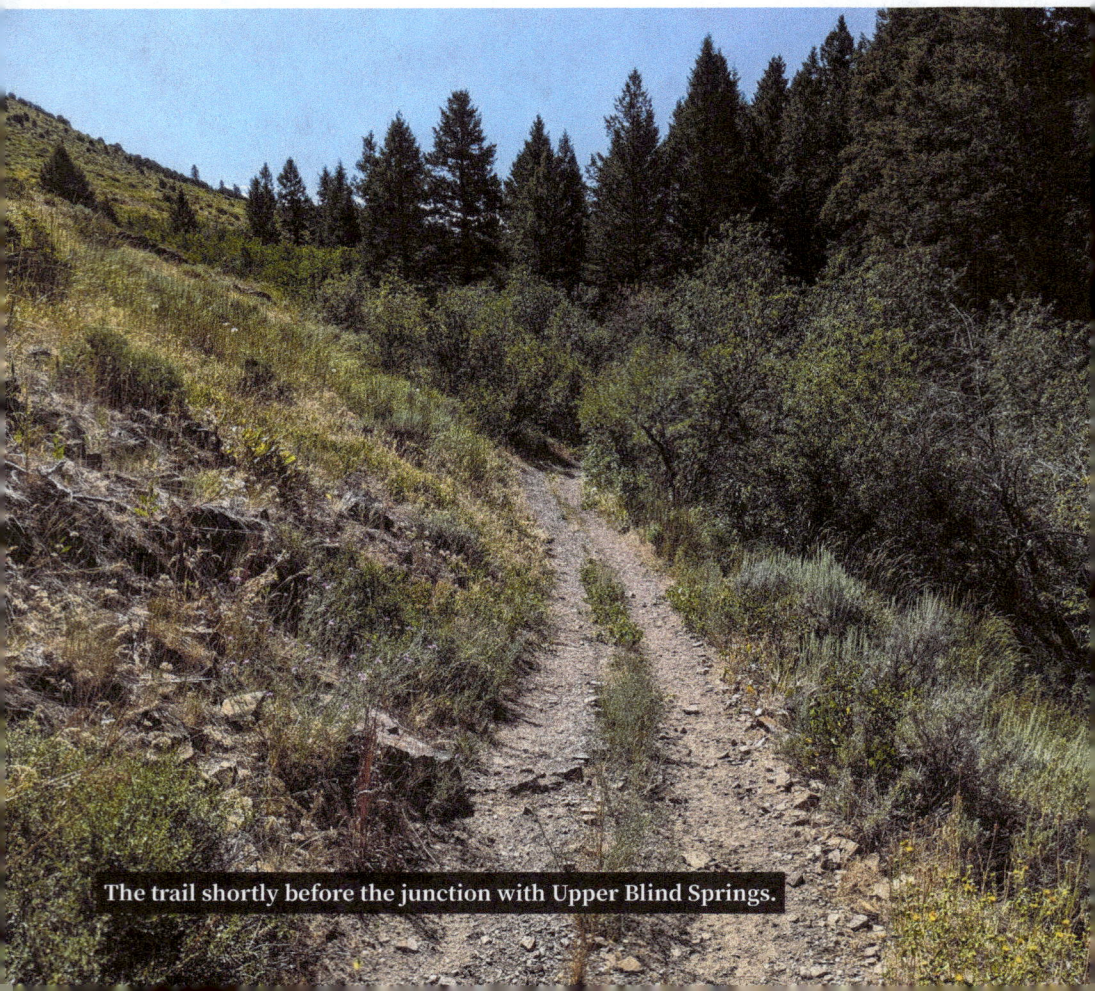

The trail shortly before the junction with Upper Blind Springs.

Blind Springs Trail

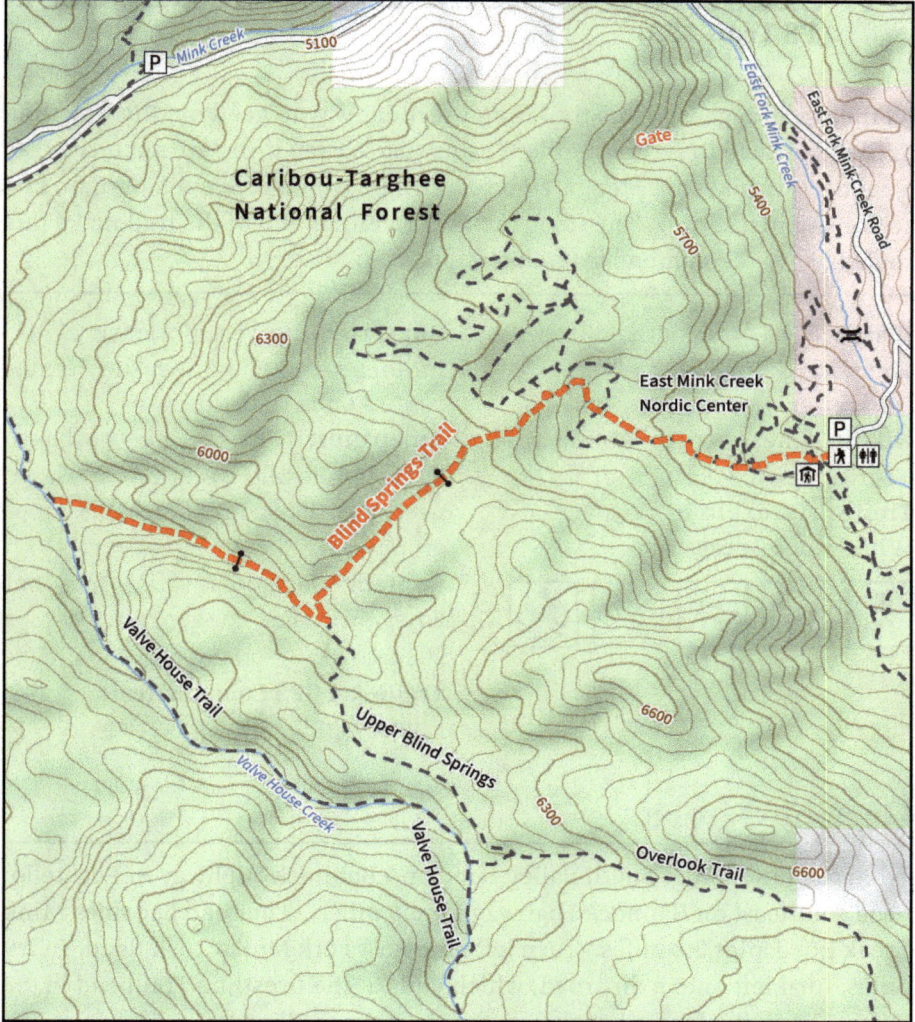

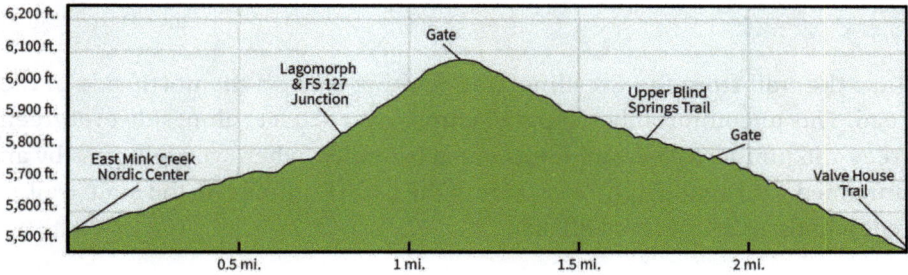

N

0.5 mi.

0.5 km.

5100

P Mink Creek

Gate

East Fork Mink Creek

East Fork Mink Creek Road

Caribou-Targhee National Forest

5400

5700

6300

East Mink Creek Nordic Center

6000

P

Blind Springs Trail

Valve House Trail

Upper Blind Springs

6600

Valve House Creek

Valve House Trail

6300

Overlook Trail

6600

6,200 ft.

6,100 ft.

6,000 ft.

5,900 ft.

5,800 ft.

5,700 ft.

5,600 ft.

5,500 ft.

Gate

Lagomorph & FS 127 Junction

Upper Blind Springs Trail

Gate

East Mink Creek Nordic Center

Valve House Trail

0.5 mi.   1 mi.   1.5 mi.   2 mi.

54. Crestline to Lead Draw Connector
(FS Trail 133)

As the name suggests, this trail is an excellent way to get from the Crestline Trail to the Lead Draw area without using roads. Even if you are not using it as a connecting hike, this steep trail offers striking views of Scout Mountain in a seldom-visited setting. The steep inclines on either end of the trail make this route hard to recommend to mountain bikers.

Distance: 4.4 miles out-and-back
Elevation Gain: 1,320 feet
Difficulty: Moderately strenuous
Hiking Time: About 2.5 hours
Nearest Town: Pocatello
Trail Surface: Dirt, rock
Wheelchair Access: None

Dog-Friendly: Yes; on-leash at the trailhead. May be off-leash if under control once on the trail
Amenities: None at the trailhead. Vault toilets and water are available nearby at the Scout Mountain Campground.
Contact: Caribou-Targhee National Forest, Westside Ranger District 208-236-7500
Trailhead GPS Coordinates: N42° 42.433' W112° 21.749'

Getting There

From the junction of South Valley Road and Bannock Highway in Pocatello, head southeast on Bannock Highway for 6.8 miles. (The road becomes Mink Creek Road after 2.3 miles.) Turn left onto East Fork Mink Creek Road. In 2.9 miles, turn left onto a dirt road, which ends at the Crestline Trailhead in 0.3 miles. The trail is located on the north side of the trailhead.

The Hike

Take the trail from the Crestline Trail parking area on the north side of the road. This uncomfortably steep trail climbs over 450 feet alongside evergreen trees and junipers. The trail levels out at 0.7 miles, where you will pass by an unnamed path on the right (east) side of the path. Continue on the main trail as it descends a sage-covered hillside.

The Crestline to Lead Draw Connector at sunset.

At around 1.1 miles, keep right (north) at the junction. Just beyond that junction, the trail shifts to the northeast and climbs a slight rise to the right of a hill. As you near the top of the rise, at 1.3 miles, you will pass over a cattle guard, where beyond that, you will continue northeast through a junction.

The remaining stretch of the route descends a steep dry creek drainage, losing over 500 feet in just under a mile. The trail ends at a junction with the Lead Draw Trail on the left (west) and the Lead Draw Motorcycle Trail on the right (east).

Sagebrush is a familiar sight on many of the hikes in this book. The big sagebrush, a species of sagebrush found in the area, can survive for more than a century and provides vital food and shelter for various species, such as sage grouse, pronghorn, and mule deer. Native Americans have used the plant for medicinal purposes throughout history.

Crestline to Lead Draw Connector

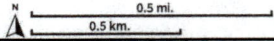

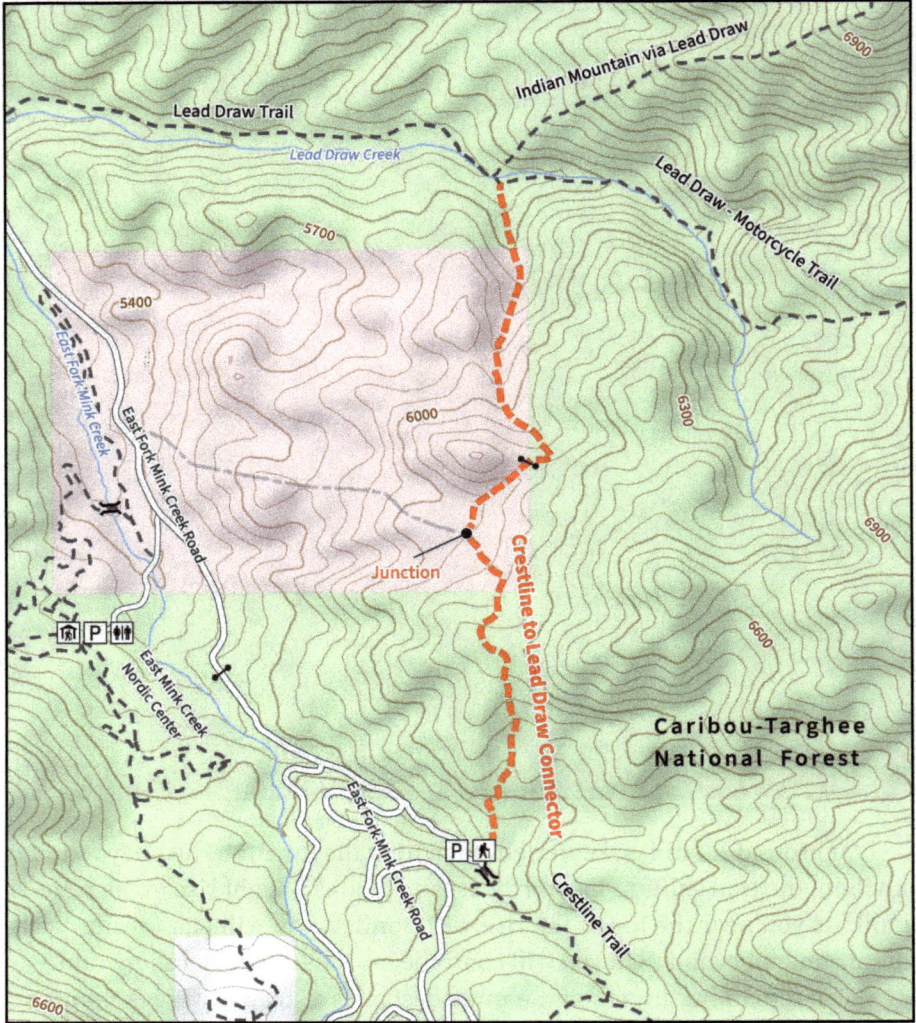

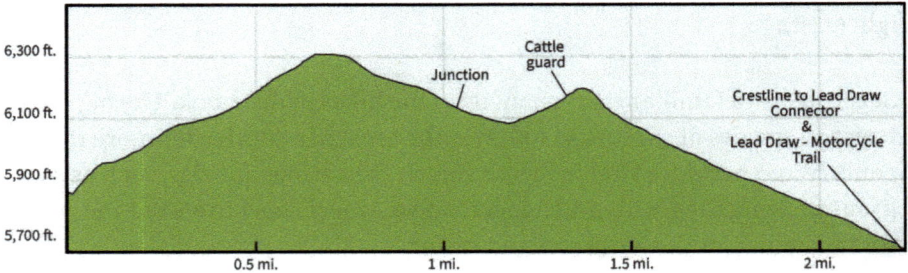

N

0.5 mi.

0.5 km.

Indian Mountain via Lead Draw

6900

Lead Draw Trail

Lead Draw Creek

Lead Draw - Motorcycle Trail

5700

5400

East Fork Mink Creek

East Fork Mink Creek Road

6300

6000

Junction

6900

Crestline to Lead Draw Connector

6600

P

East Mink Creek Nordic Center

East Fork Mink Creek Road

Caribou-Targhee National Forest

P

Crestline Trail

6600

6,300 ft.

6,100 ft.

5,900 ft.

5,700 ft.

Junction

Cattle guard

Crestline to Lead Draw Connector & Lead Draw - Motorcycle Trail

0.5 mi.   1 mi.   1.5 mi.   2 mi.

55. Crestline Trail (FS Trail 148)

Of the many hikes on Scout Mountain, Crestline Trail is the only one that runs along the mountain's eastern face, providing a unique perspective in the Bannock Range and some particularly nice views of the Bell Marsh Creek area. The first half of the trail takes you through a thick conifer forest, providing cooling shade for the hot summer months, while the upper half is mainly above the treeline alongside steep hillsides and brush. The upper section's narrow trail and loose rock can be challenging for mountain bikers, though it makes for an excellent hike.

Distance: 11.1 miles out-and-back; 7.2 miles round trip for the rocky viewpoint below the summit

Elevation Gain: 2,620 feet; 1,820 feet

Difficulty: Very Strenuous; Strenuous

Hiking Time: About 6.5 hours; about 4.5 hours

Nearest Town: Pocatello

Trail Surface: Dirt, rock

Wheelchair Access: None

Dog-Friendly: Yes; on-leash at the trailhead. May be off-leash if under control once on the trail

Amenities: None at the trailhead. Vault toilets and water are available nearby at the Scout Mountain Campground.

Contact: Caribou-Targhee National Forest, Westside Ranger District 208-236-7500

Trailhead GPS Coordinates: N42° 42.415' W112° 21.747'

Getting There

From the junction of South Valley Road and Bannock Highway in Pocatello, head southeast on Bannock Highway for 6.8 miles. (The road becomes Mink Creek Road after 2.3 miles.) Turn left onto East Fork Mink Creek Road. In 2.9 miles, turn left onto a dirt road, which ends at the Crestline Trailhead in 0.3 miles. The trail begins on the southeast side of the trailhead.

The Hike

From the trailhead, head southeast on the singletrack path and cross over the creek. The trail climbs a short but steep hill into the forest just beyond the creek. This hill signifies the start of the trail's incline, which, while not aggres-

Crestline Trail near its junction with Scout Mountain Top Road.

sively steep, is constant over the next 4 miles.

At 0.6 miles, the trail passes by the **Scout-Crestline Connector** (Forest Service Trail 151), on its right (west) side. (This side trail is about 0.3-miles long and ends at the East Fork Mink Creek Road about 1 mile below the East Fork Mink Creek Trailhead.) About 2.0 miles in, the trail exits the forest and presents you with a beautiful view of Scout Mountain's northern face. For the next mile and a half, the path weaves in and out of the open hillsides and forests as it ascends toward a large rocky outcropping. At 3.1 miles, you will pass by the South Walker Creek Trail on your left (east).

At about 3.6 miles, the trail climbs a minor hill to a rock formation, bringing Scout Mountain into view. This rocky viewpoint is an excellent resting spot as you decide whether to continue on Crestline Trail, ascend Scout Mountain, or return back to the trailhead. Two trails branch off from this viewpoint and are commonly mislabeled. The right (southwest) path, **Scout Mountain Ridge**

Trail (Forest Service Trail 165), is a 1.1 mile non-motorized trail that climbs to the summit of Scout Mountain and is frequently incorrectly referred to as Crestline Trail. The left (south) path is the actual Crestline Trail.

Take the left path to stay on Crestline Trail. For the remainder of the hike, the trail travels high on the east face of Scout Mountain, providing Southeast Idaho's equivalent of alpine views in a largely treeless environment. This section can feel exposed as it digs in along rocky ledges, making for occasionally tense terrain for mountain bikers. At about 4.0 miles, the trail reaches its high point (8,100 feet). The path remains largely level from here, though there is one downhill section that will be a welcome change for the legs. The trail ends at an intersection with Scout Mountain Top Road.

One of Pocatello's more interesting destinations is the Museum of Clean. This museum houses numerous educational exhibits that showcase the history of cleaning tools and techniques and promotes the importance of cleanliness for health and well-being. The museum, founded by Don Aslett in 2006, is home to the world's first vacuum cleaner.

Crestline Trail in autumn.

Crestline Trail

N
0.5 mi.
0.5 km.

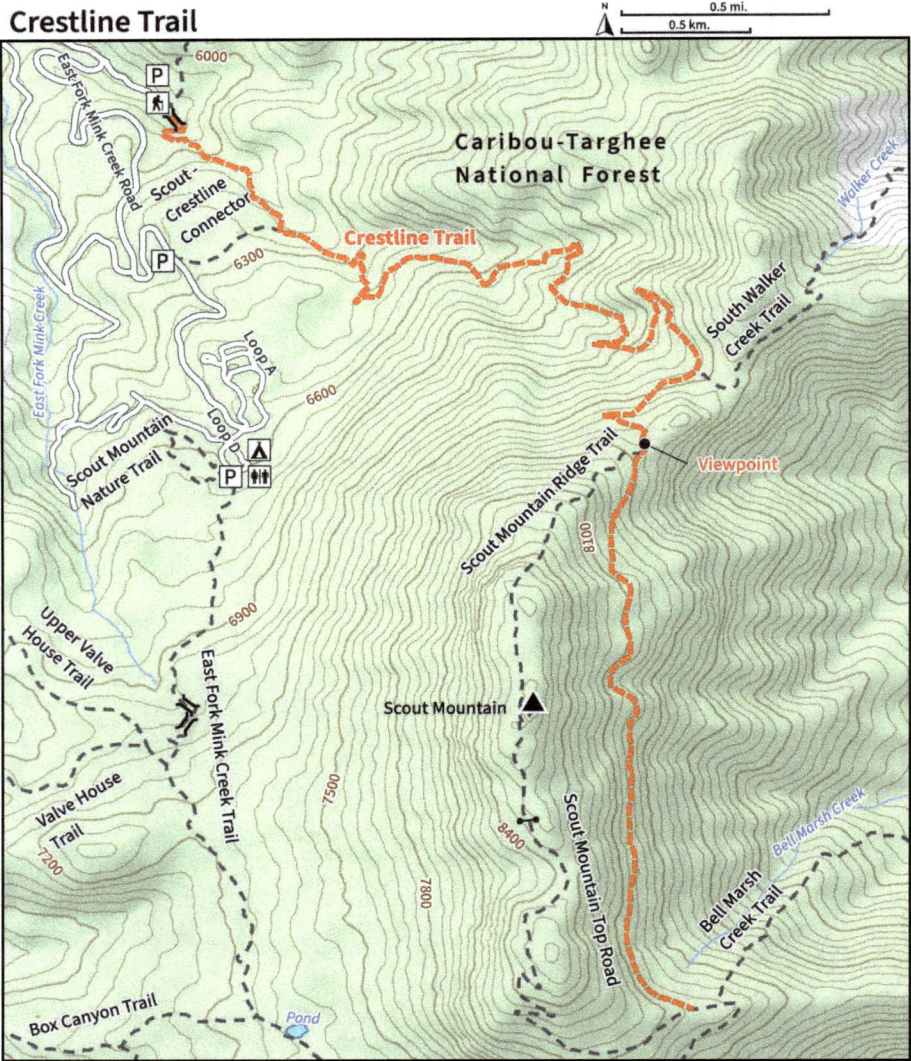

East Fork Mink Creek Road

P

Scout-Crestline Connector

Caribou-Targhee National Forest

Crestline Trail

6000
6300
6600

Loop A
Loop D

Scout Mountain Nature Trail

P

East Fork Mink Creek Trail

South Walker Creek Trail

Walker Creek

Scout Mountain Ridge Trail

Viewpoint

8100

6900

Upper Valve House Trail

7500

Scout Mountain

7200

Valve House Trail

7800

8400

Scout Mountain Top Road

Bell Marsh Creek

Bell Marsh Creek Trail

Box Canyon Trail

Pond

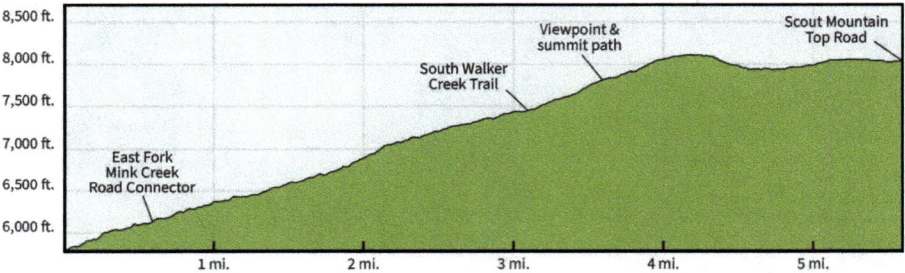

8,500 ft.
8,000 ft.
7,500 ft.
7,000 ft.
6,500 ft.
6,000 ft.

Viewpoint & summit path

Scout Mountain Top Road

South Walker Creek Trail

East Fork Mink Creek Road Connector

1 mi.   2 mi.   3 mi.   4 mi.   5 mi.

56. Scout Mountain Nature Trail
(FS Trail 172)

The Scout Mountain Nature Trail is a short, pleasant nature walk near the Scout Mountain Campground with a beautiful view of the namesake mountain. There are many benches along the path, as well as signs identifying local foliage, making it a fun route for families. An overlook at the midpoint of the loop is a particular highlight, giving a panoramic view of the East Fork Mink Creek area. Although the trail can be overgrown in some places, the easy access, informative signs, and expansive views make it easy to recommend.

Distance: 0.7-mile loop
Elevation Gain: 60 feet
Difficulty: Easy
Hiking Time: About 30 minutes
Nearest Town: Pocatello
Trail Surface: Dirt, rock
Wheelchair Access: None

Dog-Friendly: Yes; on-leash at the trailhead and at the campground. May be off-leash if under control once on the trail
Amenities: Vault toilets and water are available at the Scout Mountain Campground.
Contact: Caribou-Targhee National Forest, Westside Ranger District 208-236-7500
Trailhead GPS Coordinates: N42° 41.362' W112° 21.592'

Getting There

From the junction of South Valley Road and Bannock Highway in Pocatello, head southeast on Bannock Highway for 6.8 miles. (The road becomes Mink Creek Road after 2.3 miles.) Turn left onto East Fork Mink Creek Road, which you will stay on for 5.3 miles as it climbs toward Scout Mountain. At the roundabout, make the first right turn and then make a left turn shortly beyond that into the southern Scout Mountain Campground (Loop D). Keep right to start the loop, and then keep right again in about 200 yards to find the East Fork Mink Creek Trailhead, which has plenty of parking. The trail is about 40 yards back toward the campground, across the cattle guard on the west side of the road, next to the large "Scout Mountain Nature Trail" sign.

The Hike

From the trailhead, head west on the singletrack trail that begins next to the "Scout Mountain Nature Trail" sign. After about 100 feet, you will come to the beginning of the loop, where you can turn left or right. This family-friendly loop can be completed in either direction, though the recommended route is clockwise (left). Both directions travel through the evergreen forest before emerging from the trees in the northern stretch of the loop, where you will find a striking view of Scout Mountain and the overlook. The overlook has a wide bench, making it an excellent spot for a snack break.

The Idaho Museum of Natural History, situated at Idaho State University, houses an impressive collection of Idaho's natural wonders. The exhibits on display depict the diverse and vibrant ecosystems of the region, showcase the anthropologic history of the area, and also feature ancient fossils. One of the museum's main attractions is an exhibit on the Hagerman Horse, which is Idaho's official state fossil.

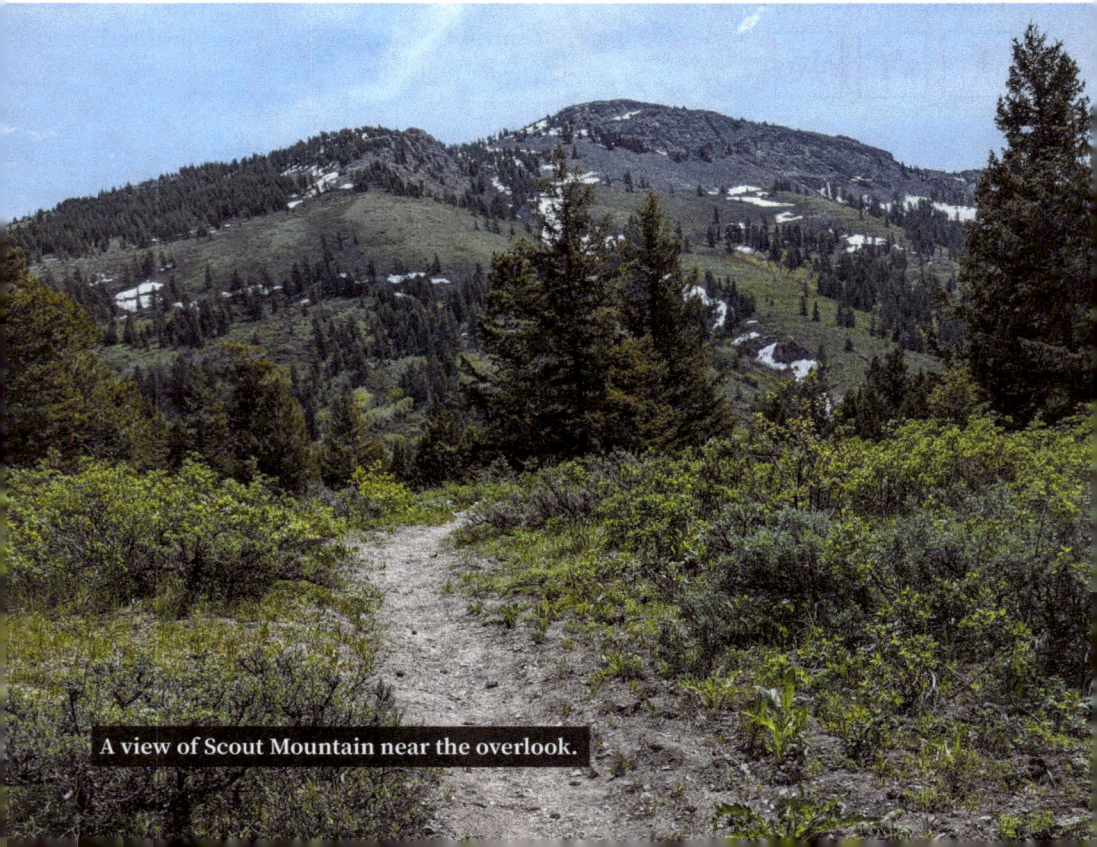

A view of Scout Mountain near the overlook.

Scout Mountain Nature Trail

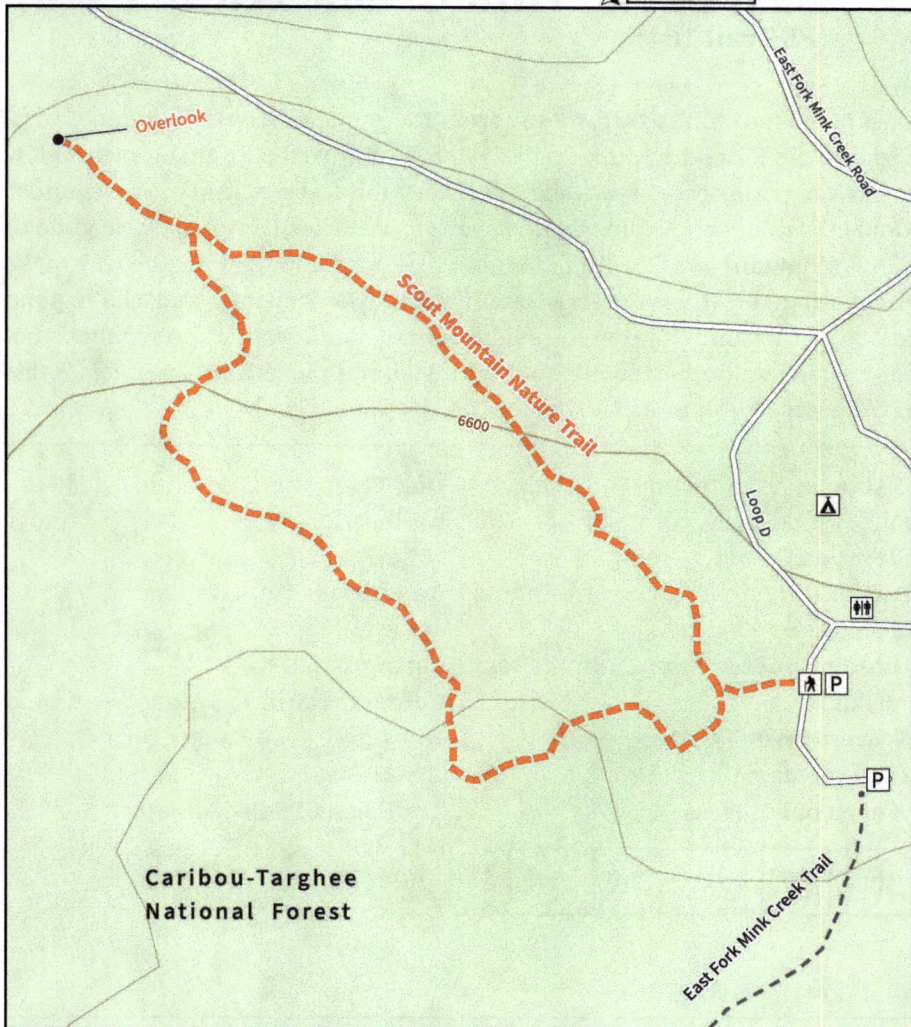

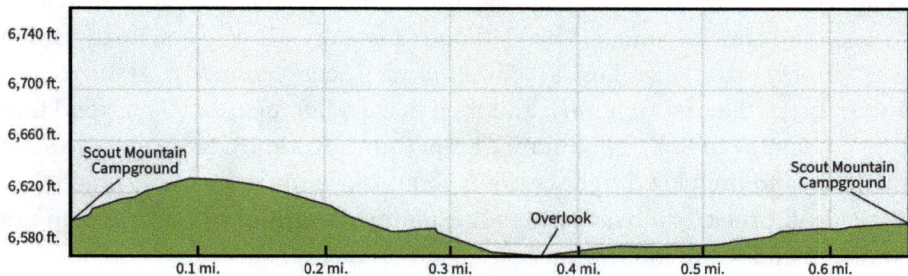

N

0.05 mi.

0.05 km.

Overlook

Scout Mountain Nature Trail

East Fork Mink Creek Road

6600

Loop D

P

East Fork Mink Creek Trail

P

Caribou-Targhee
National Forest

6,740 ft.

6,700 ft.

6,660 ft.

6,620 ft.

6,580 ft.

Scout Mountain
Campground

Overlook

Scout Mountain
Campground

0.1 mi.   0.2 mi.   0.3 mi.   0.4 mi.   0.5 mi.   0.6 mi.

57. East Fork Mink Creek Trail
(FS Trail 164)

Located just a stone's throw away from the popular Scout Mountain Campground, the East Fork Mink Creek Trail is a well-used path that travels below Scout Mountain's rocky west face. For hikers, this forested trail traverses under Douglas fir, lodgepole pines, and aspens as it makes its way to the saddle of Scout Mountain and Old Tom Mountain. High meadows along the way make for excellent locations for early-season wildflower viewings, and a large pond about 2 miles into the route provides an excellent destination for those not interested in climbing Scout Mountain. Mountain bikers will appreciate this trail's accessible approach to the top of Valve House Trail.

Distance: 7.1 miles out-and-back; 4.4 miles round trip to the pond
Elevation Gain: 1,260 feet; 750 feet
Difficulty: Moderately strenuous; Moderate
Hiking Time: About 4 hours; about 2.5 hours
Nearest Town: Pocatello
Trail Surface: Dirt, rock
Wheelchair Access: None

Dog-Friendly: Yes; on-leash at the trailhead. May be off-leash if under control once on the trail
Amenities: Vault toilets and water are available at the Scout Mountain Campground.
Contact: Caribou-Targhee National Forest, Westside Ranger District 208-236-7500
Trailhead GPS Coordinates: N42° 41.333' W112° 21.574'

Getting There

From the junction of South Valley Road and Bannock Highway in Pocatello, head southeast on Bannock Highway for 6.8 miles. (The road becomes Mink Creek Road after 2.3 miles.) Turn left onto East Fork Mink Creek Road, which you will stay on for 5.3 miles as it climbs toward Scout Mountain. At the roundabout, make the first right turn and then make a left turn shortly beyond that into the southern Scout Mountain Campground (Loop D). Keep right to start the loop, and then keep right again in about 200 yards to find the signed East Fork Mink Creek Trailhead, which has plenty of parking. The trail is on the southern end of the trailhead.

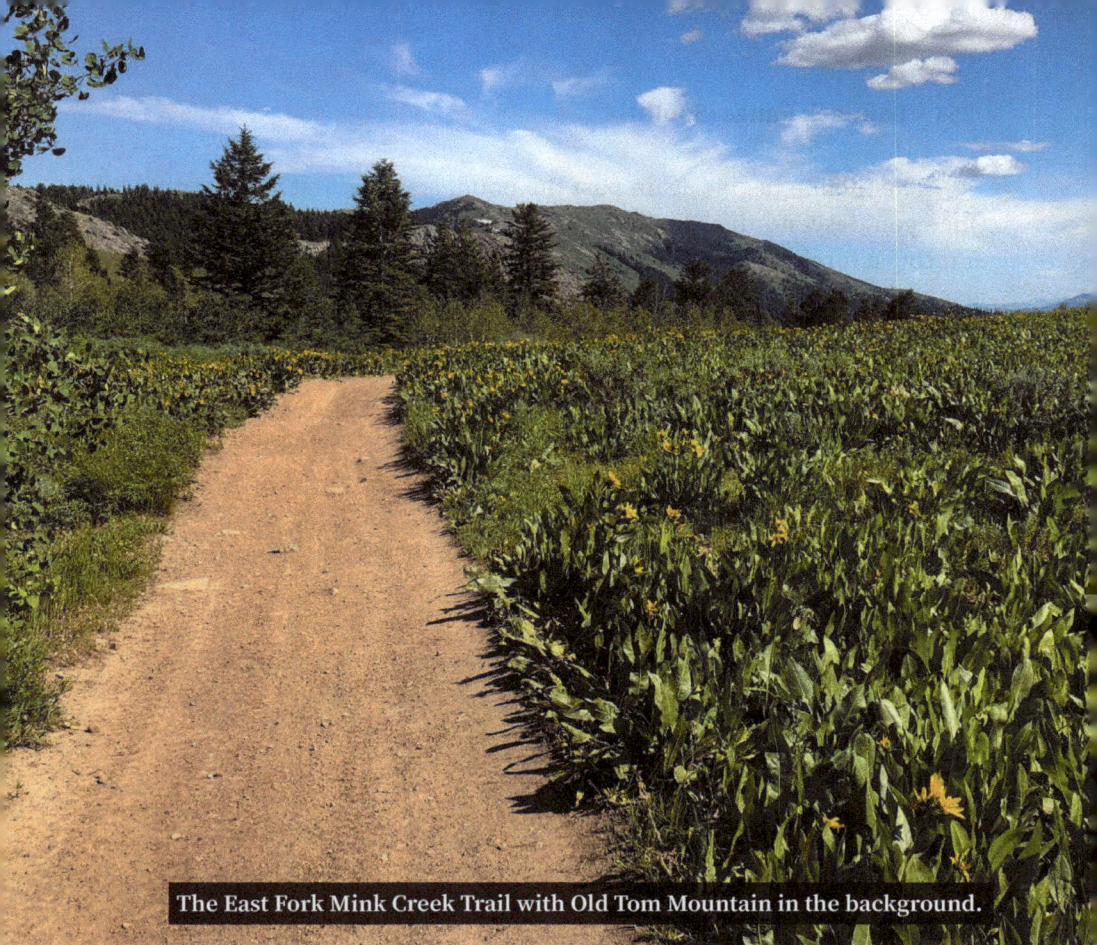
The East Fork Mink Creek Trail with Old Tom Mountain in the background.

The Hike

From the signed trailhead, head south on the well-used 4x4 path. This steadily uphill trail traverses below Scout Mountain's west face among the evergreen trees. You will cross over the creek three times on this early stretch of the hike, with the first being at about 0.8 miles, followed by two more back-to-back crossings just short of the 1.0 mile mark. At about 1.1 miles, you will come to a junction with the Valve House Trail, where you will keep left (south) to stay on the East Fork Mink Creek Trail.

At 1.3 miles, the trail plateaus as you emerge into a large meadow from the forest. In the early summer, this meadow is filled with wildflowers. About 2.1 miles into the hike, you will continue straight to pass by Box Canyon Trail. You will come to a large pond shortly past this junction at about 2.2 miles into the hike, which is a great place to rest and take in the view of Scout Mountain. For those who want to keep the elevation gain to a minimum, the pond is also a perfect point to turn around.

The incline begins again past the pond, starting first with a small hill. Once you descend this wooded hill at about 2.7 miles, the trail turns east, entering a forest. At 2.9 miles, the final stretch of the climb begins, where in just under three-quarters of a mile, the trail climbs 400 feet. This steep and often rocky climb in the trees navigates between rugged cliffs and fallen boulders as it makes its way to the saddle of Scout Mountain and Old Tom Mountain in a series of switchbacks. The trail ends at a junction with Scout Mountain Top Road. For those interested in continuing to the top of Scout Mountain from this junction, go to page 377.

> Riparian areas are land near rivers, streams, or lakes. They are crucial habitats in almost every ecosystem in the West.

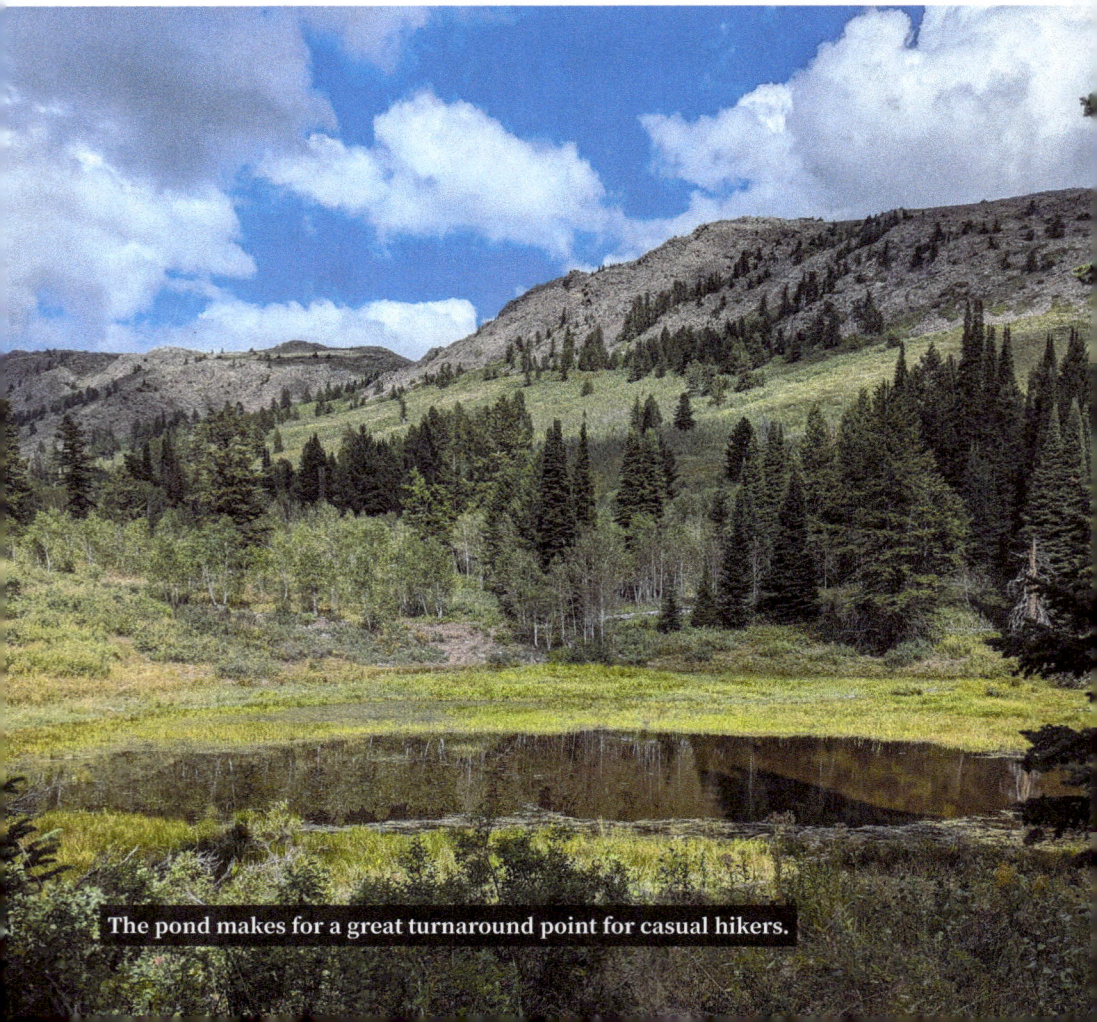

The pond makes for a great turnaround point for casual hikers.

East Fork Mink Creek Trail

N

0.5 mi.

0.5 km.

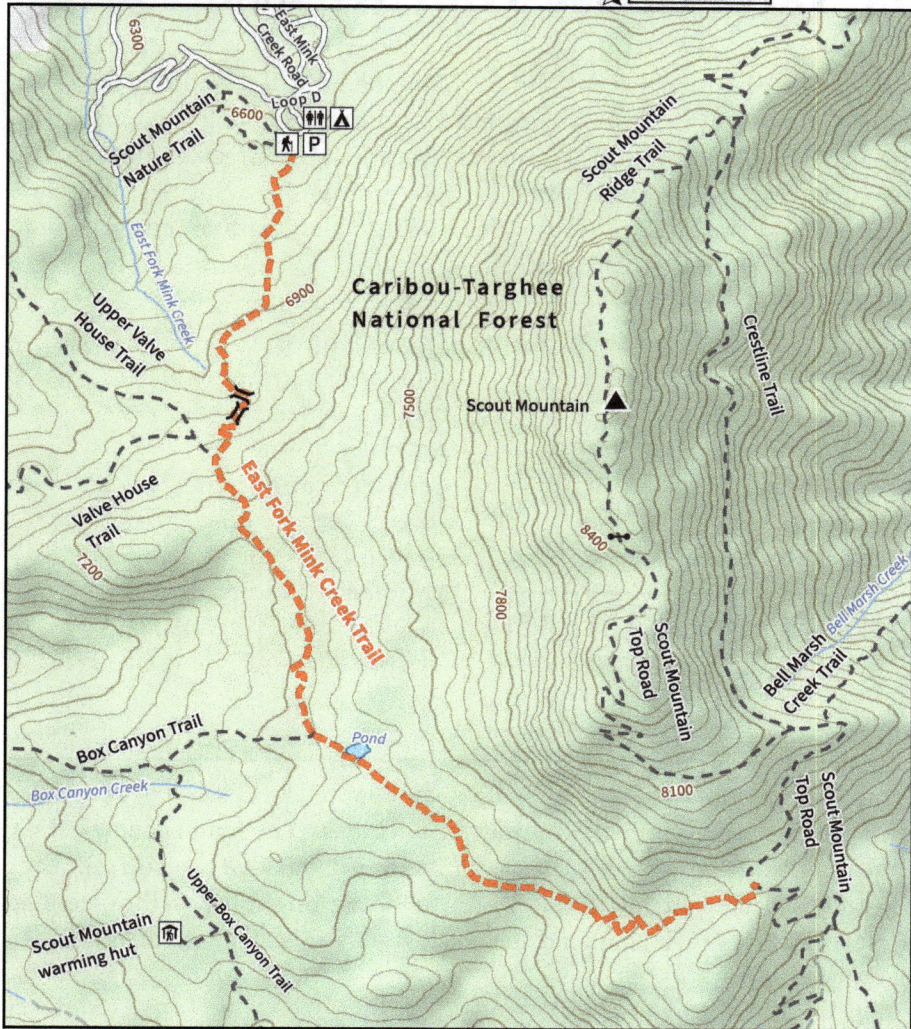

6300

East Mink Creek Road

Loop D

6600

Scout Mountain Nature Trail

East Fork Mink Creek

Upper Valve House Trail

6900

Caribou-Targhee National Forest

Scout Mountain Ridge Trail

Crestline Trail

7500

Scout Mountain ▲

Valve House Trail

7200

East Fork Mink Creek Trail

8400

7800

Scout Mountain Top Road

Bell Marsh Creek Trail

Bell Marsh Creek

Box Canyon Trail

Pond

Box Canyon Creek

8100

Scout Mountain Top Road

Upper Box Canyon Trail

Scout Mountain warming hut

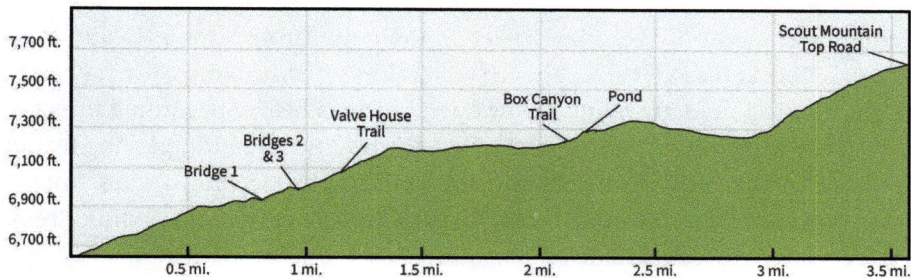

7,700 ft.
7,500 ft.
7,300 ft.
7,100 ft.
6,900 ft.
6,700 ft.

Scout Mountain Top Road

Box Canyon Trail

Pond

Valve House Trail

Bridges 2 & 3

Bridge 1

0.5 mi. 1 mi. 1.5 mi. 2 mi. 2.5 mi. 3 mi. 3.5 mi.

58. Valve House Trail (FS Trail 038)

The Valve House Trail's rocky climb from open hillsides to thick forests is a popular route for mountain bikers and trail runners looking to connect with the East Fork Mink Creek Trail from the West Fork Mink Creek Trailhead. With many side trails emerging from this path, such as Blind Springs, Wendigo, Overlook and Upper Valve House, this is an excellent path for connecting to other routes in the Scout Mountain area.

Distance: 11.9 miles out-and-back
Elevation Gain: 2,090 feet
Difficulty: Strenuous
Hiking Time: About 7 hours
Nearest Town: Pocatello
Trail Surface: Dirt, rock
Wheelchair Access: None

Dog-Friendly: Yes; on-leash at the trailhead. May be off-leash if under control once on the trail
Amenities: None
Contact: Caribou-Targhee National Forest, Westside Ranger District 208-236-7500
Trailhead GPS Coordinates: N42° 43.395' W112° 25.130'

Getting There

From the junction of South Valley Road and Bannock Highway in Pocatello, head southeast on Bannock Highway for 8.6 miles. (The road becomes Mink Creek Road after 2.3 miles.) Turn left into the small Valve House Trailhead. The trail is located on the northwest side of the parking area past the gate. The West Fork Mink Creek Trailhead, located just 100 yards to the south, is another parking option.

The Hike

From the signed trailhead, head east on the path through the gate and then immediately across a bridge. The first 3.8 miles steadily climb over 1,400 feet on a rocky 4x4 road, traveling below open hillsides before becoming forested the higher the path ascends. At 0.2 miles, the trail turns south, passing by the Slate Mountain - Valve House Connector on the path's left (north) side. Not far from there, at about 0.4 miles, you will pass by the South Fork of Mink Creek Trail on the right (south) side of the path.

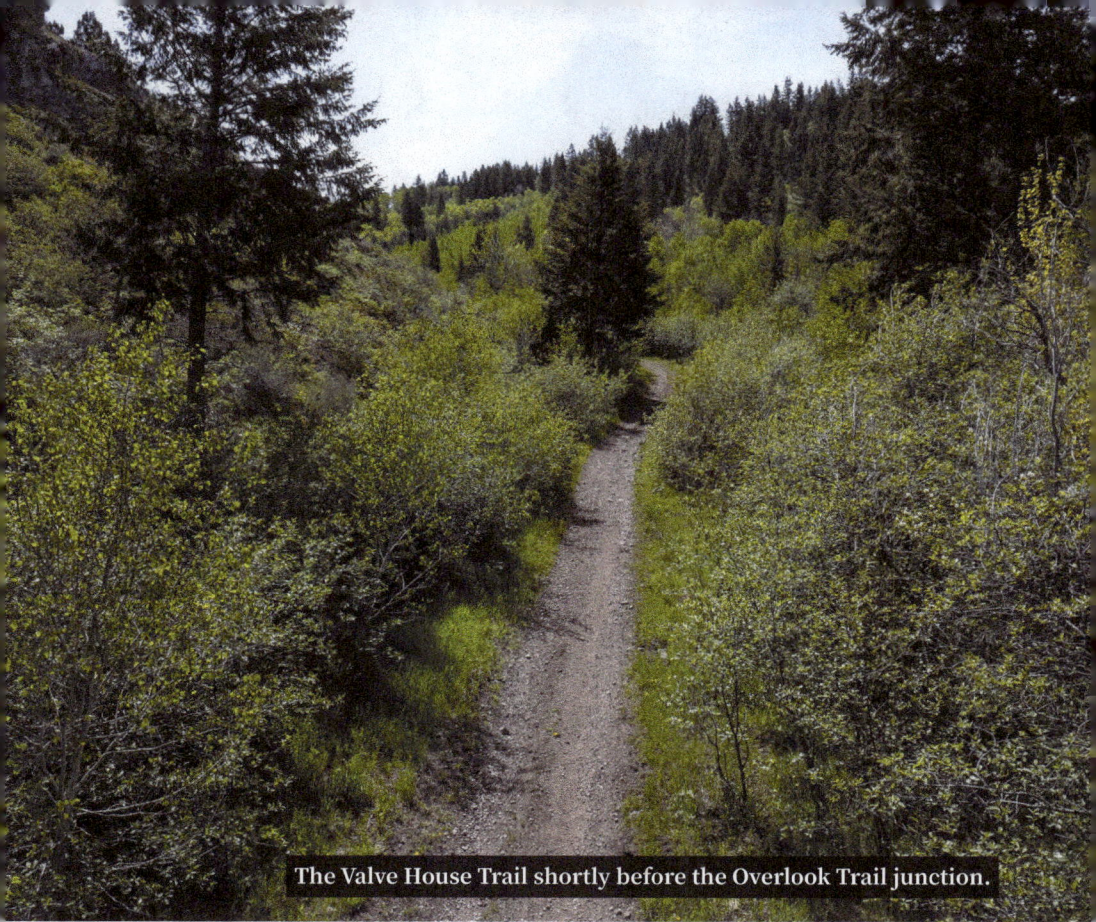

The Valve House Trail shortly before the Overlook Trail junction.

Continue up the rocky trail until you reach 0.8 miles, where you will pass by the Blind Springs Trail on the left (east) side of the path. At about 2.3 miles, you will pass by the Overlook Trail on the left (east) side of the trail. The trail becomes increasingly forested from here.

At 3.8 miles, the trail plateaus before descending a 100-foot hill. Shortly into this descent, you will pass by the Upper Valve House Trail on the left (north) side of the trail. Shortly beyond that, you will come to a cattle guard. Past the cattle guard, the aspens briefly depart from the trail, giving a clear view of Scout Mountain's western cliffs.

At 4.0 miles, you will come to the Wendigo Trail on the path's right (south) side. Wendigo is a popular turning point for mountain bikers looking to make a loop back to the trailhead. Shortly past this turnoff, the incline begins again, gaining over 550 feet in just under 2 miles. This section is mainly under shaded evergreen forests, so the elevation gain feels less taxing. At 5.9 miles, the trail turns to the southeast, passing by the Upper Valve House Trail on the left (north) side of the path. The trail ends at a junction with the East Fork Mink Creek Trail.

Keep Going

Valve House Trail has several side paths that make for fun alternate routes, each providing different viewpoints and loop options that reconnect with the main path. Two standout trails in particular are the Overlook Trail and Upper Valve House Trail.

The **Overlook Trail** (Forest Service Trail 163) begins 2.3 miles into the route. This 1.8-mile-long 4x4 trail, which can narrow at points to feel like a singletrack, gains over 750 feet in a thick forest. The first 0.6 miles can be steep and rutty, but the incline becomes more moderate after this. The ending of this trail can be tricky to specify, as it merges onto the Upper Valve House Trail with no signage. At 1.8 miles, the trail ends at a junction with the Upper Valve House Trail. Turning left (east) onto the 4x4 trail will take you to the top of Upper Valve House Trail, whereas turning right (west) onto the wild single-track will take you to the bottom.

The **Upper Valve House Trail** (Forest Service Trail 186) begins at 3.8 miles on the north side of the Valve House Trail near a pond. The trail is 1.7 miles long and gains over 450 feet, with a rather steep beginning. While the start and end of this trail are forested, the middle section travels through a large field, providing stunning views of Scout Mountain. At 0.7 miles, this singletrack trail transitions into a 4x4 path. Continue southeast on the 4x4 trail and cross over a cattle guard at 0.8 mile. The trail ends connecting to the Valve House Trail near a junction with the East Fork Mink Creek Trail.

A hiker on Upper Valve House Trail.

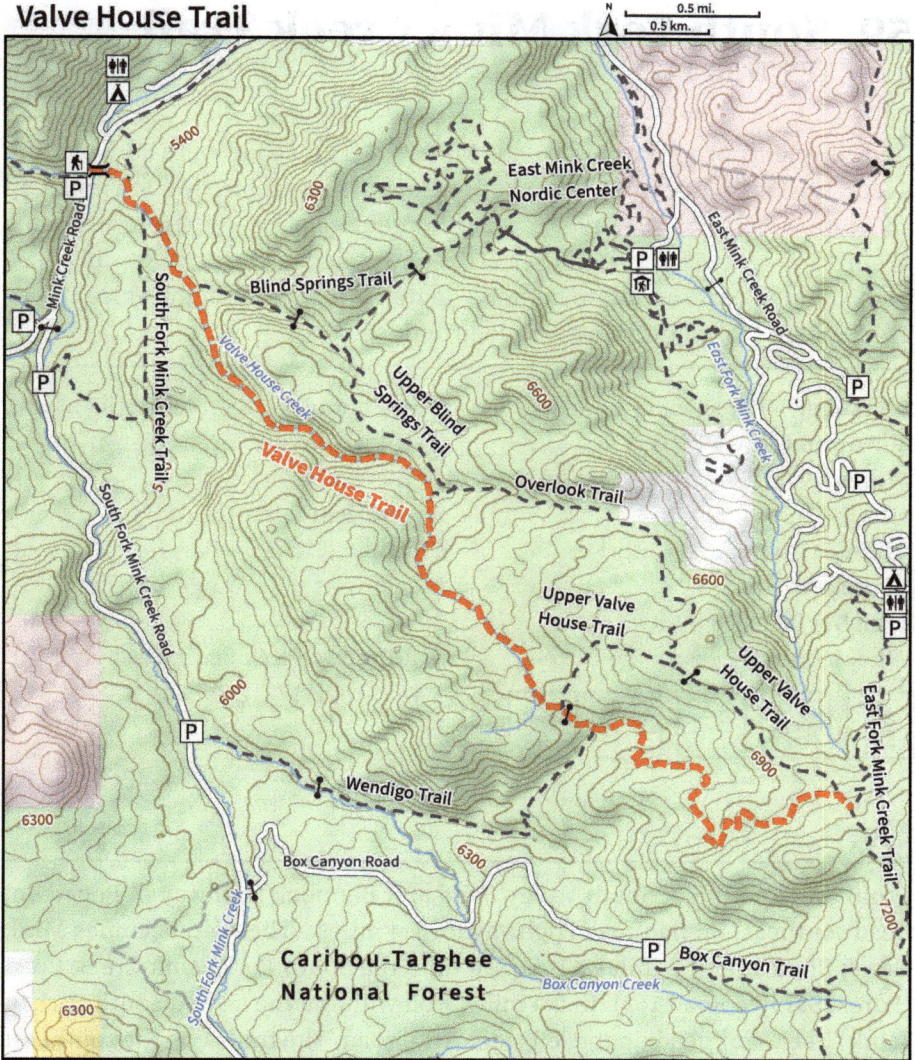

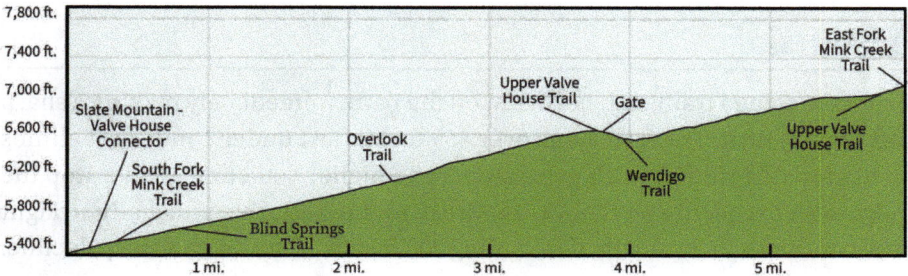

Valve House Trail

N

0.5 mi.
0.5 km.

East Mink Creek Nordic Center

Blind Springs Trail

Upper Blind Springs Trail

Valve House Trail

Overlook Trail

Upper Valve House Trail

Upper Valve House Trail

Wendigo Trail

Box Canyon Road

Box Canyon Trail

Box Canyon Creek

Mink Creek Road

South Fork Mink Creek Trail

South Fork Mink Creek Road

Valve House Creek

South Fork Mink Creek

East Fork Mink Creek Road

East Fork Mink Creek

East Fork Mink Creek Trail

Caribou-Targhee National Forest

5400
6300
6600
6600
6000
6300
6300
6900
7200

Elevation profile showing:
- 7,800 ft.
- 7,400 ft.
- 7,000 ft.
- 6,600 ft.
- 6,200 ft.
- 5,800 ft.
- 5,400 ft.

Labels: Slate Mountain - Valve House Connector, South Fork Mink Creek Trail, Blind Springs Trail, Overlook Trail, Upper Valve House Trail, Gate, Wendigo Trail, Upper Valve House Trail, East Fork Mink Creek Trail

1 mi. 2 mi. 3 mi. 4 mi. 5 mi.

59. South Fork Mink Creek Trail
(FS Trail 142)

Offering plenty of scenic views of the Mink Creek area, the South Fork of Mink Creek Trail is an uncomplicated path through the sagebrush that climbs up and down a small ridge. While the elevation gain is not huge, there are a couple of surprisingly steep hills on both sides of the ridge, which makes this hard to recommend for mountain bikers. The trail connects with the Valve House Trail, making for some interesting loop options.

Distance: 3.7 miles out-and-back
Elevation Gain: 990 feet
Difficulty: Moderate; a few very steep hills
Hiking Time: About 2.5 hours
Nearest Town: Pocatello
Trail Surface: Dirt, rock
Wheelchair Access: None

Dog-Friendly: Yes; on-leash at the trailhead. May be off-leash if under control once on the trail
Amenities: None
Contact: Caribou-Targhee National Forest, Westside Ranger District 208-236-7500
Trailhead GPS Coordinates: N42° 42.427' W112° 25.341'

Getting There

From the junction of South Valley Road and Bannock Highway in Pocatello, head southeast on Bannock Highway for 9.4 miles. (The road becomes Mink Creek Road after 2.3 miles.) Turn left onto the South Fork Mink Creek Road (Forest Service Road 163). In 0.4 miles, you will find the signed South Fork of Mink Creek Trailhead on the left side of the road. The trail is on the southeast end of the trailhead.

The Hike

From the signed trailhead, head east on the path, immediately making a sharp left (north) turn. The trail gains over 450 feet in just under 1 mile as it climbs to the top of a ridge, which gets steeper the higher you climb. Once atop the ridge with excellent views of Corral Creek to the west, this unusually straight trail continues to the north, descending 200 feet in 0.2 miles on a steep decline.

A southward view on the South Fork Mink Creek Trail.

At about 1.6 miles, the trail descends 50 feet down a short but very steep hill. The path ends, connecting with the Valve House Trail about 0.4 miles from the Valve House Trailhead.

The South, East, and West Forks of Mink Creek provide valuable riparian habitat just south of Pocatello. These tributaries eventually flow into Mink Creek, which travels northeast for 10.3 miles before joining the Portneuf River.

South Fork Mink Creek Trail

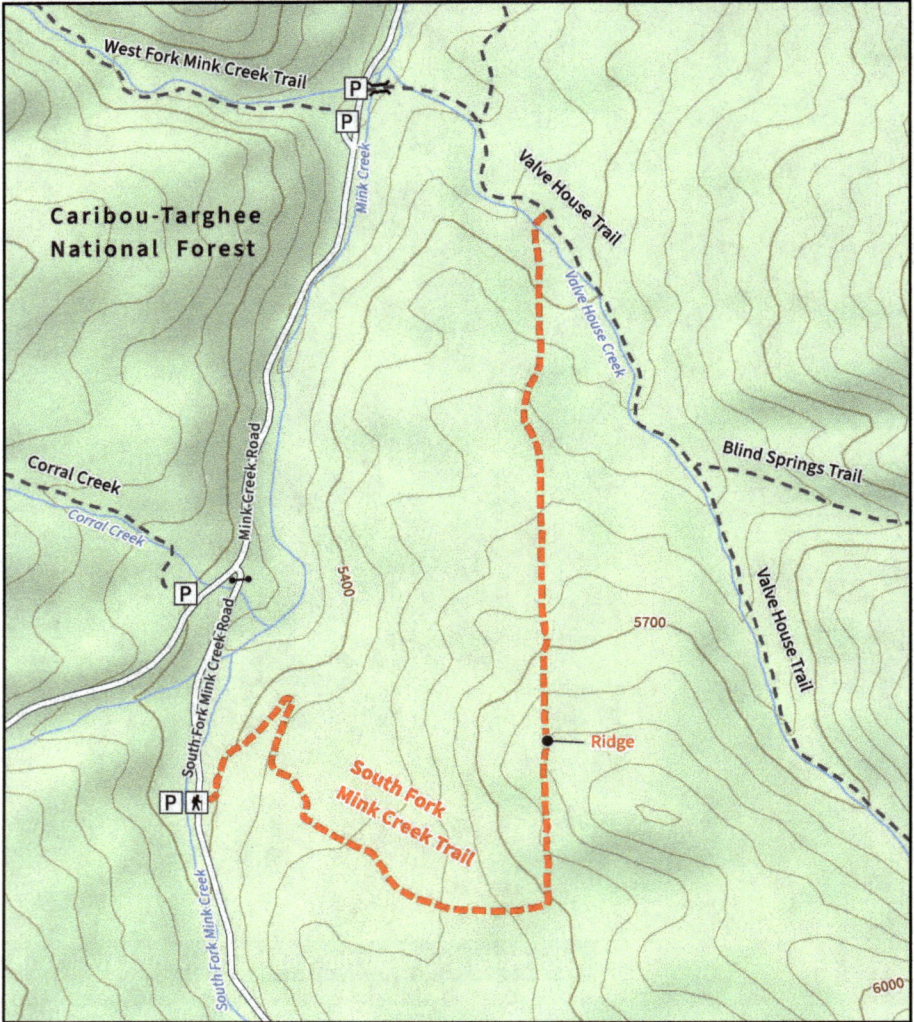

0.25 mi.
0.25 km.

West Fork Mink Creek Trail

Valve House Trail

Caribou-Targhee
National Forest

Mink Creek

Valve House Creek

Blind Springs Trail

Corral Creek

Corral Creek

Mink Creek Road

5400

5700

Valve House Trail

South Fork Mink Creek Road

Ridge

South Fork
Mink Creek Trail

South Fork Mink Creek

6000

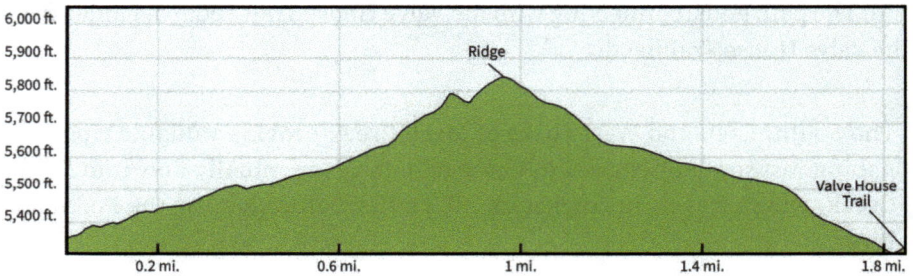

6,000 ft.
5,900 ft.
5,800 ft.
5,700 ft.
5,600 ft.
5,500 ft.
5,400 ft.

Ridge

Valve House
Trail

0.2 mi.   0.6 mi.   1 mi.   1.4 mi.   1.8 mi.

60. Wendigo Trail (FS Trail 184)

Popular with mountain bikers as a connector to the Valve House Trail, the Wendigo Trail is also a delightful and straightforward hike or trail run. This gradually uphill trail travels along a trickling creek below an open hillside before entering increasingly thick forests. Colorful wildflowers grow alongside the trail in the early summer. All in all, this is an easy path to recommend if you are looking to explore Scout Mountain's wilderness on a less-crowded trail.

Distance: 4.3 miles out-and-back
Elevation Gain: 650 feet
Difficulty: Moderate
Hiking Time: About 2.5 hours
Nearest Town: Pocatello
Trail Surface: Dirt, rock
Wheelchair Access: None

Dog-Friendly: Yes; on-leash at the trailhead. May be off-leash if under control once on the trail
Amenities: None
Contact: Caribou-Targhee National Forest, Westside Ranger District 208-236-7500
Trailhead GPS Coordinates: N42° 40.842' W112° 24.679'

Getting There

From the junction of South Valley Road and Bannock Highway in Pocatello, head southeast on Bannock Highway for 9.4 miles. (The road becomes Mink Creek Road after 2.3 miles.) Turn left onto the South Fork Mink Creek Road (Forest Service Road 163). In 2.4 miles, you will find the Wendigo Trailhead on the left side of the road. The trail is on the east end of the trailhead.

The Hike

From the trailhead, head east on the path through the grassy field as it enters the drainage. The early stretch of the trail travels alongside large shrubs and bushes, but it becomes more forested the higher you climb. At about 0.6 miles, the trail crosses over a cattle guard. At about 0.9 miles, keep left to pass by a narrow singletrack path on the trail's right (south) side. (This unofficial path connects with the Box Canyon Road and is about 0.7 miles long.)

At 1.3 miles, the trail passes below a rugged rock formation. Shortly past that rock outcropping at 1.4 miles, keep left (northeast) at the fork. The trail

Early summer wildflowers along Wendigo Trail.

heads deeper into a thick pine forest from this turn onward. A fork appears at about 1.5 miles, though both paths rejoin after a short distance. For the mileage in this book, I used the slightly longer right (east) path.

Once the trails rejoin, the path begins a largely uninterrupted northeast climb along the creek through the evergreens. For bikers, the trail can be a bit rocky and filled with roots in this upper stretch of the route, but it is usually manageable. The trail ends at a junction with the Valve House Trail.

In Algonquian Native American folklore, the "wendigo" is a malevolent spirit that possesses human beings. It is often associated with cannibalism, greed, and winter.

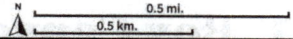

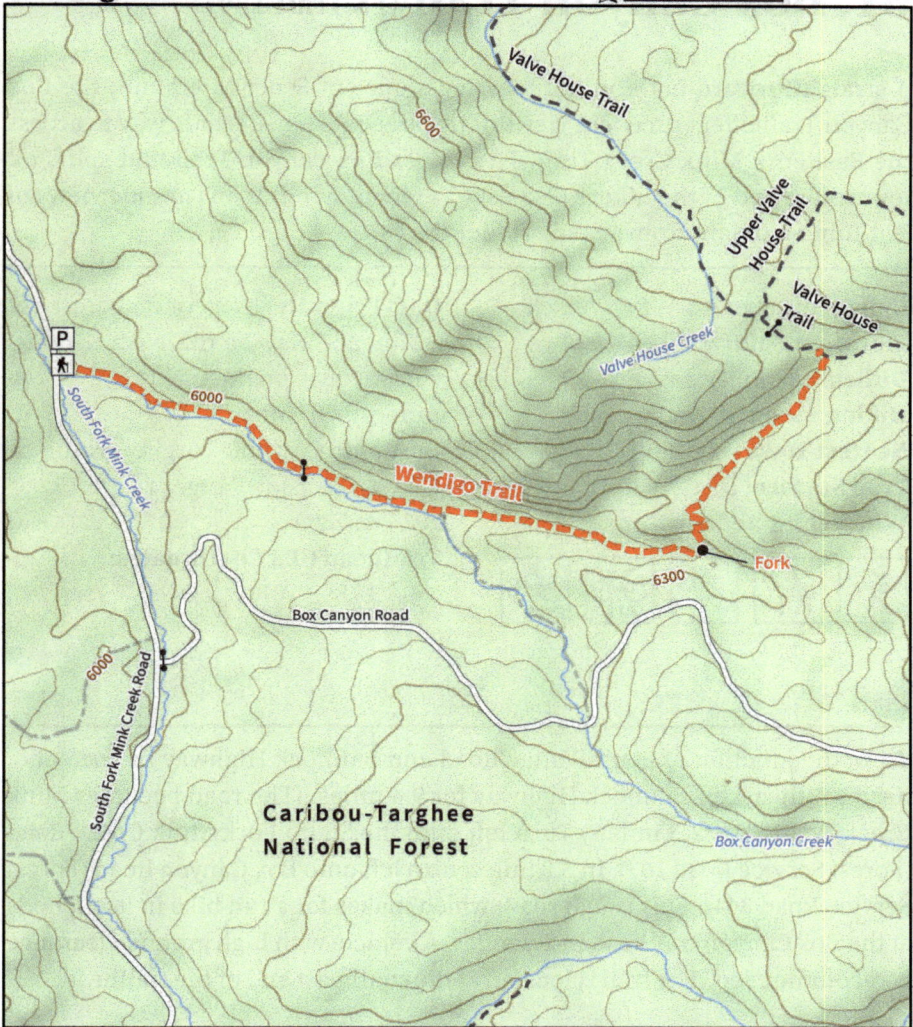

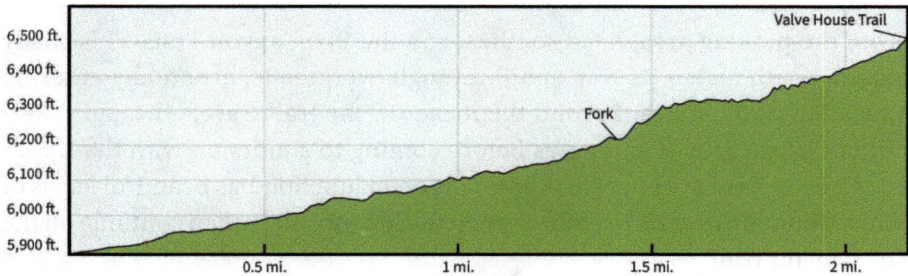

Wendigo Trail

61. Box Canyon Trail (FS Trail 189)

A straightforward path on the forested slopes of Scout Mountain, the Box Canyon Trail offers excellent views of the area and an alternate way to access the East Fork Mink Creek Trail. The Upper Box Canyon Trail that splits off toward the end of the hike is also easy to recommend. It has unique views of Old Tom Mountain from a field of wildflowers.

Distance: 2.4 miles out-and-back
Elevation Gain: 660 feet
Difficulty: Moderate
Hiking Time: About 1.5 hours
Nearest Town: Pocatello
Trail Surface: Dirt, rock
Wheelchair Access: None

Dog-Friendly: Yes; on-leash at the trailhead. May be off-leash if under control once on the trail
Amenities: None
Contact: Caribou-Targhee National Forest, Westside Ranger District 208-236-7500
Trailhead GPS Coordinates: N42° 39.862' W112° 22.626'

Getting There

From the junction of South Valley Road and Bannock Highway in Pocatello, head southeast on Bannock Highway for 9.4 miles. (The road becomes Mink Creek Road after 2.3 miles.) Turn left onto the South Fork Mink Creek Road (Forest Service Road 163). In 3.3 miles, turn left onto Box Canyon Road (Forest Service Road 344). This rough road, which makes for a fun hike in itself, ends at the Box Canyon trailhead in 2.7 miles. A vehicle with high ground clearance is recommended. The trail is located at the southeast end of the trailhead.

The Hike

From the parking area, head southeast on the Box Canyon Trail. This shady forested path makes its way uphill through evergreens, eventually entering a meadow at 0.5 miles. Beyond the meadow, the trail travels through inter-mittent aspen groves and pines before coming to a junction with the Upper Box Canyon Trail at about 0.8 miles. This open junction has beautiful views of Scout Mountains's eastern cliffs. Stay on the left (north) path to continue on the Box Canyon Trail.

Upper Box Canyon Trail heading toward Old Tom Mountain.

Past the junction, the trail enters the forest, where in 0.4 miles, the trail ends when it connects with the East Fork Mink Creek Trail.

Keep Going

At the 0.8-mile junction, you'll find the **Upper Box Canyon Trail** (Forest Service Trail 192). This southern double-wide trail is a beautiful path that connects the Box Canyon Trail to Scout Mountain Top Road. The trail is about 1-mile-long one-way and loses almost 300 feet of elevation, with most of that decline coming in the second half of the hike. Half a mile into the trail, the path enters an extensive wildflower meadow, where you will find great views of Old Tom Mountain and a western side trail leading to the Box Canyon warming hut.

Box Canyon

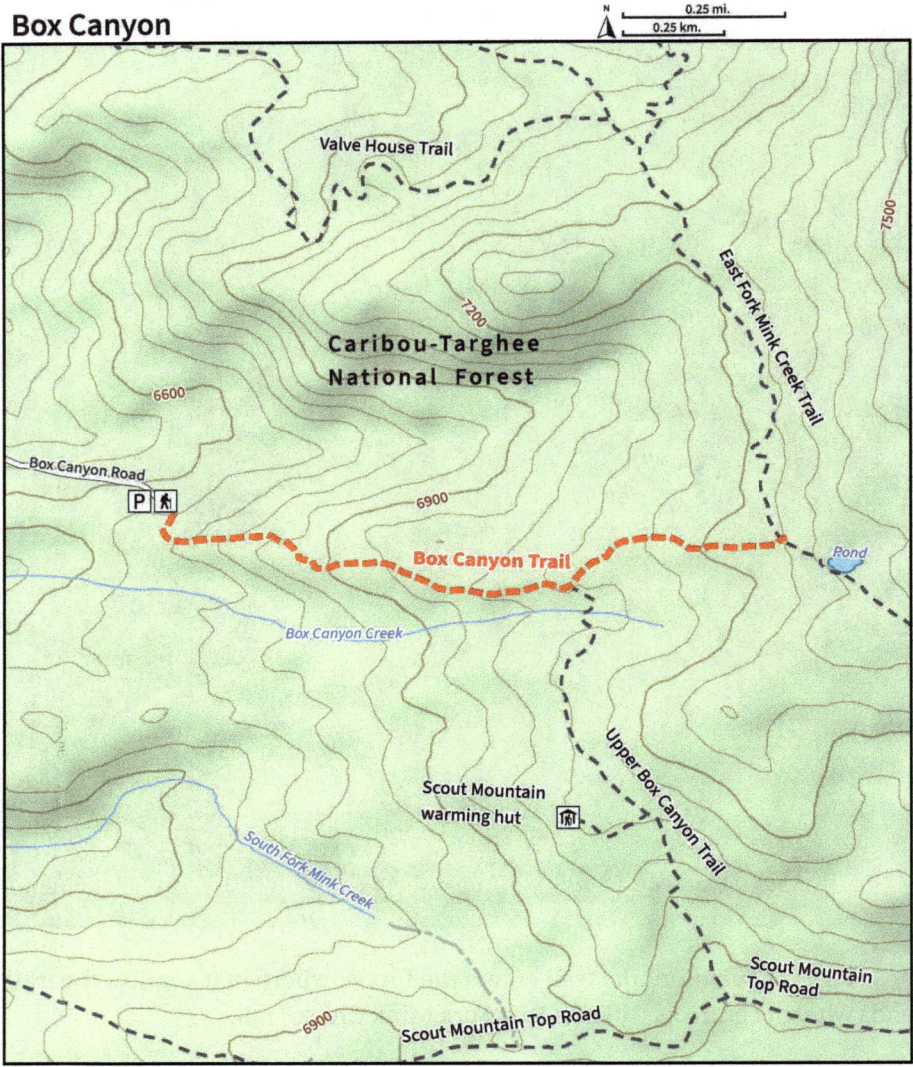

N
0.25 mi.
0.25 km.

Valve House Trail

East Fork Mink Creek Trail

7500

7200

Caribou-Targhee
National Forest

6600

Box Canyon Road

P

6900

Box Canyon Trail

Pond

Box Canyon Creek

Upper Box Canyon Trail

Scout Mountain
warming hut

South Fork Mink Creek

Scout Mountain
Top Road

6900

Scout Mountain Top Road

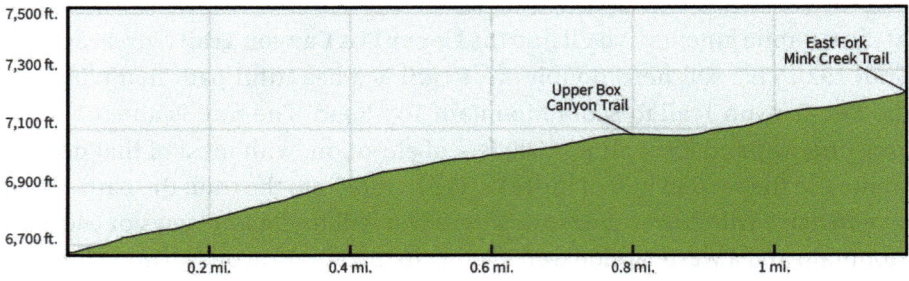

7,500 ft.

7,300 ft.
East Fork
Mink Creek Trail

7,100 ft.
Upper Box
Canyon Trail

6,900 ft.

6,700 ft.

0.2 mi.   0.4 mi.   0.6 mi.   0.8 mi.   1 mi.

62. Bull Canyon (FS Trail 190)

Bull Canyon is a short and wild trail west of Scout Mountain that leads to a meadow dotted with scenic beaver ponds. Depending on the time of year, the trail can be very overgrown, though the area's wildflowers may compensate for the increased rough vegetation.

Distance: 2.1 miles out-and-back
Elevation Gain: 220 feet
Difficulty: Easy
Hiking Time: About 1 hour
Nearest Town: Pocatello
Trail Surface: Dirt, rock
Wheelchair Access: None

Dog-Friendly: Yes; on-leash at the trailhead. May be off-leash if under control once on the trail
Amenities: None
Contact: Caribou-Targhee National Forest, Westside Ranger District 208-236-7500
Trailhead GPS Coordinates: N42° 39.122' W112° 24.421'

Getting There

From the junction of South Valley Road and Bannock Highway in Pocatello, head southeast on Bannock Highway for 9.4 miles. (The road becomes Mink Creek Road after 2.3 miles.) Turn left onto the South Fork Mink Creek Road (Forest Service Road 163). In 4.6 miles, make a sharp left turn onto the dirt road, which ends at a small parking area in about 200 yards. The trail starts on the east side of the parking area.

The Hike

From the trailhead, head east on the wild singletrack trail. As you walk the first half-mile of the trail, you will pass through a mixed forest. The path can be overgrown with grass, so make sure to go slowly and stay on the trail. At about 0.6 miles, the trail will leave the forest and lead you into a meadow, where the trail shifts to the north. The next half-mile moves alongside a series of beaver ponds, which are quite beautiful when surrounded by wildflowers. After this, the route ends shortly at a gate.

Hikers passing by one of Bull Canyon's ponds.

It is worth noting that, technically, Bull Canyon continues past the gate, but the official trail past the gate (which makes a sharp north turn) is incredibly overgrown and hard to follow. As a result, a community-made trail past the gate is commonly called the Bull Canyon Trail, which eventually ends near Scout Mountain Top Road. However, I decided against including it in the book since it is an unofficial trail.

Beavers, the largest rodents in the United States, are semi-aquatic mammals whose teeth never stop growing. They are considered a keystone species due to the impact of their dams on the ecosystem.

Bull Canyon

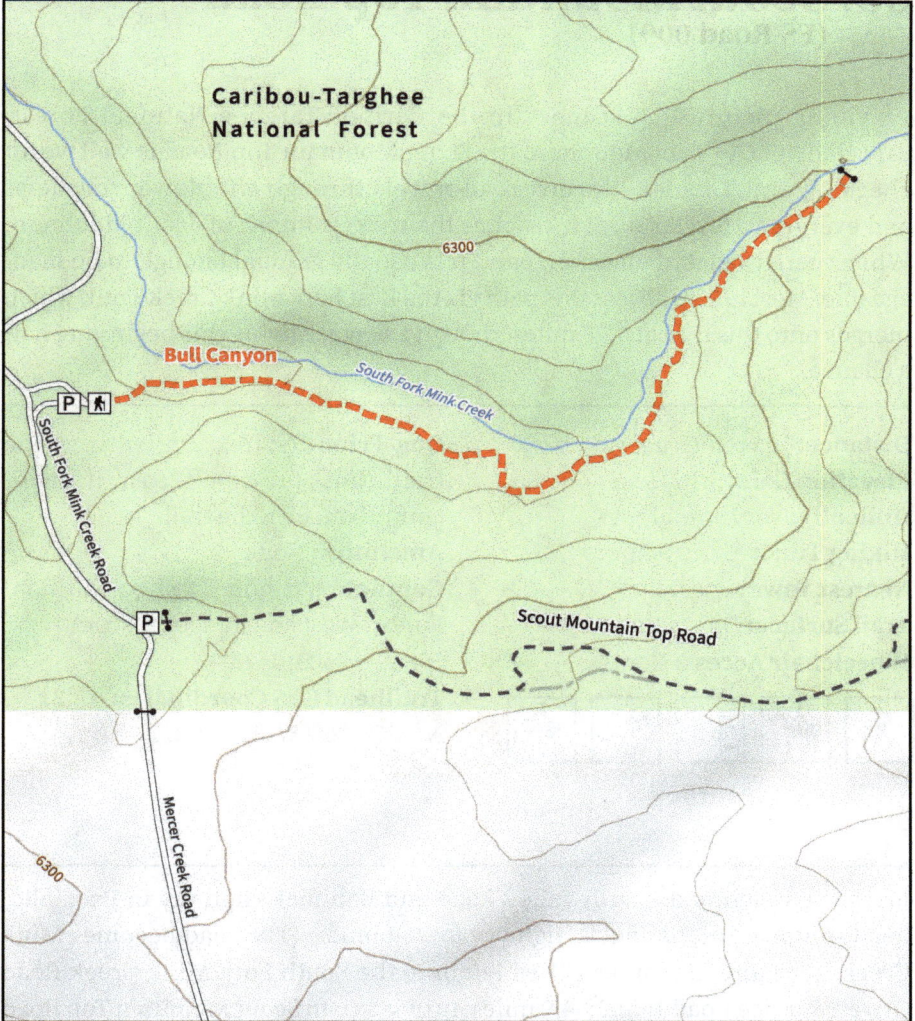

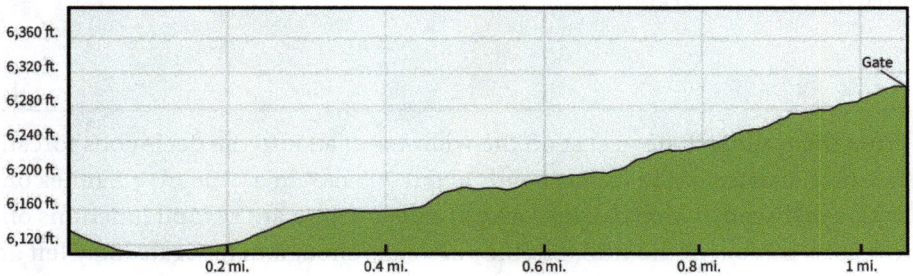

63. Scout Mountain Top Road
(FS Road 009)

Providing picturesque scenery in the Caribou-Targhee National Forest, especially of Old Tom Mountain, the Scout Mountain Top Road is well worth checking out. This lengthy dirt road travels through wildflower meadows and evergreen forests until it reaches the rocky summit of Scout Mountain. While there is a lot of elevation gain, it is usually gradual enough to be manageable. Most hikers access this path via the East Fork Mink Creek Trail, which merges onto this trail at 5.75 miles, though I suggest giving this beginning half a chance.

Distance: 16.6 miles out-and-back
Elevation Gain: 3,100 feet
Difficulty: Very strenuous
Hiking Time: About 9 hours
Nearest Town: Pocatello
Trail Surface: Dirt, rock
Wheelchair Access: None

Dog-Friendly: Yes; on-leash at the trailhead. May be off-leash if under control once on the trail
Amenities: None
Contact: Caribou-Targhee National Forest, Westside Ranger District 208-236-7500
Trailhead GPS Coordinates: N42° 38.869' W112° 24.371'

Getting There

From the junction of South Valley Road and Bannock Highway in Pocatello, head southeast on Bannock Highway for 9.4 miles. (The road becomes Mink Creek Road after 2.3 miles.) Turn left onto the South Fork Mink Creek Road (Forest Service Road 163). In 4.9 miles, turn left onto Scout Mountain Top Road (which is also the beginning of the hike) and then make an immediate right turn into a small parking area.

The Hike

From the trailhead, head east on the wide 4x4 road into the deciduous forest. The first quarter of the trail ascends about 700 feet in a little over 2 miles on a wide dirt road, which can be rocky at times. There are several junctions on this early stretch of the trail, but they are easy enough to navigate. Stay left at

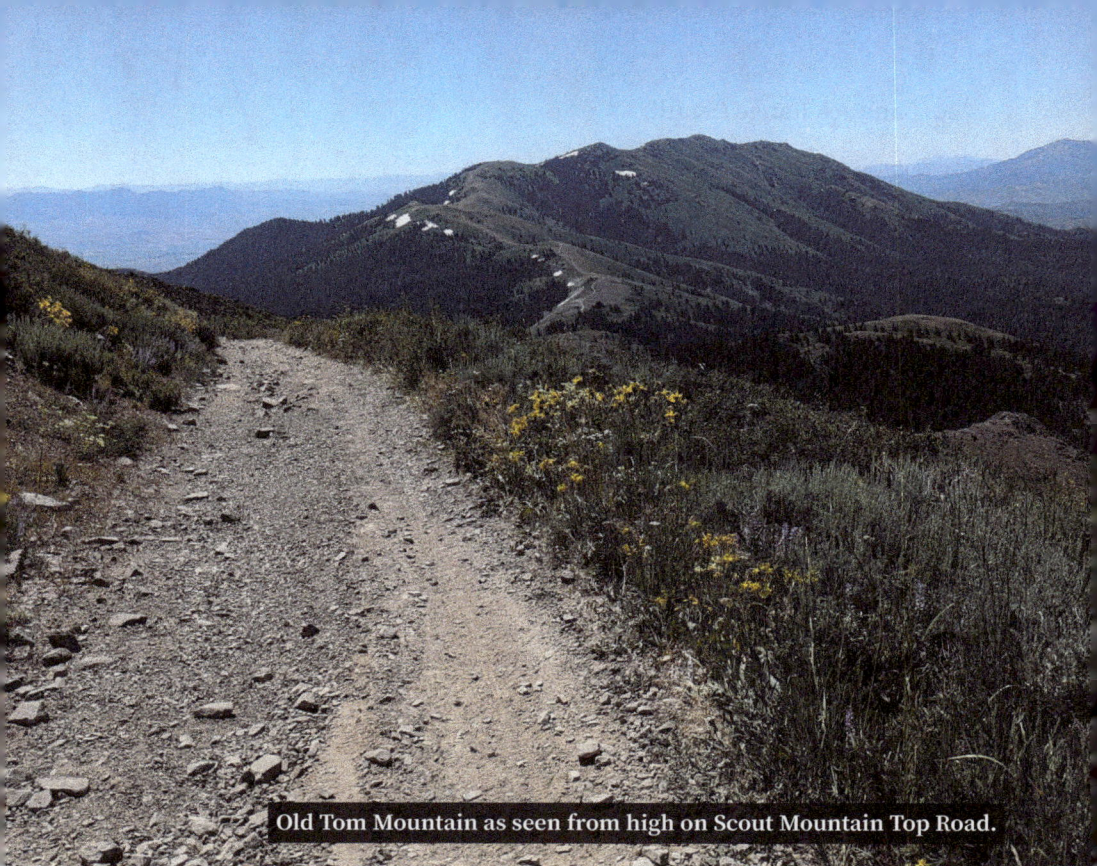

Old Tom Mountain as seen from high on Scout Mountain Top Road.

any junction during these first 2 miles. About 0.5 miles into the hike, the trail leaves the forest and enters open sage fields, with excellent views of the Fort Hall Reservation and Bannock Peak to the west.

About 2.1 miles into the trail, the initial stretch of incline ends and marks the end of the "keep left at any junction rule." Continue straight at 2.1 miles, avoiding a dead-end trail on the left (north) side of the trail. Past this side path, the trail begins a 100-foot descent into the forest, which, until the 3.5-mile mark, is an enjoyable and relatively flat stretch of trail.

At about 2.5 miles, continue straight past a 4x4 trail on the left (north) side of the trail. Shortly beyond that, at 2.6 miles, continue straight, avoiding the trail on the path's right (south) side. At about 2.9 miles, you will pass by the Upper Box Canyon Trail on the left (north) side of the trail. Beyond that junction, the trail emerges into a beautiful wildflower meadow with excellent views of Old Tom Mountain. At 3.3 miles, continue straight into the forest, avoiding the trail on your left (north).

At about 3.5 miles, just past a seasonal stream, the elevation gain begins again, gaining about 700 feet until you reach the saddle. The trail becomes a series of switchbacks at about 4.1 miles, starting a northbound climb. To avoid an alternate path that cuts between these switchbacks, keep left when encountering any side trail until you reach the saddle at 5.3 miles (7,550 feet).

You will come to a junction at the saddle with a few trails. The trail on the right (south) is the Mormon Canyon Trail, which heads toward Old Tom Mountain. The trails on the left (west and north) are the Scout Mountain Top Road and a switchback shortcut. Take the northern path (the right-most of the two) to switch back around a steep hill. At 5.75 miles, you will pass by the East Fork Mink Creek Trail (7,720 feet) on your left (west). Hikers looking to summit Scout Mountain frequently merge onto the Scout Mountain Top Road at this East Fork Mink Creek junction, so expect more traffic past this point. The summit is about 1,000 vertical feet away.

At about 6.3 miles, the trail makes a sharp left (west) turn onto a ridge. Shortly past this turn at 6.4 miles and 6.5 miles, you will pass by the Bell Marsh Creek Trail, followed by the Crestline Trail, both on the right (north) side of the trail. Past these trails, the route is largely treeless on exposed and rocky ridge tops. Bring plenty of water and sunscreen for these last 2 miles.

At 6.8 miles, the trail crosses a small ridge and becomes very rocky. From this point on, mountain bikers will have a rough time due to the large rocks in the trail. After a series of switchbacks, the trail reaches a false summit at 7.5 miles (8,540 feet). This is an excellent place to take a break and snap some photos of Scout Mountain. The true summit is about 0.9 miles away.

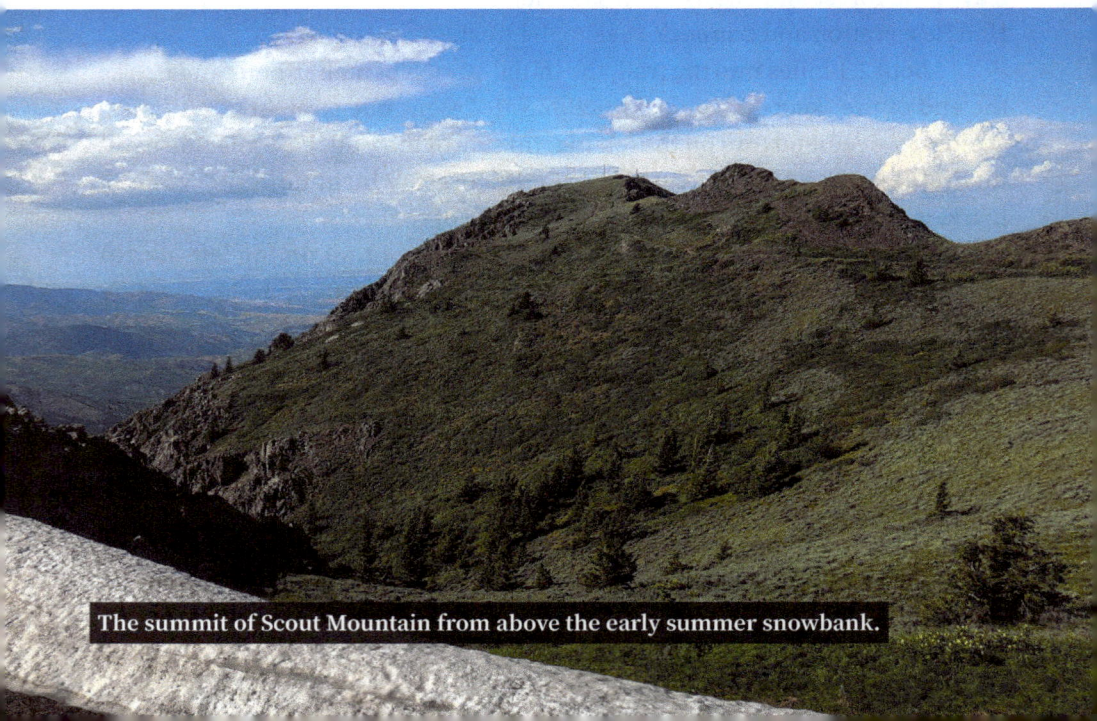

The summit of Scout Mountain from above the early summer snowbank.

A rocky stretch of the Scout Mountain Top Road.

Follow the trail north as it descends a brief hill toward the ridge. If you are hiking early in the season, this hill may be a steep snowbank, which can be challenging to descend. At about 7.9 miles, you will come across a gate. At 8.4 miles, keep right (northeast) to finish the Scout Mountain Top Trail, which ends at the fence below the tower. This location is also the true summit of the mountain (8,710 feet).

Scout Mountain Ultras is a challenging collection of early summer trail races that take place in the Caribou-Targhee National Forest, located just outside of Pocatello. The race offers several distances for runners to compete in, including the 23-miler, 50-kilometer, 50-miler and 100-miler. During the race, each course passes over the summit of Scout Mountain on the Scout Mountain Top Road.

Scout Mountain Top Road

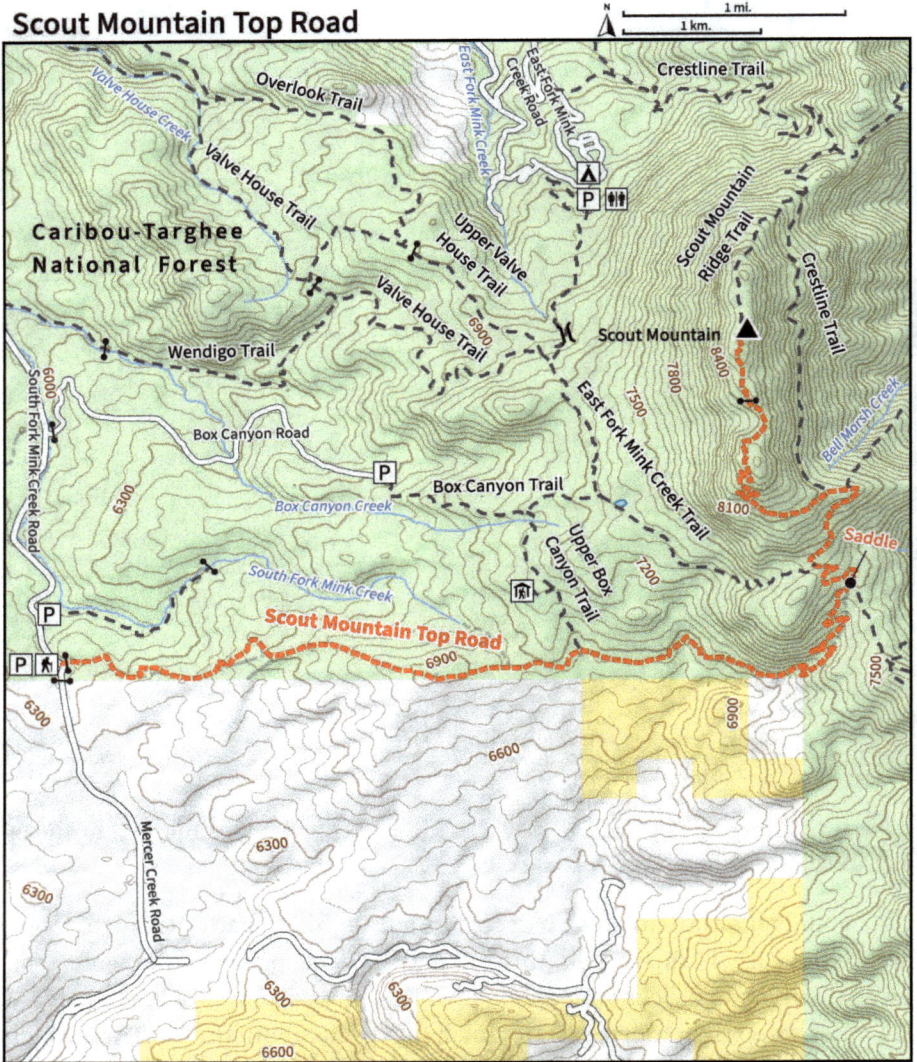

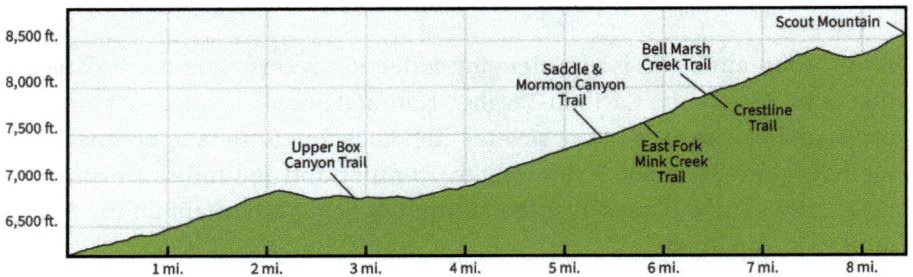

N

1 mi.

1 km.

Overlook Trail

East Fork Mink Creek Road

Crestline Trail

Valve House Creek

Valve House Trail

Scout Mountain Ridge Trail

Crestline Trail

Caribou-Targhee National Forest

Upper Valve House Trail

Valve House Trail

6900

Scout Mountain

8400

7800

Wendigo Trail

Bell Marsh Creek

7500

6000

South Fork Mink Creek Road

East Fork Mink Creek Trail

8100

Box Canyon Road

6300

Box Canyon Trail

Saddle

Box Canyon Creek

South Fork Mink Creek

Upper Box Canyon Trail

7200

P

Scout Mountain Top Road

6900

7500

6300

6600

6069

6300

Mercer Creek Road

6300

6300

6300

6600

8,500 ft.

Scout Mountain

8,000 ft.

Saddle & Mormon Canyon Trail

Bell Marsh Creek Trail

7,500 ft.

Upper Box Canyon Trail

East Fork Mink Creek Trail

Crestline Trail

7,000 ft.

6,500 ft.

1 mi.   2 mi.   3 mi.   4 mi.   5 mi.   6 mi.   7 mi.   8 mi.

64. Bell Marsh-Walker-Goodenough Trail (FS Trail 152)

Lengthy in both name and distance, the Bell Marsh - Walker - Goodenough Trail winds across sagebrush-covered hillsides, occasionally dipping into shady deciduous creek beds, with wide vistas of the Portneuf Range and the Scout Mountain foothills. Don't be deterred by its length; exploring a few miles on either end of the trail can be rewarding. The easily accessible and well-used southern end of the trail, located at the Goodenough Creek Campground, makes for a fun creek walk with excellent views of Old Tom Mountain's northeast face. Mountain bikers looking to ride this trail should be prepared for a challenging ride, especially at the rugged rock-filled northern end of the trail.

Distance: 9.9 miles one-way
Elevation Gain: 2,100 feet
Difficulty: Very strenuous
Hiking Time: About 6 hours
Nearest Town: McCammon
Trail Surface: Dirt, rock
Wheelchair Access: None
Dog-Friendly: Yes; on-leash at the trailhead. May be off-leash if under control once on the trail

Amenities: Vault toilets are available at the trailhead and Goodenough Creek Campground.
Contact: Caribou-Targhee National Forest, Westside Ranger District 208-236-7500;
Bureau of Land Management, Pocatello Field Office 208-478-6340
Trailhead GPS Coordinates:
Goodenough Trailhead
N42° 39.269' W112° 17.153'
West Walker Creek Trailhead
N42° 43.573' W112° 18.495'

Getting There

From I-15 south of Pocatello, take Exit 47 for McCammon. Turn right on East Merrill Road. In 1.2 miles, turn left onto West Portneuf Road and right onto Green Road shortly after that. Stay on Green Road for 2.7 miles. Once Green Road enters the Goodenough Campground with a right turn, it transitions into an unnamed road. Continue on the unnamed road as it turns to the left (west). In 0.4 miles, the road ends at the Goodenough Trailhead, which has plenty of parking. The trail is located on the north side of the trailhead.

The first mile of the trail is a must see in the autumn.

The Hike

From the Goodenough Canyon Trailhead, head north on the doubletrack BLM 152 trail. The beginning stretch of the path ascends alongside a creek in a heavily forested ravine, which, in the autumn, glows with a fiery mixture of red and orange leaves. At 0.6 miles, the trail emerges from the forest and crosses a hillside, where you will find excellent views of Old Tom Mountain to the southwest. At 0.8 miles, keep left (northwest) at the fork. The trail continues its uphill journey, eventually peaking at 1.1 miles (5,990 feet), a 450-foot climb from the trailhead.

The trail heads downhill for the next half mile, hugging an exposed hillside. At 1.3 miles, keep left (northwest) at the fork and head into the forest. After leaving this forested ravine at 1.6 miles, the trail makes an eastern turn, beginning a 200-foot incline that peaks in three-quarters of a mile. At about 2.3 miles, the trail intersects a lightly used 4-wheeler trail. Continue through this intersection on the well-traveled path, heading west into a forest, where at 2.5 miles (6,070 feet) it peaks before shifting downhill.

At 3.1 miles, keep right (northeast) at the fork to begin a significant 550-foot descent down a steep rocky hill. (For those looking for a casual hike, turn around atop this hill and enjoy the predominantly downhill trek back to the trailhead.) At the bottom of the hill, at about 3.6 miles, the trail makes a western turn at a fork. Stay left (west) to continue on the Bell Marsh - Walker - Goodenough Trail. Shortly past that junction at 3.7 miles, you will pass by the Bell Marsh Creek trail on the left (west) side of the path. Keep right and cross over the creek.

Continue on the trail as it heads northeast, hugging the forest before making a northern uphill turn at 4.1 miles into a dry ravine. At about 4.7 miles, after roughly 300 feet of elevation gain, the trail becomes a series of small ups and downs across juniper hillsides as it continues its northward journey. At 5.4 miles, keep left (west) at the fork, where the trail begins a 300-foot climb through a forested drainage until it tops out at 6.1 miles (5,990 feet).

For the next 0.9 miles, the trail cuts through an open sagebrush hillside, with views of the Portneuf Range and the Marsh Valley area to the east. At 7.0 miles, the trail comes to a gate. Pass through the gate and follow the trail as it makes a sharp left (west) turn. At 7.4 miles, the trail crosses over a ridge, where

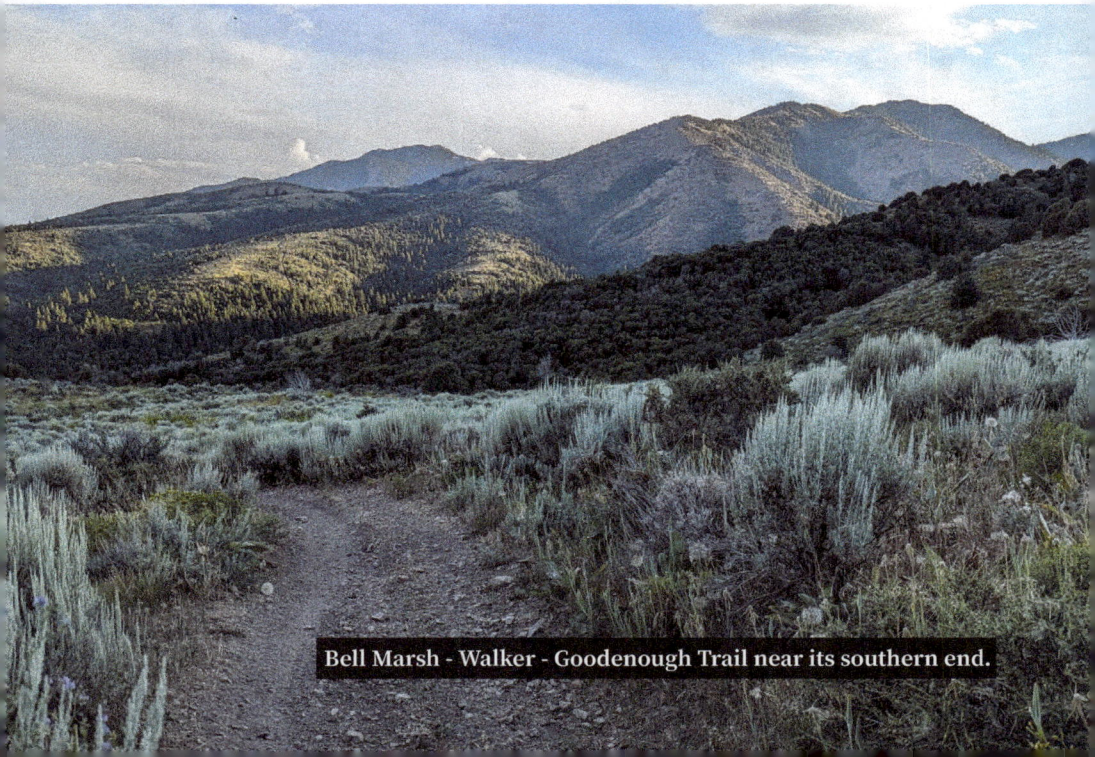

Bell Marsh - Walker - Goodenough Trail near its southern end.

you will have excellent views of the South Fork of Walker Creek and the foothills of Scout Mountain. Head southwest, beginning the rocky descent to the creek.

About 0.6 miles from the ridge, the trail makes a right (north) turn, traveling alongside the water. At about 8.1 miles, you will cross a rugged bridge over the creek, then make a left (west) turn, beginning the trail's last climb. This final incline climbs 350 feet in about 0.6 miles, eventually peaking at 8.8 miles. The final stretch of the hike heads west, hugging the forested hillside and granting views of barren foothills to the north, which look beautiful at sunset.

At about 9.5 miles, the trail heads north, making the final descent to the trailhead. The trail ends on the other side of Walker Creek at the West Walker Creek Road. There is no bridge crossing.

Keep Going

Located at the 3.7-mile mark on the west side of the main path, the **Bell Marsh Creek Trail** (Forest Service Trail 178) is a 3.8-mile-long adventurous trail that climbs 2,600 feet along the creek and ascends a steep ridge high onto Scout Mountain, with beautiful views of the area along the way. There is a bridge across the creek at the beginning of this trail, but it is almost certain that you will get your feet wet in several of the eight or more creek crossings. In fact, the trail and creek often intertwine, so I recommend stepping into the water immediately to get it over with.

After gradually ascending alongside (and often within) the forested creek for 2.7 miles, the trail begins its 1,500-foot climb to the Scout Mountain Top Road. This last mile is often filled with loose rock, so hiking poles are recommended. As you near the top, there will be several interweaving trails, but they all rejoin each other, so ascend whichever provides the best footing for you.

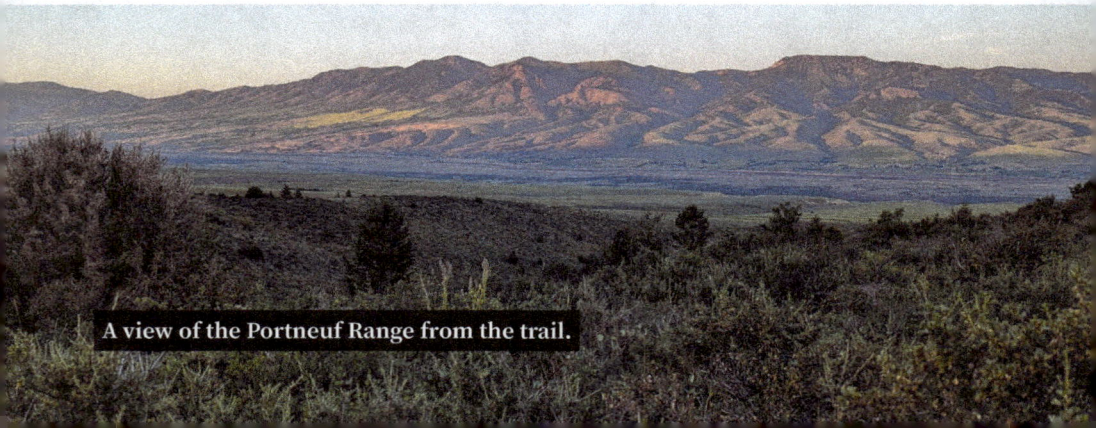

A view of the Portneuf Range from the trail.

Bell Marsh - Walker - Goodenough Trail

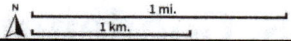

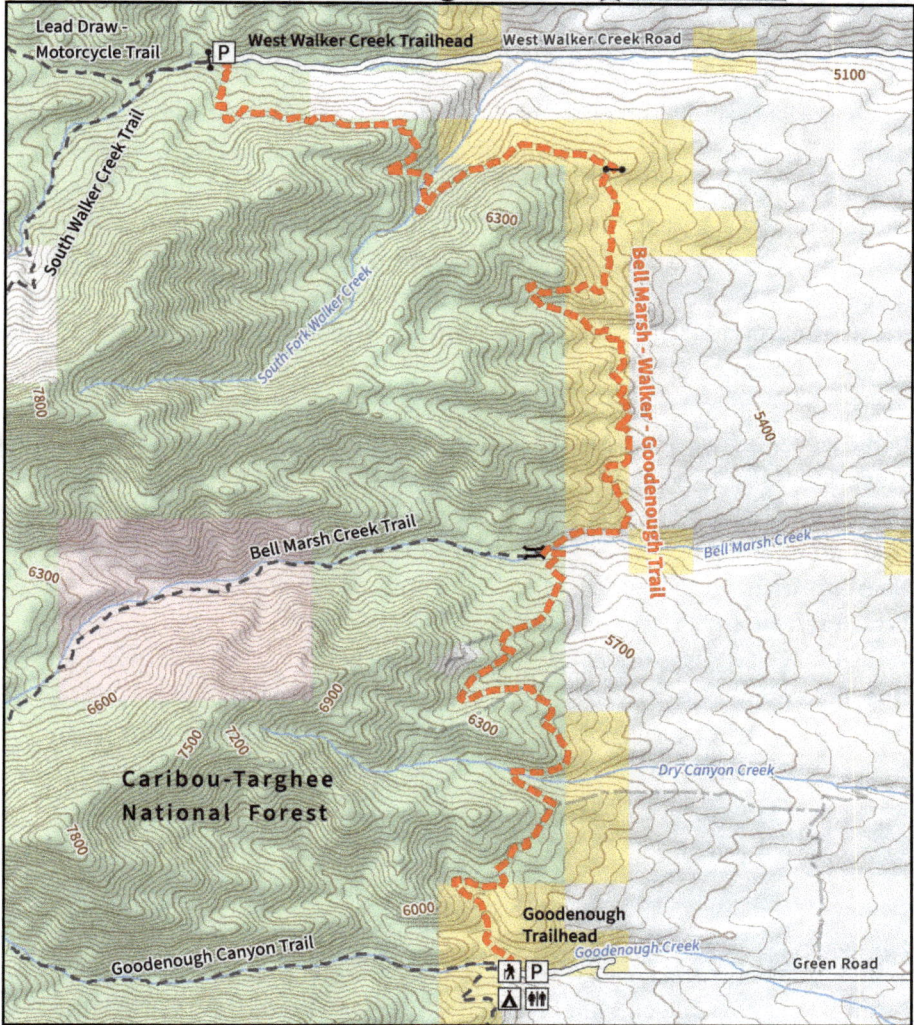

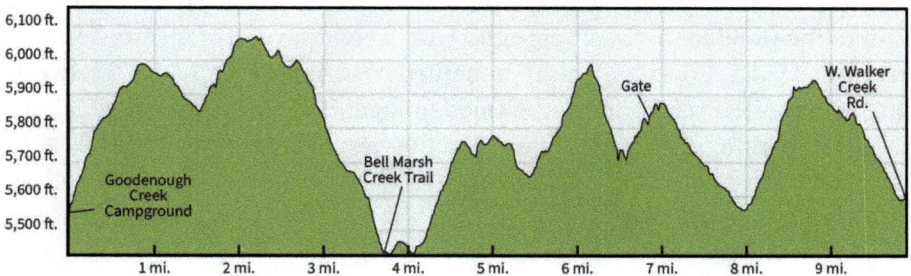

N
1 mi.
1 km.

Lead Draw -
Motorcycle Trail

West Walker Creek Trailhead

West Walker Creek Road

P

5100

South Walker Creek Trail

6300

South Fork Walker Creek

Bell Marsh - Walker - Goodenough Trail

5400

7800

Bell Marsh Creek Trail

Bell Marsh Creek

6300

5700

6600

7500

7200

6900

6300

Dry Canyon Creek

Caribou-Targhee
National Forest

7800

6000

Goodenough
Trailhead

Goodenough Creek

Goodenough Canyon Trail

P

Green Road

Elevation profile:

6,100 ft.
6,000 ft.
5,900 ft.
5,800 ft.
5,700 ft.
5,600 ft.
5,500 ft.

Goodenough
Creek
Campground

Bell Marsh
Creek Trail

Gate

W. Walker
Creek
Rd.

1 mi.   2 mi.   3 mi.   4 mi.   5 mi.   6 mi.   7 mi.   8 mi.   9 mi.

65. Goodenough Canyon Trail
(FS Trail 194)

Steep, hard to follow, and overgrown with vegetation, the shaded Goodenough Canyon Trail is a challenging path alongside a bubbling creek that often feels like bushwhacking. Those who push through this wild path are rewarded with a ridge walk near the Scout Mountain saddle with beautiful views of Goodenough Canyon. While most of the trail is hard to recommend for casual hikers, the first 0.8 miles is well-maintained and makes for a pleasant creekside stroll. Mountain biking would be very difficult on this trail, especially during the mid-summer.

Distance: 3.3 miles one-way
Elevation Gain: 2,040 feet
Difficulty: Moderately strenuous
Hiking Time: About 3 hours
Nearest Town: McCammon
Trail Surface: Dirt, rock
Wheelchair Access: None
Dog-Friendly: Yes; on-leash at the trailhead. May be off-leash if under control once on the trail

Amenities: Vault toilets are available at the trailhead and Goodenough Creek Campground.
Contact: Caribou-Targhee National Forest, Westside Ranger District 208-236-7500;
Bureau of Land Management, Pocatello Field Office 208-478-6340
Trailhead GPS Coordinates: N42° 39.259' W112° 17.164'

Getting There

From I-15 south of Pocatello, take Exit 47 for McCammon. Turn right on East Merrill Road. In 1.2 miles, turn left onto West Portneuf Road and right onto Green Road shortly after. Stay on Green Road for 2.7 miles. Once Green Road enters the Goodenough Campground with a right turn, it transitions into an unnamed road. Continue on the unnamed road as it turns to the left (west). In 0.4 miles, the road ends at the Goodenough Canyon Trailhead, which has plenty of parking. The trail is located on the west side of the trailhead.

The Goodenough Canyon Trail climbing toward the ridge.

The Hike

From the Goodenough Canyon Trailhead, head west on the singletrack trail as it passes beyond a fence. For the first 0.8 miles, the path is visible and easy to follow as it ascends a couple hundred feet next to the crackling Goodenough Creek. Beyond this, the route becomes challenging to navigate due to eroded sections of the trail, deadfall, and overgrown shrubs, trees, and grasses. There are numerous creek crossings, so be prepared to get your boots wet, especially if you are hiking this trail early in the year. Despite the difficulty, the area can be beautiful, especially when the path enters sporadic marshy meadows.

At 2.3 miles (6,480 feet), the trail turns left (southwest), beginning a climb through a conifer forest up toward the ridge. From this point on, the incline increases in steepness and is generally unrelenting until the trail's end. At around 3.0 miles, you will reach the spine of the ridge, with excellent views of Goodenough Canyon. Continue southwest on the path as it moves along the ridge through bushes and evergreens.

At about 3.3 miles, the path emerges from the trees below a rocky hillside. Seeing the path from here can be challenging, so your best bet is to head directly west, picking a manageable path. Once atop this rocky hill, the trail ends at a rock cairn shortly before connecting to the Mormon Canyon Trail.

Goodenough Canyon Trail

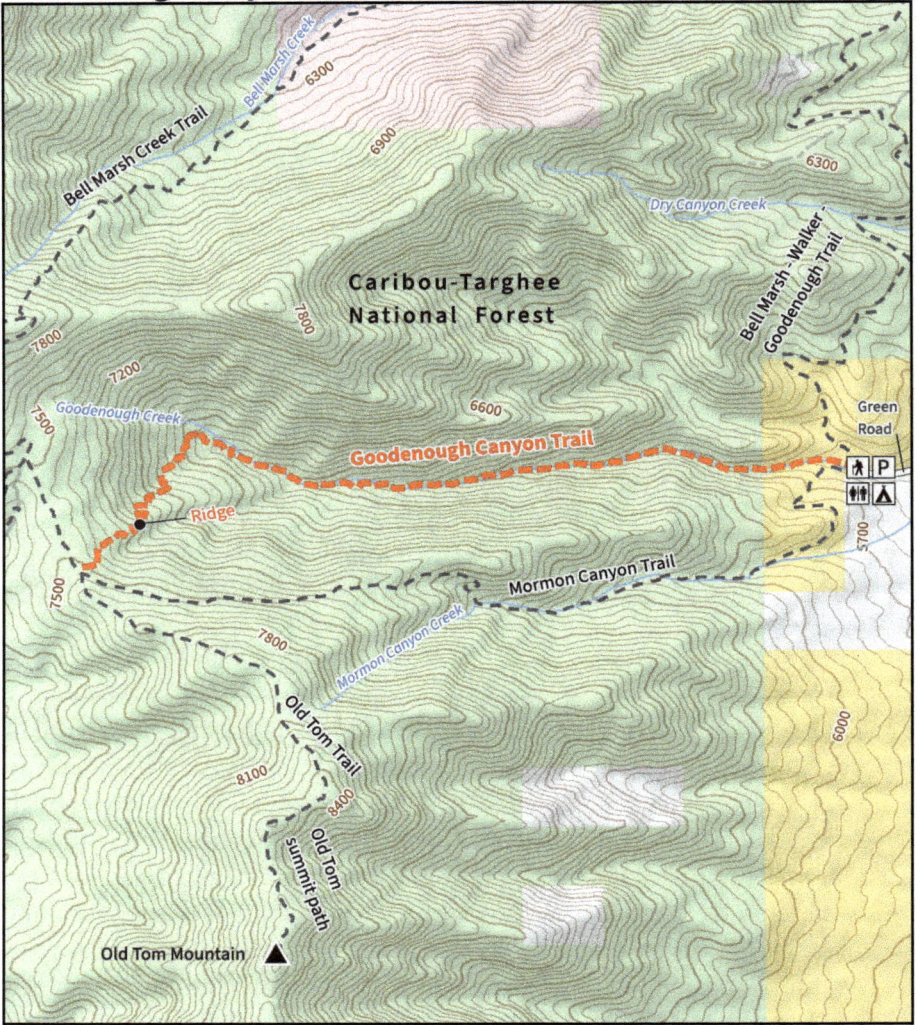

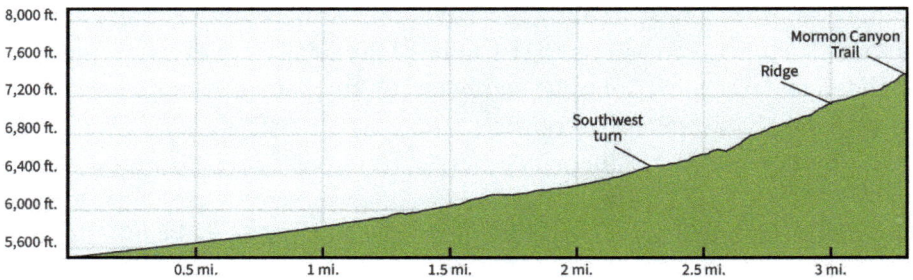

N
0.5 mi.
0.5 km.

Bell Marsh Creek Trail

6300

Bell Marsh Creek

6900

6300

Dry Canyon Creek

**Caribou-Targhee
National Forest**

Bell Marsh - Walker
Goodenough Trail

7800

7800

7200

6600

Goodenough Creek

7500

Goodenough Canyon Trail

Green
Road

Ridge

Mormon Canyon Trail

5700

7500

7800

Mormon Canyon Creek

Old Tom Trail

8100

9400

Old Tom
summit path

6000

Old Tom Mountain ▲

8,000 ft.

7,600 ft.

Mormon Canyon
Trail

7,200 ft.

Ridge

6,800 ft.

Southwest
turn

6,400 ft.

6,000 ft.

5,600 ft.

0.5 mi.   1 mi.   1.5 mi.   2 mi.   2.5 mi.   3 mi.

66. Mormon Canyon Trail (FS Trail 195)

With remarkable views of Old Tom Mountain's forested slopes along a churning creek, this steep canyon walk is an excellent way to reach the Old Tom - Scout Mountain saddle from the east. Mountain bikers will enjoy the heavily forested top and bottom of the trail, though the middle section along the creek may prove challenging for those without a sound suspension system.

Distance: 7.7 miles out-and-back
Elevation Gain: 2,150 feet
Difficulty: Strenuous
Hiking Time: About 5 hours
Nearest Town: McCammon
Trail Surface: Dirt, rock
Wheelchair Access: None
Dog-Friendly: Yes; on-leash at the trailhead. May be off-leash if under control once on the trail

Amenities: Vault toilets are available at the trailhead and Goodenough Creek Campground.
Contact: Caribou-Targhee National Forest, Westside Ranger District 208-236-7500;
Bureau of Land Management, Pocatello Field Office 208-478-6340
Trailhead GPS Coordinates: N42° 39.252' W112° 17.155'

Getting There

From I-15 south of Pocatello, take Exit 47 for McCammon. Turn right on East Merrill Road. In 1.2 miles, turn left onto West Portneuf Road and right onto Green Road shortly after that. Stay on Green Road for 2.7 miles. Once Green Road enters the Goodenough Campground with a right turn, it transitions into an unnamed road. Continue on the unnamed road as it turns to the left (west). In 0.4 miles, the road ends at the Goodenough Trailhead, which has plenty of parking. The trail is located on the southwest side of the trailhead.

The Hike

From the Goodenough Canyon Trailhead, head south on the broad path as it crosses a bridge over Goodenough Creek. The first stretch of the trail climbs up a shady forest path before crossing an open hillside at 0.4 miles. At 0.9 miles, the trail reaches the Mormon Canyon Creek, which you occasionally cross on

A mountain biker riding through an upper forest on the trail.

the climb. It is rarely an issue crossing the creek, though hiking in the early season could see you getting your boots wet.

Continue on this uneven and very rocky trail as it climbs alongside the creek, mainly under the shelter of trees. The trail's incline increases at about 1.6 miles, which can be challenging to bike up. At 2 miles (6,900 feet), the trail leaves the creek and climbs to a barren ridge. When the ridge ends at 2.5 miles, the trail enters a thick conifer forest.

The incline levels out at about 2.6 miles, giving a quarter-mile of more gradual incline to enjoy the views of Old Tom's forested slopes. At 2.9 miles, the incline picks up again for a final hill.

After about 100 feet of climbing, the steep-sided trail levels out again, making the shaded walk under the thick evergreens an enjoyable experience. At 3.3 miles, the trail reaches the saddle between Old Tom Mountain and Scout Mountain. Old Tom Trail is to your left (south), and to your right (north) is the final stretch of the Mormon Canyon Trail. The saddle makes a great spot to turn around; if you want to continue to the endpoint of Mormon Canyon Trail, head north on the last stretch of sun-exposed trail. In 0.6 miles, the trail ends once it connects with Scout Mountain Top Road.

Mormon Canyon Trail

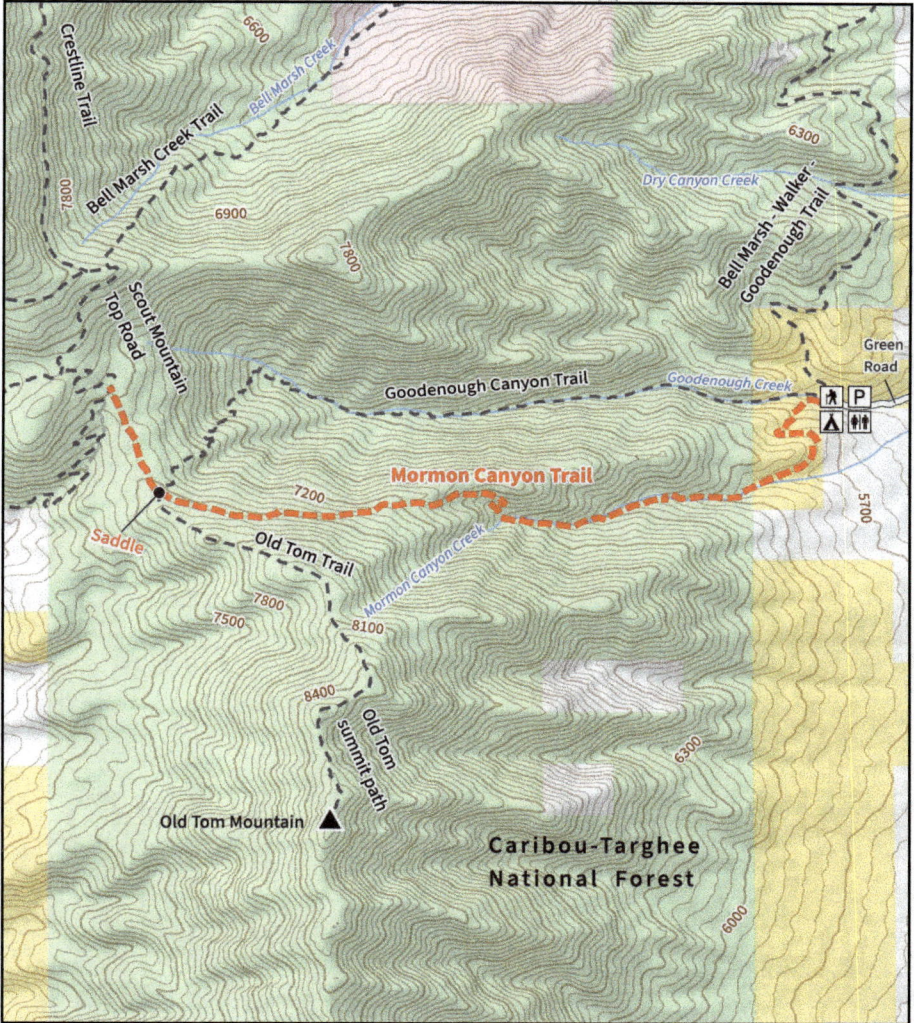

N

0.5 mi.
0.5 km.

Crestline Trail

6600

Bell Marsh Creek Trail

Bell Marsh Creek

7800

6900

7800

Dry Canyon Creek

6300

Bell Marsh - Walker - Goodenough Trail

Scout Mountain Top Road

Goodenough Canyon Trail

Goodenough Creek

Green Road

Mormon Canyon Trail

7200

Saddle

Old Tom Trail

Mormon Canyon Creek

7800

7500

8100

8400

Old Tom summit path

Old Tom Mountain ▲

5100

Caribou-Targhee National Forest

6300

6000

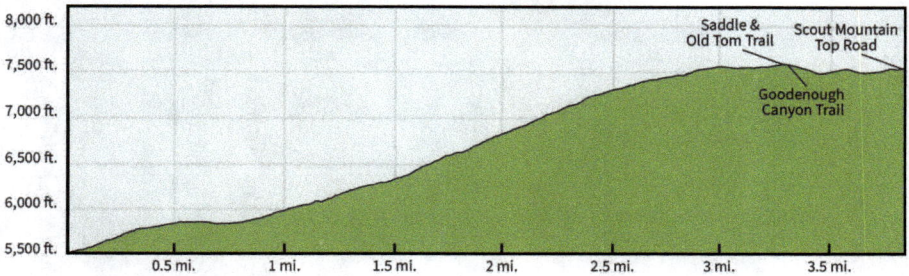

8,000 ft.

7,500 ft.

Saddle & Old Tom Trail

Scout Mountain Top Road

7,000 ft.

Goodenough Canyon Trail

6,500 ft.

6,000 ft.

5,500 ft.

0.5 mi.   1 mi.   1.5 mi.   2 mi.   2.5 mi.   3 mi.   3.5 mi.

Portneuf Range

The Portneuf Range, located along I-15 from Inkom to McCammon, has a variety of impressive trails that are some of the most remote in the book. This makes it ideal for hikers looking to escape from the busier paths closer to Pocatello. Crowd-favorite hikes in the range include the South Fork Inman Creek Trail and Robbers Roost Canyon Loop, both perfect for those seeking smaller day hikes in the area. The Portneuf Wildlife Management Area, which provides protected habitat for wintering mule deer, can be found on the western stretch of the range between Inkom and McCammon.

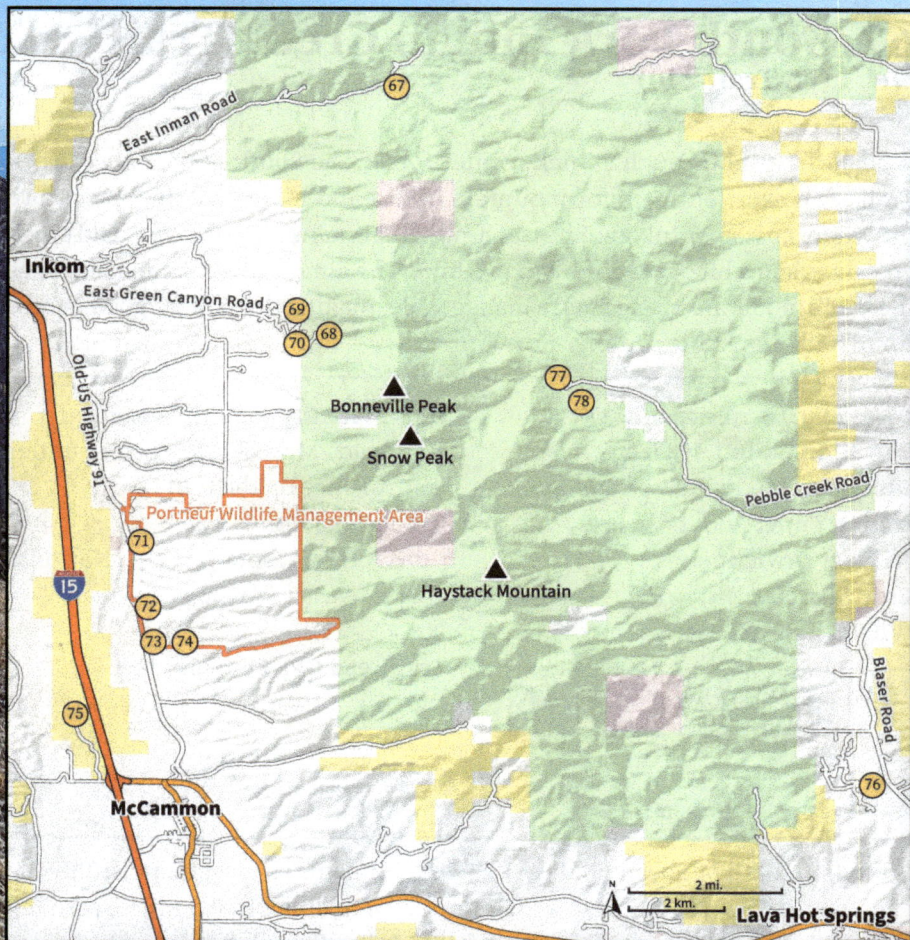

Map Labels

East Inman Road

67

Inkom

East Green Canyon Road

69

70 68

▲ Bonneville Peak

77

78

▲ Snow Peak

Pebble Creek Road

Portneuf Wildlife Management Area

71

▲ Haystack Mountain

72

73 74

75

Blaser Road

McCammon

76

N

2 mi.

2 km.

Lava Hot Springs

Haystack Mountain from a ridge on Snow Peak.

67. South Fork Inman Creek Trail
(FS Trail 240)

A beautiful trail through a thick conifer forest, the South Fork Inman Creek Trail is an excellent path for mountain bikers and hikers looking to explore the wilderness near Inkom. The trail is well maintained, though the wild creek crossings add a bit of adventure to this hike. The almost constant shade makes the trail's moderate incline more manageable, making this route a good choice for hikers even in the summer heat.

Distance: 6.8 miles one-way
Elevation Gain: 1,400 feet
Difficulty: Moderately strenuous
Hiking Time: About 4 hours
Nearest Town: Inkom
Trail Surface: Dirt, rock
Wheelchair Access: None

Dog-Friendly: Yes; on-leash at the trailhead. May be off-leash if under control once on the trail
Amenities: None
Contact: Caribou-Targhee National Forest, Westside Ranger District 208-236-7500
Trailhead GPS Coordinates:
N42° 50.714' W112° 08.489'

Getting There

From I-15 south of Pocatello, take Exit 58 for Inkom. Turn right on I-15BL/Old Highway 30 West, then make a left onto Grant Avenue. In 0.5 miles, turn left onto Main Street. Stay on Main Street for 2.5 miles (keep left at 1.1 miles to stay on Main Street). Turn right onto East Inman Road, which you will stay on for 5.0 miles until you reach the South Fork Inman Trailhead on the right side of the road. (Keep left at 2.7 miles to continue on East Inman Road.) The trail is on the southeast side of the trailhead.

The Hike

From the trailhead, head southeast on the singletrack trail, which crosses to the south side of the creek on a makeshift bridge almost immediately into the hike. For the first 3 miles, this trail climbs uphill about 1,450 feet alongside the heavily forested South Fork Inman Creek. The trail does cross the creek several times, though the crossings are usually easy to navigate without getting

An aspen grove on the South Fork Inman Creek Trail.

your feet wet. There are two old bridge crossings on the route, located about 1.6 miles and 2 miles into the trail.

At 1.4 miles, the trail shifts from the southeast to the south, where it heads for the remainder of the hike. At 2.4 miles, the trail becomes steeper, gaining over 450 feet in 0.7 miles as it climbs out of the canyon. As you approach the "summit" on the trail, the evergreens often swap out for beautiful aspen groves.

At 3.1 miles, the trail tops out (7,280 feet). The last 0.3 miles gradually descend about 150 feet through thinning trees. The trail ends in an open field when the path connects with Forest Service Road 13.

The region near Inkom was first named "Ingacom" by the Shoshone Native Americans in reference to a rock formation that still overlooks the city to this day. This rock formation, otherwise known as the "Red Hare", is featured as the logo on the City of Inkom's website.

South Fork Inman Creek Trail

N   0.5 mi.
    0.5 km.

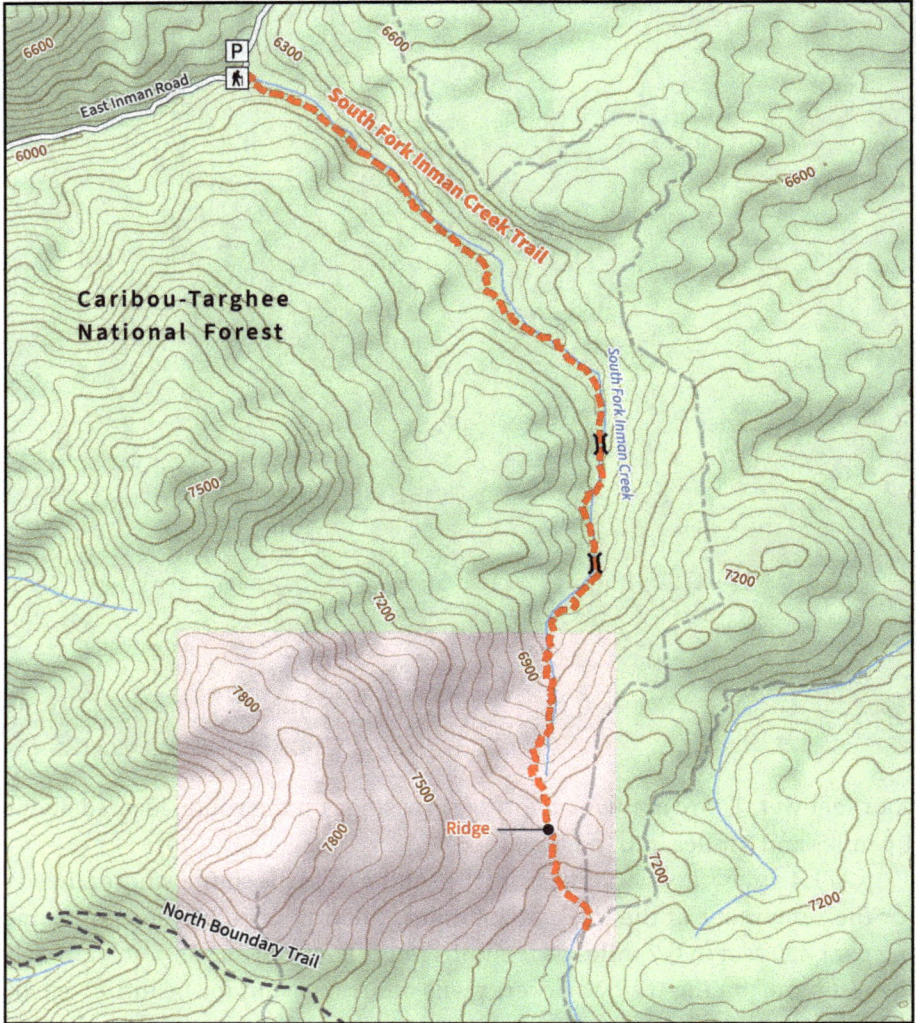

East Inman Road

South Fork Inman Creek Trail

Caribou-Targhee
National Forest

South Fork Inman Creek

Ridge

North Boundary Trail

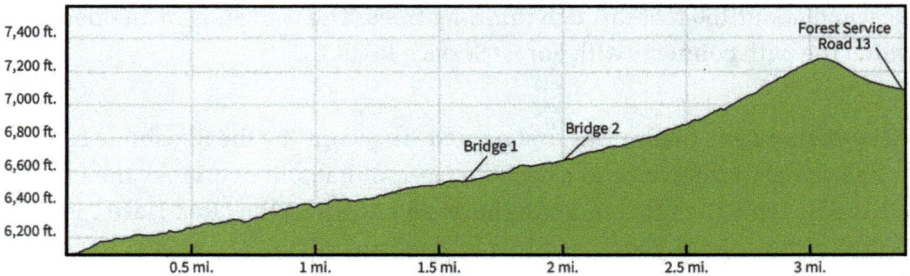

Bridge 1

Bridge 2

Forest Service
Road 13

7,400 ft.
7,200 ft.
7,000 ft.
6,800 ft.
6,600 ft.
6,400 ft.
6,200 ft.

0.5 mi.   1 mi.   1.5 mi.   2 mi.   2.5 mi.   3 mi.

68. Pebble Creek Ski Area (The Cat Track)

Beginning at the Pebble Creek Ski Resort, this trail climbs high on the forested slopes of Bonneville Peak, traveling under chair lifts and across steep hillsides to the top of the Skyline Lift, providing beautiful views along the way. This trail is steep and rocky, with a challenging workout for hikers and a miserable ride for mountain bikers. For the skiers in the community, this hike is a fun opportunity to see what some of your favorite ski trails look like without a blanket of snow covering them.

Distance: 5 miles out-and-back
Elevation Gain: 1,840 feet
Difficulty: Moderately strenuous
Hiking Time: About 3.5 hours
Nearest Town: Inkom
Trail Surface: Dirt, rock
Wheelchair Access: None

Dog-Friendly: Yes; on-leash at the trailhead. May be off-leash if under control once on the trail
Amenities: None
Contact: Caribou-Targhee National Forest, Westside Ranger District 208-236-7500;
Pebble Creek Ski Area 208-775-4452
Trailhead GPS Coordinates:
N42° 46.671' W112° 09.575'

Getting There

From I-15 south of Pocatello, take Exit 58 for Inkom. Turn right on I-15BL/Old Highway 30 West. In 0.8 miles, continue straight onto North Old Highway 91. Continue on Old Highway 91 for 1.4 miles, then turn left onto North Inkom Road. Make the second right onto East Green Canyon Road, which ends at the Pebble Creek Ski Resort in 4.3 miles. The route begins at the road on the east side of the parking lot, which crosses the front of the ticket office.

The Hike

From the east side of the upper parking lot, head north up the wide 4x4 trail toward the Pebble Creek ticket office until you reach the middle of the three ski lifts (the Skyline Lift). Continue on the trail to the left (west) of the Skyline Lift, making a right (east) turn shortly past it toward the Aspen Lift. The goal here is to connect to the Pebble Lane ski trail, also called the cat track. The stretch

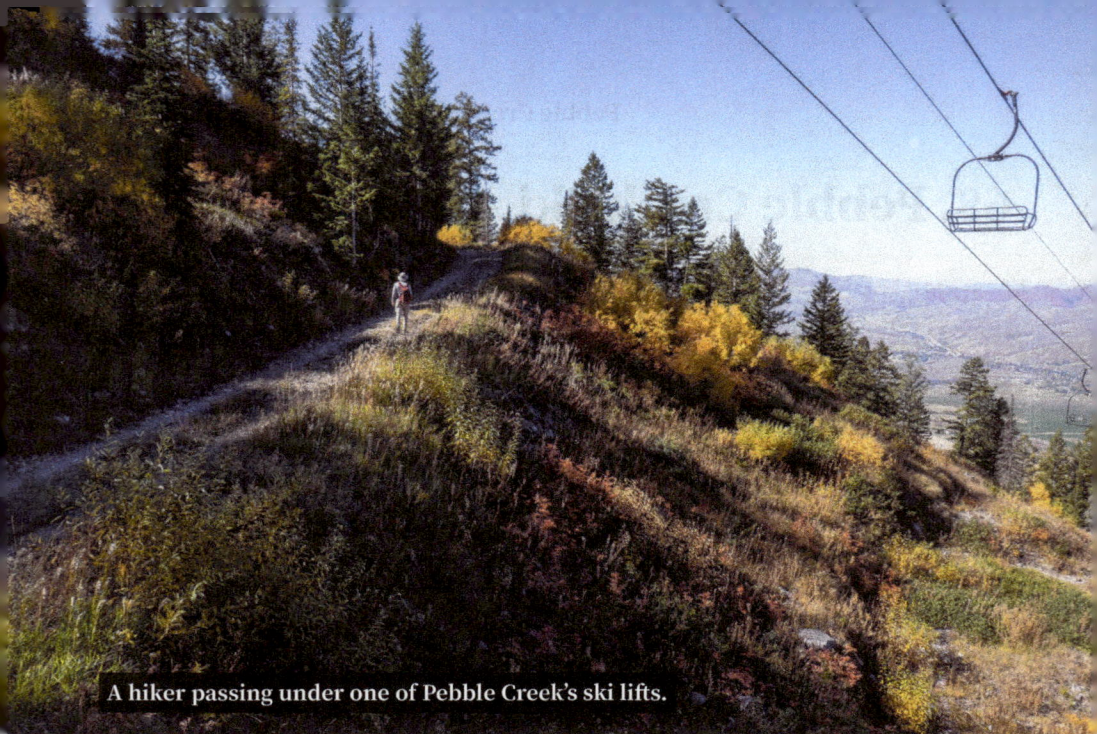
A hiker passing under one of Pebble Creek's ski lifts.

between the Skyline Lift and the first switchback is the steepest part of the trail, gaining 230 feet in just 0.2 miles.

At 0.3 miles, the rough path joins onto the wide 4x4 trail. For the next 1.3 miles, the trail climbs 850 feet on a series of very rocky switchbacks below the ski lifts through open hillsides and shady forests until it reaches the top of the Sunshine Lift. While the switchbacks alleviate some of the incline, this is still a steep trail, so be prepared for a climb.

At 1.6 miles, the trail passes by the top of the Sunshine Lift, signifying the beginning of the upper mountain. The trail rounds a hill not long past the Sunshine Lift, making a left (east) turn. At 1.7 miles, continue on the narrow 4x4 trail to stay on route. The upper stretch of the mountain is a bit steeper than the early stretch, gaining over 650 feet in 0.9 miles. The upper mountain feels more isolated than the lower mountain, mainly because of the bushes and foliage blocking many views.

The trail ends at the top of the Skyline Lift. This is an excellent spot to take a water and snack break before descending the mountain.

The Pebble Creek Ski Area is a popular winter recreation destination in Southeastern Idaho, boasting over 1,100 acres of skiable terrain and three chairlifts. However, it was not always known as Pebble Creek. When it first opened in 1949, it went by the name of Skyline and only had two tow ropes and a warming hut. The name Pebble Creek was given to the ski hill in 1979.

Pebble Creek Ski Area

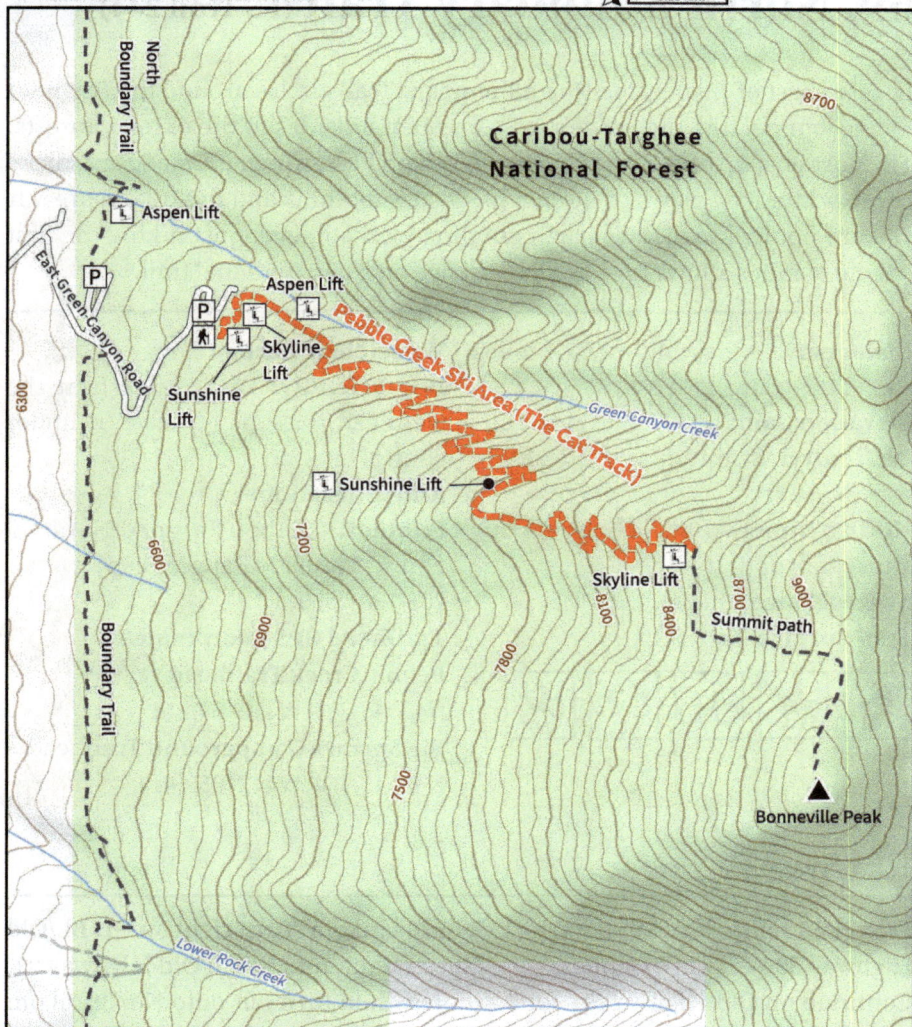

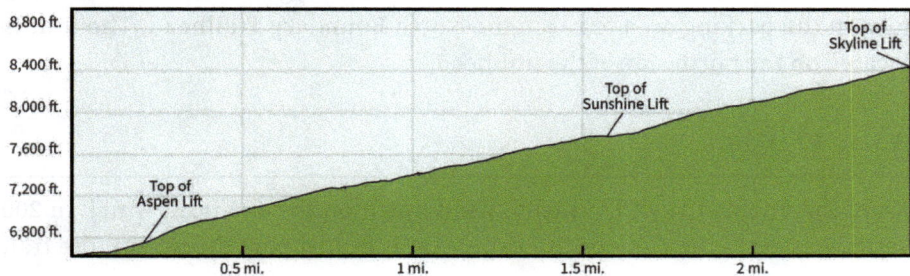

N
0.25 mi.
0.25 km.

North Boundary Trail

Caribou-Targhee National Forest

8700

Aspen Lift

P

East Green Canyon Road

Aspen Lift

P

Skyline Lift

Pebble Creek Ski Area (The Cat Track)

Sunshine Lift

Green Canyon Creek

6300

6600

7200

6900

Sunshine Lift

8100

8400

Skyline Lift

8700

9000

Summit path

Boundary Trail

7800

7500

Bonneville Peak

Lower Rock Creek

8,800 ft.

Top of Skyline Lift

8,400 ft.

8,000 ft.

Top of Sunshine Lift

7,600 ft.

7,200 ft.

Top of Aspen Lift

6,800 ft.

0.5 mi.   1 mi.   1.5 mi.   2 mi.

69. North Boundary Trail (FS Trail 244)

Located east of Inkom, the North Boundary Trail circles around the Portneuf Range, connecting the range's western open hillsides to the eastern forests. The northern tip of the route climbs to Inkom Pass, which is a steep and rocky climb with many views of Bonneville Peak's foothills and the Inkom area. If you are not looking for a heart-pounding workout, even just hiking the first couple of miles allows for a fun experience on a more gradual trail.

Distance: 7.7 miles one-way; 7.6 miles round trip to Inkom Pass
Elevation Gain: 1,530 feet; 1,430 feet
Difficulty: Strenuous; Moderately strenuous
Hiking Time: About 4.5 hours for either trail option
Nearest Town: Inkom
Trail Surface: Dirt, rock

Wheelchair Access: None
Dog-Friendly: Yes; on-leash at the trailhead. May be off-leash if under control once on the trail
Amenities: None
Contact: Caribou-Targhee National Forest, Westside Ranger District 208-236-7500
Trailhead GPS Coordinates:
Pebble Creek Trailhead
N42° 46.796' W112° 09.816'
Big Springs Campground Trailhead
N42° 45.964' W112° 05.641'

Getting There

From I-15 south of Pocatello, take Exit 58 for Inkom. Turn right on I-15BL/Old Highway 30 West. In 0.8 miles, continue straight onto North Old Highway 91. Continue on Old Highway 91 for 1.4 miles, then turn left onto North Inkom Road. Make the second right onto East Green Canyon Road, and then in 3.7 miles, turn left into the Lower Pebble Creek Parking Lot. Make the first left turn in the parking area to reach the North Boundary Trailhead. The trail is located on the north side of the trailhead.

The Hike

From the Pebble Creek Trailhead, head north on the 4x4 trail, which in 200 yards, passes to the right of the Aspen Ski Lift. Just past the ski lift, the trail

North Boundary Trail shortly before reaching Inkom Pass.

enters the forest and crosses over Green Canyon Creek. For the first 2.0 miles, this trail travels north, mainly on grassy hillsides, but occasionally dips into forested drainages. There are many small ups and downs during this stretch, though generally, the trail moves downhill, making for a fun mountain bike ride.

At about 2.0 miles, the trail crosses over Jackson Creek, and then shortly beyond that creek crossing, it makes a right (east) turn, beginning the steep climb toward Inkom Pass. The rocky trail cuts along steep hillsides, gaining over 1,400 feet in 1.8 miles. The scenery is pretty, though you may be too out of breath to fully appreciate it. Mountain bikers, in particular, will have trouble in this section due to the large amount of rocks in the trail.

The trail tops out at Inkom Pass (7,620 feet) at 3.8 miles, which sits at a junction with Inkom Pass Loop on the left (north) and Bonneville Peak Trail on the right (south). Continue east through the intersection to begin the southeast half of the route, which descends 1,250 feet in 4 miles. In contrast to the open hillsides of the western portion of the trail, the eastern half is almost entirely covered in evergreen forests. The upper portion remains relatively steep but becomes more gradual, starting at around 5.2 miles.

As you descend further down the trail, the path becomes smoother, making for a fun mountain bike ride. At 6.2 miles, the trail crosses through a junction with a Forest Service Road called Boundary Connector. Make a slight right (south) to stay on the North Boundary Trail. At 7.3 miles, turn left (southeast) onto Forest Service Road 024. At 7.6 miles, make a right (southwest) turn onto Forest Service Road 36. The route ends at the gate leading into Big Springs Campground. If you want to continue onto Boundary Trail, that route starts to the left (south) of the gate.

The Bonneville Flood, which poured through Marsh Valley about 17,400 years ago, is believed to be the second-largest flood in geologic history. The cause of the flood is not known for certain. Some theories suggest an earthquake ruptured a natural dam near Red Rock Pass. Others propose that natural erosion wore down the dam and eventually caused it to rupture.

A mountain biker descending North Boundary Trail.

North Boundary Trail

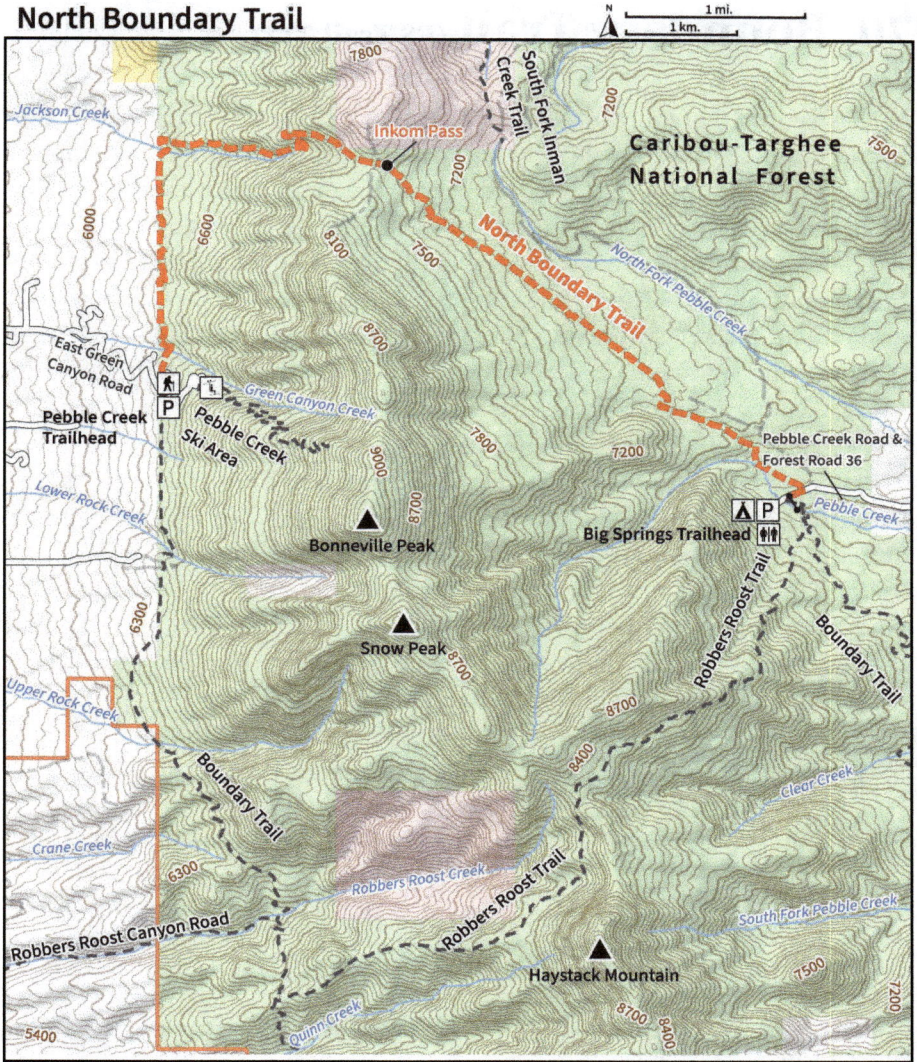

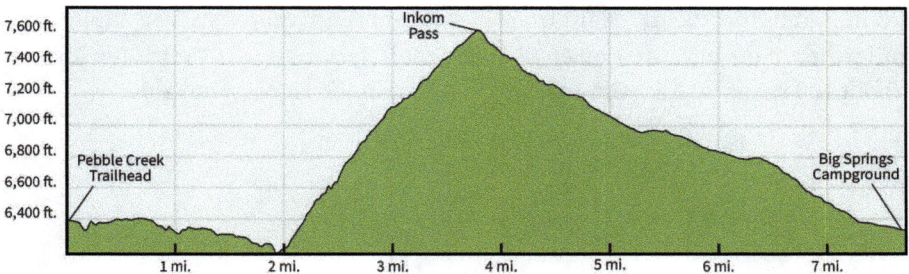

Map of the North Boundary Trail showing the route from Pebble Creek Trailhead through Inkom Pass to Big Springs Trailhead in the Caribou-Targhee National Forest. Features include Bonneville Peak, Snow Peak, Haystack Mountain, and various creeks and roads.

Elevation profile for the North Boundary Trail, from Pebble Creek Trailhead through Inkom Pass (~7,600 ft.) to Big Springs Campground, spanning approximately 7+ miles.

70. Boundary Trail (FS Trail 272)

A massive trail that tours around the Portneuf Range, Boundary Trail makes for an impressive one-way hike with excellent views throughout. Attempting to hike this in its entirety comes with a grueling amount of elevation gain on rocky trails, though trail runners and mountain bikers may be up for the challenge. There are many individual sections of the hike that are worth exploring on their own; my favorite is the southern stretch near the rocky cliffs of Haystack Mountain. I recommend hiking the first 4 miles from the Pebble Creek Trailhead on the west side of the Portneuf Range or the first 6.5 miles from Big Springs Campground on the east side.

Distance: 29 miles one-way
Elevation Gain: 7,360 feet
Difficulty: Very strenuous
Hiking Time: About 18 hours
Nearest Town: Inkom
Trail Surface: Dirt, rock
Wheelchair Access: None

Dog-Friendly: Yes; on-leash at the trailhead. May be off-leash if under control once on the trail
Amenities: None
Contact: Caribou-Targhee National Forest, Westside Ranger District 208-236-7500
Trailhead GPS Coordinates:
Pebble Creek Trailhead
N42° 46.637' W112° 09.791'
Big Springs Campground Trailhead
N42° 45.964' W112° 05.641'

Getting There

From I-15 south of Pocatello, take Exit 58 for Inkom. Turn right on I-15BL/Old Highway 30 West. In 0.8 miles, continue straight onto North Old Highway 91. Continue on Old Highway 91 for 1.4 miles, then turn left onto North Inkom Road. Make the second right onto East Green Canyon Road, and then in 3.7 miles, turn left into the Lower Pebble Creek Parking Lot. The trail is located about 100 yards up East Green Canyon Road on the right (west) side.

Boundary Trail near the Big Springs Campground.

The Hike

The western half of the trail has five large hills that must be climbed. They typically look like this: you climb a steep forested hillside above a drainage. Once you reach the top, you travel across a ridge intermixed with open hillsides and tree cover, often with excellent views of the valley and Bannock Range to the west. The trail will then descend a steep, often rocky hillside to a creek, where the process begins again. The five hills are as follows:

- ▶ Hill 1
    - ▽ Mile 2.0: Descend 300 feet in 0.5 miles
- ▶ Hill 2
    - ▽ Mile 3.0: Ascend 270 feet in 0.4 miles
    - ▽ Mile 4.2: Descend 520 feet in 0.7 miles
- ▶ Hill 3
    - ▽ Mile 5.0: Ascend 460 feet in 0.8 miles
    - ▽ Mile 5.8: Descend 530 feet in 0.6 miles
- ▶ Hill 4
    - ▽ Mile 6.4: Ascend 340 feet in 0.3 miles
    - ▽ Mile 7.7: Descend 290 feet in 0.2 miles
- ▶ Hill 5
    - ▽ Mile 7.9: Ascend 370 feet in 0.4 miles
    - ▽ Mile 9.0: Descend 720 feet in 1.0 mile

Let's jump into the route with those hill stats out of the way. From the Pebble Creek Trailhead, head southwest on the signed 272 trail. For the first 2 miles, this trail moves south across open hillsides covered in grass, sage, and shrubs. This section of the hike has several ups and downs, but there are no significant elevation changes. At about 1.4 miles, the trail crosses over Lower Rock Creek. Shortly beyond the creek, at 1.5 miles, continue straight (south) through the junction.

At about 3 miles, the now-forested trail crosses over Upper Rock Creek, and shortly beyond that, at 3.1 miles, it makes a left (east) turn at a junction. At 5.0 miles, the trail crosses over Robbers Roost Creek, passing by the Lower Robbers Roost Trail on the right (west) side of the trail. At about 5.7 miles, continue past the Robbers Roost Trail on the left (east) side of the trail. At 6.3 miles, you will pass over Quinn Creek.

At 9.5 miles, the trail joins with Harkness Canyon Road. Turn right (southwest) onto the road, which you will stay on for a little over half a mile. At 10.0 miles, make a left (southwest) turn back onto Boundary Trail, where the trail begins to climb 1,200 feet in 1.7 miles. At 10.9 miles, keep left (east) at the junction. This junction marks the beginning of the trail's southern portion, which heads east.

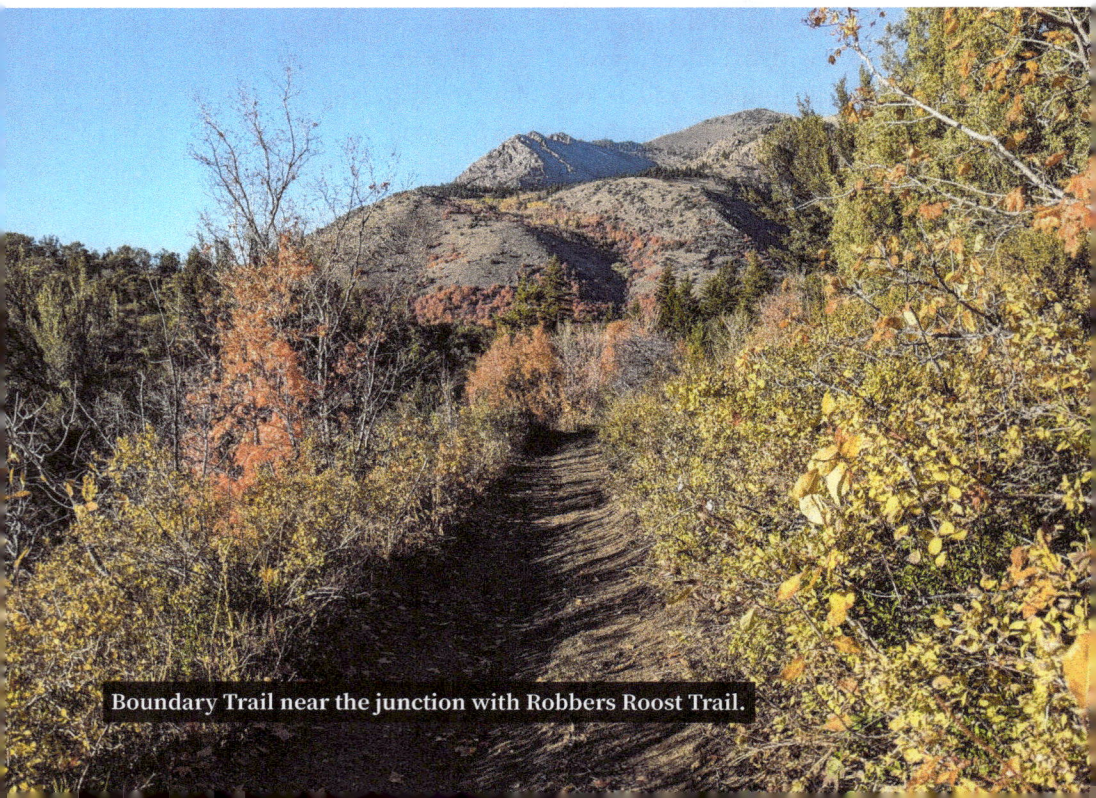

Boundary Trail near the junction with Robbers Roost Trail.

A bridge crossing over Pebble Creek.

The trail tops out on a ridge at 11.7 miles (6,870 feet), with beautiful views of the cliff faces to the northeast. After a few small climbs, the trail reaches the route's high point at 12.8 miles (6,960 feet). From this high point, the route heads southeast and begins descending the longest hill on the entire route, losing 1,460 feet in 2.6 miles. In addition to being a nice break for the legs, this significant decline also has views of the hills to the south.

At 15.4 miles, just past a bridge, the trail bottoms out at a junction with East Bob Smith Trail. Continue straight (east), following the signs for Beach Hollow. The trail quickly begins climbing up a rocky trail through a canyon, gaining 880 feet in 1.4 miles. The trail tops out at 16.8 miles (6,370 feet), where it soon begins another significant decline, this time descending 750 feet in 1.8 miles through a pleasant forest.

At 17.7 miles, you will come to the first of two back-to-back junctions on the path's right (south) side. Keep left (east and then northeast) to pass by the Beach - Bird Connector. Shortly past these junctions, the trail heads north, beginning the eastern stretch of the route.

At 18.6 miles, you will pass by the wild Bell Canyon Trail on the left (west) side of the path. From here, the trail climbs up and down several small forested hills as it continues its northward journey. At 20.5 miles, you will pass by the narrow South Fork Reed Canyon Trail on the left (west) side of the trail, and at about 20.7 miles, you will make a right (north) turn to avoid joining the Reed Canyon Trail.

At 21 miles, you will reach the last massive incline on the trail, which gains 1,150 feet in 1.5 miles on a largely treeless hillside. The trail tops out at 22.5 miles (6,610 feet), where you will find excellent views of Haystack Mountain to the west. Continue northwest to begin the last major descent on the trail, which takes you across a lovely hillside intermixed with low forests.

At 24 miles, you will come to a confusing jumble of trails. Keep right (north) initially, then 130 yards from there, make a sharp left (southwest). About 100 yards from that turn, make a right (northeast) turn, ending the confusing mess of trails. At about 25 miles, continue left (northwest) through the junction with Forest Service Road 23. At 25.7 miles, continue straight (north) to dodge Forest Service Road 23 again.

The final stretch of the trail primarily travels in a scenic evergreen and aspen forest. At about 26.1 miles, the trail passes over a cattle guard. At 27.7 miles, cross over yet another cattle guard. At about 28.5 miles, pass by the Robbers Roost Trail on the left (west) side of the trail. At 28.9 miles, make a right (northeast) turn. The trail ends in about 100 yards at the Big Springs Campground gate.

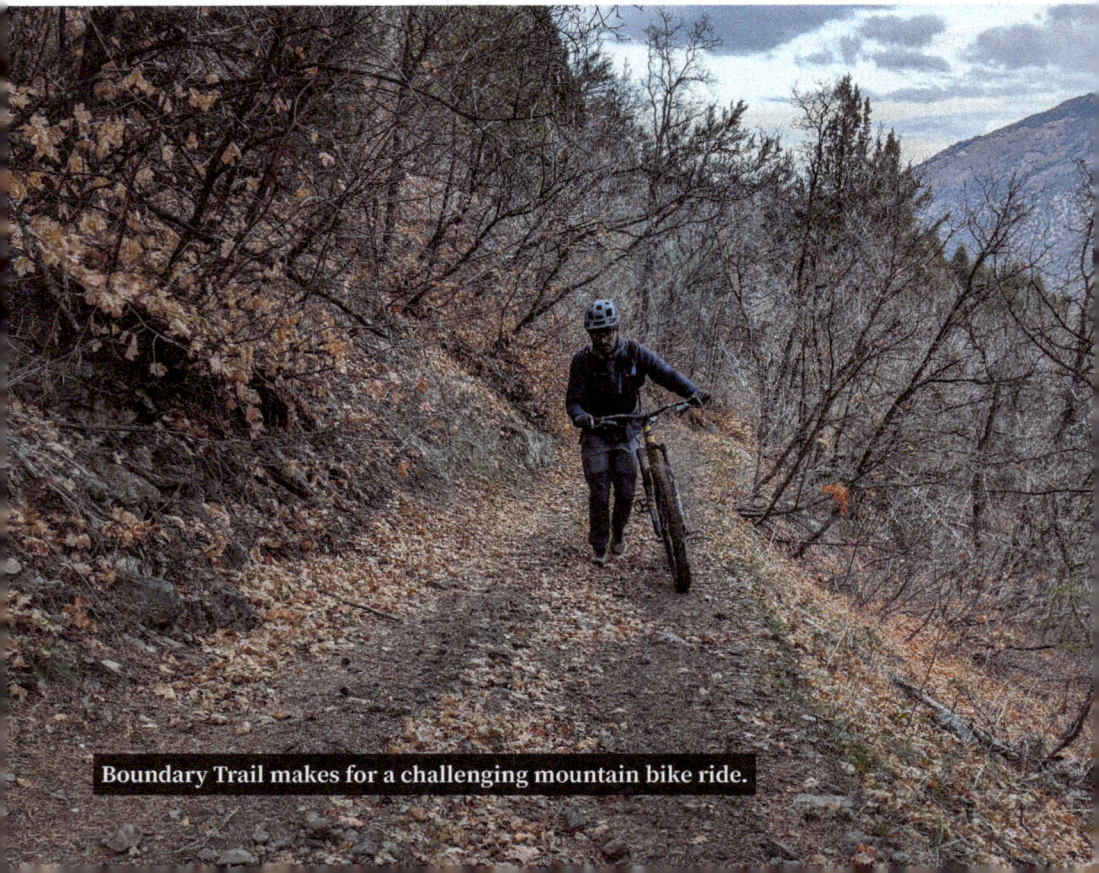

Boundary Trail makes for a challenging mountain bike ride.

Boundary Trail

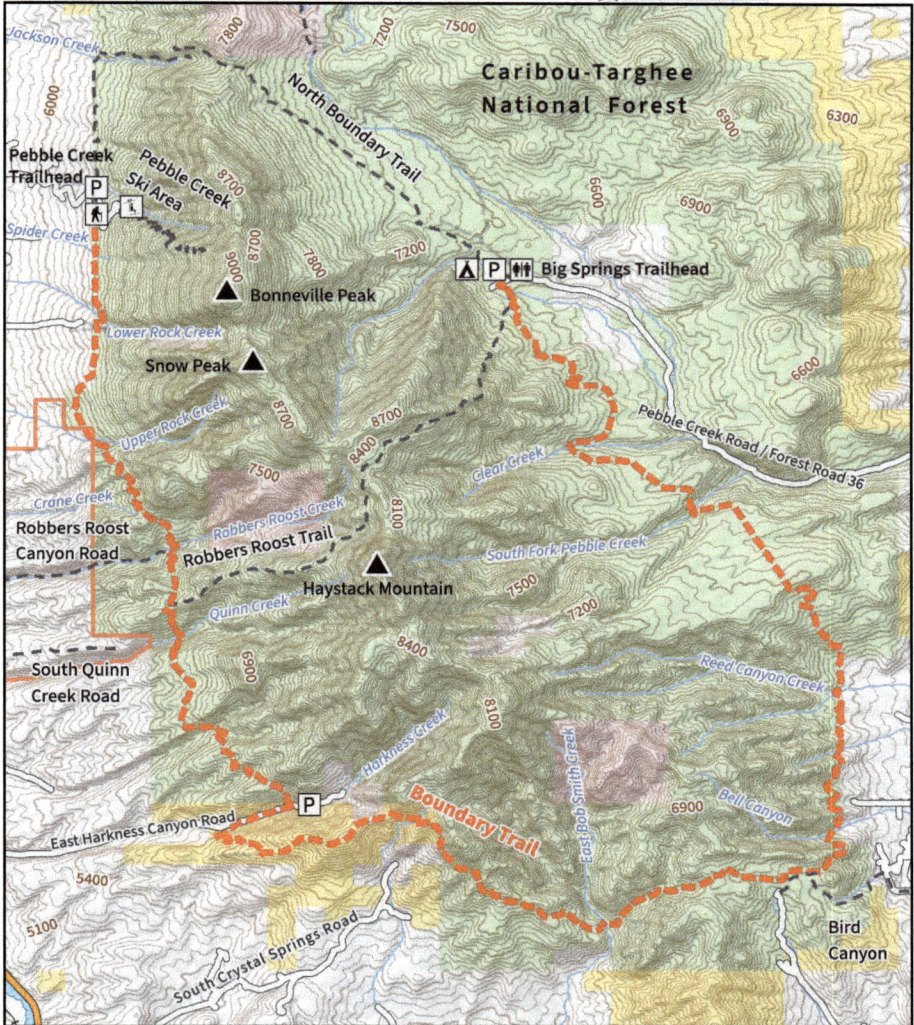

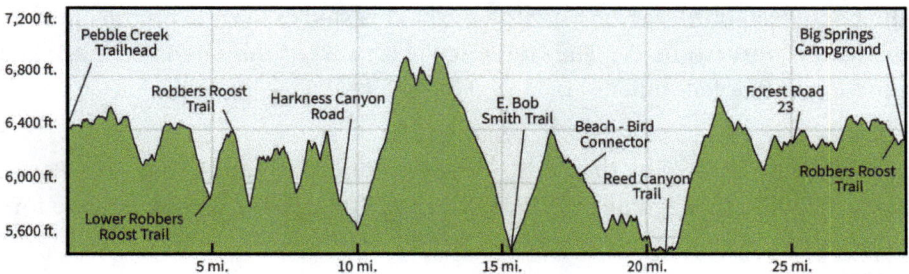

N

2 mi.

2 km.

Jackson Creek

7800

7200

7500

North Boundary Trail

Caribou-Targhee
National Forest

6000

6300

6900

Pebble Creek
Trailhead

Pebble Creek
Ski Area

8700

6600

6900

Spider Creek

8700

7800

9000

7200

Big Springs Trailhead

P

Bonneville Peak

Lower Rock Creek

6600

Snow Peak

Upper Rock Creek

8700

8700

8100

Clear Creek

Pebble Creek Road / Forest Road 36

6600

Crone Creek

7500

Robbers Roost Creek

8400

Robbers Roost
Canyon Road

Robbers Roost Trail

South Fork Pebble Creek

Haystack Mountain

7500

Quinn Creek

8400

7200

Reed Canyon Creek

South Quinn
Creek Road

6900

8100

Harkness Creek

Bell Canyon

P

East Bob Smith Creek

6900

East Harkness Canyon Road

Boundary Trail

5400

5100

South Crystal Springs Road

Bird
Canyon

7,200 ft.

Pebble Creek
Trailhead

Big Springs
Campground

6,800 ft.

Robbers Roost
Trail

Harkness Canyon
Road

Forest Road
23

6,400 ft.

E. Bob
Smith Trail

Beach - Bird
Connector

Robbers Roost
Trail

6,000 ft.

Lower Robbers
Roost Trail

Reed Canyon
Trail

5,600 ft.

5 mi.   10 mi.   15 mi.   20 mi.   25 mi.

71. Crane Creek

Crane Creek offers a brief creekside walk in the Portneuf Wildlife Management Area. With a prominent view of Snow Peak on the horizon, this slightly wild hike is a perfect bite-size adventure.

Distance: 2 miles out-and-back
Elevation Gain: 430 feet
Difficulty: Easy
Hiking Time: About 1 hour
Nearest Town: McCammon
Trail Surface: Dirt, rock

Wheelchair Access: None
Dog-Friendly: Yes; on-leash at the trailhead. May be off-leash if under control once on the trail
Amenities: None
Contact: Idaho Fish and Game, Southeast Region 208-232-4703
Trailhead GPS Coordinates: N42° 43.343' W112° 12.277'

Getting There

From I-15 south of Pocatello, take Exit 58 for Inkom. Turn right on I-15BL/Old Highway 30 West. In 0.8 miles, continue straight onto North Old Highway 91. Continue on Old Highway 91 for 5.8 miles. Turn left into the Portneuf Wildlife Management Area parking lot. The trailhead is located on the east end of the parking loop beyond a gate.

The Hike

From the trailhead, head east past the gate on the singletrack trail. The initial stretch of the trail travels on the south side of Crane Creek, though after about 150 yards, it crosses over to the north side. After the creek crossing, the remainder of the hike remains consistent. The trail continues gradually climbing northeast, bordered on one side by the forested creek and on the other by a shrub-covered hillside. The trail ends just short of the one-mile mark at a junction with a 4x4 trail.

Established in 1970 by the Idaho Department of Fish and Game, the Portneuf Wildlife Management Area (WMA) provides a critical winter range for mule deer and a habitat for sharp-tailed grouse.

A hiker on Crane Creek Trail.

Keep Going

Located about 200 yards north of the trailhead on the west side of Old Highway 91, the **Crane Creek Park** provides a fun 0.3-mile loop along the Portneuf River. With two covered picnic benches, educational signage, fishing access, and a bark-covered walking path, consider this as a family-friendly outdoor option in the Inkom area.

Crane Creek

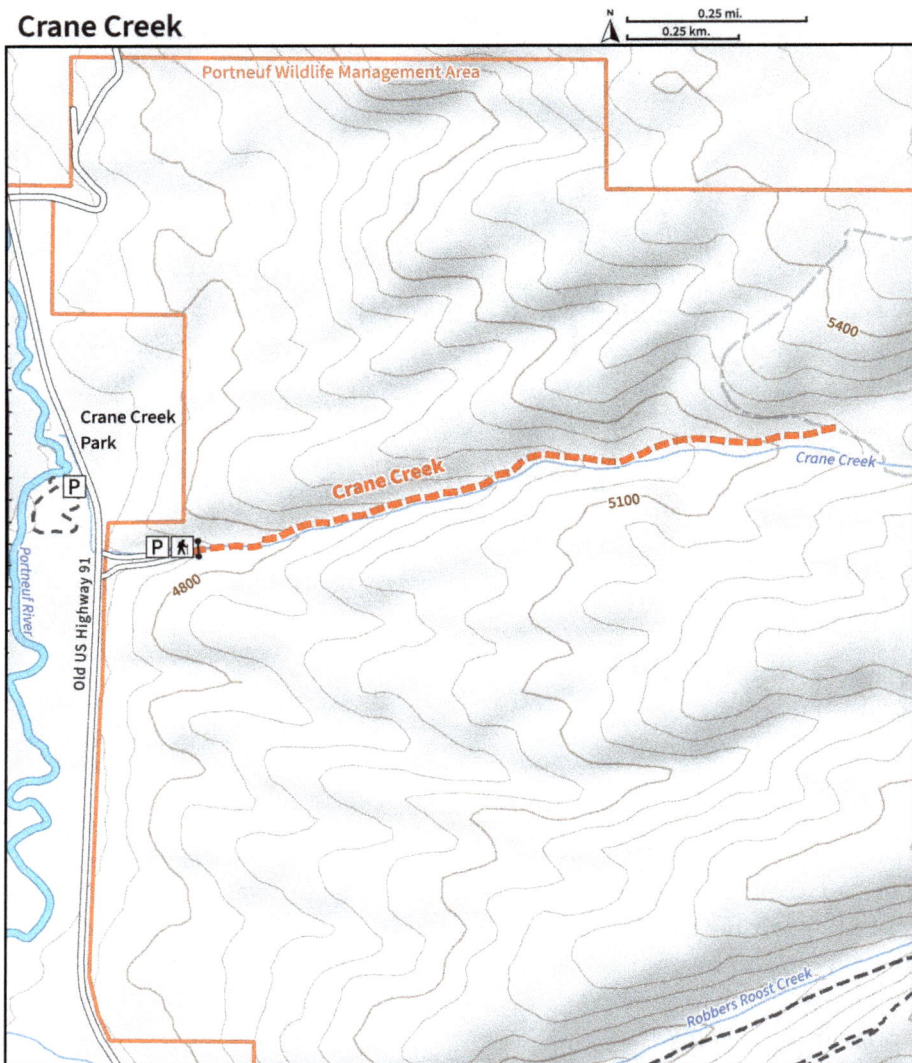

Portneuf Wildlife Management Area

Crane Creek Park

Crane Creek

Crane Creek

5400

5100

4800

Portneuf River

Old US Highway 91

Robbers Roost Creek

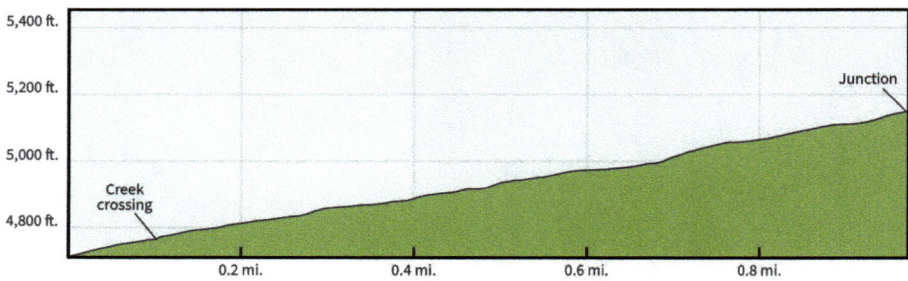

5,400 ft.

5,200 ft.

5,000 ft.

4,800 ft.

Creek crossing

Junction

0.2 mi.   0.4 mi.   0.6 mi.   0.8 mi.

72. Robbers Roost Canyon Loop

The Robbers Roost Canyon Loop is a diverse trail that winds through the Portneuf Wildlife Management Area. The trail consists of two distinct halves - the first half traverses a singletrack trail on an open ridge, offering stunning mountain vistas, while the second half follows a dirt road alongside a babbling creek. Note that motorized vehicles are only allowed on the northern half of the trail, specifically on the Robbers Roost Canyon Road.

Distance: 3-mile loop
Elevation Gain: 640 feet
Difficulty: Moderate
Hiking Time: About 2 hours
Nearest Town: McCammon
Trail Surface: Dirt, rock

Wheelchair Access: None
Dog-Friendly: Yes; on-leash at the trailhead. May be off-leash if under control once on the trail
Amenities: None
Contact: Idaho Fish and Game, Southeast Region 208-232-4703
Trailhead GPS Coordinates: N42° 42.365' W112° 12.302'

Getting There

From I-15 south of Pocatello, take Exit 58 for Inkom. Turn right on I-15BL/Old Highway 30 West. In 0.8 miles, continue straight onto North Old Highway 91. Continue on Old Highway 91 for 6.9 miles. Turn left into the Portneuf Wildlife Management Area parking lot. The trailhead is located on the north end of the parking area.

The Hike

From the trailhead, head east on the singletrack trail past the gate. At 0.1 miles, you will come to a junction where you can choose which half of the loop you would like to ascend. The path on the left (north) crosses a bridge over Robbers Roost Creek and connects with Robbers Roost Canyon Road. The right (south) path climbs onto a ridge overlooking the creek. I recommend climbing the ridge on the ascent and returning on the road for the descent.

At the junction, turn right to begin the steep climb up the ridge, which gains over 300 feet in 0.3 miles. Once atop the ridge at 0.5 miles, the trail's

Robbers Roost Canyon Road in the autumn.

incline becomes more gradual. For the next 0.7 miles, the trail continues east, paralleling North Quinn Creek Road to the south and presenting views of Haystack Mountain.

At 1.2 miles, the trail passes to the north of a dirt parking area at the end of North Quinn Creek Road. From here, the path begins its descent to Robbers Roost Canyon Road, losing 120 feet in about 0.4 miles. Once you reach the junction with the road at 1.5 miles, make a left (southwest) turn to begin the descent back to the trailhead.

Where the ridge trail provided mountain views from open sage fields, the road offers more forested views alongside a babbling creek. The road generally descends moderately, though there are occasional moments when it can be pretty steep. At 2.8 miles, turn left (south) off the road down a steep trail, which, after a bridge crossing, leads you back to the junction where you started. Turn right (west) to return to the trailhead.

Keep Going

While **Robbers Roost Canyon Road** is used for half of the loop, it makes for a fun hike on its own. At 2.3 miles in length, this rocky road travels east alongside Robbers Roost Creek in a ravine. At 2.3 miles, the road merges with the **Lower Robbers Roost Trail** (Forest Service Trail 265), which is about 0.9 miles long. Combined, this motorized trail climbs 1,300 ft in 3.2 miles and is a great way to connect with the Boundary Trail. Unless you have a vehicle with excellent ground clearance and four-wheel drive, driving on this road may be a challenge.

A creek crossing on Lower Robbers Roost Trail.

Robbers Roost Canyon Loop

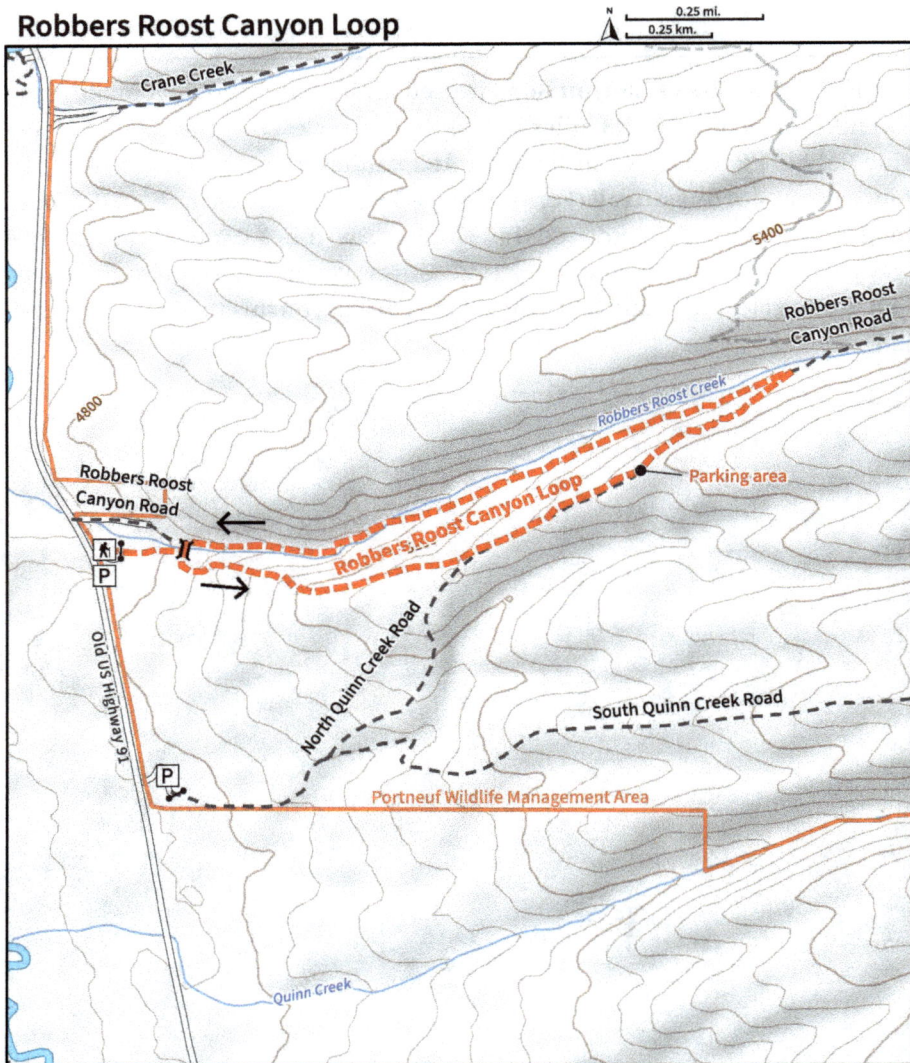

N
0.25 mi.
0.25 km.

Crane Creek

5400

Robbers Roost Canyon Road

4800

Robbers Roost Creek

Robbers Roost Canyon Road

Robbers Roost Canyon Loop

Parking area

North Quinn Creek Road

South Quinn Creek Road

Old US Highway 91

Portneuf Wildlife Management Area

Quinn Creek

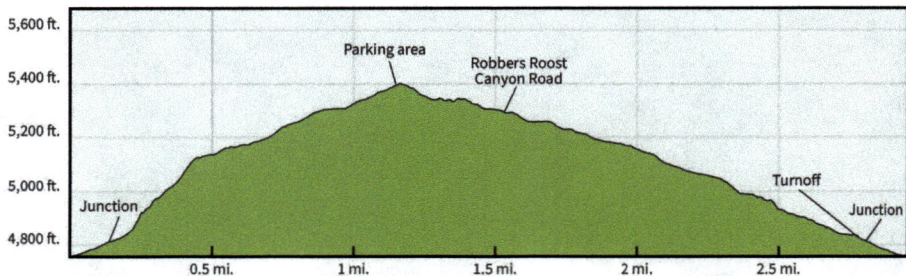

5,600 ft.

5,400 ft.

Parking area

Robbers Roost Canyon Road

5,200 ft.

5,000 ft.

Turnoff

Junction

Junction

4,800 ft.

0.5 mi.   1 mi.   1.5 mi.   2 mi.   2.5 mi.

73. North Quinn Creek Road

North Quinn Creek Road offers a brief yet captivating hiking experience in the Portneuf Wildlife Management Area. There is a small but steep hill near the midpoint of the hike that can be challenging, but the views of the surrounding mountains from the top make it worth the effort.

Distance: 2.8 miles out-and-back
Elevation Gain: 630 feet
Difficulty: Moderate
Hiking Time: About 1.5 hours
Nearest Town: McCammon
Trail Surface: Dirt, rock

Wheelchair Access: None
Dog-Friendly: Yes; on-leash at the trailhead. May be off-leash if under control once on the trail
Amenities: None
Contact: Idaho Fish and Game, Southeast Region 208-232-4703
Trailhead GPS Coordinates: N42° 41.818' W112° 12.162'

Getting There

From I-15 south of Pocatello, take Exit 58 for Inkom. Turn right on I-15BL/Old Highway 30 West. In 0.8 miles, continue straight onto North Old Highway 91. Continue on Old Highway 91 for 7.5 miles. Make a left turn into the Portneuf Wildlife Management Area parking lot. The trailhead is located on the south end of the long parking area.

The Hike

From the trailhead, head southeast past the gate on the wide 4x4 path. At 0.4 miles, keep left (northeast) at the fork to continue on North Quinn Creek Road. Shortly past the fork, the road becomes steeper, climbing almost 300 feet in 0.5 miles. At 0.9 miles, the trail levels out, making the remainder a pleasant walk with stunning views of the Portneuf Range. At 1.4 miles, the path ends in a parking area.

Keep Going

Once you reach the end of the trail in the upper parking area, consider joining the singletrack trail on the west side of the road. This trail is part of the Robbers Roost Canyon Loop, which continues northeast before descending into the canyon and joining Robbers Roost Canyon Road.

Yellow-bellied marmots, commonly known as "rock chucks," can often be spotted along the basalt flows of Southeast Idaho. These ground squirrels spend eight months hibernating every year and usually dwell in colonies of burrows that house 10 to 20 individuals.

North Quinn Creek Road heading toward Bonnevile Peak and Snow Peak.

North Quinn Creek Road

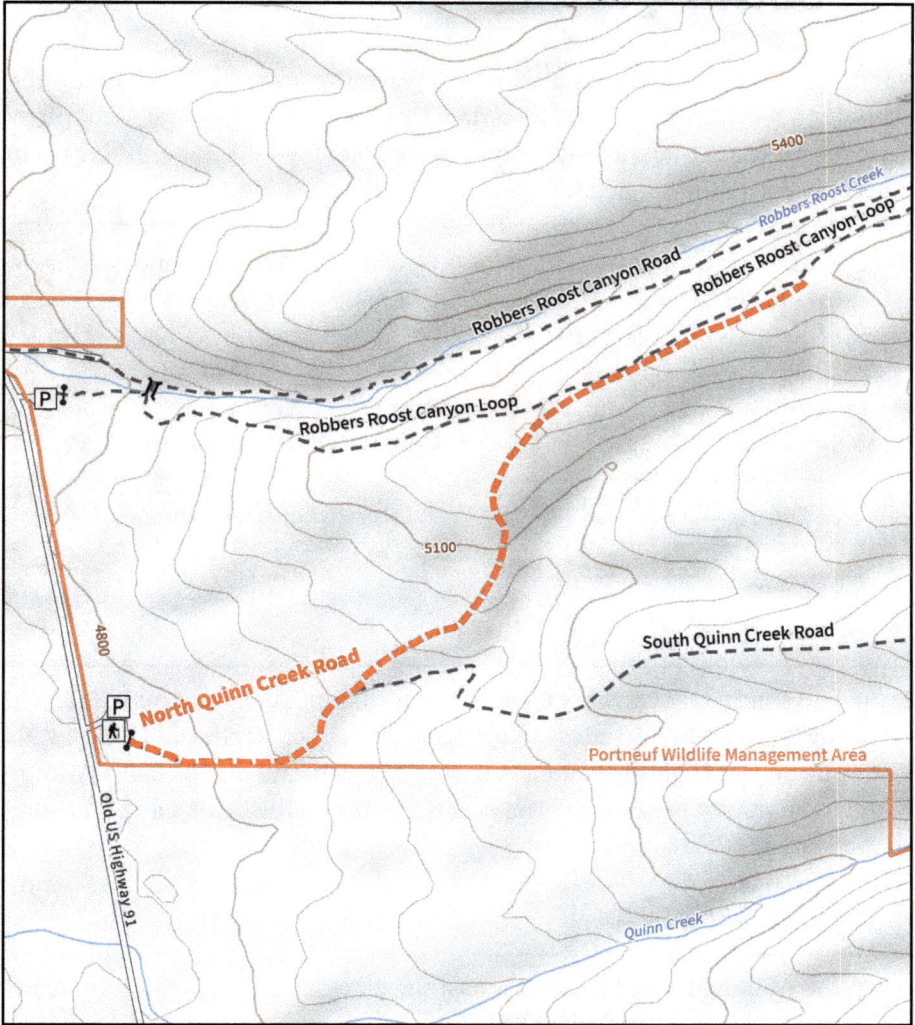

0.25 mi.
0.25 km.

N

Robbers Roost Creek
Robbers Roost Canyon Road
Robbers Roost Canyon Loop
5400
5100
Robbers Roost Canyon Loop
South Quinn Creek Road
North Quinn Creek Road
4800
Old US Highway 91
Portneuf Wildlife Management Area
Quinn Creek

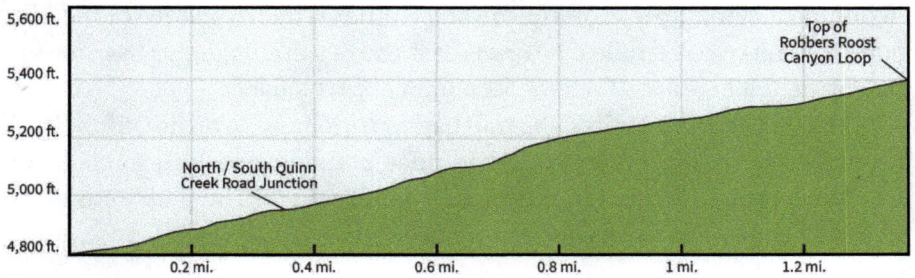

5,600 ft.
5,400 ft.
5,200 ft.
5,000 ft.
4,800 ft.

Top of
Robbers Roost
Canyon Loop

North / South Quinn
Creek Road Junction

0.2 mi. 0.4 mi. 0.6 mi. 0.8 mi. 1 mi. 1.2 mi.

74. South Quinn Creek Road

South Quinn Creek Road is a wide 4x4 trail that steadily climbs atop the sage-lined foothills on the western slopes of the Portneuf Range, with many mountain views along the way. About 2 miles into the hike, the trail begins to overlook the Quinn Creek drainage, which can be quite scenic.

Distance: 5 miles out-and-back
Elevation Gain: 1,150 feet
Difficulty: Moderately strenuous
Hiking Time: About 3 hours
Nearest Town: McCammon
Trail Surface: Dirt, rock

Wheelchair Access: None
Dog-Friendly: Yes; on-leash at the trailhead. May be off-leash if under control once on the trail
Amenities: None
Contact: Idaho Fish and Game, Southeast Region 208-232-4703
Trailhead GPS Coordinates: N42° 41.818' W112° 12.162'

Getting There

From I-15 south of Pocatello, take Exit 58 for Inkom. Turn right on I-15BL/Old Highway 30 West. In 0.8 miles, continue straight onto North Old Highway 91. Continue on Old Highway 91 for 7.5 miles. Turn left into the Portneuf Wildlife Management Area parking lot. The trail is located on the south end of the long parking area.

The Hike

From the trailhead, head southeast past the gate on the wide 4x4 path. At 0.4 miles, make a right (east) turn at the fork to continue on South Quinn Creek Road. Shortly past the fork, the road crosses over a seasonal creek before beginning a climb up a sage-hillside at 0.6 miles. The remainder of the hike gains 970 feet over 1.9 miles. It travels east above a drainage and has views of the Portneuf Range and Haystack Mountain in particular.

Starting at about 2 miles, the trail begins traveling above the Quinn Creek drainage. At this same point, the sage-sided path becomes intermixed with deciduous trees, making for a nice change of scenery. The path ends at 2.5 miles in a large parking area just short of a forest.

South Quinn Creek Road heading toward Haystack Mountain.

The City of McCammon was named after J.H. McCammon, who negotiated the purchase of the right-of-way for the Oregon Short Line Railway across the Fort Hall Indian Reservation.

South Quinn Creek Road

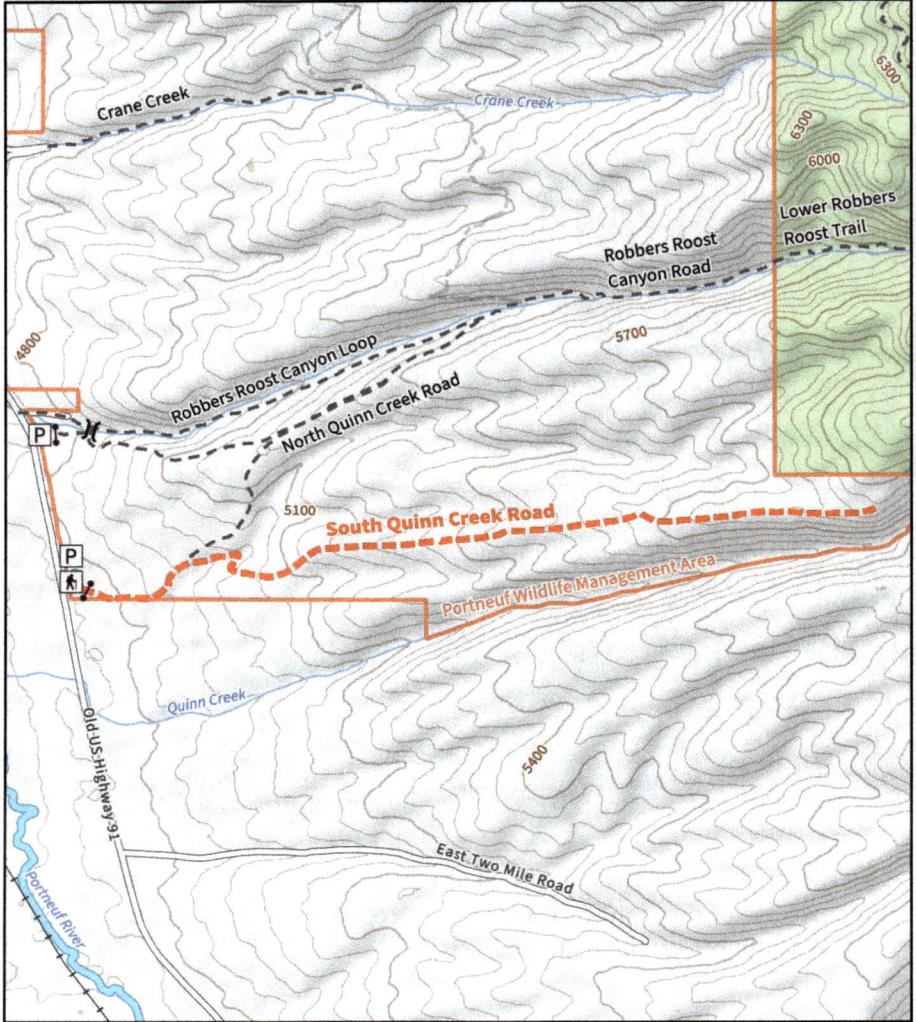

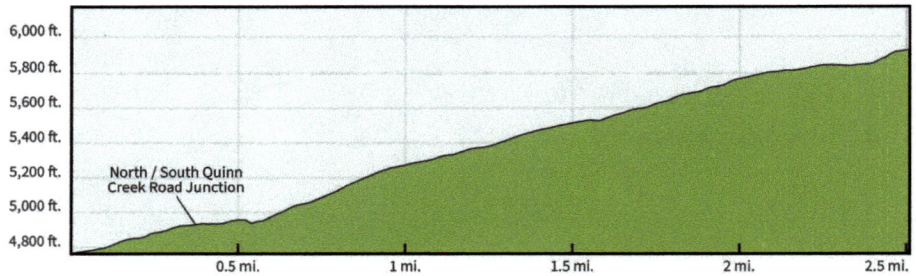

N

0.5 mi.

0.5 km.

Crane Creek

Crane Creek

6300

6300

6000

Lower Robbers
Roost Trail

Robbers Roost
Canyon Road

5700

4800

Robbers Roost Canyon Loop

North Quinn Creek Road

P

5100

South Quinn Creek Road

P

Portneuf Wildlife Management Area

Quinn Creek

5400

Old US Highway 91

Portneuf River

East Two Mile Road

6,000 ft.					
5,800 ft.					
5,600 ft.					
5,400 ft.					
5,200 ft.					
5,000 ft.					
4,800 ft.					

North / South Quinn
Creek Road Junction

0.5 mi.   1 mi.   1.5 mi.   2 mi.   2.5 mi.

75. Indian Rocks Overlook

Situated between the Bannock Range on its west and the Portneuf Range on its east, this short hike through Indian Rocks takes you alongside lava rock and sagebrush fields until you reach a panoramic clifftop viewpoint above vast basalt cliffs and massive boulders. The area was formerly the Indian Rocks State Park and Visitor Center. The park was closed in 1983 due to a state budget crisis and never reopened. Even with the park closure, the area is a popular camping destination.

Distance: 1.7 miles out-and-back
Elevation Gain: 40 feet
Difficulty: Easy
Hiking Time: About 45 minutes
Nearest Town: McCammon
Trail Surface: Dirt

Wheelchair Access: None
Dog-Friendly: Yes; on-leash at the trailhead. May be off-leash if under control once on the trail
Amenities: None
Contact: Bureau of Land Management, Pocatello Field Office 208-478-6340
Trailhead GPS Coordinates: N42° 40.767' W112° 13.202'

Getting There

From I-15 south of Pocatello, take Exit 47 for McCammon. Turn right on East Merrill Road, and then make the next right in 0.1 miles onto BLM 125. Stay on this road for 1.4 miles, keeping left at 0.5 miles and right at 1.3 miles. The trailhead, a rutted dirt road, is on the campground loop's north side. There is no designated parking area, so you will have to park in a camping spot or just off the road.

The Hike

From the trailhead, head north on the rutted dirt road as it moves through low basalt rocks and plenty of sagebrush near the interstate. Shortly into the hike, at 0.1 miles, the trail passes through a barbed wire gate. At about 0.7 miles, the trail comes to a fork. Keep left (northwest) to continue on the route. Just under a quarter of a mile from the turnoff, you will reach the endpoint of the route

The Indian Rocks Overlook not far from the trail.

at an unmarked viewpoint on the left (west) side of the road. This viewpoint overlooks a large boulder field and several seasonal ponds.

Keep Going

While the route in the book is relatively short, Indian Rocks has many miles of trails through the rocky desert. You can continue north from the viewpoint for another 2 miles on the road featured in this route, or you can cross under the interstate to explore the eastern side of Indian Rocks. To do this, turn right (north) instead of left (northwest) at the 0.7 mile turnoff found on this route.

Indian Rocks Area of Critical Environmental Concern (ACEC) was designated to protect Native American petroglyphs and other archaeological sites. You can view several petroglyphs at a signed boulder display just a short walk from the road. This display is located on the way to the trailhead about half a mile north of East Merrill Road on the right (northeast) side of BLM 125.

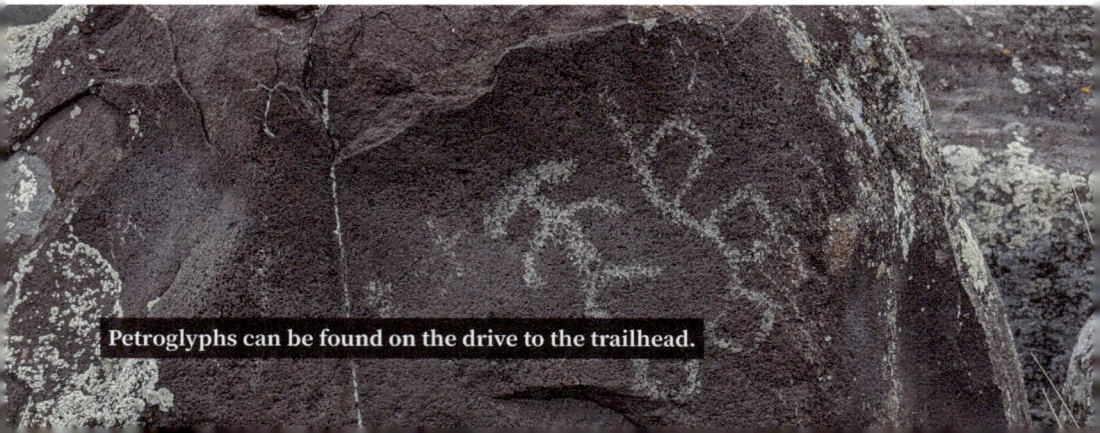
Petroglyphs can be found on the drive to the trailhead.

Indian Rocks Overlook

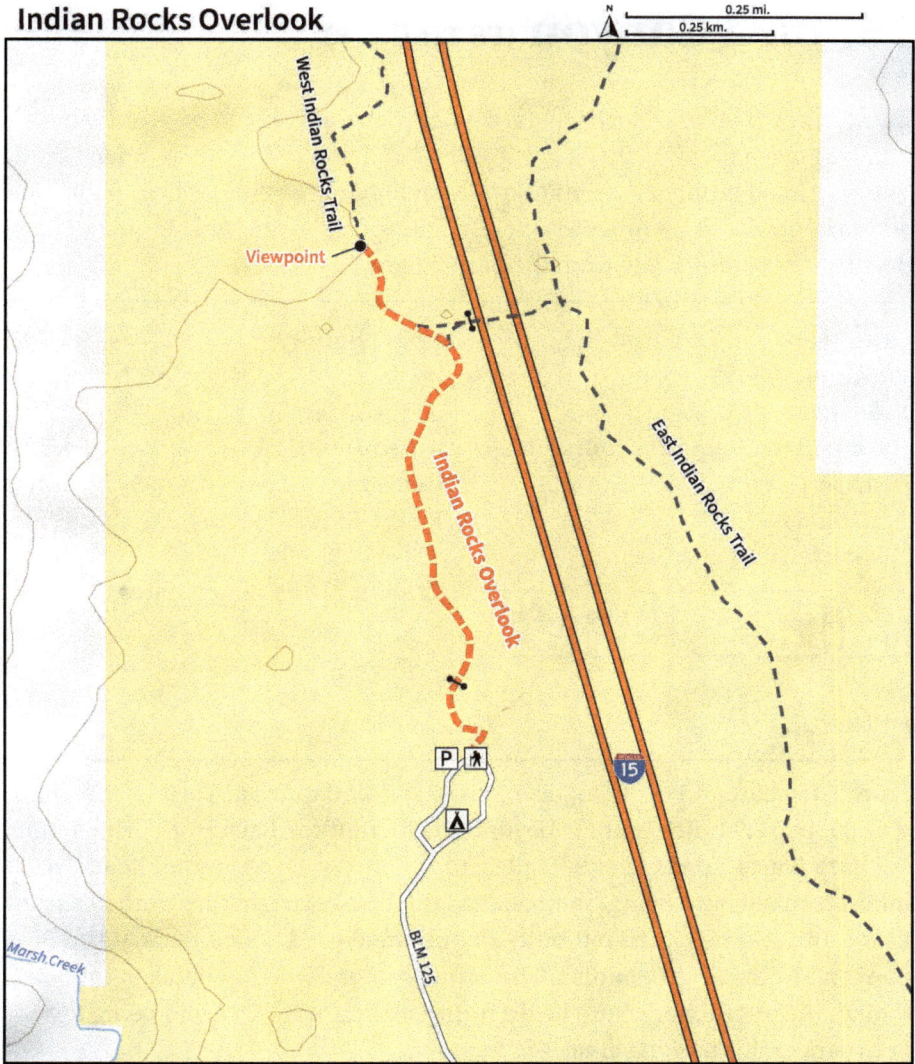

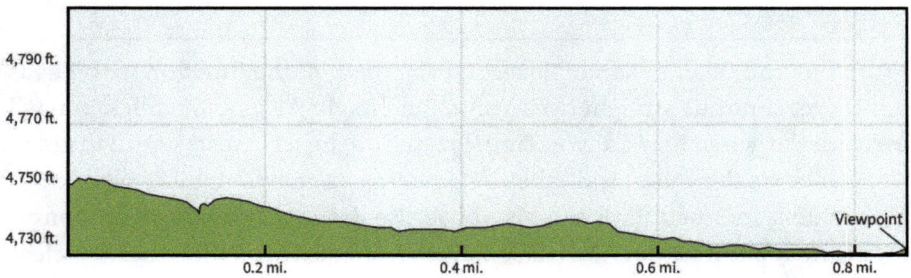

N

0.25 mi.
0.25 km.

West Indian Rocks Trail

Viewpoint

Indian Rocks Overlook

East Indian Rocks Trail

P ⊼

⛺

15

BLM 125

Marsh Creek

4,790 ft.
4,770 ft.
4,750 ft.
4,730 ft.

Viewpoint

0.2 mi.   0.4 mi.   0.6 mi.   0.8 mi.

76. Bird Canyon (FS Trail 278)

Located north of Lava Hot Springs, the Bird Canyon Trail is a pleasant forested climb above a creek that is a great way to connect with the Boundary Trail. The trail itself is only 1.1 miles one-way, though restricted parking in the area adds an additional 0.9 miles to actually gain access to the trail. As such, I have decided to start the route from the parking area.

Distance: 4 miles out-and-back
Elevation Gain: 970 feet
Difficulty: Moderate
Hiking Time: About 2.5 hours
Nearest Town: Lava Hot Springs
Trail Surface: Dirt, rock
Wheelchair Access: None

Dog-Friendly: Yes; on-leash at the trailhead. May be off-leash if under control once on the trail
Amenities: None
Contact: Caribou-Targhee National Forest, Westside Ranger District 208-236-7500
Trailhead GPS Coordinates: N42° 39.568' W112° 00.968'

Getting There

From I-15 south of Pocatello, take Exit 47 for McCammon. Turn left on Highway 30. In 12.9 miles, not far beyond the turnoff for Lava Hot Springs, turn left onto Blaser Road. After 3.9 miles, turn left onto East Symond Road. In 0.3 miles, turn left onto Byington Road, and then make a right turn onto Pheasant Drive. In 1.2 miles, turn left onto an unnamed road which ends at the Bird Canyon Trailhead in 0.3 miles. The actual trail is about 0.9 miles to the west, though the instructions here begin from this trailhead. To avoid being towed, only park at this parking area.

The Hike

From the trailhead, head northwest on the road. At the junction with Pheasant Drive, continue straight (west) onto Bald Eagle Way. At 0.9 miles, you will arrive at the actual Bird Canyon Trail, located on the left (west) side of the road.

Once on the actual trail, the route begins its constant uphill climb. This moderately inclined path travels above the creek through a thick conifer forest. At about 1.8 miles, the trail emerges from the forest into a narrow clear-

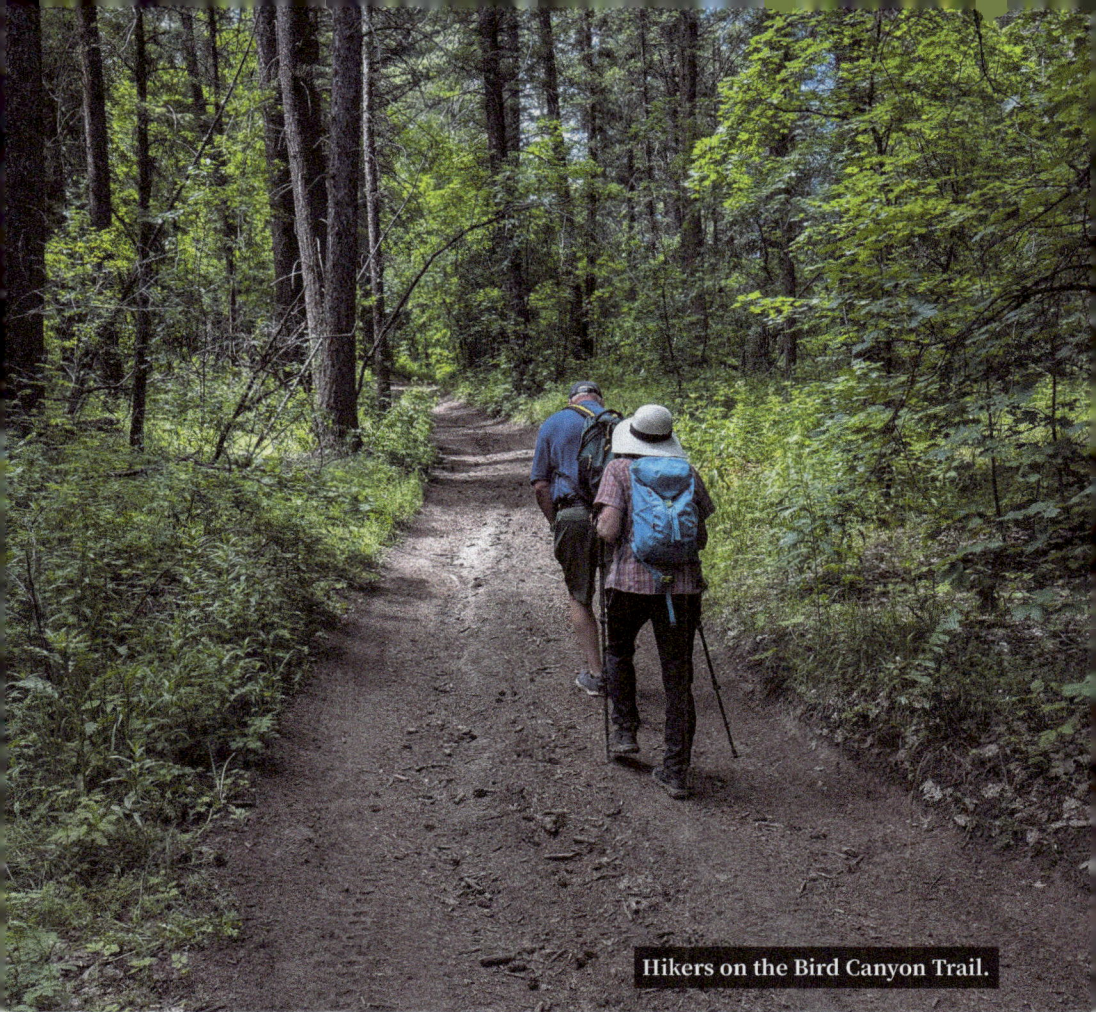

Hikers on the Bird Canyon Trail.

ing, and the incline becomes more gradual. At the end of the clearing, the trail ends at a junction with the Beach - Bird Connector Trail. If you were to go right (east) on this trail, you would connect with the Boundary Trail in about 150 yards.

Lava Hot Springs takes its name from the geothermal mineral springs that are located nearby. Even before settlers arrived in the area, the Bannock and Shoshone tribes used the springs for bathing and worship. They called the land Poha-ba or "Land of Healing Water," and believed that it was a sacred location of spiritual significance.

Bird Canyon

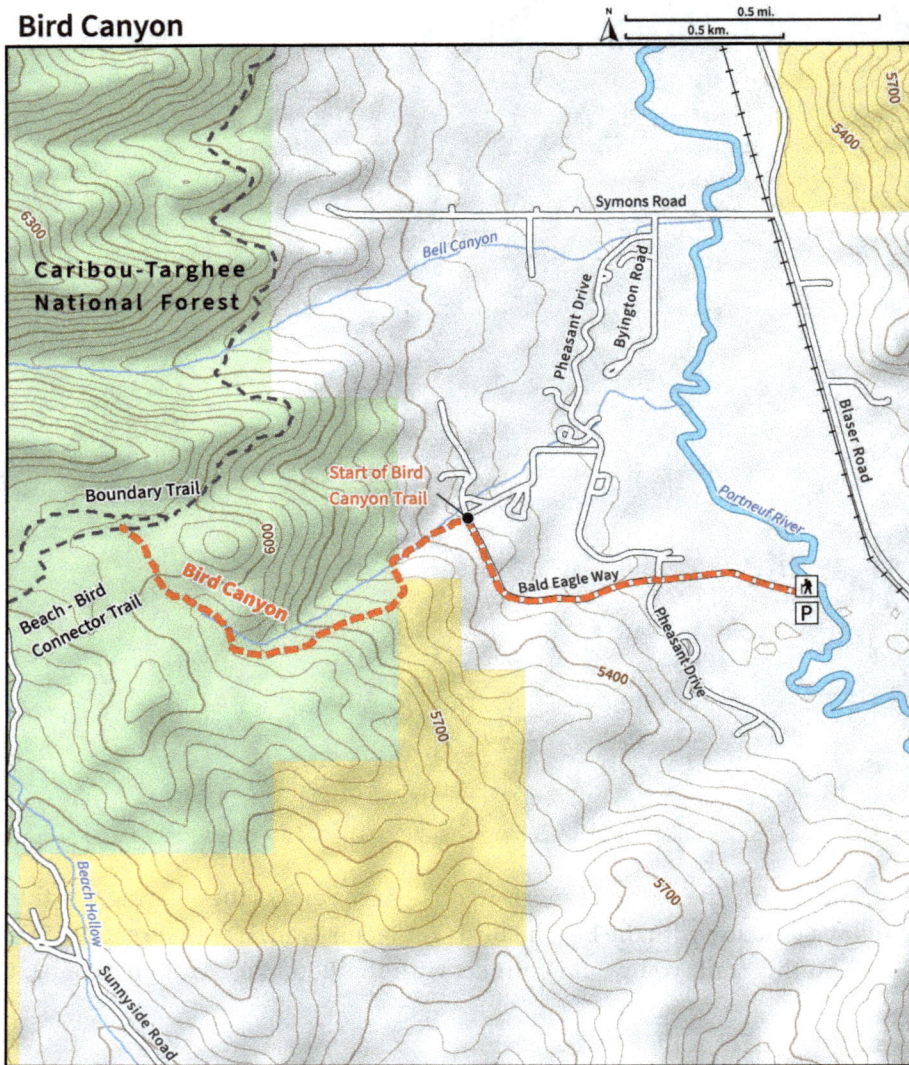

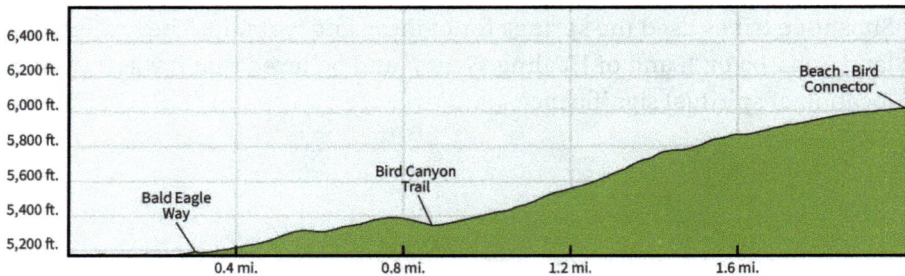

77. Big Springs Nature Trail

The Big Springs Nature Trail provides a pleasant forested creekside walk to a scenic spring near the Big Springs Campground. The old educational signage along the path is no longer in use, though the trail may still provide a nice break for families staying in the area.

Distance: 0.5-mile loop
Elevation Gain: 100 feet
Difficulty: Easy
Hiking Time: About 20 minutes
Nearest Town: Lava Hot Springs
Trail Surface: Dirt, rock
Wheelchair Access: None

Dog-Friendly: Yes; on-leash at the trailhead. May be off-leash if under control once on the trail
Amenities: Vault toilets and water are available at the Big Springs Campground.
Contact: Caribou-Targhee National Forest, Westside Ranger District 208-236-7500
Trailhead GPS Coordinates: N42° 45.898' W112° 05.848'

Getting There

From I-15 south of Pocatello, take Exit 47 for McCammon. Turn left on Highway 30. In 12.9 miles, close to the turnoff for Lava Hot Springs, turn left onto Blaser Road. After 9 miles, turn left onto Pebble Creek Road, which you will stay on for 1.1 miles. In 0.6 miles, make a left turn followed by a right turn to stay on Pebble Creek Road. At 1.1 miles, Pebble Creek Road transitions into Forest Service Road 36. Continue on FR 36 for 5.9 miles, until it arrives at the Big Springs Campground gates. Drive through the first set of gates, and continue straight through the second gate, where the road will make a right turn. Shortly past that right turn, make a left turn once you pass the vault toilet, where in under a minute, you will find the trailhead next to the "Big Springs Nature Trail" sign. Parking can be tight near the trailhead, so I recommend parking elsewhere in the campground.

The Hike

From the trailhead, head northwest past the Big Springs Nature Trail sign. The first half of the loop follows a trickling creek under the cool evergreen trees.

The spring found at the midpoint of the trail.

You will see signposts throughout the hike, but they no longer contain any information. A quarter mile in, you will reach a viewpoint looking over the crashing Big Springs. From the viewpoint, the well-defined trail makes a sharp left (south) turn up the hillside. The trail becomes wild and borderline bushwhacking from here. If you have small children, I recommend retracing your steps back to the trailhead. If you wish to continue, follow the wild trail up the hillside as it navigates around deadfall and eventually back to the trailhead.

Keep Going

While you're in the area, you might want to explore either the Boundary Trail or the North Boundary Trail. Specifically, taking a short walk along the Boundary Trail from the Big Spring Campground will lead you to a bridge that crosses the rushing Pebble Creek, which can be a refreshing sight on a hot summer day.

The cutthroat trout, Idaho's state fish, gets its name from a distinctive red mark found under its head.

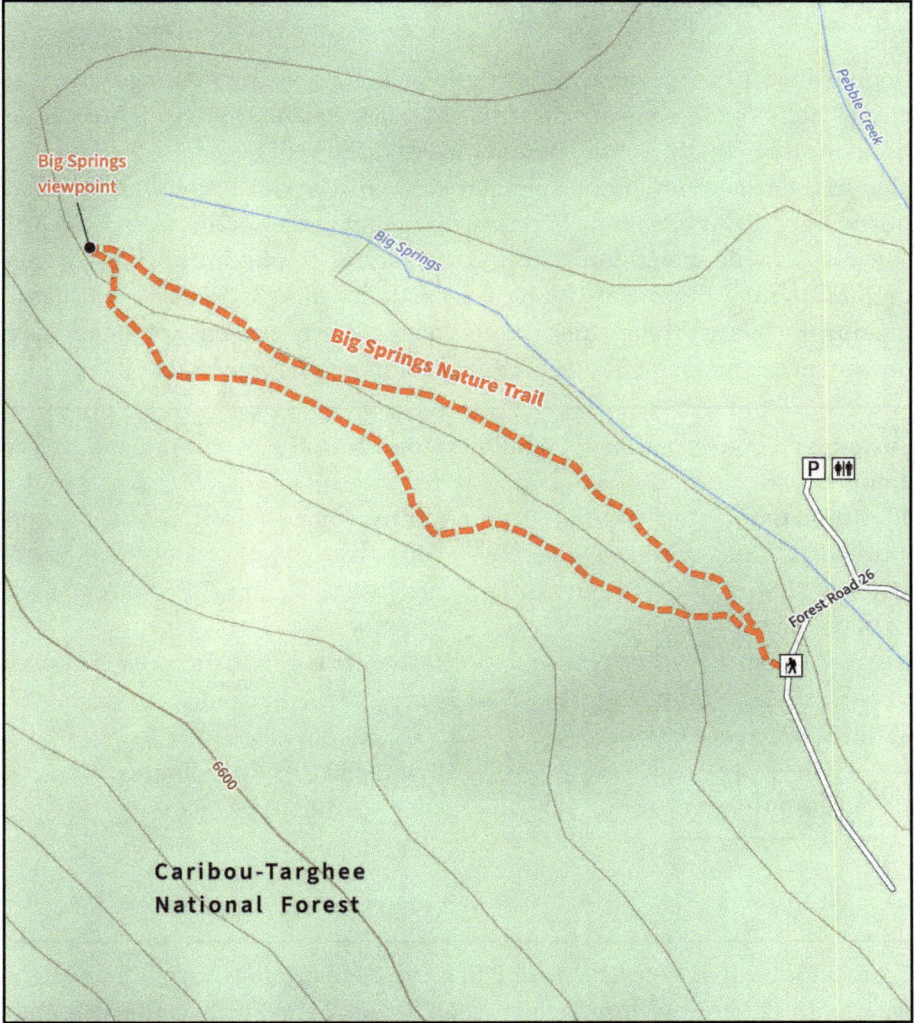

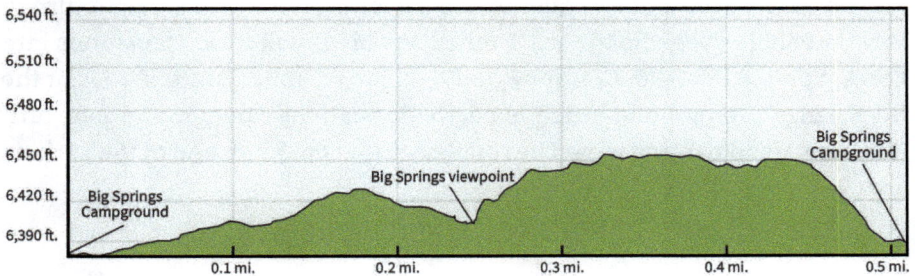

Big Springs Nature Trail

N

0.05 mi.

0.05 km.

Big Springs viewpoint

Pebble Creek

Big Springs

Big Springs Nature Trail

P

Forest Road 26

6600

Caribou-Targhee National Forest

6,540 ft.

6,510 ft.

6,480 ft.

6,450 ft.

6,420 ft.

6,390 ft.

Big Springs Campground

Big Springs viewpoint

Big Springs Campground

0.1 mi.   0.2 mi.   0.3 mi.   0.4 mi.   0.5 mi.

78. Robbers Roost Trail (FS Trail 253)

Robbers Roost Trail is a strenuous hike from the Big Springs Campground that climbs high on the eastern side of the Portneuf Range. Once atop the saddle between Haystack Mountain and Snow Peak, the trail descends the western side of the range, providing close-up views of Haystack Mountain's cliffed northwest face. While many hikers turn around at the saddle, both halves of the trail provide scenic forest views, making for a great hike for those who commit to the full trail. If you have a partner willing to park a shuttle car, making the hike a through hike is a nice option. Large stretches of the trail are deeply rutted, making this one hard to recommend for mountain bikers.

Distance: 6.1 miles one-way; 6.4 miles round trip to the saddle
Elevation Gain: 2,140 feet; 1,960 feet
Difficulty: Strenuous; Strenuous
Hiking Time: About 4 hours either option
Nearest Town: Lava Hot Springs
Trail Surface: Dirt, rock
Wheelchair Access: None

Dog-Friendly: Yes; on-leash at the trailhead. May be off-leash if under control once on the trail
Amenities: Vault toilets and water are available at the Big Springs Campground.
Contact: Caribou-Targhee National Forest, Westside Ranger District 208-236-7500
Trailhead GPS Coordinates: N42° 45.919' W112° 05.687'

Getting There

From I-15 south of Pocatello, take Exit 47 for McCammon. Turn left on Highway 30. In 12.9 miles, close to the turnoff for Lava Hot Springs, turn left onto Blaser Road. After 9 miles, turn left onto Pebble Creek Road, which you will stay on for 1.1 miles. In 0.6 miles, make a left turn followed by a right turn to stay on Pebble Creek Road. At 1.1 miles, Pebble Creek Road transitions into Forest Service Road 36. Continue on FR 36 for 5.9 miles, until it ends at the Big Springs Campground. Once you drive through the campground gate, turn left into a small parking area. The route begins at the south end of the parking area.

Robbers Roost Trail below Haystack Mountain's western cliffs.

The Hike

From the trailhead, head southeast on Boundary Trail. In about 0.2 miles, the trail crosses a bridge over Pebble Creek. At 0.3 miles, make a right (southwest) turn off Boundary Trail onto Robbers Roost Trail. Once on the official Robbers Roost Trail, the rutted path heads southwest on a singletrack trail through a thick evergreen forest. The route is very strenuous for the next 2 miles, gaining 1,850 feet as it climbs toward the saddle between Haystack Mountain and Snow Peak.

At 1.7 miles, the trail emerges from the thick forest onto a ridge. While the incline is still unrelenting, the views, largely unhindered by the forest, become quite scenic, especially those of Haystack Mountain's northeast face, which begins to stand out at the 2.0 mile mark. At 2.3 miles, the steep incline finally levels out and, for the next quarter mile, actually descends about 100 feet down a hill.

After climbing a small hill, the trail again levels out at about 2.8 miles. For the next half mile, the path continues without much elevation change toward the saddle, which you will reach at 3.2 miles. Once on the saddle (8,240 feet), keep left (south) at a junction with another trail to stay on route. (This other trail would begin the climb for Snow Peak). The saddle is an excellent turn-around point for those who do not wish to descend the western half of Robbers Roost Trail.

To continue down the western half of the hike, turn right (southwest) at 3.3 miles onto a narrow singletrack trail. The trail can be quite steep as it moves south below the saddle, descending 300 feet in 0.3 miles. At 3.6 miles, the trail levels out, allowing you to take in the cliffs of Haystack Mountain's northwest face. The trail begins another steep descent, dropping 350 feet in 0.3 miles.

The trail enters a thick forest at the bottom of the descent and heads southwest. For the next 0.7 miles, the trail flattens out quite a bit as it heads to a ridge west of Haystack Mountain. At about 4.7 miles, keep left (southwest) to stay on route.

The trail not far from the Big Springs Campground.

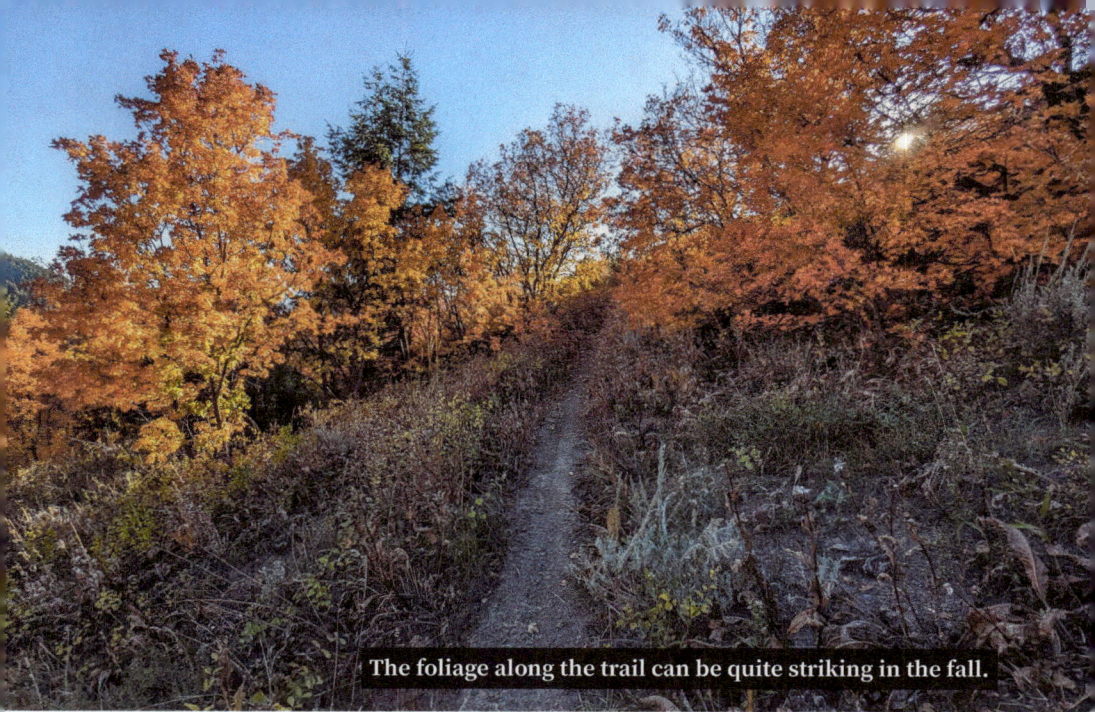

The foliage along the trail can be quite striking in the fall.

Once on the ridge at 4.8 miles, the trail begins a significant western drop, descending 800 feet in 0.8 miles. While steep, this descent has great views of Haystack Mountain behind you, the forested Quinn Creek Creek to your left (south), and the Robbers Roost Creek to your right (north). At 5.6 miles, the trail flattens out, allowing you to rest your legs as it crosses a hillside.

At 5.8 miles, the trail begins the final descent, dropping 350 feet in 0.4 miles, until it ends at a junction with the Boundary Trail.

Keep Going

If you have the option to make this a one-way hike, I highly recommend it. Once you reach the western end of Robbers Roost Trail at the junction with Boundary Trail, make a right (north) turn onto Boundary Trail. In 0.8 miles, turn left onto Lower Robbers Roost Trail, which has a route description on page 311. Eventually you will reach a parking area on Robbers Roost Canyon Road where you can park a shuttle vehicle ahead of time.

The name "Robbers Roost" was derived from the area's past as a hideout for bandits during the 1860s. Bandits are said to have used the narrow canyons and dense vegetation of the region to conceal the gold they stole from a nearby stagecoach route. As a result, the area earned the moniker "Robbers Roost."

Robbers Roost Trail

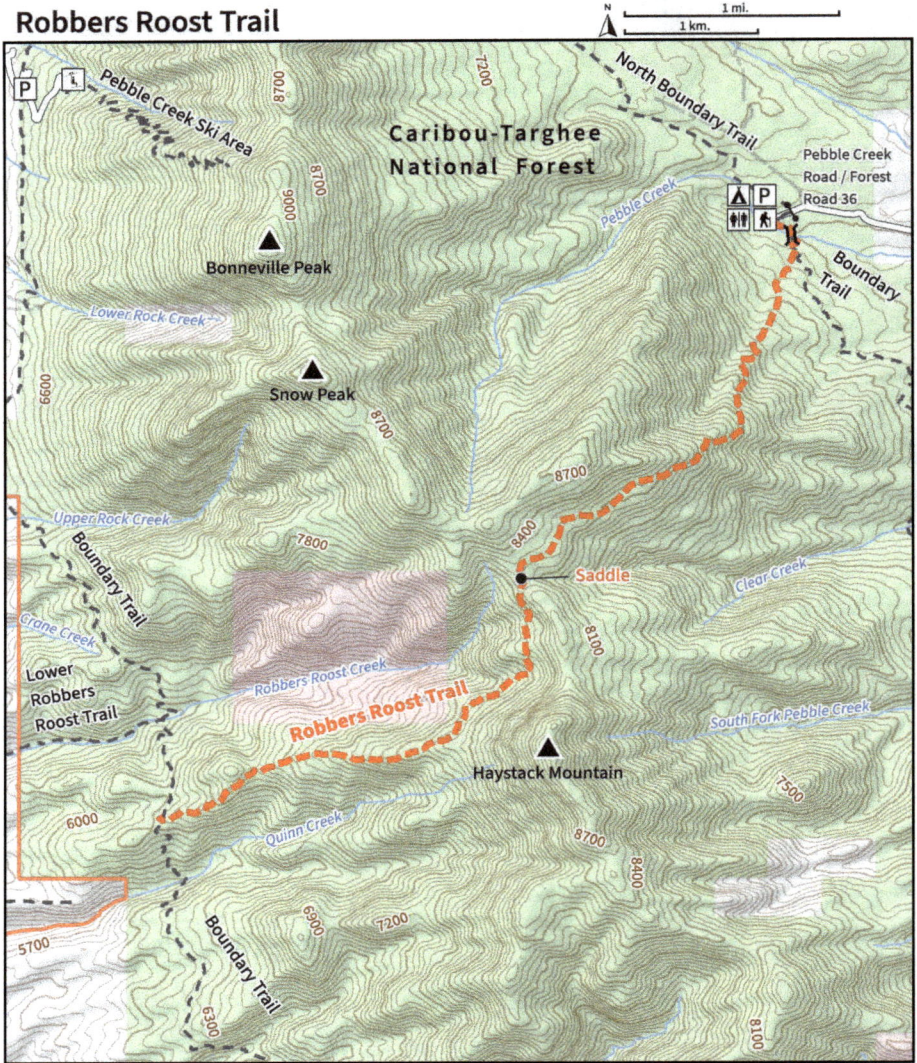

Caribou-Targhee National Forest

Pebble Creek Ski Area

Bonneville Peak

Snow Peak

Haystack Mountain

Saddle

Robbers Roost Trail

Boundary Trail

Lower Robbers Roost Trail

North Boundary Trail

Pebble Creek Road / Forest Road 36

Lower Rock Creek

Upper Rock Creek

Crane Creek

Robbers Roost Creek

Quinn Creek

Clear Creek

South Fork Pebble Creek

Pebble Creek

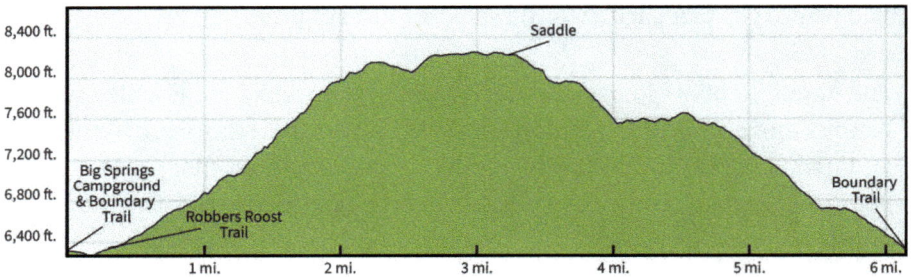

Robbers Roost Trail looking toward the Bannock Range.

Mountains

Between the Pocatello Range, Portneuf Range, and Bannock Range, Pocatello has plenty of summits to keep anyone who loves peak-bagging motivated. The most iconic peaks in Pocatello, which can be found on the redesigned city flag, are Scout Mountain, Kinport Peak, and Chinese Peak. For beginners looking to get into summit-chasing, I recommend hiking Chinese Peak. It has an easy-to-follow trail that starts close to town with beautiful city views at the top.

The Trail User Icons for these hikes indicate what users can make it to the summit, not necessarily whether the trails are motorized. For example, the route up Gibson Mountain allows motorized vehicles for the majority of the trail. However, the summit itself only allows foot traffic and horses.

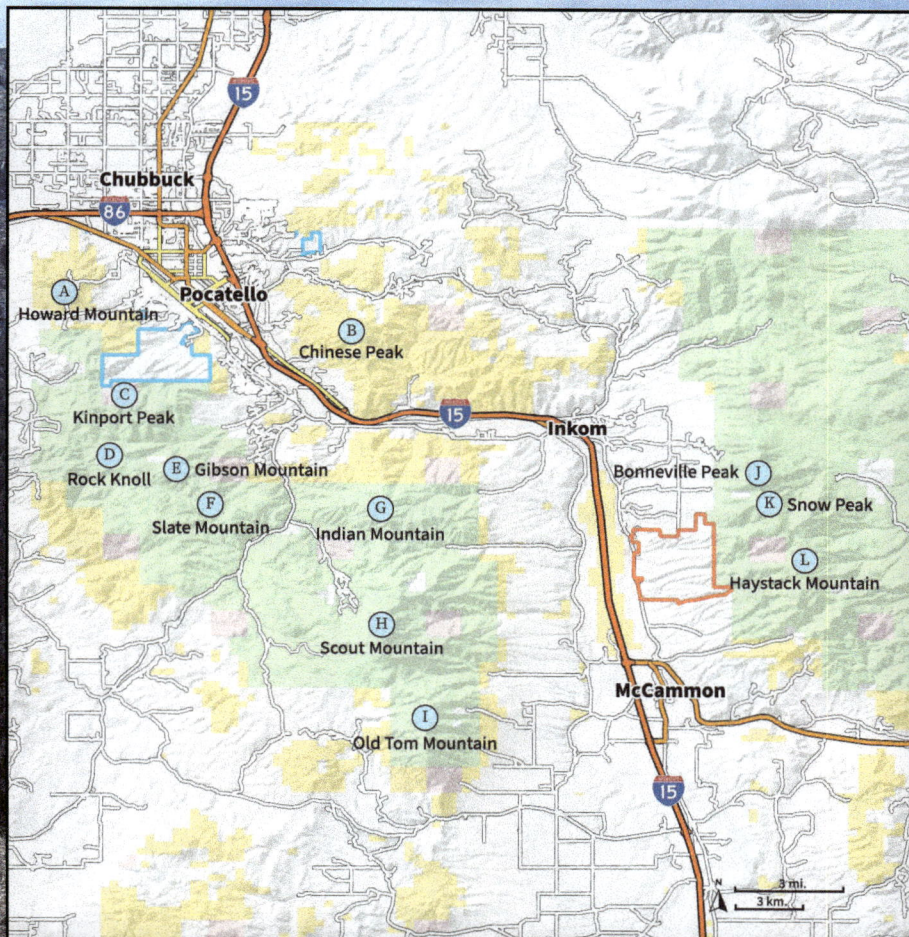

Chubbuck

Pocatello

Ⓐ Howard Mountain

Ⓑ Chinese Peak

Ⓒ Kinport Peak

Ⓓ Rock Knoll

Ⓔ Gibson Mountain

Ⓕ Slate Mountain

Ⓖ Indian Mountain

Ⓗ Scout Mountain

Ⓘ Old Tom Mountain

Inkom

Bonneville Peak Ⓙ

Ⓚ Snow Peak

Ⓛ Haystack Mountain

McCammon

3 mi.
3 km.

Scout Mountain from near the South Walker Creek Trail.

Howard Mountain

Bannock Range

5,841 feet (1,780 meters)

Located northwest of Pocatello, the dry and grassy Howard Mountain is the northernmost peak in the Bannock Range. The summit of the mountain is broad and contains several radio towers, and a large 'P' on its eastern slopes. The mountain is not a popular climb due to its low elevation and the large amounts of private property that prevent access to the peak's public land. To avoid trespassing, the hike to the top starts on BLM land just a few hundred feet below the summit and follows a dirt road. The mountain is named after William Forrest Howard and Minnie Frances Howard, two prominent historical figures from Pocatello's early years.

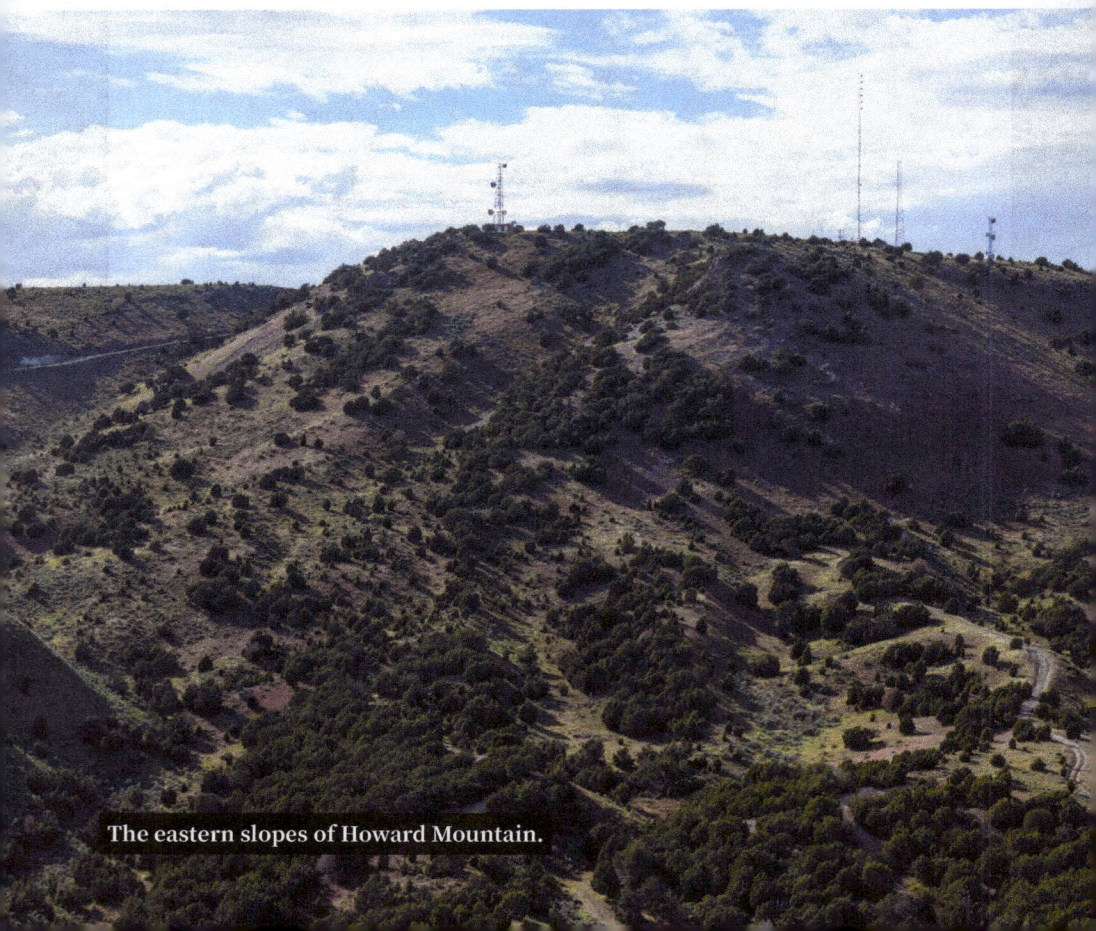

The eastern slopes of Howard Mountain.

Howard Mountain - South Ridge via BLM Road

Hiking in the Howard Mountain area is difficult due to the amount of private property blocking access points. Because of this, the hike to the summit starts on BLM land only 400 feet below the summit. Still, if you want to summit Pocatello's mountains, this short hike on a dry road may be for you.

Distance: 1.5 miles out-and-back
Elevation Gain: 380 feet
Difficulty: Easy; Class 1
Hiking Time: About 1 hour
Nearest Town: Pocatello
Trail Surface: Dirt, rock
Wheelchair Access: None

Dog-Friendly: Yes; on-leash at the trailhead. May be off-leash if under control once on the trail
Amenities: None
Contact: Bureau of Land Management, Pocatello Field Office 208-478-6340
Trailhead GPS Coordinates: N42° 51.509' W112° 30.961'

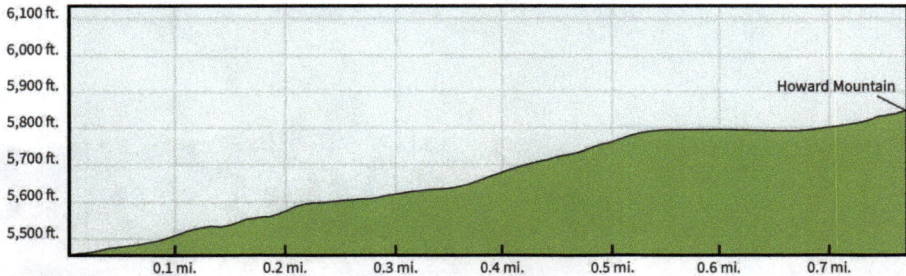

Getting There

From the junction of South Garfield Avenue and West Carson Street in Pocatello, head southwest on West Carson Street for 0.3 miles. (The road becomes Gathe Drive after crossing over the Portneuf River.) At 0.3 miles, continue straight to stay on Gathe Drive. At the stop sign at the end of Gathe Drive, make a right turn onto Foothill Boulevard. After 0.2 miles, turn left onto West Trail Creek Road.

Stay on West Trail Creek Road for 2.6 miles until it reaches the ridge below Howard Mountain. (At 1.4 miles, the paved road transitions into a dirt road at a gate.) Once on the ridge, make a right (north) turn toward Howard Mountain.

After a quarter of a mile, you will arrive on BLM land at a junction, which is where the hike begins.

The Hike

From the parking area, the hike to the summit is very straightforward. Head north on the wide road as it cuts across a dry hillside. At 0.5 miles, turn left (northwest) onto the 4x4 path up a steep hill. Once atop this short hill, continue west, where you will come to a fork at 0.6 miles. Keep left (southwest) at this fork, where in another 0.2 miles, you will find yourself at the tower-covered southwest summit of Howard Mountain.

> The Pocatello 'P' is a hillside letter on Howard Mountain that can be seen from the interstate. It is traditionally painted by Pocatello High School students during homecoming.

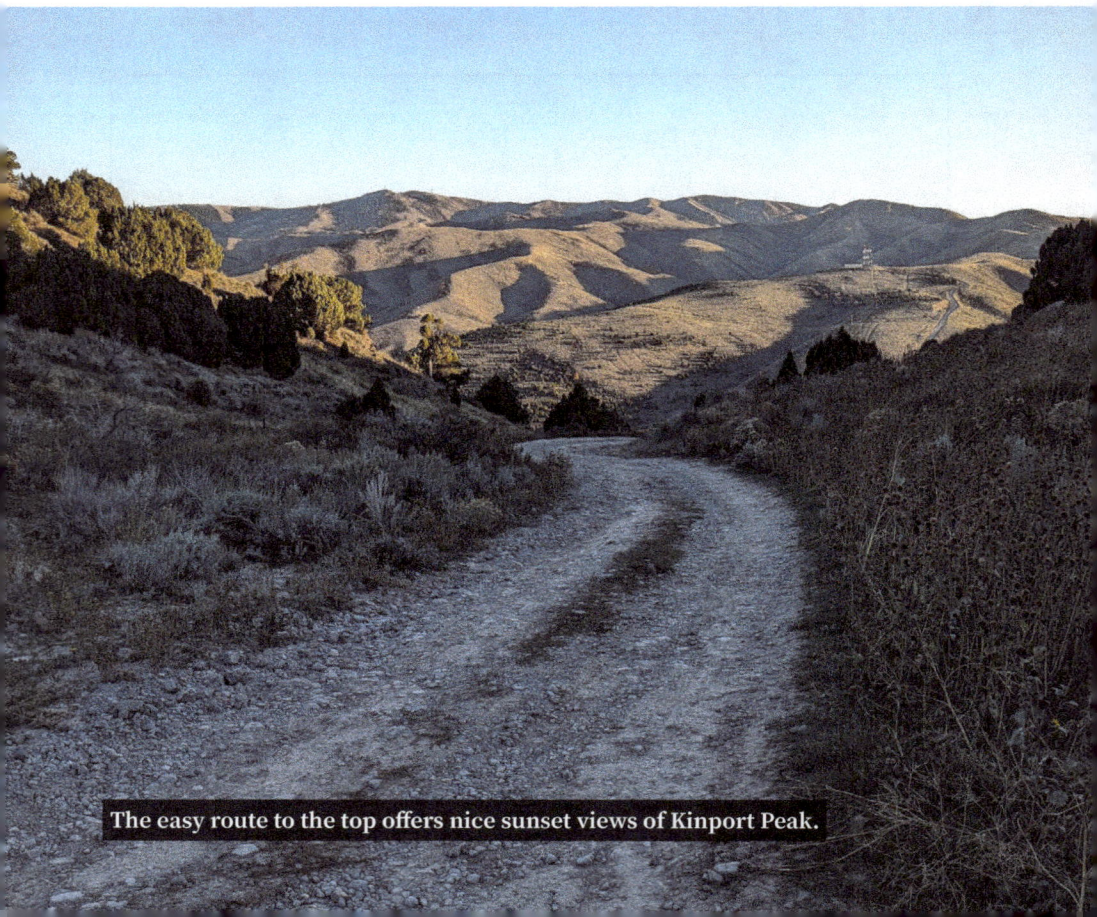

The easy route to the top offers nice sunset views of Kinport Peak.

Howard Mountain

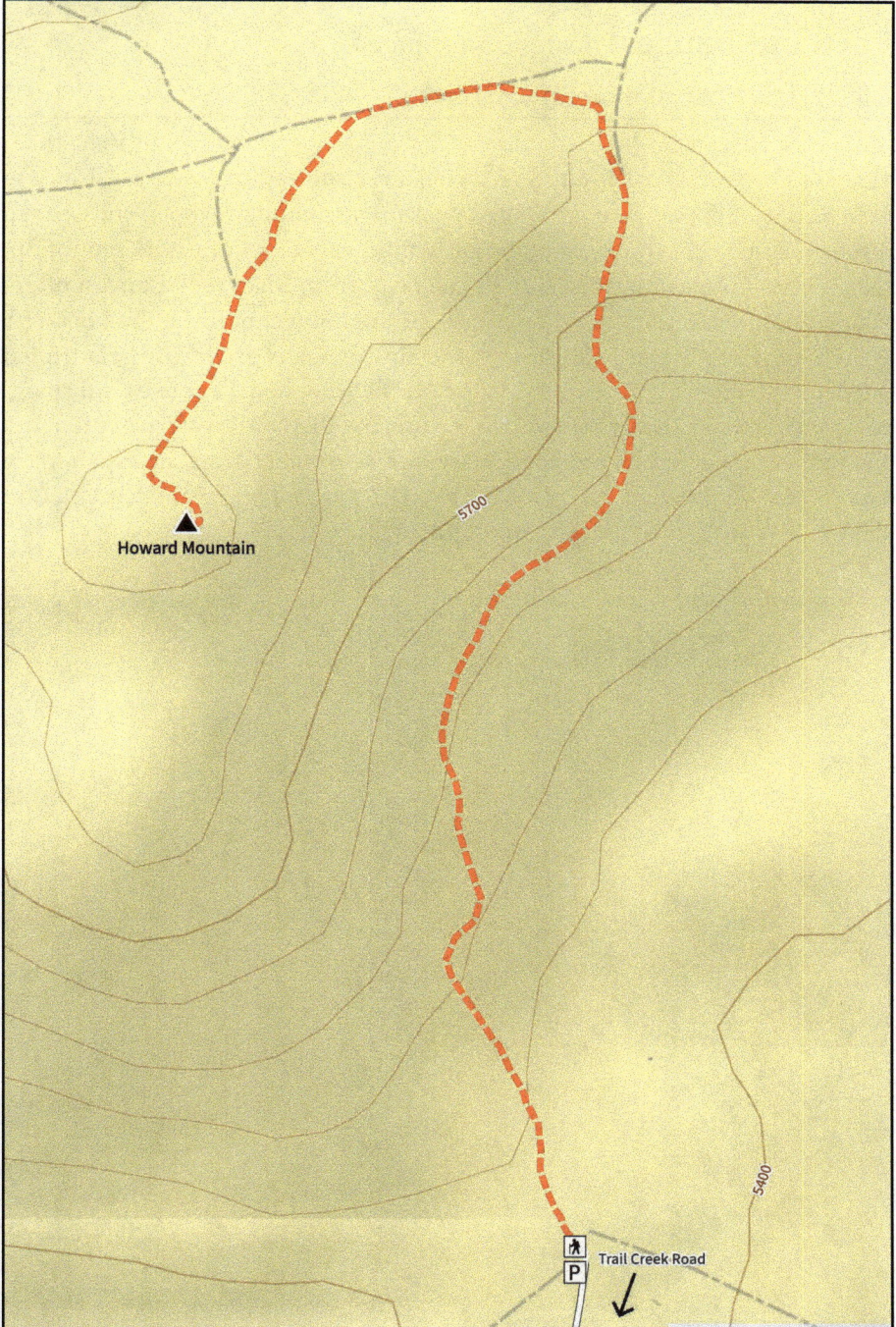

N
0.05 mi.
0.05 km.

Howard Mountain

5700

5400

Trail Creek Road

Chinese Peak

Portneuf Range (Pocatello Subrange)
6,791 feet (2,070 meters)

Due to its proximity to the city and a wide dirt road leading to the top, Chinese Peak is one of the area's most visited peaks. The mountain's open sun-soaked western slopes are the most commonly used way to summit the mountain, though the forested eastern side of the peak from Blackrock Canyon offers shaded options. The top of the mountain, the highest point in the Pocatello Range, provides a vast panorama of the city, which is especially beautiful at sunset. With an easily accessible trailhead off Barton Road, a consistently moderate incline, and an obvious path to the top, the BLM 301 western approach is the easiest way to climb the peak. However, seasoned hikers may wish to try one of the two more adventurous routes. The mountain is named after a Chinese man who died on the summit in the 1890s.

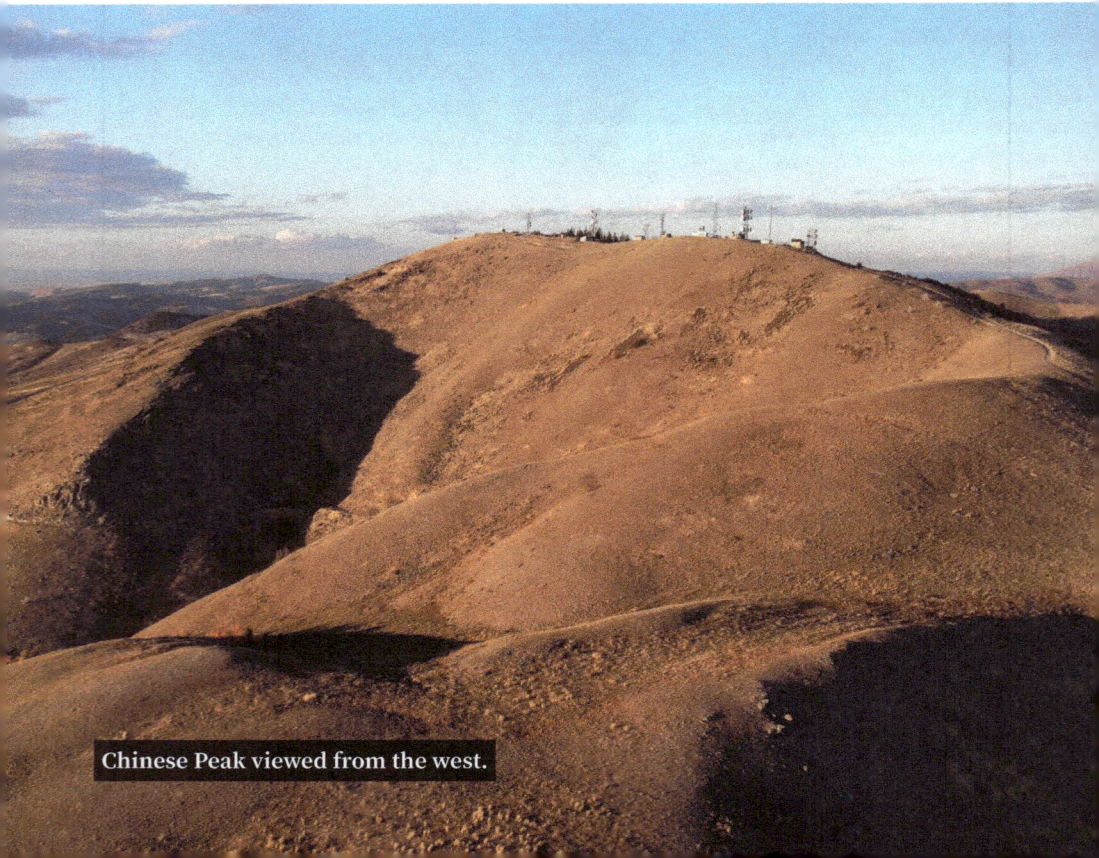

Chinese Peak viewed from the west.

Chinese Peak - West Face via Barton Road (BLM 301)

The most popular way to climb Chinese Peak, BLM 301 is an easy-to-follow dirt road that climbs through scattered juniper forests and dry grassy hillsides until it reaches the radio tower-rimmed summit.

Distance: 5.5 miles out-and-back
Elevation Gain: 1,680 feet
Difficulty: Moderately Strenuous; Class 1
Hiking Time: About 3 hours
Nearest Town: Pocatello
Trail Surface: Dirt, rock
Wheelchair Access: None

Dog-Friendly: Yes; on-leash at the trailhead. May be off-leash if under control once on the trail
Amenities: None
Contact: Bureau of Land Management, Pocatello Field Office 208-478-6340
Trailhead GPS Coordinates: N42° 51.383' W112° 23.541'

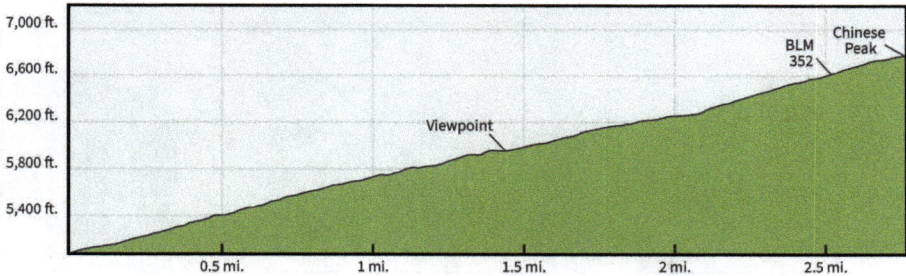

Getting There

From the junction of South 5th Avenue and Barton Road, head northeast on Barton Road for 1.8 miles until you reach a large gravel parking lot. The trailhead is located on the east end of the parking area.

The Hike

Follow the BLM 301 trail (p. 111) from Barton Road for 2.8 miles until it ends atop Chinese Peak.

Chinese Peak - Northwest Ridge via Buckskin Trailhead (BLM 352)

A more traditional hike to the top of Chinese Peak, BLM 352 challenges hikers with a very steep hill midway through the route. Once atop the mountain's northwest ridge, the path levels out and presents a beautiful view of the peak, making this arguably the most scenic way to summit the mountain.

Distance: 7.4 miles out-and-back
Elevation Gain: 2,000 feet
Difficulty: Strenuous; Class 1
Hiking Time: About 4 hours
Nearest Town: Pocatello
Trail Surface: Dirt, rock
Wheelchair Access: None

Dog-Friendly: Yes; on-leash at the trailhead. May be off-leash if under control once on the trail
Amenities: None
Contact: Bureau of Land Management, Pocatello Field Office 208-478-6340
Trailhead GPS Coordinates: N42° 52.259' W112° 24.391'

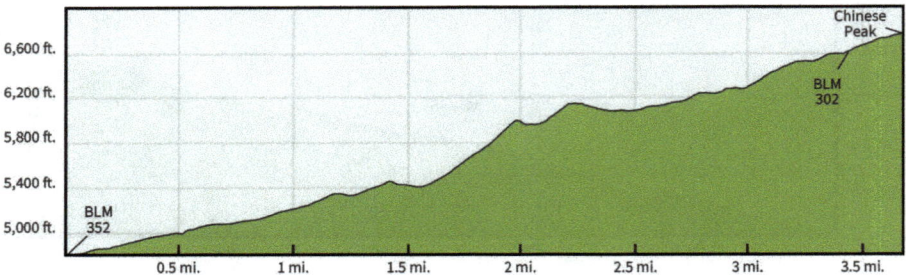

Getting There

From the junction of South 5th Avenue and East Carter Street, head northeast on East Carter Street for 0.2 miles. Turn right onto South 8th Avenue, then turn left at the light onto Martin Luther King Jr Way. Continue on Martin Luther King Jr Way for 0.3 miles until it transitions into East Terry Street at the light. Continue on East Terry Street for 1.2 miles. Turn right onto American Road, and then left immediately into the Buckskin Trailhead parking area. The trailhead is on the northeast end of the parking area.

The Hike

Follow the BLM 352 trail (p. 107) for 3.4 miles. Once the trail reaches BLM 301, turn left (northeast) onto BLM 301, which ends at the summit in about a quarter of a mile.

Did you know Healthy City, USA provides free swag to people who complete a hiking challenge every summer? Portneuf Peaks Club and Petite Peaks encourage hikers to hike three featured trails for that summer and post their pictures from the hike.

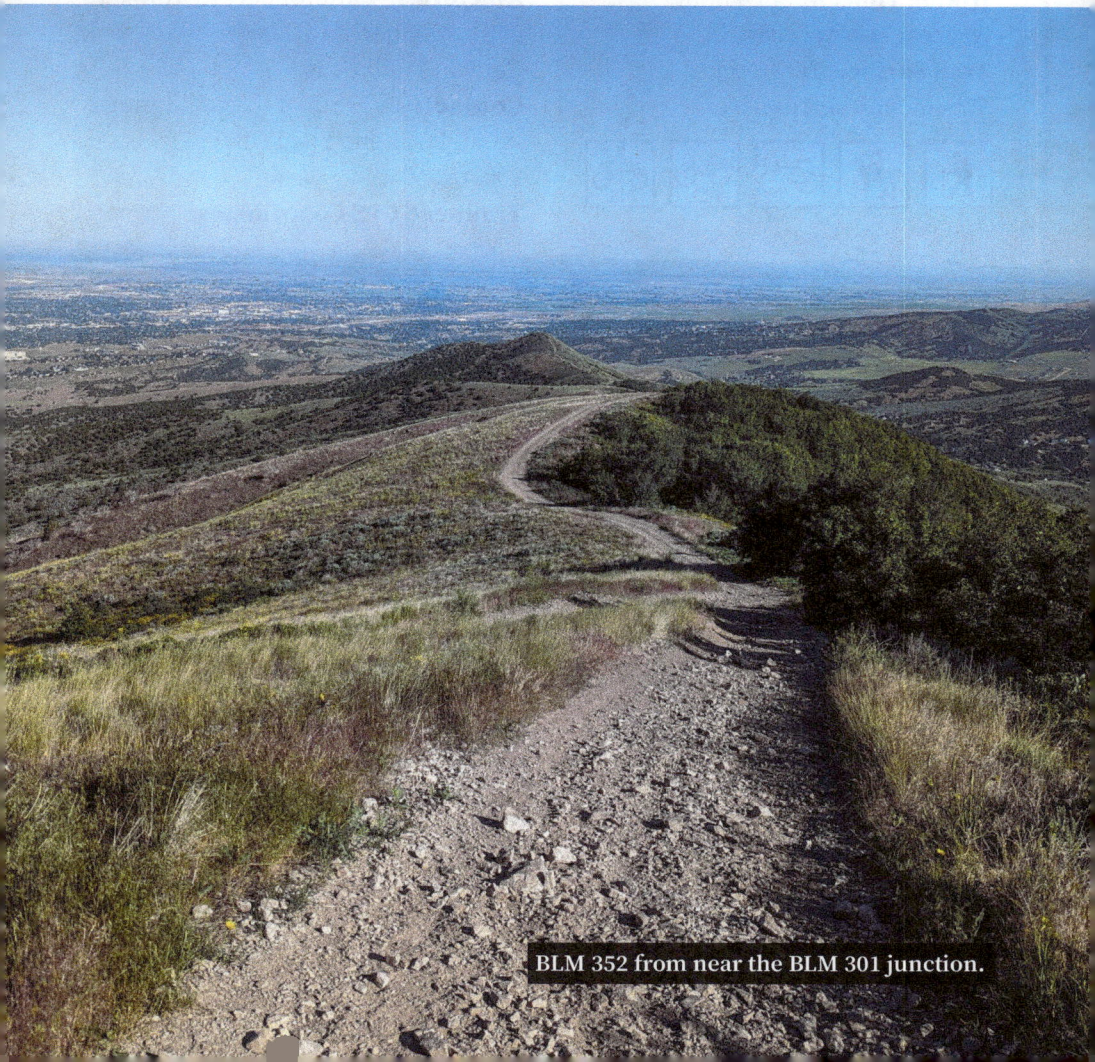

BLM 352 from near the BLM 301 junction.

Chinese Peak - Southern Ridge via Blackrock Canyon (BLM 301)

The eastern variant of BLM 301, this strenuous path travels from Blackrock Canyon up the peak's forested eastern slopes before reaching the saddle on the mountain. The last section from the saddle to the summit is incredibly steep and rocky, which makes it a more challenging route overall.

Distance: 6.4 miles out-and-back
Elevation Gain: 1,920 feet
Difficulty: Strenuous; Class 1
Hiking Time: About 4 hours
Nearest Town: Pocatello
Trail Surface: Dirt, rock
Wheelchair Access: None

Dog-Friendly: Yes; on-leash at the trailhead. May be off-leash if under control once on the trail
Amenities: Vault toilets are available at the Upper and Lower Blackrock Canyon Trailheads.
Contact: Bureau of Land Management, Pocatello Field Office
208-478-6340
Trailhead GPS Coordinates: N42° 49.248' W112° 19.672'

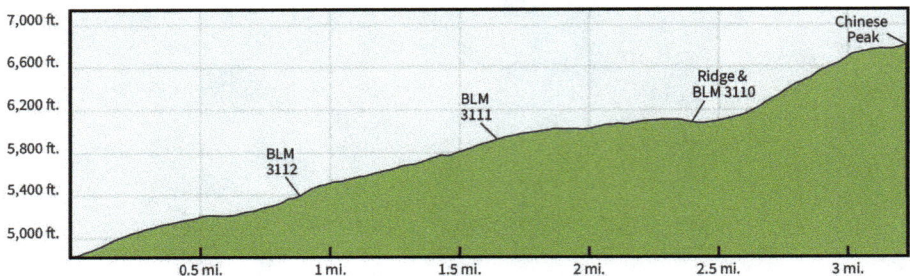

Getting There

From the junction of West Old Highway 91 and Blackrock Canyon Road, head north on Blackrock Canyon Road for 2.3 miles, making a slight left at 1 mile into Blackrock Canyon. Stay on this gravel road for another 1.3 miles until you end at the upper parking area. The trailhead is 0.1 miles southwest of the parking lot. I recommend used the southernmost starting point (the second right turn from the parking area).

The Hike

Follow the BLM 301 trail (p. 114) from Blackrock Canyon for 3.2 miles until it ends atop Chinese Peak.

BLM 301 and Chinese Peak from the saddle.

Chinese Peak

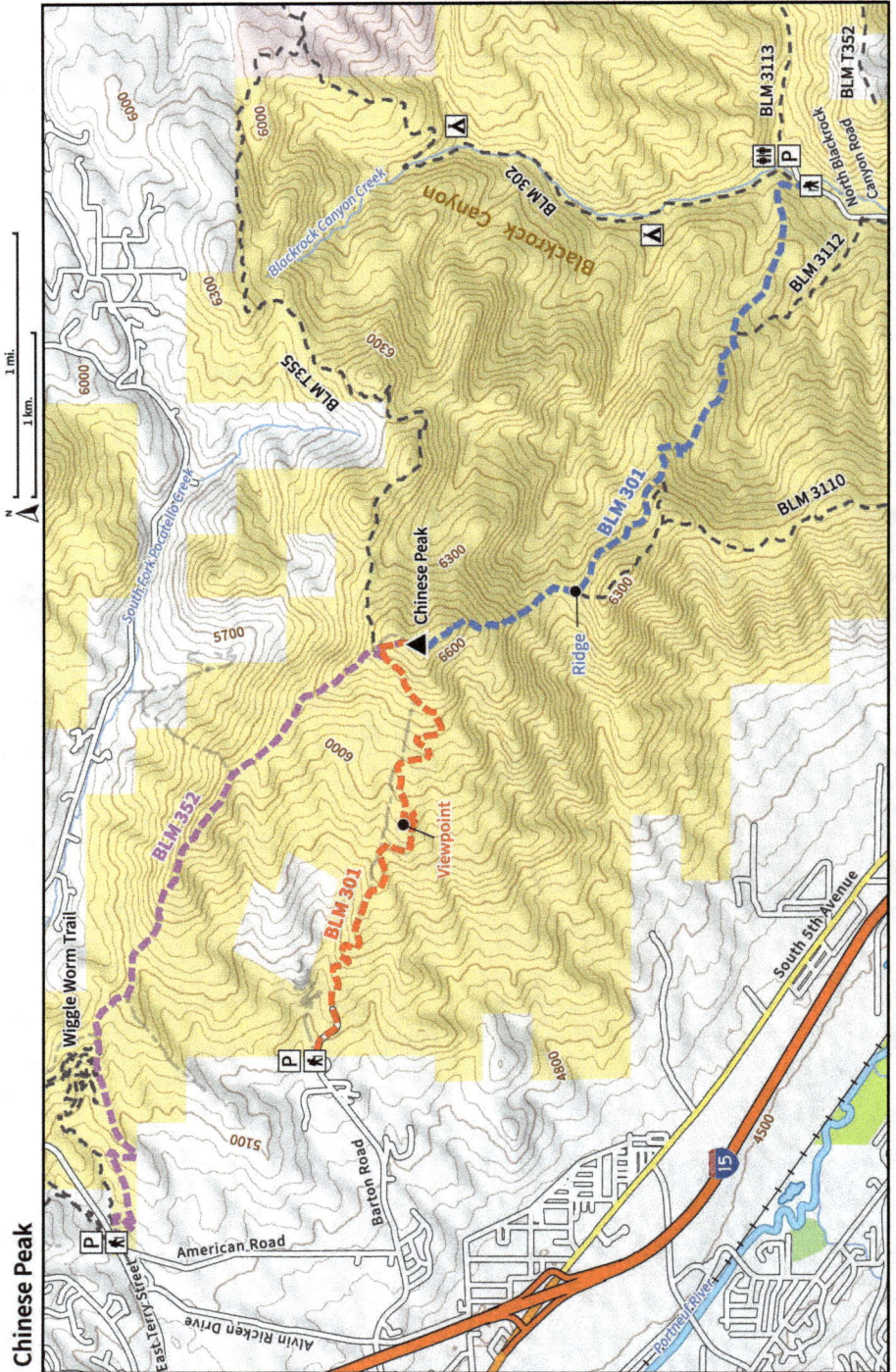

N

1 mi.

1 km.

Chinese Peak

▲ Chinese Peak

6600

6300

6000

5700

5100

4900

4800

4500

6000

6300

6000

BLM 352

BLM 301

BLM 301

BLM 302

BLM T35

BLM T355

BLM 3110

BLM 3112

BLM 3113

BLM T352

Blackrock Canyon

Blackrock Canyon Creek

South Fork Pocatello Creek

Wiggle Worm Trail

Viewpoint

Ridge

North Blackrock Canyon Road

East Terry Street

Alvin Ricken Drive

American Road

Barton Road

South 5th Avenue

Portneuf River

I-15

Kinport Peak
Bannock Range
7,222 feet (2,201 meters)

Kinport Peak and its many foothills looming large over Pocatello's west bench are a haven for outdoor enthusiasts. Many trails are found in this mountain's shadow, including those within the City Creek Management Area (CCMA). The two routes to the summit both begin in the CCMA and approach the mountain from the northeast. The mountain gets its name from Gideon R. Kinport, who planted an American flag atop the mountain in 1889 along with his two companions.

Kinport Peak from the northwest.

Kinport Peak - North Face / Southwest Ridge via Kinport Road

The most popular way to summit the mountain, the steep Kinport Road climbs directly from the forested City Creek to the top of Kinport Peak. It's not uncommon to see motorized vehicles on this broad and rocky 4x4 path, so be sure to keep an eye out when on the trail. This path is exposed to the sun for almost its entirety, so sun protection is recommended.

Distance: 5.6 miles out-and-back
Elevation Gain: 1,800 feet
Difficulty: Moderately Strenuous; Class 1
Hiking Time: About 3.5 hours
Nearest Town: Pocatello
Trail Surface: Dirt, rock
Wheelchair Access: None

Dog-Friendly: Yes; leash is required for the first mile. After one mile, may be off-leash if under control.
Amenities: None
Contact: Caribou-Targhee National Forest, Westside Ranger District 208-236-7500; City of Pocatello Parks & Recreation 208-234-6232
Trailhead GPS Coordinates: N42° 49.440' W112° 29.175'

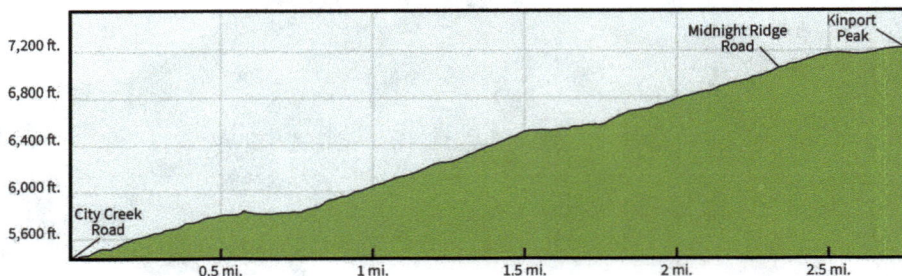

Getting There

From the junction of South 4th Avenue and Benton Street, head southwest on Benton Street for 0.7 miles. Turn right onto South Grant Avenue, and then turn left on West Whitman Street. After a few blocks, turn left onto South Lincoln Avenue, and then in 0.5 miles, turn left onto City Creek Road, following a sign for the City Creek Trails. You will reach the Upper City Creek Trailhead at the end of this paved road in 0.5 miles. From the Upper City Creek Trailhead, continue south on the dirt City Creek Road for 2.3 miles until you reach a small parking area just before the Kinport Road gate. Kinport Road begins at the gate.

The Hike

From the endpoint of City Creek Road, follow Kinport Road for 2.8 miles until you reach the summit. This route is covered in full on page 174.

Kinport Road heading toward the summit.

Kinport Peak - Northeast Face / Southwest Ridge via Cusick Creek Road

The route up Cusick Creek Road gives hikers a wilder option for summiting Kinport Peak. This scenic path follows a creek for much of the hike and spends a large amount of time in a shaded forest just below the mountain's summit. Of the two routes to the top, this is the more difficult option, though the scenic foliage and more remote experience make up for it.

Distance: 7.6 miles out-and-back
Elevation Gain: 2,210 feet
Difficulty: Strenuous; Class 1
Hiking Time: About 5 hours
Nearest Town: Pocatello
Trail Surface: Dirt, rock
Wheelchair Access: None

Dog-Friendly: Yes; leash is required for the first 1.7 miles. After 1.7 miles, may be off-leash if under control.
Amenities: None
Contact: Caribou-Targhee National Forest, Westside Ranger District 208-236-7500; City of Pocatello Parks & Recreation 208-234-6232
Trailhead GPS Coordinates: N42° 50.325' W112° 27.084'

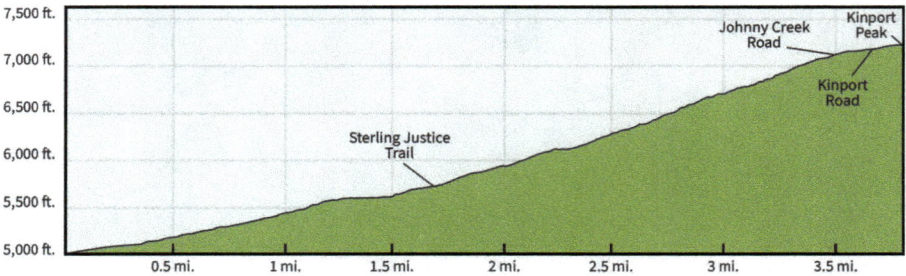

Getting There

From the junction of South 4th Avenue and Benton Street, head southwest on Benton Street for 0.7 miles. Turn left onto South Grant Avenue, and then in 0.4 miles, make a slight right turn onto Fore Road. Continue on Fore Road for 1.4 miles, turning left at 1.0 mile just before the Pocatello Women's Correctional Center to stay on Fore Road. From that turn, Fore Road transitions into a gravel road, where in 0.4 miles, you will find the Cusick Creek Trailhead and plenty of parking.

The Hike

Follow the Cusick Creek Road (p. 170) for 3.5 miles until it ends at Johnny Creek Road. Head west on Johnny Creek Road for 0.2 miles, where you will then turn right (north) onto Kinport Road. The road ends in 0.2 miles at a set of towers. The actual summit is about 70 yards to the southeast. While not the summit, the northernmost set of towers offers an excellent place for viewing the city.

Cusick Creek Road offers a quieter path to the summit.

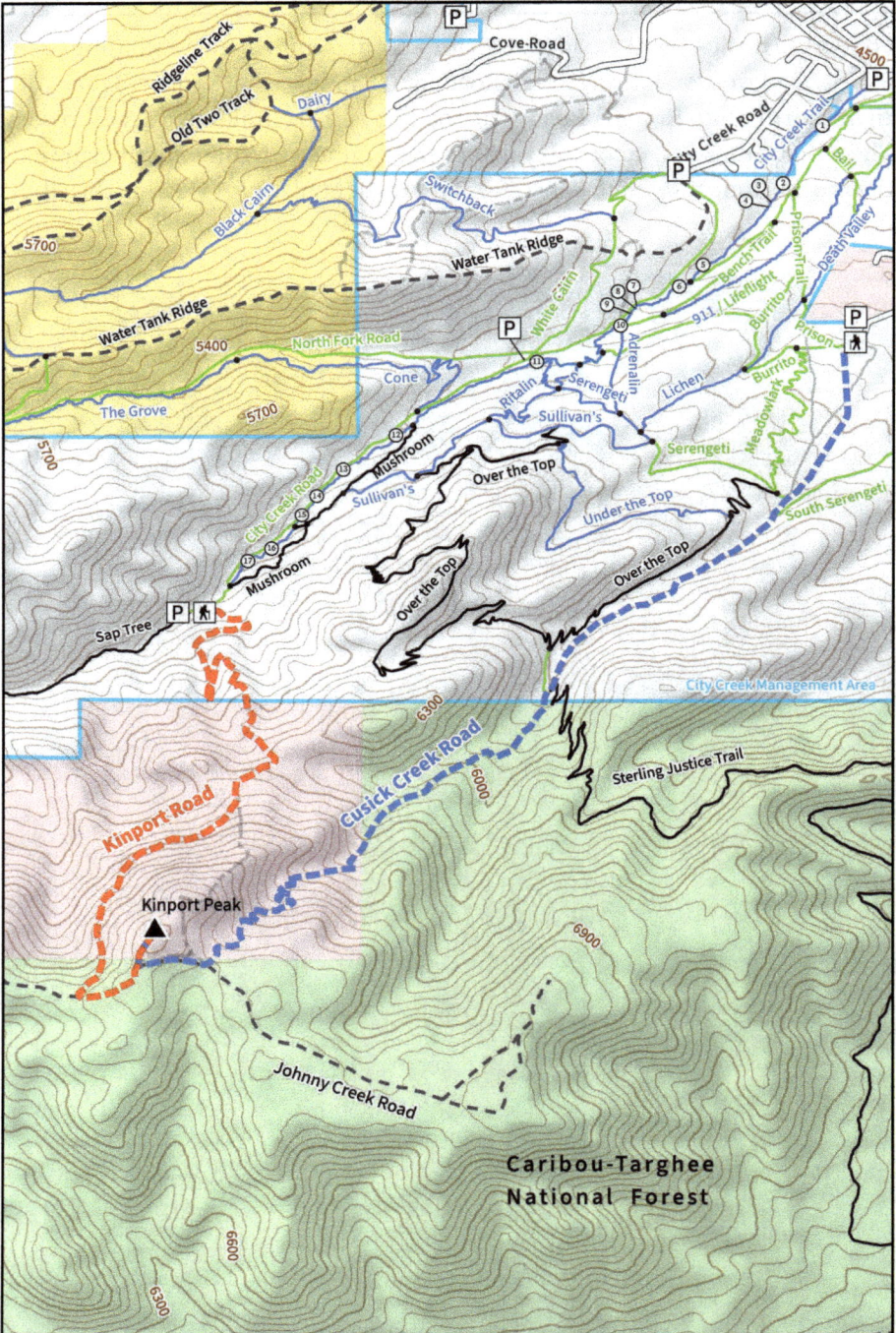

Kinport Peak

N

0.5 mi.

0.5 km.

Cove Road

Ridgeline Track

Old Two Track

Dairy

Black Cairn

5700

Switchback

City Creek Road

City Creek Trail

4500

P

P

P

Ball

Prison Trail

Death Valley

Water Tank Ridge

Bench Trail

911 / Lifeflight

White Cairn

Burrito

Prison

P

P

Water Tank Ridge

5400

North Fork Road

Cone

Adrenalin

Lichen

Serengeti

Meadowlark

Burrito

The Grove

5700

Ritalin

Sullivan's

Serengeti

Serengeti

South Serengeti

5700

Mushroom

Over the Top

Under the Top

City Creek Road

Sullivan's

Over the Top

Over the Top

Mushroom

Over the Top

Sap Tree

P

City Creek Management Area

6300

Cusick Creek Road

Sterling Justice Trail

6000

Kinport Road

6900

Kinport Peak

▲

Johnny Creek Road

Caribou-Targhee

National Forest

6600

6300

Rock Knoll

Bannock Range

7,268 feet (2,215 meters)

The aptly named Rock Knoll is an unassuming peak in southern Pocatello that is surprisingly the tallest mountain in the Bannock Range north of Mink Creek Road. The mountain provides excellent vistas of Gibson Creek and the hills of Elk Meadows. The easiest way to summit the mountain is from the Gibson Jack Trailhead. There is a trail for most of the hike, though the final half mile requires bushwhacking over manageable terrain.

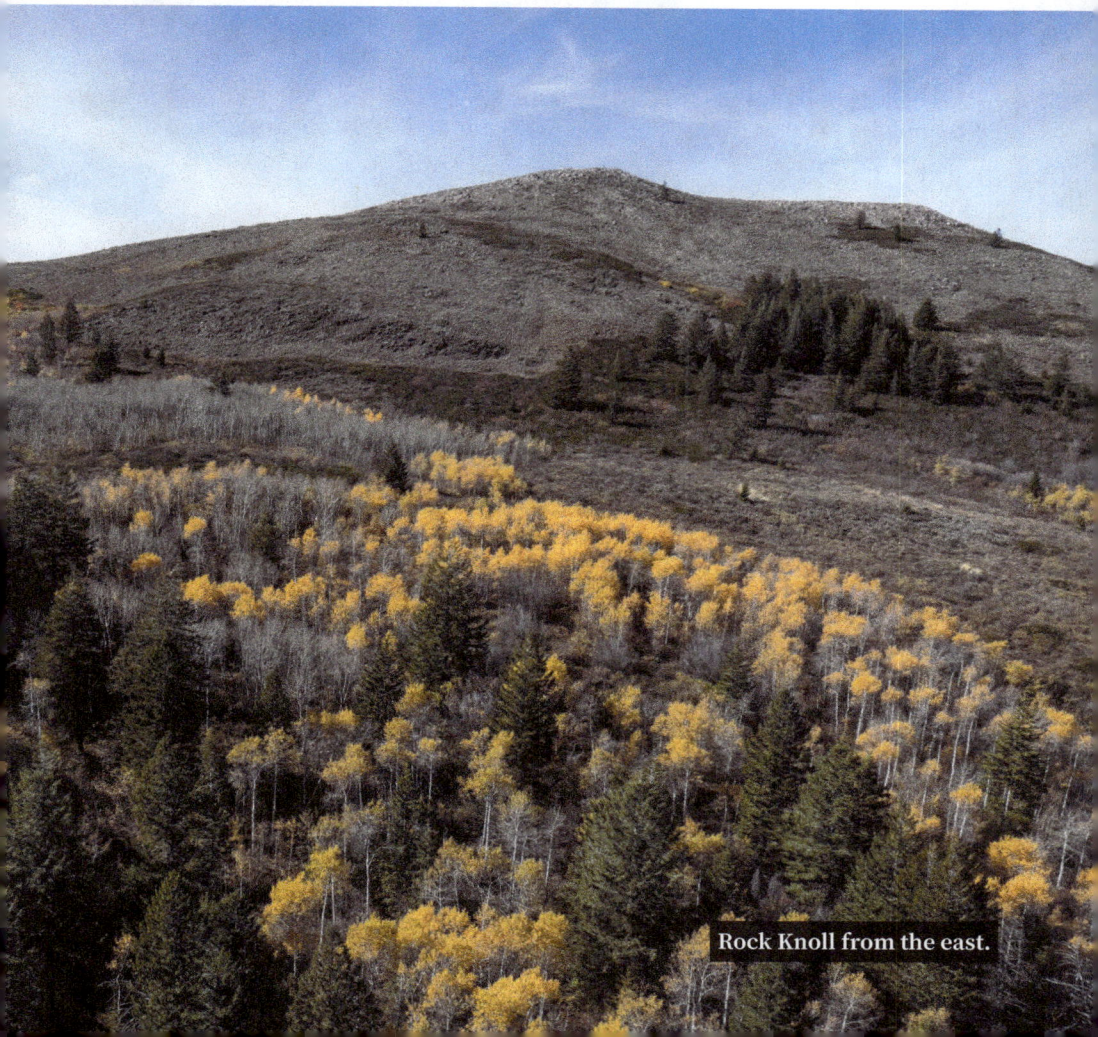

Rock Knoll from the east.

Rock Knoll - South Ridge via Gibson Jack Trail

Most of the route travels on the pleasant Gibson Jack Trail, though once the route leaves Elk Meadows and begins climbing Rock Knoll, it can be hard to follow. The end of the hike requires bushwhacking through shrubs on a rocky hillside.

Distance: 9.8 miles out-and-back
Elevation Gain: 2,100 feet
Difficulty: Moderately Strenuous; Class 1
Hiking Time: About 6 hours
Nearest Town: Pocatello
Trail Surface: Dirt, rock. Bushwhacking is required for the last 0.25 miles.
Wheelchair Access: None

Dog-Friendly: Yes; on-leash at the trailhead. May be off-leash if under control once on the trail
Amenities: A vault toilet is available at the trailhead.
Contact: Caribou-Targhee National Forest, Westside Ranger District 208-236-7500
Trailhead GPS Coordinates: N42° 47.575' W112° 25.887'

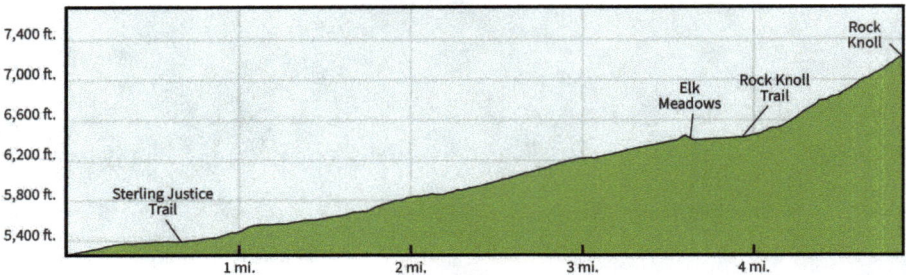

Getting There

From the junction of South Valley Road and Bannock Highway in Pocatello, head southeast on Bannock Highway for 1.4 miles, where you will turn right onto West Gibson Jack Road. Stay on this road until you reach the Gibson Jack Trailhead in 2.3 miles, which has plenty of parking. The trail is on the west side of West Gibson Jack Road just outside the parking lot.

The Hike

Follow the Gibson Jack Trail (p. 182) for 3.6 miles until it ends at Elk Meadows. Make a right (southwest) turn onto Elk Meadows. At 3.9 miles, turn right (northwest) onto the unmarked and often overgrown Rock Knoll Trail (Forest Service Trail 021). The summit is 800 vertical feet and just under a mile away from this turn. This rough 4x4 trail climbs to the left of a barbed wire fence through a mixed conifer and aspen forest and later an open hillside. At about 4.4 miles, the trail passes through a gate and leaves the fence behind.

Continue northwest atop the broad ridge, where you will soon lose the trail under tall grass and low bushes. At 4.7 miles, turn right (north) to stay atop the ridge. After another 0.2 miles of climbing over grass and large rocks, you will reach the summit, which is marked with a large rock cairn.

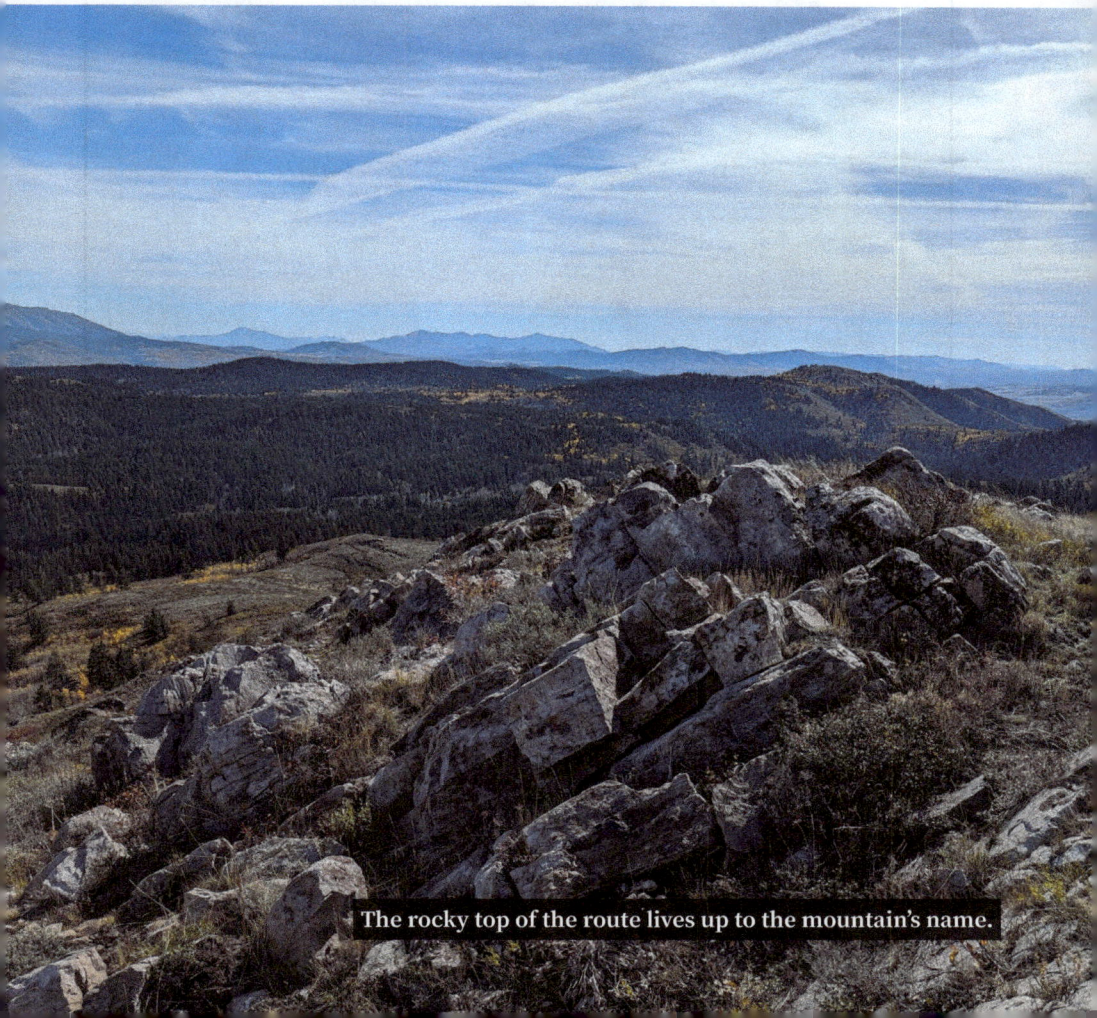

The rocky top of the route lives up to the mountain's name.

Rock Knoll

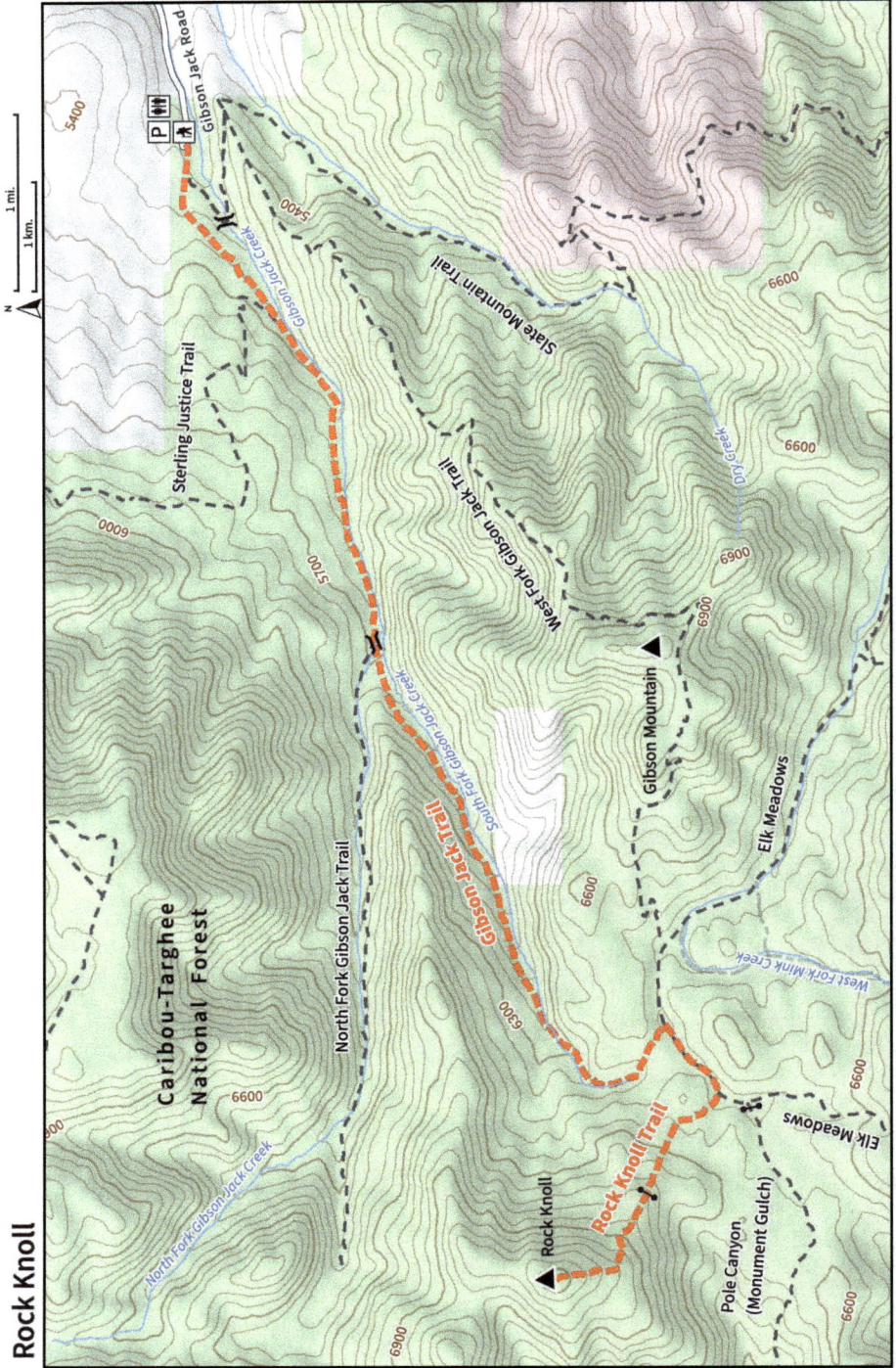

N

1 mi.

1 km.

5400

Gibson Jack Road

P

Gibson Jack Creek

5400

Slate Mountain Trail

Sterling Justice Trail

6600

Dry Creek

6000

5700

West Fork Gibson Jack Trail

6600

6900

Gibson Mountain

6900

5700

South Fork Gibson Jack Creek

Gibson Jack Trail

Elk Meadows

Caribou-Targhee
National Forest

North Fork Gibson Jack Trail

6600

6600

West Fork Mink Creek

5300

6600

North Fork Gibson Jack Creek

5900

Rock Knoll

Rock Knoll Trail

Elk Meadows

Pole Canyon
(Monument Gulch)

6600

6900

Gibson Mountain
Bannock Range
6,775 feet (2,065 meters)

The forested Gibson Mountain is a prominent landmark central to many trails in southern Pocatello. The mountain sits between the popular Elk Meadows, Gibson Jack, and Slate Mountain trails, making the peak easily accessible from a variety of trailheads. The most direct way to summit the peak is from the northeast via the Gibson Jack Trailhead. The mountain was named after Gibson Creek, which flows below the peak's forested slopes.

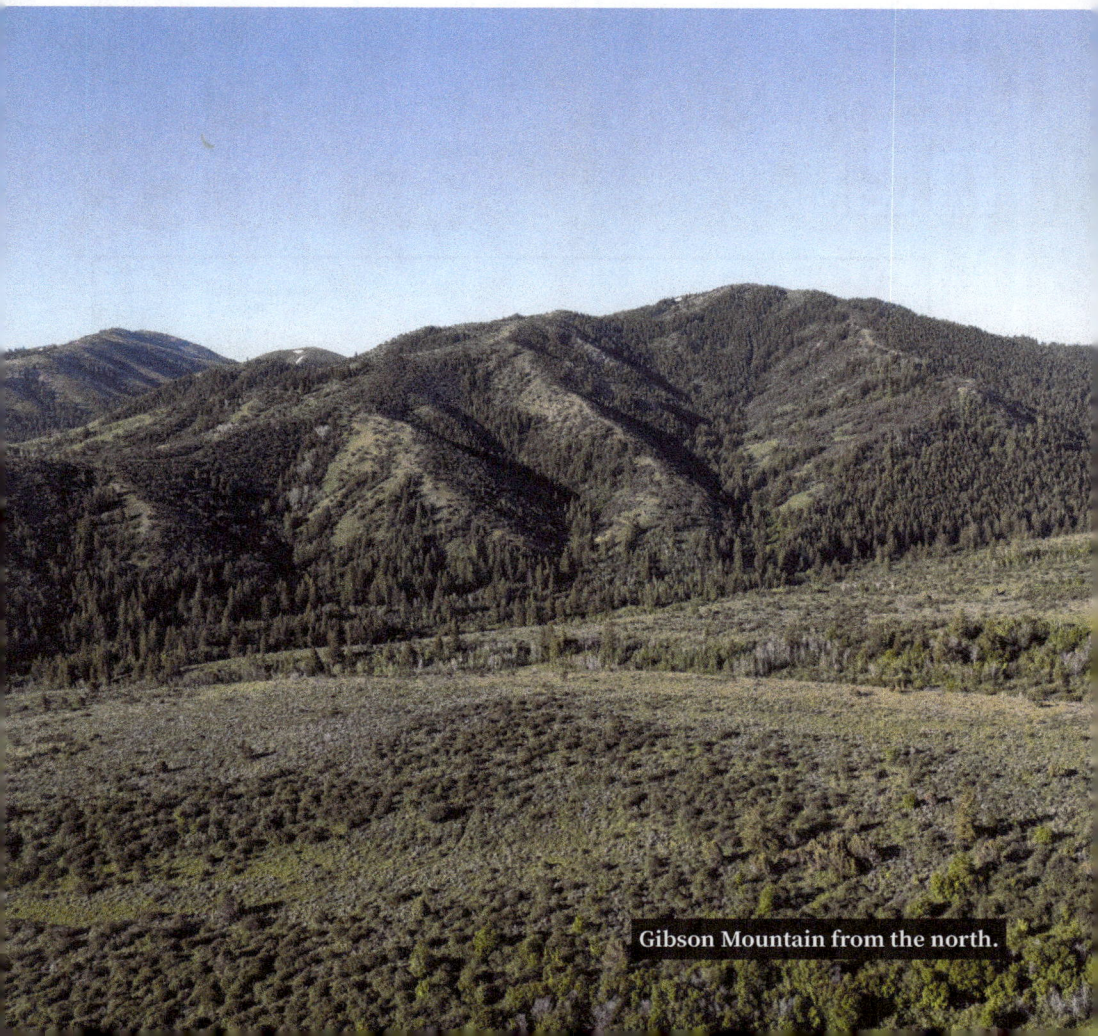

Gibson Mountain from the north.

Gibson Mountain - Southeast Ridge via West Fork Gibson Jack Trail

A strenuous climb on a rocky but highly visible 4x4 trail, this route to the top takes you through a variety of landscapes and has excellent views of Pocatello and the Caribou-Targhee National Forest. The very end of the route requires a brief section of bushwhacking.

Distance: 7.2 miles out-and-back

Elevation Gain: 1,910 feet

Difficulty: Strenuous; Class 2

Hiking Time: About 4.5 hours

Nearest Town: Pocatello

Trail Surface: Dirt, rock. The last 500 feet move off-trail.

Wheelchair Access: None

Dog-Friendly: Yes; on-leash at the trailhead. May be off-leash if under control once on the trail

Amenities: A vault toilet is available at the trailhead.

Contact: Caribou-Targhee National Forest, Westside Ranger District 208-236-7500

Trailhead GPS Coordinates: N42° 47.575' W112° 25.887'

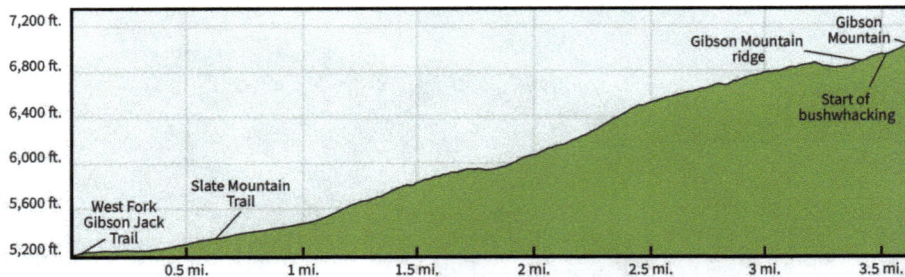

Getting There

From the junction of South Valley Road and Bannock Highway in Pocatello, head southeast on Bannock Highway for 1.4 miles, where you will turn right onto West Gibson Jack Road. Stay on this road until you reach the Gibson Jack Trailhead in 2.3 miles. A large parking lot is available. The trail is on the west side of West Gibson Jack Road just outside the parking lot.

Gibson Mountain from the West Fork Gibson Jack Trail.

The Hike

Follow the West Fork Gibson Jack Trail (p. 186) until you reach the saddle between Gibson Mountain and a sub peak at 3.4 miles. Continue on the trail northwest for about 600 feet, then make a slight right (north) turn off the trail toward the summit. The summit is just a short distance away and is marked with a large rock cairn.

Gibson Mountain

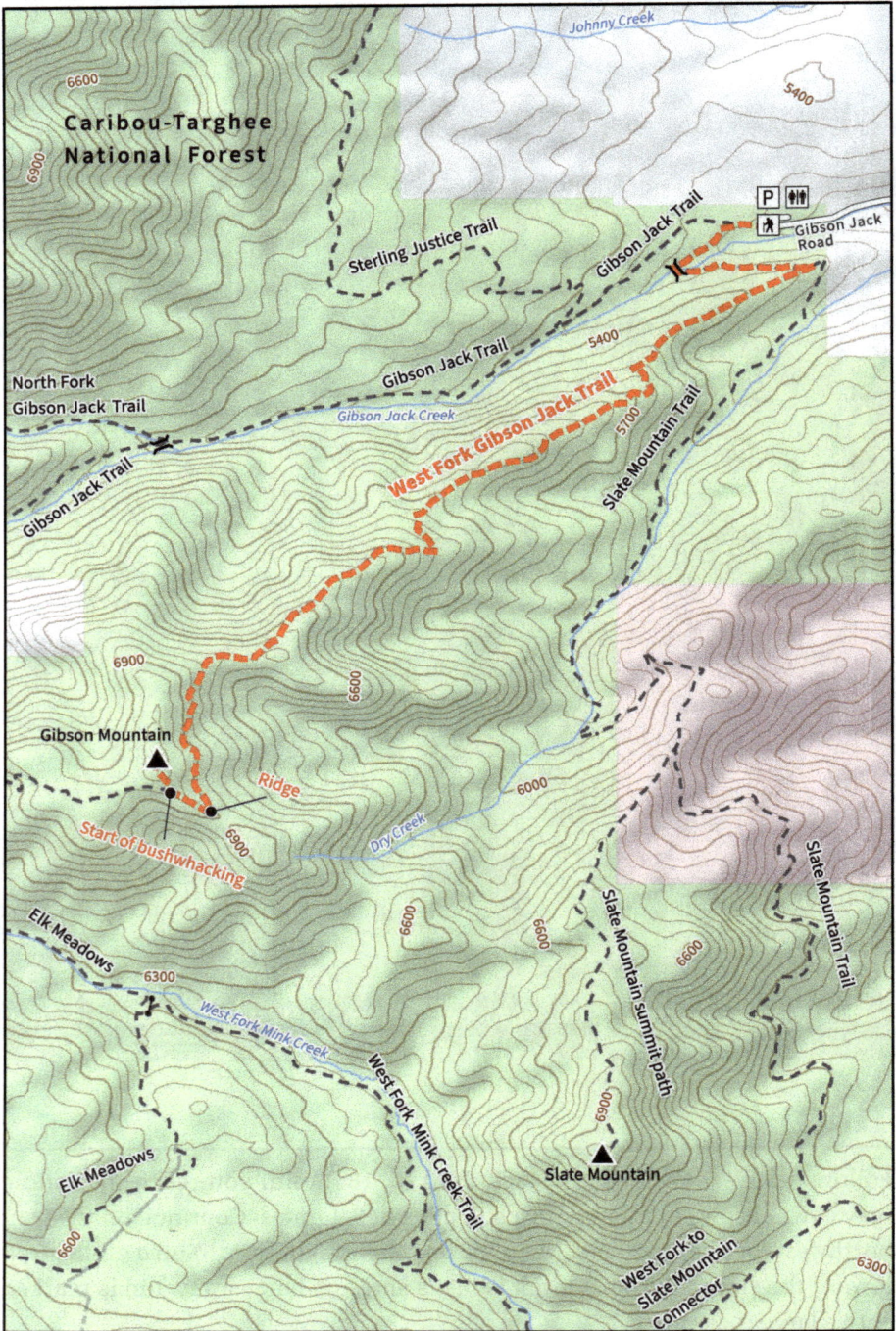

N

0.5 mi.

0.5 km.

Johnny Creek

5400

6600

Caribou-Targhee National Forest

6900

P

Gibson Jack Road

Sterling Justice Trail

Gibson Jack Trail

Gibson Jack Trail

5400

North Fork Gibson Jack Trail

Gibson Jack Creek

West Fork Gibson Jack Trail

5700

Slate Mountain Trail

Gibson Jack Trail

6900

6600

Gibson Mountain

Ridge

6600

6000

Start of bushwhacking

6900

Dry Creek

Slate Mountain Trail

Elk Meadows

6300

West Fork Mink Creek

6600

6600

Slate Mountain summit path

6600

Slate Mountain Trail

Elk Meadows

West Fork Mink Creek Trail

6000

6600

Slate Mountain

West Fork to Slate Mountain Connector

6300

Slate Mountain
Bannock Range
6,980 feet (2,128 meters)

Slate Mountain's rocky summit sits above the popular West Fork Mink Creek Trail and is highly visible to anyone driving on Mink Creek Road. The mountain has two approaches, both using the Slate Mountain Trail. The northern approach from the Gibson Jack Trailhead is a longer hike. It follows a visible path and has great views throughout. The southern approach begins on Mink Creek Road at the Slate Mountain Trailhead and, while shorter, is steeper and requires off-trail route finding.

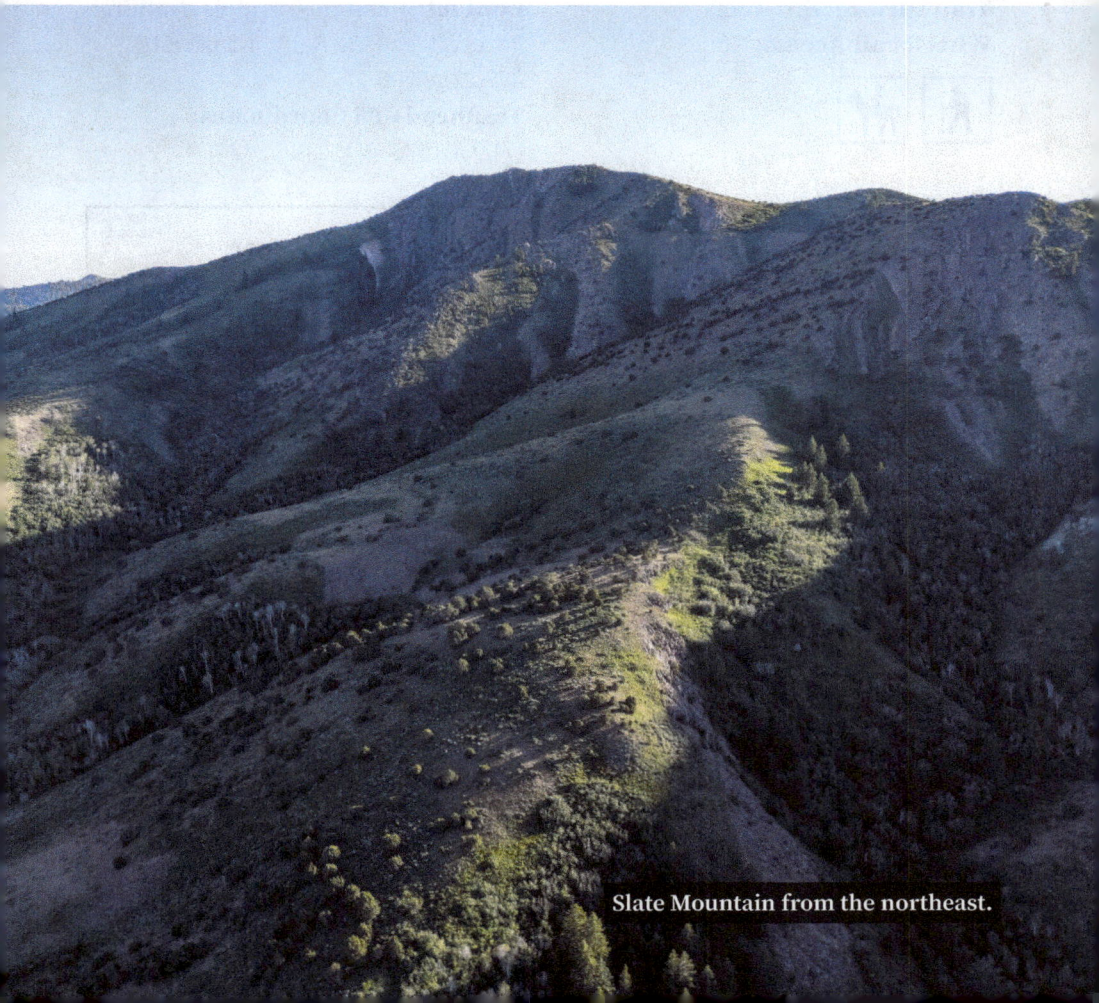

Slate Mountain from the northeast.

Slate Mountain - North Ridge via Gibson Jack Trailhead

This beautiful hike travels alongside the forested Dry Creek before climbing high onto Slate Mountain's northern ridge. While this is the longer route for summiting the mountain, the easy-to-follow trail, beautiful views, and more gradual incline make it an easier path to recommend.

Distance: 9.8 miles out-and-back
Elevation Gain: 2,150 feet
Difficulty: Very Strenuous; Class 1
Hiking Time: About 6 hours
Nearest Town: Pocatello
Trail Surface: Dirt, rock
Wheelchair Access: None

Dog-Friendly: Yes; on-leash at the trailhead. May be off-leash if under control once on the trail
Amenities: A vault toilet is available at the trailhead.
Contact: Caribou-Targhee National Forest, Westside Ranger District 208-236-7500
Trailhead GPS Coordinates: N42° 47.575' W112° 25.887'

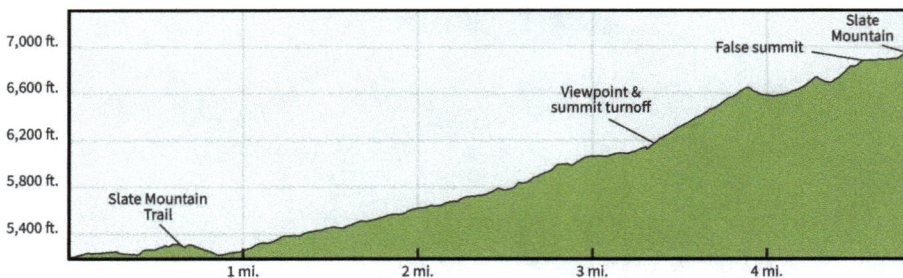

Getting There

From the junction of South Valley Road and Bannock Highway in Pocatello, head southeast on Bannock Highway for 1.38 miles, then turn right onto West Gibson Jack Road. Stay on this road until you reach the Gibson Jack Trailhead in 2.3 miles, which has plenty of parking. The trail is on the west side of West Gibson Jack Road just outside the parking lot.

The Hike

Follow the Slate Mountain Trail (p. 190) until you reach a fork at 3.3 miles, where you will turn right (southwest) onto the narrow singletrack. For the next 0.6 miles, the trail climbs 530 feet atop a dry ridge with sweeping views of Gibson Mountain to the right (west). At 3.9 miles, the trail turns southeast toward the false summit of Slate Mountain and descends a small hill, providing a brief rest before the climb continues.

At about 4.5 miles, the trail forks, where you will follow the right (south) path as it travels below the rocky ridgeline of Slate Mountain. At about 4.8 miles, the trail comes to a junction with the southern route. Keep right (southwest) and you will shortly reach the summit, marked with a rock cairn. The summit has excellent views of Scout Mountain to the southeast.

The faint trail heading toward Slate Mountain.

Slate Mountain - Southeast Face via Slate Mountain Trailhead

The southern approach is a strenuous hike that requires a significant amount of bushwhacking. This route to the top is for experienced hikers looking for the shortest path. Consider starting this route from the West Fork Mink Creek Trail for a more scenic experience.

Distance: 6.6 miles out-and-back
Elevation Gain: 2,150 feet
Difficulty: Strenuous; Class 2
Hiking Time: About 4.5 hours
Nearest Town: Pocatello
Trail Surface: Dirt, rock. Bushwhacking is required for the last 0.7 miles.

Wheelchair Access: None
Dog-Friendly: Yes; on-leash at the trailhead. May be off-leash if under control once on the trail
Amenities: None
Contact: Caribou-Targhee National Forest, Westside Ranger District 208-236-7500
Trailhead GPS Coordinates: N42° 44.025' W112° 24.448'

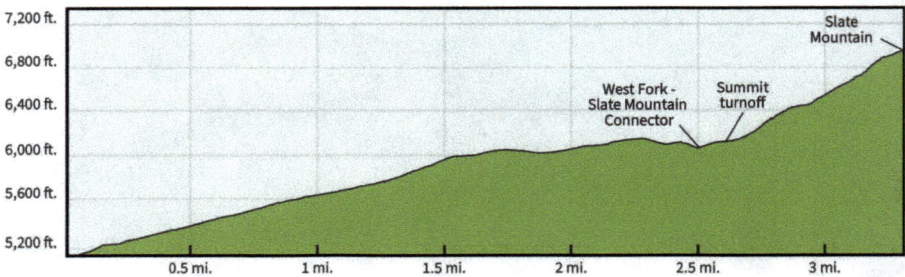

Getting There

From the junction of South Valley Road and Bannock Highway in Pocatello, head southeast on Bannock Highway for 7.7 miles. (The road becomes Mink Creek Road after 2.3 miles.) Turn right into the Slate Mountain parking lot. The trail begins on the west side of the parking area.

The Hike

Follow the Slate Mountain Trail (p. 190) north for 2.5 miles until you come to a junction with the West Fork to Slate Mountain Connector. Keep left (southwest) onto the Connector. At 2.6 miles, turn right (northwest) off the trail and continue up the hillside. The goal from here is to climb 250 feet to the top of a small ridge through thick sage and junipers, which can be a slog. Once atop the ridge, head north. At about 2.9 miles, the rocky ridge turns northwest toward Slate Mountain.

Head northwest on the ridge toward the mountain, keeping an eye out for a narrow singletrack path that helps alleviate the route finding. If you cannot find the trail, keep heading west / northwest up the mountain. You should never be on any cliff faces, so if you find yourself near them, backtrack and look for a new way up. The route does not climb directly to the summit; instead, it heads to the north around the summit and then doubles back. The summit is the southernmost highpoint on Slate Mountain and is marked with a rock cairn.

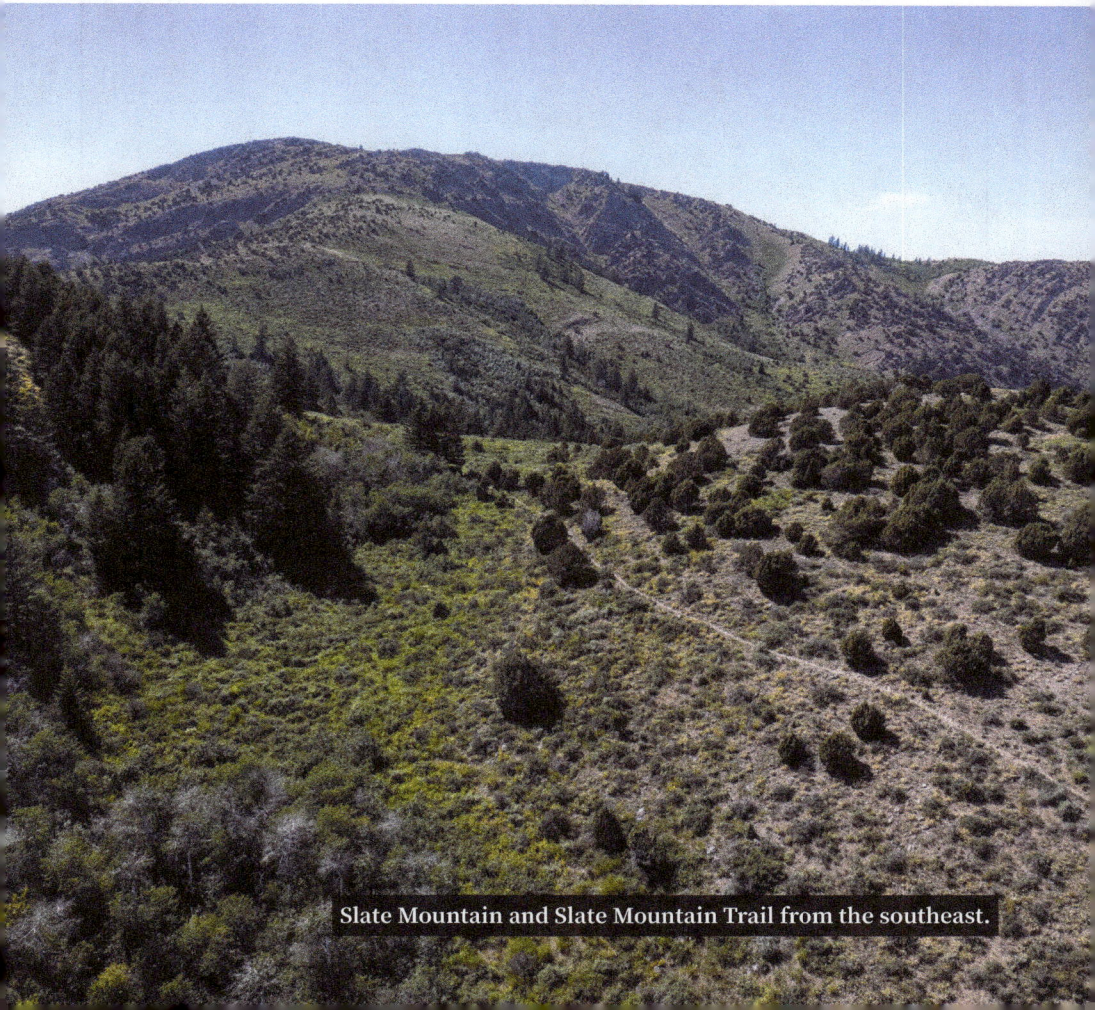

Slate Mountain and Slate Mountain Trail from the southeast.

Slate Mountain

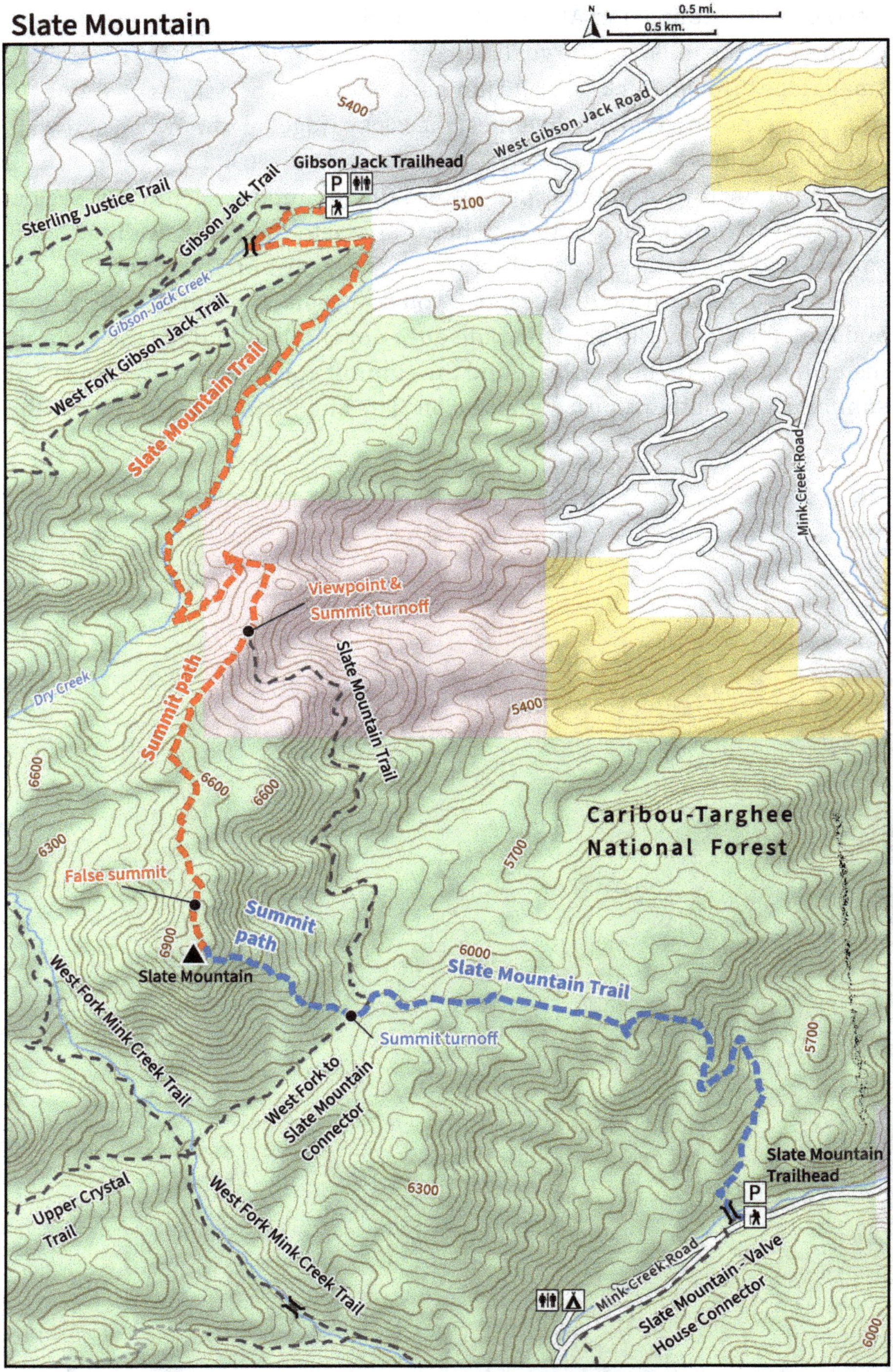

N

0.5 mi.

0.5 km.

5400

Gibson Jack Trailhead

P

West Gibson Jack Road

Sterling Justice Trail

Gibson Jack Trail

5100

Gibson-Jack Creek

West Fork Gibson Jack Trail

Slate Mountain Trail

Mink Creek Road

Viewpoint &
Summit turnoff

Slate Mountain Trail

Dry Creek

Summit path

5400

6600

6600

6600

6300

Caribou-Targhee
National Forest

5700

False summit

6900

Summit
path

Summit
path

Slate Mountain Trail

Slate Mountain

6000

West Fork Mink Creek Trail

5700

West Fork to
Slate Mountain
Connector

Summit turnoff

Slate Mountain
Trailhead

P

Upper Crystal
Trail

West Fork Mink Creek Trail

6300

Mink Creek Road

Slate Mountain - Valve
House Connector

6000

Indian Mountain
Bannock Range
7,298 feet (2,224 meters)

Visible from much of Pocatello, the barren hillsides of Indian Mountain are not typically the first place you think of for an adventurous mountain climb. Despite its lack of foliage, the mountain provides two routes through lightly traversed wilderness to the summit, where you will find a picturesque view of Scout Mountain to the south. The main route from the northwest via Kinney Creek begins in a creekside forest before starting a loop for the summit. The southwest route from Lead Draw is a steeper and wilder climb. It has a scenic direct ascent. For a more gradual hike, I recommend the Kinney Creek approach, though even that route has several very steep sections.

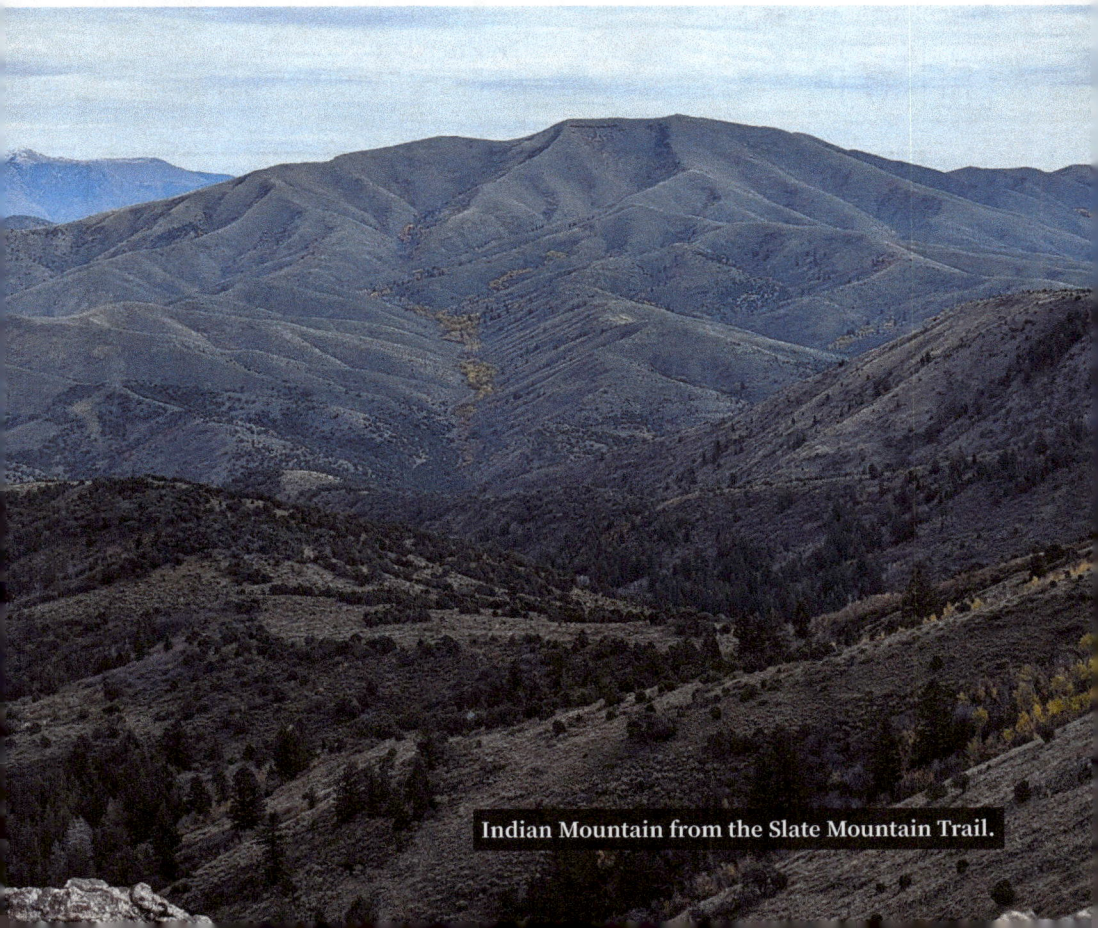

Indian Mountain from the Slate Mountain Trail.

Indian Mountain - North Ridge via Kinney Creek

The Kinney Creek route is a gradual creekside walk that utilizes a steep loop to reach the top of Indian Mountain. Once on top of the ridge, the trail becomes less defined, though a light trail is still visible. This path's relatively easy-to-follow trail has made it the default option for summiting the peak.

Distance: 6.7-mile lollipop loop
Elevation Gain: 2,400 feet
Difficulty: Moderately Strenuous; Class 2
Hiking Time: About 4.5 hours
Nearest Town: Pocatello
Trail Surface: Dirt, rock. Light bushwhacking is required near the top.
Wheelchair Access: None

Dog-Friendly: Yes; on-leash at the trailhead. May be off-leash if under control once on the trail
Amenities: None at the trailhead. A vault toilet is available nearby at the Cherry Springs Nature Area.
Contact: Caribou-Targhee National Forest, Westside Ranger District 208-236-7500
Trailhead GPS Coordinates: N42° 45.636' W112° 23.808'

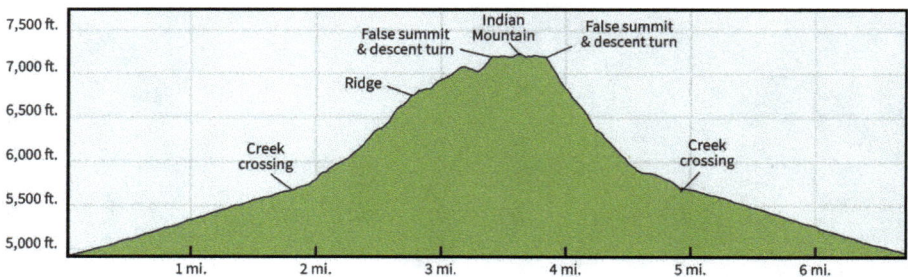

Getting There

From the junction of South Valley Road and Bannock Highway in Pocatello, head southeast on Bannock Highway for 5.4 miles. (The road becomes Mink Creek Road at 2.3 miles.) Once you see the large Caribou National Forest sign, turn left into the small Kinney Creek Trailhead parking area.

The Hike

Follow the Kinney Creek Trail (p. 222) for 1.8 miles until you reach the creek

The false summit of Indian Mountain.

crossing junction. Keep left at the junction, avoiding the creek and continuing on the singletrack trail. You will climb a small hill onto a ridge not far from the junction. Once atop this ridge at 2 miles, the path continues to the east, becoming much steeper and overgrown. This narrow singletrack climbs 980 feet over three-quarters of a mile until it reaches Indian Mountain's northern ridge. The trail is initially well-defined and moves alongside a barbed wire fence, though the fence and trail disappear the higher this steep trail climbs.

You will reach the northern ridge (6,750 feet) at 2.8 miles, which has terrific views of the area. From here, the trail follows the ridge south toward Indian Mountain. While the incline is still demanding, the ridge walk and views make for a nice change of pace. It is important to note that the peak before you is a false summit, though Indian Mountain isn't far beyond it. After a steep climb, the trail levels out atop the false summit (3.4 miles). This false summit is also where you will begin descending the mountain once you return from the summit.

Continuing south, the actual summit is only 0.2 miles away on a rocky but pleasant ridge walk. At 3.6 miles, you will reach the top of Indian Mountain, which is marked with a small rock cairn near a U.S. Geological Survey marker. Take a minute to take in the extraordinary view of Scout Mountain to the south before beginning the descent. To return to the trailhead, you could retrace your steps the way you came, but taking a different ridge back down to the creek junction is easier.

Once back at the false summit, make a left (northwest) turn down the steep hillside. The beginning stretch of the descent will require bushwhacking over shrubs, rocks, and grasses, but you should find a small trail shortly into the downclimb. This singletrack trail is the top of the Kinney Creek Trail, though it is primarily only used by those summiting the mountain.

Continue down Kinney Creek Trail as it steeply descends atop one of Indian Mountain's northwest ridges. The lower you go on this trail, the larger the surrounding shrubs become and the more difficult it is to follow. Luckily, there aren't many turns in the trail, so if you keep heading northwest, you should end up at the creek crossing. Once back at the crossing, retrace your steps another 1.8 miles back to the trailhead.

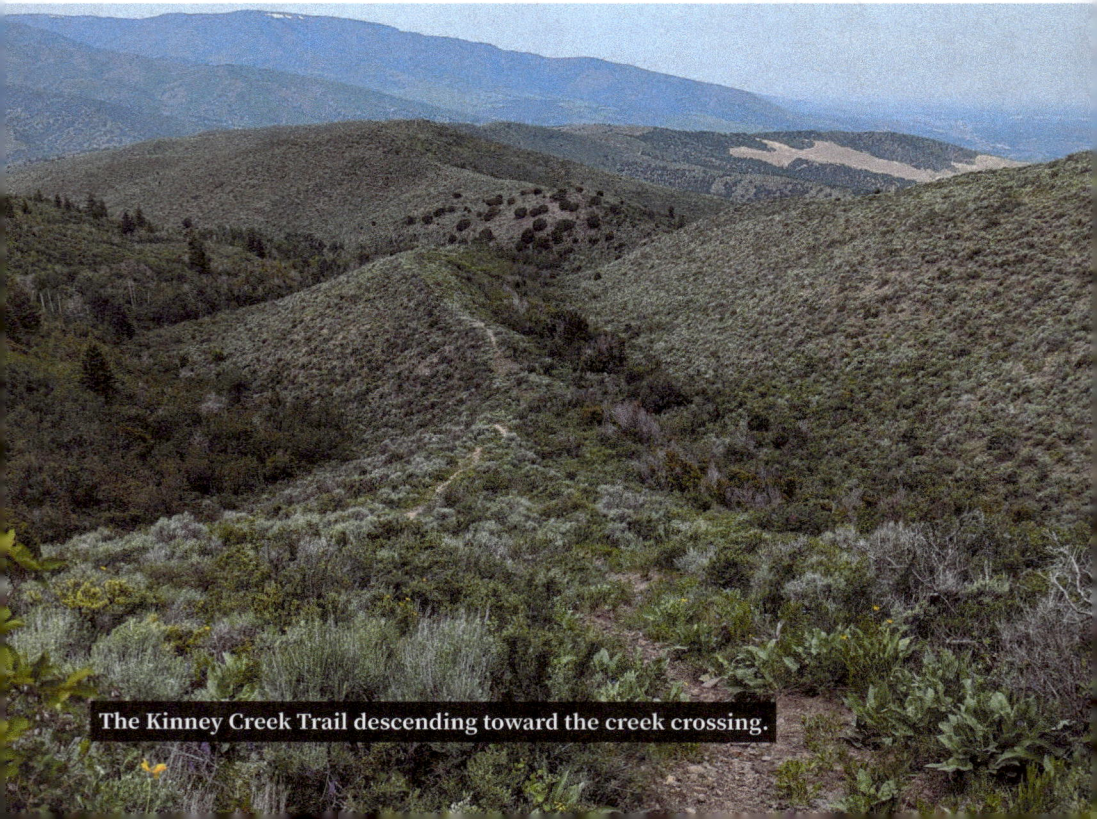

The Kinney Creek Trail descending toward the creek crossing.

Indian Mountain - Southwest Shoulder via Lead Draw Trail

This dry route passes through the Lead Draw shooting range before beginning a steep climb up Indian Mountain's southwestern sun-exposed slopes. Once the path leaves the Lead Draw Trail, the path becomes incredibly steep and overgrown. Still, the shorter overall distance and great views during the ascent may interest those looking for a less-traveled way to the summit.

Distance: 5 miles out-and-back
Elevation Gain: 2,100 feet
Difficulty: Moderately Strenuous; Class 2
Hiking Time: About 3.5 hours
Nearest Town: Pocatello
Trail Surface: Dirt, rock. Light bushwhacking is required near the top.

Wheelchair Access: None
Dog-Friendly: Yes; on-leash at the trailhead. May be off-leash if under control once on the trail
Amenities: None
Contact: Caribou-Targhee National Forest, Westside Ranger District 208-236-7500
Trailhead GPS Coordinates: N42° 44.278' W112° 23.036'

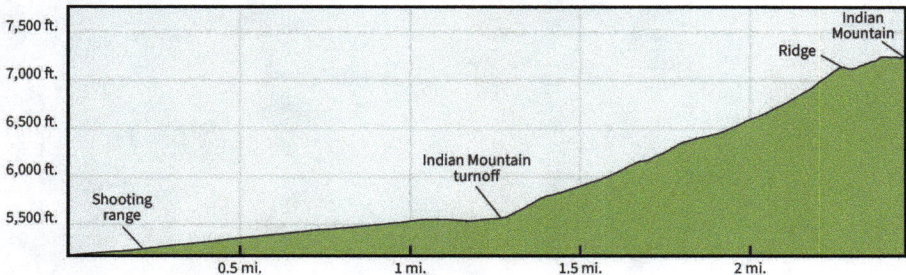

Getting There

From the junction of South Valley Road and Bannock Highway in Pocatello, head southeast on Bannock Highway for 6.8 miles. (The road becomes Mink Creek Road after 2.3 miles.) Turn left onto East Fork Mink Creek Road. In 0.6 miles, turn left into the signed Lead Draw Trailhead. The trail is located on the east side of the large parking area.

The Hike

From the trailhead, head east past the cattle guard on the Lead Draw Trail (p. 225). Stay on this trail for 1.3 miles until you reach a junction before a creek crossing. Make a left (northeast) turn up the hill on the singletrack trail, which passes alongside the old Lead Draw Ski Lodge in about 50 yards. For the next 0.6 miles, the trail steeply climbs 830 feet as it gains a ridge covered with plenty of grass and sagebrush.

At 1.9 miles, the trail shifts slightly to the east, beginning a second steep incline. After climbing 760 feet in a little over 0.5 miles, you will reach the summit ridge at 2.3 miles. Here, the trail shifts to the north and begins the final push for the summit. The path can be hard to follow at this point, though the terrain is easy to navigate across.

After climbing another 130 feet, you will reach the summit at 2.5 miles. The summit has a particularly nice view of Scout Mountain to the south.

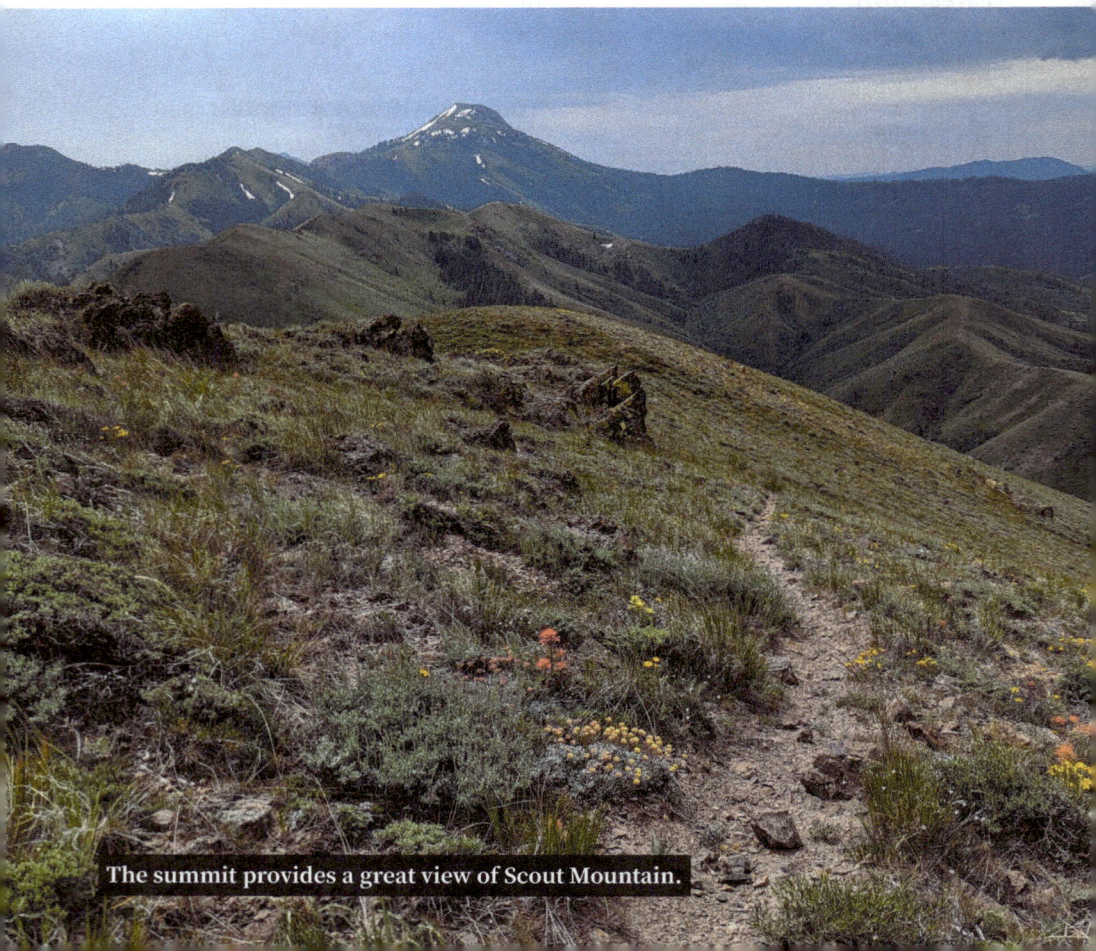

The summit provides a great view of Scout Mountain.

Indian Mountain

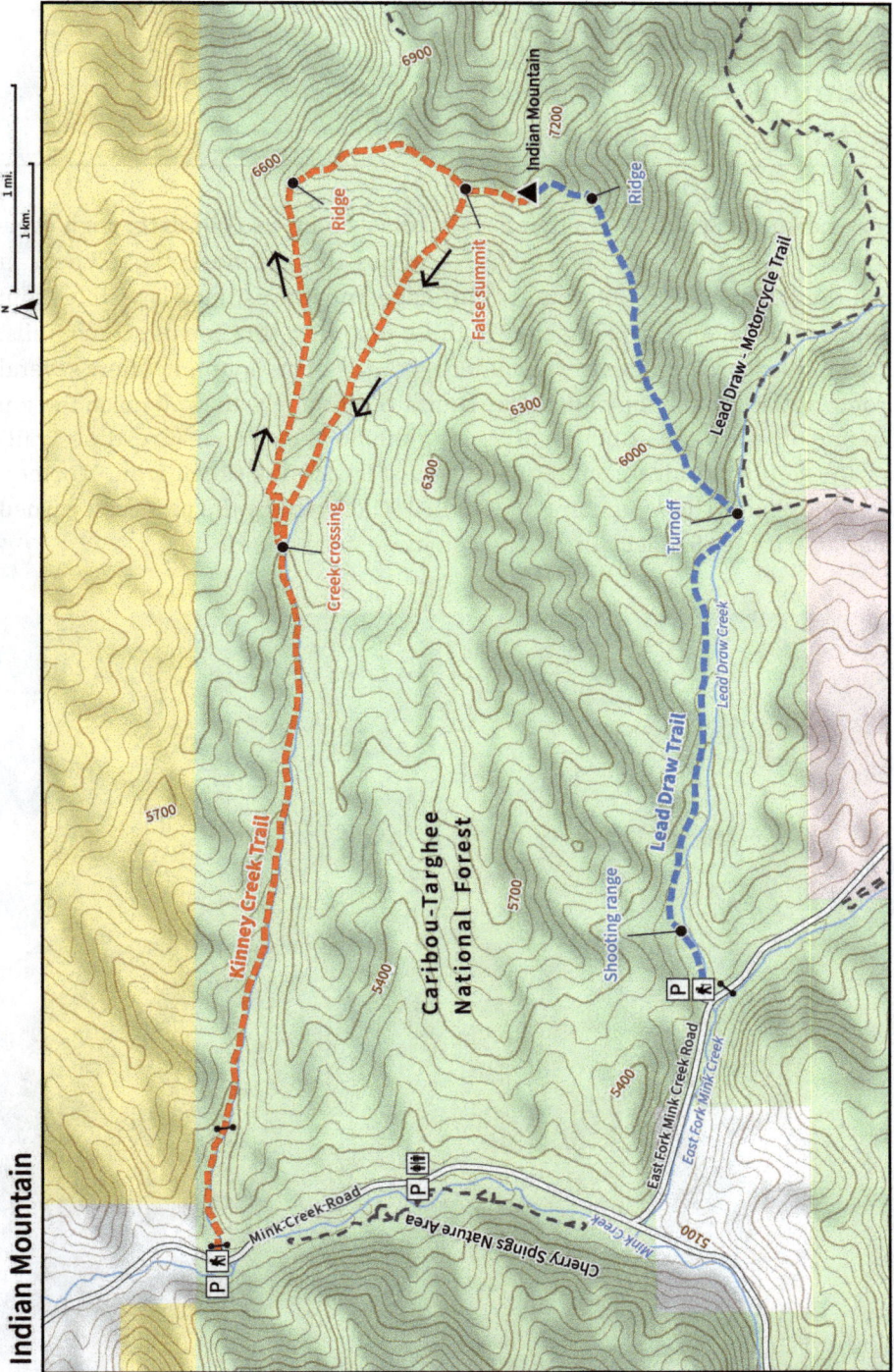

N

1 mi.
1 km.

6900

Indian Mountain
7200

Ridge

Ridge

6600

False summit

Lead Draw - Motorcycle Trail

6300

6000

6300

Creek crossing

Turnoff

Caribou-Targhee
National Forest

Lead Draw Creek

5700

Lead Draw Trail

Kinney Creek Trail

5700

Shooting range

5400

P

5400

East Fork Mink Creek Road

East Fork Mink Creek

5100

Mink Creek Road

P

Cherry Spings Nature Area

Mink Creek

P

Scout Mountain
Bannock Range
8,710 feet (2,655 meters)

The beautiful Scout Mountain offers hikers a chance to climb through evergreen forests and rocky cliffs to the top of possibly the most climbed peak in Southeast Idaho. The mountain's cliff-edged northwest face is visible from much of Pocatello, invoking envy in those unable to traverse its scenic trails. Due to the large number of surrounding trails, Scout Mountain offers several route options to the top of its rocky summit. Ultimately, they all reach the top in one of two ways: either by ascending the northeast spur (Crestline Trail) or the southern ridge from the saddle (East Fork Mink Creek Trail, Mormon Canyon Trail). The mountain, once called "Old Scab" by the pioneers, earned its name from a Scout camp situated on its western slopes.

Scout Mountain from the northwest.

Scout Mountain - Northeast Spur via Crestline Trail

Crestline Trail offers the shortest and shadiest route to the top of the mountain through a thick evergreen forest. Once you are above the trees high on Scout's northeast spur, it becomes quite steep. It isn't uncommon to see mountain bikers and dirt bikers on this trail, so be prepared to step out of the way.

Distance: 9.4 miles out-and-back
Elevation Gain: 3,000 feet
Difficulty: Very Strenuous; Class 1
Hiking Time: About 6.5 hours
Nearest Town: Pocatello
Trail Surface: Dirt, rock
Wheelchair Access: None

Dog-Friendly: Yes; on-leash at the trailhead. May be off-leash if under control once on the trail
Amenities: None
Contact: Caribou-Targhee National Forest, Westside Ranger District 208-236-7500
Trailhead GPS Coordinates: N42° 42.415' W112° 21.747'

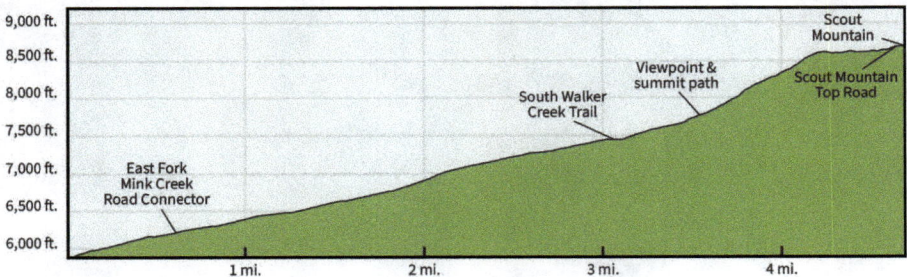

Getting There

From the junction of South Valley Road and Bannock Highway in Pocatello, head southeast on Bannock Highway for 6.8 miles. (The road becomes Mink Creek Road after 2.3 miles.) Turn left onto East Fork Mink Creek Road. In 2.9 miles, turn left onto a dirt road, which ends at the Crestline Trailhead in 0.3 miles. The trail is located on the southeast side of the parking area.

The Hike

Follow the Crestline Trail (p. 245) until you reach a junction at 3.6 miles, where you will turn right (west) off the official Crestline Trail onto the Scout Mountain Ridge Trail. This steep path gains 850 feet in just 0.7 miles as it reaches the mountain's elongated summit ridge. At about 3.8 miles, the path forks as the trail approaches a small stand of conifers. Take the path on the left (south) that stays outside the forest.

The trail tops out at 4.3 miles, and the remaining 0.4 miles gradually climbs 120 feet to the summit. At 4.7 miles, turn left onto the Scout Mountain Top Road, which in about 150 feet ends atop the mountain's summit. There is a cairn on the north end of the peak that can cause confusion, but the true summit is at the towers.

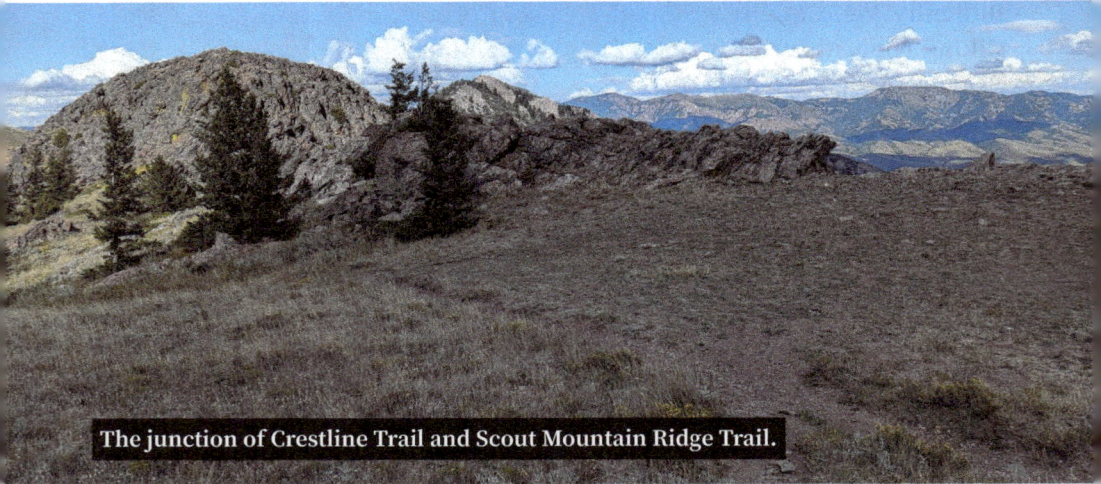

The junction of Crestline Trail and Scout Mountain Ridge Trail.

The Scout Mountain Ridge Trail heading toward the summit.

Scout Mountain - South Ridge via East Fork Mink Creek Trail

The most popular way to climb the mountain starts near the Scout Mountain Campground, at the East Fork Mink Creek Trail. The path travels through the forests below Scout Mountain's western cliffs before climbing up the saddle and eventually onto the peak's rocky southern ridge. This route is very exposed, so be sure to bring sun protection.

Distance: 12.4 miles out-and-back

Elevation Gain: 2,600 feet

Difficulty: Strenuous; Class 1

Hiking Time: About 7.5 hours

Nearest Town: Pocatello

Trail Surface: Dirt, rock

Wheelchair Access: None

Dog-Friendly: Yes; on-leash at the trailhead. May be off-leash if under control once on the trail

Amenities: None

Contact: Caribou-Targhee National Forest, Westside Ranger District 208-236-7500

Trailhead GPS Coordinates: N42° 41.333' W112° 21.574'

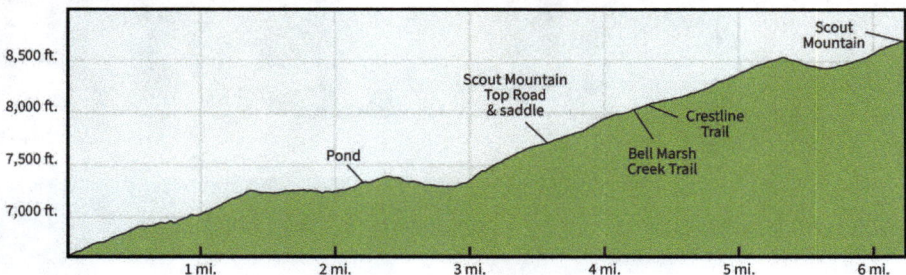

Getting There

From the junction of South Valley Road and Bannock Highway in Pocatello, head southeast on Bannock Highway for 6.8 miles. (The road becomes Mink Creek Road after 2.3 miles.) Turn left onto East Fork Mink Creek Road, which you will stay on for 5.3 miles as it climbs toward Scout Mountain. At the round-about, make the first right turn and then turn left shortly beyond that into the southern Scout Mountain Campground (Loop D). Keep right to start the loop, and then keep right again in about 200 yards to find the signed East Fork Mink Creek Trailhead, which has plenty of parking. The trail is on the southern end of the trailhead.

The Hike

Follow the East Fork Mink Creek Trail (p. 252) until it connects with the Scout Mountain Top Road at 3.6 miles. Turn left (north) onto the Scout Mountain Top Road, which, after 2.7 miles, ends at Scout Mountain's summit. Go to page 272 for an in-depth look at Scout Mountain Top Road.

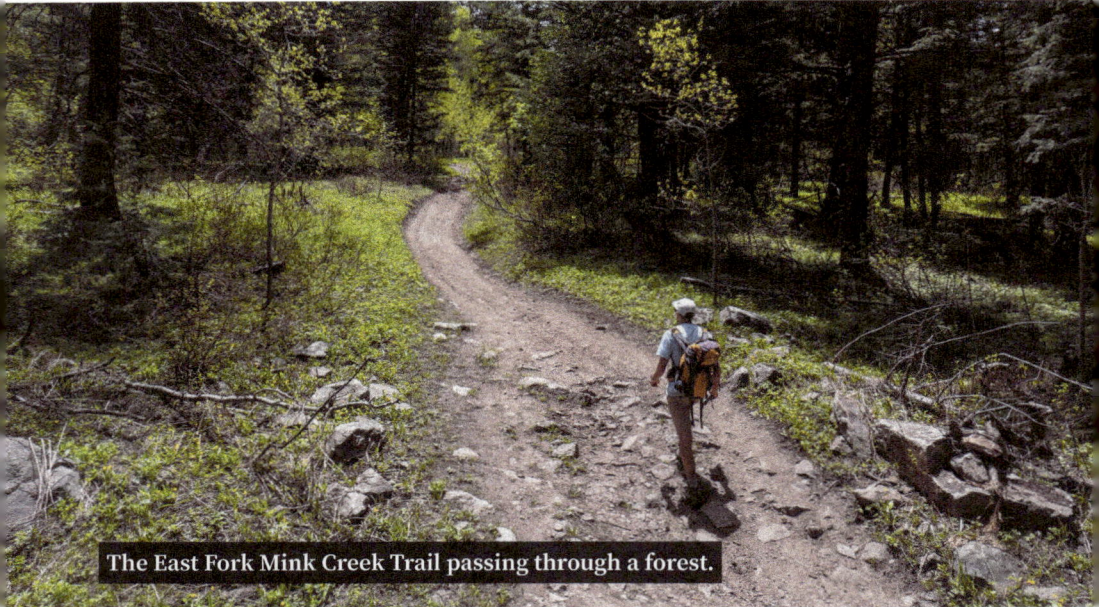

The East Fork Mink Creek Trail passing through a forest.

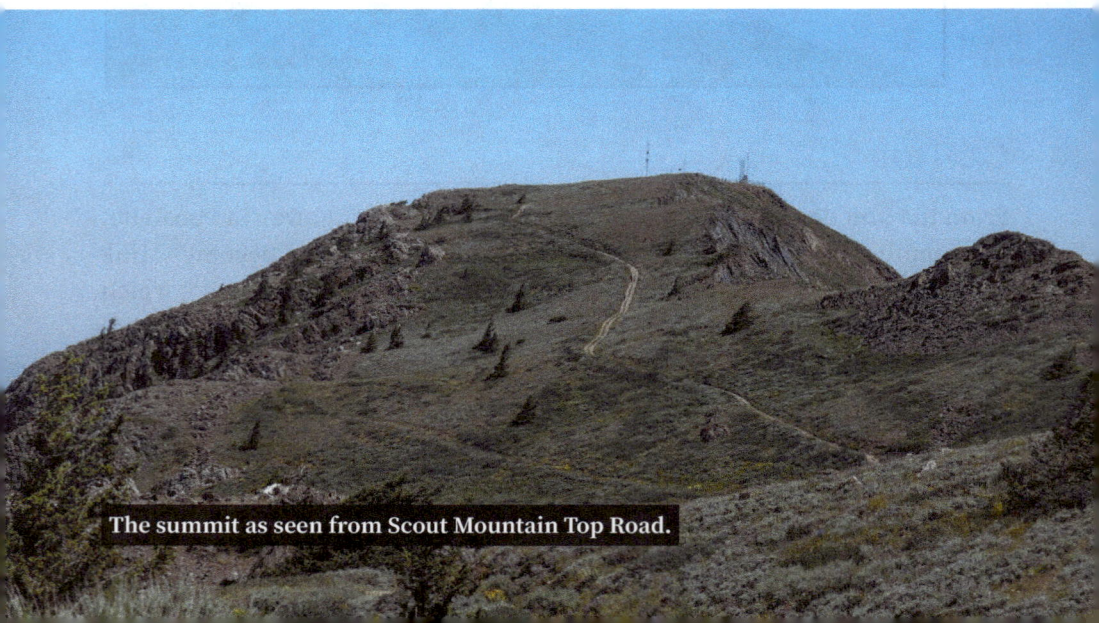

The summit as seen from Scout Mountain Top Road.

Scout Mountain - South Ridge via Mormon Canyon Trail

I recommend this eastern route for those seeking a change from their usual methods of summiting the mountain. The path begins at the Goodenough Campground and climbs along the forested Mormon Creek until reaching the saddle between Old Tom Mountain and Scout Mountain. From there, it heads north and joins Scout Mountain Top Road, climbing up the rocky southern ridge of Scout Mountain until it reaches the summit.

Distance: 13.5 miles out-and-back
Elevation Gain: 3,600 feet
Difficulty: Moderately Strenuous; Class 1
Hiking Time: About 8.5 hours
Nearest Town: McCammon
Trail Surface: Dirt, rock
Wheelchair Access: None

Dog-Friendly: Yes; on-leash at the trailhead. May be off-leash if under control once on the trail
Amenities: Vault toilets are available at the trailhead and Goodenough Creek Campground.
Contact: Caribou-Targhee National Forest, Westside Ranger District 208-236-7500
Trailhead GPS Coordinates: N42° 39.252' W112° 17.155'

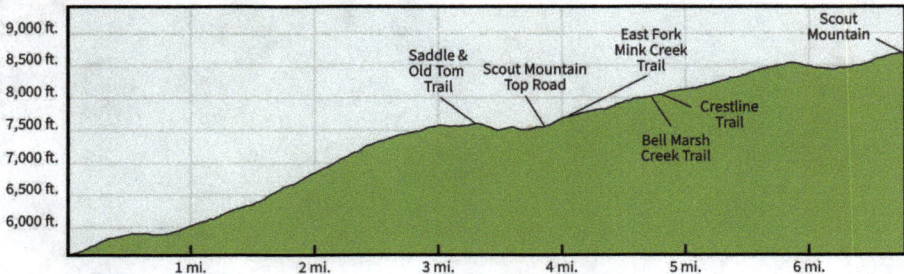

Getting There

From I-15 south of Pocatello, take Exit 47 for McCammon. Turn right on East Merrill Road. In 1.2 miles, turn left onto West Portneuf Road and then right onto Green Road. Stay on Green Road for 2.7 miles. Once Green Road enters the Goodenough Campground with a right turn, it transitions into an unnamed road. Continue on the unnamed road as it turns to the left (west). In 0.4 miles, the road ends at the Goodenough Trailhead, which has plenty of parking. The trail is located on the southwest side of the trailhead.

The Hike

Follow the Mormon Canyon Trail (p. 285) for 3.8 miles until it ends at Scout Mountain Top Road. Continue on Scout Mountain Top Road (p. 272) for about 2.9 miles until it reaches the summit.

Old Tom Mountain and Mormon Canyon Trail from Scout Mountain Top Road.

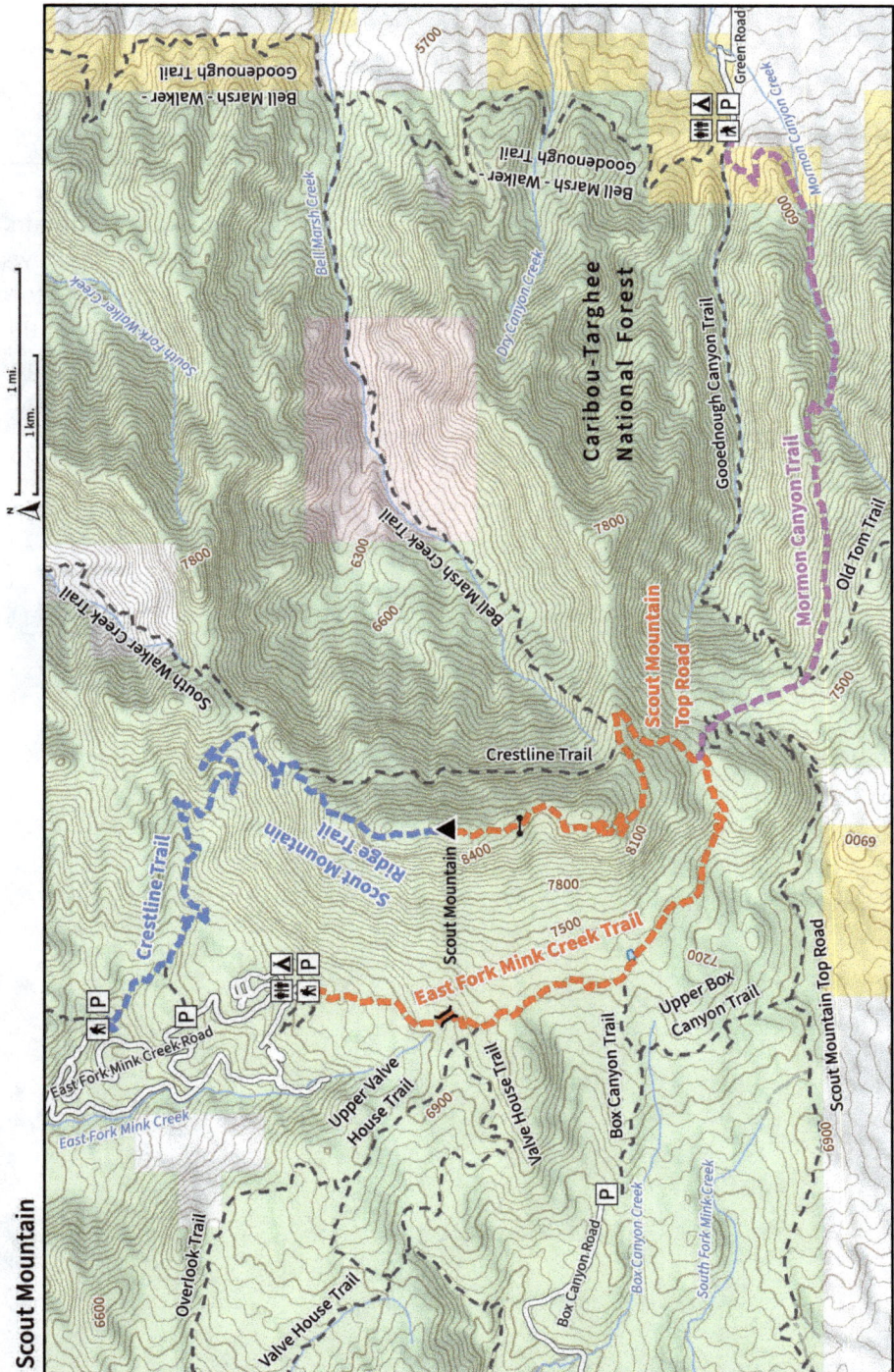

Scout Mountain

Caribou-Targhee National Forest

Bell Marsh - Walker - Goodenough Trail

Goodenough Canyon Trail

Mormon Canyon Trail

Old Tom Trail

Scout Mountain Top Road

Crestline Trail

Scout Mountain Ridge Trail

Scout Mountain

East Fork Mink Creek Trail

South Walker Creek Trail

Bell Marsh Creek Trail

Dry Canyon Creek

Bell Marsh Creek

South Fork Walker Creek

Green Road

Upper Box Canyon Trail

Box Canyon Trail

Upper Valve House Trail

Valve House Trail

Overlook Trail

East Fork Mink Creek Road

East Fork Mink Creek

Box Canyon Road

Box Canyon Creek

South Fork Mink Creek

Scout Mountain Top Road

Old Tom Mountain
Bannock Range
8,733 feet (2,662 meters)

Old Tom Mountain, the seldom-visited southern neighbor of Scout Mountain, offers a steep climb along a lightly used 4x4 path, providing sweeping views of Scout Mountain and the Portneuf Range. Both summit approaches follow well-traversed trails before joining the Old Tom Trail. The last 0.6 miles of the route requires bushwhacking on a rocky ridge. The story behind the mountain's name is my personal favorite in the state of Idaho. Old Tom Mountain is said to be named after a mountain lion that once prowled its slopes.

Old Tom Mountain from the north.

Old Tom Mountain - North Ridge via Mormon Canyon Trail

Shorter in distance than the East Fork Mink Creek approach but with slightly more elevation gain, this route is the standard path to summit Old Tom Mountain. The path begins at the forested Goodenough Campground and climbs the mountain's lower slopes before connecting to the sun-exposed Old Tom Trail. The final 0.6 miles of the hike requires bushwhacking on rocky terrain.

Distance: 11 miles out-and-back
Elevation Gain: 3,300 feet
Difficulty: Very Strenuous; Class 2
Hiking Time: About 7 hours
Nearest Town: McCammon
Trail Surface: Dirt, rock. Bushwhacking is required for the last 0.6 miles.
Wheelchair Access: None

Dog-Friendly: Yes; on-leash at the trailhead. May be off-leash if under control once on the trail
Amenities: Vault toilets are available at the trailhead and Goodenough Creek Campground.
Contact: Caribou-Targhee National Forest, Westside Ranger District 208-236-7500
Trailhead GPS Coordinates: N42° 39.252' W112° 17.155'

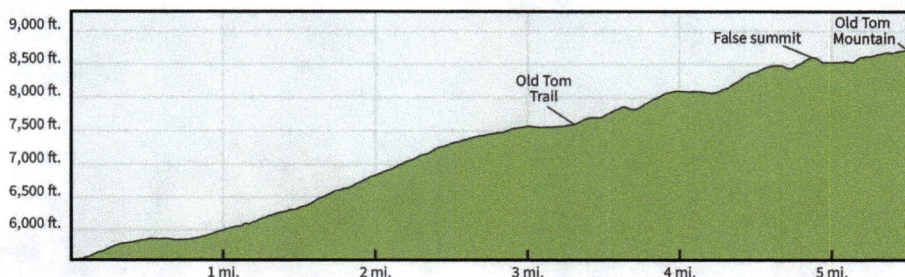

Getting There

From I-15 south of Pocatello, take Exit 47 for McCammon. Turn right on East Merrill Road. In 1.2 miles, turn left onto West Portneuf Road and then right onto Green Road. Stay on Green Road for 2.7 miles. Once Green Road enters the Goodenough Campground with a right turn, it transitions into an unnamed road. Continue on the unnamed road as it turns to the left (west). In 0.4 miles, the road ends at the Goodenough Trailhead with plenty of parking. The trail is located on the southwest side of the parking area.

The Hike

Follow the Mormon Canyon Trail for 3.3 miles (p. 285) until you come to a junction with Old Tom Trail (Forest Service Trail 193) on the saddle. From there, take a left (south) onto Old Tom Trail and continue on it for 1.6 miles as it gains 1,200 feet. The trail can be steep at times and is rocky and sun-exposed. If you're mountain biking, it's going to be a rough ride. At 4.7 miles, turn right (west) toward a false summit and follow Old Tom Trail as it disappears. Once you're atop the false summit at 4.9 miles, turn left (south) to begin the ridge walk toward Old Tom's true summit.

For the next 0.6 miles, continue south on the ridge. There isn't an official trail here, so you'll have to do some bushwhacking. Although the terrain is a mix of grass and shrubs, it's not too challenging, though you may encounter rock outcroppings that you can either go around or climb over. When you reach 5.5 miles, you will have reached the summit, which has stunning views of the surrounding area. You'll also find a U.S. Geological Survey marker and a rock cairn marking the summit.

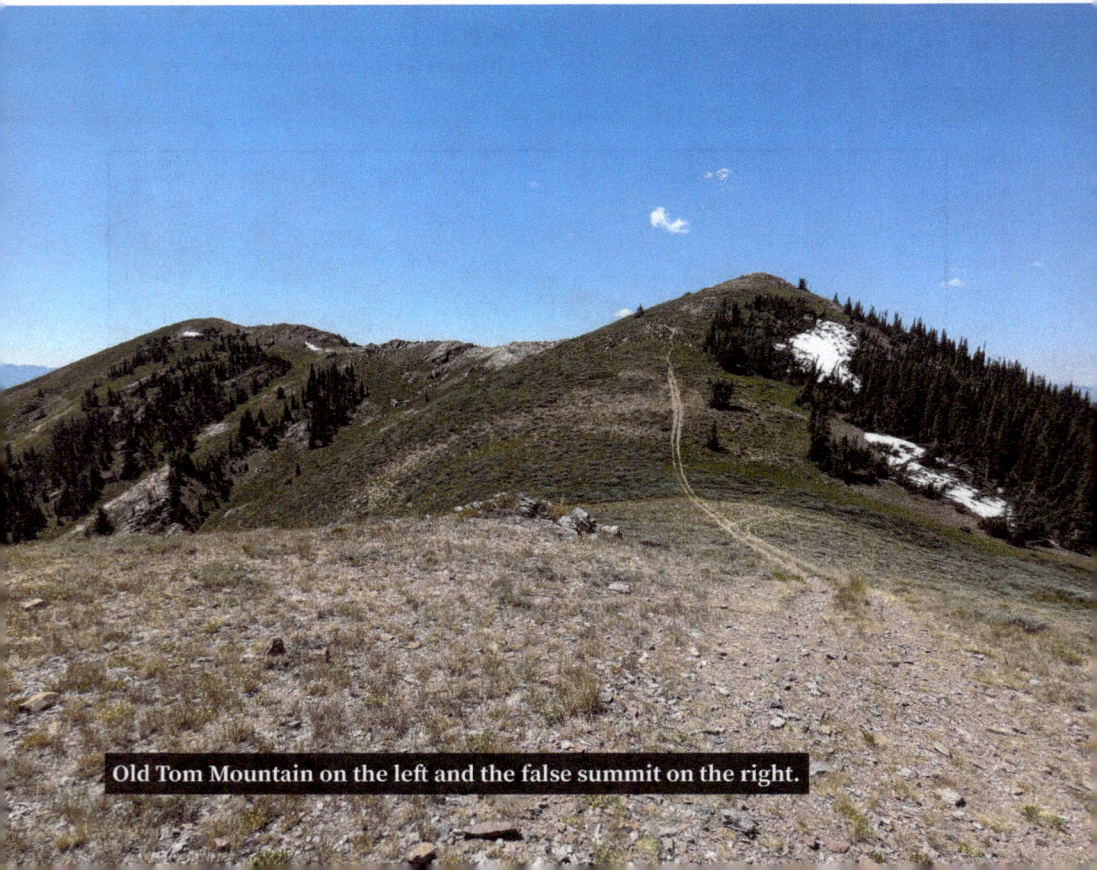

Old Tom Mountain on the left and the false summit on the right.

Old Tom Mountain - North Ridge via East Fork Mink Creek

This route is a bit longer than the standard Mormon Canyon Trail approach, but it offers a more picturesque hike. The trail begins at the East Fork Mink Creek Trailhead and ascends below Scout Mountain's western face before meeting with Scout Mountain Top Trail at the saddle. From there, the trail heads south and joins with the Mormon Canyon Trail. Both approaches converge at Old Tom Trail, which climbs the northern ridge of Old Tom Mountain and ends with a 0.6 miles section of bushwhacking.

Distance: 13.6 miles out-and-back
Elevation Gain: 3,000 feet
Difficulty: Moderately Strenuous; Class 2
Hiking Time: About 8.5 hours
Nearest Town: Pocatello
Trail Surface: Dirt, rock. Bushwhacking is required for the last 0.6 miles.
Wheelchair Access: None

Dog-Friendly: Yes; on-leash at the trailhead. May be off-leash if under control once on the trail
Amenities: Vault toilets and water are available at the Scout Mountain Campground.
Contact: Caribou-Targhee National Forest, Westside Ranger District 208-236-7500
Trailhead GPS Coordinates: N42° 41.333' W112° 21.574'

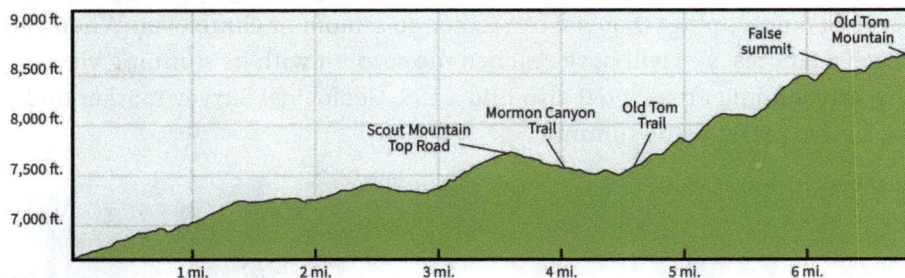

Getting There

From the junction of South Valley Road and Bannock Highway in Pocatello, head southeast on Bannock Highway for 6.8 miles. (The road becomes Mink Creek Road after 2.3 miles.) Turn left onto East Fork Mink Creek Road, which you will stay on for 5.3 miles as it climbs toward Scout Mountain. At the roundabout, make the first right turn and then make a left turn shortly beyond that into the southern Scout Mountain Campground (Loop D). Keep right to start the loop, and then keep right again in about 200 yards to find the signed East Fork Mink Creek Trailhead, which has plenty of parking. The trail is on the southern end of the parking area.

The Hike

Follow the East Fork Mink Creek Trail (p. 252) for 3.6 miles until you reach a junction with Scout Mountain Top Road on the saddle. From there, turn right (southeast) and continue on Scout Mountain Top Road for 0.5 miles, skipping the two steep shortcut paths. At the junction at 4.1 miles, keep left (southeast) onto Mormon Canyon Trail. Continue southeast on Mormon Canyon Trail for about 0.6 miles until you reach a junction with Old Tom Trail (Forest Service Trail 193). At 4.6 miles, keep right (south) on Old Tom Trail at the intersection to begin the climb.

For the next 1.6 miles, Old Tom Trail gains 1,200 feet on a steep, rocky, and sun-exposed trail. If you're mountain biking, it's going to be a rough ride. At 6.0 miles, turn right (west) toward a false summit and follow Old Tom Trail as it disappears. Once you're atop the false summit at 6.2 miles, turn left (south) to begin the ridge walk toward Old Tom's true summit.

For the next 0.6 miles, continue on the ridge south. There isn't an official trail here, so you'll have to do some bushwhacking. Although the terrain is a mix of grass and shrubs, it's not too challenging, though you may encounter rock outcroppings that you can either go around or climb over. When you reach 6.8 miles, you will have reached the summit with its stunning views of the surrounding area. You'll also find a U.S. Geological Survey marker and a rock cairn marking the summit.

Old Tom Mountain's broad summit.

Old Tom Mountain

Bonneville Peak

Portneuf Range

9,271 feet (2,826 meters)

As the highest peak in both the Portneuf Range and Bannock County, Bonneville Peak sits high on the Southeast Idaho summit baggers list. The forested slopes of the peak are home to the Pebble Creek Ski Resort, a popular winter destination for locals. The mountain sits south of the Putnam Peaks, impressive peaks in their own right on protected Fort Hall Reservation Land. The route to the top of Bonneville Peak utilizes a trail through the ski resort, although the final 0.6 miles requires bushwhacking through thick forests up a steep boulder field. The mountain was named after Benjamin Bonneville, an army officer who explored the West in the 1830s.

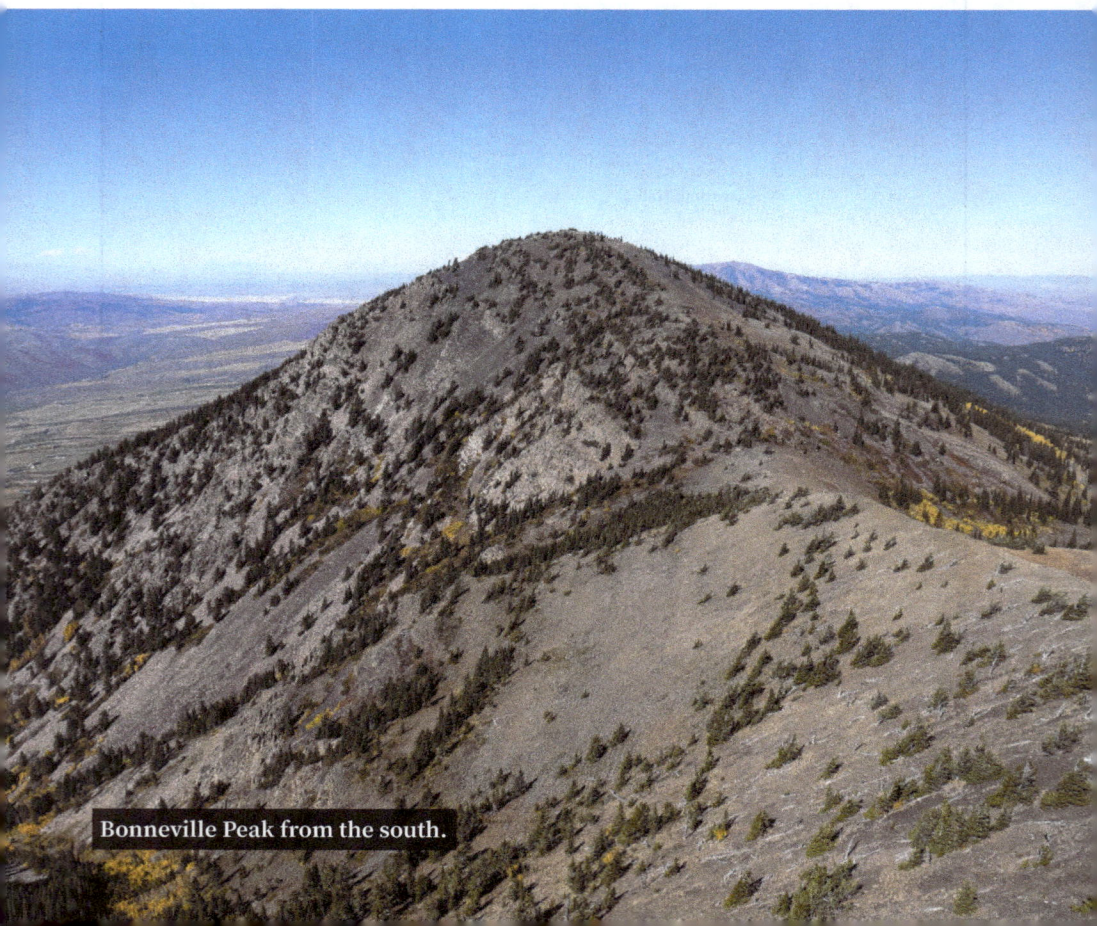

Bonneville Peak from the south.

Bonneville Peak - West Face via Pebble Creek Ski Resort

The rocky trail to the top passes below the chairlifts of Pebble Creek Ski Resort on a series of switchbacks, offering a mix of forests and open views. After reaching the top of the ski hill, the route leaves the wide path and heads directly up the steep hillside through thick evergreens and rock fields, making for a strenuous hike.

Distance: 6.6 miles out-and-back

Elevation Gain: 2,650 feet

Difficulty: Strenuous; Class 2

Hiking Time: About 5 hours

Nearest Town: Inkom

Trail Surface: Dirt, rock. Bushwhacking is required for the last 0.6 miles.

Wheelchair Access: None

Dog-Friendly: Yes; on-leash at the trailhead. May be off-leash if under control once on the trail

Amenities: None

Contact: Caribou-Targhee National Forest, Westside Ranger District 208-236-7500;

Pebble Creek Ski Area 208-775-4452

Trailhead GPS Coordinates: N42° 46.671' W112° 09.575'

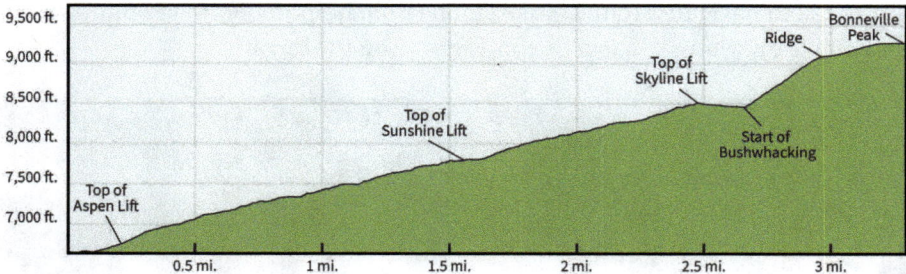

Getting There

From I-15 south of Pocatello, take Exit 58 for Inkom. Turn right on I-15BL/Old Highway 30 West. In 0.8 miles, continue straight onto North Old Highway 91. Continue on Old Highway 91 for 1.4 miles, then turn left onto North Inkom Road. Take the second right onto East Green Canyon Road, which ends at the Pebble Creek Ski Resort in 4.3 miles. The route begins at the road on the east side of the parking lot, which crosses in front of the ticket office.

The Hike

Follow the Pebble Creek Ski Area Cat Track (p. 293) until it ends at the top of the Skyline chairlift. From the chairlift, head south on the Southbound Traverse ski trail for about 0.2 miles. Once you reach the trail's end, turn left (east) off the trail, beginning the bushwhacking portion of the climb. This portion is a mix of thick forests, fallen trees, and loose boulder fields on a steep hillside, which makes for a strenuous hike. There is no specific path to follow here, so keep heading east on a manageable route until you reach the top of the ridge in 0.3 miles.

After a 640-foot climb out of the trees, you will reach the top of the open ridge at 3.0 miles. Turn right (south) to begin the last stretch toward the summit, which is about 0.3 miles away. After climbing a small hill through a forest, you will reach the summit, which is marked with a large rock cairn.

Keep Going

If you are looking for a challenge and are comfortable with Class 3 scrambling, consider climbing Snow Peak or even Haystack Mountain in the same trip as Bonneville Peak. You can descend to the saddle between Bonneville Peak and Snow Peak by continuing southeast from the summit of Bonneville Peak. Be prepared to navigate around some small cliffs. Remember, never put yourself in a situation where you feel uncomfortable on the terrain.

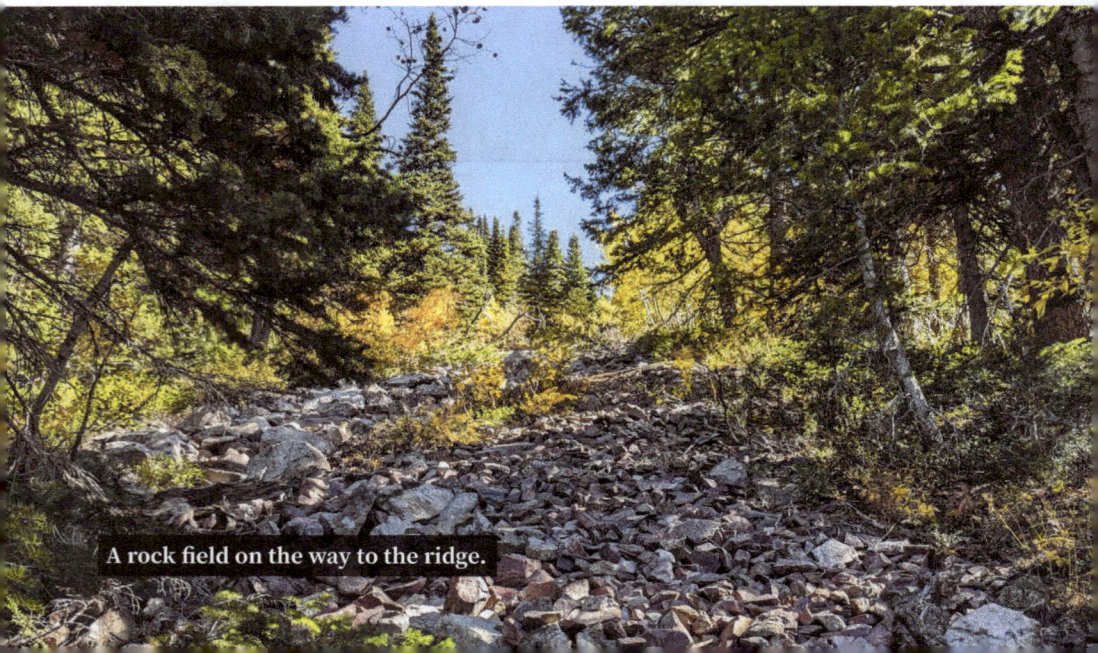
A rock field on the way to the ridge.

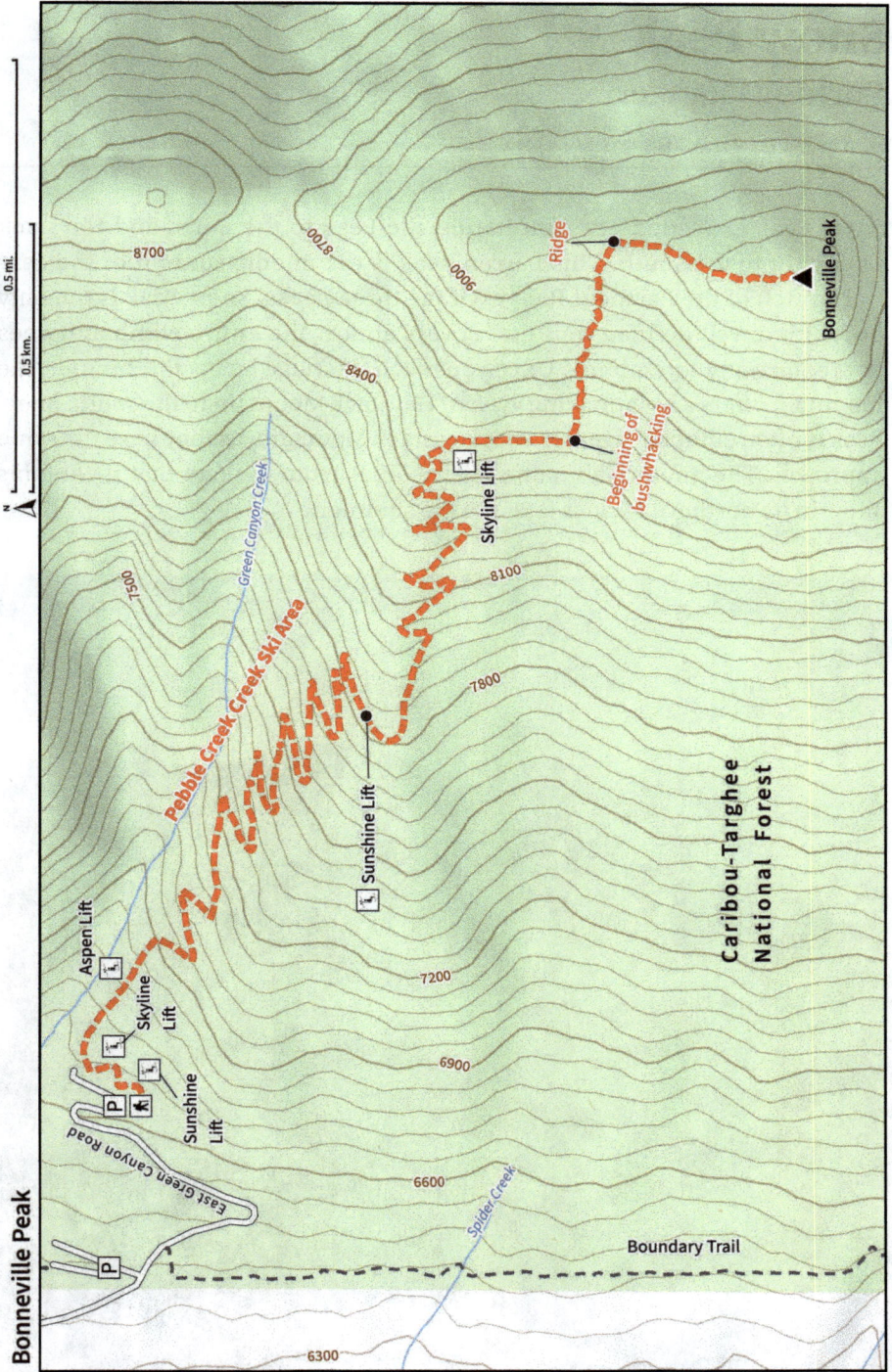

Bonneville Peak

Ridge

Beginning of bushwhacking

Bonneville Peak

Skyline Lift

Sunshine Lift

Pebble Creek Creek Ski Area

Green Canyon Creek

Aspen Lift

Skyline Lift

Sunshine Lift

East Green Canyon Road

Caribou-Targhee National Forest

Boundary Trail

Spider Creek

8700

9000

9000

8400

8100

7800

7500

7200

6900

6600

6300

0.5 mi.

0.5 km.

N

Snow Peak
Portneuf Range
9,132 feet (2,783 meters)

Snow Peak is nestled between Bonneville Peak to the north and Haystack Mountain to the south. This barren peak is the middle summit of the central stretch of the Portneuf Range. Of the three peaks, Snow Peak is the only one with a well-defined trail that covers almost the entire climb and does not require any scrambling. Once you reach the ridge below the summit, the mountain offers a breathtaking view of Haystack Mountain to the south. Snow Peak is often climbed together with Haystack Mountain, as they have the same approach. The mountain's name likely comes from the fact that it contains snow in its northern ravines late into the summer.

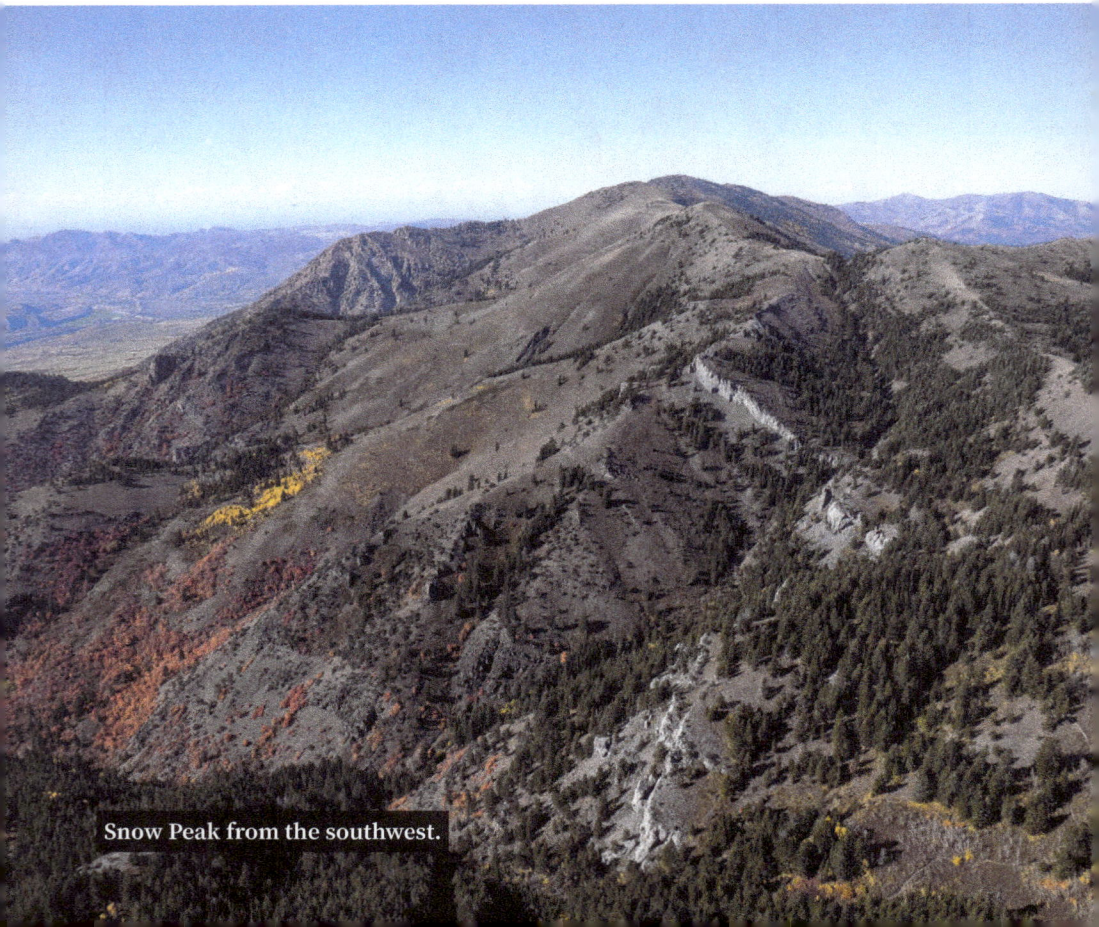

Snow Peak from the southwest.

Snow Peak - Southeast Ridge via Robbers Roost Trail

The standard route to the top, the eastern approach begins at the Big Springs Campground. The trail to the top travels on the eastern half of the Robbers Roost Trail as it climbs through winding evergreen forests and open hillsides until it reaches the saddle. Once atop the saddle, the route climbs the mountain's southern ridge toward the summit on a narrow singletrack path.

Distance: 9.9 miles out-and-back
Elevation Gain: 3,250 feet
Difficulty: Very Strenuous; Class 1
Hiking Time: About 7 hours
Nearest Town: Lava Hot Springs
Trail Surface: Dirt, rock.
Wheelchair Access: None

Dog-Friendly: Yes; on-leash at the trailhead. May be off-leash if under control once on the trail
Amenities: Vault toilets and water are available at the Big Springs Campground.
Contact: Caribou-Targhee National Forest, Westside Ranger District 208-236-7500
Trailhead GPS Coordinates: N42° 45.919' W112° 05.687'

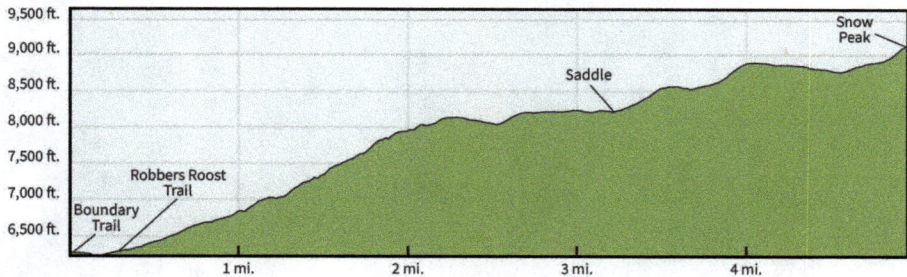

Getting There

From I-15 south of Pocatello, take Exit 47 for McCammon. Turn left on Highway 30. In 12.9 miles, close to the turnoff for Lava Hot Springs, turn left onto Blaser Road. After 9 miles, turn left onto Pebble Creek Road, which you will stay on for 1.1 miles. In 0.6 miles, make a left turn followed by a right turn to stay on Pebble Creek Road. At 1.1 miles, Pebble Creek Road transitions into Forest Service Road 36. Continue on FR 36 for 5.9 miles until it ends at the Big Spring Campground. Once you drive through the campground gate, turn left into a small parking area. The trail begins at the south end of the parking area.

The Hike

Follow the Robbers Roost Trail (p. 328) for 3.2 miles, until you reach the saddle between Haystack Mountain and Snow Peak. From there, make a right (northwest) turn onto an unofficial singletrack trail. After a steep 300-foot climb on a lightly forested ridge, turn left (northwest) at 3.5 miles. The trail levels out for the next 0.3 miles as it cuts across a hillside toward Snow Peak's southern ridge.

At 3.8 miles, the trail shifts north and you begin another steep climb, gaining 300 feet in 0.3 miles. Once you reach the top of the climb at 4.1 miles, you'll have a scenic walk atop a broad ridge toward Snow Peak. The trail may be challenging to see during this stretch, but if you go slowly, you should be able to follow it. At 4.6 miles, the trail begins its final climb toward the summit, gaining 360 feet in 0.4 miles.

Finally, at 5 miles, you will reach the summit, which is marked with a large rock cairn. The top presents a unique view of Bonneville Peak, while Haystack Mountain is mainly hidden by one of Snow Peak's lower ridges. On your way back down the mountain, you will be able to enjoy plenty of excellent views of Haystack Mountain.

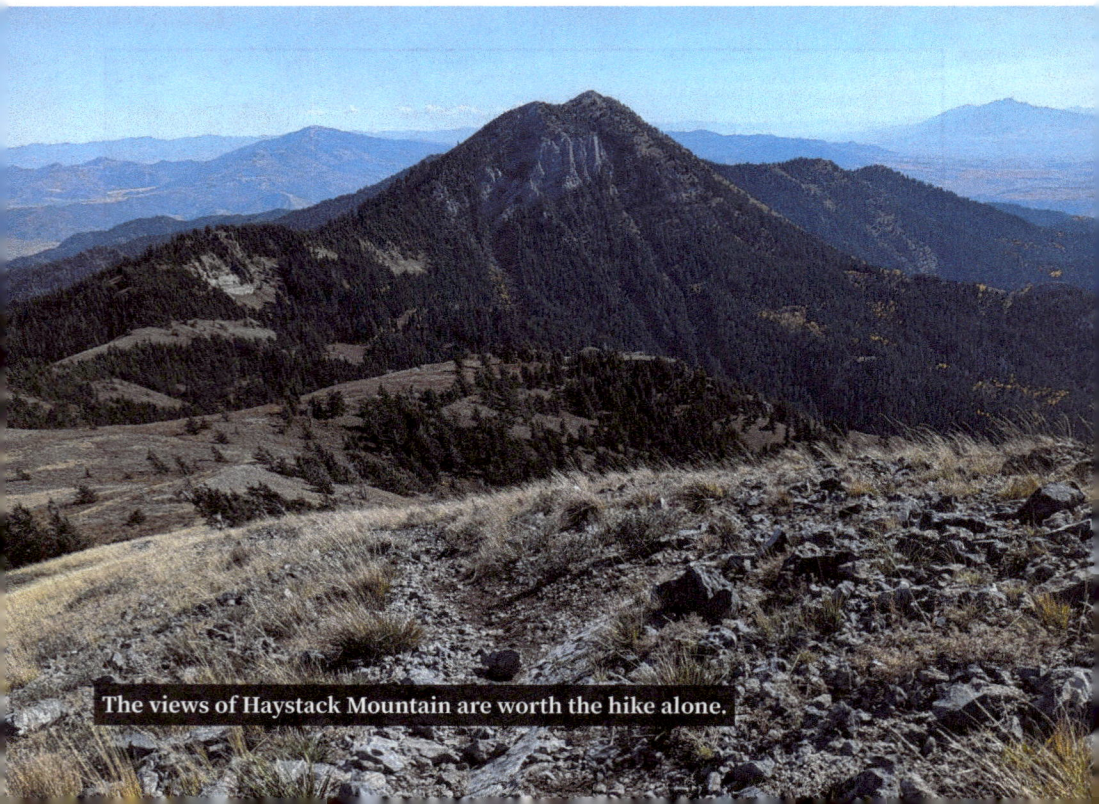

The views of Haystack Mountain are worth the hike alone.

Snow Peak - Southeast Ridge via Robbers Roost Canyon Road

The lengthy but beautiful approach from the west travels on various trails through aspen groves and evergreen forests below Haystack Mountain's cliffed west face. The trail to the saddle is easy to follow, though it is often deeply rutted and very steep. Once atop the saddle, the route climbs the mountain's southern ridge toward the summit on a narrow singletrack path.

Distance: 17.2 miles out-and-back
Elevation Gain: 4,950 feet
Difficulty: Very Strenuous; Class 1
Hiking Time: About 11 hours
Nearest Town: McCammon
Trail Surface: Dirt, rock.
Wheelchair Access: None

Dog-Friendly: Yes; on-leash at the trailhead. May be off-leash if under control once on the trail
Amenities: None
Contact: Caribou-Targhee National Forest, Westside Ranger District 208-236-7500; Idaho Fish and Game, Southeast Region 208-232-4703
Trailhead GPS Coordinates: N42° 42.365' W112° 12.302'

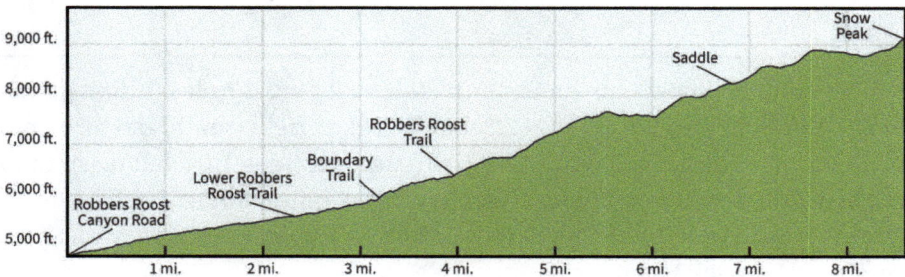

Getting There

From I-15 south of Pocatello, take Exit 58 for Inkom. Turn right on I-15BL/Old Highway 30 West. In 0.8 miles, continue straight onto North Old Highway 91. Continue on Old Highway 91 for 6.9 miles. Turn left into the Portneuf Wildlife Management Area parking lot. The trail begins about 150 yards north up the road on the right (east).

Snow Peak's lower cliffs from Robbers Roost Trail.

The Hike

Follow Robbers Roost Canyon Road (p. 311) east for 3.2 miles (it transitions into Lower Robbers Roost Trail at 2.3 miles). Make a right (southeast) turn onto Boundary Trail. After a 500-foot climb through the trees, turn left (east) onto Robbers Roost Trail at 4.0 miles. For the next 2.9 miles, follow Robbers Roost Trail as it heads northeast and climbs 2,100 feet toward the saddle with Snow Peak and Haystack Mountain.

During the first half of the Robbers Roost Trail, the path travels atop a ridge between the scenic Quinn Creek and Robbers Roost Creek, with great views of Haystack Mountain to the east. At about 5.4 miles, the trail enters a forest and continues to the northeast.

At 6.8 miles, the trail reaches the saddle at a junction. Turning right (south) takes you to Haystack Mountain. Instead, turn left (north) to begin the climb for Snow Peak. In about 100 yards, keep left at the fork. After a steep 300-foot climb on a lightly forested ridge, turn left (northwest) at 7.2 miles. The trail levels out for the next 0.3 miles as it cuts across a hillside toward Snow Peak's southern ridge.

At 7.5 miles, the trail shifts north and you will begin another steep climb, gaining 300 feet in a quarter mile. Once you reach the top of the climb at 7.7 miles, you will start a scenic walk atop a broad ridge toward Snow Peak. The trail may be challenging to see during this stretch, but if you go slowly, you should be able to follow it. At 8.3 miles, the trail will begin its final climb toward the summit, gaining 360 feet in 0.4 miles.

Finally, at 8.6 miles, you will reach the summit (9,132 feet), which is marked with a large rock cairn. The top presents a unique view of Bonneville Peak, although Haystack Mountain is mainly hidden by one of Snow Peak's lower ridges. On your way back down the mountain, you will be able to enjoy plenty of excellent views of Haystack Mountain.

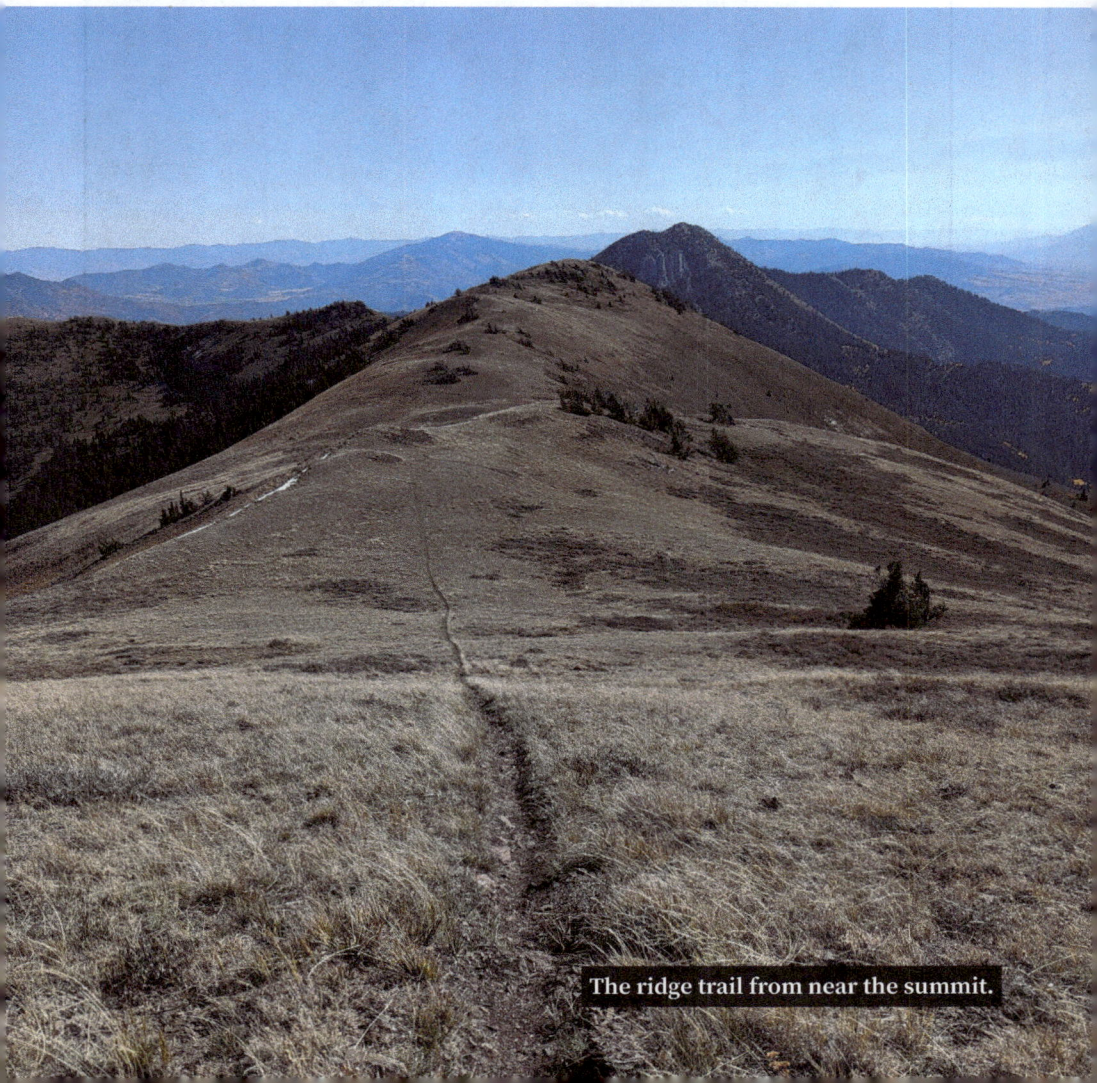

The ridge trail from near the summit.

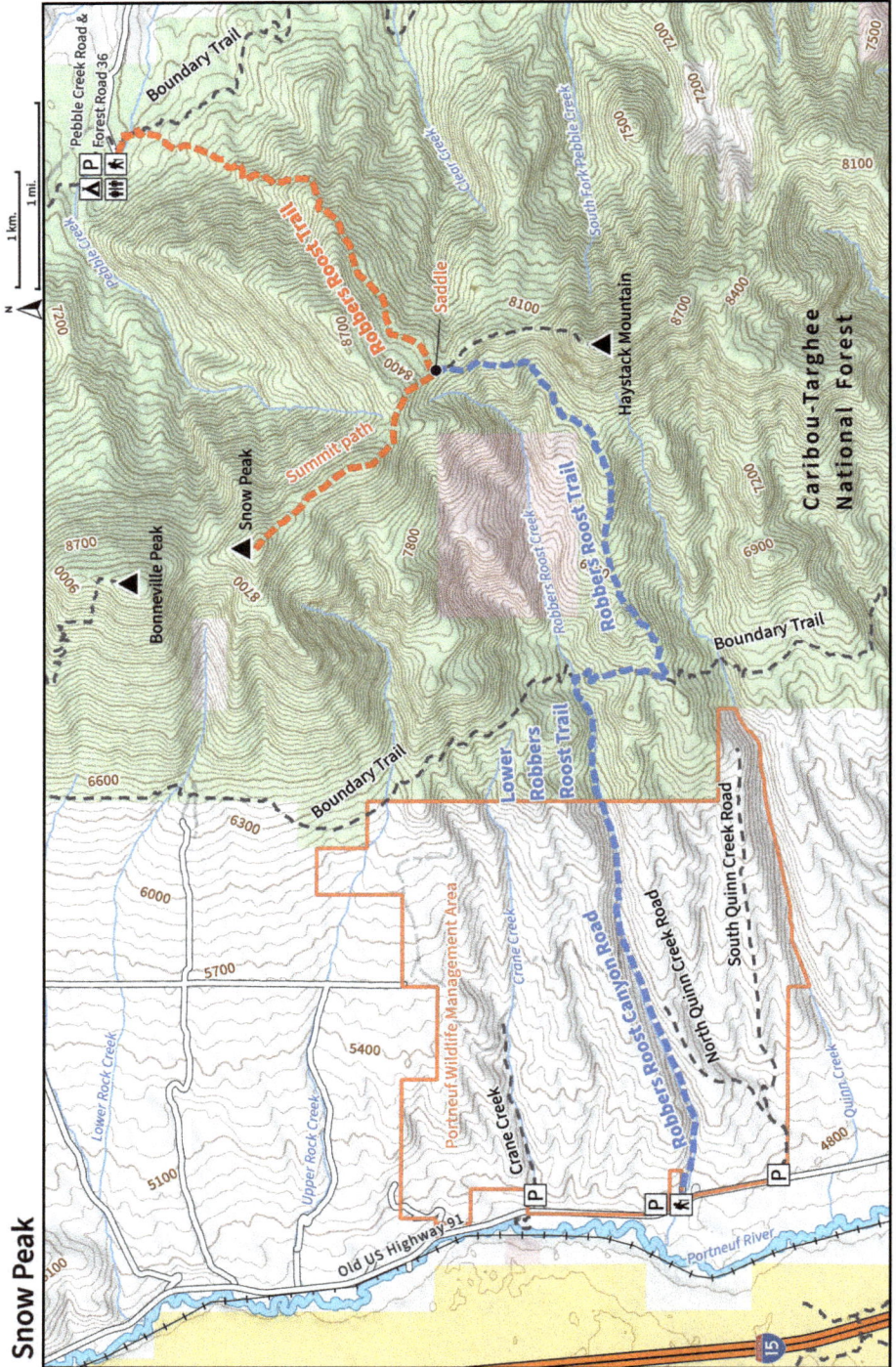

Snow Peak

Pebble Creek Road & Forest Road 36

Boundary Trail

Clear Creek

South Fork Pebble Creek

Caribou-Targhee National Forest

Saddle

8100

Haystack Mountain

8700

8400

8100

8400

8700

7200

7500

7500

7200

7200

6900

Robbers Roost Trail

Summit path

Bonneville Peak

8700

9000

Snow Peak

8100

7800

Robbers Roost Creek

Boundary Trail

Lower Robbers Roost Trail

Boundary Trail

6600

6300

6000

5700

5400

5100

Pebble Creek

Lower Rock Creek

Upper Rock Creek

Portneuf Wildlife Management Area

Crane Creek

Crane Creek

Robbers Roost Canyon Road

North Quinn Creek Road

South Quinn Creek Road

Quinn Creek

4800

Old US Highway 91

Portneuf River

15

N

1 km.

1 mi.

Haystack Mountain
Portneuf Range
9,033 feet (2,753 meters)

Located northeast of McCammon, Haystack Mountain is identifiable from the interstate because of its rocky west face. The mountain resembles a haystack from certain angles, and this is likely where it got its name. Summiting this peak is typically done by climbing Robbers Roost Trail to the saddle between it and Snow Peak to the north. As both peaks are summited from the same saddle, climbing them on the same trip isn't uncommon. While the western approach will be a shorter drive for most people, I recommend driving to the Big Springs Campground and following the eastern approach, saving you 7 miles and 1,600 feet of elevation gain during the hike.

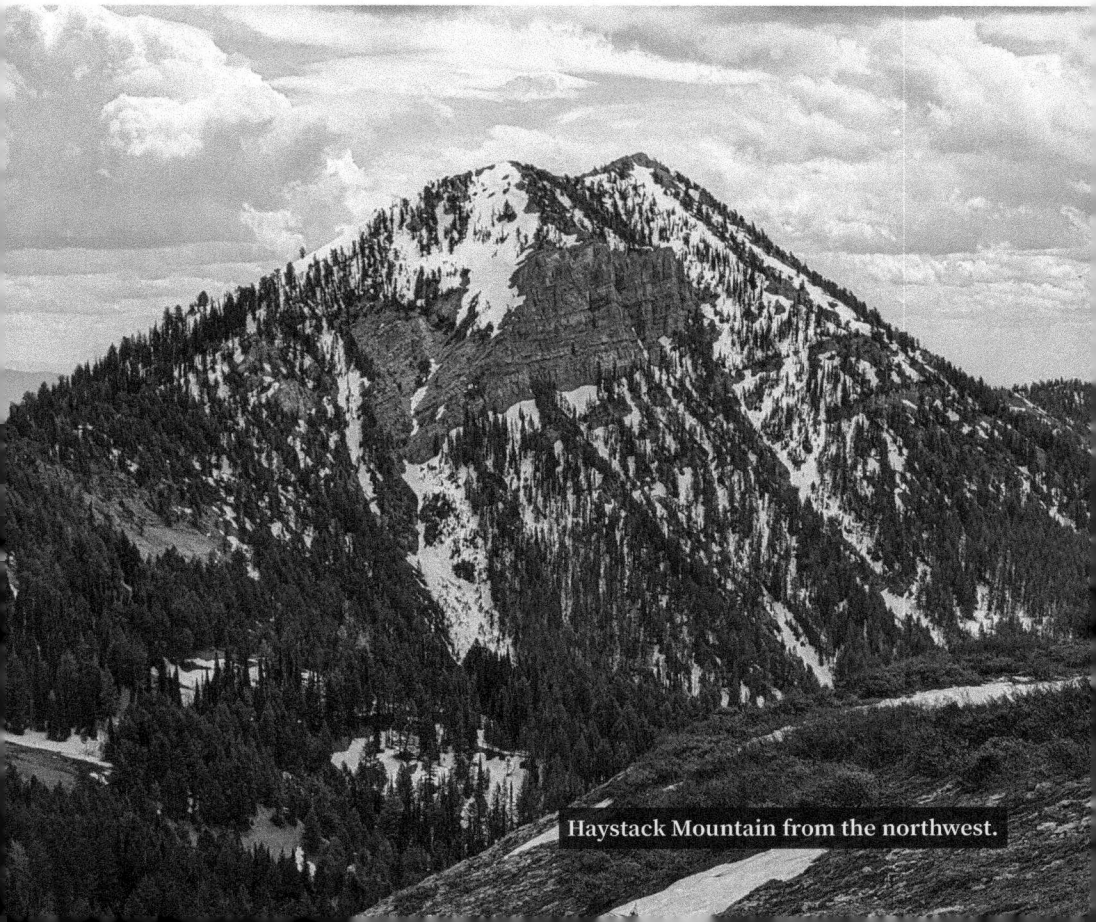

Haystack Mountain from the northwest.

Haystack Mountain - North Ridge via Robbers Roost Trail

The standard route to the top of Haystack Mountain is the eastern approach. This route begins at the Big Springs Campground. The trail travels on the eastern half of the Robbers Roost Trail as it climbs through winding evergreen forests and open hillsides until it reaches the saddle. Once atop the saddle, the route climbs the mountain's northern ridge toward the summit on a narrow singletrack path that disappears shortly below the summit. The final push for the summit requires a bit of scrambling on rocky shelves, so hiking poles and gloves are recommended.

Distance: 9 miles out-and-back
Elevation Gain: 3,200 feet
Difficulty: Very Strenuous; Class 2
Hiking Time: About 6 hours
Nearest Town: Lava Hot Springs
Trail Surface: Dirt, rock. Bushwhacking is required for the last half mile.
Wheelchair Access: None

Dog-Friendly: Yes; on-leash at the trailhead. May be off-leash if under control once on the trail
Amenities: Vault toilets and water are available at the Big Springs Campground.
Contact: Caribou-Targhee National Forest, Westside Ranger District 208-236-7500
Trailhead GPS Coordinates: N42° 45.919' W112° 05.687'

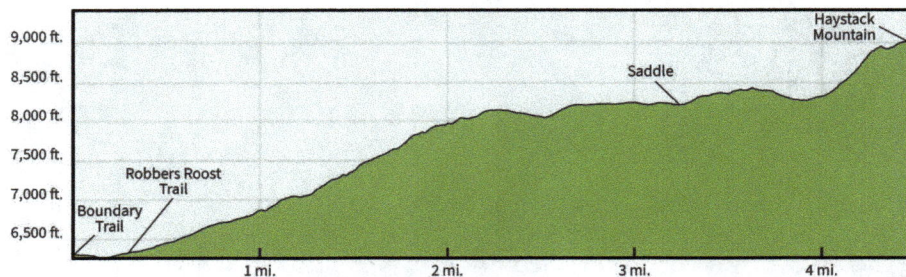

Getting There

From I-15 south of Pocatello, take Exit 47 for McCammon. Turn left on Highway 30. In 12.9 miles, close to the turnoff for Lava Hot Springs, turn left onto Blaser Road. After 9 miles, turn left onto Pebble Creek Road, which you will stay on for 1.1 miles. In 0.6 miles, make a left turn followed by a right turn to

Haystack Mountain's rocky summit.

stay on Pebble Creek Road. At 1.1 miles, Pebble Creek Road transitions into Forest Service Road 36. Continue on FR 36 for 5.9 miles until it ends at the Big Spring Campground. Once you drive through the campground gate, turn left into a small parking area. The route begins at the south end of the parking area.

The Hike

Follow the Robbers Roost Trail (p. 328) for 3.2 miles until you reach the saddle between Haystack Mountain and Snow Peak. From there, turn left (south), continuing on Robbers Roost Trail for another 100 yards. At 3.3 miles, Robbers Roost Trail makes a right (southwest) turn. Do not take this. Instead, continue south on a wild singletrack trail.

For the next 0.8 miles, the trail heads south along the cliffed northridge of Haystack Mountain. The lightly used singletrack path can be hard to follow, especially in the forested sections. It usually reappears a short while later where you would expect it to be. When in doubt, stay atop the ridge and continue south.

At 4.1 miles, the route begins a steep 0.5-mile climb toward the summit, gaining 700 feet in the process. The trail vanishes around this point, so route-finding is required. The general advice is to stick to the ridgeline and head southwest. Some light scrambling will be unavoidable. At 4.4 miles, you will find yourself near the false summit of the mountain. Continue south, slightly below it, to avoid some small cliffs.

At 4.5 miles, you will reach the summit, which is marked with a large rock cairn and has a great view of Quinn Creek to the west.

Haystack Mountain - North Ridge via Robbers Roost Canyon Road

The lengthy but beautiful approach from the west travels on various trails through aspen groves and evergreen forests below Haystack Mountain's cliffed west face. The trail to the saddle is easy to follow, though it is often deeply rutted and very steep. Once atop the saddle, the route climbs the mountain's northern ridge toward the summit on a narrow singletrack path that disappears shortly below the summit. The final push for the summit requires a bit of scrambling on rocky shelves, so hiking poles and gloves are recommended.

Distance: 16 miles out-and-back
Elevation Gain: 4,800 feet
Difficulty: Very Strenuous; Class 2
Hiking Time: About 10.5 hours
Nearest Town: McCammon
Trail Surface: Dirt, rock. Bushwhacking is required for the last half mile.
Wheelchair Access: None

Dog-Friendly: Yes; on-leash at the trailhead. May be off-leash if under control once on the trail
Amenities: None
Contact: Caribou-Targhee National Forest, Westside Ranger District 208-236-7500; Idaho Fish and Game, Southeast Region 208-232-4703
Trailhead GPS Coordinates: N42° 42.365' W112° 12.302'

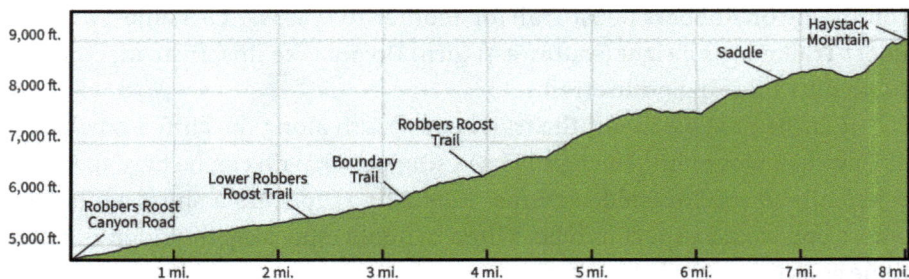

Getting There

From I-15 south of Pocatello, take Exit 58 for Inkom. Turn right on I-15BL/Old Highway 30 West. In 0.8 miles, continue straight onto North Old Highway 91. Continue on Old Highway 91 for 6.9 miles. Make a left turn into the Portneuf Wildlife Management Area parking lot. The trail begins about 150 yards north of the parking area, up the road on the right (east).

The Hike

Follow Robbers Roost Canyon Road (p. 311) east for 3.2 miles (it transitions into Lower Robbers Roost Trail at 2.3 miles). Turn right (southeast) onto Boundary Trail. After a 500-foot climb through the trees, turn left (east) onto Robbers Roost Trail at 4.0 miles. For the next 2.9 miles, follow Robbers Roost Trail as it heads northeast and climbs 2,100 feet toward the saddle between Snow Peak and Haystack Mountain.

During the first half of the Robbers Roost Trail, the path travels atop a ridge between the scenic Quinn Creek and Robbers Roost Creek, with views of Haystack Mountain to the east. At about 5.4 miles, the trail enters a forest and continues to the northeast.

At 6.8 miles, the trail reaches the saddle at a junction. Turning left (north) would take you to Snow Peak. Instead, turn right (south) to begin the climb for Haystack Mountain. For the next 0.8 miles, the trail heads south along the cliff-edged north ridge of Haystack Mountain. The lightly used singletrack path can be hard to follow, especially in the forested sections. It usually reappears a short while later where you would expect it to be. When in doubt, stay atop the ridge and continue south.

At 7.6 miles, the route begins a steep 0.5-mile climb toward the summit, gaining 700 feet in the process. The trail vanishes around this point, so route-finding is required. The general advice is to stick to the ridgeline and head southwest. Some light scrambling will be unavoidable. At 7.9 miles, you will find yourself near the false summit of the mountain. Continue south, slightly below it, to avoid some small cliffs.

At 8.1 miles, you will reach the summit, which is marked with a large rock cairn and has a great view of Quinn Creek to the west.

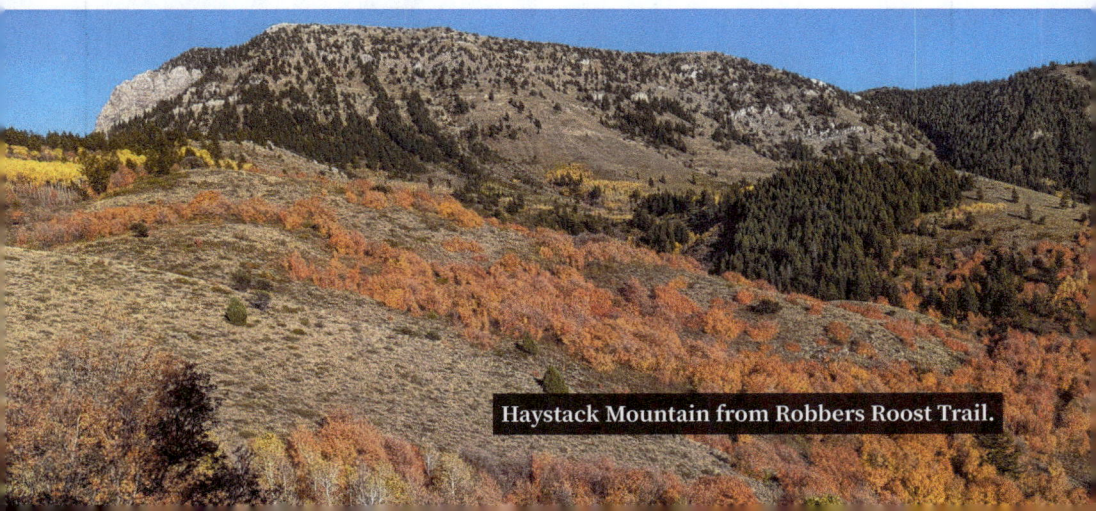

Haystack Mountain from Robbers Roost Trail.

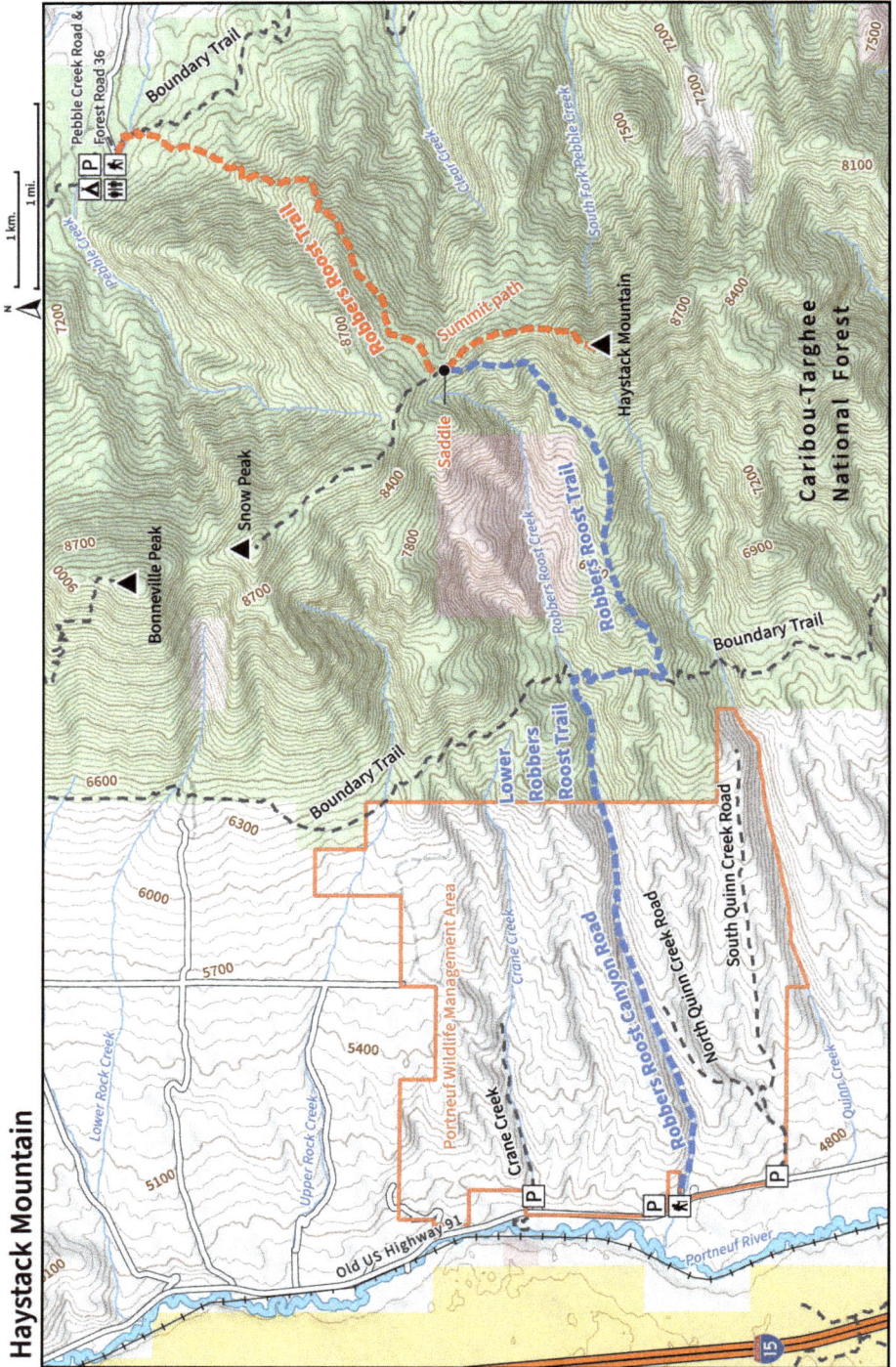

Haystack Mountain

Pebble Creek Road & Forest Road 36

Boundary Trail

Robber's Roost Trail

Summit path

Saddle

Haystack Mountain

Snow Peak

Bonneville Peak

Robbers Roost Creek

Robbers Roost Trail

Boundary Trail

Caribou-Targhee National Forest

Clear Creek

South Fork Pebble Creek

Pebble Creek

Boundary Trail

Lower Robbers Roost Trail

Portneuf Wildlife Management Area

Crane Creek

Robbers Roost Canyon Road

North Quinn Creek Road

South Quinn Creek Road

Quinn Creek

Lower Rock Creek

Upper Rock Creek

Old US Highway 91

Portneuf River

15

7700
7200
7500
8100
8700
8400
8700
8400
8700
9000
8700
8700
7800
8400
7200
6900
6600
6300
6000
5700
5400
5100
8100
4800

City Creek Management Area Trail Overview

The City Creek Management Area is a popular trail system located just minutes away from Historic Downtown Pocatello. It offers several miles of trails that wind through beautiful creeksides, rolling hills, and high ridgelines. The area can be accessed from three parking areas: the Cusick Creek Trailhead, the Lower City Creek Trailhead, and the Upper City Creek Trailhead. In addition, parking is available along City Creek Road, especially near the junction with North Fork Road and at the gate with Kinport Road.

It's important to note that the CCMA is a multi-use area, where trails are commonly shared by hikers, trail runners, and mountain bikers. Only Class 1 eBikes are allowed in the area. To ensure everyone's safety, mountain bikers are advised to follow the Biker-One-Way-Uphill designation between Bridges 1-5 on the City Creek Trail. Also, contrary to common wisdom, it's mandatory for dog owners to keep their dogs on a leash throughout the entire CCMA.

Serengeti in the fall.

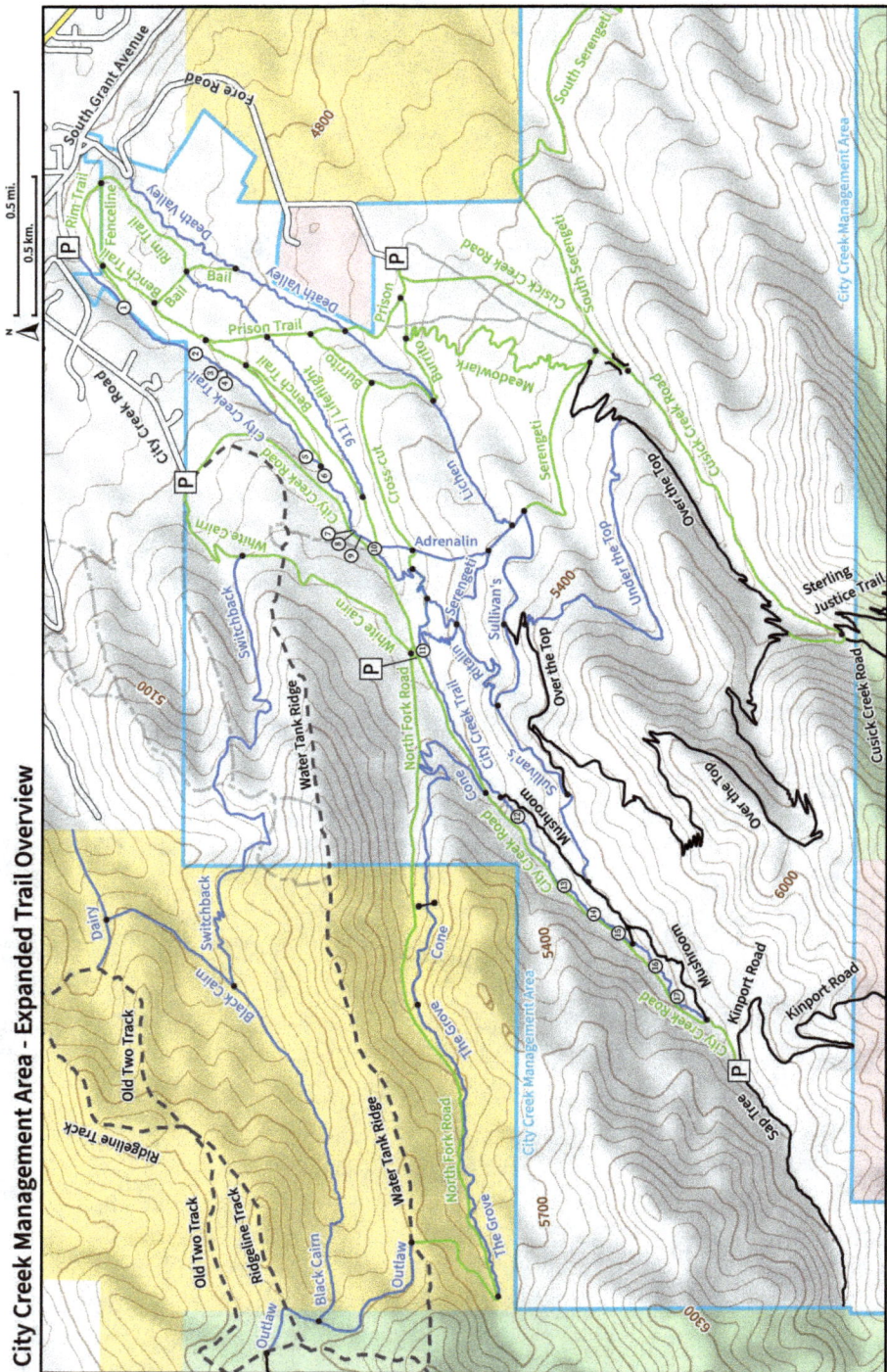

City Creek Management Area - Expanded Trail Overview

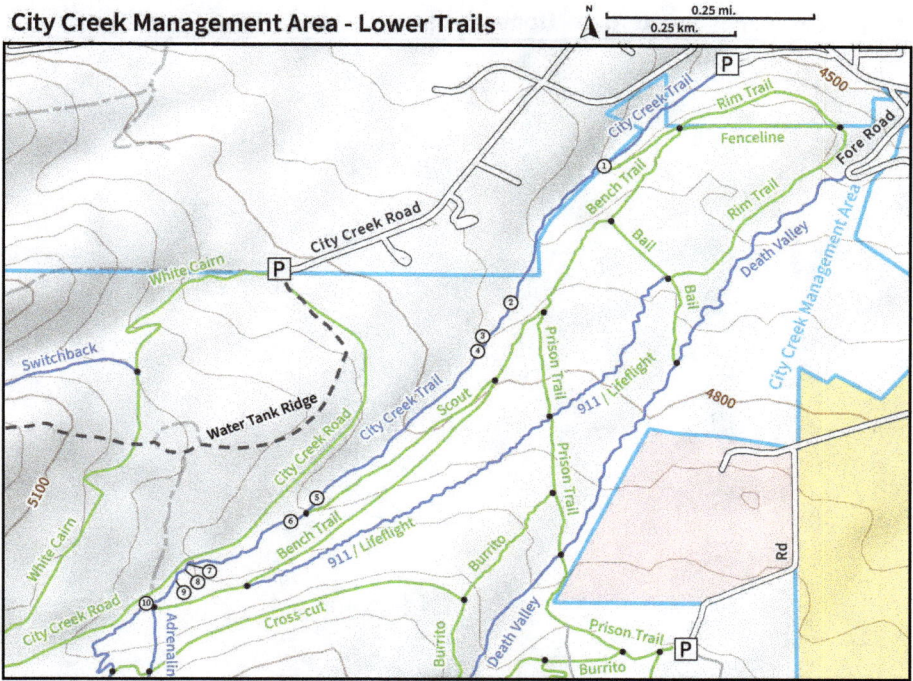

City Creek Management Area - Lower Trails

N   0.25 mi.   0.25 km.

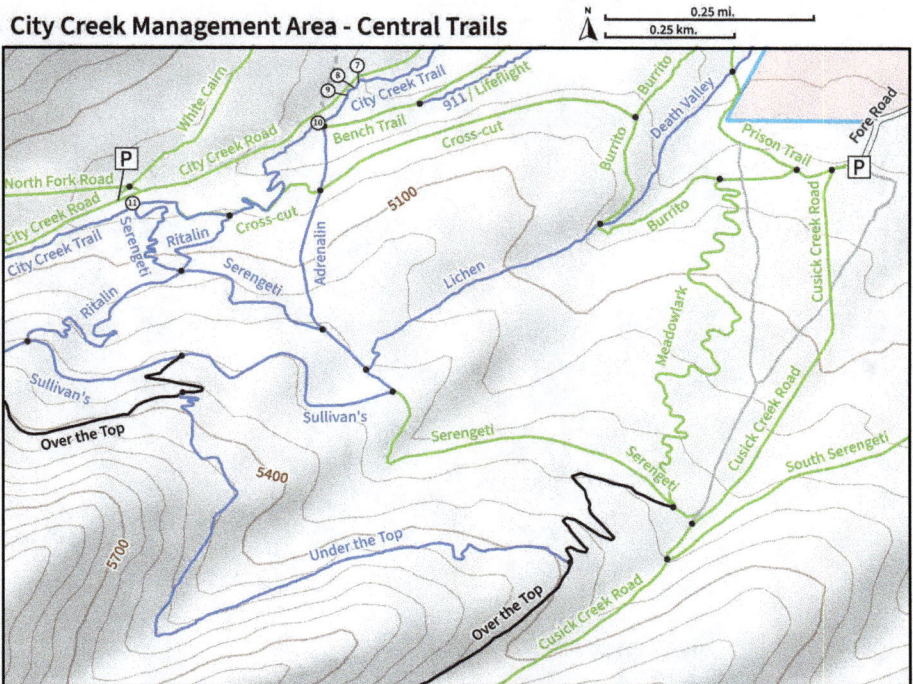

City Creek Management Area - Central Trails

N   0.25 mi.   0.25 km.

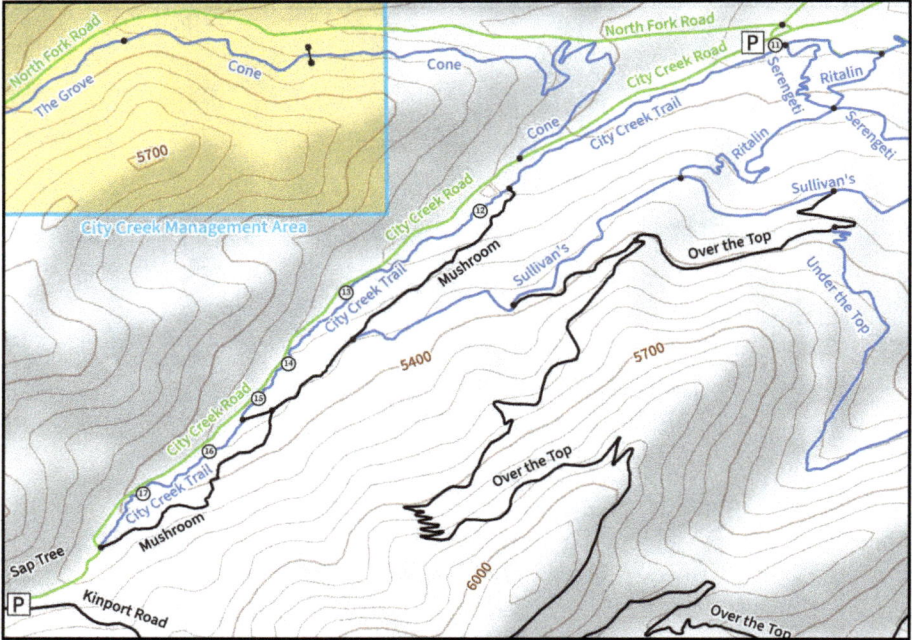

City Creek Management Area - Upper Trails

Pocatello from South Serengeti.

Adrenalin

Distance: 0.4 miles one-way   **Difficulty:** Blue square
Elevation Gain: 290 feet   **Trailhead GPS Coordinates:**
                                     N42° 50.384' W112° 27.821'

A steep and unforgiving trail that shoots straight into the gut of City Creek from Serengeti. Make sure your brakes are ready to go on this one.

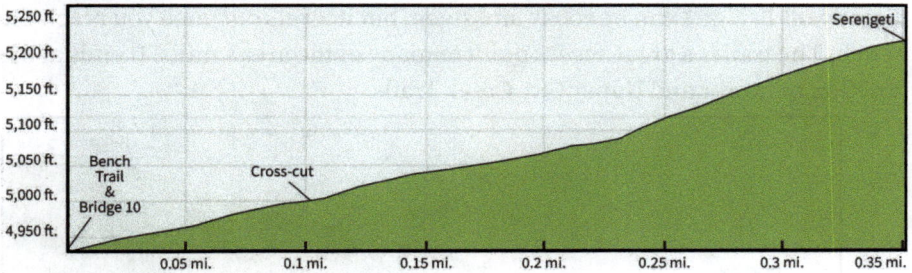

Bail

Distance: 0.3 miles one-way   **Difficulty:** Green circle
Elevation Gain: 50 feet   **Trailhead GPS Coordinates:**
                                     N42° 50.957' W112° 27.174'

A short connecting trail that bridges Death Valley to Bench Trail. The stretch between 911 and Bench Trail is well-used, but becomes wilder as you approach Death Valley.

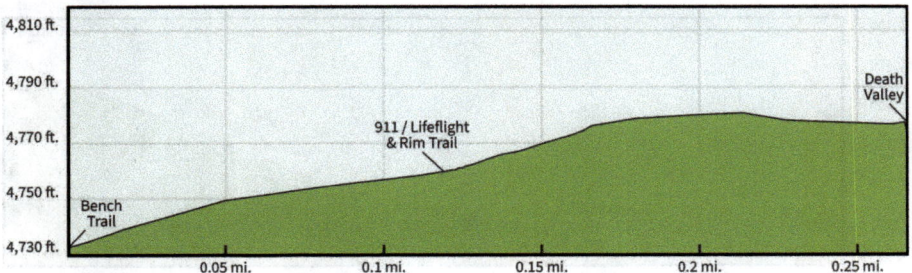

Bench Trail

Distance: 1.2 miles one-way

Elevation Gain: 340 feet

Difficulty: Green circle

Trailhead GPS Coordinates:
N42° 51.035' W112° 27.183'

An excellent alternative to riding up the Lower City Creek Trail, Bench Trail provides a well-worn uphill ride above the main creek. The lower section directly off Bridge 1 can be rocky and steep, but it levels out once you reach the bench. The trail is a great access point to many of the area's trails. It ends at the junction of Lower and Upper City Creek Trails.

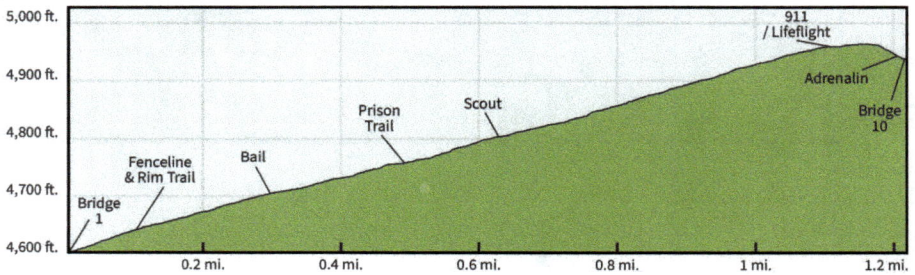

Black Cairn

Distance: 1.4 miles one-way

Elevation Gain: 600 feet

Difficulty: Blue square

Trailhead GPS Coordinates:
N42° 50.532' W112° 29.860'

A fast singletrack that winds its way downhill in a dusty creek drainage. The top can be rocky, though the trail is generally a fun ride. The path ends alongside a barbed wire fence as the trail joins with Dairy. An alternative variant I recommend is to depart the trail at the 0.9-mile mark to ride Switchback back to the Upper City Creek parking lot.

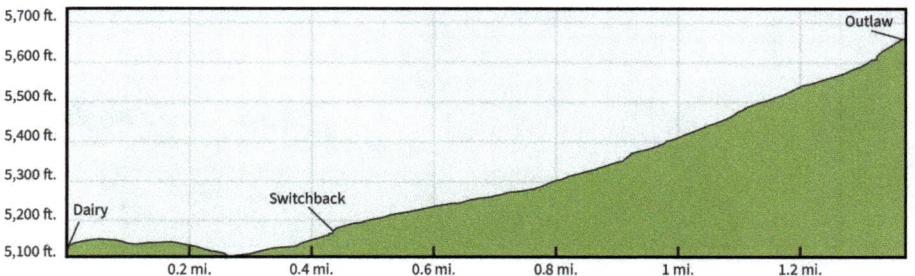

Burrito

Distance: 0.7 miles one-way

Elevation Gain: 130 feet

Difficulty: Green circle

Trailhead GPS Coordinates:
N42° 50.555' W112° 27.256'

Staying above Death Valley, this trail is an alternate ride in the Prison Trail / Death Valley area. The portion of the trail between Prison Trail and Death Valley can be slow-going and rocky, but once you pass the Lichen junction, the trail becomes a fun downhill.

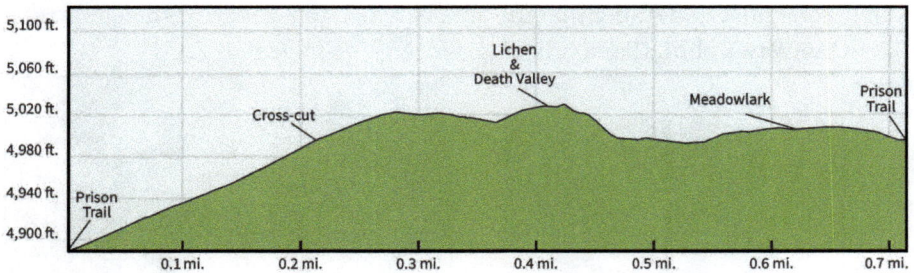

City Creek Road

Distance: 2.3 miles one-way

Elevation Gain: 630 feet

Difficulty: Green circle

Trailhead GPS Coordinates:
N42° 50.861' W112° 27.635'

A well-traveled dirt road that parallels the City Creek Trail, this road works well for mountain bikers looking to get from the Upper City Creek Trailhead to many CCMA trails. For those who dislike riding uphill on narrow singletrack paths, this is the route for you. (For a full route writeup, go to page 156.)

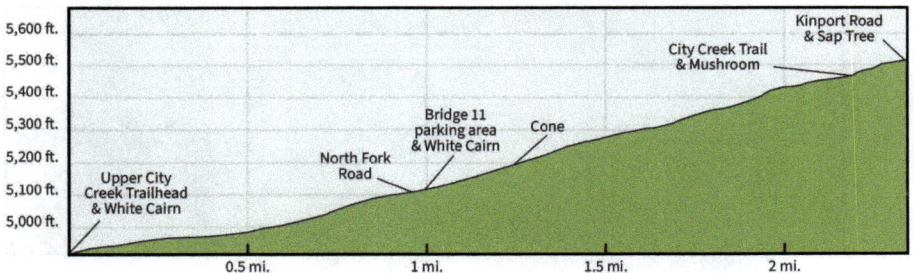

City Creek Trail

Distance: 3 miles one-way

Elevation Gain: 910 feet

Difficulty: Blue square

Trailhead GPS Coordinates: N42° 51.173' W112° 27.019'

A creekside trail just minutes from the city center, the City Creek Trail is a popular path that serves as a jumping-off point for many trails in the City Creek Management Area. The trail is generally smooth and well-packed down for the entirety of the hike, though there are rocks and roots on occasion. Mountain bikers must remember that the area between Bridges 1 - 5 is designated as Bike-One-Way-Uphill. (For a full route writeup, go to page 162.)

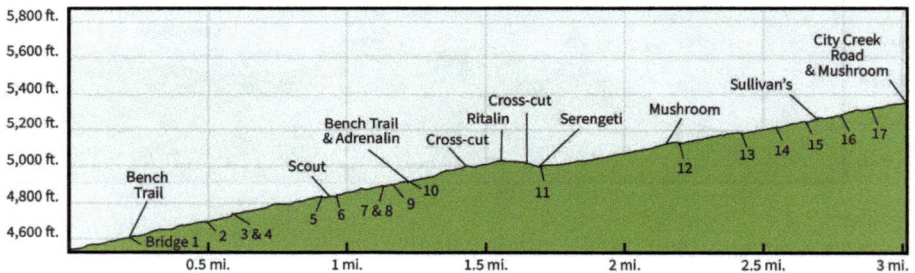

Cone

Distance: 1.1 miles one-way

Elevation Gain: 230 feet

Difficulty: Blue square

Trailhead GPS Coordinates: N42° 50.103' W112° 28.473'

Cone serves as a singletrack connector from City Creek Road (and City Creek Trail near Bridge 12) to The Grove. The first half of the trail zigzags through a grassy field before traversing across a hillside above North Fork Road.

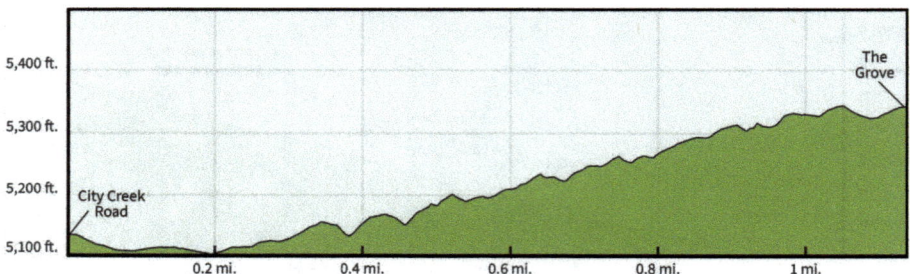

Cross-cut

Distance: 0.7 miles one-way

Elevation Gain: 40 feet

Difficulty: Green circle

Trailhead GPS Coordinates:
N42° 50.396' W112° 27.382'

A fun trail on an open hillside that is a great way to connect from Upper City Creek to Burrito. The western stretch of the trail has increased foot traffic due to the City Creek Trail merging onto Cross-cut, so be sure to watch out for hikers.

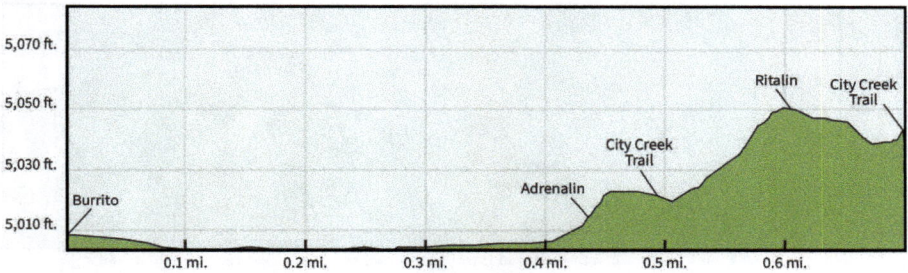

Cusick Creek Road

Distance: 3.5 miles one-way

Elevation Gain: 2,090 feet

Difficulty: Lower half: Green circle, Upper half: Black diamond

Trailhead GPS Coordinates:
N42° 50.325' W112° 27.084'

A doubletrack path that works best for mountain bikers as a connector from the Cusick Creek Trailhead over to Sterling Justice. (For a full route writeup, go to page 170.)

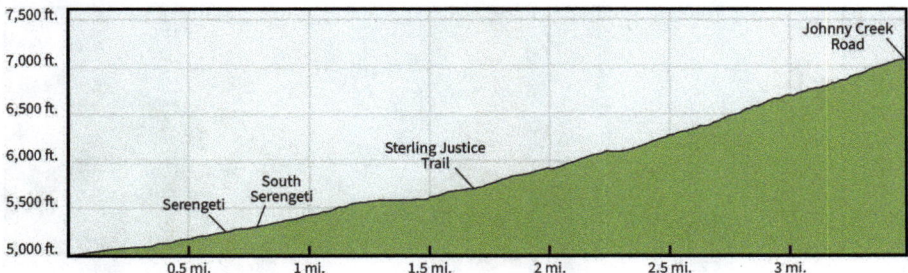

Dairy

Distance: 0.4 miles one-way

Elevation Gain: 210 feet

Difficulty: Blue square

Trailhead GPS Coordinates:
N42° 51.168' W112° 28.575'

Much of what the mountain bike community considers to be the Dairy Trail is actually on private property, and as such, will unfortunately not be featured in this book. The section that is on BLM land works best as a way to get from the lower end of Black Cairn over to Old Two Track.

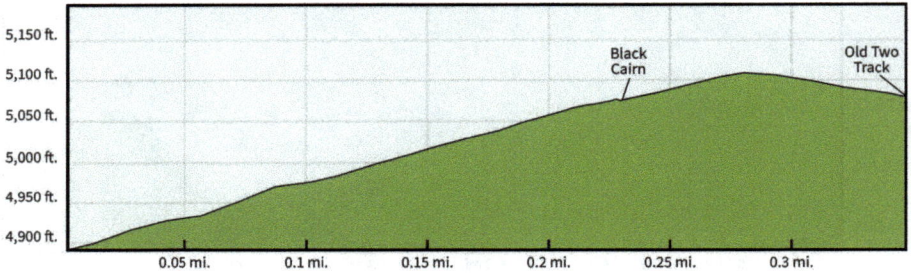

Death Valley

Distance: 1.1 miles one-way

Elevation Gain: 430 feet

Difficulty: Blue square

Trailhead GPS Coordinates:
N42° 50.994' W112° 26.880'

A twisty singletrack that navigates through a dry ravine, Death Valley offers a challenging and occasionally rocky climb that can be fun on the downhill. The lower section has plenty of shade, though most of the ride is exposed to the sun. The start of the trail can be accessed from the first U-turn on Fore Road.

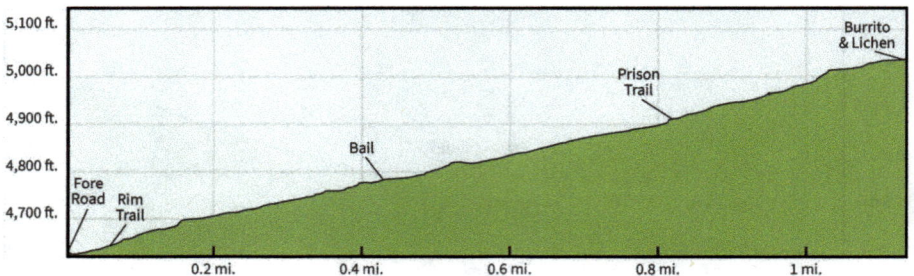

Fenceline

Distance: 0.2 miles one-way

Elevation Gain: 30 feet

Difficulty: Green circle

Trailhead GPS Coordinates:
N42° 51.090' W112° 27.073'

A brief singletrack path that acts as a shortened version of Rim Trail.

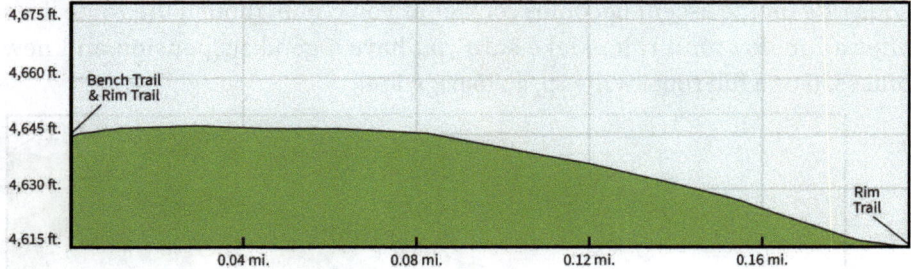

The Grove

Distance: 0.8 miles one-way

Elevation Gain: 250 feet

Difficulty: Blue square

Trailhead GPS Coordinates:
N42° 50.275' W112° 29.038'

A forested singletrack that steadily climbs alongside North Fork Road. This path is a good way to connect from City Creek to Outlaw and Black Cairn. The trail seamlessly continues off of Cone.

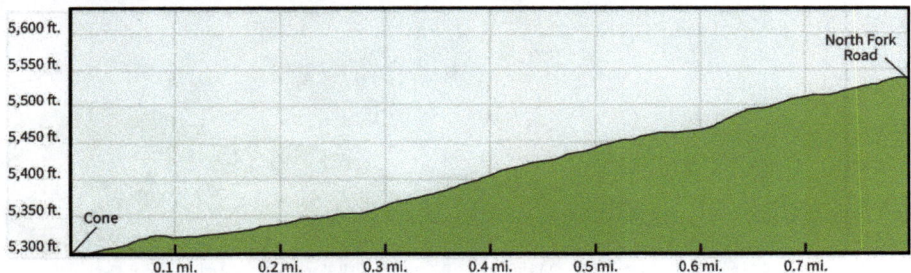

Kinport Road

Distance: 2.8 miles one-way

Elevation Gain: 1,780 feet

Difficulty: Black diamond

Trailhead GPS Coordinates: N42° 49.440' W112° 29.175'

A rocky dirt road that winds its way to the summit of Kinport Peak. The strenuous ride on the ascent becomes rockier as you climb, though the route does offer a fun downhill ride. Make sure you have a good suspension and new brakes. (For a full route writeup, go to page 174.)

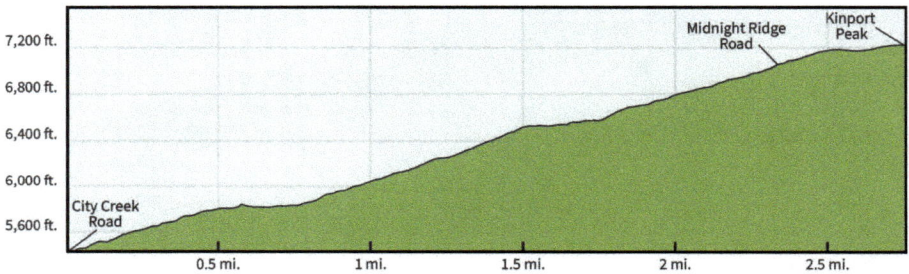

Lichen

Distance: 0.4 miles one-way

Elevation Gain: 180 feet

Difficulty: Blue square

Trailhead GPS Coordinates: N42° 50.241' W112° 27.435'

Filled with wildflowers in the early summer, Lichen is a pleasant narrow singletrack that travels through a low gully, connecting Death Valley to Serengeti.

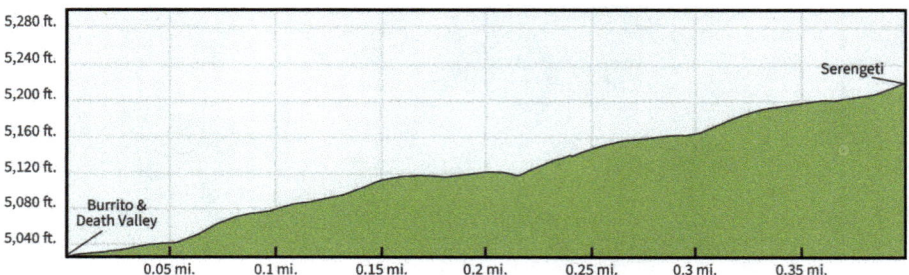

Lower Outlaw

Distance: 0.6 miles one-way

Elevation Gain: 440 feet

Difficulty: Black diamond

Trailhead GPS Coordinates:
N42° 50.666' W112° 29.951'

A rocky singletrack that continues off of Outlaw down a barren hillside until it ends at Trail Creek. This is a rough trail, so I only recommend it for people who want to access the remote trails that emerge from Trail Creek.

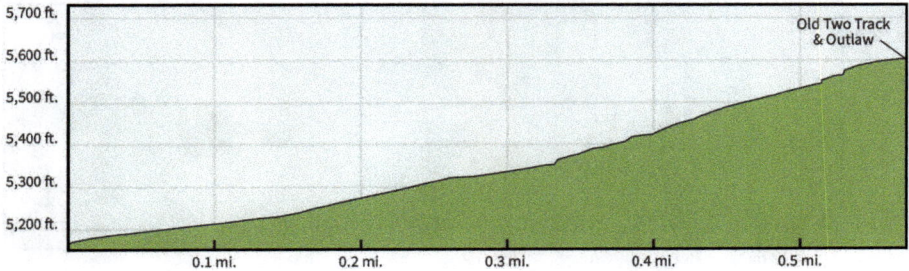

Meadowlark

Distance: 1 mile one-way

Elevation Gain: 250 feet

Difficulty: Green circle

Trailhead GPS Coordinates:
N42° 50.308' W112° 27.265'

Meadowlark offers a winding trail filled with twists and turns, making for a fun new way get from Serengeti to Burrito. The trail is a replacement for Bump Trail, which is being retired.

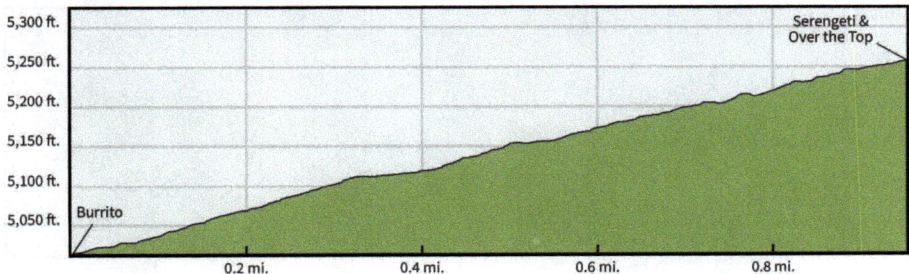

Mushroom

Distance: 0.9 miles one-way

Elevation Gain: 130 feet

Difficulty: Black diamond

Trailhead GPS Coordinates:
N42° 49.734' W112° 28.826'

A hilly singletrack that traverses the forested hillside above Upper City Creek from City Creek Road to Bridge 12. There are a few steep sections that keep this trail exciting. The lower section was previously known as DNA.

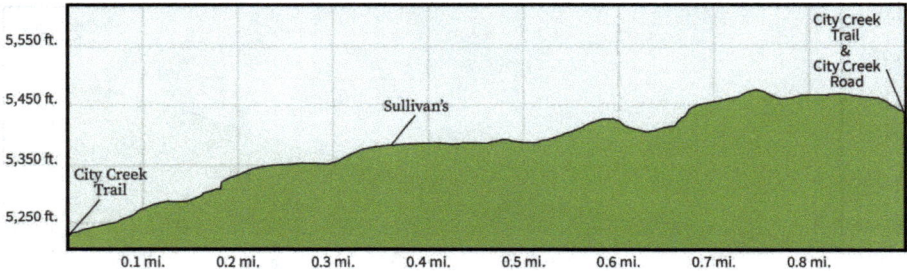

911 / Lifeflight

Distance: 0.8 miles one-way

Elevation Gain: 200 feet

Difficulty: Blue square, Green circle

Trailhead GPS Coordinates:
N42° 50.416' W112° 27.687'

911 is a classic downhill-only trail centrally located in the CCMA. This rollercoaster ride is a must for those seeking a challenge. The trail gradually becomes steeper and filled with large jumps as it progresses. A much calmer sister trail, Lifeflight, parallels 911 and makes for a nice uphill or downhill ride for anyone looking for a painless experience.

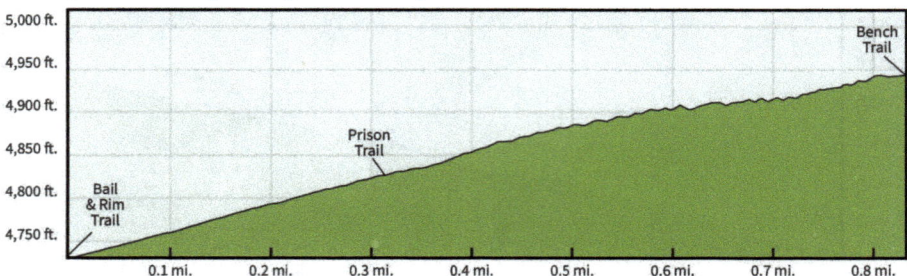

North Fork Road

Distance: 1.9 miles one-way

Elevation Gain: 660 feet

Difficulty: Green circle

Trailhead GPS Coordinates:
N42° 50.288' W112° 28.084'

A wide dirt road that works best as a way to access Black Cairn from Upper City Creek. (For a full route writeup, go to page 159.)

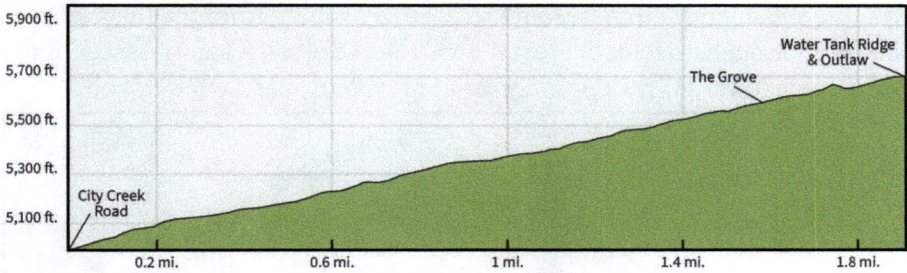

Outlaw

Distance: 0.7 miles one-way

Elevation Gain: 130 feet

Difficulty: Blue square

Trailhead GPS Coordinates:
N42° 50.290' W112° 29.659'

Outlaw provides a gentle singletrack descent to the top of Black Cairn from the end of North Fork Road. The path traverses a hillside that is covered with wildflowers in the early summer. Once past Black Cairn, the trail ascends a small hill as it makes its way to the Trail Creek area.

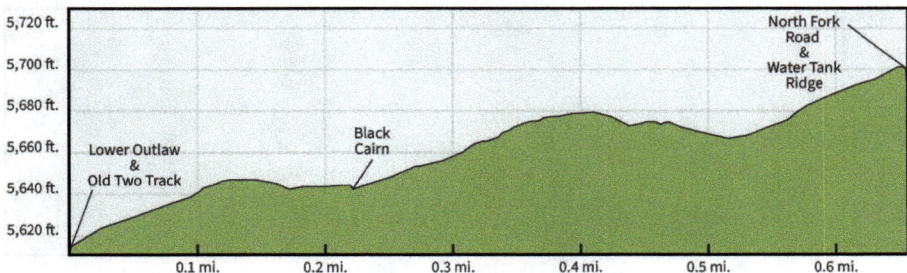

Over The Top

Distance: 4.9 miles one-way

Elevation Gain: 830 feet

Difficulty: Black diamond

Trailhead GPS Coordinates:
N42° 49.833' W112° 27.328'

Over the Top is a classic trail for mountain bikers and hikers that makes its way high onto a ridgetop with impressive views of City Creek and Cusick Creek. The trail is typically ridden from south to north, climbing from the Cusick Creek drainage through a deciduous forest high onto a dry ridge before descending a rocky slope toward City Creek on a series of switchbacks.

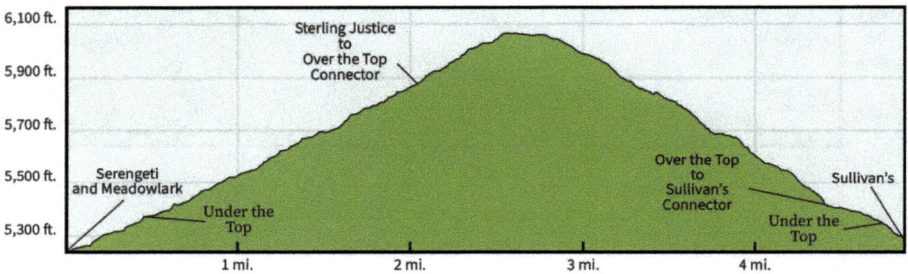

Prison Trail

Distance: 0.7 miles one-way

Elevation Gain: 250 feet

Difficulty: Green circle

Trailhead GPS Coordinates:
N42° 50.827' W112° 27.265'

Prison Trail is a fast trail on an open hillside that begins in the Cusick Creek parking lot. The trail is a great way to connect to other trails, including Death Valley, Bump Trail, Burrito, 911, and Bench Trail. This is generally an easy ride, though it can be steep as it climbs out of Death Valley.

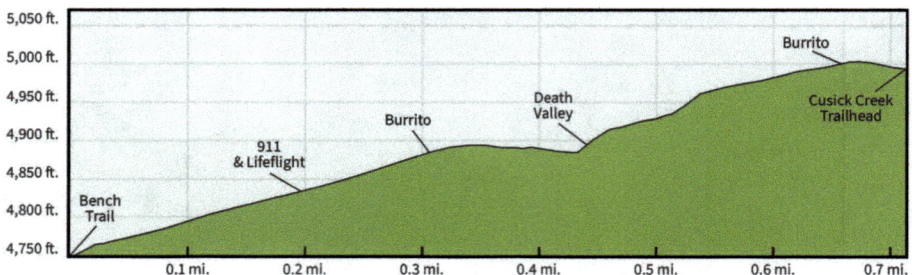

Rim Trail

Distance: 0.6 miles one-way

Elevation Gain: 110 feet

Difficulty: Green circle

Trailhead GPS Coordinates:
N42° 51.090' W112° 27.073'

Rim Trail is a short trail that serves as a way to connect with Death Valley and an alternate way to access 911. While short, the path does offer unique views of the city from atop the bench. The trail begins at a junction with Bench Trail after the climb from Bridge 1.

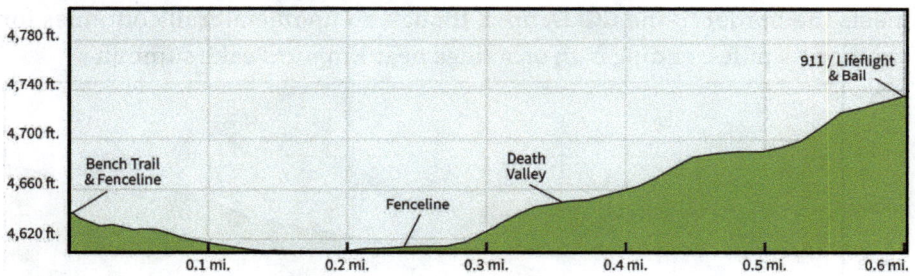

Ritalin

Distance: 0.6 miles one-way

Elevation Gain: 220 feet

Difficulty: Blue square

Trailhead GPS Coordinates:
N42° 50.255' W112° 27.954'

Ritalin is a fast bermed trail that winds its way across a small ravine. From Sullivan's, the trail crosses over Serengeti before ending at Crosscut.

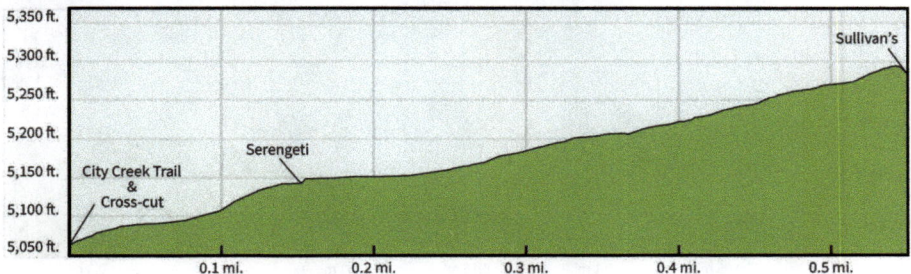

Sap Tree

Distance: 0.7 miles one-way

Elevation Gain: 280 feet

Difficulty: Double black diamond

Trailhead GPS Coordinates:
N42° 49.444' W112° 29.198'

A heavily forested and scenic creekside path that feels like a slightly rougher extension of the City Creek Trail, Sap Tree is a fun path for both hikers and mountain bikers. The trail begins across a bridge at the small parking area before the Kinport Road gate. The trail officially ends at 0.7 miles, when it meets the border of the CCMA area, though an unofficial trail continues for another 1.4 miles, ending high on a ridge near Kinport Peak's summit.

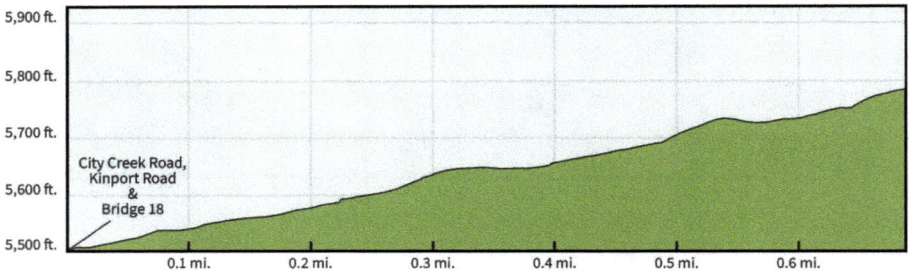

Scout

Distance: 0.3 miles one-way

Elevation Gain: 50 feet

Difficulty: Green circle

Trailhead GPS Coordinates:
N42° 50.722' W112° 27.336'

Scout is a short one-way connector that allows downhill riders to connect to Bench Trail from Bridge 6.

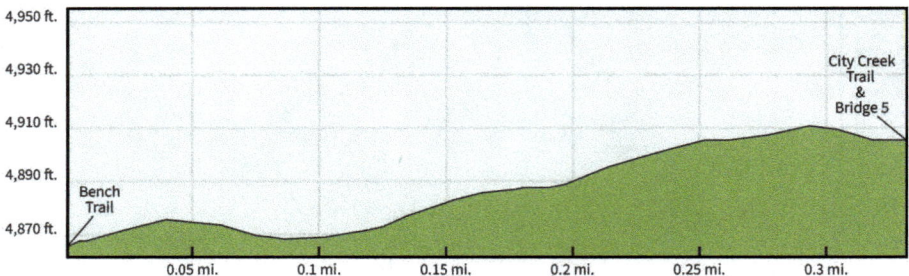

Serengeti

Distance: 1.2 miles one-way
Elevation Gain: 260 feet

Difficulty: Upper half: Green circle, Lower half: Blue square
Trailhead GPS Coordinates: N42° 50.268' W112° 28.092'

Serengeti is an excellent way to cross through the heart of the CCMA, connecting City Creek Road with Cusick Creek Road. Most of the trail traverses grassy hillsides with nice views. Serengeti is an excellent path to become familiar with, as it works well for accessing many trails in the area.

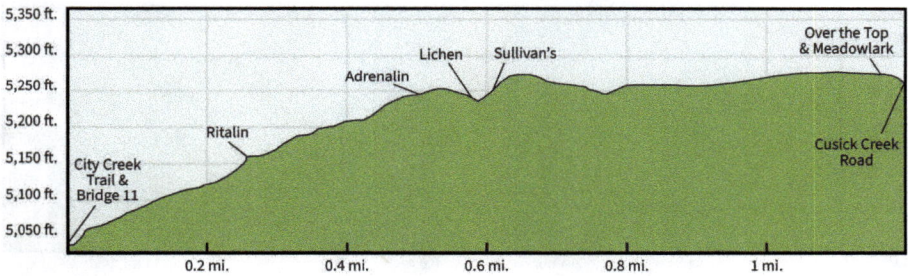

South Serengeti

Distance: 2.3 miles one-way
Elevation Gain: 340 feet

Difficulty: Green circle
Trailhead GPS Coordinates: N42° 49.758' W112° 27.337'

This lightly used doubletrack cruises downhill through grassy hillsides for the first three-quarters of a mile before turning to the southeast and leveling out. The first 1.3 miles of South Serengeti fall within the CCMA, while the remainder is on BLM land. Once on BLM land, the trail transitions into a singletrack. Overall, it is a fun trail with excellent town views, though the required backtracking to avoid private property makes it a lengthy commitment.

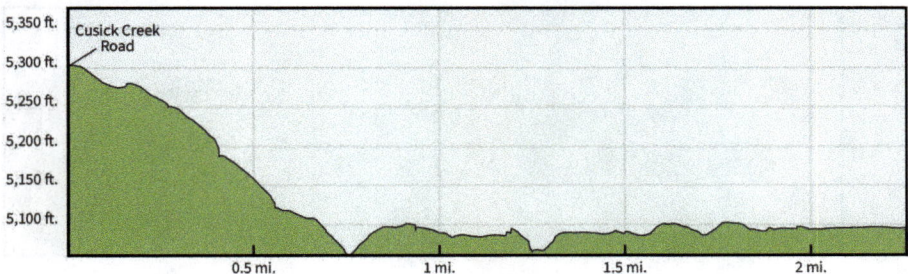

Sullivan's

Distance: 1.2 miles one-way

Elevation Gain: 140 feet

Difficulty: Blue square

Trailhead GPS Coordinates:
N42° 50.001' W112° 27.724'

A picturesque trail that is an excellent way to connect from Serengeti to various CCMA trails, Sullivan's is one of the area's highlights. This trail has many ups and downs and a few narrow stretches, so be prepared for a workout. In early summer, this path is surrounded by wildflowers.

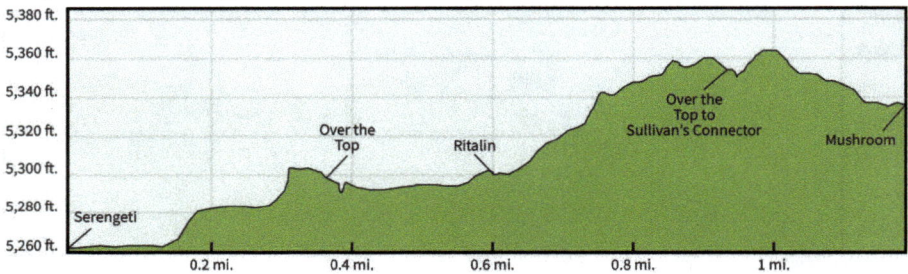

Switchback

Distance: 1.5 miles one-way

Elevation Gain: 330 feet

Difficulty: Blue square

Trailhead GPS Coordinates:
N42° 50.734' W112° 27.847'

Switchback is a challenging climb that connects Black Cairn to White Cairn. The first half of the trail, starting from Black Cairn, climbs through a series of switchbacks, but you are rewarded with a fun back half that cruises downhill. The trail crosses an unofficial 4x4 road a few times on the route, so be sure to connect with the singletrack trail on the other side when confronted with these crossings.

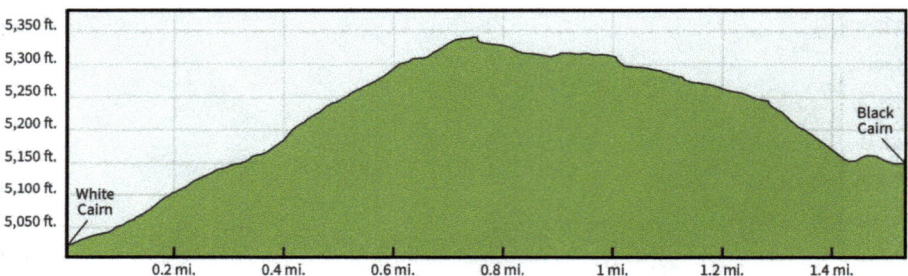

Under The Top

Distance: 1.1 miles one-way
Elevation Gain: 170 feet

Difficulty: Blue square
Trailhead GPS Coordinates:
N42° 49.753' W112° 27.475'

A scenic singletrack that traverses across a grassy hillside and through a few small forests. An easier alternative to Over The Top for those looking for a shorter ride with excellent views.

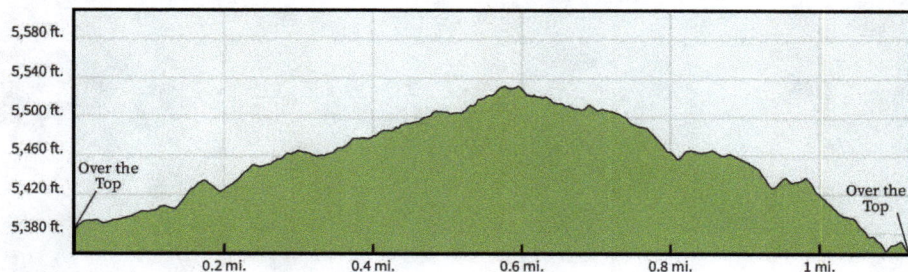

White Cairn

Distance: 1 mile one-way
Elevation Gain: 230 feet

Difficulty: Green circle
Trailhead GPS Coordinates:
N42° 50.876' W112° 27.652'

A singletrack path that connects the Upper City Creek parking lot to Bridge 11.

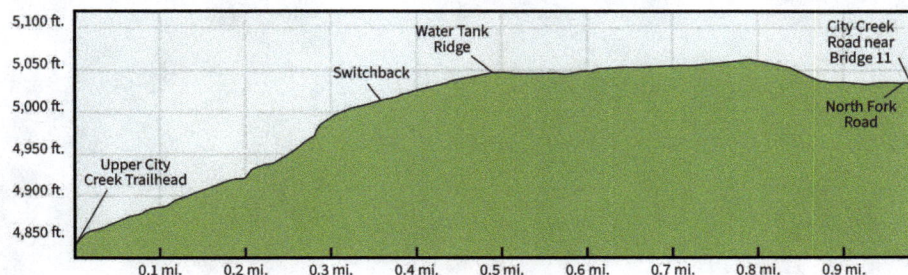

City Creek Trail in the fall.

Pioneer Ridge Trail Overview

Officially opened in the summer of 2024, Pioneer Ridge is Pocatello's newest trail system. These sage-and-juniper-lined trails climb high on the hills overlooking the city's northern stretch, granting excellent views of the Snake River Plain and the Satterfield residential area. The name comes from the local mountain bike race team, the Pocatello Pioneers, who practice in the area. This trail system was crafted for use by both hikers and mountain bikers, though the mountain biking aspect of the system was given particular attention. While the official trails are new, many intersecting preexisting side paths still exist, so be sure to watch for signage to stay on the official trails as you travel in this area. The first mile of the trail (also called Top of the First) travels through a rehabilitated section of an old landfill, so it is crucial to stay on the path due to environmental concerns along this stretch. The system is close to many residential areas, though the only official access point is off Pocatello Creek Road. For a full route description of the Pioneer Ridge Loop, go to page 96.

For a full route description of the Pioneer Ridge Loop, go to page 96.

The temple from the Pioneer Ridge area.

Pioneer Ridge Trail System

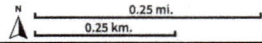

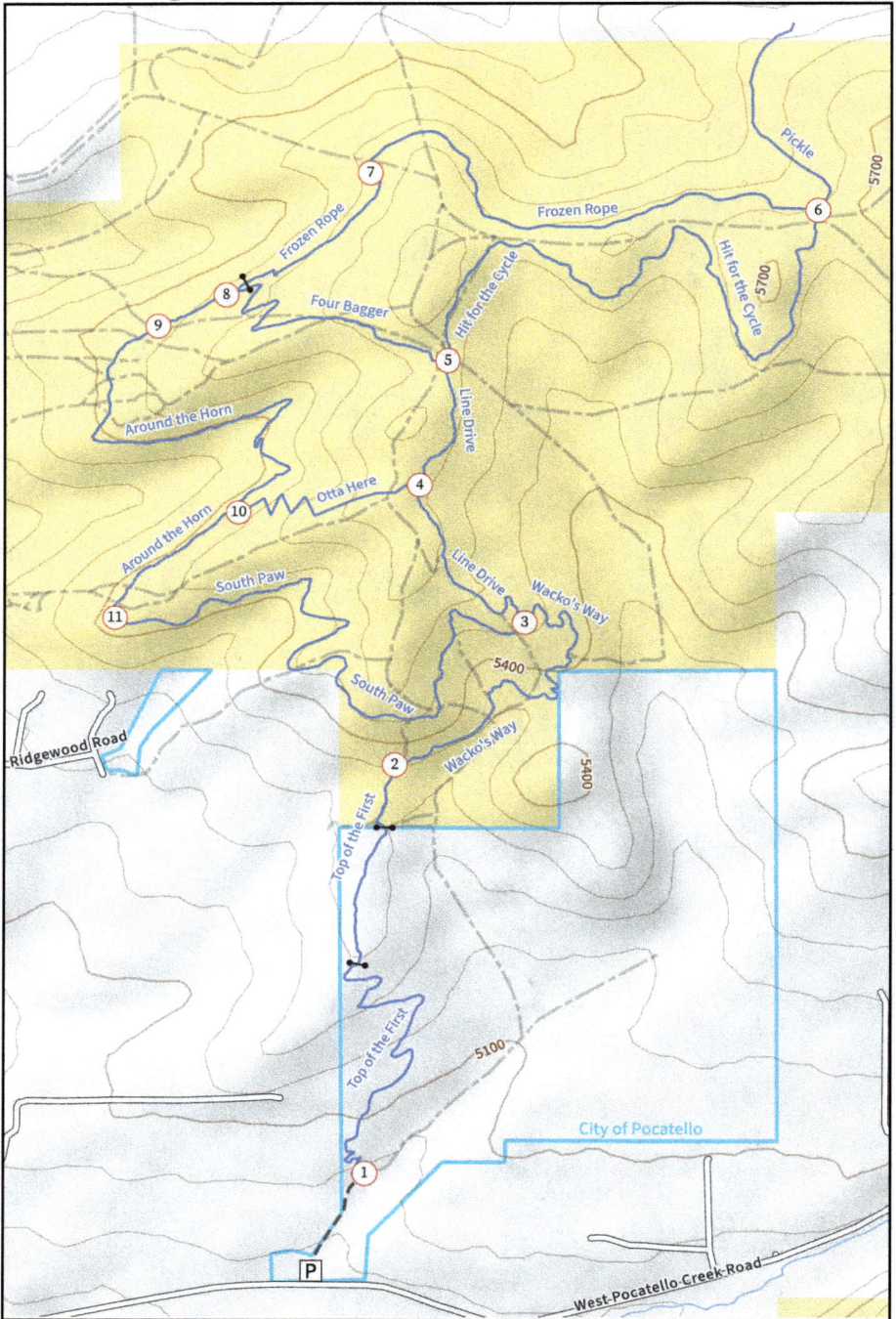

0.25 mi.
0.25 km.

Around the Horn

Distance: 1 mile one-way

Elevation Gain: 100 feet

Difficulty: Blue square

Trailhead GPS Coordinates:
N42° 54.208' W112° 23.606'

Around the Horn is a pleasant singletrack on the western side of the loop that has great views of the city. The elevation gain is minimal for most of the ride, though the northern stretch near the water tank does have a large incline.

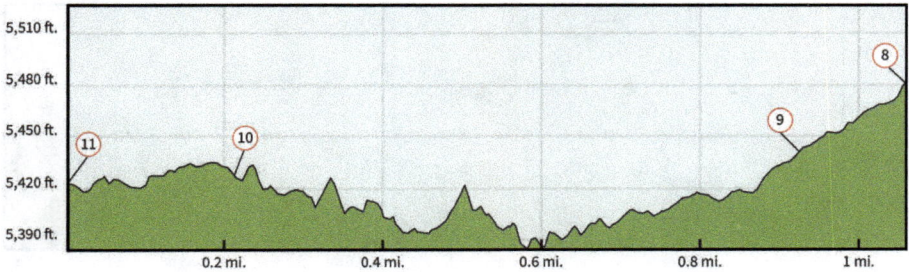

Four Bagger

Distance: 0.5 miles one-way

Elevation Gain: 140 feet

Difficulty: Blue square

Trailhead GPS Coordinates:
N42° 54.653' W112° 23.459'

This is a narrow bridge path that cuts through the center of the loop, bridging the eastern and western trails.

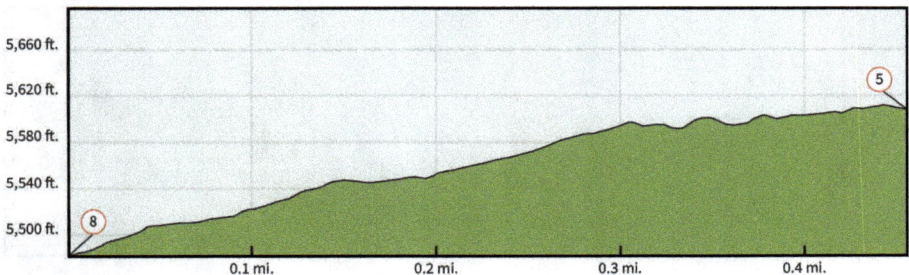

Frozen Rope

Distance: 1 mile one-way

Elevation Gain: 210 feet

Difficulty: Blue square

Trailhead GPS Coordinates:
N42° 54.653' W112° 23.459'

A consistently mild incline on the north side of the loop. This singletrack trail has views of the northern hills and ends at a junction with Pickle and Hit for the Cycle.

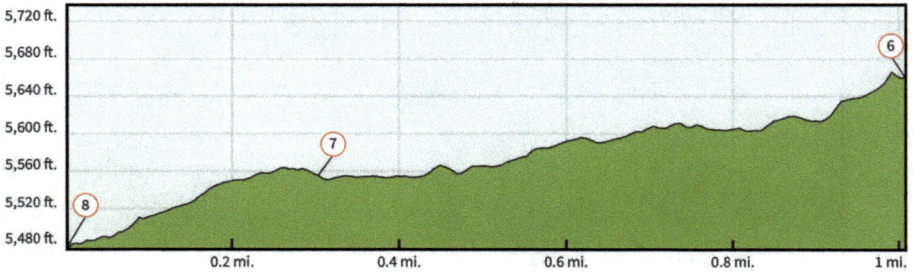

Hit for the Cycle

Distance: 1 mile one-way

Elevation Gain: 100 feet

Difficulty: Blue square

Trailhead GPS Coordinates:
N42° 54.571' W112° 23.156'

A winding sage-lined singletrack that connects the northern end of the loop back to the main ridgeline.

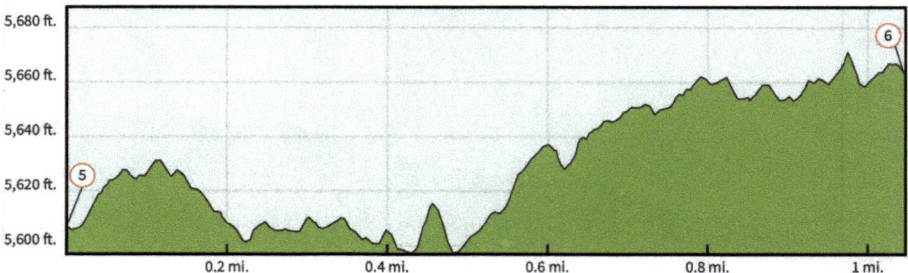

Line Drive

Distance: 0.5 miles one-way

Elevation Gain: 120 feet

Difficulty: Blue square

Trailhead GPS Coordinates:
N42° 54.198' W112° 23.049'

Line Drive travels alongside the eastern stretch of the Pioneer Ridge Loop, gaining a very manageable amount of elevation along the way. The short path length combined with both ends connecting to junctions makes this a solid trail for maneuvering around the area.

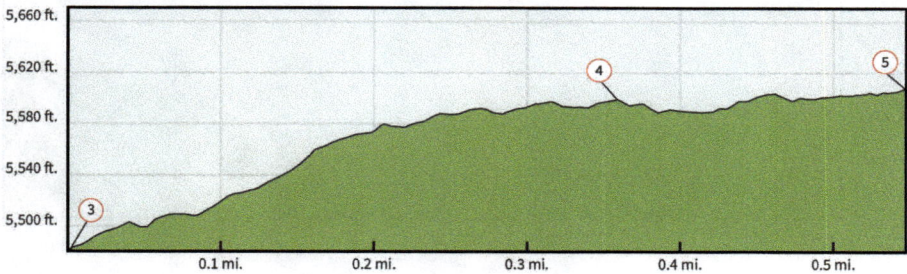

Otta Here

Distance: 0.4 miles one-way

Elevation Gain: 300 feet

Difficulty: Blue square

Trailhead GPS Coordinates:
N42° 54.394' W112° 23.194'

A brief yet occasionally steep path that allows for interesting loop options along the southern stretch of the Pioneer Ridge loop. The path bridges Line Drive with Around the Horn.

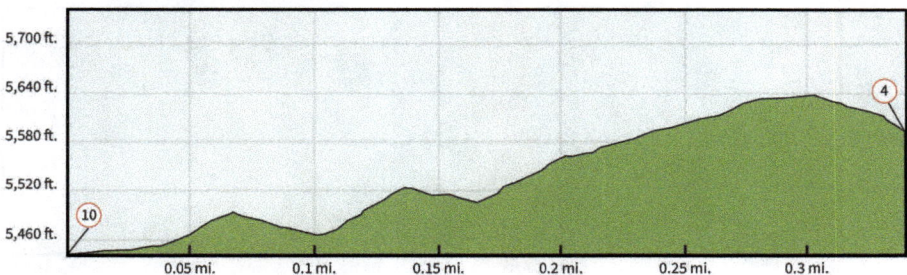

Pickle

Distance: 0.4 miles one-way

Elevation Gain: 210 feet

Difficulty: Blue square

Trailhead GPS Coordinates:
N42° 54.772' W112° 22.657'

Pickle mainly serves as a connecting route for the Pocatello Pioneers race team to connect with the Pioneer Ridge Trail System. If you ride it, be sure to avoid continuing onto private property.

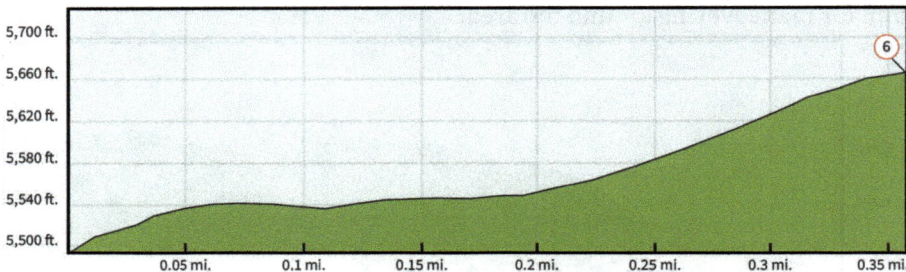

South Paw

Distance: 1 mile one-way

Elevation Gain: 150 feet

Difficulty: Blue square

Trailhead GPS Coordinates:
N42° 54.198' W112° 23.049'

This is an enjoyable singletrack that travels on the southern portion of the main Pioneer Ridge Loop. The beginning half of the trail from Wacko's Way moves up and down on small hills through a juniper forest before descending and continuing across a dry hillside and drainage connecting to Around the Horn.

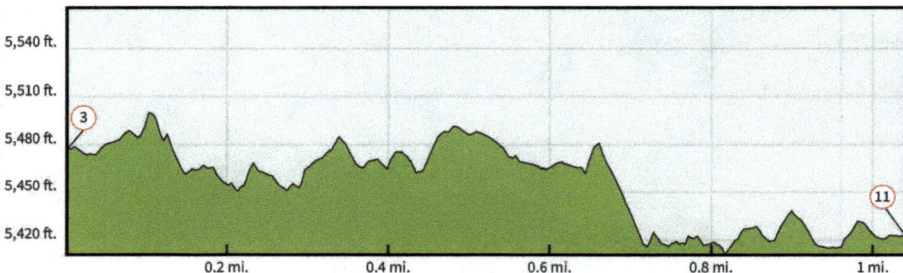

Top of the First

Distance: 1 mile one-way
Elevation Gain: 340 feet

Difficulty: Blue square
Trailhead GPS Coordinates:
N42° 53.436' W112° 23.264'

Top of the First is a nice singletrack path through junipers and sage that is primarily used as a connecting path to the main Pioneer Ridge Loop. The uphill is a moderate climb, though the return trip is a fun ride. The trail is about 0.2 miles from the parking area on Little Pocatello Creek Road's left (north) side.

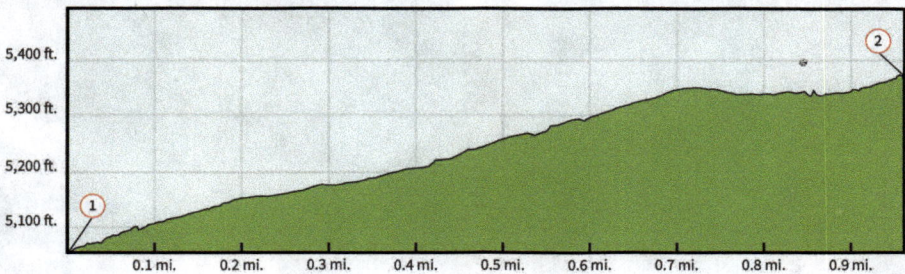

Wacko's Way

Distance: 0.6 miles one-way
Elevation Gain: 140 feet

Difficulty: Blue square
Trailhead GPS Coordinates:
N42° 54.002' W112° 23.223'

Wacko's Way works well as a short bridge path from Top of the First to the main Pioneer Ridge Loop. This path crosses a juniper-scattered hillside with a few enjoyable switchbacks, though the number of random side trails can be confusing.

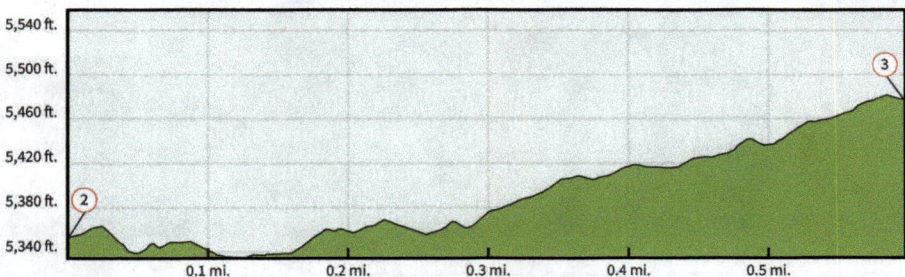

East Mink Creek Nordic Center Trail Overview

The East Mink Creek Nordic Center, located only seven miles from Pocatello, offers over 12 miles of groomed cross-country skiing trails. You can rent equipment at the Nordic Center, which is below Scout Mountain. Both classic and skate skiing are allowed on the trails, and there are also 2.5 miles of snowshoe trails available. Although most of the trails are dog-free, a few paths allow you to bring your furry friends along. These winter trails are also accessible for hiking in the summer. Additionally, the Nordic Center has a disc golf course for those who want to continue exploring the hills in the warmer months.

Lower Canyon heading toward Scout Mountain.

East Mink Creek Nordic Center

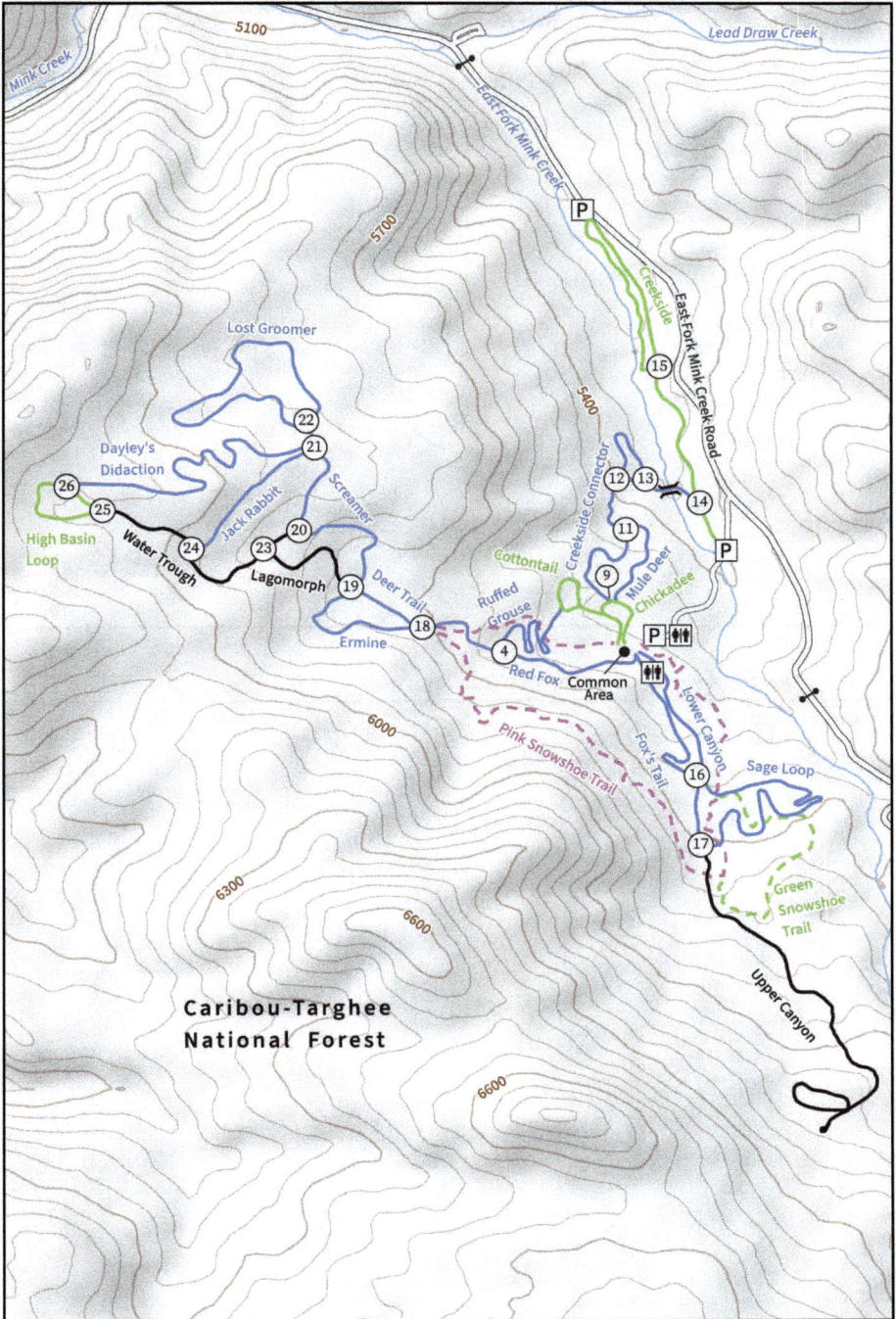

N

0.25 mi.
0.25 km.

5100

Mink Creek

Lead Draw Creek

East Fork Mink Creek

5700

Lost Groomer

Creekside

East Fork Mink Creek Road

P

15

Dayley's
Didaction

22

21

Screamer

Jack Rabbit

5400

Creekside Connector

12   13

14

P

26

25

High Basin
Loop

Water Trough

24

20

23

Lagomorph

19

Deer Trail

11

9

Cottontail

Mule Deer

Chickadee

P

Ermine

18

Ruffed
Grouse

4

Red Fox

Common
Area

6000

Pink Snowshoe Trail

Fox's Tail

Lower Canyon

16

Sage Loop

6300

6600

17

Green
Snowshoe
Trail

Caribou-Targhee
National Forest

Upper Canyon

6600

East Mink Creek Nordic Center - Upper Trails

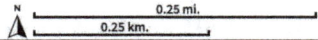

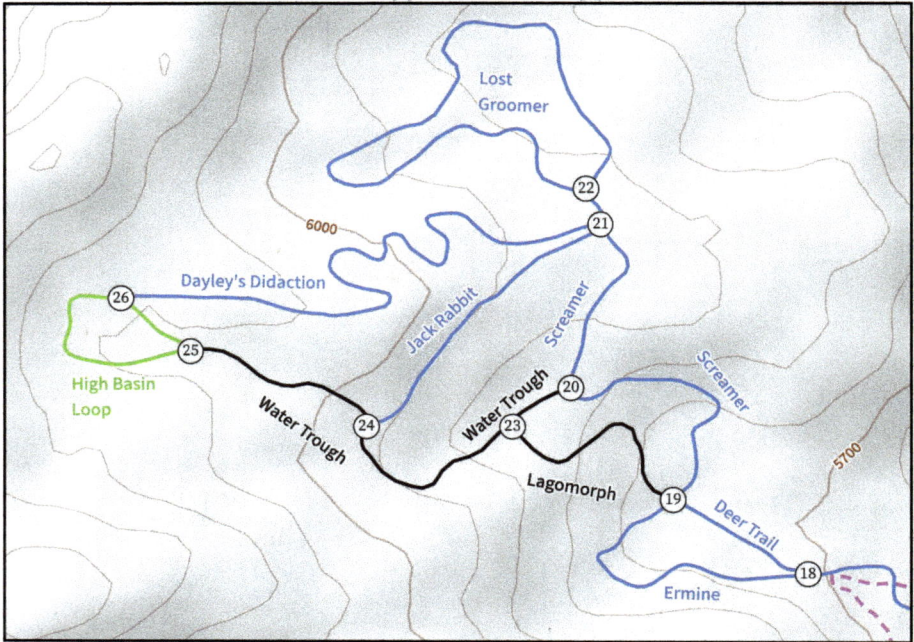

N
0.25 mi.
0.25 km.

Lost Groomer

6000

Dayley's Didaction

Jack Rabbit

Screamer

Screamer

High Basin Loop

Water Trough

Water Trough

Lagomorph

Deer Trail

Ermine

5700

22
21
26
25
24
23
20
19
18

East Mink Creek Nordic Center - Lower Trails

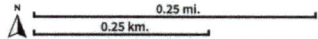

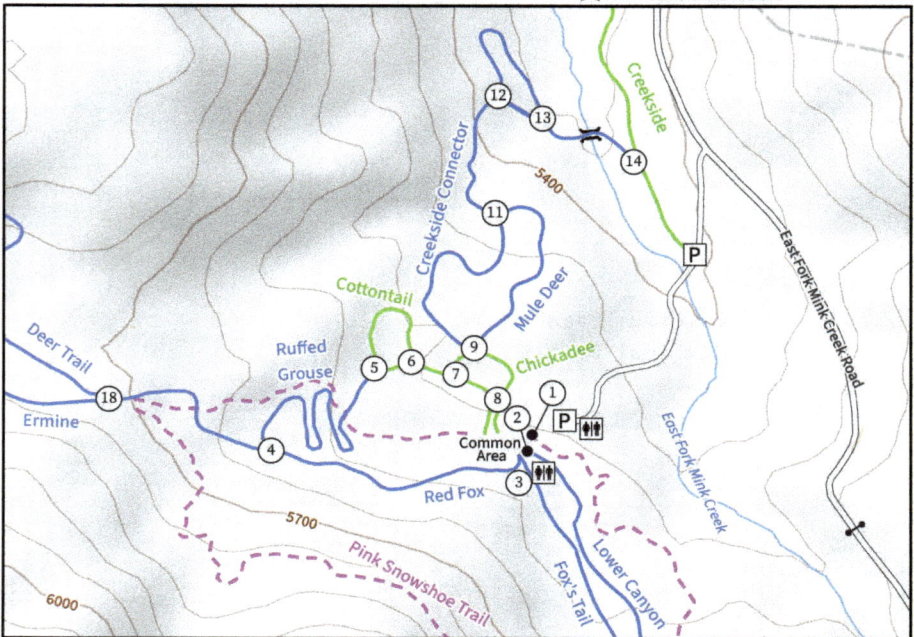

N
0.25 mi.
0.25 km.

Creekside

Creekside Connector

5400

Mule Deer

Cottontail

Chickadee

Ruffed Grouse

Deer Trail

Ermine

Red Fox

Common Area

5700

Pink Snowshoe Trail

6000

Fox's Tail

Lower Canyon

East Fork Mink Creek

East Fork Mink Creek Road

P

P

12
13
14
11
9
5
6
7
8
1
2
3
4
18

Chickadee

Distance: 0.3 miles one-way

Elevation Gain: 30 feet

Dog Friendly

Difficulty: Easy

Trailhead GPS Coordinates:
N42° 43.003' W112° 22.753'

An easy loop near the yurt that makes for a great warmup run to test gear.

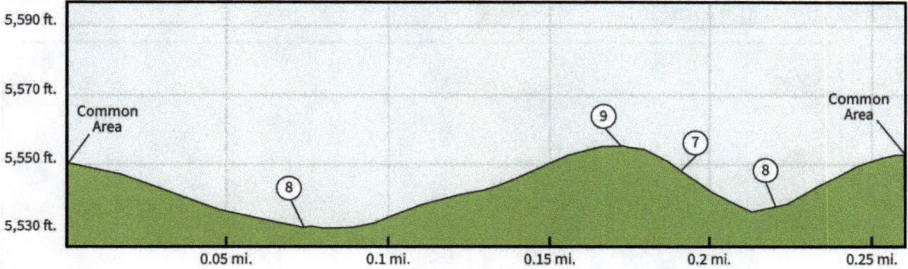

Cottontail

Distance: 0.3-mile loop

Elevation Gain: 40 feet

Dog Friendly

Difficulty: Easy

Trailhead GPS Coordinates:
N42° 43.072' W112° 22.818'

Short, forested beginner loop.

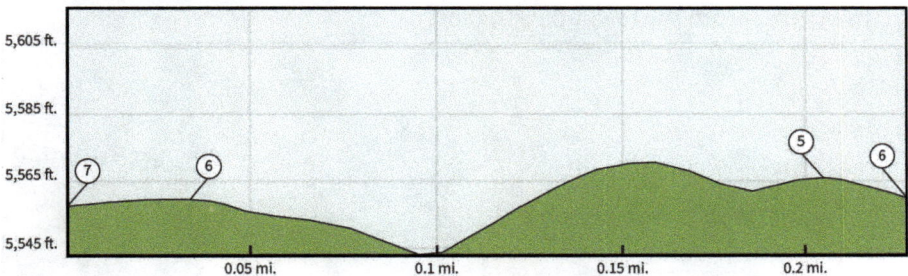

Creekside

Distance: 1.8-mile loop

Elevation Gain: 120 feet

Dog Friendly

Difficulty: Easy

Trailhead GPS Coordinates:
N42° 43.207' W112° 22.558'

A long dog friendly run that parallels the East Fork Mink Creek. Begins right off the lower parking lot.

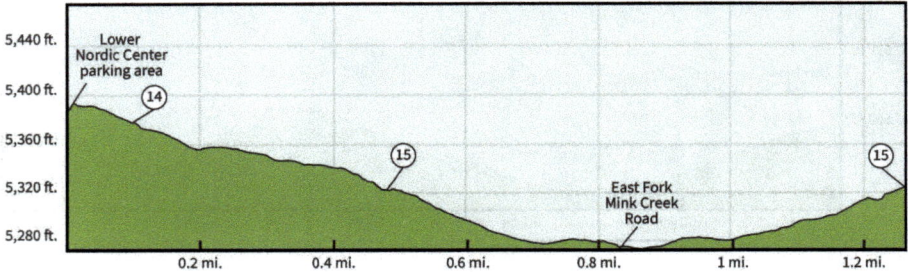

Creekside Connector

Distance: 0.8 miles one-way

Elevation Gain: 190 feet

Dog Friendly

Difficulty: Intermediate

Trailhead GPS Coordinates:
N42° 43.311' W112° 22.617'

A connecting trail with a surprising amount of incline. A great way to get to the main ski area from the lower parking lot.

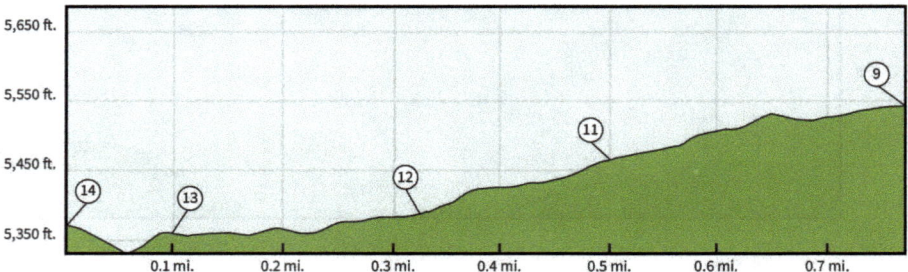

Dayley's Didaction

Distance: 0.7 miles one-way
Elevation Gain: 220 feet
No Dogs Allowed

Difficulty: Intermediate
Trailhead GPS Coordinates:
N42° 43.431' W112° 23.378'

A winding run on open hillsides with beautiful views of the area.

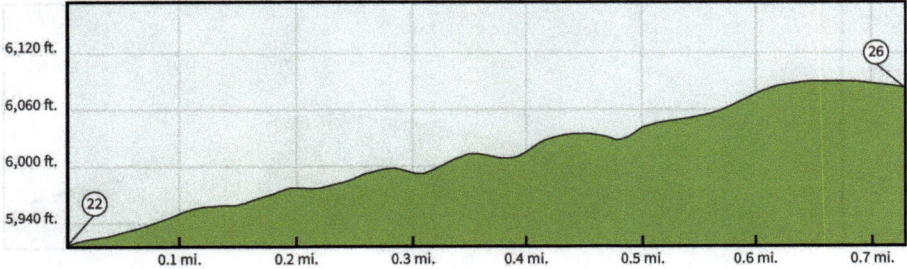

Deer Trail

Distance: 0.4 miles one-way
Elevation Gain: 120 feet
No Dogs Allowed

Difficulty: Intermediate
Trailhead GPS Coordinates:
N42° 42.990' W112° 23.006'

The main connecting path between the central trails and the upper mountain.

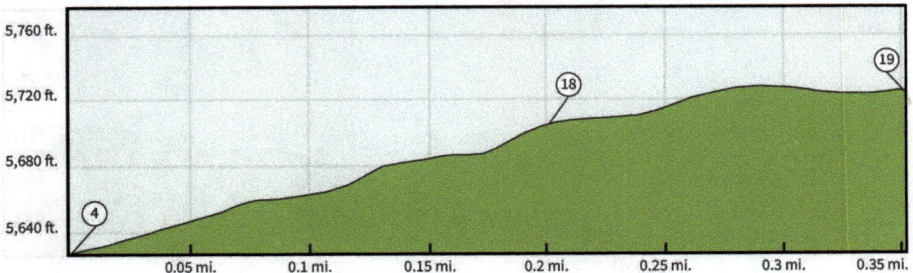

Ermine

Distance: 0.3 miles one-way

Elevation Gain: 80 feet

No Dogs Allowed

Difficulty: Intermediate

Trailhead GPS Coordinates:
N42° 43.049' W112° 23.183'

A hilly alternative to Deer Trail.

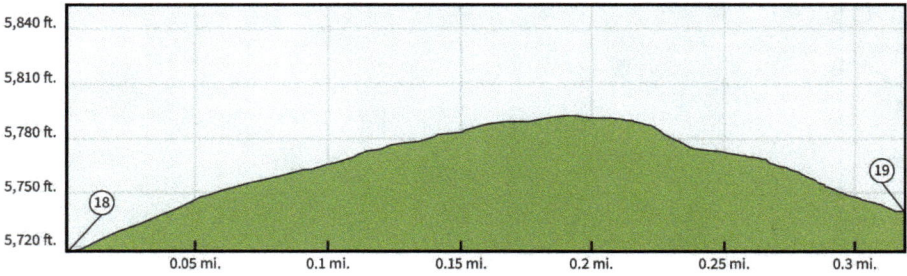

Fox's Tail

Distance: 0.4 miles one-way

Elevation Gain: 110 feet

No Dogs Allowed

Difficulty: Intermediate

Trailhead GPS Coordinates:
N42° 42.975' W112° 22.730'

A pleasant trail that connects the Common Area to Upper Canyon.

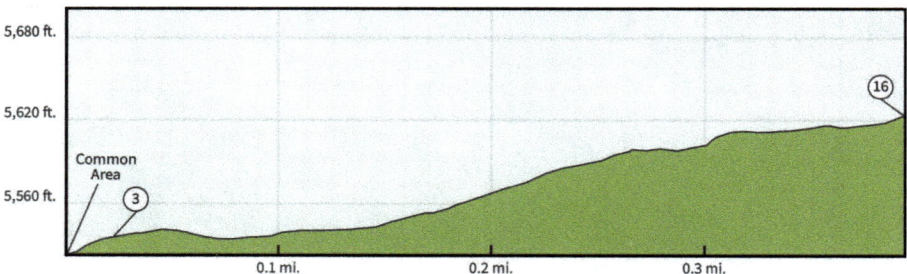

Green Snowshoe Trail

Distance: 0.7 miles one-way
Elevation Gain: 200 feet
Dog Friendly

Difficulty: Intermediate
Trailhead GPS Coordinates:
N42° 42.693' W112° 22.570'

A fun additional loop on the south end of the Pink Trail. This path can be a bit steep at times, so make sure you are comfortable on snowshoes before attempting it.

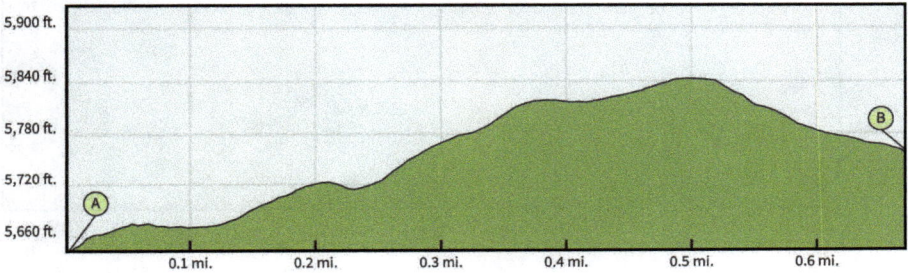

High Basin Loop

Distance: 0.3-mile loop
Elevation Gain: 30 feet
No Dogs Allowed

Difficulty: Easy
Trailhead GPS Coordinates:
N42° 43.291' W112° 23.812'

A high loop that travels on the outskirts of an aspen grove.

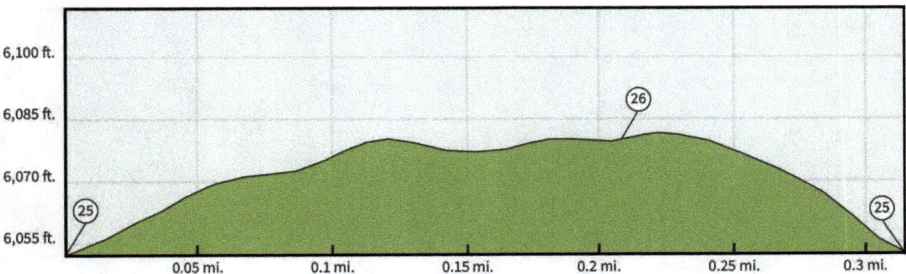

Jack Rabbit

Distance: 0.3 miles one-way

Elevation Gain: 40 feet

No Dogs Allowed

Difficulty: Intermediate

Trailhead GPS Coordinates:
N42° 43.211' W112° 23.623'

A direct connecting trail between the eastern and western upper mountain trails.

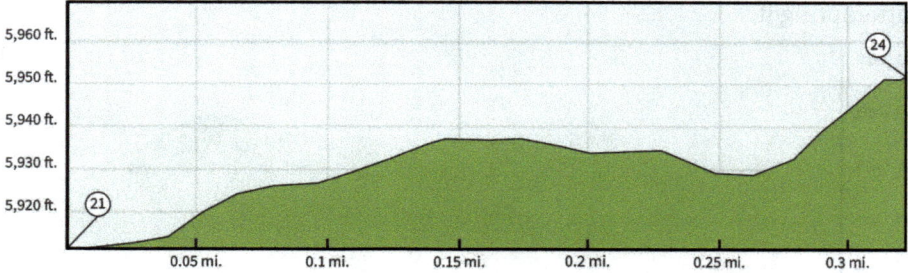

Lagomorph

Distance: 0.3 miles one-way

Elevation Gain: 120 feet

No Dogs Allowed

Difficulty: Difficult

Trailhead GPS Coordinates:
N42° 43.126' W112° 23.301'

A moderately steep forested trail that connects to Water Trough

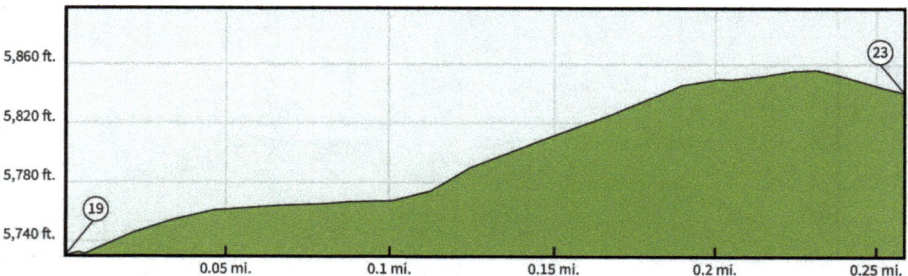

Lost Groomer

Distance: 1-mile loop

Elevation Gain: 180 feet

No Dogs Allowed

Difficulty: Intermediate

Trailhead GPS Coordinates:
N42° 43.451' W112° 23.394'

A lengthy loop on the upper mountain with plenty of uphill and downhill.

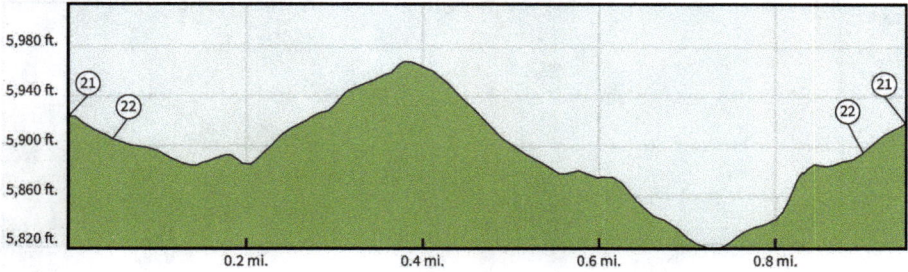

Lower Canyon

Distance: 0.3 miles one-way

Elevation Gain: 100 feet

No Dogs Allowed

Difficulty: Intermediate

Trailhead GPS Coordinates:
N42° 42.989' W112° 22.727'

A gently inclined run that connects the Common Area to the Sage Loop. It runs adjacent to the pink snowshoe trail.

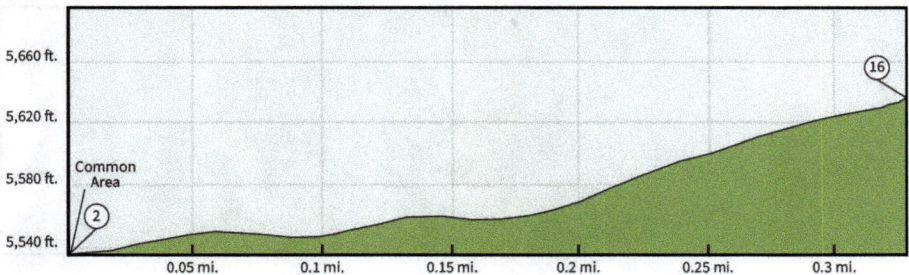

Mule Deer

Distance: 0.3 miles one-way   **Difficulty:** Intermediate
Elevation Gain: 80 feet   **Trailhead GPS Coordinates:**
Dog Friendly   N42° 43.096' W112° 22.782'

A short path with plenty of downhill that connects to the Creekside Connector.

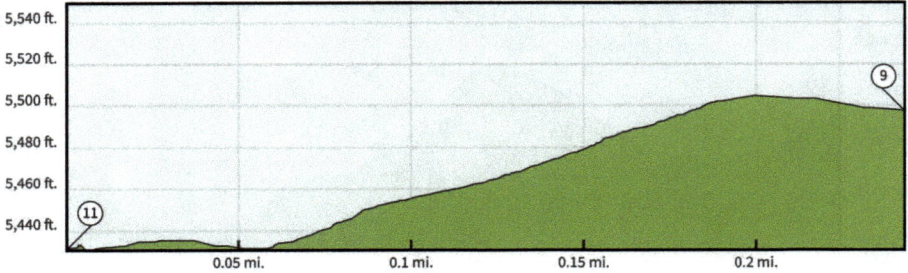

Pink Snowshoe Trail

Distance: 2.1-mile loop   **Difficulty:** Intermediate
Elevation Gain: 380 feet   **Trailhead GPS Coordinates:**
Dog Friendly   N42° 43.007' W112° 22.723'

The main snowshoe path at the Nordic Center. The trail begins near the Common Area and heads south through the evergreens before looping back around on the hillside. Once on the hillside, the trail provides excellent views of the area.

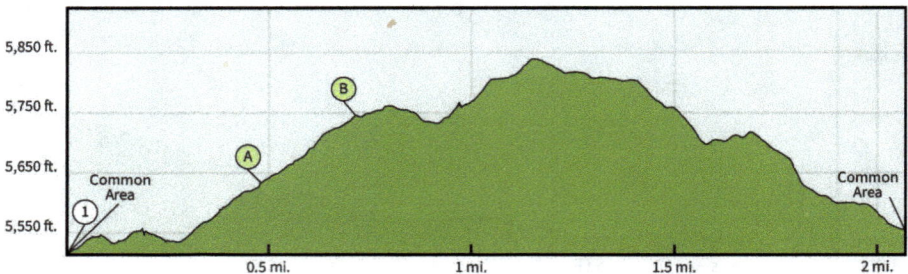

Red Fox

Distance: 0.3 miles one-way
Elevation Gain: 80 feet
No Dogs Allowed

Difficulty: Intermediate
Trailhead GPS Coordinates:
N42° 42.983' W112° 22.736'

A short trail that makes for a fun descent to the Common Area.

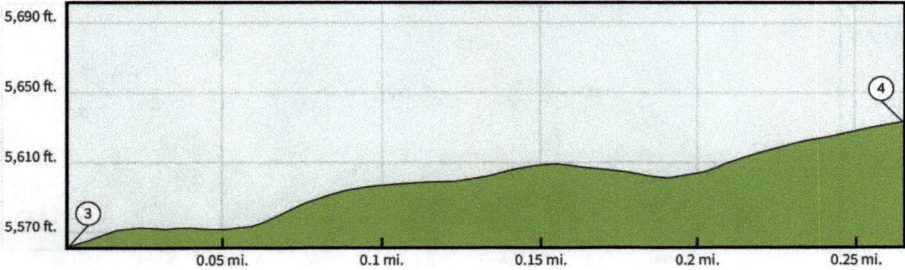

Ruffed Grouse

Distance: 0.4 miles one-way
Elevation Gain: 90 feet
No Dogs Allowed

Difficulty: Intermediate
Trailhead GPS Coordinates:
N42° 43.080' W112° 22.883'

A unique trail that uses back-to-back switchbacks to cross through a meadow.

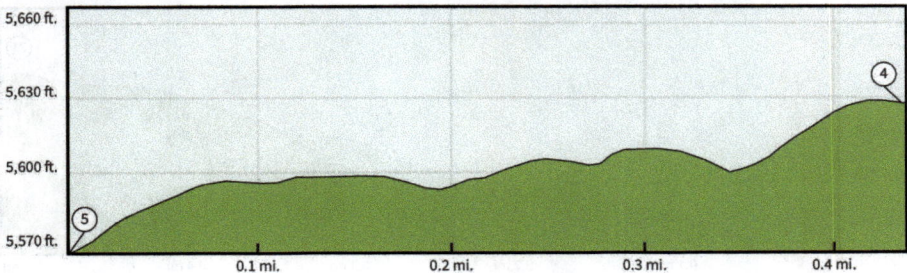

Sage Loop

Distance: 1-mile loop

Elevation Gain: 140 feet

No Dogs Allowed

Difficulty: Intermediate

Trailhead GPS Coordinates:
N42° 42.734' W112° 22.603'

A winding trail through sage fields with plenty of elevation change.

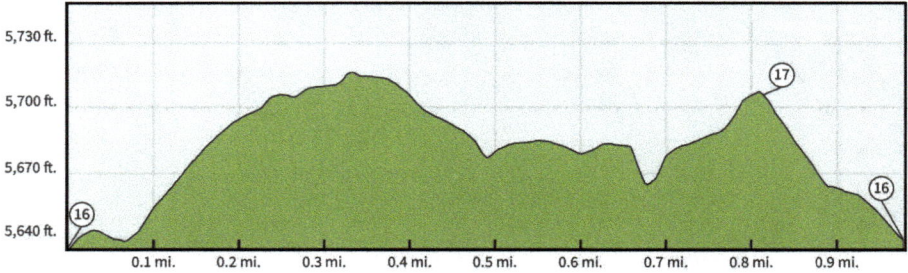

Screamer

Distance: 0.5 miles one-way

Elevation Gain: 230 feet

No Dogs Allowed

Difficulty: Intermediate

Trailhead GPS Coordinates:
N42° 43.126' W112° 23.301'

A moderate hill climb that rewards you with scenic views of the area. Makes a great way to connect to Lost Groomer.

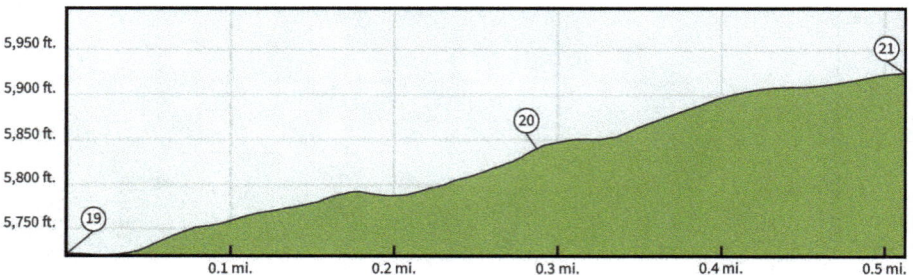

Upper Canyon

Distance: 2.3 miles out-and-back

Elevation Gain: 520 feet

No Dogs Allowed

Difficulty: Difficult

Trailhead GPS Coordinates:
N42° 42.591' W112° 22.599'

A long and isolated path at the southern end of the trail system. The beautiful evergreen forests and excellent views of Scout Mountain are well worth the tough climb.

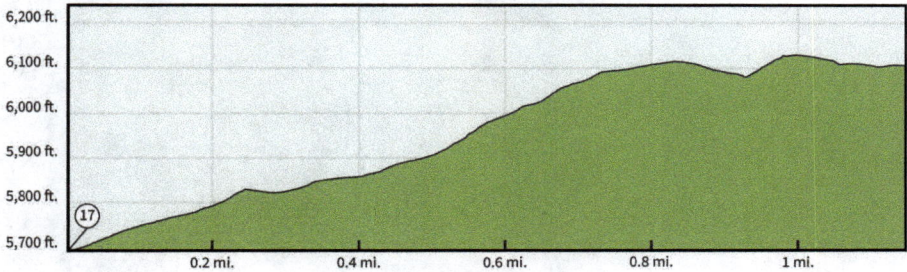

Water Trough

Distance: 0.5 miles one-way

Elevation Gain: 220 feet

No Dogs Allowed

Difficulty: Difficult

Trailhead GPS Coordinates:
N42° 43.238' W112° 23.411'

A steep trail that makes for a great way to connect to the High Basin Loop.

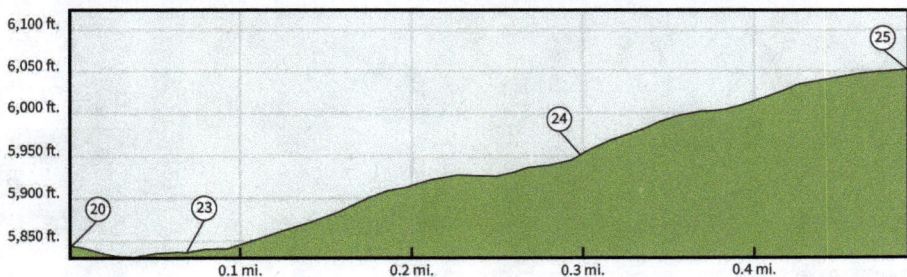

Idaho Park N' Ski - Mink Creek Trail Overview

Idaho's Park N' Ski program provides over 180 miles of cross-country skiing and snowshoeing in 14 areas around Idaho. The Park N' Ski area outside of Pocatello has 18 miles of trails on popular trails including West Fork, Corral Creek, and Valve House. The program is run primarily by the Idaho Department of Parks and Recreation, and is distinct from the East Mink Creek Nordic Center. Permits are required to access these trails.

Scout Mountain from the Porcelain Pot Loop.

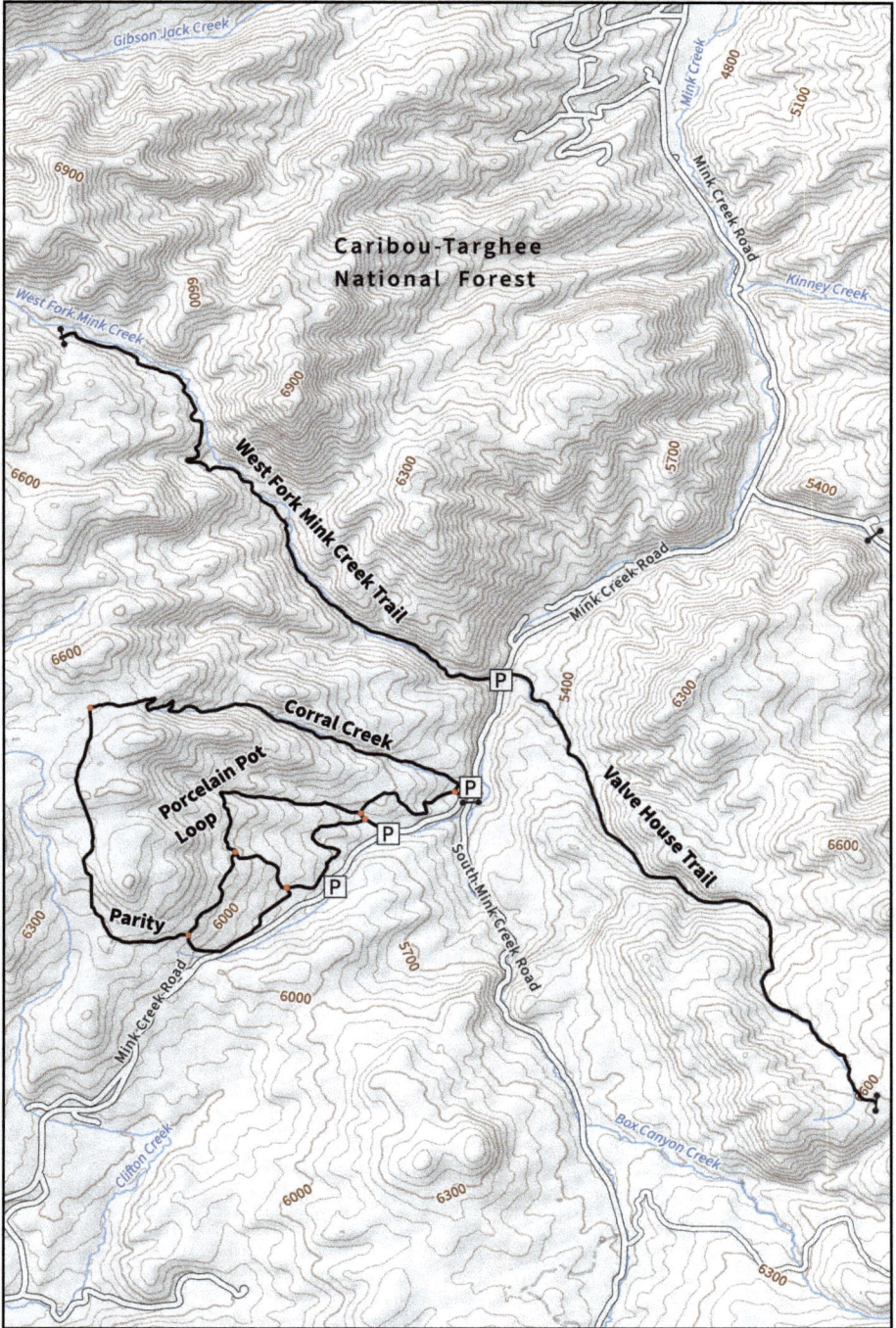

Park 'N Ski - Expanded Trail Overview

N

1 mi.
1 km.

Gibson Jack Creek

Mink Creek

4800

5100

Mink Creek Road

6900

Caribou-Targhee
National Forest

Kinney Creek

West Fork Mink Creek

6600

West Fork Mink Creek Trail

6900

6300

5700

5400

6600

Mink Creek Road

5400

Corral Creek

6300

Porcelain Pot
Loop

P

P

P

P

South Mink Creek Road

Valve House Trail

6600

Parity

6000

Mink Creek Road

6000

5700

6300

Clifton Creek

6000

6300

Box Canyon Creek

6300

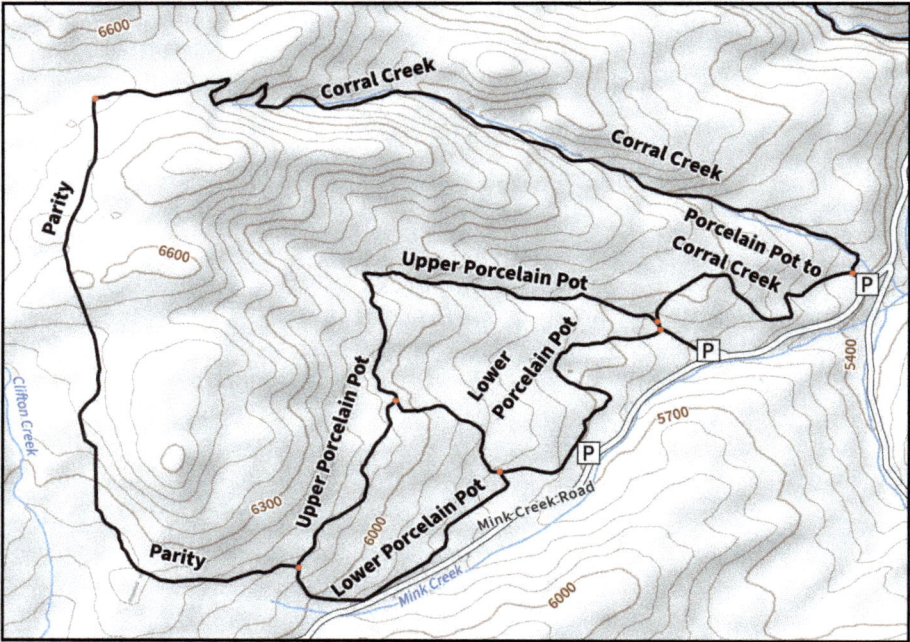

Park N' Ski - Central Trails

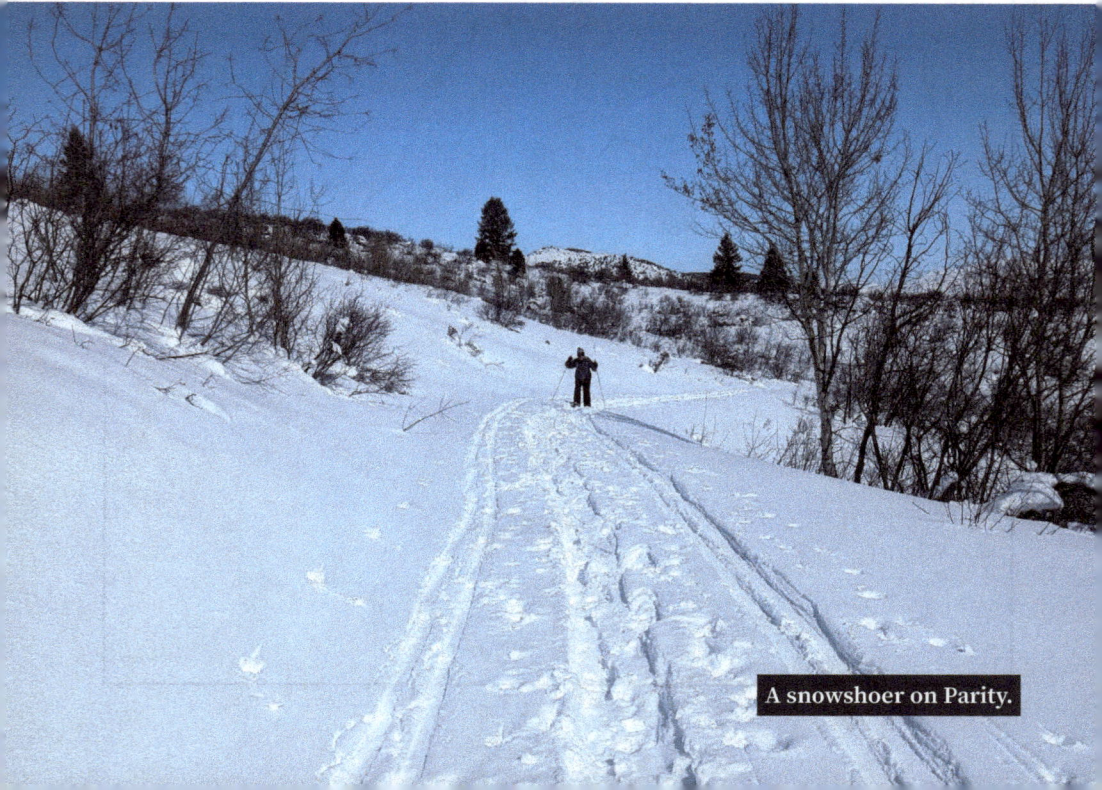

A snowshoer on Parity.

Corral Creek

Distance: 2.4 miles one-way   **Difficulty:** Difficult
Elevation Gain: 1,210 feet   **Trailhead GPS Coordinates:**
                                         N42° 42.712' W112° 25.376'

This steep trail is a forested creekside track. At the top, the trail connects with
Parity, giving the path longer loop options. (For a full route writeup, go to
page 202.)

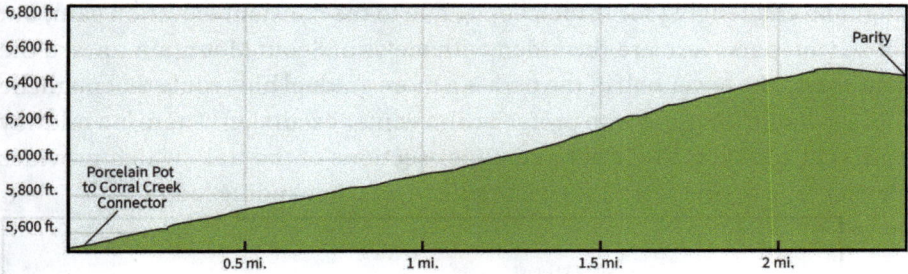

Parity

Distance: 2 miles one-way   **Difficulty:** Difficult
Elevation Gain: 630 feet   **Trailhead GPS Coordinates:**
                                         N42° 41.897' W112° 26.883'

Cutting across forested hillsides and sage meadows from the edge of the Porcelain Pot Loop, Parity makes for an easier way to reach the top of Corral Creek
than Corral Creek itself.

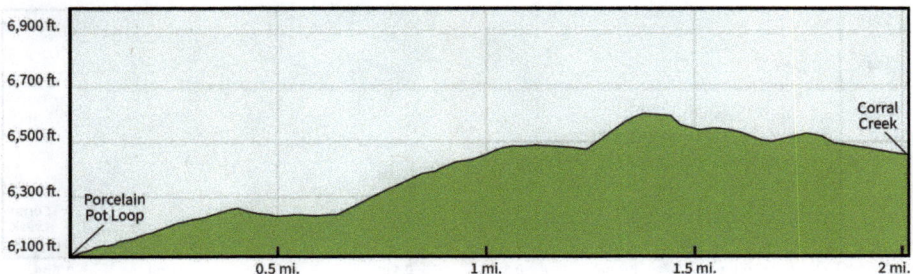

Porcelain Pot Loop

Distance: 3.7-mile loop

Elevation Gain: 900 feet

Difficulty: Difficult

Trailhead GPS Coordinates:
N42° 42.495' W112° 25.804'

The Porcelain Pot Loop is located in the heart of the Mink Creek Park N' Ski area. This path is surrounded by conifer forests and open meadows, making it a picturesque route that is easy to recommend. The upper half of the trail might be challenging for some people, due to the constant elevation gain, but those who persevere are rewarded with views of Scout Mountain toward the southeast. The lower half of the path is a more gradual hilly route that might be more suitable for those who prefer a calm winter excursion. There is a midway path that connects the lower and upper sections of the trail, which provides shorter loop options for those who prefer a less demanding loop.

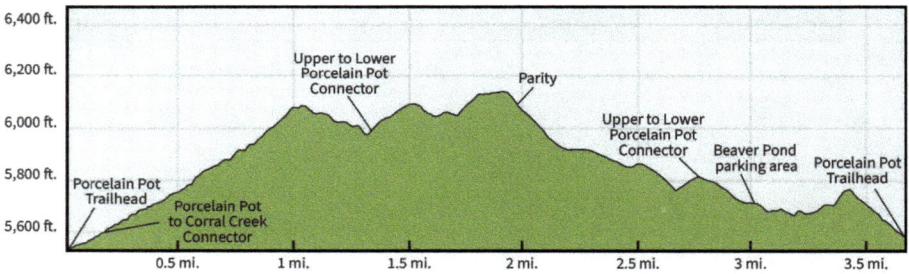

Porcelain Pot to Corral Creek Connector

Distance: 0.8 miles one-way

Elevation Gain: 280 feet

Difficulty: Difficult

Trailhead GPS Coordinates:
N42° 42.580' W112° 25.927'

A bridge path that connects Porcelain Pot to Corral Creek. This short path ascends a sage hill before descending to either trailhead.

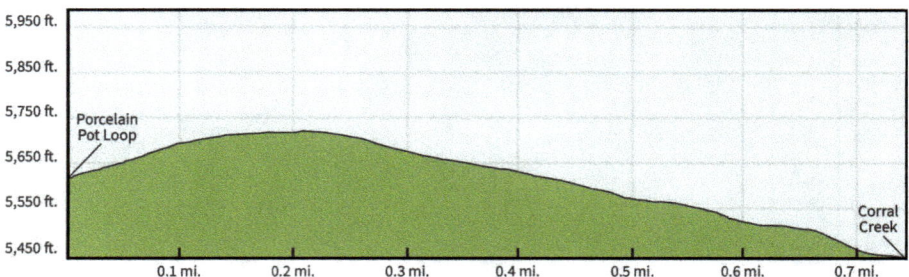

Valve House

Distance: 7.6 miles out-and-back
Elevation Gain: 1,280 feet

Difficulty: Difficult
Trailhead GPS Coordinates:
N42° 43.395' W112° 25.130'

The longest individual run in the Mink Creek Park N' Ski lineup, Valve House provides a steady climb on another classic summer trail. The path initially climbs below barren hillsides before entering a thick forest in the back half. The trail ends at the gate near the Upper Valve House turnoff. (For a full route writeup, go to page 256.)

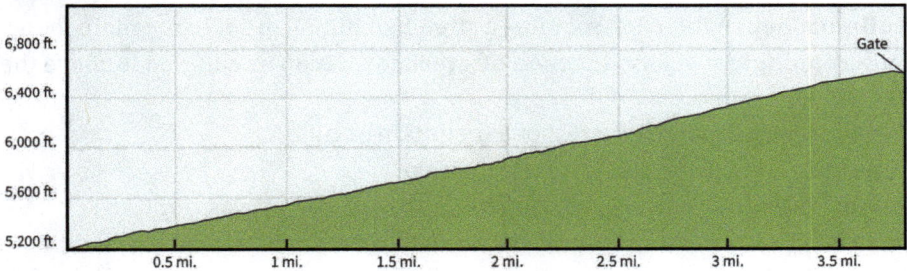

West Fork Mink Creek

Distance: 7.5 miles out-and-back
Elevation Gain: 1,070 feet

Difficulty: Difficult
Trailhead GPS Coordinates:
N42° 43.355' W112° 25.163'

This is a classic summer hike that also makes a satisfying winter ski track. The route takes you up a forested creek between steep hillsides, ending at Elk Meadows. (For a full route writeup, go to page 198.)

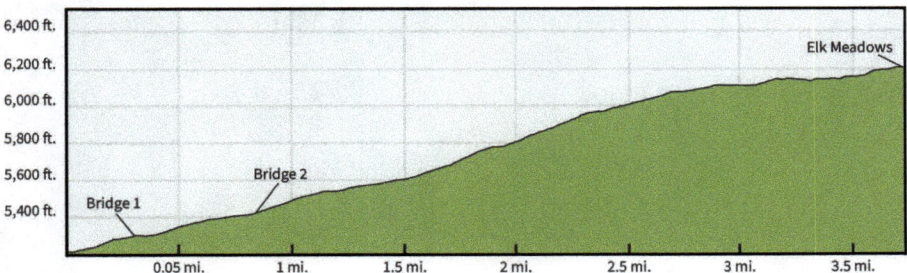

Glossary

Approach: The route to the base of a climb
BLM: Bureau of Land Management
Cairn: A distinct stack of rocks made by fellow hikers to mark a route
CCMA: City Creek Management Area
Deadfall: Fallen trees
Drainage: An area of land where water from rain or snow melt drains downhill into a body of water
FS: Forest Service
Lollipop loop: A hike that requires a stretch of hiking to get to the main loop
Outcropping: An exposed section of a rock formation or cliff that is above the ground
Ridge: A long and narrow crest of a mountain or hill
Riparian: Land near rivers, streams, or lakes
Route finding: Navigating without the use of a map, compass, or GPS
Saddle: The lowest point of a ridge connecting two mountains
Scramble: A type of climbing that requires the use of hands to continue forward
Spine: The top of a sharp ridge with defined sides
Summit: The highest point on a mountain
Switchback: A trail that forms a zigzag pattern to ease the ascent of a steep hill
Technical: In climbing, when specific gear is needed to continue. In biking, a challenging trail feature that requires cycling skill and technique to safely maneuver.
Traverse: Crossing terrain or other obstacles, such as a hillside, laterally
Watershed: An area of land that directs water, such as snowmelt and rainfall, into a common body of water
WMA: Portneuf Wildlife Management Area

Contact Information

Bureau of Land Management
Pocatello Field Office
4350 Cliffs Drive
Pocatello, ID 83204
208-478-6340
https://www.blm.gov/office/pocatello-field-office

City of Pocatello
Parks & Recreation Department
144 Wilson Avenue
Pocatello, ID 83201
208-234-6232
https://www.pocatello.gov/278/Parks-Recreation

Idaho Fish and Game
Southeast Region
1345 Barton Road
Pocatello, ID 83204
208-232-4703
https://idfg.idaho.gov/region/southeast

Idaho State University
921 S. 8th Avenue
Pocatello, ID 83209
208-282-4636
https://www.isu.edu/

U.S Forest Service
Caribou-Targhee National Forest
Westside Ranger District
4350 S. Cliffs Drive
Pocatello, ID 83204
208-236-7500
https://www.fs.usda.gov/ctnf

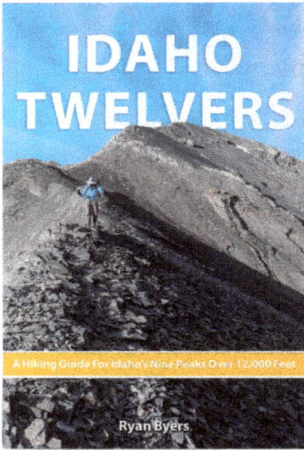

About The Author

Ryan Byers is an avid outdoorsman who has been climbing and hiking in the Idaho wilderness since childhood. An accomplished endurance athlete, his love of mountaineering has led him across the United States and internationally to collect such notable summits as Pico de Orizaba, Iztaccihuatl, Mount Rainier, and Gannett Peak. He graduated from Pocatello High School, earned his B.S. from the University of Idaho, and his MBA from Idaho State University. He is currently a videographer and writer.

www.ingramcontent.com/pod-product-compliance
Lightning Source LLC
Chambersburg PA
CBHW062111020426
42335CB00013B/920